Want to turn C's into A's?

Obviously, right?

But the right way to go about it isn't always so obvious. Go digital to get the grades. MindTap's customizable study tools and eTextbook give you everything you need all in one place.

Engage with your course content, enjoy the flexibility of studying anytime and anywhere, stay connected to assignment due dates and instructor notifications with the MindTap Mobile app...

*and most of all...***EARN BETTER GRADES.**

W9-AWW-118

CompTIA A+ Guide to Hardware: Managing, Maintaining, and Troubleshooting

NINTH EDITION

Jean Andrews, Joy Dark, Jill West

CENGAGE
Learning·

Australia • Canada • Mexico • Singapore • Spain • United Kingdom • United States

CompTIA A+ Guide to Hardware: Managing, Maintaining, and Troubleshooting, Ninth Edition, Jean Andrews, Joy Dark, Jill West

SVP, GM Skills & Global Product Management: Dawn Gerrain

Product Director: Kathleen McMahon

Product Team Manager: Kristin McNary

Senior Director, Development: Marah Bellegarde

Product Development Manager: Leigh Hefferon

Senior Content Developer: Michelle Ruelos Cannistraci

Product Assistant: Abigail Pufpaff

Vice President, Marketing Services: Jennifer Ann Baker

Marketing Director: Michele McTighe

Senior Production Director: Wendy Troeger

Production Director: Patty Stephan

Senior Content Project Manager: Brooke Greenhouse

Managing Art Director: Jack Pendleton

Cover image(s):

©iStock.com/Kotkoa

All screenshots, unless otherwise noted, are used with permission from Microsoft Corporation. Microsoft® is a registered trademark of the Microsoft Corporation.

For product information and technology assistance, contact us at
Cengage Learning Customer & Sales Support, 1-800-354-9706

For permission to use material from this text or product, submit all requests online at **www.cengage.com/permissions**
Further permissions questions can be e-mailed to
permissionrequest@cengage.com

Library of Congress Control Number: 2015957525

ISBN: 978-1-305-26645-2

Cengage Learning
20 Channel Center Street
Boston, MA 02210
USA

Cengage Learning is a leading provider of customized learning solutions with employees residing in nearly 40 different countries and sales in more than 125 countries around the world. Find your local representative at **www.cengage.com.**

Cengage Learning products are represented in Canada by Nelson Education, Ltd.

To learn more about Cengage Learning, visit **www.cengage.com**
Purchase any of our products at your local college store or at our preferred online store **www.cengagebrain.com**

Notice to the Reader

Publisher does not warrant or guarantee any of the products described herein or perform any independent analysis in connection with any of the product information contained herein. Publisher does not assume, and expressly disclaims, any obligation to obtain and include information other than that provided to it by the manufacturer. The reader is expressly warned to consider and adopt all safety precautions that might be indicated by the activities described herein and to avoid all potential hazards. By following the instructions contained herein, the reader willingly assumes all risks in connection with such instructions. The publisher makes no representations or warranties of any kind, including but not limited to, the warranties of fitness for particular purpose or merchantability, nor are any such representations implied with respect to the material set forth herein, and the publisher takes no responsibility with respect to such material. The publisher shall not be liable for any special, consequential, or exemplary damages resulting, in whole or part, from the readers' use of, or reliance upon, this material.

Printed in the United States of America
Print Number: 01   Print Year: 2016

Table of Contents

CHAPTER 5

Supporting the Power System and Troubleshooting Computers 185

CHAPTER 6

Supporting Hard Drives and Other Storage Devices 231

CHAPTER 7

Supporting I/O Devices 277

CHAPTER 8

Connecting To and Setting Up a Network 337

CHAPTER 9

Supporting Network Hardware 399

CHAPTER 10

Supporting Printers and Customizing a System 451

APPENDIX A

Safety Procedures and Environmental Concerns

APPENDIX B

APPENDIX C

CompTIA A+ 220-901 Exam Mapped to Chapters

CompTIA A+ Guide to Hardware, Ninth Edition fully meets all of CompTIA's A+ 220-901
Exam Objectives.

DOMAIN 1.0 HARDWARE

1.1 **Given a scenario, configure settings and use BIOS/UEFI tools on a PC.**

OBJECTIVES	CHAPTER	SECTION
◢ Firmware upgrades – flash BIOS	3	Flashing BIOS
◢ BIOS component information	3	Using BIOS Setup to Configure a Motherboard
• RAM	3	Using BIOS Setup to Configure a Motherboard
• Hard drive	3	Using BIOS Setup to Configure a Motherboard
• Optical drive	3	Using BIOS Setup to Configure a Motherboard
• CPU	3	Using BIOS Setup to Configure a Motherboard
◢ BIOS configurations	3	Using BIOS Setup to Configure a Motherboard
• Boot sequence	3	Using BIOS Setup to Configure a Motherboard
• Enabling and disabling devices	3	Using BIOS Setup to Configure a Motherboard
• Date/time	3	Using BIOS Setup to Configure a Motherboard
• Clock speeds	3	Using BIOS Setup to Configure a Motherboard
• Virtualization support	3	Using BIOS Setup to Configure a Motherboard
• BIOS security (passwords, drive encryption: TPM, lo-jack, secure boot)	3	Using BIOS Setup to Configure a Motherboard
◢ Built-in diagnostics	3	Configuring a Motherboard
◢ Monitoring	3	Using BIOS Setup to Configure a Motherboard
• Temperature monitoring	3	Using BIOS Setup to Configure a Motherboard
• Fan speeds	3	Using BIOS Setup to Configure a Motherboard
• Intrusion detection/notification	3	Using BIOS Setup to Configure a Motherboard
• Voltage	3	Using BIOS Setup to Configure a Motherboard
• Clock	3	Using BIOS Setup to Configure a Motherboard
• Bus speed	3	Using BIOS Setup to Configure a Motherboard

1.2 **Explain the importance of motherboard components, their purpose, and properties.**

OBJECTIVES	CHAPTER	SECTION
◢ Sizes	3	Motherboard Form Factors
• ATX	3	Motherboard Form Factors
• Micro-ATX	3	Motherboard Form Factors
• Mini-ITX	3	Motherboard Form Factors
• ITX	3	Motherboard Form Factors
◢ Expansion slots	3	Motherboard Form Factors
• PCI	3	Buses and Expansion Slots
• PCI-X	3	Buses and Expansion Slots
• PCIe	3	Buses and Expansion Slots
• miniPCI	3	Buses and Expansion Slots
◢ RAM slots	4	Memory Technologies
◢ CPU sockets	3	Processor Sockets
◢ Chipsets	3	The Chipset
• North Bridge	3	The Chipset
• South Bridge	3	The Chipset
◢ CMOS battery	3	Configuring a Motherboard
◢ Power connections and types	5	Types and Characteristics of Power Supplies

1.6   **Install various types of CPUs and apply the appropriate cooling methods.**

1.7   Compare and contrast various PC connection interfaces, their characteristics and purpose.

OBJECTIVES	CHAPTER	SECTION
⏵ Physical connections		
• USB 1.1 vs. 2.0 vs. 3.0	7	Ports and Wireless Connections Used by Peripheral Devices
○ Connector types: A, B, mini, micro	7	Ports and Wireless Connections Used by Peripheral Devices
• Firewire 400 vs. Firewire 800	7	Ports and Wireless Connections Used by Peripheral Devices
• SATA1 vs. SATA2 vs. SATA3, eSATA	6	Hard Drive Technologies and Interface Standards
• Other connector types	7	Ports and Wireless Connections Used by Peripheral Devices
○ VGA	7	Video Cards and Connectors
○ HDMI	7	Video Cards and Connectors
○ DVI	7	Video Cards and Connectors
○ Audio	7	Ports and Wireless Connections Used by Peripheral Devices
○ Analog	1	What's Inside a Desktop Case
○ Digital (Optical connector)	1	What's Inside a Desktop Case
○ RJ-45	1	What's Inside a Desktop Case
○ RJ-11	1	What's Inside a Desktop Case
○ Thunderbolt	1	First Look at Laptop Components
⏵ Wireless connections	7	Ports and Wireless Connections Used by Peripheral Devices
• Bluetooth	7	Ports and Wireless Connections Used by Peripheral Devices
• RF	7	Ports and Wireless Connections Used by Peripheral Devices
• IR	7	Ports and Wireless Connections Used by Peripheral Devices
• NFC	7	Ports and Wireless Connections Used by Peripheral Devices
⏵ Characteristics	7	Ports and Wireless Connections Used by Peripheral Devices
• Analog	7	Ports and Wireless Connections Used by Peripheral Devices
• Digital	7	Ports and Wireless Connections Used by Peripheral Devices
• Distance limitations	7	Ports and Wireless Connections Used by Peripheral Devices
• Data transfer speeds	7	Ports and Wireless Connections Used by Peripheral Devices
• Quality	7	Ports and Wireless Connections Used by Peripheral Devices
• DRM	7	Ports and Wireless Connections Used by Peripheral Devices
• Frequencies	7	Ports and Wireless Connections Used by Peripheral Devices

1.8 Install a power supply based on given specifications.

OBJECTIVES	CHAPTER	SECTION
⏵ Connector types and their voltages	1	Form Factors Used by Desktop Cases, Power Supplies, and Motherboards
	5	Types and Characteristics of Power Supplies
• SATA	1	Form Factors Used by Desktop Cases, Power Supplies, and Motherboards
	5	Types and Characteristics of Power Supplies
• Molex	1	Form Factors Used by Desktop Cases, Power Supplies, and Motherboards
	5	Types and Characteristics of Power Supplies
• 4/8-pin 12v	1	Form Factors Used by Desktop Cases, Power Supplies, and Motherboards
	5	Types and Characteristics of Power Supplies
• PCIe 6/8-pin	1	Form Factors Used by Desktop Cases, Power Supplies, and Motherboards
	5	Types and Characteristics of Power Supplies
• 20-pin	1	Form Factors Used by Desktop Cases, Power Supplies, and Motherboards
	5	Types and Characteristics of Power Supplies

1.10 Compare and contrast types of display devices and their features.

OBJECTIVES	CHAPTER	SECTION
◢ Types	7	Monitor Technologies and Features
• LCD	7	Monitor Technologies and Features
○ TN vs. IPS	7	Monitor Technologies and Features
○ Flourescent vs. LED backlighting	7	Monitor Technologies and Features
• Plasma	7	Monitor Technologies and Features
• Projector	7	Monitor Technologies and Features
• OLED	7	Monitor Technologies and Features
◢ Refresh / frame rates	7	Monitor Technologies and Features
◢ Resolution	7	Monitor Technologies and Features
◢ Native resolution	7	Monitor Technologies and Features
◢ Brightness/lumens	7	Monitor Technologies and Features
◢ Analog vs. digital	7	Monitor Technologies and Features
◢ Privacy/antiglare filters	7	Monitor Technologies and Features
◢ Multiple displays	7	Monitor Technologies and Features
◢ Aspect ratios	7	Monitor Technologies and Features
• 16:9	7	Monitor Technologies and Features
• 16:10	7	Monitor Technologies and Features
• 4:3	7	Monitor Technologies and Features

1.11 Identify common PC connector types and associated cables.

OBJECTIVES	CHAPTER	SECTION
◢ Display connector types		
• DVI-D	7	Video Cards and Connectors
• DVI-I	7	Video Cards and Connectors
• DVI-A	7	Video Cards and Connectors
• DisplayPort	1	What's Inside a Desktop Case
• RCA	7	Video Cards and Connectors
• HD15 (i.e. DE15 or DB15)	1	What's Inside a Desktop Case
• BNC	9	Ethernet Cables and Connectors
• miniHDMI	7	Video Cards and Connectors
• miniDin-6	7	Video Cards and Connectors
◢ Display cable types	1	What's Inside a Desktop Case
• HDMI	7	Video Cards and Connectors
• DVI	7	Video Cards and Connectors
• VGA	7	Video Cards and Connectors
• Component	7	Video Cards and Connectors
• Composite	7	Video Cards and Connectors
• Coaxial	9	Ethernet Cables and Connectors
◢ Device cables and connectors		
• SATA	6	Hard Drive Technologies and Interface Standards
• eSATA	6	Hard Drive Technologies and Interface Standards
• USB	6	Hard Drive Technologies and Interface Standards
• Firewire (IEEE1394)	1	What's Inside a Desktop Case
• PS/2	1	What's Inside a Desktop Case
• Audio	1	What's Inside a Desktop Case

1.14 **Compare and contrast differences between the various print technologies and the associated imaging process.**

1.15 Given a scenario, perform appropriate printer maintenance.

OBJECTIVES	CHAPTER	SECTION
◢ Laser	10	Printer Maintenance and Upgrades
• Replacing toner, applying maintenance kit, calibration, cleaning	10	Printer Maintenance and Upgrades
◢ Thermal	10	Printer Maintenance and Upgrades
• Replace paper, clean heating element, remove debris	10	Printer Maintenance and Upgrades
◢ Impact	10	Printer Maintenance and Upgrades
• Replace ribbon, replace print head, replace paper	10	Printer Maintenance and Upgrades
◢ Inkjet	10	Printer Maintenance and Upgrades
• Clean heads, replace cartridges, calibration, clear jams	10	Printer Maintenance and Upgrades

DOMAIN 2.0 NETWORKING

2.1 Identify the various types of network cables and connectors.

OBJECTIVES	CHAPTER	SECTION
◢ Fiber	9	Ethernet Cables and Connectors
• Connectors: SC, ST and LC	9	Ethernet Cables and Connectors
◢ Twisted Pair	9	Ethernet Cables and Connectors
• Connectors: RJ-11, RJ-45	9	Ethernet Cables and Connectors
• Wiring standards: T568A, T568B	9	How Twisted-Pair Cables and Connectors Are Wired
◢ Coaxial	9	Ethernet Cables and Connectors
• Connectors: BNC, F-connector	9	Ethernet Cables and Connectors

2.2 Compare and contrast the characteristics of connectors and cabling.

OBJECTIVES	CHAPTER	SECTION
◢ Fiber	9	Ethernet Cables and Connectors
• Types (single-mode vs. multi-mode)	9	Ethernet Cables and Connectors
• Speed and transmission limitations	9	Ethernet Cables and Connectors
◢ Twisted pair	9	Ethernet Cables and Connectors
• Types: STP, UTP, CAT3, CAT5, CAT5e, CAT6, CAT6e, CAT7, plenum, PVC	9	Ethernet Cables and Connectors
• Speed and transmission limitations	9	Ethernet Cables and Connectors
• Splitters and effects on signal quality	9	Ethernet Cables and Connectors
◢ Coaxial	9	Ethernet Cables and Connectors
• Types: RG-6, RG-59	9	Ethernet Cables and Connectors
• Speed and transmission limitations	9	Ethernet Cables and Connectors
• Splitters and effects on signal quality	9	Ethernet Cables and Connectors

DOMAIN 3.0 MOBILE DEVICES

3.1   Install and configure laptop hardware and components.

OBJECTIVES	CHAPTER	SECTION
◢ Expansion options		
• Express card /34	1	First Look at Laptop Components
• Express card /54	1	First Look at Laptop Components
• SODIMM	4	Types of Memory Used in Laptops
• Flash	1	First Look at Laptop Components
• Ports/Adapters	1	First Look at Laptop Components
○ Thunderbolt	1	First Look at Laptop Components
○ DisplayPort	1	First Look at Laptop Components
○ USB to RJ-45 dongle	1	First Look at Laptop Components
○ USB to WiFi dongle	1	First Look at Laptop Components
○ USB to Bluetooth	1	First Look at Laptop Components
○ USB Optical Drive	1	First Look at Laptop Components
◢ Hardware/device replacement		
• Keyboard	1	How to Work Inside a Laptop Computer
• Hard Drive	1	First Look at Laptop Components
	6	Hard Drive Technologies and Interface Standards
○ SSD vs. Hybrid vs. Magnetic disk	6	Hard Drive Technologies and Interface Standards
○ 1.8in vs. 2.5in	6	Hard Drive Technologies and Interface Standards
• Memory	1	First Look at Laptop Components
	4	How to Upgrade Memory on a Laptop
• Smart card reader	1	First Look at Laptop Components
	6	Solid-State Storage
• Optical drive	1	First Look at Laptop Components
	6	Supporting Other Types of Storage Devices
• Wireless card	1	First Look at Laptop Components
	7	Replacing Expansion Cards in a Laptop
• Mini-PCIe	7	Replacing Expansion Cards in a Laptop
• Screen	7	Video System in a Laptop
• DC jack	1	First Look at Laptop Components
	5	Problems with Laptop Power Systems
• Battery	1	First Look at Laptop Components
	5	Problems with Laptop Power Systems
• Touchpad	7	How to Work Inside a Laptop Computer
• Plastics/frames	1	First Look at Laptop Components
	5	Problems with Laptop Power Systems
• Speaker	7	How to Work Inside a Laptop Computer
• System board	1	First Look at Laptop Components
	3	Replacing a Laptop System Board
• CPU	1	First Look at Laptop Components
	4	Replacing the Processor in a Laptop

3.2   Explain the function of components within the display of a laptop.

OBJECTIVES	CHAPTER	SECTION
◢ Types	7	Video System in a Laptop
• LCD	7	Video System in a Laptop
○ TN vs. IPS	7	Video System in a Laptop
○ Flourescent vs. LED backlighting	7	Video System in a Laptop
• OLED	7	Video System in a Laptop

3.3   Given a scenario, use appropriate laptop features.

3.4   Explain the characteristics of various types of other mobile devices.

3.5   Compare and contrast accessories & ports of other mobile devices.

◢ Accessories	1	First Look at Mobile Device Hardware
• Headsets	1	First Look at Mobile Device Hardware
• Speakers	1	First Look at Mobile Device Hardware
• Game pads	1	First Look at Mobile Device Hardware
• Docking stations	1	First Look at Mobile Device Hardware
• Extra battery packs/battery chargers	1	First Look at Mobile Device Hardware
• Protective covers / water proofing	1	First Look at Mobile Device Hardware
• Credit card readers	1	First Look at Mobile Device Hardware
• Memory/MicroSD	1	First Look at Mobile Device Hardware

DOMAIN 4.0 HARDWARE AND NETWORK TROUBLESHOOTING

4.1   **Given a scenario, troubleshoot common problems related to motherboards, RAM, CPU and power with appropriate tools.**

OBJECTIVES	CHAPTER	SECTION
◢ Common symptoms	5	Troubleshooting the Motherboard, Processor, and RAM
• Unexpected shutdowns	5	Troubleshooting the Motherboard, Processor, and RAM
• System lockups	5	Troubleshooting the Motherboard, Processor, and RAM
• POST code beeps	5	Troubleshooting the Motherboard, Processor, and RAM
• Blank screen on bootup	5	Troubleshooting the Motherboard, Processor, and RAM
• BIOS time and settings resets	5	Troubleshooting the Motherboard, Processor, and RAM
• Attempts to boot to incorrect device	5	Troubleshooting the Motherboard, Processor, and RAM
• Continuous reboots	5	Troubleshooting the Motherboard, Processor, and RAM
• No power	5	Troubleshooting the Motherboard, Processor, and RAM
• Overheating	5	Troubleshooting the Motherboard, Processor, and RAM
• Loud noise	5	Troubleshooting the Motherboard, Processor, and RAM
• Intermittent device failure	5	Troubleshooting the Motherboard, Processor, and RAM
• Fans spin – no power to other devices	5	Troubleshooting the Motherboard, Processor, and RAM
• Indicator lights	5	Troubleshooting the Motherboard, Processor, and RAM
• Smoke	5	Troubleshooting the Motherboard, Processor, and RAM
• Burning smell	5	Troubleshooting the Motherboard, Processor, and RAM
• Proprietary crash screens (BSOD/pin wheel)	5	Troubleshooting the Motherboard, Processor, and RAM
• Distended capacitors	5	Troubleshooting the Motherboard, Processor, and RAM
◢ Tools	1	Tools Used by a Computer Hardware Technician
• Multimeter	1	Tools Used by a Computer Hardware Technician
• Power supply tester	1	Tools Used by a Computer Hardware Technician
• Loopback plugs	1	Tools Used by a Computer Hardware Technician
• POST card / USB	1	Tools Used by a Computer Hardware Technician

4.2   **Given a scenario, troubleshoot hard drives and RAID arrays with appropriate tools.**

OBJECTIVES	CHAPTER	SECTION
◢ Common symptoms	6	Troubleshooting Hard Drives
• Read/write failure	6	Troubleshooting Hard Drives
• Slow performance	6	Troubleshooting Hard Drives
• Loud clicking noise	5	Troubleshooting the Motherboard, Processor, and RAM
• Failure to boot	6	Troubleshooting Hard Drives
• Drive not recognized	6	Troubleshooting Hard Drives
• OS not found	6	Troubleshooting Hard Drives
• RAID not found	6	Troubleshooting Hard Drives
• RAID stops working	6	Troubleshooting Hard Drives

◢ Command line tools	9	TCP/IP Utilities Used for Troubleshooting
• PING	9	TCP/IP Utilities Used for Troubleshooting
• IPCONFIG/IFCONFIG	9	TCP/IP Utilities Used for Troubleshooting
• TRACERT	9	TCP/IP Utilities Used for Troubleshooting
• NETSTAT	9	TCP/IP Utilities Used for Troubleshooting
• NBTSTAT	9	TCP/IP Utilities Used for Troubleshooting
• NET	9	TCP/IP Utilities Used for Troubleshooting
• NETDOM	9	TCP/IP Utilities Used for Troubleshooting
• NSLOOKUP	9	TCP/IP Utilities Used for Troubleshooting

4.5   **Given a scenario, troubleshoot and repair common mobile device issues while adhering to the appropriate procedures.**

OBJECTIVES	CHAPTER	SECTION
◢ Common symptoms		
• No display	7	Video System in a Laptop
• Dim display	7	Video System in a Laptop
• Flickering display	7	Video System in a Laptop
• Sticking keys	1	Maintaining Laptops and Mobile Devices
• Intermittent wireless	9	Strategies for Troubleshooting Network Connections
• Battery not charging	5	Troubleshooting Mobile Devices
• Ghost cursor/pointer drift	7	Video System in a Laptop
• No power	5	Troubleshooting Mobile Devices
• Num lock indicator lights	7	NumLock Indicator Light
• No wireless connectivity	9	Strategies for Troubleshooting Network Connections
• No Bluetooth connectivity	9	Strategies for Troubleshooting Network Connections
• Cannot display to external monitor	7	Changing Monitor Settings
• Touchscreen non-responsive	7	Video System in a Laptop
• Apps not loading	5	Troubleshooting Mobile Devices
• Slow performance	5	Troubleshooting Mobile Devices
• Unable to decrypt email	5	Troubleshooting Mobile Devices
• Extremely short battery life	5	Troubleshooting Mobile Devices
• Overheating	5	Troubleshooting Mobile Devices
• Frozen system	5	Troubleshooting Mobile Devices
• No sound from speakers	7	Speakers in a Laptop
• GPS not functioning	9	Strategies for Troubleshooting Network Connections
• Swollen battery	5	Troubleshooting Mobile Devices
◢ Disassembling processes for proper re-assembly	2	How to Work Inside a Laptop Computer
• Document and label cable and screw locations	2	How to Work Inside a Laptop Computer
• Organize parts	2	How to Work Inside a Laptop Computer
• Refer to manufacturer resources	2	How to Work Inside a Laptop Computer
• Use appropriate hand tools	2	How to Work Inside a Laptop Computer

4.6   **Given a scenario, troubleshoot printers with appropriate tools.**

Introduction: CompTIA A+ Guide to Hardware

CompTIA A+ Guide to Hardware: Managing, Maintaining, and Troubleshooting, Ninth Edition was written to be the very best tool on the market today to prepare you to support desktop and laptop computers as well as mobile devices. The text has been updated to include the most current hardware technologies and takes you from the just-a-user level to the I-can-fix-this level for hardware matters. It achieves its goals with an unusually effective combination of tools that powerfully reinforce both concepts and hands-on, real-world experiences. It also provides thorough preparation for the content on the new CompTIA A+ 220-901 Certification exam. Competency in using a computer is a prerequisite to using this book. No background knowledge of electronics is assumed. An appropriate prerequisite course for this book would be a general course in computer applications.

This book includes:

- ◢ *Several in-depth, hands-on projects* are spaced throughout each chapter that invite you to immediately apply and reinforce critical thinking and troubleshooting skills and are designed to make certain that you not only understand the material, but also execute procedures and make decisions on your own.
- ◢ *Comprehensive review and practice end-of-chapter material*, including a chapter summary, key terms, review questions that focus on A+ content, critical thinking questions, and real-world problems to solve.
- ◢ *Step-by-step instructions* on installation, maintenance, optimization of system performance, and troubleshooting.
- ◢ *A wide array of photos, drawings, and screen shots* support the text, displaying in detail the exact features you will need to understand to set up, maintain, and troubleshoot personal computers and small networks.

In addition, the carefully structured, clearly written text is accompanied by graphics that provide the visual input essential to learning and to help students master difficult subject matter. For instructors using the book in a classroom, instructor resources are available online.

Coverage is balanced—while focusing on new hardware, the text also covers the real work of an IT support technician, where some older technology remains in widespread use and still needs support. For example, the text covers how to use and support BIOS on legacy motherboards, but also addresses the new UEFI firmware used on current motherboards and how to handle compatibility issues between the two types of firmware. Other new technologies covered include the latest Intel and AMD processor sockets, cloud printing, remote printing, virtual printing, and the latest hardware used with various types of mobile devices.

This book provides thorough preparation for CompTIA's A+ 220-901 certification examination. This certification credential's popularity among employers is growing exponentially, and obtaining certification increases your ability to gain employment and improve your salary. To get more information on CompTIA's A+ certification and its sponsoring organization, the Computing Technology Industry Association, see their website at *www.comptia.org*.

FEATURES

To ensure a successful learning experience, this book includes the following pedagogical features:

⊿ *Learning Objectives*. Every chapter opens with a list of learning objectives that sets the stage for you to absorb the lessons of the text.

⊿ *Comprehensive Step-by-Step Troubleshooting Guidance*. Troubleshooting guidelines are included in almost every chapter. In addition, the chapter, "Supporting the Power System and Troubleshooting Computers," gives insights into general approaches to troubleshooting that help apply the specifics detailed in each chapter for different hardware problems.

⊿ *Step-by-Step Procedures*. The book is chock-full of step-by-step procedures covering subjects from hardware installations and maintenance to troubleshooting the boot process or a failed network connection and optimizing performance and securing a small network.

⊿ *Art Program*. Numerous visually detailed photographs, three-dimensional art, and screen shots support the text, displaying hardware and software features exactly as you will see them in your work.

⊿ *CompTIA A+ Table of Contents*. This table of contents gives the chapter and section that provides the primary content for each certification objective on the A+ exams. This is a valuable tool for quick reference.

⊿ *Hands-On Projects*. These sections give you practice using the skills you have just studied so that you can learn by doing and know you have mastered a skill.

⊿ *Applying Concepts*. These sections offer real-life, practical applications for the material being discussed. Whether outlining a task, developing a scenario, or providing pointers, the Applying Concepts sections give you a chance to apply what you've learned to a typical computer or network problem, so you can understand how you will use the material in your professional life.

A+ Icons. All of the content that relates to CompTIA's A+ 220-901 Certification exam is highlighted with an A+ icon. The icon notes the exam name and the objective number. This unique feature highlights the relevant content at a glance, so that you can pay extra attention to the material.

Notes. Note icons highlight additional helpful information related to the subject being discussed.

A+ Exam Tip Boxes. These boxes highlight additional insights and tips to remember if you are planning to take the CompTIA A+ 220-901 exam.

Caution Icons. These icons highlight critical safety information. Follow these instructions carefully to protect the computer and its data and to ensure your own safety.

OS Differences. These boxes point you to the differences among Windows 8, Windows 7, and Vista.

◢ *End-of-Chapter Material.* Each chapter closes with the following features, which reinforce the material covered in the chapter and provide real-world, hands-on testing:

- *Chapter Summary*: This bulleted list of concise statements summarizes all major points of the chapter.

- *Key Terms*: The content of each chapter is further reinforced by an end-of-chapter key term list. The definitions of all terms are included with this text in a full-length glossary.

- *Review Questions*: You can test your understanding of each chapter with a comprehensive set of review questions. The "Reviewing the Basics" questions check your understanding of fundamental concepts focused on A+ content, while the "Thinking Critically" questions help you synthesize and apply what you've learned and also focus on A+ content.

- *Real Problems, Real Solutions*: Each comprehensive problem allows you to find out if you can apply what you've learned in the chapter to a real-life situation.

◢ *Student Companion Site.* The companion website includes older content and additional resources that still might be important in some repair situations. The content includes the following historical and older content that might still be important in some computer repair situations. The content: The Hexademical Number System and Memory Addressing, Supporting Windows XP, Electricity and Multimeters, Facts About Legacy Motherboards, How an OS Uses System Resources, Facts About Legacy Processors, All About SCSI, Behind the Scenes with DEBUG, FAT Details, and Selecting and Installing Hard Drives Using Legacy Motherboards. Other helpful online references include Frequently Asked Questions, Sample Reports, Computer Inventory and Maintenance form, and Troubleshooting Flowcharts. A video archive of clips that feature Jean Andrews illustrating concepts and providing advice on the real world of computer repair is also included.

WHAT'S NEW IN THE NINTH EDITION

Here's a summary of what's new in the *Ninth Edition*:

◢ Content maps to CompTIA's A+ 220-901 exam.

◢ There is now more focus on A+, with non-A+ content moved online to the companion website or eliminated.

◢ New content is added (all new content was also new to the A+ 220-901 exam).

- Fifth Generation (Broadwell) and Fourth Generation (Haswell) processor and chipset architectures by Intel are covered in the chapter, "Supporting Processors and Upgrading Memory."

- Enhanced content on supporting UEFI firmware is now included.

- New content on virtual printing and cloud printing is added to the chapter, "Supporting Printers and Customizing a System."

- Hands-On Projects in several chapters use virtual machines so that you get plenty of practice using this up-and-coming technology.

- New content on networking hardware devices, including patch panels, repeaters, extenders, EoP, PoE injectors, and Wi-Fi analyzers, is covered in the chapter, "Supporting Network Hardware."

- Enhanced content on mobile device hardware is covered in the chapter, "First Look at Computer Parts and Tools."

- Supporting and troubleshooting laptops is integrated throughout the text.

Chapter **objectives** appear at the beginning of each chapter, so you know exactly what topics and skills are covered.

A+ Exam Tips include key points pertinent to the A+ exams. The icons identify the sections that cover information you will need to know for the A+ certification exams.

CHAPTER

8

Connecting To and Setting Up a Network

After completing this chapter, you will be able to:

• Explain the TCP/IP protocols and standards Windows uses for networking

• Connect a computer to a wired or wireless network

• Configure and secure a multifunction router on a local network

In this chapter, you learn how Windows uses TCP/IP protocols and standards to create and manage network connections, including how computers are identified and addressed on a network. You also learn to connect a computer to a network and how to set up and secure a small wired or wireless network.

This chapter prepares you to assume total responsibility for supporting both wired and wireless networks in a small-office/home-office (SOHO) environment. In the chapter, "Supporting Network Hardware," you learn more about the hardware used in networking, including network devices, connectors, cabling, networking tools, and the types of networks used for Internet connections. So let's get started by looking at how TCP/IP works in the world of Windows networking.

★ **A+ Exam Tip** Much of the content in this chapter applies to both the A+ 220-901 exam and the A+ 220-902 exam. This text includes icons for the A+ 220-901 (hardware) exam only. For markup of content relating to the A+ 220-902 (software) exam, see the companion volume to this text, *A+ Guide to Software, 9th ed.*

⚡ **Caution** You can damage a computer component with static electricity if you touch the component when you are not grounded. Before you touch a sensitive computer component, you first need to dissipate any static electricity on your body. You learn how to do that in the appendix, "Safety Procedures and Environmental Concerns." For now, to protect a working component your instructor has on display, don't touch; just look.

Hands-On | Project 1-2 Examine the Power Supply, Motherboard, and Expansion Cards Inside a Desktop Case

A+ 220-901 1.7, 1.8, 1.11

If you have access to a desktop computer with the case cover removed, examine its components and answer the following questions. As you look, remember to not touch anything inside the case unless you are properly grounded.

1. Identify the power supply, motherboard, and any expansion cards that might be installed on the motherboard. Remember: Don't touch a component unless you are properly grounded. If the case is plugged into a power source, don't touch inside the case even if you are grounded.

2. Identify the cooler that is installed on top of the processor. This cooler is likely to have a fan on top and a heat sink that you can't see. The processor is hidden under the cooler.

3. Identify the memory modules and memory slots. How many memory slots are there? How many of these slots are populated?

4. If an expansion card is installed, what type of ports does the card provide at the rear of the case? Find the one screw that is used to attach the expansion card to the case.

5. Locate the screws that are attaching the motherboard to the case. How many screws are used? Do you see screw holes in the motherboard that are not being used? As a general rule of thumb, up to nine screws can be used to attach a motherboard to a case.

6. How many power cables are coming from the power supply? How many of these cables are connected to the motherboard? To other devices inside the computer? Identify each type of power cable the system is using.

7. Find the screws or clips that are attaching the power supply to the case. Is the power supply attached using screws, clips, or both screws and clips?

Cautions identify critical safety information.

Hands-On Projects provide practical exercises throughout each chapter so that you can practice the skills as they are learned.

Notes indicate additional content that might be of student interest or information about how best to study.

> ✎ **Notes** Be aware that a laptop might show the Bluetooth icon in the taskbar even when the laptop does not support Bluetooth.

APPLYING | CONCEPTS MAKE A STRAIGHT-THROUGH CABLE USING T568B WIRING

A+
220-901
2.1, 2.2,
2.9, 4.4

It takes a little practice to make a good network straight-through cable, but you'll get the hang of it after doing only a couple of cables. Figure 9-34 shows the materials and tools you'll need to make a network cable.

Figure 9-34 Tools and materials to make a network cable

Here are the steps to make a straight-through cable using the T568B standard:

1. Use wire cutters to cut the twisted-pair cable the correct length plus a few extra inches.

2. If your RJ-45 connectors include boots, slide two boots onto the cable.

3. Use wire strippers to strip off about two inches of the plastic jacket from the end of the wire. To do that, put the wire in the stripper and rotate the stripper around the wire to score the jacket (see Figure 9-35). You can then pull off the jacket.

Visual full-color graphics, photos, and screen shots accurately depict computer hardware and software components.

Applying Concepts sections provide practical advice or pointers by illustrating basic principles, identifying common problems, providing steps to practice skills, and encouraging creating solutions.

Chapter Summary bulleted lists of concise statements summarize all major points of the chapter, organized by primary headings.

>> CHAPTER SUMMARY

How to Work Inside a Desktop Computer Case

▲ When a hardware support technician is disassembling or reassembling a computer, it is important to stay organized, keep careful notes, and follow all the safety procedures to protect the computer equipment.

▲ Before opening a computer case, shut down the system, unplug it, disconnect all cables, and press the power button to drain residual power.

▲ An expansion card fits in a slot on the motherboard and is anchored to the case by a single screw or clip.

>> KEY TERMS

For explanations of key terms, see the Glossary for this text.

front panel connector
front panel header
spacer
standoff
ZIF connector

>> REVIEWING THE BASICS

1. When taking a computer apart, why is it important to not stack boards on top of each other?

2. Why is it important to remove loose jewelry before working inside a computer case?

3. When assembling a desktop computer, which do you install first, the drives or the motherboard?

4. What is the purpose of raised screw holes or standoffs installed between the motherboard and desktop case?

5. When installing the front panel wires to the motherboard front panel header, how do you know which pins to use for each wire if the pins on the header are not labeled?

6. How many pins does the CPU auxiliary power connector on a motherboard have?

7. Why are laptops usually more expensive than desktop computers with comparable power and features?

8. Why is the service manual so important to have when you disassemble a laptop?

9. When a laptop internal device fails, what three options can you use to deal with the problem?

10. After you have removed the AC adapter and all peripherals, what is the next component you should always remove before servicing any internal laptop components?

Key Terms are defined as they are introduced and listed at the end of each chapter. Definitions can be found in the Glossary.

Reviewing the Basics sections check understanding of fundamental concepts.

Thinking Critically sections require you to analyze and apply what you've learned.

>> THINKING CRITICALLY

1. You disassemble and reassemble a desktop computer. When you first turn it on, you see no lights and hear no sounds. Nothing appears on the monitor screen. What is the most likely cause of the problem? Explain your answer.

   a. A memory module is not seated properly in a memory slot.

   b. You forgot to plug up the monitor's external power cord.

   c. A wire in the case is obstructing a fan.

   d. Power cords to the motherboard are not connected.

>> REAL PROBLEMS, REAL SOLUTIONS

REAL PROBLEM 2-1 Taking a Lab Computer Apart and Putting It Back Together

A PC technician needs to be comfortable with taking apart a computer and putting it back together. In most situations, the essential tools you'll need for the job are an ESD strap, a Phillips-head screwdriver, a flathead screwdriver, paper, and pen.

Working with a partner and using a lab computer designated to be disassembled, take a computer apart. It is not necessary to remove the processor or memory modules from the motherboard, but be very careful to properly support the motherboard and processor as you remove them from the case. Then reassemble the system. Don't replace the computer case panel until your instructor has inspected all cable connections. Then turn on the computer and verify that all is working.

REAL PROBLEM 2-2 Setting Up a Service Center for Laptops

If you intend to set up your own computer repair shop, you might want to consider becoming a service center for a few brands of the more popular laptops. Reasons to become an authorized service center are that you have access to service manuals, parts lists, and wholesale parts for laptops. Do the following to research becoming an authorized service center:

1. Select a brand of laptops that you think you would like to service.

2. Research the website of this manufacturer and answer these questions:

   a. Where is the closest authorized service center for this brand of laptops?

   b. What are the requirements to become an authorized service center? Print the webpage showing the requirements.

   c. Is A+ certification one of those requirements?

Real Problems, Real Solutions allow you to apply what you've learned in the chapter to a real-life situation.

WHAT'S NEW WITH CompTIA® A+ CERTIFICATION

The CompTIA A+ exams include two exams, and you must pass both to become CompTIA A+ certified. The two exams are 220-901 and 220-902.

Here is a breakdown of the domain content covered on the two A+ exams. This text covers content on the 220-901 exam. Content on the 220-902 exam is covered in the companion text, *A+ Guide to Software*.

CompTIA A+ 220-901 Exam	
Domain	Percentage of Examination
1.0 Hardware	34%
2.0 Networking	21%
3.0 Mobile Devices	17%
4.0 Hardware & Network Troubleshooting	28%
Total	100%

CompTIA A+ 220-902 Exam	
Domain	Percentage of Examination
1.0 Windows Operating Systems	29%
2.0 Other Operating Systems & Technologies	12%
3.0 Security	22%
4.0 Software Troubleshooting	24%
5.0 Operational Procedures	13%
Total	100%

CompTIA.®

Becoming a CompTIA Certified IT Professional is Easy

It's also the best way to reach greater professional opportunities and rewards.

Why Get CompTIA Certified?

Growing Demand

Labor estimates predict some technology fields will experience growth of over 20% by the year 2020.* CompTIA certification qualifies the skills required to join this workforce.

Higher Salaries

IT professionals with certifications on their resume command better jobs, earn higher salaries and have more doors open to new multi-industry opportunities.

Verified Strengths

91% of hiring managers indicate CompTIA certifications are valuable in validating IT expertise, making certification the best way to demonstrate your competency and knowledge to employers.**

Universal Skills

CompTIA certifications are vendor neutral—which means that certified professionals can proficiently work with an extensive variety of hardware and software found in most organizations.

 Learn ⟩   **Certify** ⟩ 💼 **Work**

Learn more about what the exam covers by reviewing the following:

- Exam objectives for key study points.

- Sample questions for a general overview of what to expect on the exam and examples of question format.

- Visit online forums, like LinkedIn, to see what other IT professionals say about CompTIA exams.

Purchase a voucher at a Pearson VUE testing center or at CompTIAstore.com.

- Register for your exam at a Pearson VUE testing center:

- Visit pearsonvue.com/CompTIA to find the closest testing center to you.

- Schedule the exam online. You will be required to enter your voucher number or provide payment information at registration.

- Take your certification exam.

Congratulations on your CompTIA certification!

- Make sure to add your certification to your resume.

- Check out the CompTIA Certification Roadmap to plan your next career move.

Learn more: Certification.CompTIA.org/aplus

* Source: CompTIA 9th Annual Information Security Trends study: 500 U.S. IT and Business Executives Responsible for Security
** Source: CompTIA Employer Perceptions of IT Training and Certification

CompTIA AUTHORIZED QUALITY CONTENT

 CompTIA A+ Guide to Hardware, Ninth Edition has earned CompTIA's Authorized Quality Content approval. The text has been reviewed and approved by ProCert Labs, a CompTIA appointed third party. CAQC approval indicates the textbook material meets CompTIA's comprehensive coverage of the exam objectives, instructional design standards and high quality criteria.

DISCOUNTED CompTIA CERTIFICATION EXAM VOUCHERS

As a CompTIA Authorized Partner, Cengage Learning is able to provide you with a promo code that saves you 10% off the non-member price of a CompTIA Exam voucher when purchased through the CompTIA Marketplace.

Save 10% when you use coupon code **CL10Percent** during checkout. Redeeming the coupon code is easy:

1. Go to **www.comptiastore.com.**

2. Select the CompTIA Certification you want.

3. Add the voucher to the cart (note that for A+ you will need a separate voucher for each exam).

4. Enter the code **CL10Percent** on the purchase screen and click **Apply.**

INSTRUCTOR'S MATERIALS

Please visit *login.cengage.com* and log in to access instructor-specific resources on the Instructor Companion Site, which includes the Instructor's Manual, Solutions Manual, Test creation tools, PowerPoint Presentation, Syllabus, and figure files.

Instructor's Manual: The Instructor's Manual that accompanies this textbook includes additional instructional material to assist in class preparation, including suggestions for classroom activities, discussion topics, and additional projects.

Solutions: Answers to the end-of-chapter material are provided. These include the answers to the Review Questions, Thinking Critically, and to the Hands-On Projects (when applicable), as well as Lab Manual Solutions.

Cengage Learning Testing Powered by Cognero: This flexible, online system allows you to do the following:
- Author, edit, and manage test bank content from multiple Cengage Learning solutions.
- Create multiple test versions in an instant.
- Deliver tests from your LMS, your classroom, or wherever you want.

PowerPoint Presentations: This book comes with Microsoft PowerPoint slides for each chapter. These are included as a teaching aid for classroom presentation, to make available to students on the network for chapter review, or to be printed for classroom distribution. Instructors, please feel at liberty to add your own slides for additional topics you introduce to the class.

Figure Files: All of the figures in the book are reproduced on the Instructor Companion Site. Similar to the PowerPoint presentations, these are included as a teaching aid for classroom presentation, to make available to students for review, or to be printed for classroom distribution.

TOTAL SOLUTIONS FOR CompTIA A+

MINDTAP FOR A+ GUIDE TO HARDWARE, NINTH EDITION

MindTap is an online learning solution designed to help students master the skills they need in today's workforce. Research shows employers need critical thinkers, troubleshooters and creative problem-solvers to stay relevant in our fast paced technology-driven world. MindTap helps you achieve this with assignments and activities that provides hands-practice, real life relevance and certification test prep. Students are guided through assignments that help them master basic knowledge and understanding before moving on to more challenging problems.

MindTap activities and assignments are tied to CompTIA A+ certification exam objectives. The hands-on labs provide real-life application and practice. The IQ certification test prep engine allows students to quiz themselves on specific exam domains, and the pre- and post- course assessments are mock exams that measure exactly how much they have learned. Readings and "whiteboard shorts" support the lecture, while "In The News" assignments encourage students to stay current. MindTap is designed around learning objectives and provides the analytics and reporting to easily see where the class stands in terms of progress, engagement and completion rates. Use the content and learning path as-is or pick-and-choose how our materials will wrap around yours. You control what the students see and when they see it. Learn more at *http://www.cengage.com/mindtap/*.

- Instant Access Code: (ISBN: 9781305944602)
- Printed Access Code: (ISBN: 9781305944619)

LAB MANUAL FOR A+ GUIDE TO HARDWARE, NINTH EDITION

This Lab Manual contains over 65 labs to provide students with additional hands-on experience and to help prepare for the A+ exam. The *Lab Manual* includes lab activities, objectives, materials lists, step-by-step procedures, illustrations, and review questions.

- Lab Manual (ISBN: 9781305266551)

COURSENOTES

This laminated quick reference card reinforces critical knowledge for CompTIA's A+ exam in a visual and user-friendly format. CourseNotes will serve as a useful study aid, supplement to the textbook, or as a quick reference tool during the course and afterward.

- A+ Exam # 220-901 CourseNotes (ISBN: 9781305269248)
- A+ Exam # 220-902 CourseNotes (ISBN: 9781305269255)

PC TROUBLESHOOTING POCKET GUIDE, NINTH EDITION

This compact and portable volume is designed to help students and technicians diagnose any computer problem quickly and efficiently. This guide is up to date and current for today's technologies (ISBN: 9781305266537).

ACKNOWLEDGMENTS

Thank you to the wonderful people at Cengage who continue to give their best and to go the extra mile to make the texts what they are: Kristin McNary, Amy Savino, Michelle Ruelos Cannistraci, and Brooke Greenhouse. We're grateful for all you've done. Thank you, Deb Kaufmann, our Developmental Editor extraordinaire, for your careful attention to detail and your awesome commitment to excellence, and to Karen Annett, our excellent copyeditor/proofreader. Thank you, Serge Palladino, for your careful attention to the technical accuracy of the text.

Thank you to all the people who took the time to voluntarily send encouragement and suggestions for improvements to the previous editions. Your input and help is very much appreciated. The reviewers of this edition all provided invaluable insights and showed a genuine interest in the success of the text. Thank you to:

Susan Booth – Cape Fear Community College
Ron Cannon – Wichita Technical Institute
Steve Ebben – Fox Valley Technical College, Appleton
Glenn Goe – Stark State College
Abigale Trimble – Wichita Technical Institute

To the instructors and learners who use this text, we invite and encourage you to send suggestions or corrections for future editions. Please write to the author team at *jean.andrews@cengage.com*. We never ignore a good idea! And to instructors, if you have ideas for how to make a class in A+ Preparation a success, please share your ideas with other instructors! You can find us on Facebook at *http://www.facebook.com/JeanKnows*, where you can interact with the authors and other instructors.

This book is dedicated to the covenant of God with man on earth.

Jean Andrews, Ph.D.
Joy Dark
Jill West

ABOUT THE AUTHORS

Jean Andrews has more than 30 years of experience in the computer industry, including more than 13 years in the college classroom. She has worked in a variety of businesses and corporations designing, writing, and supporting application software; managing a PC repair help desk; and troubleshooting wide area networks. She has written numerous books on software, hardware, and the Internet, including the best-selling *A+ Guide to IT Technical Support, Ninth Edition* and *A+ Guide to Software: Managing, Maintaining and Troubleshooting, Ninth Edition*. She lives in northern Georgia.

Joy Dark is CompTIA A+ and HIT certified. She has worked in the IT field as a help-desk technician providing first-level support for a company with presence in 29 states, a second-tier technician in healthcare IT, and an operations specialist designing support protocols and structures. As a teacher, Joy has taught online courses in IT with the Stride Center in California and has taught English as a Second Language in the United States and South America. She has helped write several technical textbooks with Jean Andrews, her mother, and Jill West, her sister. Joy lives in Dalton, Georgia, with her two daughters and Doberman dog.

Jill West brings a unique variety of experience in writing, business, and education to the development of her innovative educational materials. She has taught multiple ages and content areas using a flipped classroom approach, distance learning, and educational counseling. Jill's résumé includes service with a nonprofit agency to inner-city disadvantaged populations, on-the-job training with a law firm, ten years working with Jean Andrews in textbook development, multiple entrepreneurial ventures, and CompTIA A+ and Network+ certifications. Her insights into the art of self-teaching provide students with effective tools for taking ownership of their own learning. Jill and her husband Mike live in the hills of northwest Georgia where they homeschool their four children.

READ THIS BEFORE YOU BEGIN

The following hardware, software, and other equipment are needed to do the Hands-On Projects in each chapter:

- ◢ You need a working desktop computer and laptop that can be taken apart and reassembled. You also need a working computer on which you can install an operating system. These computers can be the same or different computers. Use a Pentium or higher computer.
- ◢ Troubleshooting skills can better be practiced with an assortment of nonworking expansion cards that can be used to simulate problems.
- ◢ Windows 8 Professional and Windows 7 Professional are needed for some chapters.
- ◢ Internet access is needed for most chapters.
- ◢ Equipment required to work on hardware includes an ESD strap and flathead and Phillips-head screwdrivers. In addition, a power supply tester, cable tester, and can of compressed air are useful. Network wiring tools needed for the chapter, "Supporting Network Hardware," include a wire cutter, wire stripper, and crimper.
- ◢ A SOHO router that includes a wireless access point is needed for the chapter, "Connecting To and Setting Up a Network."

> ⚡ **Caution** Before undertaking any of the lab exercises, starting with the chapter, "First Look at Computer Parts and Tools," please review the safety guidelines in the appendix, "Safety Procedures and Environmental Concerns."

First Look at Computer Parts and Tools

Like many other computer users, you have probably used your personal computer to play games, update your Facebook profile, write papers, or build Excel worksheets. This text takes you from being an end user of your computer to becoming an information technology (IT) support technician able to support all types of personal computers. The only assumption made here is that you are a computer user—that is, you can turn on your machine, load a software package, and use that software to accomplish a task. No experience in electronics is assumed.

As an IT support technician, you'll want to become A+ certified, which is the industry standard certification for IT support technicians. This text prepares you to pass the A+ 220-901 exam by CompTIA (*www.comptia.org*). This exam is primarily about hardware. The A+ 220-901 exam and the A+ 220-902 exam are required by CompTIA for A+ certification. The A+ 220-902 exam is primarily about software, and content on this exam is covered in the companion book, *A+ Guide to Software: Managing, Maintaining, and Troubleshooting, Ninth Edition*. This text and the *A+ Guide to Software: Managing, Maintaining, and Troubleshooting* fully prepare you for both exams needed for CompTIA A+ certification.

In this chapter, you learn to recognize various hardware components you'll find inside desktop computer and laptop cases and about the tools you'll need to work inside the case. Later in the text, you learn to take a desktop and laptop apart and reassemble them.

> ★ **A+ Exam Tip** As you work your way through a chapter, notice the green A+ mapping icons underneath headings. These page elements help you know to which objectives on the exam the content applies. After studying each chapter, take a look at the grid at the beginning of this text and make sure you understand each objective listed in the grid that is covered in the chapter.

WHAT'S INSIDE A DESKTOP CASE

A+
220-901
1.7, 1.8,
1.11

Before we discuss the parts inside a desktop case, let's take a quick look at the case and the ports and switches on it. A computer case for any type of computer is sometimes called the chassis and houses the power supply, motherboard, processor, memory modules, expansion cards, hard drive, optical drive, and other drives. A computer case can be a tower case, a desktop case that lies flat on a desk, an all-in-one case used with an all-in-one computer, or a mobile case used with laptops and tablets. A tower case (see Figure 1-1) sits upright and can be as high as two feet and has room for several drives. Often used for servers, this type of case is also good for desktop computer users who anticipate upgrading, because tower cases provide maximum space for working inside a computer and moving components around. A desktop case lies flat and sometimes serves double-duty as a monitor stand. In the chapter, "Working Inside Desktop Computers and Laptops," you learn how to work inside a tower case, desktop case, laptop case, and all-in-one case.

© Courtesy of IN WIN Development, Inc.

Figure 1-1   This slimline tower case
              supports a microATX
              motherboard

📝 **Notes** Don't lay a tower case on its side when the computer is in use because the CD or DVD drive might not work properly. For the same reason, if a desktop case is designed to lie flat, don't set it on its end when the computer is in use.

Table 1-1 lists ports you might find on a desktop or mobile computer. Consider this table your introduction to these ports so that you can recognize them when you see them. Later in the text, you learn more about the details of each port.

⭐ **A+ Exam Tip** The A+ 220-901 exam expects you to know how to identify the ports shown in Table 1-1.

Port	Description
	A VGA (Video Graphics Array) port, also called a DB-15 port, DB15 port, HD15 port, or DE15 port, is a 15-pin, D-shaped, female port that transmits analog video. (Analog means a continuous signal with infinite variations as compared with digital, which is a series of binary values—1s and 0s.) All older monitors use VGA ports. (By the way, the HD15 [high-definition 15-pin] name for the port is an older name that distinguishes it from the early 9-pin VGA ports.)
	An S-Video port is a 4-pin or 7-pin round video port sometimes used to connect to a television. The 7-pin port is shown on the left. The 4-pin port is missing the extra pins in the middle and is the more common type.

Table 1-1   Ports used with desktop and mobile computers (continues)

Port	Description
	A DVI (Digital Video Interface) port transmits digital or analog video. Three types of DVI ports exist, which you learn about in the chapter, "Supporting I/O Devices."
	An HDMI (High-Definition Multimedia Interface) port transmits digital video and audio (not analog transmissions) and is often used to connect to home theater equipment.
	A DisplayPort transmits digital video and audio (not analog transmissions) and is slowly replacing VGA and DVI ports on personal computers.
Courtesy of Creative Commons Attribution 3.0, Macfan97	A Thunderbolt port transmits video, data, and power on the same port and cable and is popular with Apple computers. The port is shaped the same as the DisplayPort and is compatible with DisplayPort devices. Up to six peripherals (for example, monitors and external hard drives daisy-chained together) can use the same Thunderbolt port.
	A network port, also called an Ethernet port, or an RJ-45 port, is used by a network cable to connect to the wired network. Fast Ethernet ports run at 100 Mbps (megabits per second), and Gigabit Ethernet runs at 1000 Mbps or 1 Gbps (gigabits per second). A megabit is one million bits and a gigabit is one billion bits. A bit is a binary value of 1 or 0.
	A system usually has three or more round audio ports, also called sound ports, for a microphone, audio in, audio out, and stereo audio out. These types of audio ports can transmit analog or digital data. If you have one audio cable to connect to a speaker or earbuds, plug it into the lime green sound port in the middle of the three ports. The microphone uses the pink port.
	An S/PDIF (Sony/Philips Digital Interface) sound port connects to an external home theater audio system, providing digital audio output and the best signal quality. S/PDIF ports always carry digital audio and can work with electrical or optical cable. When connected to a fiber-optic cable, the port is called an optical connector.
	A USB (Universal Serial Bus) port is a multipurpose I/O port that comes in several sizes and is used by many different devices, including printers, mice, keyboards, scanners, external hard drives, and flash drives. Some USB ports are faster than others. Hi-Speed USB 2.0 is faster than regular USB, and Super-Speed USB 3.0 is faster than USB 2.0.
	A FireWire port (also called an IEEE 1394 port, pronounced "I-triple-E 1394 port") is used for high-speed multimedia devices such as digital camcorders.

Table 1-1   Ports used with desktop and mobile computers (continues)

Port	Description
	An external SATA (eSATA) port is used by an external hard drive or other device using the eSATA interface. eSATA is faster than FireWire.
	A PS/2 port, also called a mini-DIN port, is a round 6-pin port used by a keyboard or mouse. The ports look alike but are not interchangeable. On a desktop, the purple port is for the keyboard, and the green port is for the mouse. Many newer computers use USB ports for the keyboard and mouse rather than the older PS/2 ports.
	An older serial port, sometimes called a DB9 port, is a 9-pin male port used on older computers. It has been mostly replaced by USB ports. Occasionally, you see a serial port on a router where the port is used to connect the router to a device a technician can use to monitor and manage the router.
	A parallel port, also called an LPT port, is a 25-pin female port used by older printers. This older port has been replaced by USB ports.
	A modem port, also called an RJ-11 port, is used to connect dial-up phone lines to computers. A modem port looks like a network port, but is not as wide. In the photo, the right port is a modem port and the left port is a network port, shown for comparison.

Table 1-1   Ports used with desktop and mobile computers (continued)

I know you're eager to open a case and work inside it, but first let's get familiar with the major components in the case and how to work with them safely so you don't fry a motherboard or bend delicate connectors. Figure 1-2 shows the inside of a computer case.

Figure 1-2   Inside the computer case

Here is a quick explanation of the main components installed in the case, which are called internal components:

▲ *The motherboard, processor, and cooler.* The motherboard, also called the main board, the system board, or the techie jargon term, the mobo, is the largest and most important circuit board in the computer. The motherboard contains a socket to hold the processor or CPU. The central processing unit (CPU), also called the processor or microprocessor, does most of the processing of data and instructions for the entire system. Because the CPU generates heat, a fan and heat sink might be installed on top to keep it cool. A heat sink consists of metal fins that draw heat away from a component. The fan and heat sink together are called the processor cooler. Figure 1-3 shows the top view of a motherboard, and Figure 1-4 shows the ports on the side of a motherboard.

Regular PCI slot
Two PCIe ×1 slots
PCIe ×16 slot

Cooler with
CPU below

Four memory
modules
(DIMMs)

Chipset under
heat sink

Figure 1-3 All hardware components are either located on the motherboard or directly or indirectly connected to it because they must all communicate with the CPU

eSATA 2.0 port

Network port

DVI video port

FireWire port

Six audio ports

S/PDIF port
(for coaxial cable)

Two blue USB
3.0 ports

HDMI video port

DisplayPort
video port

Six USB
2.0 ports

Figure 1-4 Ports provided by a motherboard

▲ *Expansion cards.* A motherboard has expansion slots to be used by expansion cards. An expansion card, also called an adapter card, is a circuit board that provides more ports than those provided by the motherboard. Figure 1-5 shows a video card that provides three video ports. Notice the cooling fan and heat sink on the card, which help to keep the card from overheating. The trend today is for most ports in a system to be provided by the motherboard (called onboard ports) and less use of expansion cards.

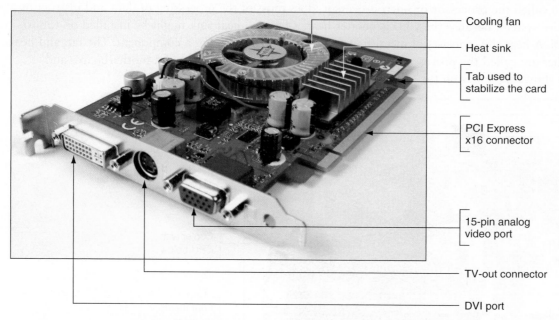

Cooling fan

Heat sink

Tab used to stabilize the card

PCI Express x16 connector

15-pin analog video port

TV-out connector

DVI port

Figure 1-5   The easiest way to identify this video card is to look at the ports on the end of the card

▲ *Memory modules.* A desktop motherboard has memory slots, called DIMM (dual inline memory module) slots, to hold memory modules. Figure 1-6 shows a memory module installed in one DIMM slot and three empty DIMM slots. Memory, also called RAM (random access memory), is temporary storage for data and instructions as they are being processed by the CPU. The memory module shown in Figure 1-6 contains several RAM chips. Video cards also contain some embedded RAM chips for video memory.

One installed DIMM

Three empty DIMM slots

Figure 1-6   A DIMM holds RAM and is mounted directly on a motherboard

▲ *Hard drives and other drives.* A system might have one or more hard drives, an optical drive, a tape drive, or, for really old systems, a floppy drive. A hard drive, also called a hard disk drive (HDD), is permanent storage used to hold data and programs. For example, the Windows 8 operating system and applications are installed on the hard drive. All drives in a system are installed in a stack of drive bays at the front of the case. The system shown in Figure 1-2 has two hard drives and one optical drive installed. These three drives are also shown in Figure 1-7. The larger hard drive is a magnetic drive, and the smaller hard drive is a solid-state drive. Each drive has two connections for cables: The power cable connects to the power supply, and another cable, used for data and instructions, connects to the motherboard.

Figure 1-7 Two types of hard drives (larger magnetic drive and smaller solid-state drive) and a DVD drive

▲ *A power supply.* A computer power supply, also known as a power supply unit (PSU), is a box installed in a corner of the computer case (see Figure 1-8) that receives and converts the house current so that components inside the case can use it. Most power supplies have a dual-voltage selector switch on the back of the computer case where you can switch the input voltage to the power supply to 115 V used in the United States or 220 V used in other countries. See Figure 1-9. The power cables can connect to and supply power to the motherboard, expansion cards, and drives.

> ✎ **Notes** If you ever need to change the dual-voltage selector switch, be sure you first turn off the computer and unplug the power supply.

Figure 1-8 Power supply with attached power cables

Dual-voltage
selector switch

Four screws hold
the power supply
in the case

Figure 1-9 The dual-voltage selector switch sets the input voltage to the power supply

FORM FACTORS USED BY DESKTOP CASES, POWER SUPPLIES, AND MOTHERBOARDS

The desktop computer case, power supply, and motherboard must all be compatible and fit together as an interconnecting system. The standards that describe the size, shape, screw hole positions, and major features of these interconnected components are called form factors. Using a matching form factor for the motherboard, power supply, and case assures you that:

◢ The motherboard fits in the case.
◢ The power supply cords to the motherboard provide the correct voltage, and the connectors match the connections on the board.
◢ The holes in the motherboard align with the holes in the case for anchoring the board to the case.
◢ The holes in the case align with ports coming off the motherboard.
◢ For some form factors, wires for switches and lights on the front of the case match up with connections on the motherboard.
◢ The holes in the power supply align with holes in the case for anchoring the power supply to the case.

The two form factors used by most desktop and tower computer cases and power supplies are the ATX and microATX form factors. Motherboards use these and other form factors that are compatible with ATX or microATX power supplies and cases. You learn about other motherboard form factors in the chapter, "All About Motherboards." Following are the important details about ATX and microATX.

ATX FORM FACTOR

ATX (Advanced Technology Extended) is the most commonly used form factor today. It is an open, nonproprietary industry specification originally developed by Intel in 1995, and has undergone several revisions since then. The original ATX form factor for cases had case fans blowing air into the case, but early revisions to the form factor had fans blowing air out of the case. Blowing air out of the case does a better job of keeping the system cool.

An ATX power supply has a variety of power connectors (see Figure 1-10). The power connectors are listed in Table 1-2 and several of them are described next.

Figure 1-10 ATX power supply with connectors

Connector	Description
	The 20-pin P1 connector is the main motherboard power connector used in the early ATX systems.
	The 24-pin P1 connector, also called the 20+4 pin connector, is the main motherboard power connector used today.

Table 1-2 Power supply connectors (continues)

Connector	Description
	The 20+4 pin P1 connector has four pins removed so the connector can fit into a 20-pin P1 motherboard connector.
	The 4-pin 12-V connector is an auxiliary motherboard connector, which is used for extra 12-V power to the processor.
	The 8-pin 12-V connector is an auxiliary motherboard connector, which is used for extra 12-V power to the processor, providing more power than the older 4-pin auxiliary connector.
	The 4-pin Molex connector is used for older IDE (PATA or Parallel ATA) drives and some newer SATA drives. It can provide +5 V and +12 V to the drive.
	The 15-pin SATA power connector is used for SATA (Serial ATA) drives. It can provide +3.3V, +5 V, and +12 V, although +3.3 V is seldom used.
	The 4-pin Berg connector is used by older floppy disk drives (FDD).
	The PCIe 6-pin connector provides an extra +12 V for high-end video cards using PCI Express, Version 1 standard.
	The PCIe 8-pin connector provides an extra +12 V for high-end video cards using PCI Express, Version 2.
	The PCIe 6/8-pin connector is used by high-end video cards using PCIe x16 slots to provide extra voltage to the card and can accommodate a 6-hole or 8-hole port. To get the 8-pin connector, combine both the 6-pin and 2-pin connectors.

Table 1-2 Power supply connectors (continued)

⭐ **A+ Exam Tip** The A+ 220-901 exam expects you to know about each connector listed in Table 1-2.

Power connectors have evolved because components using new technologies require more power. As you read about the following types of power connectors and why each came to be, you'll also learn about the evolving expansion slots and expansion cards that drove the need for more power:

◢ *20-pin P1 connector.* The first ATX power supplies and motherboards used a single 20-pin P1 power connector that provided +3.3 volts, +5 volts, +12 volts, −12 volts, and an optional and rarely used −5 volts. See Figure 1-11. This 20-pin power connector was sufficient for powering expansion cards installed in PCI (Peripheral Component Interconnect) expansion slots on the motherboard (see Figure 1-12). Several versions of PCI slots evolved over time, which you learn about in the chapter, "All About Motherboards."

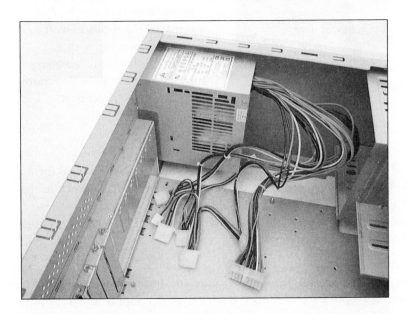

Figure 1-11   The first ATX P1 power connector used 20 pins

Pins on edge connector of expansion card

PCI slot

Bus lines

Figure 1-12   A PCI expansion card about to be installed in a PCI slot

Figure 1-13 The 4-pin 12-volt auxiliary power connector on a motherboard with power cord connected

▲ *4-pin and 8-pin auxiliary connectors.* When processors began to require more power, the ATX Version 2.1 specifications added a 4-pin auxiliary connector near the processor socket to provide an additional 12 V of power (see Figure 1-13). A power supply that provides this 4-pin 12-volt power cord is called an ATX12V power supply. Later boards replaced the 4-pin 12-volt power connector with an 8-pin motherboard auxiliary connector that provided more amps for the processor.

▲ *24-pin or 20+4-pin P1 connector.* Later, when faster PCI Express (PCIe) slots were added to motherboards, more power was required and a new ATX specification (ATX Version 2.2) allowed for a 24-pin P1 connector, also called the 20+4 power connector. The 20-pin power cable will still work in the new 24-pin connector. Looking back at Figure 1-3, you can see one long blue PCIe ×16 slot (16 lanes for 16-bit transfers on this slot) that can be used by a video card and two short black PCIe ×1 slots (for 1-bit transfers) that can be used for other expansion cards that fit this type slot.

The extra 4 pins on the 24-pin P1 connector provide +12 volts, +5 volts, and +3.3 volts pins. Motherboards that support PCI Express and have the 24-pin P1 connector are sometimes called Enhanced ATX boards. Figure 1-14 shows a 20-pin P1 power cord from the power supply and a 24-pin P1 connector on a motherboard. Figure 1-15 shows the pinouts for the 24-pin power cord connector, which is color-coded to wires from the power supply. The 20-pin connector is missing the lower four pins, which are listed in the photo and diagram.

Figure 1-14 A 20-pin power cord ready to be plugged into a 24-pin P1 connector on an ATX motherboard

Figure 1-15   P1 24-pin power connector follows ATX Version 2.2 and higher standards

Figure 1-16 shows a PCIe ×16 video card. The edge connector has a break that fits the break in the slot. The tab at the end of the edge connector fits into a retention mechanism at the end of the slot, which helps to stabilize a heavy video card.

PCIe 6-pin power connector on the end of the video card

Edge connector

Figure 1-16   This PCIe ×16 video card has a 6-pin PCIe power connector to receive extra power from the power supply

▲ *6-pin and 8-pin PCIe connectors.* Video cards draw the most power in a system, and ATX Version 2.2 provides for power cables to connect directly to a video card to provide it additional power than comes through the PCIe slot on the motherboard. The PCIe power connector might have 6 or 8 pins. PCI Express, Version 1, defined the 6-pin connector, and PCI Express, Version 2, defined the 8-pin connector. The video card shown in Figure 1-16 has a 6-pin connector on the end of the card. A PCIe 6/8-pin connector can also be located on the motherboard to supply extra power for the video card.

> ✎ **Notes** For more information about all the form factors discussed in this chapter, check out the form factor website sponsored by Intel at *www.formfactors.org*.

MICROATX FORM FACTOR

The microATX (MATX) form factor is a major variation of ATX and addresses some technologies that have emerged since the original development of ATX. MicroATX reduces the total cost of a system by reducing the number of expansion slots on the motherboard, reducing the power supplied to the board, and allowing for a smaller case size. A microATX motherboard (see Figure 1-17) will fit into a case that follows the ATX 2.1 or higher standard. A microATX power supply uses a 24-pin P1 connector and is not likely to have as many extra wires and connectors as those on an ATX power supply.

Figure 1-17   This microATX motherboard by Biostar is designed to support an AMD processor

> ★ **A+ Exam Tip** The A+ 220-901 exam expects you to recognize and know the more important features of the ATX and microATX form factors used by power supplies.

Hands-On | Project 1-1   Identify Ports and Parts

A+
220-901
1.7, 1.8,
1.11

Do the following to identify computer ports and parts that your instructor might have on display:

1. Look on the front and back of your computer case and list the type of ports the computer offers.

2. For a power supply, list the number and type of power connectors.

3. For a motherboard, list the number and type of expansion slots on the board. Does the board have a 20-pin or 24-pin P1 connector? What other power connectors are on the board? How many memory slots does the board have?

4. For expansion cards, examine the ports on the back of the card. Can you tell by the ports the purpose of the card? What type of slot does the card use?

1

> ⚡ **Caution** You can damage a computer component with static electricity if you touch the component when you are not grounded. Before you touch a sensitive computer component, you first need to dissipate any static electricity on your body. You learn how to do that in the appendix, "Safety Procedures and Environmental Concerns." For now, to protect a working component your instructor has on display, don't touch; just look.

Hands-On | Project 1-2   Examine the Power Supply, Motherboard, and Expansion Cards Inside a Desktop Case

A+
220-901
1.7, 1.8,
1.11

If you have access to a desktop computer with the case cover removed, examine its components and answer the following questions. As you look, remember to not touch anything inside the case unless you are properly grounded.

1. Identify the power supply, motherboard, and any expansion cards that might be installed on the motherboard. Remember: Don't touch a component unless you are properly grounded. If the case is plugged into a power source, don't touch inside the case even if you are grounded.

2. Identify the cooler that is installed on top of the processor. This cooler is likely to have a fan on top and a heat sink that you can't see. The processor is hidden under the cooler.

3. Identify the memory modules and memory slots. How many memory slots are there? How many of these slots are populated?

4. If an expansion card is installed, what type of ports does the card provide at the rear of the case? Find the one screw that is used to attach the expansion card to the case.

5. Locate the screws that are attaching the motherboard to the case. How many screws are used? Do you see screw holes in the motherboard that are not being used? As a general rule of thumb, up to nine screws can be used to attach a motherboard to a case.

6. How many power cables are coming from the power supply? How many of these cables are connected to the motherboard? To other devices inside the computer? Identify each type of power cable the system is using.

7. Find the screws or clips that are attaching the power supply to the case. Is the power supply attached using screws, clips, or both screws and clips?

Now let's learn about the drives you might find installed inside a system.

DRIVES, THEIR CABLES, AND CONNECTORS

A+
220-901
1.7, 1.8,
1.11

A computer might have one or more hard drives, an optical drive (CD, DVD, or Blu-ray), tape drive, or some other type of drive. A drive receives power by a power cable from the power supply, and communicates instructions and data through a cable attached to the motherboard. Most hard drives, optical drives, and tape drives today use the serial ATA (SATA) standard.

> ✎ **Notes** If you support older desktop computers, you might see some drives using the slower and older PATA (parallel ATA) standard, also called the IDE (Integrated Drive Electronics) or EIDE (Enhanced IDE) standard, for drive connections. PATA used a 40-pin connector on the motherboard and a wide ribbon cable that could accommodate one or two drives on the cable. Figure 1-18 shows two PATA ribbon cables, each connecting a drive to the motherboard.

Two 40-pin IDE cables

Connection for a second device on each cable

Hard drive

CD-ROM drive

Figure 1-18   Two PATA devices connected to a motherboard using both PATA or IDE connections and two cables

SATA and PATA standards are published by the American National Standards Institute (ANSI, see *www.ansi.org*). Figure 1-19 shows a SATA cable connecting a hard drive and motherboard. SATA cables can only connect to a SATA connector on the motherboard in one direction (see Figure 1-20). SATA drives get their power from a power cable that connects to the drive using a SATA power connector (refer back to the photo in Table 1-2).

Serial ATA cable

Power cord

Figure 1-19   A hard drive subsystem using the SATA data cable

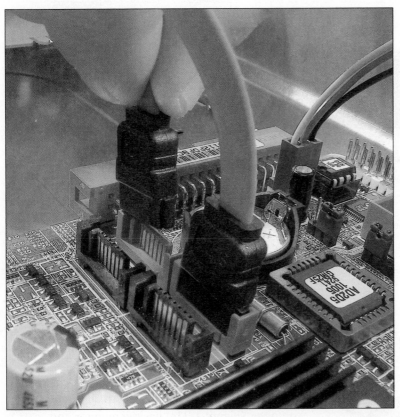

Figure 1-20 A SATA cable connects to a SATA connector in only one direction; use red connectors on the motherboard first

Hands-On | Project 1-3 Identify Drives and Their Connectors

A+ 220-901 1.7, 1.8, 1.11

If your instructor has provided a display of drives, for each drive identify the purpose of the drive (for example, a hard drive or optical drive) and the type of power connector the drive uses (for example, SATA or Molex). If you have access to a computer with the case cover removed, answer the following questions:

1. List the drives installed, the purpose of each drive, and the type of interface and power connector it uses.

2. How many connectors does the motherboard have for drives? Identify each type of connector (SATA or PATA).

Now that you know about what's inside a desktop computer case, let's take a look at laptop computers.

FIRST LOOK AT LAPTOP COMPONENTS

A+ 220-901 3.1, 3.3, 3.4, 3.5

A laptop, also called a notebook, is designed for portability (see Figure 1-21a and 1-21b) and can be just as powerful as a desktop computer. More than half of personal computers purchased today are laptops, and almost 30 percent of personal computers currently in use are laptops. Laptops use the same technology as desktops, but with modifications to use less power, take up less space, and operate on the move.

(A)   (B)   (C)

Figure 1-21   A laptop, netbook, and all-in-one computer

©iStockphoto.com/Rasslava

Figure 1-22   A laptop with a rotating display can do
double-duty as a tablet computer

Laptops come in several varieties, including some with a touch screen that also allows you to handwrite on it with a stylus and some with a rotating screen or removable screen that allows you to use the laptop as a tablet (see Figure 1-22). Another variation of a laptop is a netbook (Figure 1-21b) that is smaller and less expensive than a laptop and has fewer features. An all-in-one computer (Figure 1-21c) has the monitor and computer case built together and uses components that are common to both a laptop and desktop.

Because all-in-one computers use many laptop components and are serviced in similar ways, we include them in this chapter.

A laptop provides ports on its sides, back, or front for connecting peripherals (see Figure 1-23). Ports common to laptops as well as desktop systems include USB, FireWire, network, dial-up modem (seldom seen on newer laptops), and audio ports (for a microphone, headset, or external speakers). Video ports might include one or more VGA, DisplayPort, Thunderbolt (on Apple laptops), or HDMI ports to connect to a projector, second monitor, or television. On the side or back of the laptop, you'll see a lock connector that's used to physically secure the laptop with a cable lock (see Figure 1-24) and a DC jack to receive power from the AC adapter. Also, a laptop may have an optical drive, but netbooks usually don't have optical drives.

MagicGate slot
SD card slot
Ethernet port
VGA port

DC jack
USB 2.0 port
Two USB 3.0 ports
HDMI port

Optical drive

Speaker port
Microphone port
Cable lock

Figure 1-23   Ports and slots on a laptop computer

Source: Kensington Technology Group

Figure 1-24   Use a cable lock system to secure a notebook computer to a desk to help prevent it from being stolen

Notice the two slots in Figure 1-23 used for flash memory cards: a MagicGate slot and an SD card slot. Each can support several types of flash memory cards that you learn about later in the text.

When a laptop is missing a port or slot you need, you can usually find a USB dongle to provide the port or slot. Here are some options:

▲ *Connect to a local wired network.* Figure 1-25 shows a USB to RJ-45 dongle. Plug the dongle into a USB port and plug a network cable into the RJ-45 port the dongle provides to connect the laptop to a wired network.

▲ *Connect to a local wireless network.* Figure 1-26 shows a USB to Wi-Fi dongle, which allows you to connect a laptop that doesn't have wireless capability to a wireless network. Wi-Fi (Wireless Fidelity) is the common name for standards for a local wireless network.

Figure 1-25 USB to RJ-45 dongle provides a network port to connect to a wired network

Figure 1-26 This USB to Wi-Fi adapter plugs into a USB port to connect to a local wireless network

▲ *Connect to a cellular network.* Some laptops have embedded capability to connect to a cellular network. Figure 1-27 shows a USB cellular modem that can be used for a laptop that doesn't have the embedded technology. A cellular network consists of geographic areas of coverage called cells, each controlled by a tower, called a base station. Cell phones are called that because they use a cellular network.

LED light indicates power

LED light indicates network activity

Figure 1-27 This USB device by Sierra Wireless provides a wireless connection to a cellular network

▲ *Connect to a Bluetooth device.* When a laptop doesn't have Bluetooth capability, you can use a USB to Bluetooth adapter to connect to a Bluetooth wireless device such as a Bluetooth printer or smart phone. Bluetooth is a short-range wireless technology to connect two devices in a small personal network.

▲ *Use an external optical drive.* When a laptop or netbook doesn't have an optical drive, you can use a USB optical drive. Plug the USB optical drive into a USB port so that you can use CDs and DVDs with the laptop or netbook.

SPECIAL KEYS, BUTTONS, AND INPUT DEVICES ON A LAPTOP

A+
220-901
3.1, 3.3,
3.4, 3.5

Buttons or switches might be found above the keyboard, and the top row of keys contains the function keys. To use a function key, hold down the Fn key as you press the function key. Here are the purposes of a few keys and buttons. Some of them change Windows settings. Know that these same settings can also be changed using Windows tools:

◢ *Volume setting.* You can set the volume using the volume icon in the Windows taskbar. In addition, some laptops offer buttons or function keys to control the volume (see Figure 1-28).

Figure 1-28 On this laptop, use the Fn and the F2, F3, or F4 key to control volume; use the Fn key and the F5 or F6 key to control screen brightness; and use the Fn key and the F7 key to manage dual displays

Figure 1-29 The touch pad is the most common pointing device on a notebook

◢ *Keyboard backlight.* Function keys can be used to control the keyboard backlight to light up the keyboard.

◢ *Touch pad on or off.* Other function keys can turn on or off the touch pad, which is the most common pointing device on a laptop (see Figure 1-29). Some people prefer to use a USB wired or wireless mouse instead of a touch pad.

◢ *Screen brightness and screen orientation.* Function keys can control the screen brightness on many laptops. Screen brightness can also be controlled in Windows display settings. Some laptops allow you to use a function key to change the screen orientation to landscape or portrait so you can use the laptop turned on its end.

◢ *Dual displays.* Most laptops use a function key to control dual displays. For example, for one laptop, the combination of the Fn key and the F7 key (refer back to Figure 1-28) displays the box shown in Figure 1-30. Use arrow keys to use only the LCD panel, duplicate or extend output to the external monitor, or use only the external monitor. Dual displays can also be managed using Windows display settings.

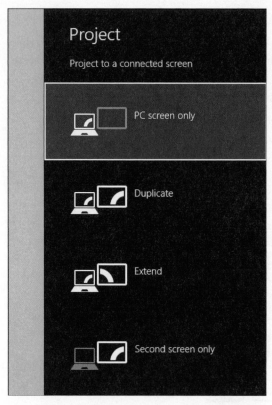

Figure 1-30   Control dual monitors on a Windows 8 laptop

▲ *Bluetooth, Wi-Fi, or cellular on or off.* Some laptops use function keys such as Fn with F5 or F6 to toggle Bluetooth, Wi-Fi, or cellular on or off, or a laptop might have a switch for this purpose. You can also control these wireless technologies using Windows settings or software utilities provided by the manufacturer. When you turn off all wireless technologies, the computer is said to be in airplane mode.

▲ *Media options.* Some laptops provide buttons or allow you to use function keys to fast forward, stop, pause, or rewind audio or video media playing in an optical drive.

▲ *GPS on or off.* If a laptop has a GPS (Global Positioning System) receiver to calculate its position on the Earth, the laptop might provide a button or function key to turn the GPS on or off. The Global Positioning System is a system of 24 or more satellites orbiting the Earth, and a GPS receiver can locate three or more of these satellites at any time and from these three locations, calculate its own position in a process called trilateration.

✎ Notes If the keyboard fails and you're not able to immediately exchange it, know that you can plug in an external keyboard to a USB port to use in the meantime.

And now onward to ExpressCard slots and docking stations.

EXPRESSCARD SLOTS

A+
220-901
3.1, 3.3,
3.4, 3.5

Most peripheral devices on today's laptops use a USB port to connect to the laptop. Before USB devices became so popular, a laptop offered ExpressCard slots to connect peripheral devices. See Figure 1-31. These slot and card standards were designed and supported by the PCMCIA (Personal Computer Memory Card International Association) and are sometimes called PCMCIA cards. The cards were used by many devices, including modems, network cards for wired or wireless networks, sound cards, FireWire (IEEE 1394) controllers, USB controllers, flash memory adapters, TV tuners, and hard disks. Most new laptops don't have these slots, but you still need to know how to support them because you'll see them on older laptops.

1

Figure 1-31 ExpressCard/54 slot has an eject button on the left side of the slot

★ **A+ Exam Tip** The A+ 220-901 exam expects you to know how to install and configure ExpressCard/34 and ExpressCard/54 cards and slots.

ExpressCard uses the PCI Express bus standard or the USB 2.0 standard. Two sizes of ExpressCards exist: ExpressCard/34 is 34mm wide and ExpressCard/54 is 54mm wide, as shown in Figure 1-32. Notice the offset in the ExpressCard/54 card. An ExpressCard/34 card can fit into an ExpressCard/54 slot, but not vice versa. An ExpressCard slot is fully hot-pluggable (you can add a card while the system is on), hot-swappable (exchange or add a card while the system is on), and supports autoconfiguration. An ExpressCard/54 card that provides two eSATA ports for external SATA drives is shown in Figure 1-33.

Figure 1-32 Dimensions of ExpressCard cards

Source: SIIG, Inc.

Figure 1-33 This ExpressCard/54 card supports two eSATA drives

Windows must provide two services for an ExpressCard: a socket service and a card service. The socket service establishes communication between the card and the laptop when the card is first inserted. The card service provides the device driver to interface with the card after the socket is created.

The first time you insert an ExpressCard in a laptop, Windows automatically guides you through the installation steps in which you can use the drivers provided by the hardware manufacturer or use Windows drivers. The next time you insert the card in the laptop, the card is detected and starts without help.

ExpressCards can be hot-swapped (inserted or removed while the system is on), but you must stop one card before inserting another. To stop the card, use the Safely Remove Hardware icon in the notification area of the Windows taskbar.

After you have stopped the card, push on the card, which causes it to pop out of the slot. Some ExpressCard slots have an eject button to pop out the card. Then you can remove the card.

> **⚡ Caution**   Inserting an ExpressCard while the laptop is shutting down or booting up can cause damage to the card and/or to the laptop. Also, a card might give problems when you insert or remove the card while the laptop is in hibernation or sleep mode.

DOCKING STATIONS

A+
220-901
3.1, 3.3,
3.4, 3.5

Some notebooks have a connector, called a docking port, on the bottom or sides of the laptop (see Figure 1-34) to connect to a docking station. A docking station provides ports to allow a laptop to easily connect to a full-sized monitor, keyboard, AC power adapter, and other peripheral devices. See Figure 1-35. Laptop manufacturers usually offer a docking station as an additional option.

Figure 1-34   The docking port and sheet battery connector on the bottom of a laptop

To use a docking station, plug all the peripherals into the docking station. Then connect your laptop to the station. No software needs installing. When you need to travel with your laptop, rather than having to unplug all the peripherals, all you have to do is disconnect the laptop from the docking station.

Courtesy of Lenovo

Figure 1-35   Docking station for a Lenovo ThinkPad

LAPTOP INTERNAL COMPONENTS

A+
220-901
3.1, 3.3,
3.4, 3.5

Figure 1-36 shows the inside of a laptop case after the cover on the bottom of the laptop has been removed. Here is a list of important components, most of which you can see in the photo:

Labels (top to bottom, right side):
- Screw to secure the optical drive installed to the left
- CPU fan
- Heat sink covering CPU underneath
- CPU partly showing
- Two installed SO-DIMMs
- Hard drive
- Wireless card
- Blue system board

Figure 1-36 Bottom of a laptop with cover removed

- ▲ *Battery pack.* The battery pack is not shown because you always remove the battery first before opening a laptop case.
- ▲ *Hard drive.* The 2.5-inch hard drive is secured in its bay with two screws. When you remove the screws, you can use the plastic tab to lift the drive from its bay.

Figure 1-37 A DIMM used in desktops compared with a SO-DIMM used in laptop computers

- ▲ *CPU, heat sink, and fan.* The CPU is hidden under the heat sink, which is labeled in the figure. The heat sink draws heat from the CPU and pipes it to the fan, also labeled in the figure. The fan blows the heat out of the laptop case.
- ▲ *Memory.* Laptops use smaller memory modules than the DIMMs used in desktop computers. In the figure, you can see two SO-DIMMs (small outline DIMMs) installed. Figure 1-37 shows a DIMM and a SO-DIMM for size comparison.

◢ *Wireless card*. The wireless card is installed to the left of the hard drive in Figure 1-36. You can see two wires leading to the wireless antennas, which are installed in the laptop lid.

◢ *System board*. Look for the blue system board (in laptop documentation, the motherboard is usually called the system board) under the heat sink, memory, and fan. If you look carefully, you can see microchips and other components on the board.

◢ *Optical drive*. The optical drive is not visible in the photo. To replace it, you first remove a single screw holding the drive in place and then slide the drive to the left and out of the case. This one screw is labeled in Figure 1-36.

Other hardware components you are likely to find in a laptop case include a small speaker and smart card reader and writer. In the chapter, "Working Inside Desktop Computers and Laptops," you learn how to disassemble and reassemble a laptop.

WHAT'S INSIDE AN ALL-IN-ONE COMPUTER

**A+
220-901
3.1, 3.3,
3.4, 3.5**

An all-in-one computer uses a mix of components sized for a desktop computer and a laptop. Let's get the general idea of what's inside the case of an all-in-one by looking at the inside of the Lenovo ThinkCentre all-in-one shown earlier in Figure 1-21. Figure 1-38 shows the computer with the case cover removed. Notice in the figure the hard drive is a 3.5-inch drive appropriate for a desktop system, and the memory modules are SO-DIMMs appropriate for a laptop. So goes the hybrid nature of an all-in-one. The fan and heat sink look more like that of a laptop computer, but the processor socket on the motherboard is a desktop processor socket, another hybrid design.

Figure 1-38   Components inside an all-in-one computer

Several components are easy to exchange in this all-in-one without further disassembly. For example, the Mini PCIe card for wireless connectivity, shown in Figure 1-39, is easy to get to, as are the SO-DIMMs you can partly see on the right side of the photo.

Figure 1-39 CMOS battery and Mini PCIe wireless card

To work inside an all-in-one, you'll need the service manual to know how to open the case and replace internal components. Also, for some components, such as the motherboard and power supply, you'll need to buy the replacement component from the all-in-one manufacturer because these components are likely to be proprietary as with many laptop components. For specific directions about replacing parts in an all-in-one, see the service manual.

MAINTAINING LAPTOPS AND MOBILE DEVICES

A+
220-901
3.1, 3.3,
3.4, 3.5

Laptops and mobile devices tend to not last as long as desktop computers because they are portable and, therefore, subject to more wear and tear. A device's user manual gives specific instructions on how to care for the device. Those instructions follow these general guidelines:

◢ LCD panels on devices are fragile and can be damaged fairly easily. Take precautions against damaging a laptop or other device's LCD panel. Don't touch it with sharp objects like ballpoint pens.

◢ Don't pick up or hold a laptop by the lid. Pick it up and hold it by the bottom. Keep the lid closed when the laptop is not in use.

◢ Only use battery packs and AC adapters recommended by the laptop manufacturer. Keep the battery pack away from moisture or heat, and don't attempt to take the pack apart. When it no longer works, dispose of it correctly. For laptops, you might consider buying an extra battery pack to use when the first one discharges. You can also buy battery chargers so that you can charge one while the other is in use.

◢ Don't tightly pack a laptop or tablet in a suitcase because the LCD panel might get damaged. Use a good-quality carrying case and make a habit of always transporting the laptop in the carrying case. Don't place heavy objects on top of the laptop case.

◢ Don't move the laptop while the hard drive is being accessed (when the drive indicator light is on). Wait until the light goes off.

◢ Don't put the laptop close to an appliance such as a TV, large audio speakers, or refrigerator that generates a strong magnetic field, and don't place your cell phone on a laptop while the phone is in use.

◢ Always use passwords to protect access to your laptop or mobile device so you are better protected when connected to a public network or the device is stolen or used by an unauthorized person.

◢ Keep your laptop or device at room temperature. For example, never leave it in a car overnight when it is cold, and don't leave it in a car during the day when it's hot. Don't expose your laptop or device to direct sunlight for an extended time.

◢ Don't leave the laptop or device in a dusty or smoke-filled area. Don't use it in a wet area such as near a swimming pool or in the bathtub. Don't use it at the beach where sand can get in it.

◢ Don't power it up and down unnecessarily.

◢ Protect the laptop from overheating by not running it when it's still inside the case, resting on a pillow, or partially covered with a blanket or anything else that would prevent proper air circulation around it.

◢ If a laptop has just come indoors from the cold, don't turn it on until it reaches room temperature. In some cases, condensation can cause problems. Some manufacturers recommend that when you receive a new laptop shipped to you during the winter, you should leave it in its shipping carton for several hours before you open the carton to prevent subjecting the laptop to a temperature shock.

◢ Protect a laptop against static electricity. If you have just come in from the cold on a low-humidity day when there is the possibility that you are carrying static electricity, don't touch the laptop until you have grounded yourself.

◢ Before placing a laptop in a carrying case for travel, remove any CDs, DVDs, or USB flash drives, and put them in protective covers. Verify that the system is powered down and not in sleep mode, which will drain the battery.

◢ If a laptop gets wet, you can partially disassemble it to allow internal components to dry. Give the laptop several days to dry before attempting to turn it on. Don't use heat to speed up the drying time.

◢ Keep current backups of important data on a laptop or device in case it fails or is stolen.

A well-used laptop, especially one that is used in dusty or dirty areas, needs cleaning occasionally. Here are some cleaning tips:

1. Clean the LCD panel with a soft dry cloth. If the panel is very dirty, you can use monitor wipes to clean it or dampen the cloth with water. Some manufacturers recommend using a mixture of isopropyl alcohol and water to clean an LCD panel. Be sure the LCD panel is dry before you close the lid.

2. Use a can of compressed air meant to be used on computer equipment to blow dust and small particles out of the keyboard, trackball, and touch pad. Turn the laptop at an angle and direct the air into the sides of the keyboard. Then use a soft, damp cloth to clean the key caps and touch pad.

3. Use compressed air to blow out all air vents on the laptop to make sure they are clean and unobstructed.

4. If keys are sticking, remove the keyboard so you can better spray under the keys with compressed air. If you can remove the key cap, remove it and clean the key contact area with contact cleaner. One example of a contact cleaner you can use for this purpose is Stabilant 22 (*www.stabilant.com*). Reinstall the keyboard and test it. If the key still sticks, replace the keyboard.

5. Remove the battery and clean the battery connections with a contact cleaner.

Hands-On | Project 1-4 Observe Laptop Features

Examine a laptop, its documentation, and the manufacturer's website, and then answer these questions:

1. What ports are on the laptop?

2. Does the laptop have an ExpressCard slot? If so, which type of ExpressCard slot does the laptop have?

3. What type of memory slots does the laptop have?

4. List the purpose of each function key on the keyboard.

5. List the purpose of each button on the top or bottom of the keyboard.

6. What is the cost of a new battery pack?

Now that you know about some of the parts and components in desktops, laptops, and all-in-ones, let's turn our attention to the components found in a few other mobile devices, including tablets, smart phones, phablets, and wearable technology devices.

FIRST LOOK AT MOBILE DEVICE HARDWARE

A+
220-901
3.1, 3.3,
3.4, 3.5

Here's a list of the mobile devices that you, as an IT support technician, might be called on to support:

▲ *Smart phone.* A smart phone is primarily a cell phone that also includes abilities to send text messages with photos, videos, or other multimedia content attached; surf the web; manage email; play games; take photos and videos; and download and use small apps. Most smart phones use touch screens for input (see Figure 1-40) and a few have a physical keyboard and a touch screen. Some smart phones allow for voice input.

©iStockphoto.com/Hocus-focus

Figure 1-40 Most smart phones don't have a keyboard and use a touch screen for input

▲ *Tablets and phablets.* A tablet is a computing device with a touch screen that is larger than a smart phone and has functions similar to a smart phone. Most tablets can connect to Wi-Fi networks and use Bluetooth or NFC (Near Field Communication) to wirelessly connect to nearby devices. Some tablets have the ability to use a cellular network for data transmissions and phone calls. Installed apps, such as Skype, can make voice phone calls, send text, and make video calls. When you can use your tablet to make a phone call, the distinction between a smart phone and a tablet is almost nonexistent, except for size.

A phablet bridges this size exception. A phablet (pronounced "*fab*-let") has the same capabilities of a smart phone or tablet, but is smaller than a tablet and larger than a smart phone.

▲ *E-readers.* An e-reader is a mobile device that holds digital versions of books, newspapers, magazines, and other printed documents, which are usually downloaded to the device from the web. An e-reader can connect to the Internet using a Wi-Fi wireless connection or a wired connection to a computer that is connected to the Internet. In addition, content can be stored on a flash memory card, which is inserted in the e-reader.

▲ *Smart cameras.* A smart camera is a digital camera that has embedded computing power to make decisions about the content of the photos or videos it records, including transmitting alerts over a wired or wireless network when it records certain content. Smart cameras, sometimes called vision sensors, can be used to initiate alerts for surveillance of a protected area or to monitor manufacturer automated assembly lines for potential problems.

▲ *Wearable technology devices.* Wearable technology devices, including smart watches (see Figure 1-41), wristbands, arm bands, eyeglasses, headsets, and clothing, can be used as computing devices to make

phone calls, send text messages, transmit data, and check email; wearable technology fitness monitors can measure heart rate, count pool laps or miles jogged or biked, and a host of other activities. These devices can sync up with a computer for power and communication, similar to how other mobile devices work. Many people believe smart watches will eventually replace smart phones as the personal communication device of choice.

©iStockphoto.com/Mutlu Kurtbas

Figure 1-41   The app screen on a smart watch by Apple, Inc.

CONNECTION TYPES

A+
220-901
3.1, 3.3,
3.4, 3.5

Here are some ways a mobile device can connect to the outside world:

▲ *Wi-Fi local wireless network and cellular network.* Most mobile devices have Wi-Fi capability and can connect to a Wi-Fi local wireless network. In addition, smart phones and some laptops, tablets, phablets, and wearable mobile devices can connect to a cellular network. To connect to a cellular network, the device must have cellular capability and a subscription to the cellular network carrier, for example, AT&T or Verizon. Two types of technologies are used to connect to cellular networks: GSM (Global System for Mobile Communication) and CDMA (Code Division Multiple Access). With GSM networks, information about your subscription is kept on a small SIM (Subscriber Identity Module) card inserted in the device. Figure 1-42 shows the slot on the side of an Apple iPad where you can insert a SIM card so that the iPad can connect to the cellular network.

Figure 1-42   A SIM card is required for a mobile device to use most cellular networks

▲ *Bluetooth and Infrared.* Mobile devices might have the capability to connect to other nearby wireless devices using a Bluetooth, IR, or NFC connection. Figure 1-43 shows an iPad connected to a keyboard using Bluetooth. Infrared (IR) is a wireless connection that requires an unobstructed "line of sight" between transmitter and receiver. Smart phones and other mobile devices sometimes offer an IR interface that can be used with an app to control a television in place of its remote control.

▲ *NFC.* Near Field Communication (NFC) is a wireless technology that establishes a communication link between two NFC devices that are within 4 inches of each other. For example, when you tap your smart phone with that of your friend, the two phones can use NFC to exchange contact information. NFC can also be used to read an NFC tag, which is a small microchip that can be embedded in just about anything, including a key chain tag, printed flyer, or billboard (see Figure 1-44). The NFC tag dispenses information to any NFC-enabled smart phone or other device that comes within 4 inches of the tag.

Figure 1-43 An iPad and a wireless keyboard can connect using Bluetooth

Figure 1-44 These programmable NFC tags have sticky backs for attaching to a flat surface like a wall, desk, or car dashboard

▲ *Wired connection.* Smart phones, tablets, phablets, and wearable devices can make a wired connection to a computer. This connection can be used to charge the device, download software updates, upload data to the computer, back up data, and restore software or data. The device's port used for power and communication may be a type of USB port or a proprietary vendor-specific port. Some USB connectors used for this purpose include microUSB (see Figure 1-45a) or the smaller miniUSB (see Figure 1-45b). Newer Apple iPhones, iPods, and iPads use the proprietary Lightning port and connector for power and communication (see Figure 1-46).

(A)   (B)

Figure 1-45 Some mobile devices may connect using a (a) microUSB or (b) miniUSB port

Figure 1-46   A Lightning cable by Apple, Inc., has a USB connector for the computer end and a Lightning connector for an iPhone or iPad

◢ **Tethering and mobile hotspots.** When a mobile device is connected to the Internet by way of its cellular network, you can allow other computers and devices to use this same connection. For example, in Figure 1-47, the smart phone is tethered by USB to a laptop so that the laptop can use the cellular

Figure 1-47   Tether your smart phone to your laptop using a USB cable

Figure 1-48   A gyroscope uses gravity to sense its relative position to the Earth

network to connect to the Internet. If the smart phone has Wi-Fi capabilities, the smart phone can create its own Wi-Fi hotspot for other computers and devices to connect to wirelessly. An app on the smart phone controls these connections, and your carrier subscription must allow for tethering and for providing mobile hotspots.

A mobile device can use an accelerometer and GPS receiver to sense its position. Here are brief details about each:

◢ **Accelerometer.** A gyroscope is a device that contains a disc that is free to move and can respond to gravity as the device is moved (see Figure 1-48). Three axes in the device sense how the disc moves and, therefore, can tell the direction of motion. An accelerometer is a type of gyroscope used in mobile devices to sense the physical position of the device. The accelerometer is used by the OS and apps to adjust the screen orientation from portrait to landscape as the user rotates the device. Apps such as a Compass, Carpenter's Leveler, and some game apps use the accelerometer to sense how the user is moving the device.

▲ *GPS receiver.* Mobile devices might contain a GPS receiver to determine its position by using the GPS satellite data or data from the position of nearby cellular towers. A cellular-enabled device with a GPS receiver is likely to use both types of data to find its position. A mobile device routinely reports its position to the owner of its operating system. For example, a device may report its position to Apple (for devices that use the iOS operating system by Apple, Inc.), Google (for devices that use the Android operating system by Google), or Microsoft (for devices that use the Windows Phone operating system by Microsoft) at least twice a day, and usually more often, which makes it possible for these companies to track your device's whereabouts, which is called geotracking. Law enforcement agencies sometimes use this data to reconstruct a person's travels.

STORAGE DEVICES

A+
220-901
3.1, 3.3,
3.4, 3.5

Mobile devices store their apps and data on a solid-state device (SSD), a type of flash memory. In addition, a device might have an external slot where you can plug in a smart card such as an SD card or MicroSD card to provide extra storage. Figure 1-49 shows a memory card slot on an Android tablet, and Figure 1-50 shows a MicroSD card. The iPhone, iPad, and iPod don't have these external slots for a smart card.

Figure 1-49   An Android device might provide a memory card slot to allow for extra storage

Figure 1-50   A mobile device might use a MicroSD card to add extra flash memory storage to the device

An Android or Microsoft device might also have a USB port that you can use to plug in a USB flash drive to provide extra storage or transfer files and folders to other devices. Apple mobile devices don't have USB ports.

MOBILE DEVICE ACCESSORIES

A+
220-901
3.1, 3.3,
3.4, 3.5

You can buy all kinds of accessories for mobile devices, such as wireless keyboards, speakers, earbuds, headsets, game pads, docking stations, printers, extra batteries, USB adapters, chargers, credit card readers for accepting payments by credit card, and protective covers for waterproofing. For example, Figure 1-51 shows a car docking station for a smart phone. Using this car dock, the smart phone is a GPS device giving driving directions.

Figure 1-51   A smart phone and a car docking station

FIELD-REPLACEABLE PARTS FOR MOBILE DEVICES

For the purposes of IT support technicians supporting mobile devices, know there are few field-replaceable units (FRU) in mobile devices because the cost of replacement, including parts and labor, generally exceeds the value of fixing rather than replacing the device. Although it is possible to replace the screens in some mobile devices, a support technician is not generally expected to take the time to do so. SIM cards and batteries can be replaced, and accessories such as a battery charger or earbuds can be attached.

Hands-On│Project 1-5   Explore www.ifixit.com

Replacing the battery in a smart phone or tablet is a handy skill for an IT support technician to have. If you have a smart phone or tablet or know a friend who has one, find out the brand and model of the device. Search the *www.ifixit.com* website, which is a wiki-based site with tons of guides for tearing down, repairing, and reassembling all kinds of products, including smart phones, tablets, and laptops. Does the site offer a guide for replacing the battery in your device or your friend's device? If so, list the high-level steps for the repair. What tools would you need to actually make the repair?

TOOLS USED BY A COMPUTER HARDWARE TECHNICIAN

Every IT support technician who plans to repair desktop or laptop computers or mobile devices needs a handy toolbox with a few essential tools. Several hardware and software tools can help you maintain a computer and diagnose and repair computer problems. The tools you choose depend on the amount of money you can spend and the level of hardware support you expect to provide.

Essential tools for computer hardware troubleshooting are listed here, and several of them are shown in Figure 1-52. You can purchase some of these tools in a computer toolkit, although most toolkits contain items you really can do without.

Figure 1-52 Tools used by IT support technicians when maintaining, repairing, or upgrading computers

One of the more important tools is an ESD strap (also called a ground bracelet), which protects against ESD when working inside the computer case. Electrostatic discharge (ESD) is another name for static electricity, which can damage chips and destroy motherboards, even though it might not be felt or seen with the naked eye. Use the strap to connect or ground your hand to the case, as shown in Figure 1-53, and any static electricity between you and the case is dissipated.

Figure 1-53 An ESD strap, which protects computer components from ESD, can clip to the side of the computer case and eliminate ESD between you and the case

Here is a list of essential tools:

◢ An ESD strap (also called a ground bracelet)

◢ Flathead screwdriver

◢ Phillips-head or crosshead screwdriver

◢ Torx screwdriver set, particularly size T15

◢ Tweezers, preferably insulated ones, for picking pieces of paper out of printers or dropped screws out of tight places

◢ Extractor, a spring-loaded device that looks like a hypodermic needle (When you push down on the top, three wire prongs come out that can be used to pick up a screw that has fallen into a place where hands and fingers can't reach.)

◢ Software, including recovery CD or DVD for any OS you might work on (you might need several, depending on the OSs you support), antivirus software on bootable CDs or USB flash drives, and diagnostic software

The following tools might not be essential, but they are very convenient:

◢ Cans of compressed air (see Figure 1-54), small portable compressor, or antistatic vacuum cleaner to clean dust from inside a computer case

◢ Cleaning solutions and pads such as contact cleaner, monitor wipes, and cleaning solutions for CDs, DVDs, tapes, and drives

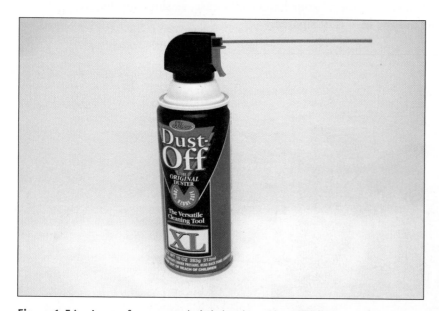

Figure 1-54   A can of compressed air is handy to blow dust from a computer case

◢ Multimeter to check cables and the power supply output

◢ Power supply tester

◢ Needle-nose pliers for removing jumpers and for holding objects (especially those pesky nuts on cable connectors) in place while you screw them in

◢ Cable ties to tie cables up and out of the way inside a computer case

◢ Flashlight to see inside the computer case

◢ AC outlet ground tester

◢ Network cable tester

◢ Loopback plugs to test ports

◢ Small cups or bags to help keep screws organized as you work

◢ Antistatic bags (a type of Faraday cage) to store unused parts

- Chip extractor to remove chips (To pry up the chip, a simple screwdriver is usually more effective, however.)
- Pen and paper for taking notes
- POST diagnostic cards

> **✎ Notes** It's important to know how to stay safe when working inside computers. Before opening a computer case and using the tools described in this section, be sure to read the appendix, "Safety Procedures and Environmental Concerns." As you work inside a computer, follow all the safety guidelines discussed in this appendix.

Keep your tools in a toolbox designated for hardware troubleshooting. If you put discs and hardware tools in the same box, be sure to keep the discs inside a hard plastic case to protect them from scratches and dents. In addition, make sure the diagnostic and utility software you use is recommended for the hardware and software you are troubleshooting.

Now let's turn our attention to the details of several IT support technician tools, including diagnostic cards, power supply testers, multimeters, and loopback plugs.

POST DIAGNOSTIC CARDS

**A+
220-901
4.1**

Although not an essential tool, a POST diagnostic card, also called a POST card, or motherboard test card, can be of great help to discover and report computer errors and conflicts that occur when you first turn on a computer and before the operating system (such as Windows 8) is launched. To understand what a POST card does, you need to know about the firmware, which is programs and data stored on the motherboard. Two types of firmware may be used on motherboards:

- The older BIOS (basic input/output system) contains system BIOS to manage essential devices (such as the keyboard, mouse, hard drive, and monitor) before the OS is launched, startup BIOS to start the computer, and BIOS setup to change the motherboard configuration or settings. Figure 1-55 shows an embedded firmware chip on a motherboard that contains the BIOS programs.

Coin battery

Firmware chip

Figure 1-55 This firmware chip contains flash ROM and CMOS RAM; CMOS RAM is powered by the coin battery located near the chip

- Newer motherboards use Unified Extensible Firmware Interface (UEFI) firmware that is more robust and secure than BIOS. Just as with BIOS, UEFI is responsible for managing essential devices before the OS is launched, starting the computer, and managing motherboard settings. UEFI can also assure that the boot is secure and no rogue operating system hijacks the system.

So now back to the usefulness of a POST card. The POST (power-on self test) is a series of tests performed by the startup UEFI/BIOS when you first turn on a computer. These tests determine if startup UEFI/BIOS can communicate correctly with essential hardware components required for a successful boot. If you have a problem that prevents the computer from booting that you suspect is related to hardware, you can install the POST card in an expansion slot on the motherboard. For laptops, some cards install in a USB port. Then attempt to boot. The card monitors the boot process and reports errors, usually as coded numbers on a small LED panel on the card. You then look up the number online or in the documentation that accompanies the card to get more information about the error and its source. Figure 1-56 shows a POST diagnostic card, the Post Code Master card by Microsystems Developments, Inc. (*www.postcodemaster.com*).

Figure 1-56 Post Code Master diagnostic card by Microsystems Developments, Inc., installs in a PCI slot

Before purchasing these or any other diagnostic tools or software, read the documentation about what they can and cannot do, and read some online product reviews. Try using Google.com and searching on "computer diagnostic card reviews."

> ✎ **Notes** Some Dell computers have lights on the case that blink in patterns to indicate a problem early in the boot before the OS loads. These blinking lights give information similar to that given by POST cards.

POWER SUPPLY TESTER

**A+
220-901
4.1**

A power supply tester is used to measure the output of each connector coming from the power supply. You can test the power supply when it is outside or inside the case. As you saw earlier in Figure 1-8, the power supply provides several cables and connectors that power various components inside the computer case. A power supply tester has plugs for each type of cable. Connect a power cable to the tester, plug up the power supply, and turn on the tester. An LCD panel reports the output of each lead (see Figure 1-57).

Figure 1-57   Use a power supply tester to test the output of each power connector on a power supply

MULTIMETER

A+
220-901
4.1

A multimeter (see Figure 1-58) is a more general-purpose tool that can measure several characteristics of electricity in a variety of devices. Some multimeters can measure voltage, current, resistance, or continuity. (Continuity determines that two ends of a cable or fuse are connected without interruption.) When set to measure voltage, you can use it to measure output of each pin on a power supply connector. Set to measure continuity, a multimeter is useful to test fuses, to determine if a cable is good, or to match pins on one end of a cable to pins on the other end.

Figure 1-58   This digital multimeter can be set to measure voltage, resistance, or continuity

LOOPBACK PLUGS

A loopback plug is used to test a port in a computer or other device to make sure the port is working and might also test the throughput or speed of the port. Figure 1-59 shows a loopback plug testing a network port on a laptop. You know both the port and the network cable are good because the lights on either side of the port are lit. You can also buy a USB loopback plug to test USB ports.

Figure 1-59   A loopback plug testing a network port and network cable

Now that you know about computer parts and their connections and the tools you need, you're ready to learn how to work inside a desktop or laptop case.

>> CHAPTER SUMMARY

What's Inside a Desktop Case

▲ Video ports a computer might have include the VGA, S-Video, DVI, DisplayPort, and HDMI ports. Other ports include RJ-45, audio, S/PDIF, USB, FireWire, eSATA, PS/2, serial, parallel, and RJ-11 ports. A Thunderbolt port can transmit video, data, and power.

▲ Internal computer components include the motherboard, processor, expansion cards, DIMM memory modules, hard drive, optical drive, tape drive, and power supply.

▲ Form factors used by cases, power supplies, and motherboards are the ATX and microATX form factors. The form factor determines how the case, power supply, and motherboard fit together and the cable connectors and other standards used by each.

▲ Power connectors used by the ATX and microATX form factors include the 20-pin P1, 24-pin P1, 4-pin and 8-pin CPU auxiliary motherboard, 4-pin Molex, 15-pin SATA, 4-pin Berg, and 6/8-pin PCIe connectors.

▲ The two main types of expansion slots in a desktop computer are PCI and PCI Express (PCIe).

▲ Most hard drives, optical drives, and tape drives today use the serial ATA (SATA) standards for the drive to interface with the motherboard and power supply.

First Look at Laptop Components

▲ Laptop computers use function keys to control display, volume, touch pad, media options, GPS, airplane mode, and other features of the laptop. A laptop docking station can make it easy to disconnect peripheral devices.

▲ A laptop may have an ExpressCard/34 or ExpressCard/54 slot for expansion. You can also use the USB ports for expansion, for example, to add a USB to RJ-45 dongle, USB to Wi-Fi dongle, Bluetooth capability, or a USB optical drive.

▲ Internal laptop components include the keyboard, hard drive, memory, smart card reader, optical drive, wireless card, screen, DC jack, battery pack, touch pad, speaker, system board, CPU, heat sink, and fan.

▲ An all-in-one computer uses a combination of components designed for desktop computers and laptops.

First Look at Mobile Device Hardware

▲ Mobile devices an IT support technician may be called on to service include smart phones, tablets, phablets, e-readers, smart cameras, GPS devices, and wearable technology devices such as smart watches, fitness monitors, glasses, and headsets.

▲ A mobile device might make a connection to the outside world using a cellular network, Wi-Fi network, Bluetooth, IR, NFC, tethering, creating its own hotspot, or wired connection. A wired connection may use a microUSB, miniUSB, or proprietary port, such as the Lightning port by Apple.

▲ A mobile device most likely will have an accelerometer to sense how the user is moving the device and a GPS receiver to sense the device's location and for geotracking.

Tools Used by a Computer Hardware Technician

▲ Common tools for a computer hardware technician include an ESD strap, screwdrivers, tweezers, flashlight, compressed air, and cleaning solutions and pads.

▲ Special tools a hardware technician might need include a POST diagnostic card, power supply tester, multimeter, and loopback plugs.

>> KEY TERMS

For explanations of key terms, see the Glossary for this text.

> ★ **A+ Exam Tip** To help you prepare for the A+ exams, the key terms in each chapter focus on the terms you need to know for the exams. Before you sit for the exams, be sure to review all the key terms in the Glossary.

4-pin 12-V connector	DB9 port	FireWire port	loopback plug
8-pin 12-V connector	DE15 port	firmware	LPT port
20-pin P1 connector	desktop case	fitness monitor	main board
24-pin P1 connector	digital	form factor	microATX (MATX)
accelerometer	DIMM (dual inline memory module)	geotracking	microprocessor
airplane mode		GPS (Global Positioning System)	microUSB
all-in-one computer	DisplayPort		miniUSB
analog	docking port	gyroscope	modem port
ATX (Advanced Technology Extended)	docking station	hard disk drive (HDD)	Molex connector
	dual-voltage selector switch	hard drive	motherboard
ATX12V power supply	DVI (Digital Video Interface) port	HD15 port	multimeter
audio port		HDMI (High-Definition Multimedia Interface) port	Near Field Communication (NFC)
base station	electrostatic discharge (ESD)		netbook
BIOS (basic input/output system)	e-reader	heat sink	network port
	Ethernet port	hotspot	notebook
BIOS setup	expansion card	IEEE 1394 port	optical connector
Bluetooth	ExpressCard	infrared (IR)	parallel port
cellular network	ExpressCard/34	internal components	PCI (Peripheral Component Interconnect)
central processing unit (CPU)	ExpressCard/54	keyboard backlight	
	external SATA (eSATA) port	laptop	PCI Express (PCIe)
chassis		Lightning port	PCIe 6/8-pin connector
DB15 port	field replaceable unit (FRU)		

PCMCIA card
phablet
POST (power-on self test)
POST card
POST diagnostic card
power supply
power supply tester
power supply unit (PSU)
processor
PS/2 port
RAM (random access memory)
RJ-11 port

RJ-45 port
SATA power connector
screen orientation
serial ATA (SATA)
serial port
SIM (Subscriber Identity Module) card
smart camera
smart phone
S/PDIF (Sony/Philips Digital Interface) sound port
SO-DIMM (small outline DIMM)

startup BIOS
S-Video port
system BIOS
system board
tablet
tethered
Thunderbolt port
touch pad
tower case
Unified Extensible Firmware Interface (UEFI)
USB (Universal Serial Bus) port

USB optical drive
USB to Bluetooth adapter
USB to RJ-45 dongle
USB to Wi-Fi dongle
VGA (Video Graphics Array) port
video memory
vision sensor
wearable technology device
Wi-Fi (Wireless Fidelity)

>> REVIEWING THE BASICS

1. List six types of video ports.

2. Which is faster, a Hi-Speed USB port or a SuperSpeed USB port?

3. What type of output does an S/PDIF port provide?

4. What is the purpose of an expansion slot on a motherboard?

5. What should be the setting for a dual-voltage selector switch on a power supply when using a computer in the United States?

6. How is the best way to determine if a cable inside a computer is a data and instruction cable or a power cable?

7. What technology standard is commonly used today for hard drives to interface with the motherboard in a system?

8. How many pins did the first P1 power connector to the motherboard have that was used with the original ATX?

9. What type of expansion slot requires extra power so that 4 more pins had to be added to the older 20-pin P1 power connector on the motherboard?

10. What device might require extra power so that it uses the 12V 6-pin power connector? In what two locations might you find the connector?

11. What is the purpose of the 4-pin auxiliary connector on a motherboard?

12. What is the purpose of the 4-pin Molex connector?

13. Why are laptops usually more expensive than desktop computers with comparable power and features?

14. Which two types of buses may be used by ExpressCard slots?

15. Which port do you use to connect a docking station to a laptop?

16. Which type of memory module is used in a desktop computer? Which type is used in a laptop computer?

17. What wireless technology is used when two smart phones in close proximity exchange contact information?

18. Which tool can a computer hardware technician use when taking apart a computer to best protect computer components against ESD?

19. What is the purpose of a POST diagnostic card?

20. What are the three purposes accomplished by the motherboard BIOS?

>> THINKING CRITICALLY

1. You purchase a new desktop computer that does not have wireless capability, and then you decide that you want to use a wireless connection to the Internet. What are the least expensive ways (choose two) to upgrade your system to wireless?

   a. Trade in the computer for another computer that has wireless installed.

   b. Purchase a second computer that has wireless capability.

   c. Purchase a wireless expansion card and install it in your system.

   d. Purchase a USB wireless adapter and connect it to the computer by way of a USB port.

2. What type of computer is likely to use SO-DIMMs, have an internal power supply, and use a desktop processor socket?

3. A friend asks you for help in determining the best product to buy: a laptop, tablet, or smart phone. She is a paralegal and spends a lot of time at the courthouse researching real estate titles. She wants a device to take notes with as she works. List three questions you would ask her to help her make her decision.

4. When troubleshooting a computer hardware problem, which tool might help with each of the following problems?

   a. You suspect the network port on a computer is not functioning.

   b. The system fails at the beginning of the boot and nothing appears on the screen.

   c. A hard drive is not working and you suspect the Molex power connector from the power supply might be the source of the problem.

>> REAL PROBLEMS, REAL SOLUTIONS

REAL PROBLEM 1-1 Planning Your Computer Repair Toolkit

Research on the web to find the following tools for sale: ESD strap, set of flathead and Phillips-head screwdrivers, can of compressed air, monitor cleaning wipes, multimeter, power supply tester, cable ties, flashlight, loopback plug to test an Ethernet port, POST diagnostic card, and toolbox.

Print or save the webpage showing each tool and its price. What is the total cost of this set of tools? If you were building your own computer repair toolkit, which tools would you purchase first if you could not afford the entire set of tools? Which tools not listed would you add to your toolbox?

Working Inside Desktop Computers and Laptops

After completing
this chapter, you
will be able to:

- Take apart a desktop computer and put it back together
- Explain the special considerations when supporting laptop computers that are different than supporting desktop computers
- Take apart a laptop computer and put it back together

Taking apart and servicing a computer are tasks that every A+ certified technician needs to know how to do. As part of your preparation to become A+ certified, try to find old desktop and laptop computers you can take apart. If you can locate the service manual for a laptop, you should be able to take it apart, repair it (assuming the parts are still available and don't cost more than the computer is worth), and get it up and running again. Have fun with this chapter and enjoy tinkering with these computers!

HOW TO WORK INSIDE A DESKTOP COMPUTER CASE

In this part of the chapter, you learn how to take apart a desktop computer and put it back together. This skill is needed in this and other chapters as you learn to add or replace computer parts inside the case and perhaps even build a system from scratch. As you read the following steps, you might want to perform the Hands-On Projects, which allow you to follow along by taking a computer apart. As you do so, be sure to follow all the safety precautions found in Appendix A "Safety Procedures and Environmental Concerns." In the steps that follow, each major computer component is identified and described. You learn much more about each component later in the text. Take your time—*don't rush*—as you take apart a computer for the first time. It can be a great learning experience or an expensive disaster! As you work, pay attention to the details, and work with care.

STEP 1: PLAN AND ORGANIZE YOUR WORK

When you first begin to learn how to work inside a computer case, make it a point to practice good organization skills. If you keep your notes, tools, screws, and computer parts well organized, your work goes smoother and is more fun. Here are some tips to keep in mind:

▲ Make notes as you work so that you can backtrack later if necessary. (When you're first learning to take a computer apart, it's really easy to forget where everything fits when it's time to put it back together. Also, in troubleshooting, you want to avoid repeating or overlooking things to try.)

▲ Remove loose jewelry that might get caught in cables and components as you work.

▲ To stay organized and not lose small parts, keep screws and spacers orderly and in one place, such as a cup or tray.

▲ Don't stack boards on top of each other: You could accidentally dislodge a chip this way. When you remove a circuit board or drive from a computer, carefully lay it on an antistatic mat or in an antistatic bag in a place where it won't get bumped.

▲ When handling motherboards, cards, or drives, don't touch the chips on the device. Hold expansion cards by the edges. Don't touch any soldered components on a card, and don't touch the edge connectors unless it's absolutely necessary. All this helps prevent damage from static electricity. Also, your fingerprints on the edge connectors can cause later corrosion.

▲ To protect a microchip, don't touch it with a magnetized screwdriver.

▲ Never ever touch the inside of a computer that is turned on. The one exception to this rule is when you're using a multimeter to measure voltage output.

▲ Consider the monitor and the power supply to be "black boxes." Never remove the cover or put your hands inside this equipment unless you know about the hazards of charged capacitors and have been trained to deal with them. The power supply and monitor contain enough power to kill you, even when they are unplugged.

▲ As you work, remember to watch out for sharp edges on computer cases that can cut you.

▲ In a classroom environment, after you have reassembled everything, have your instructor check your work before you put the cover back on and power up.

Now that you've prepared your work area and tools, put on your ESD strap and let's get started with opening the computer case.

STEP 2: OPEN THE COMPUTER CASE AND EXAMINE THE SYSTEM

Here are the steps to open a computer case:

1. *Back up important data.* If you are starting with a working computer, make sure important data is first backed up. Copy the data to an external storage device such as a flash drive or external hard drive. If something goes wrong while you're working inside the computer, at least your data will be safe.

2. *Power down the system and unplug it.* Remove discs from the optical drive. Then power down the system and unplug the power, monitor, mouse, and keyboard cables, and any other peripherals or cables attached and move them out of your way.

> ⚡ **Caution**   When you power down a computer and even turn off the power switch on the rear of the computer case, know that residual power is still on. Some motherboards even have a small light inside the case to remind you of this fact and to warn you that power is still getting to the system. Therefore, be sure to always unplug the power cord before opening a case.

3. *Press and hold down the power button for a moment.* After you unplug the computer, press the power button for about three seconds to completely drain the power supply (see Figure 2-1). Sometimes when you do so, you'll hear the fans quickly start and go off as residual power is drained. Only then is it safe to work inside the case.

Figure 2-1   Press the power button after the computer is unplugged

4. *Have a plastic bag or cup handy to hold screws.* When you reassemble the computer, you will need to insert the same screws in the same holes. This is especially important with the hard drive because screws that are too long can puncture the hard drive housing so be careful to label those screws clearly.

5. *Open the case cover.* Sometimes I think figuring out how to open a computer case is the most difficult part of disassembling. If you need help figuring it out, check the user manual or website of the case manufacturer. To remove the computer case cover, do the following:

   ◢ Some cases require you to start by laying the case on its side and removing the faceplate on the front of the case first. Other cases require you to remove a side panel first, and really older cases require you to first remove the entire sides and top as a single unit. Study your case for the correct approach.

   ◢ Most cases have panels on each side of the case that can be removed. It is usually necessary to only remove the one panel to expose the top of the motherboard. To know which panel to remove, look at where the ports are on the rear of the case. For example, in Figure 2-2, the ports on this motherboard are on the left side of the case, indicating the bottom of the motherboard is on the left. Therefore, you will want to remove the right panel to expose the top of this motherboard. Lay the case down to its left so that the ports and the motherboard are sitting on the bottom. Later, depending on how drives are installed, it might become necessary to remove the bottom panel in order to remove the screws that hold the drives in place.

Motherboard is
mounted to
this side
of the case

Figure 2-2   Decide which side panel to remove

▲ Locate the screws or clips that hold the side panel in place. Be careful not to unscrew any screws besides these. The other screws probably are holding the power supply, fan, and other components in place (see Figure 2-3). Place the screws in the cup or bag used for that purpose. Some cases use clips on a side panel in addition to or instead of screws (see Figure 2-4).

Figure 2-3   Locate the screws that hold the side panel in place

Figure 2-4 On this system, clips hold the side panel in place

▲ After the screws are removed, slide the panel toward the rear, and then lift it off the case (see Figure 2-5).

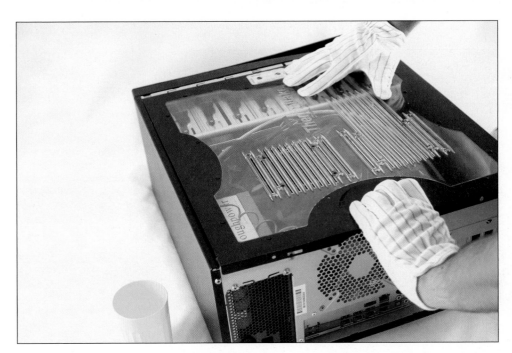

Figure 2-5 Slide the panel to the rear of the case

▲ Some cases require you to pop the front panel off the case before removing the side panels. Look for a lever on the bottom of the panel and hinges at the top. Squeeze the lever to release the front panel and lift it off the case (see Figure 2-6).

Figure 2-6 Some cases require you to remove the front panel before removing the side panel of a computer case

◢ Then remove a single screw (see Figure 2-7) and slide the side panel to the front and then off the case.

Figure 2-7 One screw holds the side panel in place

6. ***Clip your ESD strap to the side of the computer case.*** To dissipate any charge between you and the computer, put on your ESD strap if you have not already done so. Then clip the alligator clip on the strap cable to the side of the computer case (see Figure 2-8).

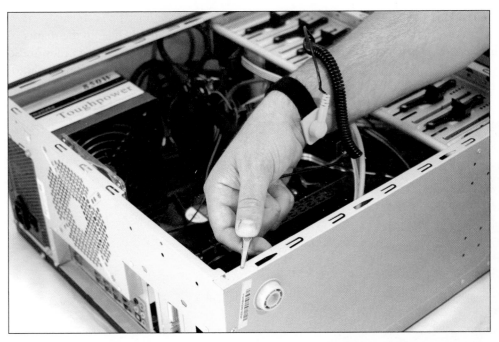

Figure 2-8　Attach the alligator clip of your ground bracelet to the side of the computer case

After you open a computer case, the main components you see inside are the power supply, motherboard, and drives installed in drive bays. You also see a lot of cables and wires connecting various components. These cables are power cables from the power supply to various components, or cables carrying data and instructions between components. The best way to know the purpose of a cable is to follow the cable from its source to its destination.

Hands-On | Project 2-1　Open a Computer Case

Using a desktop or tower computer, identify all the ports on the front or rear of the case. If you need help, see Table 1 in the chapter, "First Look at Computer Parts and Tools." Look at the rear of the case. On which side is the motherboard? Examine the case and determine how to open it. Shut down the system, and unplug the power cable. Disconnect all other cables. Press the power button on the front of the case to discharge residual power. Carefully open the case. Remember to not touch anything inside the case unless you are using an ESD strap or antistatic gloves to protect components against ESD.

Draw a diagram of the inside of the case and label all drives, the motherboard, the cooler, DIMM memory modules, the power supply, and any expansion cards installed. Leave the case open so you'll be ready for Hands-On Project 2-2 coming up later.

STEP 3: REMOVE EXPANSION CARDS

A+
220-901
1.2, 1.4,
1.5, 1.8

If you plan to remove several components, draw a diagram of all cable connections to the motherboard, expansion cards, and drives. You might need this cable connection diagram to help you reassemble. Note where each cable begins and ends, and pay particular attention to the small wires and connectors that connect the lights, switches, and ports on the front of the case to the motherboard front panel connectors. It's important to be careful about diagramming these because it is so easy to connect them in the wrong position later when you reassemble. If you want, use a felt-tip marker to make a mark across components, to indicate a cable connection, board placement, motherboard orientation, speaker connection, brackets, and so on, so that you can simply line up the marks when you reassemble. This method, however, probably won't work for the front case wires because they are so small. For these, consider writing down the color of the wires and their position on the pins or taking a photo of the wires in their positions with a digital camera (see Figure 2-9).

Figure 2-9   Diagram the pin locations of the color-coded wires that connect to the front of the case

> ✏️ **Notes** A connector on a motherboard that consists of pins that stick up from the board is called a header. For example, the group of pins shown in Figure 2-9 is called the front panel header.

Computer systems vary in so many ways, it's impossible to list the exact order to disassemble one. Most likely, however, you need to remove the expansion cards first. Do the following to remove the expansion cards:

1. Remove any wire or cable connected to the card.

2. Remove the screw holding the card to the case (see Figure 2-10).

Figure 2-10   Remove the screw holding an expansion card to the case

3. Grasp the card with both hands and remove it by lifting straight up. If you have trouble removing it from the expansion slot, you can *very slightly* rock the card from end to end (*not* side to side). Rocking the card from side to side might spread the slot opening and weaken the connection.

4. As you remove the card, don't put your fingers on the edge connectors or touch a chip, and don't stack the cards on top of one another. Lay each card aside on a flat surface, preferably in an antistatic bag.

> **Notes** Cards installed in PCI Express × 16 slots use a latch that helps to hold the card securely in the slot. To remove these cards, use one finger to hold the latch back from the slot, as shown in Figure 2-11, as you pull the card up and out of the slot.

Figure 2-11 Hold the retention mechanism back as you remove a video card from its expansion slot

Hands-On | Project 2-2 Identify Connectors Used on an Installed Motherboard

If necessary, remove the case cover to your desktop computer. Next, remove the expansion cards from your system. With the expansion cards out of the way, you can more clearly see the power cables and other cables and cords connected to the motherboard. Diagrams and notes are extremely useful when disassembling and reassembling a system. To practice this skill, draw a large rectangle that represents the motherboard. On the rectangle, label every header or connector that is used on the board. Include on the label the type of cable that is used and where the other end of the cable connects.

STEP 4: REMOVE THE MOTHERBOARD, POWER SUPPLY, AND DRIVES

A+
220-901
1.2, 1.4,
1.5, 1.8

Depending on the system, you might need to remove the motherboard next or remove the drives next. My choice is to first remove the motherboard. It and the processor are the most expensive and easily damaged parts in the system. I like to get them out of harm's way before working with the drives. However, in some cases, you must remove the drives or the power supply before you can get to the motherboard. Study your situation and decide which to do first. To remove the motherboard, do the following:

1. Unplug the power supply lines to the motherboard.

2. Unplug SATA cables connected to the motherboard.

3. The next step is to disconnect wires leading from the front or top of the computer case to the motherboard, which are called the front panel connectors. If you don't have the motherboard manual handy, be very careful to diagram how these wires connect because they are rarely labeled well on a motherboard. Make a careful diagram and then disconnect the wires. Figure 2-12 shows five leads and the pins on the motherboard front panel header that receive these leads. The pins are color-coded and cryptically labeled on the board.

Figure 2-12   Five leads from the front panel connect to two rows of pins on the motherboard front panel header

4. Disconnect any other cables or wires connected to the motherboard. A case fan might be getting power by a small wire connected to the motherboard. In addition, USB ports on the front of the computer case might be connected by a cable to the motherboard.

5. You're now ready to remove the screws that hold the motherboard to the case. A motherboard is installed so that the bottom of the board does not touch the case. If the fine traces or lines on the bottom of the board were to touch the case, a short would result when the system is running. To keep the board from touching the case, screw holes are elevated, or you'll see spacers, also called standoffs, which are round plastic or metal pegs that separate the board from the case. Carefully pop off these spacers and/or remove the screws (up to nine) that hold the board to the case (see Figure 2-13) and then remove the board. Set it aside in a safe place. Figure 2-14 shows a motherboard sitting to the side of these spacers. One spacer is in place and the other is lying beside its case holes. Also notice in the photo the two holes in the motherboard where screws are used to connect the board to the spacers.

Figure 2-13 Remove up to nine screws that hold the motherboard to the case

Figure 2-14 This motherboard connects to a case using screws and spacers that keep the board from touching the case

📝 **Notes** When you're replacing a motherboard in a case that is not the same size as the original board, you can use needle-nose pliers to unplug a standoff so you can move it to a new hole.

6. The motherboard should now be free and you can carefully remove it from the case, as shown in Figure 2-15. Lift the board by its edges, as shown in the figure.

> ⚡ **Caution**   Never lift a motherboard by the cooler because doing so might create an air gap between the cooler and the processor, which can cause the processor to later overheat.

Figure 2-15   Remove the motherboard from the case

> ⚡ **Caution**   Some processors have heavy cooling assemblies installed on top of them. For these systems, it is best to remove the cooler before you take the motherboard out of the case because the motherboard is not designed to support this heavy cooler when the motherboard is not securely seated in the case. How to remove the cooler is covered in the chapter, "Supporting Processors and Upgrading Memory."

7. To remove the power supply from the case, look for screws that attach the power supply to the computer case, as shown in Figure 2-16. Be careful not to remove any screws that hold the power supply housing together. You do not want to take the housing apart. After you have removed the screws, the power supply still might not be free. Sometimes, it is attached to the case on the underside by recessed slots. Turn the case over and look on the bottom for these slots. If they are present, determine in which direction you need to slide the power supply to free it from the case.

Figure 2-16   Removing the power supply mounting screws

8. Remove each drive next, handling the drives with care. Here are some tips:

   ◢ Some drives have one or two screws on each side of the drive attaching the drive to the drive bay. After you remove the screws, the drive slides to the front or to the rear and then out of the case.

   ◢ Sometimes, there is a catch underneath the drive that you must lift up as you slide the drive forward.

   ◢ Some drive bays have a clipping mechanism to hold the drive in the bay. First release the clip and then pull the drive forward and out of the bay (see Figure 2-17). Handle the drives with care. Some drives have an exposed circuit board on the bottom of the drive. Don't touch this board.

Figure 2-17   To remove this CD drive, first pull the clip forward to release the drive from the bay

◢ Some cases have a removable bay for small drives (see Figure 2-18). These bays can hold narrow drives such as hard drives and tape drives. The bay is removed first and then the drives are removed from the bay. To remove the bay, first remove the screws or release the clip holding the bay in place and then slide the bay out of the case. The drives are usually installed in the bay with two screws on each side of each drive. Remove the screws and then the drives (see Figure 2-19).

Figure 2-18   Push down on the clip and then slide the removable bay forward and out of the case

Figure 2-19   Drives in this removable bay are held in place with screws on each side of the bay

STEPS TO PUT A COMPUTER BACK TOGETHER

A+
220-901
1.2, 1.4,
1.5, 1.8

To reassemble a computer, reverse the process of disassembling. Here is where your diagrams will be really useful and having the screws and cables organized will also help. In the directions that follow, we're also considering the possibility that you are installing a replacement part as you reassemble the system. Do the following:

1. Install components in the case in this order: power supply, drives, motherboard, and cards. When installing drives, know that for some systems, it's easier to connect data cables to the drives and then slide the drives into the bay. If the drive is anchored to the bay with screws or latches, be careful to align the front of the drive flush with the front of the case before installing screws or pushing in the latches (see Figure 2-20).

Push in two latches to secure the drive

Figure 2-20 Align the front of the drive flush with the case front and then anchor with a screw

2. Place the motherboard inside the case. Make sure the ports stick out of the I/O shield at the rear of the case and the screw holes line up with screw holes on the bottom of the case. Figure 2-21 shows how you must align the screw holes on the motherboard with those in the case. There should be at least six screw sets, and there might be as many as nine. Use as many screws as there are holes in the motherboard. Figure 2-22 shows one screw being put in place.

Raised screw holes on the case

Screw holes on motherboard

Figure 2-21 Align screw holes in the case with those on the motherboard

Figure 2-22 Use one screw in each screw hole on the motherboard

3. Connect the power cords from the power supply to the motherboard. A system will always need the main P1 power connector and most likely will need the 4-pin auxiliary connector for the processor. Other power connectors might be needed depending on the devices you later install in the system. Here are the details:

▲ Connect the P1 power connector from the power supply to the motherboard (see Figure 2-23).

Figure 2-23 The 24-pin connector supplies power to the motherboard

◢ Connect the 4-pin auxiliary power cord coming from the power supply to the motherboard, as shown in Figure 2-24. This cord supplies the supplemental power required for the processor.

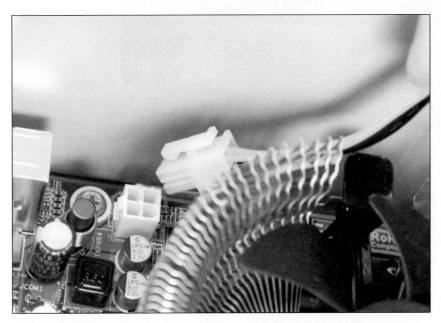

Figure 2-24 The auxiliary 4-pin power cord provides power to the processor

◢ A board might have a 6-pin or 8-pin PCIe power connector (see Figure 2-25). If the board has either connector, connect the 6-pin or 8-pin cord from the power supply to the connector. If a power supply doesn't have this connector, you can use an adapter to convert two Molex connectors to a PCIe connector.

8-pin connector

Figure 2-25 8-pin PCIe Version 2.0 power connector

◢ Some boards designed to support multiple PCIe video cards will have additional power connectors on the board to power these wattage-hungry cards. For example, Figure 2-26(a) shows a Molex-style connector on one board that provides auxiliary power to PCIe graphics cards. This same board offers a SATA-style connector, shown in Figure 2-26(b). The motherboard documentation says to use just one of these auxiliary power connectors to provide additional wattage for PCIe video cards.

SATA-style power connector

Molex-style power connector

Figure 2-26   Auxiliary power connectors to support PCIe

◢ To power the case fan, connect the power cord from the fan to pins on the motherboard labeled Fan Header. Alternately, some case fans use a 4-pin Molex connector that connects to a power cable coming directly from the power supply.

◢ If a CPU and cooler are already installed on the motherboard, connect the power cord from the CPU fan to the pins on the motherboard labeled CPU Fan Header.

4. Connect the wire leads from the front panel of the case to the front panel header on the motherboard. These are the wires for the switches, lights, and ports on the front or top of the computer. Because your case and your motherboard might not have been made by the same manufacturer, you need to pay close attention to the source of the wires to determine where they connect on the motherboard. For example, Figure 2-27 shows a computer case that has seven connectors from the front panel that connect to the motherboard. Figure 2-28 shows the front panel header on the motherboard for these lights and switches. If you look closely at the board in Figure 2-28, you can see labels identifying the pins.

Triangle used to orient connector on pins

Figure 2-27   Seven connectors from the front panel connect to the motherboard

Labels on the board identify the pins

Figure 2-28   Front panel header uses color-coded pins and labels

The five smaller connectors on the right side of Figure 2-27 from right to left are labeled as follows:

- ▲ *Power SW*. Controls power to the motherboard; must be connected for the PC to power up
- ▲ *HDD LED*. Controls the drive activity light on the front panel that lights up when any SATA or IDE device is in use (HDD stands for hard disk drive; LED stands for light-emitting diode; and an LED is a light on the front panel.)
- ▲ *Power LED+*. Positive LED controls the power light and indicates that power is on
- ▲ *Power LED−*. Negative LED controls the power light; the two positive and negative leads indicate that power is on
- ▲ *Reset SW*. Switch used to reboot the computer

> ✎ **Notes**   Positive wires connecting the front panel to the motherboard are usually a solid color, and negative wires are usually white or striped.

To help orient the larger connectors on the motherboard pins, look for a small triangle embedded on the connector that marks one of the outside wires as pin 1 (see Figure 2-27). Look for pin 1 to be labeled on the motherboard as a small 1 embedded to either the right or the left of the group of pins. If the labels on the board are not clear, turn to the motherboard user guide for help. The diagram in Figure 2-29 shows what you can expect from one motherboard user guide. Notice pin 1 is identified as a square pin in the diagram, rather than round like the other pins.

Pin	Assignment	Function	Pin	Assignment	Function
1	+5 V	Speaker connector	9	N/A	N/A
2	N/A		10	N/A	
3	N/A		11	N/A	N/A
4	Speaker		12	Power LED (+)	Power LED
5	HDD LED (+)	Hard drive LED	13	Power LED (+)	
6	HDD LED (–)		14	Power LED (–)	
7	Ground	Reset button	15	Power button	Power-on button
8	Reset control		16	Ground	

Figure 2-29   Documentation for front panel header connections

> ✎ **Notes**   If the user guide is not handy, you can download it from the motherboard manufacturer's website. Search on the brand and model number of the board, which is imprinted somewhere on the board.

Sometimes the motherboard documentation is not clear, but guessing is okay when connecting a wire to a front panel header connection. If it doesn't work, no harm is done. Figure 2-30 shows all front panel wires in place and the little speaker also connected to the front panel header pins.

Speaker connected to front panel header

Figure 2-30   Front panel header with all connectors in place

5. Connect wires to ports on the front panel of the case. Depending on your motherboard and case, there might be cables to connect audio ports or USB ports on the front of the case to headers on the motherboard. Audio and USB connectors are the two left connectors shown in Figure 2-27. You can see these ports for audio and USB on the front of the case in Figure 2-31. Look in the motherboard documentation for the location of these connectors. The audio and USB connectors are labeled for one board in Figures 2-32(a) and (b).

Audio-out and microphone ports

USB ports

Figure 2-31   Ports on the front of the computer case

Front audio header

Three USB headers

Figure 2-32   Connectors for front panel ports

6. Install the video card and any other expansion cards. Push the card straight down into the slot, being careful to not rock side to side, and install the screw to secure the card to the case.

7. Take a few minutes to double-check each connection to make sure it is correct and snug. Verify all required power cords are connected correctly and the video card is seated solidly in its slot. Also verify that no wires or cables are obstructing fans. You can use cable ties to tie wires up and out of the way.

8. Plug in the keyboard, monitor, and mouse.

9. In a classroom environment, have the instructor check your work before you close the case and power up.

10. Turn on the power and check that the PC is working properly. If the PC does not work, most likely the problem is a loose connection. Just turn off the power and go back and check each cable connection and each expansion card. You probably have not solidly seated a card in the slot. After you have double-checked, try again.

Now step back and congratulate yourself on a job well done! By taking a computer apart and putting it back together, you've learned much about how computer parts interconnect and work.

Hands-On | Project 2-3   Close the Case

The case cover to your desktop computer is off from doing the previous exercises. Before you close your case, it's always a good idea to quickly clean it first. Using a can of compressed air, blow the dust away from fans and other components inside the case. Be careful to not touch components unless you are properly grounded. When you're done, close the case cover.

Now we turn our attention to laptops.

SPECIAL CONSIDERATIONS WHEN SUPPORTING LAPTOPS

A+
220-901
3.1, 4.5

Laptops and their replacement parts cost more than desktop computers with similar features because their components are designed to be more compact and stand up to travel. They use compact hard drives, small memory modules, and CPUs that require less power than regular components. Whereas a desktop computer is often assembled from parts made by a variety of manufacturers, laptop computers are almost always sold by a vendor that either manufactured the laptop or had it manufactured as a consolidated system. Factors to consider that generally apply more to laptop than desktop computers are the original equipment manufacturer's warranty, the service manuals and diagnostic software provided by the manufacturer, the customized installation of the OS that is unique to laptops, and the advantage of ordering replacement parts directly from the laptop manufacturer or other source authorized by the manufacturer.

In many situations, the tasks of maintaining, upgrading, and troubleshooting a laptop require the same skills, knowledge, and procedures as when servicing a desktop computer. However, you should take some special considerations into account when caring for, supporting, upgrading, and troubleshooting laptops. These same concerns apply to netbooks and all-in-one computers. Let's begin with warranty concerns.

WARRANTY CONCERNS

A+
220-901
3.1, 4.5

Most manufacturers or retailers of laptops offer at least a one-year warranty and the option to purchase an extended warranty. Therefore, when problems arise while the laptop is under warranty, you are dealing with a single manufacturer or retailer to get support or parts. After the laptop is out of warranty, this manufacturer or retailer can still be your one-stop shop for support and parts.

⚡ **Caution**   The warranty often applies to all components in the system, but it can be voided if someone other than an authorized service center services the laptop. Therefore, you, as a service technician, must be very careful not to void a warranty that the customer has purchased. Warranties can be voided by opening the case, removing part labels, installing other-vendor parts, upgrading the OS, or disassembling the system unless directly instructed to do so by the authorized service center help desk personnel.

Before you begin servicing a laptop, to avoid problems with a warranty, always ask the customer, "Is the laptop under warranty?" If the laptop is under warranty, look at the documentation to find out how to get technical support. Options are chat sessions on the web, phone numbers, and email. Use the most appropriate option. Before you contact technical support, have the laptop model and serial number ready (see Figure 2-33). You'll also need the name, phone number, and address of the person or company that made the purchase. Consider asking the customer for a copy of the receipt and warranty so that you'll have the information you need to talk with support personnel.

Figure 2-33   The model and serial number stamped on the bottom of a laptop are used to identify the laptop to service desk personnel

Based on the type of warranty purchased by the laptop's owner, the manufacturer might send an on-site service technician, ask you to ship or take the laptop to an authorized service center, or help you solve the problem by an online chat session or over the phone. Table 2-1 lists some popular manufacturers of laptops, netbooks, and all-in-ones. Manufacturers of laptops typically also produce all-in-ones because of the features they have in common.

Manufacturer	Website
Acer	*us.acer.com* and *us.acer.com/ac/en/US/content/support*
Apple Computer	*www.apple.com* and *www.apple.com/support*
ASUS	*usa.asus.com* and *www.asus.com/us/support/*
Dell Computer	*www.dell.com* and *support.dell.com*
Fujitsu/Fuji	*www.fujitsu.com* and *www.fujitsu.com/support*
Gateway	*www.gateway.com* and *support.gateway.com*
Hewlett Packard (HP)	*www.hp.com* and *www8.hp.com/us/en/support.html*
Lenovo (formerly IBM ThinkPad)	*www.lenovo.com* and *support.lenovo.com*
Microsoft	*www.microsoft.com*
Samsung	*www.samsung.com* and *www.samsung.com/support*
Sony (VAIO)	*store.sony.com* and *esupport.sony.com*
Toshiba America	*www.toshiba.com/tai/* and *www.toshiba.com/tai/support.jsp*

Table 2-1   Laptop, netbook, and all-in-one manufacturers

SERVICE MANUALS AND OTHER SOURCES OF INFORMATION

A+
220-901
3.1, 4.5

Desktop computer cases tend to be similar to one another, and components in desktop systems are usually interchangeable among manufacturers. Not so with laptops. Laptop manufacturers typically take great liberty in creating their own unique computer cases, buses, cables, connectors, drives, circuit boards, fans, and even screws, all of which are likely to be proprietary in design.

Every laptop model has a unique case. Components are installed in unique ways and opening the case for each laptop model is done differently. Because of these differences, servicing laptops can be very complicated and time consuming. For example, a hard drive on one laptop is accessed by popping open a side panel and sliding the drive out of its bay. However, to access the hard drive on another model laptop, you must remove the keyboard. If you are not familiar with a particular laptop model, you can damage the case frame or plastics as you pry and push trying to open it. Trial and error is likely to damage a case. Even though you might successfully replace a broken component, the damaged case will result in an unhappy customer.

Fortunately, a laptop service manual can save you much time and effort—if you can locate one (see Figure 2-34). Most laptop manufacturers closely guard these service manuals and release them only to authorized service centers. Two laptop manufacturers, Lenovo (formerly IBM ThinkPad) and Dell, provide their service manuals online free of charge. HP also does an excellent job of offering online support. For example, in Figure 2-35, you can see a video in progress showing you the steps to replace the optical drive in an HP laptop. I applaud Lenovo, Dell, and HP for the generous documentation about how their laptops are disassembled and the options to purchase proprietary parts without first being an authorized service center.

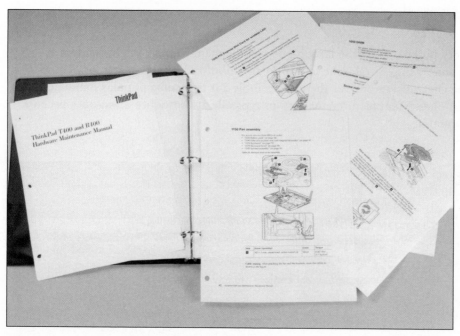

Figure 2-34   A laptop service manual tells you how to use diagnostic tools, troubleshoot a laptop, and replace components

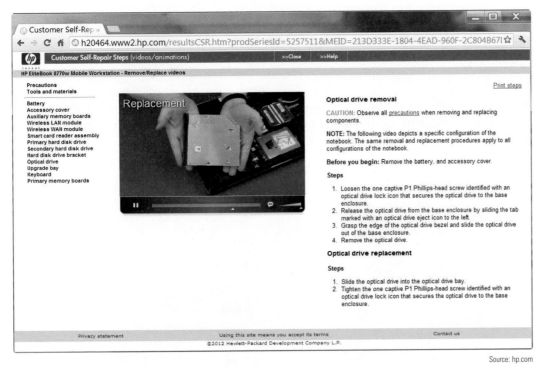

Figure 2-35   The HP website (*www.hp.com*) provides detailed instructions and videos for troubleshooting and replacing components

 Notes   The wiki-type website *ifixit.com* does an excellent job of providing its own teardown and reassemble instructions for many brands and models of laptops.

For all laptop manufacturers, check the Support or FAQ pages of their websites for help in tasks such as opening a case without damaging it and locating and replacing a component. Be aware that some manufacturers offer almost no help at all. Sometimes, you can find service manuals on the web. To find your manual, search on the model of laptop, for example, search on "Sony VGN-CR120E laptop service manual".

Don't forget about the user manuals. They might contain directions for upgrading and replacing components that do not require disassembling the case, such as how to upgrade memory or install a new hard drive. User manuals also include troubleshooting tips and procedures and possibly descriptions of UEFI/BIOS settings. In addition, you can use a web search engine to search on the computer model, component, or error message, which might give you information about the problem and solution.

DIAGNOSTIC TOOLS PROVIDED BY MANUFACTURERS

A+
220-901
3.1, 4.5

Most laptop manufacturers provide diagnostic software that can help you test components to determine which component needs replacing. As one of the first steps when servicing a laptop, check the user manual, service manual, or manufacturer's website to determine if diagnostic software exists and how to use it. Use the software to pinpoint the problem component, which can then be replaced.

> ✎ **Notes** When you purchase a replacement part for a laptop from the laptop's manufacturer, most often the manufacturer also sends you detailed instructions for exchanging the part.

Check the manufacturer's website for diagnostics software that can be downloaded for a particular model laptop or stored on the hard drive or on CDs bundled with the laptop. Figure 2-36 shows a window provided by the diagnostics program installed on the hard drive of one laptop.

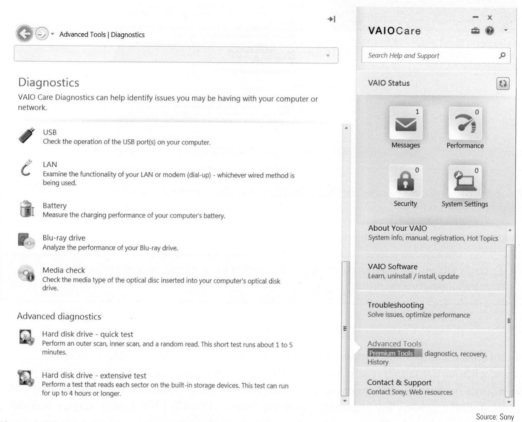

Source: Sony

Figure 2-36   Use diagnostics software provided by a laptop manufacturer to troubleshoot hardware problems

One example of diagnostic software is PC-Doctor, which is used by several manufacturers, including Lenovo, Fujitsu, and HP laptops. The diagnostic software is stored on the hard drive or on CD. If stored on CD, you can boot from the CD to run the tests. If the software is stored on the hard drive, you can run it from the Windows Start menu or by pressing a function key at startup before Windows loads. Either way, PC-Doctor can run tests on the keyboard, video, speakers, touch pad, optical drive, wireless LAN, motherboard, processor, ports, hard drive, and memory. To learn how to use the software, see the laptop's service manual or user manual.

Lenovo offers PC-Doctor for DOS that you can download from their website at *www.lenovo.com/support* and burn to a CD. Boot from the CD and use the command-line interface of the older DOS operating system to run the tests. You can also find a stand-alone version of PC-Doctor for DOS and PC-Doctor for Windows at *www.pc-doctor.com*. You can purchase it at this site; it's expensive but might be worth it if you plan to service many laptops.

Hands-On | Project 2-4 Research Laptop Service Manuals

Do the following to find a service manual for a laptop that you have access to, such as one belonging to you or a friend:

1. What are the brand, model, and serial number of the laptop?

2. What is the website of the laptop manufacturer? Print a webpage on that site that shows the documentation and/or drivers available for this laptop.

3. If the website provides a service manual for disassembling the laptop, download the manual. Print two or three pages from the manual showing the title page and table of contents for the manual.

4. If the website does not provide a service manual, search the Internet for the manual. If you find it, download it and print the title page and table of contents.

Now let's turn our attention to how to disassemble and reassemble a laptop.

HOW TO WORK INSIDE A LAPTOP COMPUTER

**A+
220-901
3.1, 4.5**

Sometimes it is necessary to open a laptop case so you can upgrade memory, exchange a hard drive, or replace a failed component such as the LCD panel, video inverter, keyboard, touch pad, processor, optical drive, DC jack, fan, motherboard, CMOS battery, Mini-PCIe card, wireless card, or speaker. Most laptops sold today are designed so that you can easily purchase and exchange memory modules or hard drives. However, replacing a broken LCD panel or motherboard can be a complex process, taking several hours. Most likely, you will choose to replace the entire laptop rather than doing these labor-intensive and costly repairs.

Screws and nuts on a laptop are smaller than a desktop system and therefore require smaller tools. Figure 2-37 shows a display of several tools used to disassemble a laptop, although you can get by without several of them. Here's the list:

Figure 2-37 Tools for disassembling a laptop

▲ ESD strap
▲ Small flathead screwdriver
▲ Number 1 Phillips-head screwdriver
▲ Dental pick (useful for prying without damaging plastic cases, connectors, and screw covers such as the one in Figure 2-38)

Figure 2-38 Use a small screwdriver or dental pick to pry up the plastic cover hiding a screw

- Torx screwdriver set, particularly size T5
- Something such as a pillbox to keep screws and small parts organized
- Notepad for note taking or digital camera (optional)
- Flashlight (optional)
- Three-prong extractor to pick up tiny screws (optional)

Working on laptops requires extra patience. Just as when you are working with desktop systems, before opening the case of a laptop or touching sensitive components, you should always wear an ESD strap to protect the system against ESD. You can attach the alligator clip end of the strap to an unpainted metallic surface on the laptop. This surface could be, for instance, a port on the back of the laptop (see Figure 2-39). If a ground strap is not available, first dissipate any ESD between you and the laptop by touching a metallic unpainted part of the laptop, such as a port on the back, before you touch a component inside the case.

Figure 2-39 To protect the system against ESD, attach the alligator clip of a ground strap to an I/O port on the back of the laptop

Laptops contain many small screws of various sizes and lengths. When reassembling, put screws back where they came from so that when you reassemble the system, you won't use screws that are too long and that can protrude into a sensitive component and damage it. As you remove a screw, store or label it so you know where it goes when reassembling. One way to do that is to place screws in a pillbox with each compartment labeled. Another way is to place screws on a soft padded work surface and use white labeling tape to label each set of screws. A third way to organize screws is to put them on notebook paper and write beside them where the screw belongs (see Figure 2-40). My favorite method of keeping up with all those screws is to tape the screw beside the manufacturer documentation that I'm following to disassemble the laptop (see Figure 2-41). Whatever method you use, work methodically to keep screws and components organized so you know what goes where when reassembling.

Figure 2-40 Using a notepad can help you organize screws so you know which screw goes where when reassembling

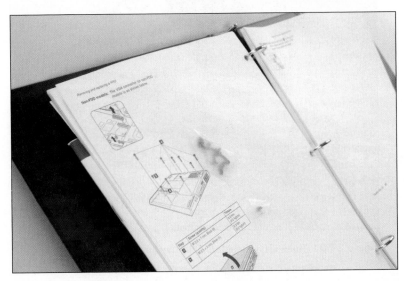

Figure 2-41 Tape screws beside the step in the manufacturer documentation that told you to remove the screw

★ **A+ Exam Tip** The A+ 220-901 exam expects you to know the importance of keeping parts organized when disassembling a laptop as well as the importance of having manufacturer documentation to know the steps to disassembly.

As you disassemble the computer, if you are not following directions from a service manual, keep notes as you work to help you reassemble later. Draw diagrams and label things carefully. Include in your drawings cable orientations and screw locations. You might consider using a digital camera. Photos that you take at each step in the disassembly process will be a great help when it's time to put the laptop back together.

When disassembling a laptop, consider the following tips:

▲ Make your best effort to find the hardware service manual for the particular laptop model you are servicing. The manual should include all the detailed steps to disassemble the laptop and a parts list of components that can be ordered from the laptop manufacturer. If you don't have this manual, your chances of successfully replacing an internal component are greatly reduced! And, if you don't have much experience disassembling a laptop, it is not wise to attempt to do so without this manual.

▲ Consider the warranty that might still apply to the laptop. Remember that opening the case of a laptop under warranty most likely will void the warranty. Make certain that any component you have purchased to replace an internal component will work in the model of laptop you are servicing.

▲ Take your time. Patience is needed to keep from scratching or marring plastic screw covers, hinges, and the case.

▲ As you work, don't force anything. If you find yourself forcing something, you're likely to break it.

▲ Always wear an ESD strap or use other protection against ESD.

▲ When removing cables, know that sometimes cable connectors are ZIF connectors. To disconnect a cable from a ZIF connector, first pull up on the connector and then remove the cable, as shown in Figure 2-42. Figure 2-43 shows a laptop using three ZIF connectors that hold the three keyboard cables in place.

Figure 2-42 To disconnect a ZIF connector, first push up on the connector to release the latch, and then remove the cable

Figure 2-43 Three ZIF connectors hold the three keyboard cables in place

▲ Again, use a dental pick or very small screwdriver to pry up the plastic cover hiding a screw.

▲ Some laptops use plastic screws that are intended to be used only once. The service manual will tell you to be careful to not overtighten these screws and to always use new screws when reassembling a laptop.

◢ Disassemble the laptop by removing each field replaceable unit (FRU) in the order given by the service manual for your laptop. For example, one manufacturer says that to replace the motherboard for a laptop, remove components in this order: battery pack, RAM door, keyboard, middle cover, hinge cover, DVD drive and bracket, mini PCIe adapter, keyboard bezel assembly, fan assembly, CPU, CPU fixture, and DVD drive bracket. After all these components are removed, you can then remove the motherboard. Follow the steps to remove each component in the right order.

When reassembling a laptop, consider these general tips:

◢ Reassemble the laptop in the reverse order of the way you disassembled it. Follow each step carefully.

◢ Be sure to tighten, but not overtighten, all screws. Loose screws or metal fragments in a laptop can be dangerous; they might cause a short as they shift about inside the laptop.

◢ Before you install the battery or AC adapter, verify that there are no loose parts inside the laptop. Pick it up and gently shake it. If you hear anything loose, open the case and find the loose component, screw, spring, or metal flake, and fix the problem.

>> CHAPTER SUMMARY

How to Work Inside a Desktop Computer Case

◢ When a hardware support technician is disassembling or reassembling a computer, it is important to stay organized, keep careful notes, and follow all the safety procedures to protect the computer equipment.

◢ Before opening a computer case, shut down the system, unplug it, disconnect all cables, and press the power button to drain residual power.

◢ An expansion card fits in a slot on the motherboard and is anchored to the case by a single screw or clip.

Special Considerations When Supporting Laptops

◢ Laptop computers are designed for travel. They use the same technology as desktop computers, with modifications for space, portability, and power conservation. A laptop generally costs more than a desktop with comparable power and features. Special concerns when supporting a laptop also apply to supporting a netbook or all-in-one computer.

◢ When supporting laptops, pay careful attention to what the warranty allows you to change on the computer.

◢ The laptop manufacturer documentation, including the service manual, diagnostic software, and recovery media, is useful when disassembling, troubleshooting, and repairing a laptop.

How to Work Inside a Laptop Computer

◢ Field replaceable units in a laptop can include the memory modules, hard drive, LCD panel, video inverter, keyboard, touch pad, processor, optical drive, DC jack, fan, motherboard, CMOS battery, Mini-PCIe card, wireless card, or speakers.

◢ When an internal component needs replacing, consider the possibility of disabling the component and using an external peripheral device in its place. Don't jeopardize the warranty on a laptop by opening the case or using components not authorized by the manufacturer.

◢ Replacing the laptop might be more cost effective than performing labor-intensive repairs, such as replacing the motherboard.

◢ When disassembling a laptop, the manufacturer's service manual is essential.

◢ When upgrading components on a laptop, including memory, use components that are the same brand as the laptop, or use only components recommended by the laptop's manufacturer.

◢ Follow the directions in a service manual to disassemble a laptop. Keep small screws organized as you disassemble a laptop because the laptop will have a variety of sizes and lengths of screws. Some manufacturers use plastic screws and recommend you use new screws rather than reuse the old ones.

>> KEY TERMS

For explanations of key terms, see the Glossary for this text.

front panel connector
front panel header
spacer
standoff
ZIF connector

>> REVIEWING THE BASICS

1. When taking a computer apart, why is it important to not stack boards on top of each other?

2. Why is it important to remove loose jewelry before working inside a computer case?

3. When assembling a desktop computer, which do you install first, the drives or the motherboard?

4. What is the purpose of raised screw holes or standoffs installed between the motherboard and desktop case?

5. When installing the front panel wires to the motherboard front panel header, how do you know which pins to use for each wire if the pins on the header are not labeled?

6. How many pins does the CPU auxiliary power connector on a motherboard have?

7. Why are laptops usually more expensive than desktop computers with comparable power and features?

8. Why is the service manual so important to have when you disassemble a laptop?

9. When a laptop internal device fails, what three options can you use to deal with the problem?

10. After you have removed the AC adapter and all peripherals, what is the next component you should always remove before servicing any internal laptop components?

>> THINKING CRITICALLY

1. You disassemble and reassemble a desktop computer. When you first turn it on, you see no lights and hear no sounds. Nothing appears on the monitor screen. What is the most likely cause of the problem? Explain your answer.

   a. A memory module is not seated properly in a memory slot.

   b. You forgot to plug up the monitor's external power cord.

   c. A wire in the case is obstructing a fan.

   d. Power cords to the motherboard are not connected.

2. You are looking to buy a laptop on a budget and want to save money by not purchasing an extended service agreement with the manufacturer beyond the first year. What should you consider when choosing manufacturers to limit your search? Which manufacturers would you choose and why?

3. A four-year-old laptop will not boot and presents error messages on screen. You have verified with the laptop technical support that these error messages indicate the motherboard has failed and needs replacing. What is the first question you should ask yourself before performing the repair?

   a. Will replacing the motherboard be more costly than purchasing a new laptop?

   b. Can you find a replacement motherboard?

   c. Can you find the service manual to show you how to replace the motherboard?

   d. Is the laptop still under warranty?

>> REAL PROBLEMS, REAL SOLUTIONS

REAL PROBLEM 2-1 Taking a Lab Computer Apart and Putting It Back Together

A PC technician needs to be comfortable with taking apart a computer and putting it back together. In most situations, the essential tools you'll need for the job are an ESD strap, a Phillips-head screwdriver, a flathead screwdriver, paper, and pen.

Working with a partner and using a lab computer designated to be disassembled, take a computer apart. It is not necessary to remove the processor or memory modules from the motherboard, but be very careful to properly support the motherboard and processor as you remove them from the case. Then reassemble the system. Don't replace the computer case panel until your instructor has inspected all cable connections. Then turn on the computer and verify that all is working.

REAL PROBLEM 2-2 Setting Up a Service Center for Laptops

If you intend to set up your own computer repair shop, you might want to consider becoming a service center for a few brands of the more popular laptops. Reasons to become an authorized service center are that you have access to service manuals, parts lists, and wholesale parts for laptops. Do the following to research becoming an authorized service center:

1. Select a brand of laptops that you think you would like to service.

2. Research the website of this manufacturer and answer these questions:

   a. Where is the closest authorized service center for this brand of laptops?

   b. What are the requirements to become an authorized service center? Print the webpage showing the requirements.

   c. Is A+ certification one of those requirements?

   d. Some laptop manufacturers offer a program that falls short of becoming an authorized service center but does provide support for IT professionals so that repair technicians can order laptop parts. Does the manufacturer offer this service? If so, what must you do to qualify?

If you try one brand of laptop and can't find the information you need, try another brand. Sometimes this information can only be obtained by contacting the manufacturer directly. And one more hint: To use *www.google.com* to search a particular site, begin the search string with *site:hostname.com*.

REAL PROBLEM 2-3 Taking Apart a Laptop

If you enjoy putting together a thousand-piece jigsaw puzzle, you'll probably enjoy working on laptop computers. With desktop systems, replacing a component is not a time-consuming task, but with laptops, the job could take half a day. If you take the time to carefully examine the laptop's case before attempting to open it, you will probably find markings provided by the manufacturer to assist you in locating components that are commonly upgraded. If you have a service manual, your work will be much easier than without one.

The best way to learn to disassemble a laptop is to practice on an old one that you can afford to break. Find an old Dell or Lenovo or IBM ThinkPad for which you can download the service manual from the Dell or Lenovo website. Carefully and patiently follow the disassembly instructions and then reassemble it. When done, you can congratulate yourself and move on to newer laptops.

All About Motherboards

After completing
this chapter, you
will be able to:

- Describe and contrast various types and features of motherboards

- Configure a motherboard using BIOS or UEFI firmware

- Maintain a motherboard, including updating drivers, flashing UEFI/BIOS, and replacing the CMOS battery

- Select, install, and replace a motherboard

- Replace a laptop system board

In previous chapters, you learned how to work inside a computer and began the process of learning about each major component or subsystem in a computer case. In this chapter, we build on all that knowledge to learn about motherboards, which techies sometimes call the mobo. You'll learn about the many different features of a motherboard, including motherboard sockets, chipsets, buses, expansion slots, and onboard ports and connectors. Then you'll learn how to support a motherboard, and that includes configuring, maintaining, installing, and replacing it. A motherboard is considered a field replaceable unit, so it's important to know how to replace one, but the good news is you don't need to know how to repair one that is broken. Troubleshooting a motherboard works hand in hand with troubleshooting the processor and other components that must work to boot up a computer, so we'll leave troubleshooting the motherboard until later chapters.

MOTHERBOARD TYPES AND FEATURES

A+
220-901
1.2, 1.4,
1.6

A motherboard is the most complicated component in a computer. When you put together a computer from parts, generally you start with deciding which processor and motherboard you will use. Everything else follows these two decisions. Take a look at the details of Figure 3-1, which shows a microATX motherboard by Intel that can hold an Intel Core i7, Core i5, or Core i3 processor in the LGA1155 processor socket. When selecting a motherboard, generally you'd need to pay attention to the form factor, processor socket, chipset, buses and number of bus slots, and other connectors, slots, and ports. In this part of the chapter, we'll look at the details of each of these features so that you can read a technical motherboard ad with the knowledge of a pro and know how to select the right motherboard when replacing an existing one or when building a new system.

Regular PCI slot
Two PCIe ×1 slots
PCIe ×16 slot

Cooler with CPU below

Four memory modules (DIMMs)

Chipset under heat sink

Figure 3-1   The Intel desktop motherboard DH67GD uses the microATX form factor and has the processor, cooler, and memory modules installed

MOTHERBOARD FORM FACTORS

A+
220-901
1.2

Recall from the chapter, "First Look at Computer Parts and Tools," that a motherboard form factor determines the size of the board and its features that make it compatible with power supplies and cases. The most popular motherboard form factors are ATX, microATX (a smaller version of ATX), and Mini-ITX (a smaller version of microATX). You saw a microATX motherboard in Figure 3-1. Figure 3-2 shows an ATX board, and a Mini-ITX board is shown in Figure 3-3. The Mini-ITX board is also commonly referred to as an ITX board.

Socket LGA1366

X58 North
Bridge

South Bridge

Four DDR3
DIMM slots

PCIe x16 slots for two
video cards

Figure 3-2   The Intel DX58SO motherboard uses the ATX form factor and is designed with the gamer in mind

Courtesy of ASUSTeK Computer, Inc.

Figure 3-3   A Mini-ITX motherboard

Table 3-1 lists the popular and not-so-popular form factors used by motherboards, and Figure 3-4 shows a comparison of the sizes and hole positions of the ATX, microATX, and Mini-ITX boards. Each of these three boards can fit into an ATX computer case and use an ATX power supply.

Form Factor	Motherboard Size	Description
ATX, full size	Up to 12" × 9.6" (305mm × 244mm)	A popular form factor that has had many revisions and variations.
MicroATX	Up to 9.6" × 9.6" (244mm × 244mm)	A smaller version of ATX.
Mini-ITX (aka ITX)	Up to 6.7" × 6.7" (170mm × 170mm)	A small form factor (SFF) board used in low-end computers and home theater systems. The boards are often used with an Intel Atom processor and are sometimes purchased as a motherboard-processor combo unit.
NLX	Up to 9" × 13.6" (229mm × 345mm)	A low profile form factor used in low-end systems with a riser card.

Table 3-1   Motherboard form factors

Rear of motherboard

Figure 3-4   Sizes and hole positions for the ATX, microATX, and Mini-ITX motherboards

⭐ **A+ Exam Tip**   The A+ 220-901 exam expects you to know about the ATX, microATX, Mini-ITX, and ITX motherboard form factors.

PROCESSOR SOCKETS

Another important feature of a motherboard is the processor socket. This socket and the chipset determine which processors a board can support. A socket for a desktop or laptop computer is designed to hold either an Intel processor or an AMD processor. Some older processors were installed on the motherboard in a long narrow slot, but all processors sold today use sockets. Now let's look at sockets for Intel and AMD processors.

SOCKETS FOR INTEL PROCESSORS

Table 3-2 lists the sockets used by Intel processors for desktop systems. The first two sockets are currently used by new Intel processors. The last six sockets in the table have been discontinued by Intel, but you still need to be able to support them because you might be called on to replace a processor or motherboard that uses one of these legacy sockets. The types of memory listed in the table that are used with these sockets are explained in detail in the chapter, "Supporting the Power System and Troubleshooting Computers." Intel also makes several Itanium and Xeon processors designed for servers. These server processors might use different sockets than those listed in the table. Mobile processor sockets are also not included in the table.

Intel Socket Name	Used by Processor Family	Description
LGA1150 (aka Socket H3)	Fourth Generation (Haswell) Core i7, Core i5, Core i3, Pentium, and Celeron	◢ 1150 pins in the socket touch 1150 lands on the processor. ◢ LGA1150 (see Figure 3-5) supports DDR3 memory.

Table 3-2   Sockets for Intel processors used for desktop computers (continues)

Intel Socket Name	Used by Processor Family	Description
LGA1155 and FCLGA1155 (aka Socket H2)	Third Generation (Ivy Bridge) Core i7 Extreme, Core i7, Core i5, Core i3, Pentium, and Celeron	◢ 1155 pins in the socket touch 1155 lands on the processor. ◢ The LGA1155 (see Figure 3-6) works with DDR3 memory and was designed to replace the LGA1156 socket.
LGA2011 (aka Socket R)	Second Generation (Sandy Bridge) Core i7 Extreme, Core i7, Core i5, Core i3, Pentium, and Celeron	◢ 2011 pins in the socket touch 2011 lands on the processor, which uses a flip-chip land grid array (FCLGA). ◢ Supports DDR3 and DDR4 memory. ◢ Designed to replace LGA1366, used in high-end gaming and server computers and may require a liquid cooling system.
LGA1156 (aka Socket H or H1)	Core i7, Core i5, Core i3, Pentium, and Celeron	◢ 1156 pins in the socket touch 1156 lands on the processor, which uses a flip-chip land grid array (FCLGA). ◢ Works with DDR3 memory.
LGA1366 (aka Socket B)	Core i7, Core i7 Extreme	◢ 1366 pins in the socket touch 1366 lands on the processor. ◢ Works with DDR3 memory.
LGA771 (aka Socket J)	Core 2 Extreme	◢ 771 pins in the socket touch 771 lands on the processor. ◢ Used on high-end workstations and low-end servers. ◢ Works with DDR2 memory on boards that have two processor sockets.
LGA775 (aka Socket T)	Core 2 Extreme, Core 2 Quad, Core 2 Duo, Pentium Dual-Core, Pentium Extreme Edition, Pentium D, Pentium Pentium 4, Pentium 4 Extreme Edition, and Celeron	◢ 775 pins in the socket touch 775 lands on the processor. ◢ Works with DDR3 and DDR2 memory.

Table 3-2   Sockets for Intel processors used for desktop computers (continued)

★ A+ Exam Tip   The A+ 220-901 exam expects you to know about Intel LGA sockets, including the 775, 1155, 1156, 1366, 1150, and 2011 LGA sockets.

Figure 3-5   Socket LGA1150 with protective cover installed

Processor
installed in
socket

Socket lever
used to open
and close the
socket

Figure 3-6   The LGA1155 socket is used by a variety of Intel processors

Sockets and processors use different methods to make the contacts between them. Here is a list of the more important methods:

◢ A pin grid array (PGA) socket has holes aligned in uniform rows around the socket to receive the pins on the bottom of the processor. Early Intel processors used PGA sockets, but they caused problems because the small delicate pins on the processor were easily bent as the processor was installed in the socket. Some newer Intel mobile processors, including the Second Generation Core i3, Core i5, and Core i7 processors, use the PGA988 socket or the FCPGA988 socket in laptops.

◢ A land grid array (LGA) socket has blunt protruding pins on the socket that connect with lands or pads on the bottom of the processor. The first LGA socket was the LGA775 socket. It has 775 pins and is shown with the socket lever and top open in Figure 3-7. Another LGA socket is the LGA1366 shown in Figure 3-8. LGA sockets generally give better contacts than PGA sockets, and the processor doesn't have the delicate pins so easily damaged during an installation. You learn how to use both sockets in the chapter, "Supporting the Power System and Troubleshooting Computers."

Plastic cover
protects the
socket when
it's not in use

Figure 3-7   Socket LGA775 is the first Intel socket to use lands rather than pins

3

Figure 3-8 The LGA1366 socket with socket cover removed and load level lifted ready to receive a processor

Notes Figure 3-9 shows a close-up photo of the LGA775 socket and the bottom of a Pentium processor. Can you make out the pads or lands on the processor and the pins in the socket?

Figure 3-9 Socket LGA775 and the bottom of a Pentium processor

▲ Some sockets can handle a processor using a flip-chip land grid array (FCLGA) processor package or a flip-chip pin grid array (FCPGA) package. The chip is flipped over so that the top of the chip is on the bottom and makes contact with the socket. The LGA1155 socket has a flip-chip version, which is called the FCLGA1155 socket. The two sockets are not compatible.

▲ A staggered pin grid array (SPGA) socket has pins staggered over the socket to squeeze more pins into a small space.

▲ A ball grid array (BGA) connection is not really a socket. The processor is soldered to the motherboard, and the two are always purchased as a unit. For example, the little Atom processors often use this technology with a Mini-ITX motherboard in low-end computers or home theater systems.

Caution When a processor is installed in a socket, extreme care must be taken to protect the socket and the processor against ESD and from damage caused by bending the pins or scratching the socket holes during the installation. Take care to not touch the bottom of the processor or the pins or holes of the socket, which can leave finger oil on the gold plating of the contact surfaces. This oil can later cause tarnishing and lead to a poor contact.

So that even force is applied when inserting the processor in the socket, all current processor sockets have one or two levers on the sides of the socket. These sockets are called zero insertion force (ZIF) sockets, and this lever is used to lift the processor up and out of the socket. Push the levers down and the processor moves into its pin or hole connectors with equal force over the entire housing. Because the socket and processor are so delicate, processors generally should not be removed or replaced repeatedly.

SOCKETS FOR AMD PROCESSORS

Table 3-3 lists the AMD sockets for desktop systems. AMD has chosen to use the PGA socket architecture for its desktop processors. (Some of AMD's server processors use Socket F, which is an LGA socket.) Figure 3-10 shows the AM2+ socket. The lever on the side of the socket is lifted, and an Athlon 64 processor is about to be inserted. If you look closely near the lower edge of the processor, you can see the small delicate pins that will seat into the holes of the socket.

AMD Socket	Used by Processor Family	Description
FM2+	Used with the A10-, A8-, and A6-Series of processors	◢ 906 holes for pins (PGA) ◢ Uses AMD Steamroller architecture with integrated graphics controller in the processor ◢ Works with DDR3 memory
FM2	Used with the Trinity line of processors	◢ 904 holes for pins (PGA) ◢ Uses AMD Piledriver architecture with integrated graphics controller in the processor ◢ Works with DDR3 memory
FM1	AMD A4, A6, A8, E2, Athlon II	◢ 905 holes for pins (PGA) ◢ Works with DDR3 memory
AM3+	AMD FX	◢ 942 holes for pins (PGA) ◢ Uses Bulldozer architecture and is compatible with AM3 processors ◢ Works with DDR3 memory
AM3 or AMD3	Phenom II	◢ 941 holes for pins (PGA) ◢ Works with DDR3 or DDR2 memory

Table 3-3   Sockets for AMD processors used for desktop computers

Figure 3-10   AMD Athlon 64 processor to be inserted into an AM2+ socket

⭐ **A+ Exam Tip** The A+ 220-901 exam expects you to know about these AMD sockets: AM3, AM3+, FM1, FM2, and FM2+.

MATCH A PROCESSOR TO THE SOCKET AND MOTHERBOARD

As you glance over Tables 3-2 and 3-3, you'll notice the same processor family listed under several different sockets. For example, the AMD Athlon family of processors offers many versions of the Athlon. Among these are the Athlon X2 Dual-Core, the Athlon Neo, and the Athlon 64 X2 Dual-Core. Because these various processors within the same processor family use different sockets, you must be careful when matching a processor to a motherboard. To be certain you have a good match, search the Intel (*www.intel .com*) or AMD (*www.amd.com*) website for the exact processor you are buying and make sure the socket it uses is the same as the socket on the motherboard you plan to use.

Also, look at the motherboard manufacturer's website or user guide for a list of processors that the motherboard supports. It's not likely to support every processor that uses its socket because the motherboard chipset is designed to work only with certain processors.

⭐ **A+ Exam Tip** The A+ 220-901 exam does not expect you to be familiar with the processor sockets used by laptop computers. For laptops, generally, it is more cost effective to replace a laptop that has a damaged processor than to replace the processor. If you are called on to replace a laptop processor, however, always use a processor the laptop manufacturer recommends for the particular laptop model and system board CPU socket.

THE CHIPSET

A+
220-901
1.2

A chipset is a set of chips on the motherboard that works closely with the processor to collectively control the memory, buses on the motherboard, and some peripherals. The chipset must be compatible with the processor it serves. The two major chipset manufacturers are Intel (*www.intel.com*) and AMD (*www.amd.com*).

Intel dominates the chipset market for several reasons: It knows more about its own Intel processors than other manufacturers do, and it produces the chipsets most compatible with the Intel family of processors.

INTEL CHIPSETS

Intel has produced far too many chipsets to list them here. To see a complete comparison chart of all Intel chipsets, start at the Intel link *ark.intel.com*.

Here is a list of the more significant chipset families by Intel:

▲ *North Bridge and South Bridge use a hub architecture.* Beginning with the release in 2006 of the Intel i800 series of chipsets, a hub using the Accelerated Hub Architecture is used to connect buses (see Figure 3-11). This hub has a fast and slow end, and each end is a separate chip on the motherboard. The fast end of the hub, called the North Bridge, contains the graphics and memory controller, and connects directly to the processor by way of a 64-bit bus, called the Front Side Bus (FSB), system bus, or host bus. The slower end of the hub, called the South Bridge, contains the I/O controller hub (ICH). All I/O (input/output) devices, except video, connect to the hub by using the slower South Bridge. Notice that in Figure 3-11, the primary PCI Express slot, the slot designated for the video card, has direct access to the North Bridge, but other PCI Express slots must access the processor by way of the slower South Bridge. On a motherboard, when you see two major chip housings for the chipset, one is controlling the North Bridge and the other is controlling the South Bridge (refer to Figure 3-2). Other chipset manufacturers besides Intel also use the North Bridge and South Bridge architecture for their chipsets.

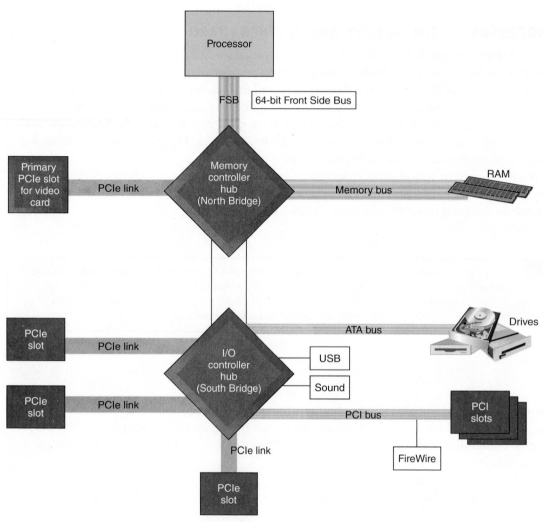

Figure 3-11   The chipset's North Bridge and South Bridge control access to the processor for all components

◢ *Nehalem chipsets with the memory controller in the processor.* The release of the X58 chipset in 2008 was significant because, with previous chipsets, the memory controller was part of the North Bridge. But beginning with the X58, the memory controller was contained in the processor housing. For example, in Figure 3-12, the Core i7 processor contains the memory controller. Notice that memory connects directly to the processor rather than to the North Bridge. Another significant change is the 64-bit Front Side Bus was replaced with a technology called the QuickPath Interconnect (QPI). The QPI has 16 lanes for data packets and works similar to how PCI Express works. All Intel chipsets since the X58 use QuickPath Interconnects. A motherboard using the X58 chipset is shown in Figure 3-13. The board comes with a fan that can be clipped to the top of the North Bridge to help keep the chipset cool.

Nehalem chipsets, which Intel has begun to call the previous generation of chipsets, support the Intel LGA1366 socket, the Core i7 processors, and PCI Express Version 2. They can also support either SLI or CrossFire technologies. (SLI and CrossFire are two competing technologies that allow for multiple video cards installed in one system.)

Figure 3-12 X58 chipset architecture

Figure 3-13 The X58 chipset uses heat sinks to stay cool

✎ **Notes** For an interesting white paper by Intel on QuickPath Interconnect, including a brief history of processor interfaces, go to *www.intel.com* and search on "An Introduction to the Intel QuickPath Interconnect."

▲ *Sandy Bridge chipsets with the memory and graphics controller in the processor.* In 2011, Intel introduced its second-generation chipsets and sockets, which it code-named Sandy Bridge technologies. Rather than using the traditional North Bridge and South Bridge, only one chipset housing is needed, which houses the Platform Controller Hub. The processor interfaces directly with the faster graphics PCI Express 2.0 bus as well as with memory (see Figure 3-14). Therefore, both the memory controller and graphics controller are contained within all Sandy Bridge processors. Sandy Bridge processors, such as the Second Generation Core i7, use the LGA1155 or the LGA2011 socket, and Sandy Bridge motherboards use DDR3 memory. The Sandy Bridge H67 chipset on an Intel motherboard is shown in Figure 3-15 and earlier in Figure 3-1.

Figure 3-14 The Sandy Bridge architecture uses a single chipset hub, called the Platform Controller Hub

Figure 3-15 The Sandy Bridge H67 chipset on the Intel DH67GD motherboard sits under a heat sink to keep it cool

▲ *Ivy Bridge chipsets.* Third-generation processors and chipsets by Intel, released in 2012 and code-named Ivy Bridge, use less power, squeeze more transistors into a smaller space, and perform better than earlier products. Ivy Bridge chipsets include B75, Q75, Q77, H77, Z75, and Z77. Several Ivy Bridge processors use the LGA1155 socket for backward compatibility with earlier motherboards. The Ivy Bridge chipset uses a single Platform Controller Hub.

▲ *Haswell and Broadwell chipsets.* In 2013, Intel introduced the Haswell chipsets, which work with the LGA1150 and LGA2011 sockets in desktops and servers and also work with low-power processors in laptops and ultrabooks (very thin laptops). The chipsets work with DDR3 and DDR4 memory and use less power than previous chipset architectures. Broadwell chipsets, released in 2015, are a little faster than the Haswell chipsets and can also use the LGA1150 socket.

> ✎ **Notes** The Skylake chipset architecture is expected to be released by the time this text is published. The chipset will use the new LGA1151 socket and will support DDR3 and DDR4 memory.

AMD CHIPSETS

AMD specializes in chipsets and graphics processors (called a graphics processor unit or GPU) that target the gaming and hobbyist markets. The two current chipset families by AMD are:

▲ *A-Series chipsets.* These chipsets are designed to support the AMD Accelerated Processing Unit (APU). An APU is a combination of a CPU and a graphics processor unit (GPU) in the same processor housing. In traditional desktops with high graphics needs, the CPU is installed on the motherboard and a GPU is embedded on a video card, also called a graphics adapter, installed in the system. The A-Series chipsets also support AMD CrossFire technology, which uses dual video cards in the same system.

▲ *9-Series chipsets.* These chipsets are designed to support AMD processors that can have up to eight cores. You'll learn more about processor cores in the chapter, "Supporting Processors and Upgrading Memory."

Hands-On | Project 3-1 Identify the Intel Chipset and Processor on Your Computer

A+
220-901
1.4

Intel offers two utilities you can download and run to identify an installed Intel processor or chipset. Do the following to use the utilities:

▲ If you are using a computer with an Intel processor, download and run the Processor Identification Utility available at: *www.intel.com/p/en_US/support/highlights/processors/toolspiu*

▲ If you are using a computer with an Intel processor and your operating system is a 32-bit OS, download and run the Chipset Identification Utility available at: *www.intel.com/support/chipsets/sb/CS-009266.htm*

Websites change often, so if these links don't work, try searching the Intel website for each utility. What information does each utility provide about your processor and chipset?

Hands-On | Project 3-2 Research the Intel ARK Database

A+
220-901
1.4

Intel provides an extensive database of all its processors, chipsets, motherboards, and other products at *ark.intel.com*. Research the database and answer these questions:

1. List three Fourth Generation Core i7 processors. For each processor, list the Processor Number (model), the maximum memory it supports, the PCI Express version it supports (version 1.1, 2.0, 3.0, or 4.0), and the socket it uses.

2. List three Intel motherboards for desktops: An ATX board, a microATX board, and a Mini-ITX board. For each motherboard, list the processor socket it provides, the chipset it uses, the maximum memory it supports, and the number of PCIe slots it has.

(continues)

3. The X99 chipset is designed for gaming computers using the Core i7 processor. What is the launch date for theX99 chipsets?

Find the block diagram for the X99 chipset and answer the following:

4. Which processor socket does the X99 chipset support?

5. Do PCI Express 3.0 graphics adapters connect directly to the processor or to the X99 chipset?

6. Do High-Speed USB ports connect directly to the processor or to the X99 chipset?

BUSES AND EXPANSION SLOTS

**A+
220-901
1.2**

When you look carefully at a motherboard, you see many fine lines on both the top and the bottom of the board's surface (see Figure 3-16). These lines, sometimes called traces, are circuits or paths that enable data, instructions, and power to move from component to component on the board. This system of pathways used for communication and the protocol and methods used for transmission are collectively called the bus. (A protocol is a set of rules and standards that any two entities use for communication.) The parts of the bus that we are most familiar with are the lines of the bus that are used for data; these lines are called the data bus. A bus can also carry electrical power (to power components on the motherboard), control signals (to coordinate activity), and memory addresses (for one program to tell another program where to find data or instructions).

One bus line

Bottom of the CPU socket

Figure 3-16   On the bottom of the motherboard, you can see bus lines terminating at the CPU socket

All data and instructions inside a computer exist in binary, which means there are only two states: on and off. Binary data is put on a line of a bus by placing voltage on that line. We can visualize that bits are "traveling" down the bus in parallel, but in reality, the voltage placed on each line is not "traveling"; rather, it is all over the line. When one component at one end of the line wants to write data to another component, the two components get in sync for the write operation. Then, the first component places voltage on several lines of the bus, and the other component immediately reads the voltage on these lines. The CPU or other devices interpret the voltage, or lack of voltage, on each line on the bus as binary digits (0s or 1s).

The width of a data bus is called the data path size. Some buses have data paths that are 8, 16, 32, 64, 128, or more bits wide. For example, a bus that has eight wires, or lines, to transmit data is called an 8-bit bus. Figure 3-17 shows an 8-bit bus between the CPU and memory that is transmitting the letter A (binary 0100 0001). All bits of a byte are placed on their lines of the bus at the same time: no voltage for binary zero and voltage for binary one. For every eight bits of a bus, a bus might use a ninth bit for error checking. Adding a check bit for each byte allows the component reading the data to verify that it is the same data written to the bus.

Figure 3-17   A data bus has traces or lines that carry voltage interpreted by the CPU and other devices as bits

One of the most interesting lines, or circuits, on a bus is the system clock or system timer, which is dedicated to timing the activities on the motherboard much like a metronome helps a musician with timing. The chipset sends out a continuous pulsating electrical signal on one line of the system bus. This one system clock line, dedicated to carrying the pulse, is read by other components on the motherboard (including the processor, bus slots, memory slots, and so forth) and ensures that all activities are synchronized. Remember that everything in a computer is binary, and this includes the activities themselves. Instead of continuously working to perform commands or move data, the CPU, bus, and other devices work in a binary fashion—do something, stop, do something, stop, and so forth. Each device works on a clock cycle or beat of the clock. Some devices, such as the CPU, do two or more operations on one beat of the clock, and others do one operation for each beat. Some devices might even do something on every other beat, but most components inside the system work according to these beats or cycles.

You can think of this as similar to children jumping rope. The system clock (child turning the rope) provides the beats or cycles, while devices (children jumping) work in a binary fashion (jump, don't jump). In the analogy, some children jump two or more times for each rope pass.

> ✎ **Notes**   If the processor requests something from a slow device and the device is not ready, the device issues a wait state, which is a command to the processor to wait for slower devices to catch up.

The speed of memory, Front Side Bus, processor, or other component is measured in hertz (Hz), which is one cycle per second; megahertz (MHz), which is one million cycles per second; and gigahertz (GHz), which is one billion cycles per second. Common ratings for memory are 1333 MHz and 1866 MHz. Common ratings for Front Side Buses are 2600 MHz, 2000 MHz, 1600 MHz, 1333 MHz, 1066 MHz, 800 MHz, 533 MHz, or 400 MHz. A CPU operates from 166 MHz to almost 4 GHz. The CPU can put data or instructions on its internal bus at a much higher rate than does the motherboard. Although we often refer to the speed of the CPU and memory, talking about the frequency of these devices is more accurate, because the term *speed* implies a continuous flow, while the term *frequency* implies a digital or binary flow: on and off, on and off.

> **✎ Notes** Rather than measuring the frequency of a system bus, sometimes you see a system bus measured in performance such as the GA-990FXA-UD3 motherboard by GIGABYTE (see *www.gigabyte.us*). This system bus is rated at 5.2 GT/s or 5200 MT/s. One GT/s is one billion transfers per second, and one MT/s is one million transfers per second.

A motherboard can have more than one bus, each using a different protocol, speed, data path size, and so on. Table 3-4 lists the various buses used on motherboards today, in order of throughput speed from fastest to slowest. (Throughput is sometimes called bandwidth.) Looking at the second column of Table 3-4, you can see that a bus is called an expansion bus, local bus, local I/O bus, or local video bus. A bus that does not run in sync with the system clock is called an expansion bus. For chipsets that use a South Bridge, expansion buses always connect here. Most buses today are local buses, meaning they run in sync with the system clock. If a local bus connects to the slower I/O controller hub or South Bridge of the chipset, it is called a local I/O bus. Because the video card needs to run at a faster rate than other adapter cards, this one slot always connects to the faster end of the chipset, the North Bridge, or directly to the processor when using Sandy Bridge or later technologies. Today's boards use PCI Express x16 slots for video cards. These video buses that connect to the older North Bridge or directly to the processor are called local video buses.

Bus	Bus Type	Data Path in Bits	Address Lines	Throughput(Bandwidth)
PCI Express Version 4.0 (not yet released)	Local video and local I/O	Serial with up to 32 lanes	Up to 32 lanes	Up to 64 GB/sec for 16 lanes
PCI Express Version 3.0	Local video and local I/O	Serial with up to 32 lanes	Up to 32 lanes	Up to 32 GB/sec for 16 lanes
PCI Express Version 2.0	Local video and local I/O	Serial with up to 32 lanes	Up to 32 lanes	Up to 16 GB/sec for 16 lanes
PCI Express Version 1.1	Local video and local I/O	Serial with up to 16 lanes	Up to 16 lanes	Up to 8 GB/sec for 16 lanes
PCI-X	Local I/O	64	32	Up to 8.5 GB/sec
PCI	Local I/O	32 or 64	32 or 64	133, 266, or 532 MB/sec
FireWire 400 and 800	Local I/O or expansion	1	Serial	Up to 3.2 Gbps (gigabits per second)
USB 1.1, 2.0, and 3.0	Expansion	1	Serial	12 or 480 Mbps (megabits per second) or 5.0 Gbps (gigabits per second)

Table 3-4 Buses listed by throughput

> **★ A+ Exam Tip** The 220-901 exam expects you to know about the PCI, PCI-X, PCIe, and MiniPCI expansion slots.

So now let's look at the details of the PCI, PCI-X, and PCIe expansion slots used in desktops. We'll also discuss the MiniPCI expansion slots used in laptops. The FireWire and USB buses are discussed in the chapter, "Supporting I/O Devices."

CONVENTIONAL PCI

The first PCI bus had a 32-bit data path, supplied 5 V of power to an adapter card, and operated at 33 MHz. It was the first bus that allowed adapter cards to run in sync with the CPU. PCI Version 2.x introduced the 64-bit, 3.3-V PCI slot, doubling data throughput of the bus. Because a card can be damaged if installed in the wrong voltage slot, a notch in a PCI slot distinguishes between a 5-V slot and a 3.3-V slot. A Universal PCI card can use either a 3.3-V or 5-V slot and contains both notches (see Figure 3-18). Conventional PCI is no longer evolving and ended up with four types of slots and six possible PCI card configurations to use these slots. These slots and cards include 32-bit PCI and 64-bit PCI-X, all shown in Figure 3-19.

Figure 3-18 A 32-bit, 5-V PCI network card and a 32-bit, universal PCI wireless card show the difference in PCI notches set to distinguish voltages in a PCI slot

Figure 3-19 With PCI Version 2.x, there are four possible types of expansion slots and six differently configured PCI expansion cards to use these slots

PCI-X

The next evolution of PCI is PCI-X, which uses a 64-bit data path and had three major revisions; the last and final revision is PCI-X 3.0. All PCI-X revisions are backward compatible with conventional PCI cards and slots, except 5-V PCI cards are not supported. PCI-X focused on the server market; therefore, it's unlikely you'll see PCI-X slots in desktop computers. Motherboards that use PCI-X tend to have several different PCI slots with some 32-bit or 64-bit slots running at different speeds. For example, Figure 3-20 shows a server motherboard with three types of slots. The two long white slots are PCI-X; the two shorter white slots are PCI, and the two black slots are PCIe. The two PCI-X slots can use most 32-bit and 64-bit PCI or PCI-X cards.

Courtesy of Super Micro Computer, Inc.

Figure 3-20   The two long white PCI-X slots can support PCI cards

PCI EXPRESS

PCI Express (PCIe) uses an altogether different architectural design than conventional PCI and PCI-X and is not backward compatible with either. PCI Express will ultimately replace both these buses, although it is expected PCI Express will coexist with conventional PCI for some time to come (see Figure 3-21). Whereas PCI uses a 32-bit or 64-bit parallel bus, PCI Express uses a serial bus, which is faster than a parallel bus because it transmits data in packets similar to how Ethernet, USB, and FireWire transmit data. A PCIe expansion slot can provide one or more of these serial lanes.

Two PCIe x16 slots

PCIe x4 slot

Conventional PCI slot

Two PCIe x1 slots

Figure 3-21   Three types of PCIe slots and one conventional PCI slot

Another difference in PCI Express is how it connects to the processor. One or more PCI Express slots used for video cards have a direct link to the North Bridge or to the processor (using Sandy Bridge or later architecture). Refer back to Figures 3-10, 3-11, and 3-13.

PCI Express currently comes in four different slot sizes called PCI Express ×1 (pronounced "by one"), ×4, ×8, and ×16. Figure 3-21 shows three of these slots. Notice in the photo how the PCIe slots are not as tall and the pins are closer together than the conventional PCI slot. A PCI Express ×1 slot contains a single lane for data; this lane is actually four wires. One pair of wires is used to send data and the other pair receives data, one bit at a time. The ×16 slot contains 16 lanes, with each lane timed independently of other lanes. The more lanes you have, the more data gets transmitted in a given time. Therefore, a ×16 slot is faster than a ×4 slot, which is faster than a ×1 slot. A shorter PCI Express card (such as a ×1 card) can be installed in a longer PCI Express slot (such as a ×4 slot).

Revisions of PCIe include PCIe version 1.1, PCIe version 2.0 and 2.1, PCIe version 3.0, and PCIe version 4.0. Here are important facts about each PCIe version:

▲ **PCIe version 1.0.** The original PCIe version 1.0 allowed for 150 W to PCIe cards. Pins on the expansion card provide 75 W, and a new 6-pin PCIe connector from the power supply provides an additional 75 W.

▲ **PCIe version 1.1.** PCIe version 1.1 allowed for more wattage to PCIe cards, up to 225 W. The standard allows for two 6-pin PCIe connectors from the power supply to the card. Therefore, the total 225 W comes as 75 W from the slot and 150 W from the two connectors.

▲ **PCIe version 2.0.** PCIe version 2.0 doubled the frequency of the PCIe bus and allows for up to 32 lanes on one slot (though few motherboards or cards actually use 32 lane slots). The allowed wattage to one PCIe 2.0 card was increased to a total of 300 W by using a new 8-pin PCIe power connector that provides 150 W (see Figure 3-22). The 300 W to the card come from the slot (75 W), from the 8-pin connector (150 W), and an additional 75 W come from a second auxiliary connector on the motherboard. This second connector can be a 6-pin PCIe connector, a Molex-style connector, or a SATA-style connector. You'll see an example of these connectors later in this chapter.

Figure 3-22 8-pin PCIe Version 2.0 power connector

▲ **PCIe versions 3.0 and 4.0.** PCIe version 3.0 roughly doubles the speed of PCIe version 2.0 and is backward compatible with PCIe version 2.0 components. PCIe version 4.0 doubles the speed of PCIe version 3.0 and is also backward compatible with earlier PCIe standards; PCIe version 4.0 devices are not yet available on the market.

MINI PCI AND MINI PCIe IN LAPTOP COMPUTERS

Smaller versions of the PCI and PCIe slots are used in laptops, all-in-one computers, and with small form factor motherboards such as the Mini-ITX board. The Mini PCI slot follows the PCI standards and the Mini PCI Express slot follows the PCI Express standards. To save space, the slots lay flat on the motherboard and hold an expansion card parallel to the board.

Mini PCIe slots have 52 or 54 pins on the edge connector and have one notch offset from the center of the slot (see Figure 3-23). One screw holds the card securely in the slot. The Mini PCI slot is wider and has 100 or 124 pins and a notch slightly offset from the end of the slot (see Figure 3-24).

Notch in Mini PCIe slot and card

Figure 3-23   Mini PCIe slot with a Wireless Mini PCIe card installed

Figure 3-24   A Mini PCI card has a notch near the side of the edge connector

PCI RISER CARDS USED TO EXTEND THE SLOTS

A+
220-901
1.4

Suppose you are installing a Mini-ITX or microATX motherboard into a low-profile or slimline case that does not give you enough room to install a PCI card standing up in an expansion slot. In this situation, a PCI riser card can solve the problem. The riser card installs in the slot and provides another slot at a right angle (see Figure 3-25). When you install an expansion card in this riser card slot, the card sits parallel to the motherboard, taking up less space. These riser cards come for all types of PCI slots, including PCIe, PCI-X, and conventional PCI.

3

Figure 3-25 PCI riser card provides a 3.3-V slot or 5-V slot depending on which direction the card is inserted in the PCI slot

ONBOARD PORTS AND CONNECTORS

**A+
220-901
1.2**

In addition to expansion slots, a motherboard might also have several ports and internal connectors. Ports coming directly off the motherboard are called onboard ports or integrated components. Almost all motherboards have two or more USB ports and sound ports. Boards might also offer a network port, FireWire (IEEE 1394) port, one or more video ports, one or more eSATA ports (for external SATA hard drives), parallel port, serial port, a port for a wireless antenna, and PS/2 ports for a mouse and keyboard. Older motherboards might have a modem port. Figure 3-26 shows ports on an entry-level desktop motherboard.

Figure 3-26 A motherboard provides ports for common I/O devices

When you purchase a motherboard, the package includes an I/O shield, which is the plate that you install in the computer case that provides holes for these I/O ports. The I/O shield is the size designed for the case's form factor, and the holes in the shield are positioned for the motherboard ports (see Figure 3-27). When you first install a motherboard, you might need to install the drivers that come on the DVD or CD bundled with the board before some of the motherboard ports will work. How to install the motherboard drivers is covered later in this chapter.

Figure 3-27   The I/O shield fits the motherboard ports to the computer case

A motherboard might have several internal connectors, including SATA, USB, and FireWire (IEEE 1394) connectors. When you purchase a motherboard, look in the package for the motherboard manual either printed or on DVD or CD. It will show a diagram of the board with a description of each connector. For example, the connectors for the motherboard in Figure 3-28 are labeled as the manual describes them. If a connector is a group of pins sticking up on the board, the connector is called a header. You will learn to use most of these connectors in later chapters.

- S/PDIF header
- Six SATA headers
- Two USB headers
- FireWire header
- High-definition audio header

Figure 3-28   Internal connectors on a motherboard for drives and ports on the front of the case

APPLYING | CONCEPTS   FIND THE MOTHERBOARD DOCUMENTATION

A+ 220-901 1.4

The motherboard user guide is essential to identifying components on a board and knowing how to support the board. This guide can be a PDF file stored on the CD or DVD that came bundled with the motherboard. If you don't have the CD, you can download the user guide from the motherboard manufacturer's website.

To find the correct user guide online, you need to know the board manufacturer and model. If a motherboard is already installed in a computer, you can use the Windows System Information utility (msinfo32.exe) to report the brand and model of the board. To access the utility, for Windows 8.x, from the desktop, right-click **Start**, click **Run**, and type **msinfo32.exe** in the Run box. (For Windows 7/Vista, click **Start**, type **msinfo32.exe** in the Search box, and press **Enter**.) In the System Information window, click **System Summary**. In the System Summary information in the right pane, look for the motherboard information labeled as the System Manufacturer and System Model (see Figure 3-29).

Figure 3-29 Use the System Information window to identify the motherboard brand and model

If the motherboard is not installed or the system is not working, look for the brand and model imprinted somewhere on the motherboard (see Figure 3-30). Next, go to the website of the motherboard manufacturer and download the user guide. Websites for several motherboard manufacturers are listed in Table 3-5. The diagrams, pictures, charts, and explanations of settings and components in the user guide will be invaluable to you when supporting this board.

Figure 3-30 The motherboard brand and model are imprinted somewhere on the board

(continues)

Manufacturer	Web Address
ASUS	*www.asus.com*
Evga	*www.evga.com*
ASRock	*www.asrock.com*
Gigabyte Technology Co., Ltd.	*www.gigabyte.com*
Intel Corporation	*www.intel.com*
Micro-Star International (MSI)	*www.msicomputer.com*
Super Micro Computer, Inc.	*www.supermicro.com*

Table 3-5   Major manufacturers of motherboards

Hands-On | Project 3-3   Examine a Motherboard in Detail

A+
220-901
1.4

1. Look at the back of a desktop computer. Without opening the case, list the ports that you believe come directly from the motherboard.

2. Remove the cover of the case, which you learned to do in the chapter, "Working Inside Desktop Computers and Laptops." List the different expansion cards in the expansion slots. Was your guess correct about which ports come from the motherboard?

3. To expose the motherboard so you can identify its parts, remove all the expansion cards.

4. Draw a diagram of the motherboard and label these parts:

   ◢ Processor socket
   ◢ Chipset
   ◢ RAM (each DIMM slot)
   ◢ CMOS battery
   ◢ Expansion slots (Identify the slots as PCI, PCIe x1, PCIe x4, or PCIe x16.)
   ◢ Each port coming directly from the motherboard
   ◢ Power supply connections
   ◢ SATA drive connectors

5. What is the brand and model of the motherboard?

6. Locate the manufacturer's website. If you can find the motherboard manual on the site, download it. Find the diagram of the motherboard in the manual and compare it with your diagram. Did you label components correctly?

7. Reassemble the computer, as you learned to do in the chapter, "Working Inside Desktop Computers and Laptops."

Hands-On | Project 3-4 Examine Motherboard Documentation

A+
220-901
1.4

Using the motherboard brand and model installed in your computer, or another motherboard brand and model assigned by your instructor, download the user guide from the motherboard manufacturer and answer these questions:

1. What processors does the board support?

2. What type of RAM does the board support?

3. What is the maximum RAM the board can hold?

4. If the board has a PCIe slot, what version of PCIe does the board use?

5. What chipset does the board use?

Now that you know what to expect when examining or selecting a motherboard, let's see how to configure a board.

CONFIGURING A MOTHERBOARD

Firmware on the motherboard is used to enable or disable a connector, port, or component; control the frequency of the CPU, security features, and what happens when the PC first boots; and monitor various activities of the board. Today's motherboards may use these types of firmware:

▲ *BIOS.* BIOS is used on older motherboards.
▲ *UEFI.* Unified Extensible Firmware Interface (UEFI) is replacing BIOS and is used on most motherboards made after 2012. Microsoft requires UEFI in order for the system to be certified for Windows 8 and later. UEFI is also required for hard drives larger than 2 TB. (One terabyte or TB equals 1000 gigabytes or GB.)
▲ *UEFI with BIOS.* Most personal computer motherboards contain UEFI firmware with BIOS also provided for backward compatibility with older devices.

As an IT support technician, you need to know how to configure the BIOS or UEFI firmware settings. We first look at how to configure BIOS settings and then we'll see how to configure UEFI settings.

USING BIOS SETUP TO CONFIGURE A MOTHERBOARD

The motherboard settings don't normally need to be changed except, for example, when there is a problem with hardware, or a power-saving feature or security feature (such as a power-on password) needs to be disabled or enabled.

★ **A+ Exam Tip** The A+ 220-901 exam expects you to know about BIOS settings regarding RAM, the hard drive, optical drive, CPU, boot sequence, enabling and disabling devices, system date and time, virtualization support, passwords, drive encryption, and monitoring temperature, fan speeds, intrusion detection, voltage, and clock and bus speeds. All these settings are covered in this part of the chapter.

ACCESS THE BIOS SETUP PROGRAM

You access the BIOS setup program by pressing a key or combination of keys during the boot process. For most motherboards, you press F2 or Del during the boot. For a few older motherboards, you press Ctrl+Alt+Esc. See the motherboard documentation to know for sure which keys to press. A message such as the following usually appears on the screen near the beginning of the boot:

```
Press DEL to change Setup
```

or

```
Press F2 for Setup
```

When you press the appropriate key or keys, a setup screen appears with menus and Help features that are often very user-friendly. Although the exact menus depend on the BIOS maker, the sample screens that follow will help you become familiar with the general contents of BIOS setup screens. Figure 3-31 shows a main menu for setup. On this menu, you can view information about the BIOS version, processor model and speed, memory speed, total memory, and the amount of memory in each memory slot. You can also change the system date and time.

```
                              System Setup
   Main    Configuration    Performance    Security   Power    Boot    Exit

   BIOS Version              BLH6710H.86A.0105.2011.0301.1654    Number of cores to
                                                                 enable in each
   Processor Type           Intel(R)  Core(TM) i5-2320 CPU @     processor package
                            3.00GHz
   Active Processor Cores               <ALL>
   Host Clock Frequency                 100 MHz
   Processor Turbo Speed                3.30 GHz
   Memory Speed                         1333 MHz

   L2 Cache RAM                         4 x 256 KB
   L3 Cache RAM                         6 MB
   Total Memory                         16 GB
   DIMM3 (Memory Channel A Slot 0)      4 GB
   DIMM1 (Memory Channel A Slot 1)      4 GB
   DIMM4 (Memory Channel B Slot 0)      4 GB
   DIMM2 (Memory Channel B Slot 1)      4 GB

   System Identification Information

   System Date                          <Mon 02/19/2016>
   System Time                          <12:05:32>




                                                        → ←: Select Screen
                                                        ↑ ↓: Select Item
                                                        Enter:Select
                                                        +/-: Change Opt.
                                                        F9: Load Defaults
                                                        F10:Save ESC:Exit
```

Source: Intel

Figure 3-31   BIOS setup main menu

> ✎ **Notes** For a comprehensive list of BIOS manufacturers and links to their websites, visit *support.microsoft.com/en-us/kb/243909*.

Now let's examine setup screens that apply to the boot sequence, virtualization, built-in diagnostics, monitoring the system, and security.

CHANGE THE BOOT SEQUENCE

Figure 3-32 shows an example of a boot menu in BIOS setup. Here, you can set the order in which the system tries to boot from certain devices (called the boot sequence or boot priority). Most likely when you first install a hard drive or an operating system, you will want to have the BIOS attempt to first boot from a DVD so that you can install Windows from the setup DVD. After the OS is installed, to prevent accidental boots from a DVD or other media, change setup BIOS to boot first from the hard drive. Notice in Figure 3-32 the option to perform a UEFI Boot. This particular motherboard holds both BIOS and UEFI firmware.

```
                            System Setup
  Main    Configuration   Performance   Security   Power    Boot     Exit

  Boot Menu Type                    <Advanced>                Select how the bot menu is
  Boot Device Priority              <P0: KINGSTON SVP200S3120>  displayed. Select Normal
                                    <P1: ST1000DM003-9YN162 >  to display boot devices by
                                    <P3: TSSTcorp CDDVDW SH-2>  category. Select Advanced
                                    <IBA GE Slot 00C8 v1365>   to display individual boot
  Boot to Optical Devices           <Enable>                   devices.
  Boot to Removable Devices         <Enable>
  Boot to Network                   <Enable>
  USB Boot                          <Enable>
  Boot USB Devices First            <Enable>
  UEFI Boot                         <Disable>

  HyperBoot
     General Optimization           <Disable>
     USB Optimization               <Disable>
     Video Optimization             <Disable>              → ←: Select Screen
                                                           ↑ ↓: Select Item
  Boot Display Options                                     Enter:Select
                                                           +/-: Change Opt.
                                                           F9: Load Defaults
                                                           F10:Save ESC:Exit
```
Source: Intel

Figure 3-32 Set the boot priority order in BIOS setup

Also, the BIOS setup boot screens might give you options regarding built-in diagnostics that occur at the boot. Recall from the chapter, "First Look at Computer Parts and Tools," that these tests are called the POST (power-on self test). You can configure some motherboards to perform a quick boot and bypass the extensive POST. For these systems, if you are troubleshooting a boot problem, be sure to set BIOS to perform the full POST.

CONFIGURE ONBOARD DEVICES

You can enable or disable some onboard devices (for example, a network port, FireWire port, USB ports, or video ports) using setup BIOS. For one system, the Configuration screen shown in Figure 3-33 does the job. On this screen, you can enable or disable a port or group of ports, and you can configure the Front Panel Audio ports for Auto, High Definition audio, and Legacy audio, or you can disable these audio ports. What you can configure on your system depends on the onboard devices the motherboard offers.

```
                            System Setup
  Main    Configuration   Performance   Security   Power    Boot     Exit

  Onboard Devices                                          Enables or Disables
                                                           Enhanced Consumer Infrared
  Enhanced Consumer IR              <Disable>              (CIR)
  Audio                             <Enable>
     Front Panel Audio              <Auto>
  HDMI/DisplayPort Audio            <Enable>
  LAN                               <Enable>
  1394                              <Enable>

  USB                               <Enable>
  Num Lock                          <On>
  PCI Latency Timer                 <32>




                                                           → ←: Select Screen
                                                           ↑ ↓: Select Item
                                                           Enter:Select
                                                           +/-: Change Opt.
                                                           F9: Load Defaults
                                                           F10:Save ESC:Exit
```
Source: Intel

Figure 3-33 Enable and disable onboard devices

> **Notes** You don't have to replace an entire motherboard if one port fails. For example, if the network port fails, use BIOS setup to disable the port. Then use an expansion card for the port instead.

VIEW HARD DRIVE AND OPTICAL DRIVE INFORMATION

Using setup BIOS, you can view information about installed hard drives and optical drives. For example, in Figure 3-34, one system shows five internal SATA and eSATA ports and one external eSATA port. One 120-GB hard drive is installed on SATA port 0, and another 1000-GB hard drive is installed on SATA port 1. Both ports are internal SATA connectors on the motherboard. Notice the optical drive is installed on SATA port 3, also an internal connector on the motherboard.

```
                              System Setup
   Main    Configuration    Performance   Security   Power   Boot   Exit

   SATA Drives                                       Enables of disables the
                                                     Chipset SATA Controller.
   Chipset SATA Controller Configuration             The Chipset SATA
   Chipset SATA                <Enable>              controller supports the 2
    Chipset SATA Mode          <AHCI>                blue internal SATA ports
    S.M.A.R.T.                 <Enable>              (up to 6Gb/s supported per
    SATA Port 0                KINGSTON SUP20(120.0GB-6.0Gb/s)  port) and the 2 black and
    SATA Port 1                ST1000DM003-9Y(1000.2GB-6.0Gb/s) 2 red internal and
    SATA Port 2                [Not Installed]       external SATA ports (up to
    SATA Port 3                TSSTcorp CDDVD(1.5GB/s)  3Gb/s supported per port).

   eSATA Ports                 <Enable>
    Internal eSATA Port 4      [Not Installed]
    External eSATA Port 5      [Not Installed]

   Hard Disk Pre-Delay         <No>
                                                     → ←: Select Screen
                                                     ↑ ↓: Select Item
                                                     Enter:Select
                                                     +/-: Change Opt.
                                                     F9: Load Defaults
                                                     F10:Save ESC:Exit
```

Source: Intel

Figure 3-34   A BIOS setup screen showing a list of drives installed on the system

PROCESSOR AND CLOCK SPEEDS

Overclocking is running a processor, memory, motherboard, or video card at a higher speed than the manufacturer recommends. Some motherboards allow overclocking. If you decide to overclock a system, pay careful attention to the temperature of the processor so it does not overheat; overheating can damage the processor. Figure 3-35 shows one BIOS setup screen for adjusting performance. Notice on the screen the Host Clock Frequency. This is the basic system clock provided by the chipset, by which all other components synchronize activities. The Core Max Multiplier on this screen is 33. (This value is sometimes called the bus/core ratio.) When you multiply 100 MHz by 33, you get 3.30 GHz, which is the frequency of the processor. This board uses the QuickPath Interconnect. For older boards that use a Front Side Bus, you can change the speed of the FSB to overclock the system, which affects the processor and memory speeds. On some boards, you can change the processor multiplier to change the processor speed and/or change the memory multiplier to affect memory speed.

```
                              System Setup
  Main    Configuration    Performance    Security  Power    Boot    Exit

                            Proposed    Active     Default
  Host Clock Frequency        100        100        100     (MHz)
  Processor Overrides
    Intel® Turbo Boost Technology  Enable    Enable    Enable
    Core Max Multiplier       33         33         33
    Speed                     3.30       3.30       3.30    (GHz)
    Graphic Max Multiplier    22         22         22
  Memory Overrides
    Multiplier                10         10         10
    Speed                     1333       1333       1333    (MHz)
  Voltage Overrides
    Memory                  <1.5000>   <1.5000>   <1.5000> (V)      → ←: Select Screen
    Graphics                <Default>   Default    Default  (V)     ↑ ↓: Select Item
                                                                    Enter:Select
                                                                    +/-: Change Opt.
                                                                    F9: Load Defaults
                                                                    F10:Save ESC:Exit

                                                              Source: Intel
```

Figure 3-35 A motherboard might give options for changing the clock speed or multipliers for the processor and memory

MONITOR TEMPERATURES, FAN SPEEDS, AND VOLTAGES

Using BIOS setup screens, you can monitor temperatures inside the case, fan speeds, and voltages. One BIOS screen that allows you to monitor these values and also control fan speeds is shown in Figure 3-36. Case and CPU fans on modern computers adjust their speeds based on the temperatures of the CPU, memory, and motherboard. You can also install software (for example, SpeedFan by Alfredo Comparetti at *www .almico.com/speedfan.php*) in Windows to monitor temperatures and control fan speeds. To use the software, you might need to change a BIOS setting to allow software to control the speeds. For this system, when you select Processor Temperature, you can set the threshold temperatures that software uses to create an alert.

```
                              System Setup
  Main    Configuration    Performance    Security  Power    Boot    Exit

  Fan Control & Real-Time Monitoring

  CPU Fan                        1008 RPM
  Front Fan                         0 RPM
  Rear Fan                        659 RPM


  Processor Temperature            63  °C
  PCH Temperature                  53  °C
  Memory Temperature               36  °C
  VR Temperature                   41  °C

  +12.0V                         11.96 V
  +5.0V                           5.07 V
  +3.3V                           3.36 V
  Memory Vcc                      1.54 V
  Processor Vcc                   1.20 V
  PCH Vcc                         1.07 V
  +3.3V Standby                   3.39 V                    → ←: Select Screen
                                                            ↑ ↓: Select Item
  Restore Default Fan Control Configuration                 Enter:Select
                                                            +/-: Change Opt.
  Warning: Setting items on these screens to incorrect values may cause  F9: Load Defaults
  system to overheat and/or produce undesired acoustics!    F10:Save ESC:Exit

                                                              Source: Intel
```

Figure 3-36 Monitor temperatures, fan speeds, and voltages in a system

INTRUSION DETECTION

BIOS settings might offer several security features, and one of these is an intrusion-detection alert. For example, for the BIOS setup screen shown in Figure 3-37, you can enable event logging, which logs when the case is opened. To use the feature, you must use a cable to connect a switch on the case to a header on the motherboard.

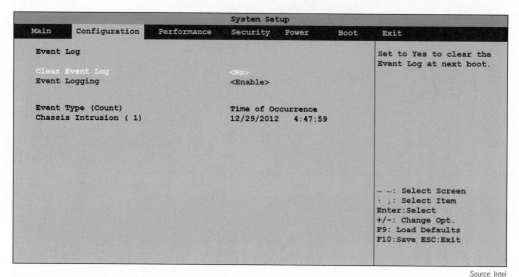

Figure 3-37   BIOS is enabled to log a chassis intrusion

When the security measure is in place and the case is opened, BIOS displays an alert the next time the system is powered up. For example, the alert message at startup might be "Chassis Intruded! System has halted." If you see this message, know that the case has been opened. Reboot the system and the system should start up as usual. To make sure the alert was not tripped by accident, verify that the case cover is securely in place. Also, sometimes a failed CMOS battery can trip the alert. Intrusion-detection devices are not a recommended best practice for security. False alerts are annoying, and criminals generally know how to get inside a case without tripping the alert.

POWER-ON PASSWORDS

Another security feature is power-on passwords assigned in BIOS setup to prevent unauthorized access to the computer and/or the BIOS setup utility. For one motherboard, this security screen looks like the one shown in Figure 3-38, where you can set a supervisor password and a user password. In addition, you can configure how the user password works.

Figure 3-38   Set supervisor and user passwords in BIOS setup to lock down a computer

The choices under User Access Level are **No Access** (the user cannot access the BIOS setup utility), **View Only** (the user can access BIOS setup, but cannot make changes), **Limited** (the user can access BIOS setup and make a few changes such as date and time), and **Full Access** (the user can access the BIOS setup utility and make any changes). When supervisor and user passwords are both set and you boot the system, a box to enter a password is displayed. What access you have depends on which password you enter. Also, if both passwords are set, you must enter a valid password to boot the system. By setting both passwords, you can totally lock down the computer from unauthorized access.

> ★ **A+ Exam Tip** The A+ 220-901 exam expects you to know how to use BIOS setup to secure a workstation from unauthorized use.

> ✎ **Notes** For added protection, configure the BIOS setup utility so that a user cannot boot from a removable device such as a CD, USB device, or floppy disk.

> ⚡ **Caution** In the event that passwords are forgotten, know that supervisor and user passwords to the computer can be reset by setting a jumper (group of pins) on the motherboard to clear all BIOS customized settings and return BIOS setup to its default settings. To keep someone from using this technique to access the computer, you can use a computer case with a lockable side panel and install a lock on the case. How to use jumpers is covered later in this chapter.

BIOS SUPPORT FOR VIRTUALIZATION

Virtualization is when one physical machine hosts multiple activities that are normally done on multiple machines. One type of virtualization is the use of virtual machines. A virtual computer or virtual machine (VM) is software that simulates the hardware of a physical computer. Each VM running on a computer works like a physical computer and is assigned virtual devices such as a virtual motherboard and virtual hard drive. Examples of VM software are Windows Virtual PC, Microsoft Hyper-V, and Oracle VirtualBox. For most VM software to work, virtualization must be enabled in BIOS setup. Looking back at Figure 3-38, you can see the option to enable Intel VT. Intel VT is the name that Intel gives to its virtualization technology.

LOJACK FOR LAPTOPS TECHNOLOGY

LoJack is a technology embedded in the BIOS of many laptops to protect a system against theft. When you subscribe to the LoJack for Laptops service by Absolute (*www.absolute.com*), the Computrace Agent software is installed. The software and BIOS work together to protect the system. The company can locate your laptop whenever it connects to the Internet, and you can give commands through the Internet to lock the laptop or delete all data on it.

DRIVE ENCRYPTION AND DRIVE PASSWORD PROTECTION

Some motherboards and hard drives allow you to set a password that must be entered before someone can access the hard drive. This password is kept on the drive and works even if the drive is moved to another computer. Some manufacturers of storage media offer similar products. For example, Seagate (*www.seagate.com*) offers Maxtor BlackArmor, a technology that encrypts an entire external storage device that is password protected.

> ✎ **Notes** Drive lock password protection might be too secure at times. I know of a situation where a hard drive with password protection became corrupted. Normally, you might be able to move the drive to another computer and recover some data. However, this drive asked for the password, but then could not confirm it. Therefore, the entire drive, including all the data, was inaccessible.

THE TPM CHIP AND HARD DRIVE ENCRYPTION

Many high-end computers have a chip on the motherboard called the TPM (Trusted Platform Module) chip. The BitLocker Encryption tool in Windows 8/7/Vista is designed to work with this chip; the chip holds the BitLocker encryption key (also called the startup key). The TPM chip can also be used with other encryption software that may be installed on the hard drive other than BitLocker. If the hard drive is stolen from the computer and installed in another computer, the data would be safe because BitLocker has encrypted all contents on the drive and would not allow access without the startup key stored on the TPM chip. Therefore, this method assures that the drive cannot be used in another computer. However, if the motherboard fails and is replaced, you'll need a backup copy of the startup key to access data on the hard drive.

★ **A+ Exam Tip** The A+ 220-901 exam expects you to know about drive encryption and the TPM chip.

When you use Windows to install BitLocker Encryption, the initialization process also initializes the TPM chip. Initializing the TPM chip configures it and turns it on. After BitLocker is installed, you can temporarily turn off BitLocker, which also turns off the TPM chip. For example, you might want to turn off BitLocker to test the BitLocker recovery process. Normally, BitLocker will manage the TPM chip for you, and there is no need for you to manually change TPM chip settings. However, if you are having problems installing BitLocker, one thing you can do is clear the TPM chip. *Be careful!* If the TPM chip is being used to hold an encryption key to protect data on the hard drive and you clear the chip, the encryption key will be lost. That means all the data will be lost, too. Therefore, don't clear the TPM chip unless you are certain it is not being used to encrypt data.

APPLYING | CONCEPTS MANAGE THE TPM CHIP

A+
220-901
1.1

To manage the TPM chip, follow these steps:

1. Log on to Windows using an administrator account.

2. In the Windows 8 Run box or the Windows 7/Vista Search box, enter the **tpm.msc** command and respond to the User Account Control box. The TPM Management console opens.

3. If no TPM chip is present, the console reports that. If your system has a TPM chip that is not yet initialized, the console will have the option under the Actions pane to Initialize TPM. If the TPM chip is already initialized and ready for use, the console looks similar to the one shown in Figure 3-39.

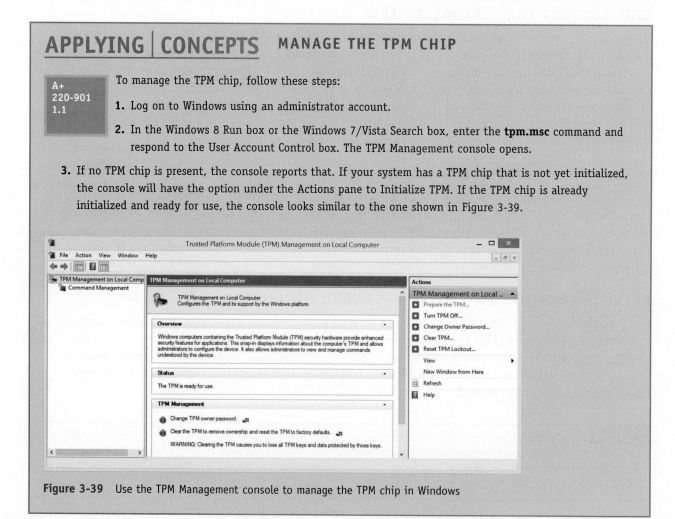

Figure 3-39 Use the TPM Management console to manage the TPM chip in Windows

4. Using the console, you can change the TPM owner password, turn TPM on or off, reset the TPM when it has locked access to the hard drive, and clear the TPM, which resets it to factory defaults. After you have made changes to the TPM chip, you will most likely be asked to restart the computer for the changes to take effect.

EXITING THE BIOS SETUP MENUS

When you finish with BIOS setup, an exit screen such as the one shown in Figure 3-40 gives you various options, such as exit and save your changes or exit and discard your changes. Notice in the figure that you also have the option to load BIOS default settings. This option can sometimes solve a problem when a user has made several inappropriate changes to the BIOS settings.

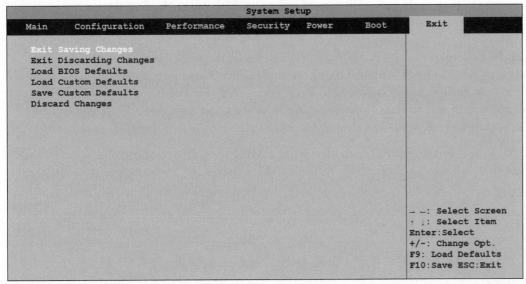

Source: Intel

Figure 3-40 BIOS setup Exit menu

Hands-On | Project 3-5 Examine BIOS Settings

**A+
220-901
1.1**

Access the BIOS setup program on your computer and answer the following questions:

1. What key(s) did you press to access BIOS setup?

2. What brand and version of BIOS are you using?

3. What is the frequency of your processor?

4. What is the boot sequence order of devices?

5. Do you have an optical drive installed? What are the details of the installed drive?

6. What are the details of the installed hard drive(s)?

7. Does the BIOS offer the option to set a supervisor or power-on password? What is the name of the screen where these passwords are set?

8. Does the BIOS offer the option to overclock the processor? If so, list the settings that apply to overclocking.

9. Can you disable the onboard ports on the computer? If so, which ports can you disable, and what is the name of the screen(s) where this is done?

10. List three BIOS settings that control how power is managed on the computer.

USING UEFI SETUP TO CONFIGURE A MOTHERBOARD

Extensible Firmware Interface (EFI), the original version of UEFI, was first developed by Intel. Today, Unified EFI (UEFI) is managed by several manufacturers and developers under the Unified EFI Forum (see *www.uefi.org*). UEFI firmware on the motherboard working with an operating system that supports UEFI improves on legacy BIOS in these ways:

◢ *Faster and better booting.* UEFI does a faster and better job of booting the system, handing over the boot to the OS, and loading device drivers and applications before the OS loads.

◢ *Mouse-enabled interface.* The mouse-enabled UEFI interface is more user friendly to get information about system components; configure the boot sequence, clock speed, virtualization, and power-on passwords; and monitor temperature, fan speeds, voltage, and bus speeds.

◢ *Secure boot.* UEFI version 2.3 and higher offers a secure boot, which prevents a system from booting up with drivers or an OS that are not digitally signed and trusted by the motherboard or computer manufacturer. For secure boot to work, the OS, such as Windows 8 or Linux Ubuntu version 14, must support UEFI.

◢ *Support for hard drives larger than 2 TB.* UEFI allows booting from hard drives larger than 2 TB. A hard drive uses one of two methods for partitioning the drive: The Master Boot Record (MBR) method is older, allows for four partitions and is limited to 2-TB drives. The GUID Partition Table (GPT) method is newer, allows for any size hard drive, and, for Windows, can have up to 128 partitions on the drive. GPT is required for drives larger than 2 TB or for systems that boot using UEFI firmware.

UEFI allows for backward compatibility. It can boot from a MBR hard drive and provides a BIOS boot through its Compatibility Support Module (CSM) feature. CSM is backward compatible with devices and drivers that use BIOS.

APPLYING | CONCEPTS   EXPLORE UEFI SETUP

Let's explore a few important UEFI setup screens that you need to be aware of. If you need help using UEFI setup, refer to the documentation for the motherboard manufacturer. Here are the steps for one system, but your UEFI screens might be different:

1. As with BIOS setup, to access the UEFI firmware, press a key, such as F12, F2, or Del, during the boot. A UEFI main screen appears. Figure 3-41 shows the main screen for one system, but yours might be different. On this screen, you can view information about the CPU and memory and change the language, date, or time. You can use your mouse or arrow keys to navigate through menus at the top of the screen to view and change information. Use the Ai Tweaker screen to overclock the CPU, the Advanced screen to configure the CPU, SATA, USB, onboard devices, power, and network settings, and the Monitor screen to monitor temperature, fans, and voltages. On the Boot screen, you can change the boot sequence and other boot settings. The Tool screen is used to flash UEFI and BIOS.

Source: American Megatrends, Inc.

Figure 3-41 UEFI main screen in Advanced Mode by Asus

2. To manage the CSM and Secure boot, click the **Boot** menu. On the Boot menu, first make sure Fast Boot is disabled (see Figure 3-42). Notice the two setup modes that are listed in the figure. Select CSM for backward compatibility with older BIOS devices and drivers and MBR hard drives. Select Secure Boot to boot using UEFI secure boot. For secure boot to work, CSM must be disabled, Windows 8 or another UEFI-aware OS must be installed, and the hard drive used for the boot must be partitioned using GPT.

Source: American Megatrends, Inc.

Figure 3-42 Use CSM to boot a legacy BIOS system or disable it to implement UEFI secure boot

3. To manage Secure boot, click **Secure Boot**. On the next screen, you can select the operating system that will be loaded when you have more than one OS installed on the system. To manage the keys used for a Secure boot, click **Key Management**. The screen in Figure 3-43 appears.

Source: American Megatrends, Inc.

Figure 3-43   Manage the UEFI secure boot keys and databases

4. A Secure boot uses the following keys, databases, and drivers, which are stored in flash memory on the motherboard and/or on the hard drive and can be managed using commands shown in Figure 3-43:

  ◢ The signature database (db) holds a list of digital signatures of approved operating systems, applications, and drivers that can be loaded by UEFI. Notice in Figure 3-43, the option to delete the db, load it from a file, or append to it.

  ◢ The revoked signature database (dbx) is a blacklist of signatures for software that has been revoked and is no longer trusted.

  ◢ The Key-exchange Key (KEK), also called the Key-enrollment Key (KEK), database is another database that holds digital signatures provided by OS manufacturers, such as Microsoft and Red Hat (a Linux manufacturer). The OS manufacturer or vendor that owns the keys can update them, which will in turn update the db or dbx. For example, an update may occur when a new OS is released or to revoke a bad release of an OS.

  ◢ The Platform Key (PK) is a digital signature belonging to the motherboard or computer manufacturer. The PK authorizes turning on or off Secure boot and updating the KEK database.

  ◢ Option ROMs are UEFI drivers, for example, video, keyboard, and mouse drivers required as the computer first boots, that are digitally signed and identified in the signature database.

Just as with BIOS, UEFI loads an OS and drivers at the beginning of the boot and then turns the control of the computer over to the OS. When UEFI secure boot is active, it checks the OS and each UEFI driver or application before it is loaded to verify it is signed and identified in the secure boot databases. The OS, drivers, and applications that are loaded by UEFI are stored in a system partition on the hard drive named efi. After the OS is launched, it can load additional drivers and applications that UEFI secure boot does not verify.

For normal operation, you would not be required to change secure boot settings unless you want to install hardware that is not certified by the OS or computer manufacturer. In this situation, you could disable secure boot, assuming the PK allows you to do so. When you disable secure boot, the system is no longer protected from rogue drivers or OS installing at the boot. Before you make any changes to the secure boot screen, be sure to use the option to Save Secure Boot Keys, which saves all the databases to a USB flash drive so that you can backtrack your changes later if need be.

📝 **Notes** On laptops and other computers that carry the Windows 8 logo imprinted on the computer, the computer manufacturer is required to configure secure boot so that it cannot be disabled, which assures that only certified OS and drivers can be loaded by UEFI.

Now let's see what other tasks you might need to do when you are responsible for maintaining a motherboard.

MAINTAINING A MOTHERBOARD

A+
220-901
1.1

To maintain a motherboard, you need to know how to update the motherboard drivers, flash BIOS or UEFI, and replace the CMOS battery. All these skills are covered in this part of the chapter.

⭐ **A+ Exam Tip** The A+ 220-901 exam expects you to know how to update drivers and firmware and replace the CMOS battery.

UPDATING MOTHERBOARD DRIVERS

A+
220-901
1.1, 1.2

Device drivers are small programs stored on the hard drive that an operating system, such as Windows or Linux, uses to communicate with a specific hardware device, for example, a printer, network port on the motherboard, or scanner. The CD or DVD that comes bundled with the motherboard contains a user guide and drivers for its onboard components (for example, chipset, graphics, audio, network, and USB drivers), and these drivers need to be installed in the OS. For a motherboard, after installing the board, you can install the drivers from CD or DVD and later update drivers by downloading updates from the motherboard manufacturer's website. Updates are sometimes included in updates to Windows.

📝 **Notes** The motherboard CD or DVD or the manufacturer's website might contain useful utilities, for example, a utility to monitor the CPU temperature and alert you if overheating occurs or a diagnostics utility for troubleshooting.

If a motherboard or one of its components is giving problems, try downloading and installing updated drivers from the motherboard manufacturer website. Figure 3-44 shows the download page for one Asus motherboard where you can download drivers and BIOS updates. When you download the drivers using the system with the motherboard installed, Asus selects the correct OS, as shown in the figure.

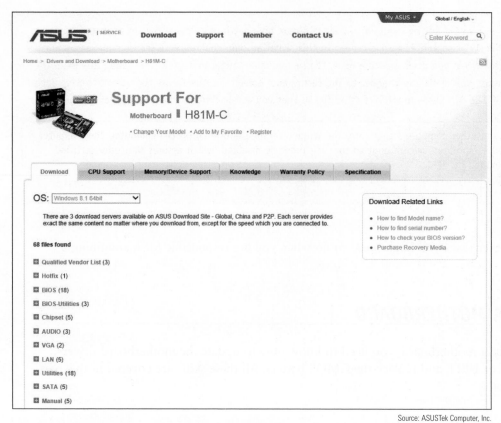

Figure 3-44   Download drivers, BIOS updates, documentation, utilities, and other help software from the motherboard manufacturer's website

If you must download the drivers from a computer that does not have the motherboard installed, be sure to select the correct OS (for example, Windows 7) and the correct type (32 bit or 64 bit). Always use 32-bit drivers with a 32-bit OS and 64-bit drivers with a 64-bit OS. The bit number is the number of bits the driver or OS can process at one time, and you want that to match up. To know what edition and type of Windows you are using, on the Windows 8 desktop, right-click **Start** and click **System**. For Windows 7/Vista, click **Start**, right-click **Computer**, and select **Properties**. The System window appears, giving you details about the Windows installation (see Figure 3-45).

Figure 3-45   The System window reports the edition and type of OS installed

FLASHING BIOS

Recall that BIOS includes the BIOS setup program, the startup BIOS that manages the startup process, and the system BIOS that manages basic I/O functions of the system. All these programs are stored on a firmware chip. The process of upgrading or refreshing the programming stored on the firmware chip is called updating the BIOS or flashing BIOS. Here are some good reasons you might want to flash the BIOS:

- The system hangs at odd times or during the boot.
- Some motherboard functions have stopped working or are giving problems. For example, the onboard video port is not working.
- You want to incorporate some new features or component on the board. For example, a BIOS upgrade might be required before you upgrade the processor.

> ⚡ **Caution** Be sure you use the correct motherboard brand and model when selecting the BIOS update on the manufacturer's website. Trying to use the wrong update can cause problems.

The BIOS updates are downloaded from the motherboard manufacturer's website. To flash BIOS, always follow the directions that you can find in the user guide for your motherboard. Here are four methods that most motherboards can use:

- *Express BIOS update.* Some motherboards allow for an express BIOS update, which is done from Windows. Download the update file to your hard drive. Close all open applications. Double-click the file, which runs the update program, and follow the directions on screen. The system will reboot to apply the update.
- *Update from a USB flash drive using BIOS setup.* Copy the downloaded update file to a USB flash drive. Then restart the system and press a key at startup that launches the BIOS update process. (For some motherboard brands, you press F7.) A screen appears where you can select the USB flash drive. BIOS finds the update file on the flash drive, completes the update, and restarts the system.
- *Update using a bootable CD.* You can download an ISO file from the motherboard manufacturer's website that contains the BIOS update. An ISO file has an .iso file extension and contains an ISO image of a CD. You can use an ISO image to create a bootable CD with software and data on it. After you have created the bootable CD, boot from it and follow the directions on screen to flash the BIOS.

> ✏️ **Notes** To use Windows to burn a CD from an ISO file, first insert a blank CD in the optical drive. Then right-click the .iso file, select **Burn disc image**, and follow the directions on screen.

If the BIOS update is interrupted or the update gives errors, you are in an unfortunate situation. You might be able to revert to the earlier version. To do this, generally, you download the recovery file from the website and copy the file to a USB flash drive. Then set the jumper on the motherboard to recover from a failed BIOS update. Reboot the system and the BIOS automatically reads from the device and performs the recovery. Then reset the jumper to the normal setting and boot the system.

> ✏️ **Notes** To identify the BIOS version installed, look for the BIOS version number displayed on the main menu of BIOS setup. Alternately, you can use the System Information utility (msinfo32.exe) in Windows to display the BIOS version.

Makers of BIOS code are likely to change BIOS frequently because providing the upgrade on the Internet is so easy for them. Generally, however, follow the principle that "if it's not broke, don't fix it." Update your BIOS only if you're having a problem with your motherboard or there's a new BIOS feature you want to use. Also, don't update the BIOS unless the update is a later version than the one installed. One last word of caution: It's very important the update not be interrupted while it is in progress. A failed update can make your motherboard totally unusable. Be sure you don't interrupt the update, and make sure there are no power interruptions. For laptops, make sure the AC adapter is plugged in and powering the system.

> **⚡ Caution**   Be very careful that you upgrade BIOS with the correct upgrade and that you follow the manufacturer's instructions correctly. Upgrading with the wrong file could make your system BIOS useless. If you're not sure that you're using the correct upgrade, *don't guess*. Check with the technical support for your BIOS before moving forward. Before you call technical support, have the information that identifies your BIOS and motherboard available.

FLASHING UEFI

UEFI updates are more secure than BIOS updates because they require digital signatures for the update to be verified. UEFI firmware, drivers, and databases can be updated by way of a USB flash drive or from within Windows. The process using a USB flash drive works like this:

1. Follow the motherboard manufacturer's directions to make the USB drive bootable and download the UEFI update files to the drive.

2. If secure boot is enabled, enter UEFI setup and disable secure boot. Also make sure the USB device is listed in the boot priority order before the hard drive.

3. For a laptop, plug the AC adapter into an external power source so that the power won't fail during the update.

4. Reboot the system, this time from the USB flash drive. Follow the manufacturer's directions to flash UEFI. For one manufacturer, you enter the **flash** command at a command prompt.

5. When prompted, reboot the system. For a secure boot system, go back to UEFI setup and enable secure boot.

Windows updates sometimes include UEFI updates that are handled similarly to driver updates published by hardware manufacturers. When Windows receives an update that it recognizes to be a UEFI update, it hands off the update to UEFI. On the next reboot, the Windows loader verifies the update against the UEFI signature database. If the signature is validated, the update passes to the UEFI firmware. The firmware is then responsible for applying the update and displays a screen letting the user know to not disturb the system while the update is in progress. After the update is completed, the Windows loader continues loading the OS.

> **✎ Notes**   If a UEFI update fails to complete, UEFI may reboot and try again up to three times. After the third attempt, the update will be discarded and UEFI will roll back a partial update.

USING JUMPERS TO CLEAR BIOS SETTINGS

A motherboard may have jumpers that you can use to clear BIOS/UEFI settings, which returns BIOS/UEFI setup to factory default settings. You might want to clear settings when flashing BIOS didn't work or failed to complete correctly or a power-on password is forgotten and you cannot boot the system.

A jumper is two small posts or metal pins that stick up on the motherboard, used to hold configuration information. An open jumper has no cover, and a closed jumper has a cover on the two pins (see Figure 3-46). Look at the jumper cover in Figure 3-46(b) that is "parked," meaning it is hanging on a single pin for safekeeping, but is not being used to turn a jumper setting on.

A   B   C

Figure 3-46 A 6-pin jumper group on a circuit board: (a) has no jumpers set to on, (b) has a cover parked on one pin, and (c) is configured with one jumper setting turned on

Most motherboards today allow you to set a supervisor password (to make changes in BIOS setup) or a power-on password (to get access to the system). Know that these passwords are not the same password that can be required by a Windows OS at startup. If both passwords are forgotten, you cannot use the computer. However, jumpers can be set to clear both passwords. Also, if flashing BIOS fails, a jumper can be set to undo the update.

For example, Figure 3-47 shows a group of three jumpers on one board. (The tan jumper cap is positioned on the first two jumper pins on the left side of the group.) Figure 3-48 shows the motherboard documentation on how to use these jumpers. When jumpers 1 and 2 are closed, which they are in the figure, normal booting happens. When jumpers 2 and 3 are closed, passwords to BIOS setup can be cleared on the next boot. When no jumpers are closed, on the next boot, the BIOS will recover itself from a failed update. Once set for normal booting, the jumpers should be changed only if you are trying to recover when a power-up password is lost or flashing BIOS has failed. To know how to set jumpers, see the motherboard documentation.

BIOS jumper group

Figure 3-47 This group of three jumpers controls the BIOS configuration

Jumper Position	Mode	Description
1 ▢ ● ● 3	Normal (default)	The current BIOS configuration is used for booting.
1 ▢ ● ● 3	Configure	After POST, the BIOS displays a menu in CMOS setup that can be used to clear the user and supervisor power-on passwords.
1 ▢ ● ○ 3	Recovery	Recovery is used to recover from a failed BIOS update. Details can be found on the motherboard CD.

Figure 3-48 BIOS configuration jumper settings

REPLACING THE CMOS BATTERY

Motherboard settings may be stored in flash memory in the firmware or in CMOS RAM. CMOS (complementary metal-oxide semiconductor) is a method of manufacturing microchips, and CMOS RAM is a small amount of memory stored on the motherboard that retains the data even when the computer is turned off because it is charged by a nearby lithium coin-cell battery (see Figure 3-49). If the CMOS battery is disconnected or fails, setup information is lost. An indication that the battery is getting weak is that the system date and time are incorrect after power has been disconnected to the PC. A message about a low battery can also appear at startup.

Figure 3-49   The coin-cell battery powers CMOS RAM when the system is turned off and unplugged

⭐ **A+ Exam Tip**   The A+ 220-901 exam expects you to know about the CMOS battery.

The CMOS battery on the motherboard is considered a field replaceable unit. The battery is designed to last for years and recharges when the motherboard has power. However, on rare occasions, you might need to replace one if the system loses BIOS settings when it is unplugged. Make sure the replacement battery is an exact match to the original or is one the motherboard manufacturer recommends for the board. Power down the system, unplug it, press the power button to drain the power, and remove the case cover. Use your ESD strap to protect the system against ESD. The old battery can be removed with a little prying using a flathead screwdriver. The new battery pops into place. For more specific directions, see the motherboard documentation.

Hands-On | Project 3-6   Examine How to Clear BIOS Settings

A+
220-901
1.1

You can complete the following activity only if you have the documentation for a motherboard: Locate the jumper on the board that returns BIOS setup to default settings and label this jumper on your diagram. It is often found near the CMOS battery. Some boards might have more than one, and some have none.

Now let's turn our attention to installing or replacing a motherboard.

INSTALLING OR REPLACING A MOTHERBOARD

A motherboard is considered a field replaceable unit, so you need to know how to replace one when it goes bad. In this part of the chapter, you learn how to select a motherboard and then how to install or replace one in a desktop or laptop computer.

HOW TO SELECT A DESKTOP MOTHERBOARD

Because the motherboard determines so many of your computer's features, selecting the motherboard is, in most cases, your most important decision when you purchase a desktop computer or assemble one from parts. Depending on which applications and peripheral devices you plan to use with the computer, you can take one of three approaches to selecting a motherboard. The first approach is to select the board that provides the most room for expansion, so you can upgrade and exchange components and add devices easily. A second approach is to select the board that best suits the needs of the computer's current configuration, knowing that when you need to upgrade, you will likely switch to new technology and a new motherboard. The third approach is to select a motherboard that meets your present needs with moderate room for expansion.

Ask the following questions when selecting a motherboard:

1. What form factor does the motherboard use?

2. Which brand (Intel or AMD) and model processors does the board support? Which chipset does it use? How much memory can it hold? What memory speeds does the board support?

3. What type and how many expansion slots are on the board (for example, PCI Express 3.0 or PCI)?

4. How many and what hard drive controllers and connectors are on the board (for example, SATA or eSATA)?

5. What are the embedded devices on the board, and what internal slots or connections does the board have? (For example, the board might provide a network port, wireless antenna port, FireWire port, two or more USB ports, video port, and so forth.)

6. Does the board fit the case you plan to use?

7. What are the price and the warranty on the board? Does the board get good reviews?

8. How extensive and user friendly is the documentation?

9. How much support does the manufacturer supply for the board?

Sometimes a motherboard contains an onboard component more commonly offered as a separate device. One example is support for video. The video port might be on the motherboard or might require a video card. The cost of a motherboard with an embedded component is usually less than the combined cost of a motherboard with no embedded component and an expansion card. If you plan to expand, be cautious about choosing a proprietary board that has many embedded components. Often such boards do not easily accept add-on devices from other manufacturers. For example, if you plan to add a more powerful video card, you might not want to choose a motherboard that contains an onboard video port. Even though you can likely disable the video port in UEFI/BIOS setup, there is little advantage to paying the extra money for it.

> **Notes** If you have an embedded component, make sure you can disable it so you can use another external component if needed. Components are disabled in UEFI/BIOS setup.

Table 3-5 shown earlier in the chapter lists some manufacturers of motherboards and their web addresses. For motherboard reviews, check out *www.motherboards.org* and *www.pcmag.com*, or do a general search of the web.

HOW TO INSTALL OR REPLACE A MOTHERBOARD

When you purchase a motherboard, the package comes with the board, I/O shield, documentation, drivers, and various screws, cables, and connectors. When you replace a motherboard, you pretty much have to disassemble an entire computer, install the new motherboard, and reassemble the system, which you learned to do earlier. The following list is meant to be a general overview of the process and is not meant to include the details of all possible installation scenarios, which can vary according to the components and case you are using. The best place to go for detailed instructions on installing a motherboard is the motherboard user guide.

> ⚡ **Caution** As with any installation, remember the importance of using an ESD strap to ground yourself when working inside a computer case to protect components against ESD.

The general process for replacing a motherboard is as follows:

1. *Verify that you have selected the right motherboard to install in the system.* The new motherboard should have the same form factor as the case, support the RAM modules and processor you want to install on it, and have other internal and external connectors you need for your system.

2. *Get familiar with the motherboard documentation, features, and settings.* Especially important are any connectors and jumpers on the motherboard. It's a great idea to read the motherboard user guide from cover to cover. At the least, get familiar with what it has to offer and study the diagrams in it that label all the components on the board. Learn how each connector and jumper is used. You can also check the manufacturer's website for answers to any questions you might have.

3. *Remove components so you can reach the old motherboard.* Use an ESD strap. Turn off the system and disconnect all cables and cords. Press the power button to dissipate the power. Open the case cover and remove all expansion cards. Disconnect all internal cables and cords connected to the old motherboard. To safely remove the old motherboard, you might have to remove drives. If the processor cooler is heavy and bulky, you might remove it from the old motherboard before you remove the motherboard from the case.

4. *Install the I/O shield.* The I/O shield is a metal plate that comes with the motherboard and fits over the ports to create a well-fitting enclosure for them. A case might come with a standard I/O shield already in place. Hold the motherboard up to the shield and make sure the ports on the board will fit the holes in the shield (see Figure 3-50). If the holes in the shield don't match up with the ports on the board, punch out the shield and replace it with the one that came bundled with the motherboard.

I/O shield installed
on the back
of the case

Figure 3-50 Make sure the holes in the I/O shield match up with the ports on the motherboard

5. *Install the motherboard.* Place the motherboard into the case and, using spacers or screws, securely fasten the board to the case. Because coolers are heavy, most processor instructions say to install the motherboard before installing the processor and cooler to better protect the board or processor from being damaged. On the other hand, some motherboard manufacturers say to install the processor and cooler and then install the motherboard. Follow the order given in the motherboard user guide. The easiest approach is to install the processor, cooler, and memory modules on the board and then place the board in the case (see Figure 3-51).

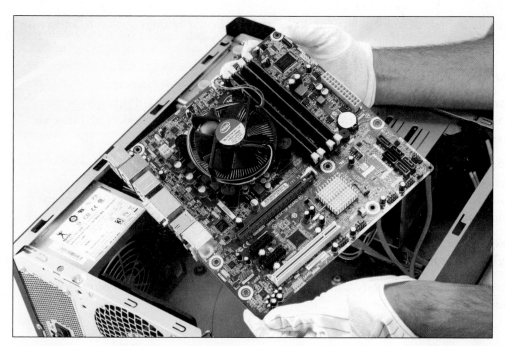

Figure 3-51 Motherboard with processor, cooler, and memory modules installed is ready to go in the case

6. *Install the processor and processor cooler.* The processor comes already installed on some motherboards, in which case you just need to install the cooler. How to install a processor and cooler is covered in the chapter, "Supporting Processors and Upgrading Memory."

7. *Install RAM into the appropriate slots on the motherboard.* How to install RAM is covered in the chapter, "Supporting Processors and Upgrading Memory."

8. *Attach cabling that goes from the case switches to the motherboard, and from the power supply and drives to the motherboard.* Pay attention to how cables are labeled and to any information in the documentation about where to attach them. The chapter, "First Look at Computer Parts and Tools," can help you identify the types of power connectors. You'll need to connect the P1 connector, the fan connectors, and the processor auxiliary power connector. Position and tie cables neatly together to make sure they don't obstruct the fans and the airflow.

9. *Install the video card on the motherboard.* This card should go into the primary PCI Express ×16 slot. If you plan to install multiple video cards, install only one now and check out how the system functions before installing the second one.

10. *Plug the computer into a power source, and attach the monitor, keyboard, and mouse.* Initially install only the devices you absolutely need.

11. *Boot the system and enter UEFI/BIOS setup.* Make sure settings are set to the default. If the motherboard comes new from the manufacturer, it will already be at default settings. If you are salvaging a motherboard from another system, you might need to reset settings to the default. You will need to do the following while you are in UEFI/BIOS setup:

    ◢ Check the time and date.

    ◢ Make sure fast boot (also called abbreviated POST) is disabled. While you're installing a motherboard, you generally want it to do as many diagnostic tests as possible. After you know the system is working, you can choose fast boot.

    ◢ Set the boot order to the hard drive, and then the optical drive, if you will be booting the OS from the hard drive.

    ◢ Leave everything else at their defaults unless you know that particular settings should be otherwise.

    ◢ Save and exit.

12. *Observe POST and verify that no errors occur.*

13. *Verify Windows starts with no errors.* If Windows is already installed on the hard drive, boot to the Windows desktop. Use Device Manager to verify that the OS recognizes all devices and that no conflicts are reported.

14. *Install the motherboard drivers.* If your motherboard comes with a CD that contains some motherboard drivers, install them now. You will probably need Internet access so that the setup process can download the latest drivers from the motherboard manufacturer's website. Reboot the system one more time, checking for errors.

15. *Install any other expansion cards and drivers.* Install each device and its drivers, one device at a time, rebooting and checking for conflicts after each installation.

16. *Verify that everything is operating properly, and make any final OS and UEFI/BIOS adjustments, such as setting power-on passwords.*

3

Notes Whenever you install or uninstall software or hardware, keep a notebook with details about the components you are working on, configuration settings, manufacturer specifications, and other relevant information. This helps if you need to backtrack later and can also help you document and troubleshoot your computer system. Keep all hardware documentation for this system together with the notebook in an envelope in a safe place.

Hands-On | Project 3-7   Insert and Remove Motherboards

A+
220-901
4.1

Using old or defective expansion cards and motherboards, practice inserting and removing expansion cards and motherboards. In a lab or classroom setting, the instructor can provide extra cards and motherboards for exchange.

REPLACING A LAPTOP SYSTEM BOARD

A+
220-901
3.1

Replacing the system board (motherboard) on a laptop probably means you'll need to fully disassemble the entire laptop except the LCD assembly in the lid. Therefore, before you tackle the job, consider alternatives. If available, use diagnostic software from the laptop manufacturer to verify that the problem is a failed system board. If a port or component on the system board has failed, consider installing an external device rather than replacing the entire board. Replacing the system board is a big deal, so consider that the cost of repair, including parts and labor, might be more than the laptop is worth. A new laptop might be your best solution.

If you do decide to replace a system board, use a replacement purchased from the laptop manufacturer. Here is the general procedure for replacing the system board in one laptop:

1. Remove the keyboard, optical drive, and mini PCIe card.

2. The next step is to remove the laptop lid and keyboard bezel assembly. To do this, first remove two screws on the back of the laptop (see Figure 3-52) and the screws on the bottom of the laptop. You can then crack the case by lifting the laptop lid and keyboard bezel from the case (see Figure 3-53).

Figure 3-52   Remove two screws on the back of the notebook

Figure 3-53   Cracking the notebook case

3. Lift up the assembly and look underneath to see two cables connecting the assembly to the motherboard (see Figure 3-54). Disconnect these two cables and set the assembly aside.

Figure 3-54   Lift the assembly to locate the two cable connections

4. To remove the CPU fan assembly, remove screws (see Figure 3-55) and then lift the fan assembly up. Then open the CPU socket and remove the CPU.

Figure 3-55   Remove the screws holding the CPU fan assembly in place

5. The DVD drive can now be removed, and the motherboard is fully exposed.

6. Remove a single screw that holds the motherboard in place (see Figure 3-56) and lift the board out of the case. Figure 3-57 shows the bottom of the board. Both top and bottom are packed with components. When reassembling the system, all steps are done in reverse.

Figure 3-56   Remove the single screw attaching the system board to the case

Figure 3-57   Bottom of the system board

>> CHAPTER SUMMARY

Motherboard Types and Features

▲ The motherboard is the most complicated of all components inside the computer. It contains the processor socket and accompanying chipset, firmware holding the UEFI/BIOS, memory slots, expansion slots, jumpers, ports, and power supply connections. The motherboard you select determines both the capabilities and limitations of your system.

▲ The most popular motherboard form factors are ATX, microATX, and Mini-ITX.

◢ A motherboard will have one or more Intel sockets for an Intel processor or one or more AMD sockets for an AMD processor.

◢ The chipset embedded on the motherboard determines what kind of processor and memory the board can support.

◢ Major advancements in past Intel chipsets included the Accelerated Hub Architecture (using the North Bridge and South Bridge), Nehalem chipsets (using the memory controller on the processor), and Sandy Bridge chipsets (using the memory and graphics controller on the processor). All later chipsets use the memory and graphics controller in the processor package.

◢ Buses used on motherboards include conventional PCI, PCI-X, and PCI Express. PCI Express is replacing all the other bus types.

◢ Some components can be built into the motherboard, in which case they are called onboard components. Other components can be attached to the system in some other way, such as on an expansion card.

Configuring a Motherboard

◢ The firmware that controls a motherboard and the boot is the older BIOS or the newer UEFI. Most UEFI firmware provides for backward compatibility with BIOS devices.

◢ Motherboard settings that can be configured using UEFI/BIOS setup include changing the boot priority order, enabling or disabling onboard devices, support for virtualization, and security settings (for example, power-on passwords and intrusion detection). You can also view information about the installed processor, memory, and storage devices and temperatures, fan speeds, and voltages.

Maintaining a Motherboard

◢ Motherboard drivers might need updating to fix a problem with a board component or to use a new feature provided by the motherboard manufacturer.

◢ To flash BIOS, use a utility program in Windows, a USB flash drive, or a bootable CD.

◢ To update UEFI, you can boot from a USB flash drive that holds the updates, or Windows can receive an update during the normal Windows update process and then pass it on to the UEFI firmware, which applies the update.

◢ Jumpers on the motherboard may be used to clear UEFI/BIOS settings, restoring them to factory default. The CMOS battery that powers CMOS RAM might need replacing.

Installing or Replacing a Motherboard

◢ When selecting a motherboard, pay attention to the form factor, chipset, expansion slots, and memory slots used and the processors supported. Also notice the internal and external connectors and ports the board provides.

◢ When installing a motherboard, first study the motherboard and its manual, and set jumpers on the board. Sometimes the processor and cooler are best installed before installing the motherboard in the case. When the cooling assembly is heavy and bulky, it is best to install it after the motherboard is securely seated in the case.

Replacing a Laptop System Board

◢ For laptops, it's usually more cost effective to replace the laptop than to replace a failed system board.

>> KEY TERMS

For explanations of key terms, see the Glossary for this text.

Accelerated Processing Unit (APU)
ball grid array (BGA)
BitLocker Encryption
bus
chipset
CMOS (complementary metal-oxide semiconductor)
CMOS battery
CMOS RAM
Compatibility Support Module (CSM)
data bus
data path size
device driver
EFI (Extensible Firmware Interface)
flashing BIOS

flip-chip land grid array (FCLGA)
flip-chip pin grid array (FCPGA)
Front Side Bus (FSB)
gigahertz (GHz)
GUID Partition Table (GPT)
hertz (Hz)
I/O shield
ISO image
ITX
jumper
Key-enrollment Key (KEK)
Key-exchange Key (KEK)
land grid array (LGA)
LoJack
Master Boot Record (MBR)

megahertz (MHz)
Mini-ITX
PCI
PCI Express
North Bridge
onboard port
option ROM
overclocking
PCI Express (PCIe)
PCI-X
pin grid array (PGA)
Platform Key (PK)
protocol
QuickPath Interconnect (QPI)
revoked signature database (dbx)
riser card

secure boot
signature database (db)
small form factor (SFF)
South Bridge
staggered pin grid array (SPGA)
system bus
system clock
TPM (Trusted Platform Module) chip
trace
Unified Extensible Firmware Interface (UEFI)
virtual machine (VM)
virtualization
wait state
zero insertion force (ZIF) socket

>> REVIEWING THE BASICS

1. What are the three most popular form factors used for motherboards?

2. Which type of Intel chipsets was the first to support the graphics controller to be part of the processor?

3. How many pins does the Intel Socket B have? What is another name for this socket?

4. What type of memory does the LGA1155 socket work with? Which socket was it designed to replace?

5. Does the Sandy Bridge chipset family use two chipset housings on the motherboard or a single chipset housing? The Nehalem chipset?

6. How many pins does the AMD socket AM3 have?

7. Which part of a Nehalem chipset connects directly to the processor, the North Bridge or the South Bridge?

8. How does the throughput of PCI Express Version 3.0 compare to PCIe Version 2.0?

9. What is the maximum wattage that a PCIe Version 2.0 expansion card can draw?

10. What type of power connector on the motherboard was introduced with PCIe Version 1.0? How much power does this connector provide?

11. What type of power connector was introduced with PCIe Version 2.0? How much power does this connector provide?

12. If you are installing an expansion card into a case that does not have enough clearance above the motherboard for the card, what device can you use to solve the problem?

13. Which chip on the motherboard does Windows BitLocker Encryption use to secure the hard drive?

14. How can you find out how many memory slots are populated on a motherboard without opening the computer case?

15. What are two reasons you might decide to flash BIOS?

16. What is the easiest way to obtain the latest software to upgrade BIOS?

17. What can you do if the power-on password and the supervisor password to a system have been forgotten?

18. How is CMOS RAM powered when the system is unplugged?

19. Describe how you can access the BIOS setup program.

20. Does Windows 7 support a secure boot in UEFI? Windows 8? Linux Ubuntu version 14?

21. Which partitioning method must be used for partitioning a 4-TB hard drive?

22. If a USB port on the motherboard is failing, what is one task you can do that might fix the problem?

23. What might the purpose be for a SATA-style power connector on a motherboard?

24. What is the purpose of installing standoffs or spacers between the motherboard and the case?

25. When installing a motherboard, suppose you forget to connect the wires from the case to the front panel header. Will you be able to power up the system? Why or why not?

>> THINKING CRITICALLY

1. Why don't all buses on a motherboard operate at the same speed?

2. When you turn off the power to a computer and unplug it at night, it loses the date, and you must reenter it each morning. What is the problem and how do you solve it?

3. Why do you think the trend is to put more control such as the graphics controller and the memory controller in the processor rather than in the chipset?

4. When troubleshooting a desktop motherboard, you discover the network port no longer works. What is the best and least expensive solution to this problem? If this solution does not work, which solution should you try next?

   a. Replace the motherboard.

   b. Disable the network port and install a network card in an expansion slot.

   c. Use a wireless network device in a USB port to connect to a wireless network.

   d. Return the motherboard to the factory for repair.

   e. Update the motherboard drivers.

5. A computer freezes at odd times. At first you suspect the power supply or overheating, but you have eliminated overheating and replaced the power supply without solving the problem. What do you do next?

   a. Replace the processor.

   b. Replace the motherboard.

   c. Reinstall Windows.

   d. Replace the memory modules.

   e. Flash BIOS.

>> REAL PROBLEMS, REAL SOLUTIONS

REAL PROBLEM 3-1 Labeling the Motherboard

Figure 3-58 shows a blank diagram of an ATX motherboard. Using what you learned in this chapter and in the chapter, "First Look at Computer Parts and Tools," label as many components as you can. If you would like to print the diagram, look for "Figure 3-58" in the online content that accompanies this text at *www.cengagebrain.com*. For more information on accessing this content, see the Preface.

Figure 3-58   Label the motherboard

REAL PROBLEM 3-2 Selecting a Replacement Motherboard

When a motherboard fails, you can select and buy a new board to replace it. Suppose the motherboard in your computer has failed and you want to buy a replacement and keep your repair costs to a mum. Try to find a replacement motherboard on the web that can use the same case, power supply, processor, memory, and expansion cards as your current system. If you cannot find a good match, what other components might have to be replaced (for example, the processor or memory)? What is the total cost of the replacement parts? Save or print webpages showing what you need to purchase.

REAL PROBLEM 3-3 Researching Maintaining a Motherboard

Using the motherboard user guide that you downloaded in Hands-On Project 3-4, answer the following questions:

1. How many methods can be used to flash UEFI/BIOS on the motherboard? Describe each method. If your system uses BIOS rather than UEFI, what can you do to recover the system if flashing BIOS fails?

2. Locate the CMOS battery on the diagram of the motherboard. What are the steps to replace this battery?

Using a computer in your school lab, do the following to practice replacing the CMOS battery:

1. Locate the CMOS battery on your motherboard. What is written on top of the battery? Using the web, find a replacement for this battery. Print the webpage showing the battery. How much does the new battery cost?

2. Enter BIOS setup on your computer. Write down any BIOS settings that are not default settings. You'll need these settings later when you reinstall the battery.

3. Turn off and unplug the computer, press the power button to drain the system of power, open the case, remove the battery, and boot the PC. What error messages appear? What is the system date and time?

4. Power down the computer, unplug it, press the power button to drain the power, replace the battery, and boot the PC. Close up the case and return BIOS settings to the way you found them. Make sure the system is working normally.

Supporting Processors and Upgrading Memory

Previously, you learned about motherboards. In this chapter, you learn about the two most important components on the motherboard, which are the processor and memory. You learn how a processor works, about the many different types and brands of processors, and how to match a processor to the motherboard.

Memory technologies have evolved over the years. When you support an assortment of desktop and laptop computers, you'll be amazed at all the different variations of memory modules used not only in newer computers, but also in older computers still in use. A simple problem of replacing a bad memory module can become a complex research project if you don't have a good grasp of current and past memory technologies.

The processor and memory modules are considered field replaceable units (FRUs), so you'll learn how to install and upgrade a processor and memory modules. Upgrading the processor or adding more memory to a system can sometimes greatly improve performance. How to troubleshoot problems with the processor or memory is covered in the chapter, "Supporting the Power System and Troubleshooting Computers."

TYPES AND CHARACTERISTICS OF PROCESSORS

A+
220-901
1.1, 1.6 The processor installed on a motherboard is the primary component that determines the computing power of the system (see Figure 4-1). Recall that the two major manufacturers of processors are Intel (*www.intel.com*) and AMD (*www.amd.com*).

Figure 4-1   An AMD Athlon 64 X2 installed in socket AM2+ with cooler not yet installed

In this chapter, you learn a lot of details about processors. As you do, try to keep these nine features of processors at the forefront. These features affect performance and compatibility with motherboards:

▲ *Feature 1: Processor speed.* The processor frequency is the speed at which the processor operates internally and is measured in gigahertz, such as 3.3 GHz. Current Intel and AMD processors run at 1.8 GHz up to more than 4.4 GHz.

▲ *Feature 2: Socket and chipset the processor can use.* Recall that important Intel sockets for desktop systems are the LGA1150, LGA1155, LGA1156, LGA2011, LGA1366, and LGA775. AMD's important desktop sockets are AM3+, AM3, AM2+, AM2, FM1, FM2+, and FM2 sockets.

▲ *Feature 3: Processor architecture (32 bits or 64 bits).* All desktop and laptop processors sold today from either Intel or AMD are hybrid processors, which can process 64 bits or 32 bits at a time. A hybrid processor can use a 32-bit operating system (OS) or a 64-bit OS. Windows 8 and most editions of Windows 7 come in either type.

▲ *Feature 4: Multiprocessing abilities.* The ability of a system to do more than one thing at a time is accomplished by several means:

　▲ *Multiprocessing.* Two processing units (called arithmetic logic units or ALUs) installed within a single processor is called multiprocessing. The Pentium was the first processor that contained two ALUs, which means the processor can execute two instructions at the same time.

　▲ *Multithreading.* Each processor or core processes two threads at the same time. When Windows hands off a task to the CPU, it is called a thread and might involve several instructions. To handle two threads, the processor requires extra registers, or holding areas, within the processor housing that it uses to switch between threads. In effect, you have two logical processors for each physical processor or core. Intel calls this technology Hyper-Threading and AMD calls it HyperTransport. The feature must be enabled in UEFI/BIOS setup and the operating system must support the technology.

▲ *Multicore processing.* Multiple processors can be installed in the same processor housing (called multicore processing). A processor package might contain up to eight cores (dual-core, triple-core, quad-core, and so forth). In Figure 4-2, this quad-core processor contains four cores or CPUs. Using multithreading, each core can handle two threads. Therefore, the processor appears to have up to eight logical processors as it can handle eight threads from the operating system.

Figure 4-2 This quad-core processor has four cores and each core can handle two threads

▲ *Dual processors.* A server motherboard might have two processor sockets, called dual processors or a multiprocessor platform (see Figure 4-3). A processor (for example, the Xeon processor for servers) must support this feature.

▲ *Feature 5: Memory cache, which is the amount of memory included within the processor package.* Today's processors all have some memory on the processor chip (called a die). Memory on the processor die is called Level 1 cache (L1 cache). Memory in the processor package, but not on the processor die, is called Level 2 cache (L2 cache). Some processors use a third cache farther from the processor core, but still in the processor package, which is called Level

3 cache (L3 cache). Memory used in a memory cache is static RAM (SRAM; pronounced "S-Ram"). Memory used on the motherboard loses data rapidly and must be refreshed often. It is, therefore, called volatile memory or dynamic RAM (DRAM; pronounced "D-Ram"). SRAM is faster than DRAM because it doesn't need refreshing; it can hold its data as long as power is available.

Two processor sockets

Courtesy of Intel Corporation

Figure 4-3 This motherboard for a server has two processor sockets, which allow for a multiprocessor platform

▲ *Feature 6: Security.* Execute Disable Bit (EDB) (also called eXecute Disable [XD] by Intel, Enhanced Virus Protection by AMD, and disable execute bit by CompTIA) is security built into a processor so that it can work with the operating system to designate an area of memory for holding data or instructions. When an area is designated for data, instructions stored in this area are not executed, thus preventing a buffer overflow attack by malicious software, which attempts to run its code from an area of memory assigned to another program for its data. EDB requires a compatible OS. You can enable EDB using the BIOS or UEFI setup screen (see Figure 4-4). It is important to remember that even though EDB can stop malware from executing, it cannot remove it. You still need to use anti-malware software to remove the malware.

Source: American Megatrends, Inc.

Figure 4-4   The Execute Disable Bit is enabled using the UEFI setup screen

▲ *Feature 7: The memory features on the motherboard that the processor can support.* DRAM memory modules that might be used on a motherboard include DDR, DDR2, DDR3, or DDR4. Besides the type of memory, a processor can support certain amounts of memory, memory speeds, and number of memory channels (single, dual, triple, or quad channels). All these characteristics of memory are discussed later in the chapter.

▲ *Feature 8: Support for virtualization.* A computer can use software to create and manage multiple virtual machines and their virtual devices. Most processors sold today support virtualization, and the feature must be enabled in UEFI/BIOS setup.

▲ *Feature 9: Integrated graphics.* A processor might include an integrated GPU. A graphics processing unit (GPU) is a processor that manipulates graphic data to form the images on a monitor screen. The GPU might be on a video card, on the motherboard, or embedded in the CPU package. When inside the CPU package, it is called integrated graphics. Many AMD processors and all the Intel second generation and higher processors have integrated graphics.

⭐ **A+ Exam Tip**   The A+ 220-901 exam expects you to be familiar with the characteristics of processors. Know the purposes and characteristics of Hyper-Threading, core processing, types of cache, virtualization, integrated GPU, disable execute bit (CompTIA's name for EDB), and 32-bit versus 64-bit processing.

Let's now turn our attention to a discussion of how a processor works, including several of the processor features just listed. Then you'll learn about the families of Intel and AMD processors.

HOW A PROCESSOR WORKS

A+
220-901
1.1, 1.6

Although processors continue to evolve, they all have some common elements. These elements are diagrammed in Figure 4-5 for the Pentium processor. The Pentium made several major advances in processor technologies when it was first introduced. Because of its historical significance and the foundation it created for today's processors, it's a great place to start when learning how a processor works.

Figure 4-5   Since the Pentium processor was first released in 1993, the standard has been for a processor core to have two arithmetic logic units so that it can process two instructions at once

A processor contains these basic components diagrammed in Figure 4-5 for the Pentium processor:

- An input/output (I/O) unit manages data and instructions entering and leaving the processor.
- A control unit manages all activities inside the processor itself.
- One or more arithmetic logic units (ALUs) do all logical comparisons and calculations inside the processor. All desktop and laptop processors sold today contain two ALUs in each processor core within the processor package.
- Registers, which are small holding areas on the processor chip, work much like RAM does outside the processor to hold counters, data, instructions, and addresses that the ALU is currently processing.
- Internal memory caches (L1, L2, and possibly L3 or L4) hold data and instructions waiting to be processed by the ALU.
- Buses inside the processor connect components within the processor housing. These buses run at a much higher frequency than the motherboard buses that connect the processor to the chipset and memory on the motherboard.

If the processor operates at 3.2 GHz internally and the Front Side Bus is operating at 800 MHz, the processor operates at four times the FSB speed. This factor is called the multiplier. As you learned in the chapter, "All About Motherboards," you can view the actual processor frequency and the clock speed using the UEFI/BIOS setup screens. You can also change the multiplier or the clock speed in order to overclock or throttle the processor.

In Figure 4-5, you can see the internal data bus for the Pentium was only 32 bits wide. More important, however, than the width of the internal bus is the fact that each ALU and register in the early Pentiums could process only 32 bits at a time. All desktop and laptop processors sold today from either Intel or AMD contain ALUs and registers that can process 32 bits or 64 bits at a time. To know which type of operating system to install, you need to be aware of three categories of processors currently used on desktop and laptop computers:

▲ *32-bit processors.* These older processors are known as x86 processors because Intel used the number 86 in the model number of these processors. If you are ever called on to install Windows on one of these old Pentium computers, you must use a 32-bit version of Windows. These processors can handle only 32-bit instructions from the OS.

▲ *Processors that can process 32 bits or 64 bits.* These hybrid processors are known as x86-64 bit processors. AMD was the first to produce one (the Athlon 64) and called the technology AMD64. Intel followed with a version of its Pentium 4 processors and called the technology Extended Memory 64 Technology (EM64T). Because of their hybrid nature, these processors can handle a 32-bit OS or a 64-bit OS. All desktop or laptop processors made after 2007 are of this type.

▲ *64-bit processors.* Intel makes several 64-bit processors for workstations or servers that use fully implemented 64-bit processing, including the Itanium and Xeon processors. Intel calls the technology IA64, but they are also called x64 processors. They require a 64-bit operating system and can handle 32-bit applications only by simulating 32-bit processing.

> ✎ **Notes** To know which type of operating system is installed (32-bit or 64-bit) and other information about the Windows installation, recall from the chapter, "All About Motherboards," that you can use the System window. To open the System window in Windows 8, press **Win+X** and click **System**. In Windows 7, click **Start**, right-click **Computer**, and select **Properties**.

Each core in a processor has its own cache and can also share a cache. Figure 4-6 shows how quad-core processing can work if the processor uses an L3 cache and an internal memory controller. Each core within a processor has its own independent internal L1 and L2 caches. The L1 cache is on the die and the L2 cache is off the die. In addition, all the cores might share an L3 cache within the processor package. Recall that prior to the memory controller being in the processor package, it was part of the North Bridge chipset. Putting the controller inside the processor package resulted in a significant increase in system performance.

Figure 4-6   Quad-core processing with L1, L2, and L3 cache and the memory controller within the processor housing

INTEL PROCESSORS

A+
220-901
1.1, 1.6

Intel's current families of processors for the desktop include the Core, Atom, Celeron, and Pentium families of processors. In addition, Intel groups its processors into Sixth Generation, Fifth Generation, Fourth Generation, Third Generation, Second Generation, and Previous Generation processors. Each generation improves on how the processor and chipset are integrated in the system. Processors in each family are listed in Table 4-1. Some significant retired processors are also listed. Later in the chapter, you'll learn about the memory technologies mentioned in the table.

Processor	Speed	Description
Fifth-Generation (Broadwell) Processors		
Core i7	Up to 3.8 GHz	6-MB cache, quad core 1333/1600/1866 MHz DDR3 memory Dual-channel memory
Core i5	Up to 3.6 GHz	4-MB cache, quad core 1333/1600/1866 MHz DDR3 memory Dual-channel memory
Fourth-Generation (Haswell) Processors		
Core i7	Up to 4.4 GHz	8-MB cache, quad core 1333/1600 MHz DDR3 memory Dual-channel memory
Core i5	Up to 3.6 GHz	4- to 6-MB cache, quad or dual core 1333/1600 MHz DDR3 memory Dual-channel memory
Core i3	Up to 3.8 GHz	3- to 4-MB cache, dual core 1333/1600 MHz DDR3 memory Dual-channel memory
Third-Generation (Ivy Bridge) Processors		
Core i7	Up to 3.9 GHz	8-MB cache, quad core 1333/1600 MHz DDR3 memory Dual-channel memory
Core i5	Up to 3.8 GHz	6-MB cache, quad core 1333/1600 MHz DDR3 memory Dual-channel memory
Core i3	Up to 3.5 GHz	3-MB cache, dual core 1333/1600 MHz DDR3 memory Dual-channel memory
Second-Generation (Sandy Bridge) Processors		
Core i7 Extreme	Up to 3.9 GHz	15-MB cache, six cores 1066/1333/1600 MHz DDR3 memory Quad-channel memory
Core i7	Up to 3.9 GHz	8- to 12-MB cache, four or six cores 1066/1333/1600 MHz DDR3 memory Dual- or quad-channel memory
Core i5	Up to 3.8 GHz	3- to 6-MB cache, dual or quad core 1066/1333 MHz DDR3 memory Dual-channel memory
Core i3	Up to 3.4 GHz	3-MB cache, dual core 1066/1333 MHz DDR3 memory Dual-channel memory
Pentium	Up to 3.0 GHz	3-MB cache 1066/1333 MHz DDR3 memory Dual-channel memory
Previous-Generation Processors		
Core i7 Extreme	Up to 3.4 GHz	8- or 12-MB cache 1066 MHz DDR3 memory Triple-channel memory
Core i7	Up to 3.3 GHz	8- or 12-MB cache, four or six cores 800/1066/1333 MHz DDR3 memory Dual- or triple-channel memory

Table 4-1   Current Intel processors (continues)

Processor	Speed	Description
Core i5	Up to 3.3 GHz	4- or 8-MB cache, dual or quad core 1066/1333 MHz DDR3 memory Dual-channel memory
Core i3	Up to 3.3 GHz	Dual core, 4-MB cache 1066/1333 MHz DDR3 memory Dual-channel memory
Atom	Up to 2.1 GHz	Up to 1-MB cache, some dual core 800/1066 MHz DDR3 memory 667/800 MHz DDR2 memory Single-channel memory
Celeron, Celeron Desktop, Celeron D	1.6 to 3.6 GHz 533/667/800 MHzFSB	128-KB to 1-MB cache
Core 2 Extreme, Core 2 Quad, Core 2 Duo	Up to 3.2 GHz 533 to 1600 MHz FSB	2- to 12-MB cache Dual or quad core
Pentium Extreme, Pentium, Pentium 4, Pentium D	Up to 3.7 GHz	Up to 4-MB cache, some dual core

Table 4-1   Current Intel processors (continued)

An Intel Sandy Bridge Core i5 processor is shown in Figure 4-7. You can purchase a processor with or without the cooler. When it's purchased with a cooler, it's called a boxed processor. The cooler is also shown in the photo. If you purchase the cooler separately, make sure it fits the socket you are using.

Figure 4-7   The Intel Core i5 processor (processor number i5-2320)
with boxed cooler

Each processor listed in Table 4-1 represents several processors that vary in performance and functionality. To help identify a processor, Intel uses a processor number. For example, two Core i7 processors are identified as i7-940 and i7-920. To find details about an Intel processor, search the Intel ARK database at *ark.intel.com* (see Figure 4-8).

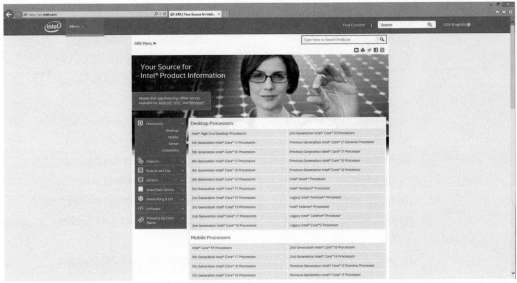

Figure 4-8 The Intel ARK database at *ark.intel.com* lists details about all Intel products

Some of the Intel mobile processors are packaged in the Centrino processor technology. Using the Centrino technology, the Intel processor, chipset, and wireless network adapter are all interconnected as a unit, which improves laptop performance. Several Intel mobile processors have been packaged as a Centrino processor. You also need to be aware of the Intel Atom processor, which is Intel's low-powered processor and is used in low-cost desktops, laptops, and netbooks.

AMD PROCESSORS

A+
220-901
1.1, 1.6

Processors by Advanced Micro Devices, Inc., or AMD (*www.amd.com*) are popular in the game and hobbyist markets, and are generally less expensive than comparable Intel processors. Recall that AMD processors use different sockets than do Intel processors, so the motherboard must be designed for one manufacturer's processor or the other, but not both. Many motherboard manufacturers offer two comparable motherboards—one for an Intel processor and one for an AMD processor.

The current AMD processor families are the FX, Phenom, Athlon, Sempron, A Series, and E Series for desktops and the Athlon, Turion, V Series, Phenom, and Sempron for laptops. Table 4-2 lists the current AMD processors for desktops. Figure 4-9 shows an FX processor by AMD.

Processor	Core Speed	Description
FX Black Edition Family		
FX 4-Core Black Edition	Up to 3.6 GHz	Quad-core uses AM3+ socket
FX 6-Core Black Edition	Up to 3.3 GHz	Six-core uses AM3+ socket
FX 8-Core Black Edition	Up to 3.6 GHz	Eight-core uses AM3+ socket
Phenom Family		
Phenom II X6	Up to 3 GHz	Six-core uses AM3 socket
Phenom II X6 Black	Up to 3.2 GHz	Six-core uses AM3 socket
Phenom II X4	Up to 3.2 GHz	Quad-core uses AM3 socket
Phenom II X3	Up to 2.5 GHz	Triple-core uses AM3 socket

Table 4-2 Current AMD processors (continues)

Processor	Core Speed	Description
Phenom II X2	Up to 3.1 GHz	Dual-core uses AM3 socket
Phenom X4	Up to 2.6 GHz	Quad-core uses AM2+ socket
Phenom X3	Up to 2.4 GHz	Triple-core uses AM2+ socket
Athlon Family		
Athlon II X4	Up to 2.3 GHz	Quad-core uses AM3 socket
Athlon X4	Up to 3.2 GHz	Quad-core uses FM2 socket
Athlon II X3	Up to 3.4 GHz	Triple-core uses AM3 socket
Athlon II X2	Up to 3 GHz	Dual-core uses AM3 socket
Athlon X2	Up to 2.3 GHz	Dual-core uses AM3 socket
Athlon	Up to 2.4 GHz	Single-core uses AM2 socket
Sempron Family		
Sempron	Up to 2.3 GHz	Single-core uses AM2 socket

Table 4-2   Current AMD processors (continued)

Courtesy of Advanced Micro Devices, Inc.

Figure 4-9   The AMD FX processor can have up to eight cores

In the next part of the chapter, you learn the detailed steps to select and install a processor in several of the popular Intel and AMD sockets used by desktop computers.

SELECTING AND INSTALLING A PROCESSOR

A+
220-901
1.6

A hardware technician is sometimes called on to assemble a desktop computer from parts, exchange a processor that is faulty, add a second processor to a dual-processor system, or upgrade an existing processor to improve performance. In each situation, it is necessary to know how to match a processor for the system in which it is installed. And then you need to know how to install the processor on the motherboard for each of the current Intel and AMD sockets used for desktop and laptop systems. In this part of the chapter, you learn about selecting and installing processors in desktops. Later in the chapter, you learn about selecting and installing processors in laptops.

SELECT A PROCESSOR TO MATCH SYSTEM NEEDS

A+
220-901
1.6

When selecting a processor, the first requirement is to select one that the motherboard is designed to support. Among the processors the board supports, you need to select the best one that meets the general requirements of the system and the user's needs. To get the best performance, use the highest-performing processor the board supports. However, sometimes you need to sacrifice performance for cost.

APPLYING | CONCEPTS   SELECT A PROCESSOR

Your friend, Alice, is working toward her A+ certification. She has decided the best way to get the experience she needs before she sits for the exam is to build a system from scratch. She has purchased an Asus motherboard and asked you for some help selecting the right processor. She tells you that the system will later be used for light business needs and she wants to install a processor that is moderate in price to fit her budget. She says she doesn't want to install the most expensive processor the motherboard can support, but neither does she want to sacrifice too much performance or power.

The documentation on the Asus website (*support.asus.com*) for the ASUS H81M-C motherboard gives this information:

- ◢ The microATX board contains the H81 chipset and socket LGA1150 and uses DDR3 memory.
- ◢ CPUs supported include a long list of Fourth-Generation Core i3, Core i5, and Core i7 processors and Celeron and Pentium processors. Here are five processors found in this list:
  - ◢ Intel Core i7-4790, 3.6 GHz, 8-MB cache
  - ◢ Intel Core i5-4590, 3.3 GHz, 6-MB cache
  - ◢ Intel Core i3-4350, 3.6 GHz, 4-MB cache
  - ◢ Intel Celeron G1850, 2.9 GHz, 2-MB cache
  - ◢ Intel Pentium G3260, 3.3 GHz, 3-MB cache

Based on what Alice has told you, you decide to eliminate the most expensive processors (the Core i7) and the least-performing processors (the Celerons and Pentiums). That decision narrows your choices down to the Core i3 and Core i5. Before you select one of these processors, you need to check the list on the Asus site to make sure the specific Core i3 or Core i5 processor is in the list. Look for the exact processor number, for example, the Core i3-4350. Also double-check and make sure the processor uses the correct socket and is a Fourth-Generation processor.

You will also need a cooler assembly. If your processor doesn't come boxed with a cooler, select a cooler that fits the processor socket and gets good reviews. You'll also need some thermal compound if it is not included with the cooler.

The cooler is bracketed to the motherboard using a wire or plastic clip. A creamlike thermal compound is placed between the bottom of the cooler heat sink and the top of the processor. This compound eliminates air pockets, helping to draw heat off the processor. The thermal compound transmits heat better than air and makes an airtight connection between the fan and the processor. When processors and coolers are boxed together, the cooler heat sink might have thermal compound already stuck to the bottom (see Figure 4-10).

Preapplied thermal compound

Figure 4-10   Thermal compound is already stuck to the bottom of this cooler that was purchased boxed with the processor

INSTALL A PROCESSOR

Now let's look at the details of installing a processor in Intel LGA1150, LGA1155, LGA1366, LGA775, and AMD AM2+ sockets.

INSTALLING AN INTEL PROCESSOR IN SOCKET LGA1150

We're installing the Intel Core i5-4440 processor in Socket LGA1150 shown in Figure 4-11. In the photo, the socket has its protective cover in place.

Figure 4-11   Intel socket LGA1150 with protective cover in place

> ★ **A+ Exam Tip**   The A+ 220-901 exam expects you to know how to install a processor in these Intel processor sockets: LGA775, LGA1150, LGA1155, LGA1156, LGA1366, and LGA2011.

When building a new system, if the motherboard is not already installed in the case, follow the directions of the motherboard manufacturer to install the motherboard and then the processor or to install the processor and then the motherboard. The order of installation varies among manufacturers. When replacing a processor in an existing system, power down the system, unplug the power cord, press the power button to drain the system of power, and open the case. Follow these steps to install the processor and cooler using socket LGA1150:

1. Read all directions in the motherboard user guide about installing the processor and carefully follow them in order.

2. Use an ESD strap or antistatic gloves to protect the processor, motherboard, and other components against ESD.

3. Remove the socket protective cover. Keep this cover in a safe place. If you ever remove the processor, put the cover back on the socket to protect the socket. While the socket is exposed as in Figure 4-12, be *very careful* to not touch the pins in the socket.

Figure 4-12   The exposed socket is extremely delicate

4. Open the socket by pushing down on the socket lever and gently pushing it away from the socket to lift the lever. As you fully open the socket lever, the socket load plate opens, as shown in Figure 4-13.

Figure 4-13   The load plate is open, and ready for the processor

5. Remove the clear plastic protective cover from the processor. While the processor contacts are exposed, take extreme care to not touch the bottom of the processor. Hold it only at its edges. (It's best to use antistatic gloves as you work, but the gloves make it difficult to handle the processor.) Put the processor cover in a safe place and use it to protect the processor if you ever remove the processor from the socket.

6. Hold the processor with your index finger and thumb and orient the processor so that the two notches on the edge of the processor line up with the posts embedded on the socket. Gently lower the processor straight down into the socket. Don't allow the processor to tilt, slide, or shift as you put it in the socket. To protect the pads, it needs to go straight down into the socket.

7. Check carefully to make sure the processor is aligned correctly in the socket. Closing the socket without the processor fully seated can destroy the socket. Figure 4-14 shows the processor fully seated in the socket. Close the socket load plate so that it catches under the screw head at the front of the socket.

Notches

Figure 4-14   Orient the processor so the notches line up with the posts on the socket

8. Push down on the lever and gently return it to its locked position.

We are now ready to install the cooler. Before installing a cooler, read the directions carefully and make sure you understand them. Clips that hold the fan and heat sink to the processor frame or housing are sometimes difficult to install. The directions might give you important tips. Follow these general steps:

1. The motherboard has four holes to anchor the cooler. You can see them labeled in Figure 4-15. Examine the cooler posts that fit over these holes and the clips, screws, or wires that will hold the cooler firmly in place. Make sure you understand how this mechanism works.

2. If the cooler has thermal compound preapplied, remove the plastic from the compound. If the cooler does not have thermal compound applied, put a small dot of compound (about the size of a small pea) in the center of the processor (see Figure 4-15). When the cooler is attached and the processor

Thermal compound

Four holes to attach cooler

Figure 4-15 If the cooler does not have preapplied thermal compound, apply it on top of the processor

is running, the compound spreads over the surface. Don't use too much—just enough to later create a thin layer. If you use too much compound, it can slide off the housing and damage the processor or circuits on the motherboard. To get just the right amount, you can buy individual packets that each contain a single application of the thermal compound.

> ✏️ **Notes** When removing and reinstalling a processor, use a soft dry cloth to carefully remove all the old thermal compound from both the processor and the cooler. Don't try to reuse the compound.

3. Verify the locking pins on the cooler are turned as far as they will go in a counterclockwise direction. (Make sure the pins don't protrude into the hollow plastic posts that go down into the motherboard holes.) Align the cooler over the processor so that all four posts fit into the four holes on the motherboard and the fan power cord can reach the fan header on the motherboard.

4. Push down on each locking pin until you hear it pop into the hole. To help keep the cooler balanced and in position, push down two opposite pins and then push the remaining two pins in place. Using a flathead screwdriver, turn the locking pin clockwise to secure it (see Figure 4-16). (Later, if you need to remove the cooler, turn each locking pin counterclockwise to release it from the hole.)

Fan header

Figure 4-16 The pins are turned clockwise to secure the cooler to the motherboard

5. Connect the power cord from the cooler fan to the 4-pin CPU fan header on the motherboard near the processor, as shown in Figure 4-17.

Figure 4-17 Connect the cooler fan power cord to the motherboard CPU fan header

After the processor and cooler are installed and the motherboard is installed in the case, make sure cables and cords don't obstruct fans or airflow, especially airflow around the processor and video card. Use cable ties to tie cords and cables up and out of the way.

Make one last check to verify that all power connectors are in place and other cords and cables connected to the motherboard are correctly done. You are now ready to plug back up the system, turn it on, and verify all is working. If the power comes on (you hear the fan spinning and see lights), but the system fails to work, most likely the processor is not seated solidly in the socket or some power cord has not yet been connected or is not solidly connected. Turn everything off, unplug the power cord, press the power button to drain power, open the case, and recheck your installation. If the system comes up and begins the boot process, but suddenly turns off before the boot is complete, most likely the processor is overheating because the cooler is not installed correctly. Turn everything off, unplug the power cord, press the power button to drain power, open the case, and verify that the cooler is securely seated and connected.

After the system is up and running, you can check UEFI/BIOS setup to verify that the system recognized the processor correctly. The setup screen for one processor is shown in Figure 4-18.

Also check in UEFI/BIOS setup the CPU and motherboard temperatures to verify the CPU is not overheating. For the UEFI setup in this system, this screen is under the Monitor menu, as shown in Figure 4-19.

Source: American Megatrends, Inc.

Figure 4-18 Verify the CPU is recognized correctly by UEFI setup

Source: American Megatrends, Inc.

Figure 4-19 Verify the processor temperature is within an acceptable range

The maximum processor temperature varies by processor; to know the maximum, download the datasheet specifications for the processor from the Intel website (*ark.intel.com*). For the Intel Core i5-4440, the processor will stop execution if the temperature rises above 130 degrees. If you see the temperature rising this high, open the case cover and verify that the processor fan is running. Perhaps a wire is in the way and preventing the fan from turning or the fan wire is not connected. Other troubleshooting tips for processors are covered in the chapter, "Supporting the Power System and Troubleshooting Computers."

INSTALLING AN INTEL PROCESSOR IN SOCKET LGA1155

The installations of all processors and sockets in this part of the chapter are similar to that of installing a processor in Socket LGA1150, so we will not repeat many of those steps. Listed next are the differences when installing a processor in the LGA1155 socket. These socket pins are delicate, so work slowly and take care. Here is how to work with this socket:

1. Open the socket by pushing down on the socket lever and gently pushing it away from the socket to lift the lever (see Figure 4-20). You can then lift the socket load plate, as shown in Figure 4-21. Next, remove the socket protective cover.

Figure 4-20 Release the lever from the socket

Figure 4-21 Lift the socket load plate to expose the processor socket

2. To install the processor, hold the processor with your index finger and thumb and orient the processor so that the gold triangle on the corner of the processor lines up with the right-angle mark embedded on the motherboard just outside a corner of the socket (see Figure 4-22). Gently lower the processor straight down into the socket. Don't allow the processor to tilt, slide, or shift as you put it in the socket. To protect the pads, it needs to go straight down into the socket.

4

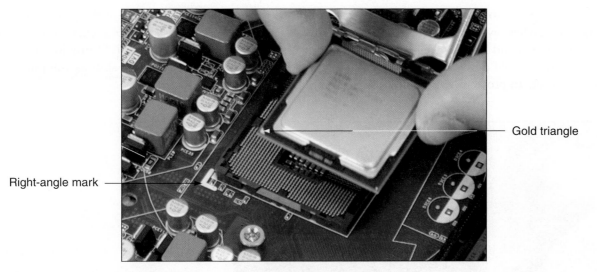

Right-angle mark

Gold triangle

Figure 4-22   Align the processor in the socket using the gold triangle and the right-angle mark

3. You can now lower the socket load plate and return the lever to its locked position (see Figure 4-23).

Socket screw

Figure 4-23   The socket screw head secures the socket load plate

Figure 4-24   Lift the socket load plate

INSTALLING AN INTEL PROCESSOR IN SOCKET LGA1366

Listed next are the differences when installing a processor in the LGA1366 socket:

1. To open the socket, press down on the socket lever and gently push it away from the socket to lift the lever. You can then lift the socket load plate, as shown in Figure 4-24. Next, remove the socket protective cover.

2. To install the processor, hold the processor with your index finger and thumb and orient the processor so that the notches on the two edges of the processor line up with the two posts on the socket. You can see the notch and post on the right side of the processor and socket in Figure 4-25. Gently lower the processor straight down into the socket. Don't allow the processor to tilt, slide, or shift as you put it in the socket. To protect the pins, it needs to go straight down into the socket.

— Right notch

— Right post

Figure 4-25   Orient the processor over the socket so that the notches on each side of the processor match the posts on each side of the socket

3. You can now lower the socket load plate and return the lever to its locked position.

INSTALLING AN INTEL PROCESSOR IN SOCKET LGA775

Socket LGA775 is shown in Figure 4-26 along with a Pentium processor and cooler. In the photo, the socket is open and the protective cover removed. The processor is lying upside down in front of the cooler. When installing a processor in socket LGA775, do the following:

1. Push down on the lever and gently push it away from the socket to lift it. Lift the socket load plate. Remove the socket protective cover.

Figure 4-26   A Pentium, cooler, and open socket 775

2. Orient the processor so that the notches on the two edges of the processor line up with the two notches on the socket. Gently place the processor in the socket. Socket LGA775 doesn't have those delicate pins that Socket LGA1366 has, but you still need to be careful to not touch the top of the socket or the bottom of the processor as you work.

3. Close the socket cover. Push down on the lever and gently return it to its locked position.

INSTALLING AN AMD PROCESSOR IN SOCKET AM2+

When installing an AMD processor in AMD socket AM2, AM2+, or other AMD sockets, do the following:

1. Open the socket lever. If there's a protective cover over the socket, remove it.

2. Holding the processor very carefully so you don't touch the bottom, orient the four empty positions on the bottom with the four empty positions in the socket (see Figure 4-27). For some AMD sockets, a gold triangle on one corner of the processor matches up with a small triangle on a corner of the socket. Carefully lower the processor into the socket. Don't allow it to tilt or slide as it goes into the socket. The pins on the bottom of the processor are very delicate, so take care as you work.

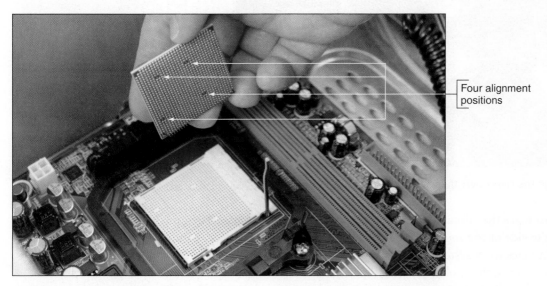

Four alignment positions

Figure 4-27   Orient the four alignment positions on the bottom of the processor with those in the socket

3. Check carefully to make sure the pins in the processor are sitting slightly into the holes. Make sure the pins are not offset from the holes. If you try to use the lever to put pressure on these pins and they are not aligned correctly, you can destroy the processor. You can actually feel the pins settle into place when you're lowering the processor into the socket correctly.

4. Press the lever down and gently into position (see Figure 4-28).

Figure 4-28   Lower the lever into place, which puts pressure on the processor

5. You are now ready to apply the thermal compound and install the cooler assembly. For one system, the black retention mechanism for the cooler is already installed on the motherboard (see Figure 4-29). Set the cooler on top of the processor, aligning it inside the retention mechanism.

Black retention mechanism is preattached

Figure 4-29   Align the cooler over the retention mechanism

6. Next, clip into place the clipping mechanism on one side of the cooler. Then push down firmly on the clip on the opposite side of the cooler assembly; the clip will snap into place. Figure 4-30 shows the clip on one side in place for a system that has a yellow retention mechanism and a black cooler clip. Later, if you need to remove the cooler, use a Phillips screwdriver to remove the screws holding the retention mechanism in place. Then remove the retention mechanism along with the entire cooler assembly.

Cooler clip

Retention mechanism

Figure 4-30   The clips on the cooler attach the cooler to the retention mechanism on the motherboard

7. Connect the power cord from the fan to the 4-pin CPU fan header on the motherboard next to the processor.

Notes   How to troubleshoot problems with the processor, motherboard, and RAM is covered in the chapter, "Supporting the Power System and Troubleshooting Computers."

Hands-On | Project 4-1   Research a Processor Upgrade or Replacement

To identify your motherboard and find out the processor and processor socket a motherboard is currently using, you can use UEFI/BIOS setup, Windows utilities, or third-party software such as Speccy at *www.periform.com/speccy*. To research processors a board can support, you can use the motherboard user guide, the website of the motherboard manufacturer, and for Intel processors, the Intel site at *ark.intel.com*. Research the current processor and processor socket of your computer's motherboard and which processors your board can support, and answer the following questions:

1. What is the brand and model of your motherboard? What processor socket does it use? How did you find your information?

2. Identify the currently installed processor, including its brand, model, speed, and other important characteristics. How did you find your information?

3. List three or more processors the board supports according to the motherboard documentation or website.

4. Search the web for three or more processors that would match this board. Save or print three webpages showing the details and prices of a high-performing, moderately performing, and low-performing processor the board supports.

5. If your current processor fails, which processor would you recommend for this system? Explain your recommendation.

Now assume the Core i7 920 processor that you saw installed in Figure 4-25 has gone bad. The motherboard in which it is installed is the Intel DX58SO desktop board. The owner of the motherboard has requested that you keep the replacement cost as low as possible. What processor would you recommend for the replacement? Save or print a webpage showing the processor and its cost.

Hands-On | Project 4-2   Insert and Remove a Processor

In this project, you remove and install a processor. As you work, be very careful to not bend pins on the processor or socket, and protect the processor and motherboard against ESD. Do the following:

1. Verify the computer is working. Turn off the system, unplug it, press the power button, and open the computer case. Put on your ESD strap. Remove the cooler assembly. Remove all the thermal compound from the cooler and processor.

2. Reinstall the processor and thermal compound. Have your instructor check the thermal compound. Install the cooler.

3. Replace the case cover, power up the system, and verify all is working.

REPLACING THE PROCESSOR IN A LAPTOP

A+ 220-901 3.1

Before replacing the processor in a laptop, consider the laptop might still be under warranty. Also consider it might be more cost effective to replace the laptop rather than replacing the processor, including the cost of parts and labor. If you do decide to replace a processor in a laptop, be sure to select a processor supported by the laptop manufacturer for the particular model laptop. The range of processors supported by a laptop does not usually include as many options as those supported by a desktop motherboard.

For many laptops, removing the cover on the bottom of a laptop exposes the processor fan and heat sink assembly. When you remove this assembly, you can then open the socket and remove the processor. For example, looking at the laptop shown in Figure 4-31, you can see the processor heat sink and fan assembly exposed. To remove the assembly, remove the seven screws and the fan power connector (see Figure 4-32). Then lift the assembly straight up, being careful not to damage the processor underneath.

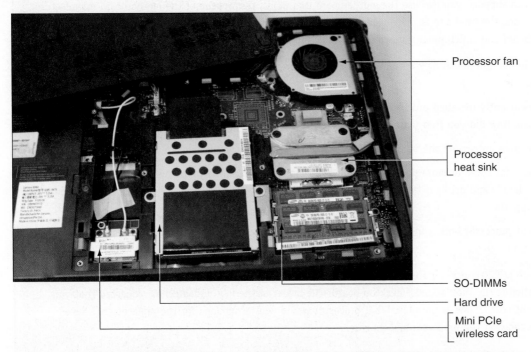

Processor fan

Processor heat sink

SO-DIMMs

Hard drive

Mini PCIe wireless card

Figure 4-31   The cover is removed from the bottom of a laptop exposing several internal components

For another laptop, the heat sink and fan assembly is also exposed when you remove the cover on the bottom of the laptop (see Figure 4-33). Notice the heat sink on this laptop extends to the processor and chipset. You remove several screws and then lift the entire assembly out as a unit. For both laptops, the heat sink fits on top of the processor and the fan sits to the side of the processor. This design is typical of many laptops. However, some laptops require you to remove the keyboard and the keyboard bezel to reach the fan assembly and processor under the bezel.

Seven screws secure the fan and heat sink assembly

Figure 4-32   Seven screws hold the processor heat sink and fan assembly in place

Processor socket is under this portion of the heat sink

Figure 4-33   Remove the cover from the bottom of the laptop to expose the heat sink and fan assembly and to reach the processor

Figure 4-34 shows the heat sink and fan assembly removed in one laptop, exposing the processor. Notice the thermal compound on the processor. To remove the processor, turn the CPU socket screw 90 degrees to open the socket, as shown in the figure. Most Intel and AMD sockets have this socket screw on the side of the socket, as shown in Figure 4-34, although other sockets have the screw on the corner of the socket.

Figure 4-34   Open the CPU socket

Lift the CPU from the socket. Be careful to lift straight up without bending the CPU pins. Figure 4-35 shows the processor out of the socket. If you look carefully, you can see the missing pins on one corner of the processor and socket. This corner is used to correctly orient the processor in the socket, which is socket 478B.

Before you place the new processor into the socket, be sure the socket screw is in the open position. Then delicately place the processor into its socket. If it does not drop in completely, consider that the screw might not be in the full open position. Be sure to use thermal compound on top of the processor. Intel recommends

Figure 4-35   The processor removed from socket 478B

0.2 grams of compound, which is about the size of a small pea. To make sure you use just the right amount of compound, consider buying it in individual packets that are measured for a single application.

Now let's turn our attention to the various memory technologies used in personal computers, and how to upgrade memory.

MEMORY TECHNOLOGIES

A+
220-901
1.2, 1.3

Recall that random access memory (RAM) temporarily holds data and instructions as the CPU processes them and that the memory modules used on a motherboard are made of dynamic RAM or DRAM. DRAM loses its data rapidly, and the memory controller must refresh it several thousand times a second. RAM is stored on memory modules, which are installed in memory slots on the motherboard (see Figure 4-36).

One populated
black slot and
one empty
black slot

Two empty
blue slots

Figure 4-36   RAM on motherboards today is stored in DIMMs

⭐ **A+ Exam Tip**   The A+ 220-901 exam expects you to know the purposes and characteristics of DDR, DDR2, and DDR3 memory technologies.

Several variations of DRAM have evolved over the years. Here are the four major categories of memory modules:

▲ All new motherboards for desktops sold today use a type of memory module called a DIMM (dual inline memory module).

▲ Laptops use a smaller version of a DIMM called a SO-DIMM (small outline DIMM and pronounced "sew-dim"). MicroDIMMs are used on subnotebook computers and are smaller than SO-DIMMs.

▲ An older type of module is a RIMM, which is designed by Rambus, Inc.

▲ Really old computers used SIMMs (single inline memory modules). You're unlikely to ever see these modules in working computers.

The major differences among these modules are the width of the data path that each type of module accommodates and the way data moves from the system bus to the module. DIMMs have seen several evolutions. Five versions of DIMMs, one RIMM, and two types of SIMMs are shown in Table 4-3. Notice the notches on the modules, which prevent the wrong type of module from being inserted into a memory slot on the motherboard. The table includes older and current memory technologies.

Description of Module	Example
288-pin DDR4 DIMM is currently the fastest memory with lower voltage requirements. It can support quad or dual channels or function as single DIMMs. It has one notch near the center of the edge connector.	Source: kingston.com
240-pin DDR3 DIMM can support quad, triple, or dual channels or function as single DIMMs. It has an offset notch farther from the center than a DDR2 DIMM.	
240-pin DDR2 DIMM can support dual channels or function as single DIMMs. It has one notch near the center of the edge connector.	
184-pin DDR DIMM can support dual channels or function as a single DIMM. It has one offset notch.	
168-pin SDRAM DIMM has two notches on the module. The positions of these notches depend on the memory features the DIMM uses.	
RIMM has 184 pins and two notches near the center of the edge connector.	
72-pin SIMMs were installed in groups of two modules to each bank of memory.	
30-pin SIMMs were installed in groups of four modules to each bank of memory.	

Table 4-3   Types of memory modules

In this chapter, you see tons of different technologies used by RAM and so many can get a little overwhelming. You need to know about them because each motherboard you might support requires a specific type of RAM. Figure 4-37 is designed to help you keep all these technologies straight. You might find it a useful road map as you study each technology in the chapter. And who keeps up with all these technologies? JEDEC (*www.jedec.org*) is the organization responsible for standards used by solid-state devices, including RAM technologies. The goal of each new RAM technology approved by JEDEC is to increase speed and performance without greatly increasing the cost.

Figure 4-37 Timeline of memory technologies

Even though an older RAM technology is no longer used by new motherboards, RAM manufacturers continue to produce the older RAM because older motherboards require these replacement modules. In Figure 4-37, the dotted lines for SIMMs and RIMMs indicate these technologies are now obsolete. All new motherboards today use DIMMs. However, if you check some retail websites, you can see that RIMMs can still be purchased.

> **✎ Notes** For an interesting discussion on how RAM works, complete with animation, see the webpage by HowStuff Works, Inc., at *www.howstuffworks.com/ram.htm*.

We'll now look at each of the types of DIMM and SO-DIMM modules and the technologies they use.

DIMM TECHNOLOGIES

DIMMs use a 64-bit data path. (Some early DIMMs had a 128-bit data path, but they're now obsolete.) A DIMM (dual inline memory module) gets its name because it has independent pins on opposite sides of the module.

Early DIMMs did not run in sync with the system clock because they were too slow to keep up. Their speeds are measured in nanoseconds (ns), which is how long it takes for the module to read or write data. The first DIMM to run synchronized with the system clock was synchronous DRAM (SDRAM), which has two notches, and uses 168 pins. (Don't confuse SDRAM with SRAM. SRAM is static RAM used in processor memory caches, and SDRAM is dynamic RAM used on DIMMs.) Synchronized memory runs in step with the processor and system clock, and its speeds are measured just as processor and bus speeds are measured in MHz.

Double Data Rate SDRAM (DDR SDRAM, or SDRAM II, or simply DDR) is an improved version of SDRAM. DDR runs twice as fast as regular SDRAM, has one notch, and uses 184 pins. Instead of processing data for each beat of the system clock, as regular SDRAM does, it processes data when the beat rises and again when it falls, doubling the data rate of memory. If a motherboard runs at 200 MHz, DDR memory runs at 400 MHz. Three other improvements over DDR are DDR2, DDR3, and DDR4. DDR2 is faster and uses less power than DDR. DDR3 is faster and uses less power than DDR2. The trend continues with DDR4 being faster and using less power than DDR3. Both DDR2 and DDR3 use 240 pins. They are not compatible because their notches are not in the same position, and the different notch positions keep someone from installing a DDR2 or DDR3 DIMM in the wrong memory slot. DDR4 uses 288 pins.

Factors that affect the capacity, features, and performance of DIMMs include the number of channels they use, how much RAM is on one DIMM, the speed, error-checking abilities, and buffering. All these factors are discussed next.

SINGLE, DUAL, TRIPLE, AND QUAD CHANNELS

When you look at a motherboard, you might notice the DIMM slots are different colors. This color coding is used to identify the channel each slot uses. Channels have to do with how many DIMM slots the memory controller can address at a time. Early DIMMs only used a single channel, which means the memory controller can access only one DIMM at a time. To improve overall memory performance, dual channels allow the memory controller to communicate with two DIMMs at the same time, effectively doubling the speed of memory access. A motherboard that supports triple channels can access three DIMMs at the same time. Sandy Bridge technology introduced quad channels where the processor can access four DIMMs at the same time. DDR, DDR2, DDR3, and DDR4 DIMMs can use dual channels. DDR3 DIMMs can also use triple channels. DDR3 and DDR4 DIMMs can use quad channels. For dual, triple, or quad channels to work, the motherboard and the DIMM must support the technology.

Figure 4-38 shows how dual channeling works on a board with four DIMM slots. The board has two memory channels, Channel A and Channel B. With dual channeling, the two DIMMs installed in the two slots labeled Channel A can be addressed at the same time. If two more DIMMs are installed in the Channel B slots, they can be accessed at the same time.

Figure 4-38   Using dual channels, the memory controller can read from two DIMMs at the same time

When setting up dual channeling, know that the pair of DIMMs in a channel must be equally matched in size, speed, and features, and it is recommended they come from the same manufacturer. A motherboard supporting dual channels was shown in Figure 4-36. The two black DIMM slots make up the first channel, and the two blue slots make up the second channel. To use dual channeling, matching DIMMs must be installed in the black slots and another matching pair in the blue slots, as shown in Figure 4-39. Know that the second pair of DIMMs does not have to match the first pair of DIMMs because the first channel runs independently of the second channel. If the two DIMM slots of a channel are not populated with matching pairs of DIMMs, the motherboard will revert to single channeling.

Figure 4-39 Matching pairs of DIMMs installed in four DIMM slots that support dual channeling

> ⭐ **A+ Exam Tip** The A+ 220-901 exam expects you to be able to distinguish between single-channel, dual-channel, and triple-channel memory installations.

For a triple-channel installation, three DIMM slots must be populated with three matching DDR3 DIMMs (see Figure 4-40). The three DIMMs are installed in the three blue slots on the board. This motherboard has a fourth black DIMM slot. You can barely see this black slot behind the three filled slots in the photo. If the fourth slot is used, then triple channeling is disabled, which can slow down performance. If a matching pair of DIMMs is installed in the first two slots and another matching pair of DIMMs is installed in the third and fourth slots, then the memory controller will use dual channels. Dual channels are not as fast as triple channels, but certainly better than single channels.

Figure 4-40 Three identical DDR3 DIMMs installed in a triple-channel configuration

The latest memory technology is quad channeling that was introduced with Intel Sandy Bridge chipsets and processors. Figure 4-41 shows an Intel motherboard that has the LGA2011 socket and eight memory slots. The processor can access four slots at the same time. The four black slots can be addressed by the processor on one memory channel and the four blue slots on another channel. Second Generation Sandy Bridge and later processors contain the memory controller within the processor package rather than on the chipset. To get the highest performance, memory slots are placed on either side of the processor in order to shorten the length of the memory bus. Because of the high performance of processors that use the LGA2011 socket, Intel recommends that systems using this socket use liquid cooling methods.

Courtesy of Intel Corporation

Figure 4-41   The Intel Desktop Board DX79TO has eight memory slots and supports two quad channels

DIMM SPEEDS

DIMM speeds are measured either in MHz (such as 1333 MHz or 800 MHz) or PC rating (such as PC6400). A PC rating is a measure of the total bandwidth in MB/second of data moving between the module and the CPU. To calculate the PC rating for a DDR DIMM, multiply the speed by 8 bytes because a DIMM has an 8-byte or 64-bit data path. For example, a DDR DIMM that runs at 800 MHz has a bandwidth or transfer rate of 800×8 or 6400 MB/second, which is expressed as a PC rating of PC6400. A DDR2 PC rating is usually labeled PC2, a DDR3 PC rating is labeled PC3, and a DDR4 PC rating is labeled PC4. In Figure 4-42, this memory ad shows the PC rating and lists speed as the DDR rate. Table 4-4 lists some current PC ratings.

Source: crucial.com

Figure 4-42   Memory speed is expressed in PC rating and lists speed as DDR rating

> ★ **A+ Exam Tip**   The A+ 220-901 exam expects you to be able to calculate PC ratings, given the transfers per second. To get the PC rating, multiply the transfers per second by eight. To get the speed, divide the PC rating by eight.

SINGLE-SIDED AND DOUBLE-SIDED DIMMs

A DIMM can have memory chips installed on one side of the module (called single-sided) or both sides of the module (called double-sided). Most desktop and laptop processors address memory 64 bits at a time. A memory bank is the memory a processor addresses at one time and is 64 bits wide, and a DIMM

Type of Memory	Speed	PC Rating
DDR4 DIMM	2666 MHz	PC4-21300
DDR4 DIMM	3000 MHz	PC4-24000
DDR4 DIMM	2133 MHz	PC4-17000
DDR3 DIMM	2000 MHz	PC3-16000
DDR3 DIMM	1800 MHz	PC3-14400
DDR3 DIMM	1333 MHz	PC3-10600
DDR2 DIMM	800 MHz	PC2-6400
DDR2 DIMM	667 MHz	PC2-5400
DDR DIMM	500 MHz	PC4000

Table 4-4   PC ratings for current memory modules

slot provides a 64-bit data path. However, some double-sided DIMMs provide more than one bank, which means the chips on the DIMM are grouped so that the memory controller addresses one group and then addresses another. These DIMMs are said to be dual ranked, and don't perform as well as DIMMs where all the memory is addressed at one time. Figure 4-43 shows some examples of DDR dual-ranked memory modules used in servers.

Figure 4-43   Memory ad lists dual-ranked DDR4 memory

Source: crucial.com

ERROR CHECKING AND PARITY

Because DIMMs intended to be used in servers must be extremely reliable, error-checking technology called ECC (error-correcting code) is sometimes used. The memory modules shown in Figure 4-43 are ECC memory. Some DDR, DDR2, DDR3, and DDR4 memory modules support ECC. A DIMM normally has an even number of chips on the module, but a DIMM that supports ECC has an odd number of chips on the module. The odd extra chip is the ECC chip. ECC compares bits written to the module to what is later read from the module, and it can detect and correct an error in a single bit of the byte. If there are errors in 2 bits of a byte, ECC can detect the error but cannot correct it. The data path width for DIMMs is normally 64 bits, but with ECC, the data path is 72 bits. The extra 8 bits are used for error checking. ECC memory costs more than non-ECC memory, but it is more reliable. For ECC to work, the motherboard and all installed modules must support it. Also, it's important to know that you cannot install a mix of ECC and non-ECC memory on the motherboard because such a mixture causes the system to not work.

As with most other memory technologies discussed in this chapter, when buying memory to add to a motherboard, match the type of memory to the type the board supports. To see if your motherboard supports ECC memory, look for the ability to enable or disable the feature in UEFI/BIOS setup, or check the motherboard documentation.

Older SIMMs used an error-checking technology called parity. Using parity checking, a ninth bit is stored with every 8 bits in a byte. If memory is using odd parity, it makes the ninth or parity bit either a 1 or a 0, to make the number of 1s in the nine bits odd. If it uses even parity, it makes the parity bit a 1 or a 0 to make the number of 1s in the 9 bits even.

> ⭐ **A+ Exam Tip** The A+ 220-901 exam expects you to know that parity memory uses 9 bits (8 bits for data and 1 bit for parity). You also need to be familiar with ECC and non-ECC memory technologies.

Later, when the byte is read back, the memory controller checks the odd or even state. If the number of bits is not an odd number for odd parity or an even number for even parity, a parity error occurs. A parity error always causes the system to halt. On the screen, you see the error message "Parity Error 1" or "Parity Error 2" or a similar error message about parity. Parity Error 1 is a parity error on the motherboard; Parity Error 2 is a parity error on an expansion card.

Figure 4-44 shows a SIMM for sale. It's pricy because this old technology is hardly ever used. Notice the module is non-parity memory. In the ad, the SIMM is called EDO memory. EDO (extended data out) is a technology used by SIMMs.

Figure 4-44 A SIMM appears in a memory ad as EDO memory

> ✏️ **Notes** RAM chips that have become undependable and cannot hold data reliably can cause errors. Sometimes this happens when chips overheat or power falters.

BUFFERED AND REGISTERED DIMMs

Buffers and registers hold data and amplify a signal just before the data is written to the module. (Using buffers is an older technology than using registers.) Some DIMMs use buffers, some use registers, and some use neither. If a DIMM doesn't support registers or buffers, it's referred to as an unbuffered DIMM. Looking at the ad in Figure 4-42 for value memory used in desktops, you can see all the modules are unbuffered. However, in Figure 4-43, two of the kits of expensive server memory are registered DIMMs.

CAS LATENCY AND RAS LATENCY

Two other memory features are CAS Latency (CAS stands for "column access strobe") and RAS Latency (RAS stands for "row access strobe"), which are two ways of measuring access timing. Both features refer to the number of clock cycles it takes to write or read a column or row of data off a memory module. CAS Latency is used more than RAS Latency. Lower values are better than higher ones. For example, CL8 is a little faster than CL9.

> ✎ **Notes** In memory ads, CAS Latency is sometimes written as CL, and RAS Latency might be written as RL.

Ads for memory modules might give the CAS Latency value within a series of timing numbers, such as 5-5-5-15. The first value is CAS Latency, which means the module is CL5. The second value is RAS Latency. Looking back at Figure 4-42, you can see CL ratings vary from 2.5 to 11.

> ✎ **Notes** When selecting memory, use the memory type that the motherboard manufacturer recommends.

TYPES OF MEMORY USED IN LAPTOPS

Today's laptops use DDR4, DDR3L, DDR3, or DDR2 SO-DIMM (small outline DIMM) memory. Table 4-5 lists current SO-DIMMs. All of these memory modules are smaller than regular DIMMs.

> 💡 **A+ Exam Tip** The A+ 220-901 exam expects you to know that DDR3, DDR2, and DDR memory can be found on SO-DIMMs.

Memory Module Description	Sample Memory Module
2.74" 260-pin SO-DIMM contains DDR4 memory. The one notch on the module is offset from the center of the module.	Source: crucial.com
2.66" 204-pin SO-DIMM contains DDR3 memory. The one notch on the module is offset from the center of the module. A DDR3L SO-DIMM uses less power than a regular DDR3 SO-DIMM.	Courtesy of Kingston Technology Corporation
2.66" 200-pin SO-DIMM contains DDR2 SDRAM. One notch is near the side of the module.	Courtesy of Kingston Technology Corporation
2.66" 200-pin SO-DIMM contains DDR SDRAM. One notch near the side of the module is slightly offset from the notch on a DDR2 SDRAM module.	Courtesy of Micron Consumer Products

Table 4-5 Memory modules used in laptop computers (continues)

Memory Module Description	Sample Memory Module
2.66" 144-pin SO-DIMM contains SDRAM. One notch is slightly offset from the center of the module.	Courtesy of Micron Consumer Products
2.35" 72-pin SO-DIMM has no notch on the edge connector.	
160-pin SO-RIMM contains Rambus memory and has two notches.	Courtesy of High Connection Density, Inc.

Table 4-5 Memory modules used in laptop computers (continued)

Just as with memory modules used in desktop computers, you can only use the type of memory the laptop is designed to support. The number of pins and the position of the notches on a SO-DIMM keep you from inserting the wrong module in a memory slot.

Now, onward to upgrading memory.

HOW TO UPGRADE MEMORY

A+
220-901
1.3, 3.1

To upgrade memory means to add more RAM to a computer. Adding more RAM might solve a problem with slow performance, applications refusing to load, or an unstable system. When Windows does not have adequate memory to perform an operation, it gives an "Insufficient memory" error or it slows down to a painful crawl.

When first purchased, many computers have empty slots on the motherboard, allowing you to add DIMMs or SO-DIMMs to increase the amount of RAM. Sometimes a memory module goes bad and must be replaced.

When you add more memory to your computer, you need answers to these questions:

▲ How much RAM do I need and how much is currently installed?
▲ How many and what kind of memory modules are currently installed on my motherboard?
▲ How many and what kind of modules can I fit on my motherboard?
▲ How do I select and purchase the right modules for my upgrade?
▲ How do I physically install the new modules?

All these questions are answered in the following sections.

HOW MUCH MEMORY DO I NEED AND HOW MUCH IS CURRENTLY INSTALLED?

A+
220-901
1.3, 3.1

With the demands today's software places on memory, the answer is probably, "All you can get." Windows 8 and Windows 7 need at least 2 GB, but more is better. The limit for a 32-bit OS is 4 GB installed RAM. A 64-bit Windows installation can handle more. For example, a 64-bit installation of Windows 8 can use up to 128 GB of RAM, and a 64-bit installation of Windows 7 Home Premium can use up to 16 GB of RAM.

APPLYING | CONCEPTS   HOW MUCH MEMORY IS CURRENTLY INSTALLED?

In Windows, you can use the System Information window to report the amount of physical memory installed. From the Windows 8 desktop, right-click **Start**, click **Run**, and then type **msinfo32**. For Windows 7, click **Start** and type **msinfo32** in the Search box. The System Information window shown in Figure 4-45 reports the amount of installed physical memory. Notice on the window that 16 GB is installed.

Figure 4-45   The System Information window reports installed physical memory

The BIOS setup screen shows more information about installed memory than does Windows. Reboot the computer and access BIOS setup (you learned how to do that in the chapter, "All About Motherboards"). The BIOS setup main menu for one system is shown in Figure 4-46. This screen shows the number of memory slots and how much RAM is installed in each slot. Notice the system has two memory channels of two slots each. You can, therefore, conclude this system is using dual channels.

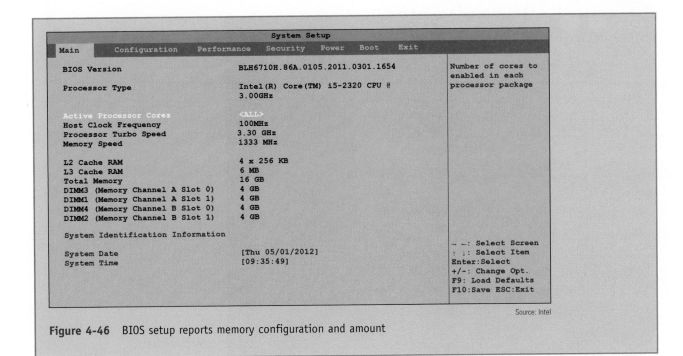

Source: Intel

Figure 4-46 BIOS setup reports memory configuration and amount

HOW MANY AND WHAT KIND OF MEMORY MODULES ARE CURRENTLY INSTALLED?

**A+
220-901
1.3, 3.1**

The next step to upgrading memory is to determine what type of memory modules the motherboard is currently using. If the board already has memory installed, you want to do your best to match the new modules with whatever is already installed. To learn what type of memory modules are already installed, do the following:

1. Open the case and look at the memory slots. How many slots do you have? How many are filled? Remove each module from its slot and look on it for imprinted type, size, and speed. For example, a module might say "PC2-4200/512MB." The PC2 tells you the memory is DDR2, the 4200 is the PC rating and tells you the speed, and the 512 MB is the size. This is not enough information to know exactly what modules to purchase, but it's a start.

2. Examine the module for the physical size and position of the notches. Compare the notch positions to those in Table 4-3.

3. Read your motherboard documentation. If the documentation is not clear (and some are not) or you don't have the documentation, look on the motherboard for the imprinted manufacturer and model (see Figure 4-47). With this information, you can search a good memory website such as Kingston (*www.kingston.com*) or Crucial (*www.crucial.com*), which can tell you what type of modules this board supports.

Figure 4-47   Look for the manufacturer and model of a motherboard imprinted somewhere on the board

4. Look in the documentation to see if the board supports dual channel, triple channel, or quad channels. If it does, most likely the memory slots on the board will be color-coded in pairs (for dual channels) or groups of three slots (for triple channels) or four slots (for quad channels). If the board supports multiple channels and modules are already installed, verify that matching DIMMs are installed in each channel.

5. If you still have not identified the module type, you can take the motherboard and the old memory modules to a good computer parts store and they should be able to match it for you.

Hands-On | Project 4-3   Use an Online Memory Scanner

A great shortcut to research a memory upgrade is an online memory scanner. Go to *www.crucial.com/systemscanner* by Crucial. Download and run the Crucial System Scanner, which scans your system and reports what type of memory is installed and can be installed. Using the Crucial report, answer these questions:

1. Which motherboard do you have installed? How much memory is installed? How many memory slots does the board have? How many are populated?

2. What is the maximum memory the board supports? What type of memory does the board support? What would be the total cost of the memory upgrade if you were to max out the total memory on the board?

HOW MANY AND WHAT KIND OF MODULES CAN FIT ON MY MOTHERBOARD?

A+
220-901
1.3, 3.1

Now that you know what memory modules are already installed, you're ready to decide how much and what kind of modules you can add to the board. Keep in mind that if all memory slots are full, sometimes you can take out small-capacity modules and replace them with larger-capacity modules, but you can only use the type, size, and speed of modules that the board can support. Also, if you must discard existing modules, the price of the upgrade increases.

To know how much memory your motherboard can physically hold, read the documentation that comes with the board. You can always install DIMMs as single modules, but you might not get the best performance by doing so. For best performance, install matching DIMMs in all the slots (two, three, or four slots) on one channel. Now let's look at a few examples. The examples are ordered from a more recent motherboard to an older motherboard. As you study these examples, notice that the older the board, the more complicated the configuration can be and the harder it is to understand the documentation. Is life with computers getting simpler or what?

MOTHERBOARD USING DDR3 DUAL-CHANNEL DIMMs

The Intel Desktop Board DH67GD shown earlier in Figure 4-21 has four memory slots that use dual channeling. These slots are numbered in the user guide, as shown in Figure 4-48. The slots can hold Dual Channel DDR3 1333 MHz and 1066 MHz non-ECC, 1.35-V modules for up to 32 GB of RAM on this board. To use four DIMMs and dual channeling, install matching DIMMs in the two blue slots and matching DIMMs in the two black slots.

Figure 4-48 Documentation shows four DIMM slots that use dual channels

The motherboard user guide says it is possible to use only three DIMMs and dual channeling if you install matching DIMMs in the two blue slots and install a third DIMM in a black slot. This third DIMM must be equal in speed and total size of the DIMMs in the blue slots. For example, you can install two 4-GB DIMMs in the two blue slots and one 8-GB DIMM in a black slot for a total of 16-GB of RAM. If you install only a single DIMM on this board, it must go in the first blue slot, which is the blue slot closest to the processor.

MOTHERBOARD USING DDR3 TRIPLE-CHANNEL DIMMs

The Intel motherboard shown earlier in Figure 4-40 has four DDR3 memory slots that can be configured for single, dual, or triple channeling. The four empty slots are shown in Figure 4-49. If triple channeling is used, three matching DIMMs are used in the three blue slots. If the fourth slot is populated, the board reverts to single channeling. For dual channeling, install two matching DIMMs in the two blue slots farthest from the processor and leave the other two slots empty. If only one DIMM is installed, it goes in the blue slot in the farthest position from the processor.

Figure 4-49   Four DDR3 slots on a motherboard

The motherboard documentation says that these types of DIMMs can be used:

- The DIMM voltage rating no higher than 1.6 V
- Non-ECC DDR3 memory
- Serial Presence Detect (SPD) memory only
- Gold-plated contacts (some modules use tin-plated contacts)
- 1333 MHz, 1066 MHz, or 800 MHz (best to match the system bus speed)
- Unbuffered, nonregistered single- or double-sided DIMMs
- Up to 16 GB total installed RAM

The third item in the list needs an explanation. Serial Presence Detect (SPD) is a DIMM technology that declares to system UEFI/BIOS at startup the module's size, speed, voltage, and data path width. If the DIMM does not support SPD, the system might not boot or boot with errors. Today's memory always supports SPD.

MOTHERBOARD USING DDR DIMMs WITH DUAL CHANNELING

Let's look at another example of a DIMM installation. The Pentium motherboard allows you to use three different speeds of DDR DIMMs in one to four sockets on the board. The board supports dual channeling and has two blue slots for one channel and two black slots for the other channel. For dual channeling to work, matching DIMMs must be installed in the two blue sockets. If two DIMMs are installed in the two black sockets, they must match each other.

This board supports up to 4 GB of unbuffered, 184-pin, non-ECC memory running at PC3200, PC2700, or PC2100. The documentation says the system bus can run at 800 MHz, 533 MHz, or 400 MHz, depending on the speed of the processor installed. Therefore, the speed of the processor determines the system bus speed, which determines the speed of memory modules.

Figure 4-50 outlines the possible configurations of these DIMM modules, showing that you can install one, two, or four DIMMs and which sockets should hold these DIMMs. To take advantage of dual channeling on this motherboard, you must populate the sockets according to Figure 4-50, so that identical DIMM pairs are working together in DIMM_A1 and DIMM_B1 sockets (the blue sockets), and another pair can work together in DIMM_A2 and DIMM_B2 sockets (the black sockets).

The board has two installed DDR DIMMs. The label on one of these DIMMs is shown in Figure 4-51. The important items on this label are the size (256 MB), the speed (400 MHz or 3200 PC rating), and the CAS Latency (CL3). With this information and knowledge about what the board can support, we are now ready to select and buy the memory for the upgrade. For example, if you decide to upgrade the system to

		Sockets			
Mode		DIMM_A1	DIMM_A2	DIMM_B1	DIMM_B2
Single channel	(1)	Populated	—	—	—
	(2)	—	Populated	—	—
	(3)	—	—	Populated	—
	(4)	—	—	—	Populated
Dual channel*	(1)	Populated	—	Populated	—
	(2)	—	Populated	—	Populated
	(3)	Populated	Populated	Populated	Populated

Use only identical DDR DIMM pairs

Figure 4-50 Motherboard documentation shows that one, two, or four DIMMs can be installed

Figure 4-51 Use the label on this DIMM to identify its features

1 GB of memory, you would buy two DDR, 400 MHz, CL3 DIMMs that support dual channeling. For best results, you need to also match the manufacturer and buy Elixir memory.

HOW DO I SELECT AND PURCHASE THE RIGHT MEMORY MODULES?

You're now ready to make the purchase. As you select your memory, you might find it difficult to find an exact match to DIMMs already installed on the board. If necessary, here are some compromises you cannot or can make:

▲ Mixing unbuffered memory with buffered or registered memory won't work.
▲ When matching memory, for best results, also match the module manufacturer. But in a pinch, you can try using memory from two different manufacturers.
▲ If you mix memory speeds, know that all modules will perform at the slowest speed.

Now let's look at how to use a website or other computer ad to search for the right memory.

USING A WEBSITE TO RESEARCH YOUR PURCHASE

When purchasing memory from a website such as Crucial Technology's site (*www.crucial.com*) or Kingston Technology's site (*www.kingston.com*), look for a search utility that will match memory modules to your motherboard (see Figure 4-52). These utilities are easy to use and help you confirm you have made the right decisions about type, size, and speed to buy. They can also help if motherboard documentation is inadequate, and you're not exactly sure what memory to buy.

Source: kingston.com

Figure 4-52   The Kingston website DIMM recommendations for a particular motherboard

Let's look at one example on the Crucial site where we are looking to install memory in the Intel DH67GD motherboard discussed earlier in the chapter. The search results are shown in Figure 4-53.

Source: crucial.com

Figure 4-53   Selecting memory off the Crucial website

Modules faster than the board supports are listed. They will work on the board, running at a slower speed, but it's not necessary to spend the money for speed you won't use. The best buy is the second item listed; these DIMMs are rated at 1333 MHz, which is the maximum speed the board supports.

Hands-On | Project 4-4   Plan and Price a Memory Upgrade

Using the information you gained about your computer in Hands-On Project 4-3, research the web to determine the total cost of the memory upgrade in order to max out the total memory on your computer. You can keep the cost down by using the modules you already have, but don't forget to match the speed of the modules already installed. Print two webpages from two sites other than the Crucial site that show the modules you would purchase. How much will the upgrade cost?

HOW DO I INSTALL THE NEW MODULES?

A+
220-901
1.3, 3.1

When installing RAM modules, be careful to protect the chips against static electricity, as you learned to do in the "Working Inside Desktop Computers and Laptops" chapter. Follow these precautions:

- Always use an ESD strap as you work.
- Turn off the power, unplug the power cord, press the power button, and remove the case cover.
- Handle memory modules with care.
- Don't touch the edge connectors on the memory module or on the memory slot.
- Don't stack cards or modules because you can loosen a chip.
- Usually modules pop into place easily and are secured by spring catches on both ends. Make sure that you look for the notches on one side or in the middle of the module that orient the module in the slot.

Let's now look at the details of installing a DIMM.

INSTALLING DIMMs

For DIMM modules, small clips latch into place on each side of the slot to hold the module in the slot, as shown in Figure 4-54. Some newer motherboards have only one latch on the slot. To install a DIMM, first pull the supporting arms on the sides of the slot outward. Look on the DIMM edge connector for the notches,

Clip holds module in place

Open clip on empty slot

Figure 4-54   Clips on each side of a slot hold a DIMM in place which help you orient the DIMM correctly over the slot, and insert the DIMM straight down into the slot. When the DIMM is fully inserted, the supporting clips should pop back into place. Figure 4-55 shows a DIMM being inserted into a slot on a motherboard. Apply pressure on both ends of the DIMM at the same time.

Figure 4-55 Insert the DIMM into the slot by pressing down until the support clips lock into position

Most often, placing memory on the motherboard is all that is necessary for installation. When the computer powers up, it counts the memory present without any further instruction and senses the features that the modules support, such as ECC or buffering. For some really old computers, you must tell BIOS setup the amount of memory present. Read the motherboard documentation to determine what yours requires. If the new memory is not recognized, power down the system and reseat the module. Most likely it's not installed solidly in the slot.

Hands-On | Project 4-5 Examine UEFI/BIOS Settings

On your home or lab computer, use UEFI/BIOS setup to answer these questions:

1. Which processor is installed? What is the processor frequency?

2. What are the UEFI/BIOS settings that apply to the processor and how is the processor configured?

3. What information does UEFI/BIOS report about total memory installed and how each memory slot is populated? Does the board support dual, triple, or quad channeling? How do you know?

Hands-On | Project 4-6 Upgrade Memory

To practice installing additional memory in a computer in a classroom environment, remove the DIMMs from one computer and place them in another computer. Boot the second computer and check that it counts the additional memory. When finished, return the borrowed modules to the original computer.

HOW TO UPGRADE MEMORY ON A LAPTOP

A+ 220-901 3.1 Before upgrading memory, make sure you are not voiding the laptop's warranty. Search for the best buy, but make sure you use memory modules made by or authorized by your laptop's manufacturer and designed for the exact model of your laptop. Installing generic memory might save money but might also void the laptop's warranty.

Upgrading memory on a laptop works about the same way as with upgrading memory on a desktop: Decide how much memory you can upgrade and what type of memory you need, purchase the memory, and install it. As with a desktop computer, be sure to match the type of memory to the type the laptop supports.

4

Hands-On | Project 4-7 Upgrade Laptop Memory

A friend has a Lenovo ThinkPad X200 laptop and is looking for ways to improve its performance. He's cleaned up the hard drive and is now considering the possibility of upgrading memory. Windows reports the system has 2 GB of RAM. He opens the cover on the bottom of the case and discovers that both SO-DIMM slots are filled. How much will the upgrade cost to bring total RAM in the system to 4 GB? Print the webpage to support your answer. What type and speed of SO-DIMMs does this laptop use?

APPLYING | CONCEPTS UPGRADE MEMORY ON A LAPTOP

Most laptops are designed for easy access to memory. Follow these steps to exchange or upgrade memory for one laptop:

1. Back up data and shut down the system. Remove peripherals, including the AC adapter. Remove the battery. Be sure to use a ground bracelet as you work.

2. Many laptops have a RAM door on the bottom of the laptop. For some laptops, this door is in the battery cavity. Turn the laptop over and loosen the screws on the RAM door. (It is not necessary to remove the screws.)

3. Raise the door (see Figure 4-56) and remove the door from its hinges. The two memory slots are exposed.

Figure 4-56 Raise the DIMM door on the bottom of the notebook

(continues)

4. Notice in Figure 4-57 that one slot is filled and one is available for a memory upgrade. Also notice in the figure that when you remove the RAM door, the CMOS battery is exposed. This easy access to the battery makes exchanging it very easy. To remove a SO-DIMM, pull the clips on the side of the memory slot apart slightly (see Figure 4-58). The SO-DIMM will pop up out of the slot and can then be removed. If it does not pop up, you can hold the clips apart as you pull the module up and out of the slot.

Installed SO-DIMM

Empty SO-DIMM slot

CMOS battery

Figure 4-57 SO-DIMM slots, one installed SO-DIMM, and the CMOS battery are exposed

Figure 4-58 Pull apart the clips on the memory slot to release the SO-DIMM

5. To install a new SO-DIMM, insert the module at an angle into the slot (see Figure 4-59) and gently push it down until it snaps into the clips (see Figure 4-60). Replace the RAM door.

Figure 4-59   Insert a new SO-DIMM into a memory slot

Figure 4-60   Push down on the SO-DIMM until it pops into the clips

6. Replace the battery, plug in the power adapter, and power up the laptop.

>> CHAPTER SUMMARY

Types and Characteristics of Processors

▲ The most important component on the motherboard is the processor, or central processing unit. The two major manufacturers of processors are Intel and AMD.

▲ Processors are rated by the processor speed, the socket and chipset the processor can use, processor architecture (32-bit or 64-bit), multicore rating, how much internal memory cache the processor has, amount and type of RAM the processor can support, and the computing technologies the processor can use.

▲ A processor's memory cache inside the processor housing can be an L1 cache (contained on the processor die), L2 cache (off the die), and L3 cache (farther from the core than L2 cache).

▲ The core of a processor has two arithmetic logic units (ALUs). Multicore processors have two, three, or more cores (called dual core, triple core, quad core, and so forth). Each core can process two threads at once if the feature is enabled in UEFI/BIOS setup.

▲ The current families of Intel processors for desktops include the Core, Atom, Celeron, and Pentium families of processors. Several different processors are within each family.

▲ The current AMD desktop processor families are the FX, Phenom, Athlon, and Sempron. Several processors exist within each family.

Selecting and Installing a Processor

▲ Select a processor that the motherboard supports. A board is likely to support several processors that vary in performance and price.

▲ When installing a processor, always follow the directions given in the motherboard user guide and be careful to protect the board and processor against ESD. Current Intel sockets LGA1150, LGA1155, LGA1366, and LGA775 use a socket lever and socket load plate. When opening these sockets, lift the socket lever and then the socket load plate, install the processor, and then close the socket. Many AMD sockets have a socket lever, but not a socket load plate.

Memory Technologies

◢ DRAM is stored on DIMMs for desktop computers and SO-DIMMs for laptops.

◢ Types of current DIMMs are DDR4 with 288 pins, DDR3 and DDR2 DIMMs that have 240 pins, and DDR DIMMs with 184 pins.

◢ DIMMs can be single-sided or double-sided. Some double-sided DIMMs provide more than one memory bank and are called dual ranked or quad ranked. A memory bank has a 64-bit data path and is accessed by the processor independently of other banks.

◢ DIMMs can work together in dual channels, triple channels, and quad channels so that the memory controller can access more than one DIMM at a time to improve performance. In a channel, all DIMMs must match in size, speed, and features. DDR3 DIMMs can use dual, triple, or quad channeling, but DDR and DDR2 DIMMs can only use dual channels. DDR4 DIMMs can use dual or quad channels.

◢ DIMM speeds are measured in MHz (for example, 1333 MHz) or PC rating (for example, PC3-10600).

◢ The memory controller can check memory for errors and possibly correct those errors using ECC (error-correcting code). Using parity, an older technology, the controller could only recognize an error had occurred, but not correct it.

◢ Buffers and registers are used to hold data and amplify a data signal. A DIMM is rated as a buffered, registered, or unbuffered DIMM.

◢ CAS Latency (CL) and RAS Latency (RL) measure access time to memory. The lower values are faster than the higher values.

◢ Today's laptops use DDR4, DDR3L, DDR3, or DDR2 SO-DIMMs.

How to Upgrade Memory

◢ When upgrading memory, use the type, size, and speed the motherboard supports and match new modules to those already installed. Features to match include DDR4, DDR3, DDR2, DDR, size in MB or GB, speed (MHz or PC rating), buffered, registered, unbuffered, single-sided, double-sided, CL rating, tin or gold connectors, support for dual, triple, or quad channeling, ECC, and non-ECC. Using memory made by the same manufacturer is recommended.

◢ When upgrading components on a laptop, including memory, use components that are the same brand as the laptop, or use only components recommended by the laptop's manufacturer.

>> KEY TERMS

For explanations of key terms, see the Glossary for this text.

buffer overflow attack	dual channels	Level 3 cache (L3 cache)	SIMM (single inline memory module)
CAS Latency	dual processors	memory bank	single channel
Centrino	dual ranked	multicore processing	single-sided
DDR	dynamic RAM (DRAM)	multiplier	SO-DIMM (small outline DIMM)
DDR2	ECC (error-correcting code)	multiprocessing	static RAM (SRAM)
DDR3		multiprocessor platform	synchronous DRAM (SDRAM)
DDR3L	Execute Disable Bit (EDB)	parity	thermal compound
DDR4	graphic processing unit (GPU)	parity error	thread
DIMM (dual inline memory module)	Hyper-Threading	processor frequency	triple channels
Double Data Rate SDRAM (DDR SDRAM)	Hyper Transport	quad channels	x86 processor
	Level 1 cache (L1 cache)	RAS Latency	x86-64 bit processor
double-sided	Level 2 cache (L2 cache)	RIMM	
		SDRAM II	

>> REVIEWING THE BASICS

1. Who are the two major manufacturers of processors?

2. What is the name of the memory cache that is on the same die as the processor?

3. What is the name of the memory cache that is closest to the processor die but is not housed on the die?

4. What is the name of the Intel technology that allows a processor to handle two threads at the same time?

5. How many threads can a quad-core processor handle at once?

6. Which two Intel processor sockets use a screw head to hold down the socket load plate?

7. What is the purpose of the Execute Disable Bit?

8. Which is faster, SRAM or DRAM? Why?

9. How many pins are on a DDR3 DIMM? DDR2 DIMM?

10. How many pins are on a DDR DIMM?

11. How many notches does a DDR3 DIMM have?

12. Which DIMM performs better, a double-sided dual-ranked DIMM or a double-sided single-ranked DIMM?

13. What prevents a DDR DIMM from being installed in a DDR2 DIMM slot on a motherboard?

14. Which module, a DDR3 or DDR2 DIMM, uses lower voltage?

15. In a memory ad for DIMMs, you notice 64Meg ×72 for one DIMM and 64Meg ×64 for another DIMM. What does the 72 tell you about the first DIMM?

16. What type of DIMM supports triple channeling?

17. If 2 bits of a byte are in error when the byte is read from ECC memory, can ECC detect the error? Can it fix the error?

18. A DIMM memory ad displays 5-5-5-15. What is the CAS Latency value of this DIMM?

19. What is the most amount of RAM that can be used by a 32-bit installation of Windows 7 Professional?

20. A motherboard uses dual channeling, but you have four DIMMs available that differ in size. The motherboard supports all four sizes. Can you install these DIMMs on the board? Will dual channeling be enabled?

21. How many pins does a DDR3 SO-DIMM have? A DDR2 SO-DIMM?

22. Which is faster, CL3 memory or CL5 memory?

23. You are looking to purchase two DIMMs running at 400 MHz. You find DIMMs advertised at PC4000 and PC3200. Which do you purchase?

24. You need to find out how much RAM is installed in a system. What command do you execute to launch the System Information utility?

25. Although ECC memory costs more than non-ECC memory, why would you choose to use it? Which type of computer typically requires ECC memory?

>> THINKING CRITICALLY

1. You need to upgrade memory in a system but you don't have the motherboard documentation available. You open the case and notice that the board has four DIMM slots; three slots are colored yellow and one slot is black. What type of DIMM does the board likely use? How can you be sure?

2. If your motherboard supports DIMM memory, will RIMM memory still work on the board?

3. If your motherboard supports ECC DDR3 memory, can you substitute non-ECC DDR3 memory?

4. You have just upgraded memory on a computer from 1 GB to 2 GB by adding one DIMM. When you first turn on the PC, the memory count shows only 1 GB. Which of the following is most likely the source of the problem? What can you do to fix it?

   a. Windows is giving an error because it likely became corrupted while the computer was disassembled.

   b. The new DIMM you installed is faulty.

   c. The new DIMM is not properly seated.

   d. The DIMM is installed in the wrong slot.

5. Your motherboard supports dual channeling and you currently have two slots used in Channel A on the board; each module holds 1 GB. You want to install an additional 1 GB of RAM. Will your system run faster if you install two 512-MB DIMMs or one 1-GB DIMM? Explain your answer.

>> REAL PROBLEMS, REAL SOLUTIONS

REAL PROBLEM 4-1 Understanding Dual-Processor Motherboards

Print the webpage of a picture of a motherboard that supports dual processors. Use one of these websites to find the picture:

▲ ASUS at *www.asus.com*

▲ Intel at *www.intel.com*

Answer these questions about the motherboard:

1. What is the manufacturer and model number of the motherboard?

2. What type of memory and how much memory does the board support?

3. What operating systems does the board support?

4. What processors does the board support?

REAL PROBLEM 4-2 Troubleshooting Memory

Follow the rules outlined earlier in the text to protect the computer against ESD as you work. Remove the memory module in the first memory slot on a motherboard, and boot the PC. Did you get an error? Why or why not?

REAL PROBLEM 4-3 Playing the Memory Research Game

In a group of four players with Internet access and a fifth person who is the scorekeeper, play the Memory Research Game. The scorekeeper asks a question and then gives players one minute to find the best answer. Five points are awarded to the player who has the best answer at the end of each one-minute play. The scorekeeper can use these questions or make up his or her own. If you use these questions, mix up the order:

1. What is the fastest DDR3 DIMM sold today?

2. What is the largest size DDR2 DIMM sold today?

3. What is the largest size fully buffered ECC 240-pin DDR2 DIMM sold today?

4. What is the lowest price for an 8-GB 240-pin ECC DDR3 DIMM?

CHAPTER 5

Supporting the Power System and Troubleshooting Computers

After completing this chapter, you will be able to:

- Describe the methods and devices for keeping a system cool

- Select a power supply to meet the power needs of a system

- Demonstrate an organized approach to solving any computer problem, especially hardware problems occurring during the boot

- Troubleshoot problems with the electrical system

- Troubleshoot problems with the motherboard, processor, and RAM

- Troubleshoot hardware problems with mobile devices

In the first chapters of this text, you learned much about the motherboard, processor, and RAM. This chapter focuses on how to keep these heat-producing components cool. You learn about the fans, heat sinks, and other devices needed to keep a system cool. You also learn about one more essential component of a computer system, the power supply, including how to select a power supply to meet the wattage needs of a system.

Then we focus on troubleshooting these various hardware subsystems and components. You study the troubleshooting techniques and procedures to get the full picture of what it's like to have the tools and knowledge in hand to solve any computer hardware-related problem. Then you learn to practically apply these skills to troubleshooting the electrical system, motherboard, processor, and memory. Finally, you learn about troubleshooting the hardware in mobile devices. By the end of this chapter, you should feel confident that you can face a problem with hardware and understand how to zero in on the source of the problem and its solution.

COOLING METHODS AND DEVICES

**A+
220-901
1.6**

The processor, motherboard, memory modules, expansion cards, and other components in the case produce heat, and, if they get overheated, the system can get unstable and components can fail or be damaged. As a hardware technician, you need to know how to keep a system cool. Devices that are used to keep a system cool include CPU fans, case fans, coolers, heat sinks, and liquid cooling systems.

In this part of the chapter, you learn about these several methods to keep the system cool. We begin with keeping the processor cool.

PROCESSOR COOLERS, FANS, AND HEAT SINKS

**A+
220-901
1.6**

Because a processor generates so much heat, computer systems use a cooling assembly designed for a specific processor to keep temperatures below the processor maximum temperature. If a processor reaches its maximum temperature, it automatically shuts down.

Good processor coolers maintain a temperature of 90–110 degrees F (32–43 degrees C). The cooler (see Figure 5-1) sits on top of the processor and consists of a fan and a heat sink. A heat sink is made of metal that draws the heat away from the processor into the fins. The fan can then blow the heat away. You learned to install a cooler in the chapter, "Supporting Processors and Upgrading Memory."

Figure 5-1   A cooler sits on top of a processor to help keep it cool

Figure 5-2   The Thermaltake V1 copper cooler fits Intel LGA1366 and LGA775 and AMD AM2 and AM2+ sockets

A cooler is made of aluminum, copper, or a combination of both. Copper is more expensive, but does a better job of conducting heat. For example, the Thermaltake (*www.thermaltake. com*) multisocket cooler shown in Figure 5-2 is made of copper and has an adjustable fan control.

Recall that the cooler is bracketed to the motherboard using a wire or plastic clip and thermal compound is placed between the bottom of the cooler heat sink and the top of the processor. To get its power, the cooler fan power cord connects to a 4-pin fan header on the motherboard (see Figure 5-3). The fan connector will have three or four holes. A three-hole connector can fit onto a 4-pin header; just ignore the last pin. A 4-pin header on the motherboard supports pulse width modulation (PWM) that controls fan speed in order to reduce the overall noise in a system. If you use a cooler fan power cord with three pins, know that the fan will always operate at the same speed.

—— 3-pin CPU fan power cord

—— 4-pin CPU fan header

Figure 5-3 A cooler fan gets its power from a 4-pin PWM header on the motherboard

© BonD80/Shutterstock.com

Figure 5-4 A passive or fanless cooler uses heat pipes to dissipate heat from the CPU

For enthusiasts trying to run a desktop computer with less noise, a fanless CPU cooler, also called a passive CPU cooler, can help (see Figure 5-4). These coolers contain heat pipes, which contain a small amount of liquid that becomes a vapor when heated, and the vapor draws the heat away from the CPU toward the fins on the cooler. There the heat can be blown away by case fans. Most passive CPU coolers are very large, so before you buy one, be sure it will fit in your computer case with all other components installed. Also, most motherboards give a startup error if a cable is not attached to the CPU fan header. Because these coolers don't have a fan cable, you will need to attach another cable to the header. For some systems, you can connect a case fan to the header.

CASE FANS AND OTHER FANS AND HEAT SINKS

A+
220-901
1.6

To prevent overheating, you can also install additional case fans. Most cases have one or more positions on the case to hold a case fan to help draw air out of the case. Figure 5-5 shows holes on the rear of a case designed to hold a case fan.

—— Install case fan here

—— Install power supply here

Figure 5-5 Install a case fan on the rear of this case to help keep the system cool

A computer case might need as many as seven or eight fans mounted inside the case; however, the trend is to use fewer and larger fans. Generally, large fans tend to perform better and run quieter than small fans.

Figure 5-6 A PCI fan card by Vantec can be used next to a high-end graphics card to help keep it cool

Processors and video cards, also called graphics cards, are the two highest heat producers in a system. Some graphics cards come with a fan on the side of the card. You can also purchase heat sinks and fans to mount on a card to keep it cool. Another solution is to use a fan card mounted next to the graphics card. Figure 5-6 shows a PCI fan card. Be sure you select the fan card that fits the expansion slot you plan to use, and make sure there's enough clearance beside the graphics card for the fan card to fit.

For additional cooling, consider a RAM cooler such as the one shown in Figure 5-7. It clips over a DIMM. A fan might be powered by a SATA power connector or 4-pin Molex power connector. The fan shown in Figure 5-7 uses a Molex connector. You can use an adapter to convert a SATA or Molex connector to whichever the power supply provides.

4-pin power connector

DIMM cover

Figure 5-7 A RAM cooler keeps memory modules cool

When selecting any fan or cooler, take into consideration the added noise level and the ease of installation. Some coolers and fans can use a temperature sensor that controls the fan. Also consider the guarantee made by the cooler or fan manufacturer.

LIQUID COOLING SYSTEMS

**A+
220-901
1.6**

In addition to using fans, heat sinks, and thermal compound to keep a processor cool, a liquid cooling system can be used. For the most part, they are used by hobbyists attempting to overclock to the max a processor in a gaming computer. For example, Intel recommends a liquid cooling system for processors that use the LGA2011 socket, which is typically used on hobbyist and gaming computers. (You learned about this socket in the chapter, "All About Motherboards.") Liquid cooling systems tend to run quieter than other cooling methods. They might include a PCIe or PCI card that has a power supply, temperature sensor, and processor to control the cooler.

Using liquid cooling, a small pump sits inside the computer case, and tubes move liquid around components and then away from them to a place where fans can cool the liquid, similar to how a car radiator works. Figure 5-8 shows one liquid cooling system where the liquid is cooled by fans sitting inside a large case. Sometimes, however, the liquid is pumped outside the case, where it is cooled.

Courtesy of Thermaltake (USA) Inc.

Figure 5-8   A liquid cooling system pumps liquid outside and away from components where fans can then cool the liquid

Figure 5-9   This case comes with a power supply, power cord, and bag of screws

Now let's turn our attention to the power supply.

SELECTING A POWER SUPPLY

A+
220-901
1.2, 1.8

In the chapter, "Working Inside Desktop Computers and Laptops," you learned how to uninstall and install a power supply unit (PSU). Reasons you might need to replace a power supply are when a power supply fails, or the power supply in an existing system is not adequate for the system. When building a new system, you can purchase a computer case with the power supply already installed (see Figure 5-9), or you can purchase a power supply separate from the case.

5

TYPES AND CHARACTERISTICS OF POWER SUPPLIES

A+
220-901
1.2, 1.8

As you select the right power supply for a system, you need to be aware of the following power supply features:

▲ *ATX or microATX form factor.* The form factor of a power supply determines the size of the power supply and the placement of screw holes and slots used to anchor the power supply to the case.

▲ *Wattage ratings.* A power supply has a wattage rating for total output maximum load (for example, 500 W, 850 W, or 1000 W) and individual wattage ratings for each of the voltage output circuits. These wattage capacities are listed in the documentation and on the side of a power supply, as shown in Figure 5-10.

Figure 5-10   Consider the number and type of power connectors and the wattage ratings of a power supply

When selecting a power supply, pay particular attention to the capacity for the +12 V rail. (A *rail* is the term used to describe each circuit provided by the power supply.) The +12 V rail is the most used, especially in high-end gaming systems. Notice in Figure 5-10, the +12 V rail gets 360 W of the maximum 525 W load. Sometimes you need to use a power supply with a higher-than-needed overall wattage to get enough wattage on this one rail. Also, a PSU rated 1000 W and higher might have a second +12 V rail and is called a dual rail power supply. The extra rail is used for safety to ensure that a single +12 V rail is not overloaded.

▲ *Number and type of connectors.* Consider the number and type of power cables and connectors the unit provides. Connector types are shown in Table 1-2 in the chapter, "First Look at Computer Parts and Tools." Table 5-1 lists some common connectors and the voltages they supply. Some power supplies include detached power cables that you can plug into connectors on the side of the unit. By using only the power cables you need, extra power cables don't get in the way of airflow inside the computer case.

Connector	Voltages	Description
SATA	+3.3 V, +5 V, +12 V	Power to SATA drives, 5 pin
Molex	+5 V, +12 V	Power to older IDE drives and used with some older SATA drives, 4 pin
4/8-pin 12 V	+12 V	Auxiliary power to CPU
PCIe 6/8 pin	+12 V	Auxiliary power to PCIe cards
20-pin P1	+3.3 V, ±5 V, ±12 V	Older main power connector to motherboard
24-pin P1	+3.3 V, ±5 V, ±12 V	Newer main power connector to motherboard

Table 5-1   Power supply connectors and voltages

Figure 5-11 This adapter converts two Molex cables to a single 12 V 6-pin PCIe connector

▲ *Fans inside the PSU*. Every power supply has a fan inside its case; some have two fans. The fan can be mounted on the back or top of the PSU. Fans range in size from 80mm to 150mm wide. The larger the fan, the better job it does and the quieter it runs. Some PSUs can automatically adjust the fan speed based on the internal temperature of the system.

▲ *Dual voltage options*. Expect a power supply to have a dual-voltage selector switch on the back where you can switch input voltage to 115 V for the United States or 220 V for other countries.

▲ *Extra features*. Consider the warranty of the power supply and the overall quality. Some power supplies are designed to support two video cards used in a gaming computer. Two technologies used for dual video cards are SLI by NVIDIA and Crossfire by AMD. If you plan to use dual video cards, use a PSU that supports SLI or Crossfire used by the video cards. Know that more expensive power supplies are quieter, last longer, and don't put off as much heat as less expensive ones. Also, expect a good power supply to protect the system against overvoltage. A power supply rated with Active PFC runs more efficiently and uses less electricity than other power supplies.

HOW TO CALCULATE WATTAGE CAPACITY

A+
220-901
1.2, 1.8

When deciding what wattage capacity you need for the power supply, consider the total wattage requirements of all components inside the case as well as USB and FireWire devices that get their power from ports connected to the motherboard.

Keep these two points in mind when selecting the correct wattage capacity for a power supply:

▲ *Video cards draw the most power*. Video cards draw the most power in a system, and they draw from the +12 V output. If your system has a video card, pay particular attention to the +12 V rating.

The current trend is for the motherboard to provide the video components and video port, thus reducing the overall wattage needs for a system. Video cards are primarily used in gaming computers or other systems that require high-quality graphics.

▲ *The power supply should be rated about 30 percent higher than expected needs.* Power supplies that run at less than peak performance last longer and don't overheat. In addition, a power supply loses some of its capacity over time. Also, don't worry about a higher-rated power supply using too much electricity. Components only draw what they need. For example, a power supply rated at 1000 W and running at a 500 W draw will last longer and give off less heat than a power supply rated at 750 W and running at a 500 W draw.

To know what size power supply you need, add up the wattage requirements of all components, and add 30 percent. Technical documentation for these components should give you the information you need. Table 5-2 lists appropriate wattage ratings for common devices. Alternately, you can use a wattage calculator provided on the website of many manufacturers and vendors. Using the calculator, you enter the components in your system and then the calculator will recommend the wattage you need for your power supply.

Devices	Approximate Wattage
Motherboard, processor, memory, keyboard, and mouse	200–300 W
Fan	5 W
SATA hard drive	15–30 W
DVD/CD drive	20–30 W
PCI video card	50 W
PCI card (network card, FireWire card, or other PCI card)	20 W
PCIe ×16 video card	150–300 W
PCIe ×16 card other than a video card	100 W

Table 5-2   To calculate the power supply rating you need, add up total wattage

⚡ **Caution**   Some older Dell motherboards and power supplies do not use the standard P1 pinouts for ATX, although the power connectors look the same. For this reason, never use a Dell power supply with a non-Dell motherboard, or a Dell motherboard with a non-Dell power supply, without first verifying that the power connector pinouts match; otherwise, you might destroy the power supply, the motherboard, or both.

Table 5-3 lists a few case and power supply manufacturers.

Manufacturer	Website
Antec	www.antec.com
Cooler Master	www.coolermaster.com
EVGA	www.evga.com
FirePower Technology	www.firepower-technology.com
Rosewill	www.rosewill.com
Sentey	www.sentey.com
Silverstone	www.silverstonetek.com
Thermaltake	www.thermaltakeusa.com
Zalman	www.zalman.com

Table 5-3   Manufacturers of cases and power supplies for personal computers

Hands-On | Project 5-1 Calculate Wattage Capacity for Your System

A+
220-901
1.8

Do the following to compare the wattage capacity of the power supply installed in your computer with the recommended value:

1. Search the web for a power supply wattage calculator. Be sure the one you use is provided by a reliable website. For example, the ones at *newegg.com* and *extreme.outervision.com* are reliable. (At *newegg.com*, click **Computer Hardware** and then click **Power Supply Wattage Calculator**. At *extreme. outervision.com*, click **eXtreme Power Supply Calculator**.)

2. Enter the information about your computer system. Print or save the webpage showing the resulting calculations.

3. What is the recommended wattage capacity for a power supply for your system?

4. Look on the printed label on the power supply currently installed in your computer. What is its wattage capacity?

5. If you had to replace the power supply in your system, what wattage capacity would you select?

Hands-On | Project 5-2 Shop for a Power Supply

A+
220-901
1.8

Shop online for a power supply to meet the needs of each of the following systems. Print or save the webpage showing the power supply, its features, and its price:

1. A regular desktop system for light computing has a moderately priced motherboard and processor, onboard video, two SATA hard drives, a DVD-RW drive, and two case fans. The system needs a microATX power supply rated at least 450 W.

2. A file server has a high-end motherboard and processor using the LGA2011 socket, 8 modules of DDR4 RAM, onboard video, one SSD SATA hard drive, five magnetic SATA hard drives, DVD-RW drive, tape drive, PCI RAID card, and four fans. The system needs an ATX power supply rated at about 550 W.

3. A gaming system has a high-end motherboard and processor, two high-end video cards using SLI technology, two SATA hard drives, a Blu-ray drive, and four fans. The system needs an ATX power supply rated at about 800 W. The two high-end video cards require about 275 W each.

4. Suppose the gaming system in Number 3 is generating extra heat because of overclocking and a liquid cooling system has been installed. To account for the needs of the liquid cooling system, the power supply needs to be upgraded to 1800 W.

So far in the text, you have learned about motherboards, processors, RAM, and the electrical system, which are the principal hardware components of a computer. With this hardware foundation in place, you're ready to learn about computer troubleshooting. Let's start with an overview of how to approach any hardware problem, and then we'll turn our attention to the details of troubleshooting the electrical system, motherboard, RAM, and CPU.

HOW TO APPROACH A HARDWARE PROBLEM

A+
220-901
3.0, 4.1

A good IT support technician over time builds a strong network of resources he or she can count on when solving computer problems. Here are some resources to help you get started with your own list of reliable and time-tested sources of help:

▲ *The web.* Do a web search on an error message, short description of the problem, or model and manufacturer of a device to get all sorts of help on the web. Check out the website of the product manufacturer or search a support forum. It's likely that others have encountered the same problem and posted the question and answer. If you search and cannot find your answer, you can post a new question. *Youtube.com* videos might help. Many technicians enjoy sharing what they know online, but be careful, however. Not all technical advice is correct or well intentioned.

▲ *Chat, forums, or email technical support.* Support from the hardware and software manufacturers can help you interpret an error message or provide general support in diagnosing a problem. Most technical support is available during working hours by way of an online chat session.

▲ *Manufacturer's diagnostic software.* Many hardware device manufacturers provide diagnostic software, which is available for download from their websites. For example, you can download Diagnostic Tools (can be used to copy all data from a drive that won't boot to another device), SeaTools for Windows (must be installed in Windows), or SeaTools for DOS (used to create a bootable CD that contains the software) and use the software to diagnose problems with Seagate and Maxtor drives. See Figure 5-12. Search the support section of a manufacturer's website to find diagnostic software and guidelines for using it.

✎ Notes   Always check compatibility between utility software and the operating system you plan to use.

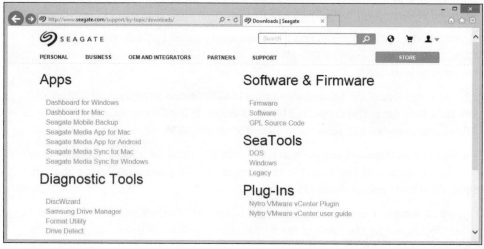

Source: www.seagate.com

Figure 5-12   Download diagnostic software tools from a manufacturer's website

---

▲ *User manuals.* Refer to your user manuals, which often list error messages and their meanings. They also might contain a troubleshooting section and list any diagnostic tools available.

▲ *Technical associates in your organization can help.* Be sure to ask for advice when you're stuck. Also, after making a reasonable and diligent effort to resolve a problem, getting the problem fixed could become more important than resolving it yourself. There comes a time when you might need to turn the problem over to a more experienced technician. (In an organization, this process is called escalating the problem.)

Next, let's examine the six-step model for computer troubleshooting. You'll learn much more about these steps in later chapters. Keep in mind, however, that these steps are only the beginning of computer troubleshooting. As an IT technician, expect that you will build your own style and steps for troubleshooting based on your own experiences over time.

STEP 1: INTERVIEW THE USER

When an end user brings any computer problem to you, begin the troubleshooting process by interviewing the user. When you interview the user, you might want to include these questions:

▲ Can you describe the problem and describe when the problem first started and when it occurs?
▲ Was the computer recently moved?

▲ Was any new hardware or software recently installed?
▲ Was any software recently reconfigured or upgraded?
▲ Did someone else use your computer recently?
▲ Does the computer have a history of similar problems?
▲ Is there important data on the drive that is not backed up?
▲ Can you show me how to reproduce the problem?

After you gather this basic information, you can prioritize what to do and begin diagnosing and addressing the problem. If the computer will not start or starts with errors so that you cannot reach the Windows desktop, setting priorities helps focus your work. For most users, data is the first priority unless they have a recent backup.

STEP 2: BACK UP DATA AS NEEDED

If the hard drive has important data on it that has not been backed up, your first priority is most likely to recover the data. Here are three options for doing that:

▲ *Move the hard drive to another system.* If a system won't boot from the hard drive, consider removing the drive and installing it as a second drive in a working system. If the file system on the problem drive is intact, you might be able to copy data from the drive to the primary drive in the working system.

To move the hard drive to a working computer, you don't need to physically install the drive in the drive bay. Open the computer case. Carefully lay the drive on the case and connect a power cord and data cable (see Figure 5-13). Then turn on the computer. While you have the computer turned on, be *very careful* to not touch the drive or touch inside the case. Also, while a tower case is lying on its side like the one in Figure 5-13, don't use the optical drive.

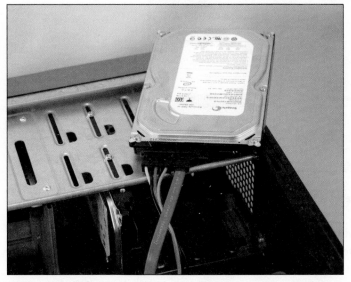

Start the computer and sign in to Windows using an Administrator account. (If you don't sign in with an Administrator account, you must provide the password to an Administrator account before you can access the files on the newly connected hard drive.) When Windows finds the new drive, it assigns it a drive letter. Use Explorer in Windows 8/7/Vista or third-party software to copy files from this drive to the primary hard drive in this system or to another storage media. Then return the drive to the original system and turn your attention to solving the original problem.

Figure 5-13 Move a hard drive to a working computer to recover data on the drive

> ✏ **Notes** An easier way to temporarily install a hard drive in a system is to use a USB port. Figure 5-14 shows a SATA-to-USB converter kit. The SATA connector can be used for desktop or laptop hard drives because a SATA connector is the same for both. A SATA-to-USB converter is really handy when recovering data and troubleshooting problems with hard drives that refuse to boot.

Figure 5-14 Use a USB-to-SATA converter to recover data from a drive using a SATA connector

▲ *Use file recovery software.* File recovery software is third-party software that can help recover deleted and corrupted files. On the Internet, do a search on "data recovery" for lots of examples. One good product is GetDataBack by Runtime Software (*www.runtime.org*), which can recover data and program files even when Windows cannot recognize the drive. Another example is Seagate Recovery Services (see Figure 5-15), which includes various tools and services, including file recovery software PC Trial.

Source: www.seagate.com

Figure 5-15 File recovery software made available by Seagate, a hard drive manufacturer

▲ *Hire a professional file recovery service.* If your data is extremely valuable and other methods have failed, you might want to consider a professional data recovery service. They're expensive, but getting the data back might be worth it. To find a service, do a web search on "data recovery." Before selecting a service, be sure to read reviews, understand the warranty and guarantees, and perhaps get a recommendation from a satisfied customer. For example, in Figure 5-15, click **Data Recovery** to see a description of the service offered by Seagate.

STEP 3: EXAMINE THE SYSTEM AND ESTABLISH A THEORY

A+
220-901
4.1

After data is secure, you're ready to tackle the problem and its solution. Most computer problems are simple and can be simply solved, but you do need a game plan. That's how Figure 5-16 can help. The flowchart focuses on problems that affect the boot. As you work your way through it, you're eliminating one major computer subsystem after another until you zero in on the problem. After you've discovered the problem, many times the solution is obvious.

5

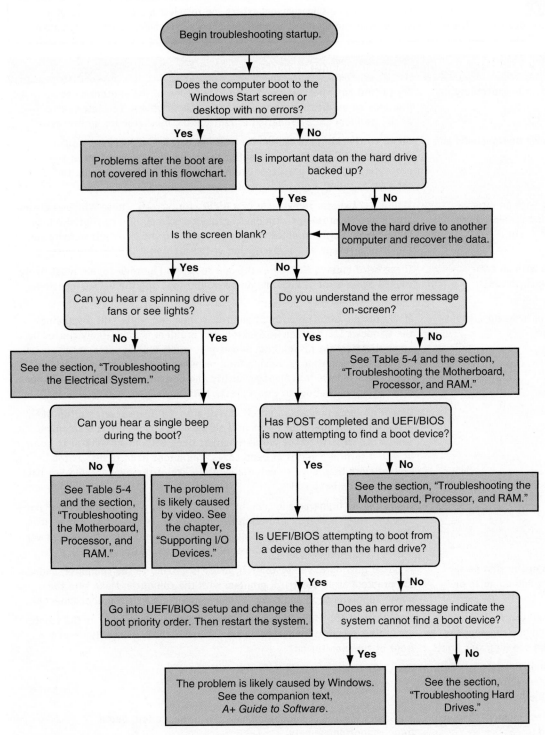

Figure 5-16 Use this flowchart when first facing a computer problem

As Figure 5-16 indicates, troubleshooting a computer problem is divided into problems that occur during the boot and those that occur after the Windows Start screen or desktop has successfully loaded. Problems that occur during the boot might happen before Windows starts to load or during Windows startup. Read the flowchart in Figure 5-16 very carefully to get an idea of the symptoms you might be faced with that would cause you to suspect each subsystem.

Also, Table 5-4 can help as a general guideline for the primary symptoms and what are likely to be the sources of a problem.

> ★ **A+ Exam Tip** The A+ 220-902 exam might give you a symptom and expect you to select a probable source of a problem from a list of sources. These examples of what can go wrong can help you connect problem sources to symptoms.

Symptom or Error Message	What to Do About the Problem
System shuts down unexpectedly	Try to find out what was happening at the time of the shutdowns to pinpoint an application or device causing the problem. Possible sources of the problem are overheating or faulty RAM, motherboard, or processor.
System shuts down unexpectedly and starts back up	Begin by checking the system for overheating. Is the processor cooler fan working? Go to UEFI/BIOS setup and check the temperature of the processor. When the processor overheats and the system restarts, the problem is called a processor thermal trip error.
System locks up with an error message on a blue screen, called a blue screen of death (BSOD)	Figure 5-17 shows an example of a BSOD error screen. These Windows errors are caused by problems with devices, device drivers, or a corrupted Windows installation. Begin troubleshooting by searching the Microsoft website for the error message and a description of the problem.
System locks up with an error message on a black screen	These error messages, such as the one shown in Figure 5-18, are most likely caused by an error at POST. Begin by troubleshooting the device mentioned in the error message.
System freezes or locks up without an error message	If the system locks up without an error screen and while still displaying the Windows Start screen or desktop, the problem is most likely caused by an application not responding. Sometimes you'll see the Windows pinwheel indicating the system is waiting for a response from a program or device. Open the Windows Task Manager utility and end any application that is not responding. If that doesn't work, restart Windows.
POST code beeps	One or no beep indicates that all is well after POST. However, startup UEFI/BIOS communicates POST errors as a series of beeps before it tests video. Search the website of the motherboard or UEFI/BIOS manufacturer to know how to interpret a series of beep codes. You might need to restart the system more than once so you can carefully count the beeps. Table 5-5 lists some common beep codes.
No power	If you see no lights on the computer case and hear no spinning fans, make sure the surge protector or wall outlet has power. Is the switch on the rear of the case on? Is the dual voltage selector switch set correctly? Are power supply connectors securely connected? Is the power supply bad?
Blank screen when you first power up the computer, and no noise or indicator lights	Is power getting to the system? If power is getting to the computer, address the problem as an electrical problem with the computer. Make sure the power supply is good and power supply connectors are securely connected.
Blank screen when you first power up the computer, and you can hear the fans spinning and see indicator lights	Troubleshoot the video subsystem. Is the monitor turned on? Is the monitor data cable securely connected at both ends? Is the indicator light on the front of the monitor on?
BIOS loses its time and date settings "CMOS battery low" error message appears during the boot	The CMOS battery is failing. Replace the battery.
System reports less memory than you know is installed	A memory module is not seated correctly or has failed. Begin troubleshooting memory.

Table 5-4 Symptoms or error messages caused by hardware problems and what to do about them (continues)

Symptom or Error Message	What to Do About the Problem
System attempts to boot to the wrong boot device	Go into UEFI/BIOS setup and change the boot device priority order.
Fans spin, but no power to other devices	Begin by checking the power supply. Are connectors securely connected? Use a power supply tester to check for correct voltage outputs.
Smoke or burning smell	Consider this a serious electrical problem. Immediately unplug the computer.
Loud whining noise	Most likely the noise is made by the power supply or a failing hard drive. There might be a short. The power supply might be going bad or is underrated for the system.
Clicking noise	A clicking noise likely indicates the hard drive is failing. Replace the drive as soon as possible.
Intermittent device failures	Failures that come and go might be caused by overheating or failing RAM, the motherboard, processor, or hard drive. Begin by checking the processor temperature for overheating. Then check RAM for errors and run diagnostics on the hard drive.
Distended capacitors	Failed capacitors on the motherboard or other circuit board are sometimes distended and discolored on the top of the capacitor. Replace the motherboard.
Error appears during boot: *Intruder detection error*	An intrusion detection device installed on the motherboard has detected that the computer case was opened. Suspect a security breach.
Error appears during boot: *Overclocking failed. Please enter setup to reconfigure your system*	Overclocking should be discontinued. However, this error might not be related to overclocking; it can occur when the power supply is failing.
Possible error messages: *No boot device available* *Hard drive not found* *Fixed disk error* *Invalid boot disk* *Inaccessible boot device or drive* *Invalid drive specification*	Startup BIOS did not find a device to use to load the operating system. Make sure the boot device priority order is correct in BIOS setup. Then begin troubleshooting the hard drive.
Possible error messages: *Missing operating system* *Error loading operating system*	Windows startup programs are missing or corrupted. How to troubleshoot Windows startup is covered in the companion text, *A+ Guide to Software*.
Continuous reboots	See explanation later in this chapter.

Table 5-4 Symptoms or error messages caused by hardware problems and what to do about them (continued)

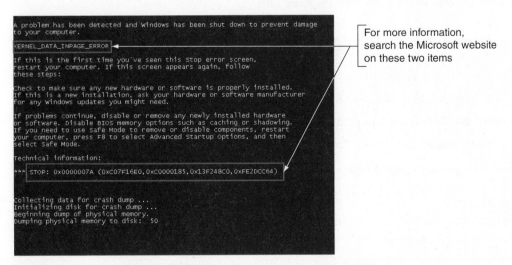

For more information, search the Microsoft website on these two items

Figure 5-17 Search the Microsoft website for information about a BSOD error

```
HardWare Monitor


CPU Vcore      :      1.32V           NB/SB Voltage   :      1.24V
+ 3.3 V        :      3.37V           + 5.0 V         :      5.13V
+12.0 V        :      12.22V          VDIMM           :      2.01V
HT Voltage     :      1.26V           5V(SB)          :      5.05V
Voltage Bat    :      3.08V           CPU Temp        :      32°C
CPU FAN        :      2755 RPM        System FAN      :      0 RPM


Verifying DMI Pool Data . . . . . . . . . . Update Success

A disk read error occurred

Press Ctrl+Alt+Del to restart
```

Source: Intel

Figure 5-18   A POST error message on a black screen shown early in the boot

Beeps During POST	Description
1 short beep or no beep	The computer passed all POST tests
1 long and 2 short beeps	Award BIOS: A video problem, no video card, bad video memory Intel BIOS: A video problem
Continuous short beeps	Award BIOS: A memory error Intel BIOS: A loose card or short
1 long and 1 short beep	Intel BIOS: Motherboard problem
1 long and 3 short beeps	Intel BIOS: A video problem
3 long beeps	Intel BIOS: A keyboard controller problem
Continuous 2 short beeps and then a pause	Intel BIOS: A video card problem
Continuous 3 short beeps and then a pause	Intel BIOS: A memory error
8 beeps followed by a system shutdown	Intel BIOS: The system has overheated
Continuous high and low beeps	Intel BIOS: CPU problem

Table 5-5   Common beep codes and their meanings for Intel and Award BIOS

APPLYING | CONCEPTS   FOUR TROUBLESHOOTING RULES

A+
220-901
4.1

Here are four important rules that can help you solve many hardware problems:

Rule 1: Check the Obvious and Check Simple Things First

Check for obvious and simple solutions first. Here are some tips:

◢ Is the external device plugged in and turned on? Are the data cable connections solid at both ends? Is there a wall light switch controlling the power, and is it turned on? Is the surge suppressor you're using plugged in and turned on?

◢ For expansion cards and memory modules, are they seated solidly in their slots? For sound, is the volume knob turned up? For video, is the monitor getting power, turned on, connected, and is the screen resolution correct?

◢ Consider the application using the device. For example, if you are having problems trying to use a USB scanner, try scanning using a different application.

Rule 2: Trade Known Good for Suspected Bad

When diagnosing hardware problems, this method works well if you can draw from a group of parts that you know work correctly. Suppose, for example, video does not work. The parts of the video subsystem are the video card, the power cord to the monitor, the cord from the monitor to the computer case, and the monitor itself. Also, don't forget that the video card is inserted into an expansion slot on the motherboard, and the monitor depends on electrical power. As you suspect each of these five components to be bad, you can try them one at a time beginning with the easiest one to replace: the monitor. Trade the monitor for one that you know works. If this theory fails, trade the power cord, trade the cord to the computer's video port, move the video card to a new slot, and trade the video card. When you're trading a good component for a suspected bad one, work methodically by eliminating one component at a time.

Rule 3: Trade Suspected Bad for Known Good

An alternate approach works well in certain situations. If you have a working computer that is configured similarly to the one you are troubleshooting (a common situation in many corporate or educational environments), rather than trading good for suspected bad, you can trade suspected bad for good. Take each component that you suspect is bad and install it in the working computer. If the component works on the good computer, then you have eliminated it as a suspect. If the working computer breaks down, then you have probably identified the bad component.

Rule 4: Divide and Conquer

Isolate the problem. In the overall system, remove one hardware or software component after another, until the problem is isolated to a small part of the whole system. As you divide a large problem into smaller components, you can analyze each component separately. You can use one or more of the following to help you divide and conquer on your own system:

◢ In Windows, stop all nonessential services running in the background to eliminate them as the problem.

◢ Boot from a bootable DVD to eliminate the OS and startup files on the hard drive as the problem.

◢ Remove any unnecessary hardware devices, such as a second video card, optical drive, and even the hard drive.

Once down to the essentials, start exchanging components you know are good for those you suspect are bad, until the problem goes away. You don't need to physically remove the optical drive or hard drive from the bays inside the case. Simply disconnect the data cable and the power cable.

STEPS 4, 5, AND 6: FIX THE PROBLEM, VERIFY THE FIX, AND DOCUMENT THE OUTCOME

A+
220-901
4.1

After you understand the problem, you're ready to plan steps to resolve the problem. After the fix, be sure to verify the system works. Perform one last hard boot and make sure everything works as expected. If you're working with a user, ask the user to also verify the problem is fixed. In addition, ask yourself if anything could have been done to prevent the problem from happening in the first place. If so, take preventive action. Finally, most organizations require troubleshooting a computer problem be documented in a call tracking or help desk application where you are expected to record your findings, actions, and outcomes. Throughout the rest of this text, you'll have many opportunities to practice the troubleshooting skills introduced here.

Hands-On | Project 5-3   Research Beep Codes

A+
220-901
4.1   Identify the motherboard and UEFI/BIOS version installed in your computer. Locate the motherboard user guide on the web and find the list of beep codes that the UEFI/BIOS might give at POST. If the manual doesn't give this information, search the support section on the website of the motherboard manufacturer or search the website of the UEFI/BIOS manufacturer. List the beep codes and their meanings for your motherboard.

SPECIAL CONCERNS WHEN TROUBLESHOOTING MOBILE DEVICE HARDWARE

A+
220-901
3.0   When a component on a laptop or other mobile device needs replacing or upgrading, first you need to consider the warranty and how much time the repair will take. Before you decide to upgrade or repair an internal component, take into consideration these three alternatives:

▲ *Return the mobile device to the manufacturer or another service center for repair.* If the mobile device is under warranty, you need to return it to the manufacturer to do any serious repair work such as fixing a broken LCD panel on a laptop. However, for simple repair and upgrade tasks, such as upgrading memory or exchanging a hard drive on a laptop, most likely you can do these simple jobs by yourself without concern for voiding a warranty. Manufacturers allow a user to exchange the hard drive or memory when these components are accessible by way of a door or cover on the bottom of the laptop and it's not necessary to open the case. If you're not sure about the possibility of voiding the warranty, check with the manufacturer before you begin working on the mobile device. If the device is not under warranty and you don't have the experience or time to fix a broken component, find out how much the manufacturer will charge to do the job. Also, consider taking the device to a mobile device repair shop. Know that some mobile device manufacturers refuse to sell internal components or service manuals that explain how to take the device apart except to authorized service centers. In this case, you have few options but to use the authorized service center for repairs.

> **⚡ Caution**   Before you send a laptop or other device for repairs, if possible, back up any important data on the device. It's possible the service center will format the hard drive or install a new drive on a laptop or do a factory reset for a mobile device.

▲ *Substitute an external component for an internal component.* Replacing components on mobile devices can be time consuming and require a lot of patience. For a laptop, consider using BIOS setup to disable an internal component and then use an external device in its place. For example, if a keyboard fails, you can use a wireless keyboard with an access point connected to the USB port. Also, if the Ethernet port fails, the simplest solution might be to disable the port and use a USB network adapter to provide the Ethernet port.

▲ *Replace the internal device.* Before deciding to replace an internal device that is not easy to get to, such as an LCD panel in a laptop, first find out if you can get the manufacturer documentation necessary to know how to open the laptop case and exchange the component. Also consider if the cost of parts and labor is worth more than the value of the device. Buying a new device might be the best solution for your customer.

> **✎ Notes**   Check out *www.ifixit.com* for directions for device teardowns and repairs. You can also buy on the site the specific tools you might need for a teardown.

Now you're ready to look at how to troubleshoot each subsystem that is critical to booting up the computer. We begin with the electrical system.

TROUBLESHOOTING THE ELECTRICAL SYSTEM

APPLYING | CONCEPTS

A+
220-901
4.1

Your friend Sharon calls to ask for your help with a computer problem. Her system has been working fine for over a year, but now strange things are happening. Sometimes the system powers down for no apparent reason while she is working, and sometimes Windows locks up. As you read this section, look for clues as to what the problem might be. Also, as you read, think of questions to ask your friend that will help you diagnose the problem.

5

A+
220-901
4.1

Electrical problems can occur before or after the boot and can be consistent or intermittent. Many times repair technicians don't recognize the cause of a problem to be electrical because of the intermittent nature of some electrical problems. In these situations, the hard drive, memory, the OS, or even user error might be suspected as the source of the problem and then systematically eliminated before the electrical system is suspected. This section will help you to be aware of symptoms of electrical problems so that you can zero in on the source of an electrical problem as quickly as possible.

Possible symptoms of a problem with the electrical system are:

- The computer appears "dead"—no indicator lights and no spinning drive or fan.
- The computer sometimes locks up during booting. After several tries, it boots successfully.
- Error codes or beeps occur during booting, but they come and go.
- You smell burnt parts or odors. (Definitely not a good sign!)
- The computer powers down at unexpected times.
- The computer appears dead, but you hear a whine coming from the power supply.

Without opening the computer case, the following list contains some questions you can ask and things you can do to solve a problem with the electrical system. The rule of thumb is "try the simple things first." Most computer problems have simple solutions.

- If you smell any burnt parts or odors, don't try to turn the system on. Identify the component that is fried and replace it.
- When you first plug up power to a system and hear a whine coming from the power supply, the power supply might be inadequate for the system or there might be a short. Don't press the power button to start up the system. Unplug the power cord so that the power supply will not be damaged. The next step is to open the case and search for a short. If you don't find a short, consider upgrading the power supply.
- Is the power cord plugged in? If it is plugged into a power strip or surge suppressor, is the device turned on and also plugged in?
- Is the power outlet controlled by a wall switch? If so, is the switch turned on?
- Are any cable connections loose?
- Is the circuit breaker blown? Is the house circuit overloaded?
- Are all switches on the system turned on? Computer? Monitor? Surge suppressor or UPS (uninterruptible power supply)?
- Is there a possibility the system has overheated? If so, wait a while and try again. If the system comes on, but later turns itself off, you might need additional cooling fans inside the unit. How to solve problems with overheating is covered later in this chapter.
- Older computers might be affected by electromagnetic interference (EMI). Check for sources of electrical or magnetic interference such as fluorescent lighting or an electric fan or copier sitting near the computer case.

> ⚡ **Caution**   Before opening the case of a brand name computer, such as a Gateway or Dell, consider the warranty. If the system is still under warranty, sometimes the warranty is voided if the case is opened. If the warranty prevents you from opening the case, you might need to return the system to a manufacturer's service center for repairs.

If the problem is still not solved, it's time to look inside the case. First, turn off the computer, unplug it, press the power button to drain residual power, and then open the case. Next, do the following:

- Check all power connections from the power supply to the motherboard and drives. Also, some cases require the case's front panel be in place before the power-on button will work. Are all cards securely seated?
- If you smell burnt parts, carefully search for shorts and frayed and burnt wires. Disassemble the parts until you find the one that is damaged.
- If you suspect the power supply is bad, test it with a power supply tester.

PROBLEMS THAT COME AND GO

If a system boots successfully to the Windows Start screen or desktop, you still might have a power system problem. Some problems are intermittent; that is, they come and go. Generally, intermittent problems are more difficult to solve than a dead system. There can be many causes of intermittent problems, such as an inadequate power supply, overheating, and devices and components damaged by ESD. Here are some symptoms that might indicate an intermittent problem with the electrical system after the boot:

- The computer stops or hangs for no reason. Sometimes it might even reboot itself.
- Memory errors appear intermittently.
- Data is written incorrectly to the hard drive.
- The keyboard stops working at odd times.
- The motherboard fails or is damaged.
- The power supply overheats and becomes hot to the touch.
- The power supply fan whines and becomes very noisy or stops.

Here is what to do to eliminate the electrical system as the source of an intermittent problem:

1. *Consider the power supply is inadequate.* If the power supply is grossly inadequate, it will whine when you first plug up the power. If you have just installed new devices that are drawing additional power, verify the wattage rating of the power supply is adequate for the system.

   You can also test the system to make sure you don't have power problems by making all the devices in your system work at the same time. For instance, you can make two hard drives and the DVD drive work at the same time by copying files from one hard drive to the other while playing a movie on the DVD. If the new drive and the other drives each work independently, but data errors occur when all work at the same time, suspect a shortage of electrical power.

2. *Suspect the power supply is faulty.* You can test it using either a power supply tester (the easier method) or a multimeter (the more tedious method). However, know that a power supply that gives correct voltages when you measure it might still be the source of problems because power problems can be intermittent. Also be aware that an ATX power supply monitors the range of voltages provided to the motherboard and halts the motherboard if voltages are inadequate. Therefore, if the power supply appears "dead," your best action is to replace it.

3. *The power supply fan might not work.* Don't operate the computer if the fan does not work because computers without cooling fans can quickly overheat. Usually just before a fan stops working, it hums or whines, especially when the computer is first turned on. If this has just happened, replace the power supply. After you replace the power supply, if the new fan does not work, you have to dig deeper to find

the source of the problem. You can now assume the problem wasn't the original fan. A short somewhere else in the system drawing too much power might cause the problem. To troubleshoot a nonfunctional fan, which might be a symptom of another problem and not a problem of the fan itself, follow these steps:

a. Turn off the power and remove all power cord connections to all components except the motherboard. Turn the power back on. If the fan works, the problem is with one of the systems you disconnected, not with the power supply, the fan, or the motherboard.

b. Turn off the power and reconnect one card or drive at a time until you identify the device with the short.

c. If the fan does not work when all devices except the motherboard are disconnected, the problem is the motherboard or the power supply. Because you have already replaced the power supply, you can assume the problem is the motherboard and it's time to replace it.

POWER PROBLEMS WITH THE MOTHERBOARD

A+
220-901
4.1

A short might occur if some component on the motherboard makes improper contact with the chassis. This short can seriously damage the motherboard. For some cases, check for missing standoffs (small plastic or metal spacers that hold the motherboard a short distance away from the bottom of the case). A missing standoff most often causes these improper connections. Also check for loose standoffs or screws under the board that might be touching a wire on the bottom of the board and causing a short.

Shorts in the circuits on the motherboard might also cause problems. Look for damage on the bottom of the motherboard. These circuits are coated with plastic, and quite often damage is difficult to spot. Also look for burned-out capacitors that are spotted brown or corroded. You'll see examples of burned-out capacitors later in the chapter.

APPLYING | CONCEPTS

Back to Sharon's computer problem. Here are some questions that will help you identify the source of the problem:

A+
220-901
4.1

- ◢ Have you added new devices to your system? (These new devices might be drawing too much power from an overworked power supply.)
- ◢ Have you moved your computer recently? (It might be sitting beside a heat vent or electrical equipment.)
- ◢ Does the system power down or hang after you have been working for some time? (This symptom might have more than one cause, such as overheating or a power supply, processor, memory, or motherboard about to fail.)
- ◢ Has the computer case been opened recently? (Someone working inside the case might not have used a ground bracelet and components are now failing because of ESD damage.)
- ◢ Are case vents free so that air can flow? (The case might be close to a curtain covering the vents.)

Intermittent problems like the one Sharon described are often heat related. If the system only hangs but does not power off, the problem might be caused by faulty memory or bad software, but because it actually powers down, you can assume the problem is related to power or heat.

If Sharon tells you that the system powers down after she's been working for several hours, you can probably assume overheating. Check that first. If that's not the problem, the next thing to do is replace the power supply.

⚡ **Caution** Never replace a damaged motherboard with a good one without first testing or replacing the power supply. You don't want to subject another good board to possible damage.

PROBLEMS WITH OVERHEATING

A+
220-901
4.1

As a repair technician, you're sure to eventually face problems with computers overheating. Overheating can happen as soon as you turn on the computer or after the computer has been working a while. Overheating can cause intermittent errors, the system to hang, or components to fail or not last as long as they normally would. (Overheating can significantly shorten the life span of the CPU and memory.) Overheating happens for many reasons, including improper installation of the CPU cooler or fans, overclocking, poor airflow inside the case, an underrated power supply, a component going bad, or the computer's environment (for example, heat or dust).

Here are some symptoms that a system is overheating:

◢ The system hangs or freezes at odd times or freezes just a few moments after the boot starts.

◢ A Windows BSOD error occurs during the boot.

◢ You cannot hear a fan running or the fan makes a whining sound.

◢ You cannot feel air being pulled into or out of the case.

Source: SpeedFan by Alfredo Milani Comparetti

Figure 5-19   SpeedFan monitors fan speeds and system temperatures

If you suspect overheating, go into UEFI/BIOS screens and view the temperature monitors for the system. To protect the expensive processor and other components, you can also purchase a temperature sensor. The sensor plugs into a power connection coming from the power supply and mounts on the side of the case or in a drive bay. The sensor sounds an alarm when the inside of the case becomes too hot. To decide which temperature sensor to buy, use one recommended by the case manufacturer. You can also install utility software that can monitor system temperatures. For example, SpeedFan by Alfredo Comparetti is freeware that can monitor fan speeds and temperatures (see Figure 5-19). A good website to download the freeware is *www.filehippo.com/ download_speedfan*. Be careful to not download other freeware available on the site.

Here are some simple things you can do to solve an overheating problem:

1. If the system refuses to boot or hangs after a period of activity, suspect overheating. Immediately after the system hangs, go into UEFI/BIOS setup and find the screen that reports the CPU temperature. The temperature should not exceed that recommended by the CPU manufacturer.

2. Excessive dust insulates components and causes them to overheat. Use compressed air, a blower, or an antistatic vacuum to remove dust from the power supply, the vents over the entire computer, and the processor cooler fan (see Figure 5-20). To protect the fan, don't allow it to spin as you blow air into it. Overspinning might damage a fan.

Figure 5-20 Dust in this cooler fan can cause the fan to fail and the processor to overheat

✎ Notes When working in a customer's office or home, be sure you clean up any mess you create from blowing dust out of a computer case.

3. Check airflow inside the case. Are all fans running? You might need to replace a fan. Is there an empty fan slot on the rear of the case? If so, install a case fan in the slot (see Figure 5-21). Orient the fan so that it blows air out of the case. The power cord to the fan can connect to a fan header on the motherboard or to a power connector coming directly from the power supply.

Figure 5-21 Install one exhaust fan on the rear of the case to help pull air through the case

4. If there are other fan slots on the side or front of the case, you can also install fans in these slots. However, don't install more fans than the case is designed to use.

5. Can the side of the case hold a chassis air guide that guides outside air to the processor? If it has a slot for the guide and the guide is missing, install one. However, don't install a guide that obstructs the CPU cooler. How to install an air guide is covered later in this section.

6. A case is generally designed for optimal airflow when slot openings on the front and rear of the case are covered and when the case cover is securely in place. To improve airflow, replace missing faceplates over empty drive bays and replace missing slot covers over empty expansion slots. See Figure 5-22.

7. Are cables in the way of airflow? Use tie wraps to secure cables and cords so that they don't block airflow across the processor or get in the way of fans turning. Figure 5-23 shows the inside of a case where cables are tied up and neatly out of the way of airflow from the front to the rear of the case.

Figure 5-22 For optimum airflow, don't leave empty expansion slots and bays uncovered

Figure 5-23 Use cable ties to hold cables out of the way of fans and airflow

8. A case needs some room to breathe. Place it so there are at least a few inches of space on both sides and the top of the case. If the case is sitting on carpet, put it on a computer stand so that air can circulate under the case and also to reduce carpet dust inside the case. Many cases have a vent on the bottom front of the case and carpet can obstruct airflow into this vent (see Figure 5-24). Make sure drapes are not hanging too close to fan openings.

Figure 5-24 Keep a tower case off carpet to allow air to flow into the bottom air vent

9. Verify the cooler is connected properly to the processor. If it doesn't fit well, the system might not boot and certainly the processor will overheat. If the cooler is not tightly connected to the motherboard and processor or the cooler fan is not working, the processor will quickly overheat as soon as the computer is turned on. Has thermal compound been installed between the cooler and processor?

10. After you close the case, leave your system off for at least 30 minutes. When you power up the computer again, let it run for 10 minutes, go into UEFI/BIOS setup, check the temperature readings, and reboot. Next, let your system run until it shuts down. Power it up again and check the temperature in UEFI/BIOS setup again. A significant difference in this reading and the first one you took after running the computer for 10 minutes indicates an overheating problem.

11. Check UEFI/BIOS setup to see if the processor is being overclocked. Overclocking can cause a system to overheat. Try restoring the processor and system bus frequencies to default values.

12. Have too many peripherals been installed inside the case? Is the case too small for all these peripherals? Larger tower cases are better designed for good airflow than smaller slimline cases. Also, when installing cards, try to leave an empty slot between each card for better airflow. The same goes for drives. Try not to install a group of drives in adjacent drive bays. For better airflow, leave empty bays between drives. Take a close look at Figure 5-23, where you can see space between each drive installed in the system.

13. Flash UEFI/BIOS to update the firmware on the motherboard. How to flash UEFI/BIOS is covered in the chapter, "All About Motherboards."

14. Thermal compound should last for years, but eventually it will harden and need replacing. If the system is several years old, replace the thermal compound.

> ★ **A+ Exam Tip** The A+ 220-902 exam expects you to recognize that a given symptom is possibly power or heat related.

If you try the preceding list of things to do and still have an overheating problem, it's time to move on to more drastic solutions. Consider whether the case design allows for good airflow; the problem might be caused by poor air circulation inside the case. The power supply fan in ATX cases blows air out of the case, pulling outside air from the vents in the front of the case across the processor to help keep it cool. Another exhaust fan is usually installed on the back of the case to help the power supply fan pull air through the case. In addition, most processors require a cooler with a fan installed on top of the processor. Figure 5-25 shows a good arrangement of vents and fans for proper airflow and a poor arrangement.

Good arrangement for proper airflow   Poor arrangement for proper airflow

Figure 5-25 Vents and fans need to be arranged for best airflow

For better ventilation, use a power supply that has vents on the bottom and front of the power supply, as shown in Figure 5-26. Compare that with the power supply in Figure 5-21 that has vents only on the front and not on the bottom.

Figure 5-26   This power supply has vents on the bottom to provide better airflow inside the case

An intake fan on the front of the case might help pull air into the case. Intel recommends you use a front intake fan for high-end systems, but AMD says a front fan for ATX systems is not necessary. Check with the processor and case manufacturers for specific instructions as to the placement of fans and what type of fan and heat sink to use.

Intel and AMD both recommend a chassis air guide (CAG) as part of the case design. This air guide is a round air duct that helps to pull and direct fresh air from outside the case to the cooler and processor (see Figure 5-27). The guide should reach inside the case very close to the cooler, but not touch it. Intel recommends the clearance be no greater than 20mm and no less than 12mm. If the guide obstructs the cooler, you can remove the guide, but optimum airflow will not be achieved.

Figure 5-27   Use a chassis air guide to direct outside air over the cooler

5

Be careful when trying to solve an overheating problem. Excessive heat can damage the CPU and the motherboard. Never operate a system if the case fan, power-supply fan, or cooler fan is not working.

Hands-On | Project 5-4 Identify Airflow Through a Case

A+
220-901
4.1

Turn on a computer and feel the front and side vents to decide where air is flowing into and out of the case. Identify where you believe fans are working to produce the airflow. Power down the computer, unplug it, and press the power button to completely drain the power. Then open the computer case. Are fans located where you expected? Which fans were producing the strongest airflow through the case when the system was running? In which direction is each case fan drawing air, into the case or out of the case?

Hands-On | Project 5-5 Blow Dust Out of a Case

A+
220-901
4.1

If necessary, open the case cover to your desktop computer. Using a can of compressed air, blow the dust away from all fans and other components inside the case. Be careful to not touch components unless you are properly grounded. When you're done, close the case cover.

PROBLEMS WITH LAPTOP POWER SYSTEMS

A laptop can be powered by an AC adapter (which uses regular house current to power the laptop) or an installed battery pack. Battery packs today use lithium ion technology. Most AC adapters today are capable of auto-switching from 110 V to 220 V AC power. Figure 5-28 shows an AC adapter that has a green light that indicates the adapter is receiving power.

Figure 5-28 This AC adapter for a laptop uses a green light to indicate power

Some mobile users like to keep an extra battery on hand in case the first one uses up its charge. When the laptop signals that power is low, shut down the system, remove the old battery, and replace it with a charged one. To remove a battery, generally, you release a latch and then remove the battery, as shown in Figure 5-29.

Thumb latch
releases
the battery

Figure 5-29   Release a latch to remove the battery from a laptop

For best battery charge times, some laptops can use two batteries. For example, the laptop in Figure 5-30 uses a second battery called a sheet battery that fits on the bottom of the laptop. The two batteries together give about 12 hours of use between charges. The sheet battery comes with an adapter so you can charge it when it's disconnected from the laptop.

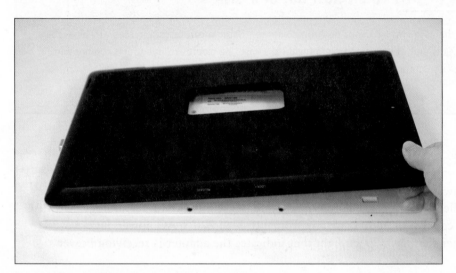

Figure 5-30   The second battery for this laptop is a sheet battery that attaches to the bottom of the laptop and adds up to six hours to the battery charge

> **Notes** If you're using the AC adapter to power your laptop when the power goes out, the installed battery serves as a built-in UPS. The battery immediately takes over as your uninterruptible power supply (UPS). Also, a laptop has an internal surge protector. However, for extra protection, you might want to use a power strip that provides surge protection.

Here are some problems you might encounter with laptop power systems and their solutions:

▲ If power is not getting to the system or the battery indicator light is lit when the AC adapter should be supplying power, verify the AC adapter is plugged into a live electrical outlet. Is the light on the AC adapter lit? Check if the AC adapter's plug is secure in the electrical outlet. Check the connections on both sides of the AC adapter transformer. Check the connection at the DC jack on the laptop. Try exchanging the AC adapter for one you know is good. The DC jack might need replacing. Most laptops allow you to replace the DC jack without replacing the entire system board. Check the service manual for the laptop to see how labor-intensive is the repair before you decide to proceed.

▲ If the battery is not charging when the AC adapter is plugged in, the problem might be with the battery or the motherboard. A hot battery might not charge until it cools down. If the battery is hot, remove it from the computer and allow it to cool to room temperature. Check the battery for physical damage. If the battery is swollen or warped, replace it. If it shows no physical signs of damage, try to recharge it. If it does not recharge, replace the battery pack. If a known-good battery does not recharge, you have three options: (1) Replace the system board, (2) replace the laptop, or (3) use the laptop only when it's connected to power using the AC adapter.

APPLYING | CONCEPTS   TEST AN AC ADAPTER

A+
220-901
4.1

If the system fails only when the AC adapter is connected, it might be defective. Try a new AC adapter, or, if you have a multimeter, use it to verify the voltage output of the adapter. Do the following for an adapter with a single center pin connector:

1. Unplug the AC adapter from the computer, but leave it plugged into the electrical outlet.

2. Using a multimeter set to measure voltage in the 1 to 20 V DC range, place the red probe of the multimeter in the center of the DC connector that would normally plug into the DC outlet on the laptop. Place the black probe on the outside cylinder of the DC connector (see Figure 5-31).

3. The voltage range should be plus or minus 5 percent of the accepted voltage. For example, if a laptop is designed to use 16 V, the voltage should measure somewhere between 15.2 and 16.8 V DC.

Figure 5-31   To use a multimeter to test this AC adapter, place the red probe (which, in the photo, is in the person's left hand) in the center connector and the black probe on the outside

Hands-On | Project 5-6   POST Diagnostics Cards for Laptops

A+
220-901
4.1

Suppose you spend much of your day diagnosing problems with laptop computers. Laptops have a Mini PCI or Mini PCIe slot that works in a similar way to PCI and PCIe slots on desktop systems. Search the web for diagnostic cards that you can use in a mini PCI or mini PCIe slot that can help you diagnose hardware problems with laptops. Print the webpages showing your findings. Which diagnostic card would you choose to buy and why?

TROUBLESHOOTING THE MOTHERBOARD, PROCESSOR, AND RAM

The field replaceable units (FRUs) on a motherboard are the processor, the processor cooler assembly, RAM, and the CMOS battery. Also, the motherboard itself is an FRU. As you troubleshoot the motherboard and discover that some component is not working, such as a network port, you might be able to disable that component in UEFI/BIOS setup and install a card to take its place.

> ★ **A+ Exam Tip**   The A+ 220-901 exam expects you to know how to troubleshoot problems with motherboards, processors, and RAM.

When you suspect a bad component, a good troubleshooting technique is to substitute a known-good component for the one you suspect is bad. Be cautious here. A friend once had a computer that wouldn't boot. He replaced the hard drive, with no change. He replaced the motherboard next. The computer booted up with no problem; he was delighted, until it failed again. Later he discovered that a faulty power supply had damaged his original motherboard. When he traded the bad one for a good one, the new motherboard also got zapped! If you suspect problems with the power supply, check the voltage coming from the power supply before putting in a new motherboard.

Symptoms that a motherboard, processor, or memory module is failing can appear as:

◢ The system begins to boot but then powers down.

◢ An error message is displayed during the boot. Investigate this message.

◢ The system reports less memory than you know is installed.

◢ The system becomes unstable, hangs, or freezes at odd times. (This symptom can have multiple causes, including a failing power supply, RAM, hard drive, motherboard or processor, Windows errors, and overheating.)

◢ Intermittent Windows or hard drive errors occur.

◢ Components on the motherboard or devices connected to it don't work.

Remember the troubleshooting principle to check the simple things first. The motherboard and processor are expensive and time consuming to replace. Unless you're certain the problem is one of these two components, don't replace either until you first eliminate other components as the source of the problem.

If you can boot the system, follow these steps to eliminate Windows, software, RAM, BIOS settings, and other software and hardware components as the source of the problem:

1. If an error message appears, Google the error message. Pay particular attention to hits on the motherboard or processor manufacturer or Microsoft websites. Search forums for information about the error.

2. The problem might be a virus. If you can boot the system, run a current version of antivirus software to check for viruses.

3. A memory module might be failing. In Windows 8/7/Vista, use the Memory Diagnostics tool to test memory. Even if Windows is not installed, you can still run the tool by booting the system from the Windows setup DVD. How to use the Memory Diagnostics tool is coming up later in this chapter.

> 🖉 **Notes**   Other than the Windows Memory Diagnostics tool, you can use the Memtest86 utility to test installed memory modules. Check the site *www.memtest86.com* to download this program.

4. Suspect the problem is caused by an application or by Windows. In Windows, the best tool to check for potential hardware problems is Device Manager.

5. In Windows, download and install any Windows updates or patches. These updates might solve a hardware or application problem.

5

> **Notes** Another useful Windows tool for troubleshooting hardware problems is Event Viewer, which reports logs of hardware and application errors. A Real Problems, Real Solutions activity at the end of this chapter gives you experience using Event Viewer.

6. Ask yourself what has changed since the problem began. If the problem began immediately after installing a new device or application, uninstall the device or applications.

7. A system that does not have enough RAM can sometimes appear to be unstable. Using the System window, find out how much RAM is installed, and compare that with the recommended amounts. Consider upgrading RAM.

8. The UEFI/BIOS might be corrupted or have wrong settings. Check UEFI/BIOS setup. Have settings been tampered with? Is the CPU speed set incorrectly or is it overclocked? Reset UEFI/BIOS setup to restore default settings.

9. Disable any quick booting features in UEFI/BIOS so that you get a thorough report of POST. Then look for errors reported on the screen during the boot.

10. Flash BIOS to update the firmware on the board.

11. Check the motherboard manufacturer's website for diagnostic software that might identify a problem with the motherboard.

12. Update all drivers of motherboard components that are not working. For example, if the USB ports are not working, try updating the USB drivers with those downloaded from the motherboard manufacturer's website. This process can also update the chipset drivers.

13. If an onboard port or device isn't working, but the motherboard is stable, follow these steps:

    a. Verify the problem is not with the device using the port. Try moving the device to another port on the same computer or move the device to another computer. If it works there, return it to this port. The problem might have been a bad connection.

    b. Go into UEFI/BIOS setup and verify the port is enabled.

    c. Check Device Manager and verify Windows recognizes the device or port with no errors. For example, Device Manager shown in Figure 5-32 reports the onboard Wi-Fi adapter is disabled. Try to enable the device.

Figure 5-32 Device Manager reports a problem with an onboard port

    d. Next try updating the motherboard drivers for this device from the motherboard manufacturer's website.

    e. If you have a loopback plug, use it to test the port.

    f. If the problem is still not solved, disable the port in BIOS setup and install an expansion card to provide the same type of port or connector.

14. Suspect the problem is caused by a failing hard drive. How to troubleshoot a failing drive is covered in the chapter, "Supporting Hard Drives and Other Storage Devices."

15. Suspect the problem is caused by overheating. How to check for overheating is covered earlier in this chapter.

16. Verify the installed processor is supported by the motherboard. Perhaps someone has installed the wrong processor.

APPLYING | CONCEPTS   USE WINDOWS MEMORY DIAGNOSTICS

**A+
220-901
4.1**

Errors with memory are often difficult to diagnose because they can appear intermittently and might be mistaken as application errors, user errors, or other hardware component errors. Sometimes these errors cause the system to hang, a blue screen error might occur, or the system continues to function with applications giving errors or data getting corrupted. You can quickly identify a problem with memory or eliminate memory as the source of a problem by using the Windows 8/7/Vista Memory Diagnostics tool. Use one of these two methods to start the utility:

▲ *Use the mdsched.exe command from within Windows.* To open a command prompt window from the Windows 8 desktop, right-click **Start** and click **Command Prompt**. (In Windows 7, click **Start**, enter **command** or **cmd**, and press **Enter**.) In the command prompt window, enter **mdsched.exe** and press **Enter**. A dialog box appears (see Figure 5-33) asking if you want to run the test now or on the next restart.

Figure 5-33   Use the mdsched.exe command to test memory

▲ *Boot from the Windows setup DVD.* If Windows is not the installed operating system or you cannot boot from the hard drive, boot the computer from the Windows setup DVD. On the opening screen, select your language. On the next screen (see Figure 5-34), click **Repair your computer**. For Windows 8, in the following boxes, click **Troubleshoot** and then **Advanced options**. On the Advanced options screen, click **Command Prompt**. At the command prompt, enter **mdsched.exe** and press **Enter**. For Windows 7, select the Windows installation to repair. On the System Recovery Options screen (see Figure 5-35), click **Windows Memory Diagnostic**.

Figure 5-34 Opening menu when you boot from the Windows 8 setup DVD

Figure 5-35 Test memory using the Windows 7 System Recovery Options menu

If the tool reports memory errors, replace all memory modules installed on the motherboard.

APPLYING | CONCEPTS   USE DEVICE MANAGER TO DELETE THE DRIVER STORE

**A+
220-901
4.1**

One thing you can do to solve a problem with a device is to uninstall and reinstall the device. When you first install a device, Windows stores a copy of the driver package in a driver store. When you uninstall the device, you can tell Windows to also delete the driver store. If you don't delete the driver store, Windows uses it when you install the device again. That's why the second time you install the same device Windows does not ask you for the location of the drivers. Windows might also use the driver store to automatically install the device on the next reboot without your involvement.

All this is convenient unless there is a problem with the driver store. To get a true fresh start with an installation, you need to delete the driver store. To do that, first sign in to Windows using an account with administrative privileges and then follow these steps:

1. To open Device Manager from the Windows 8 desktop, right-click **Start** and click **Device Manager**. (In Windows 7, click **Start** and click **Control Panel**. In Control Panel Classic icon view, click **Device Manager**.) Device Manager opens.

> ★ **A+ Exam Tip**   The A+ 220-902 exam expects you to be familiar with Control Panel in Classic icon view. If Control Panel is showing Category view, click **Category**, and then click **Large icons** or **Small icons**.

2. Right-click the device and click **Properties** in the shortcut menu. Click the **Driver** tab and click **Uninstall**. In the Confirm Device Uninstall box, check **Delete the driver software for this device**, and click **OK**. See Figure 5-36. The installed drivers and the driver store are both deleted. When you reinstall the device, you'll need the drivers on CD or downloaded from the web.

Figure 5-36   Use Device Manager to uninstall the drivers and delete the driver store for a device

Also know if the check box is missing on the Confirm Device Uninstall box, the drivers are embedded in Windows and you cannot delete the driver store for these devices. Examples of these devices are the optical drive, hard drive, and generic keyboard, which all have embedded Windows drivers.

We're working our way through what to do when the system locks up, gives errors, or generally appears unstable. Another problem that can occur at the boot is continuous reboots, which can be caused by overheating, a failing processor, motherboard, or RAM, or a corrupted Windows installation. For Windows 8, many continuous restart errors can be solved by performing a Startup Repair process. Follow these steps:

1. Boot from the Windows 8 setup DVD. (You might need to first change the boot priority order in UEFI/BIOS setup to boot first from the optical drive.)

2. On the opening screen, select your language. On the next screen (refer back to Figure 5-34), click **Repair your computer**. Next click **Troubleshoot** and then **Advanced options**. On the Advanced options screen (see Figure 5-37), click **Startup Repair** and follow directions on screen.

Figure 5-37   Startup Repair on the Advanced options menu can solve problems launching Windows 8

For Windows 7/Vista, error messages disappear before they can be read as the system reboots. To disable these automatic restarts, press F8 as Windows starts up. The Advanced Boot Options menu appears (see Figure 5-38). Select Disable automatic restart on system failure. When you restart Windows,

Figure 5-38   Press F8 during the boot to see the Windows 7 Advanced Boot Options menu

the error message stays on screen long enough for you to read it. Search the Microsoft websites (*support .microsoft.com* and *technet.microsoft.com*) for information about the hardware component causing the problem and what to do about it. BSOD errors might apply to the motherboard, video card, RAM, processor, hard drive, or some other device for which Windows is trying to load device drivers.

If you have checked Windows and UEFI/BIOS settings and searched the web for help and still have not identified the source of the problem, it's time to open the case and check inside. As you do so, be sure to use an ESD strap and follow other procedures to protect the system against ESD. With the case open, follow these steps:

1. Check that all the power and data cables the system is using are securely connected. Try reseating all expansion cards and DIMM modules.

2. Look for physical damage on the motherboard. Look for frayed traces on the bottom of the board or discolored, distended, or bulging capacitors on the board.

3. Reduce the system to essentials. Remove any unnecessary hardware, such as expansion cards, and then watch to see if the problem goes away. If the problem goes away, replace one component at a time until the problem returns and you have identified the component causing the trouble.

4. Try using a POST diagnostic card. It might offer you a clue as to which component is giving a problem.

5. Suspect the problem is caused by a failing power supply. It's less expensive and easier to replace than the motherboard or processor, so eliminate it as a cause before you move on to the motherboard or processor.

6. Exchange the processor.

7. Exchange the motherboard, but before you do, measure the voltage output of the power supply or simply replace it, in case it is producing too much power and has damaged the board.

APPLYING | CONCEPTS   DISCOLORED CAPACITORS

A+ 220-901 4.1

Jessica complained to Wally, her IT support technician, that Windows was occasionally giving errors, data would get corrupted, or an application would not work as it should. At first, Wally suspected Jessica might need a little more training on how to open and close an application or save a file, but he discovered user error was not the problem. He tried reinstalling the application software Jessica most often used, and even reinstalled Windows, but the problems persisted.

> ✎ **Notes** Catastrophic errors (errors that cause the system to not boot or a device to not work) are much easier to resolve than intermittent errors (errors that come and go).

Wally began to suspect a hardware problem. Carefully examining the motherboard revealed the source of the problem: failing capacitors. Look carefully at Figure 5-39 and you can see five bad discolored capacitors with bulging heads. (Know that sometimes a leaking capacitor can also show crusty corrosion at the base of the capacitor.) When Wally replaced the motherboard, the problems went away.

Bad capacitors

Figure 5-39 These five bad capacitors have bulging and discolored heads

---

Hands-On | Project 5-7 Troubleshoot Memory

A+
220-901
4.1

Do the following to troubleshoot memory:

1. Open the Windows System window and record the amount of memory in your system.

2. Follow the rules to protect a computer against ESD as you work. Remove the memory module in the first memory slot on the motherboard, and boot the computer. Did you get an error? Why or why not? Replace the module and verify the system starts with no errors and that the full amount of memory is recognized by Windows.

3. Use the Windows 8/7/Vista Memory Diagnostics tool to test memory. About how long did the test take? Were any errors reported?

Hands-On | Project 5-8 Sabotage and Repair a Computer

A+
220-901
4.1

Open the computer case and create a hardware problem with your computer that prevents the system from booting without damaging a component. For example, you can disconnect a data cable or power cable or loosen a DIMM in a memory slot. Close the computer case and restart the system. Describe the problem as a user would describe it who does not know much about computer hardware. Power down the system and fix the problem. Boot up the system and verify all is well.

TROUBLESHOOTING MOBILE DEVICES

A+
220-901
4.5

Here is what to do for problems with a cell phone that is overheating:

◢ Check if the heat is coming from the bottom of the cell phone where the battery is located. If so, try these things:

  ◢ Use a different AC adapter to charge the battery.

  ◢ If the phone is not under warranty, open the case and examine the battery for damage. Is it swollen or warped? If so, replace the battery. If the phone is under warranty, lay the phone on a flat surface. If the phone appears warped, take it in for repair.

> ✎ **Notes** Some Android cell phones will provide information about the device when you enter *#*#4636#*#* in the phone keypad. In the screen that appears, select Battery Information. If the Battery Health screen reports "unknown," suspect a bad battery. The temperature of the battery is also reported on this screen, which should be less than 40°C.

◢ If heat is coming from other areas of the phone, try these things:

  ◢ Too many apps might be open. Close all apps you're not currently using.

  ◢ Follow troubleshooting steps for your phone's operating system to resolve the problem. These steps include updating the OS.

  ◢ The phone processor might be overworked by streaming data (watching a movie online), playing a game, or texting. Allow the phone to rest and cool down.

  ◢ Consider removing the phone from a case that doesn't allow heat to dissipate.

If you decide the battery is the problem, check if the phone is under warranty. If not, you are likely to find teardown directions to replace the battery online. For example, at *ifixit.com* the kit to replace the iPhone 5 battery includes the battery, tools, and directions (see Figure 5-40). You can also watch videos on the site to step you through the process.

Source: IFIXIT

Figure 5-40   At *www.ifixit.com*, you can purchase tools, parts, and instructions to replace an iPhone battery

Here are some other problems and solutions for cell phones and phablets:

◢ For a frozen system, do the following:

  ◢ For the iPhone or iPad, reset the device. To do so, hold down the Wake/sleep button and the Home button at the same time for at least 10 seconds until the Apple logo appears.

◢ For a frozen Android device, you can reboot the system by following manufacturer directions for a reboot for the specific device. As a last resort, you can open the back of the device and remove and reinstall the battery.

◢ For Windows Phone, first try holding down the Power button and then swipe Slide down to power off. Power back up your phone. If that doesn't work, press and hold the Volume Down and Power buttons at the same time for at least 10 seconds until you feel a vibration. If that doesn't work, open the back of the device and remove and reinstall the battery.

◢ When the battery charge lasts an extremely short time, first try exchanging the AC adapter (charger). If that doesn't work, exchange the battery unless the device is under warranty.

◢ When installing apps that don't load or load slowly, a hot or failing battery might be the problem. Other problems might be a failing network connection. Reset the Wi-Fi or Bluetooth connection. If your device is connected to your computer with a USB connection, check the USB connection.

◢ For slow performance, close apps you're not using, clean Android cached data, and disable live wallpapers. Consider performing a factory reset and start over by installing only the apps you actually use.

◢ Email encryption is done using a public key and private key. You distribute your public key to those who want to send you encrypted email and you keep the private key on your device. If your device is unable to decrypt email, most likely you'll need to generate a new public key and private key and distribute your new public key to those who send you encrypted email.

5

APPLYING | CONCEPTS   LESSONS LEARNED

**A+
220-901
4.1**

Sophia is putting together a computer from parts for the first time. She has decided to keep costs low and is installing an AMD processor on a microATX motherboard, using all low-cost parts. She installed the hard drive, optical drive, and power supply in the computer case. Then she installed the motherboard in the case, followed by the processor, cooler, and memory. Before powering up the system, she checked all connections to make sure they were solid and read through the motherboard documentation to make sure she did not forget anything important. Next, she plugs in the monitor to the onboard video port and then plugs in the keyboard and power cord. She takes a deep breath and turns on the power switch on the back of the computer. Immediately, she hears a faint whine, but she's not sure what is making the noise. When she presses the power button on the front of the case, nothing happens. No fans, no lights. Here are the steps Sophia takes to troubleshoot the problem:

1. She turns off the power switch and unplugs the power cord. She remembers to put on her ground bracelet and carefully checks all power connections. Everything looks okay.

2. She plugs in the system and presses the power button again. Still all she hears is the faint whine.

3. She presses the power button a second and third time. Suddenly a loud pop followed by smoke comes from the power supply, and the strong smell of electronics fills the room! Sophia jumps back in dismay.

4. She removes a known-good power supply from another computer, disconnects the blown power supply, and connects the good one to the computer. When she turns on the power switch, she hears that same faint whine. Quickly she turns off the switch and unplugs the power cord. She does not want to lose another power supply!

5. Next, Sophia calls technical support of the company that sold her the computer parts. A very helpful technician listens carefully to the details and tells Sophia that the problem sounds like a short in the system. He explains that a power supply might whine if too much power is being drawn. As Sophia hangs up the phone, she begins to think that the problem might be with the motherboard installation.

(continues)

6. She removes the motherboard from the case, and the source of the problem is evident: She forgot to install spacers between the board and the case. The board was sitting directly on the bottom of the case, which had caused the short.

7. Sophia installs the spacers and reinstalls the motherboard. Using the good power supply, she turns on the system. The whine is gone, but the system is dead.

8. Sophia purchases a new power supply and motherboard, and this time, carefully uses spacers in every hole used by the motherboard screws. Figure 5-41 shows one installed spacer and one ready to be installed. The system comes up without a problem.

Figure 5-41   Spacers installed in case holes keep the motherboard from causing a short

In evaluating her experience with her first computer build, Sophia declares the project a success. She was grateful she had decided to use low-cost parts for her first build. She learned much from the experience and will never, ever forget to use spacers. She told a friend, "I made a serious mistake, but I learned from it. I feel confident I know how to put a system together now, and I'm ready to tackle another build. When you make mistakes and get past them, your confidence level actually grows because you learn you can face a serious problem and solve it."

>> CHAPTER SUMMARY

Cooling Methods and Devices

◢ Devices that are used to keep a processor and system cool include CPU coolers and fans, thermal compound, case fans, heat sinks, and liquid cooling.

◢ Liquid cooling systems use liquids pumped through the system to keep it cool and are sometimes used by hobbyists when overclocking a system.

Selecting a Power Supply

◢ Important features of a power supply to consider when purchasing it are its form factor, wattage capacity, number and type of connectors it provides, and warranty.

◢ To decide on the wattage capacity of a power supply, add up the wattage requirements for all components in a system and then increase that total by about 30 percent. The wattage provided by the +12 V rail is also important.

How to Approach a Hardware Problem

⊿ If possible, always begin troubleshooting a computer problem by interviewing the user. Find out when the problem started and what happened about the time it started. You also need to know if important data on the computer is not backed up. When troubleshooting, set your priorities based on user needs.

⊿ Sources that can help with hardware troubleshooting are the web, online technical support and forums, diagnostic software, user manuals, and your network of technical associates.

⊿ When troubleshooting, check the simple things first. For example, you can scan for viruses, test RAM, and run diagnostic software before you begin the process of replacing expensive components.

⊿ Decide if a computer problem occurs before or after a successful boot and if it is caused by hardware or software. After you have fixed the problem, verify the fix and document the outcome.

⊿ When troubleshooting mobile devices, consider the warranty and that replacing a component might cost more than replacing the device. If possible, substitute an external component for an internal one.

Troubleshooting the Electrical System

⊿ To determine if a system is getting power, listen for spinning fans or drives and look for indicator lights.

⊿ Use a power supply tester to test the power supply.

⊿ Intermittent problems that come and go are the most difficult to solve and can be caused by hardware or software. The power supply, motherboard, RAM, processor, hard drive, and overheating can cause intermittent problems.

⊿ Removing dust from a system, providing for proper ventilation, and installing extra fans can help to keep a system from overheating.

⊿ The battery and the DC jack are considered field replaceable units in a laptop that pertain to the power system.

⊿ Use a multimeter to check the voltage output of an AC adapter.

Troubleshooting the Motherboard, Processor, and RAM

⊿ UEFI/BIOS gives beep codes when a POST error occurs during the boot before it tests video.

⊿ Error messages on a black screen during the boot are usually put there by startup UEFI/BIOS during POST.

⊿ Error messages on a blue screen during or after the boot are put there by Windows and are called the blue screen of death (BSOD).

⊿ The motherboard, processor, RAM, processor cooler assembly, and CMOS battery are field replaceable units.

⊿ An unstable system that freezes or hangs at odd times can be caused by a faulty power supply, RAM, hard drive, motherboard, or processor, Windows error, or overheating.

⊿ A POST diagnostic card can troubleshoot problems with the motherboard.

Troubleshooting Mobile Devices

⊿ A mobile device battery that overheats or quickly loses its charge might need replacing, but first try replacing the AC adapter (charger).

⊿ For a frozen system, try resetting an iPhone or iPad, rebooting an Android device, or resetting Windows Phone. You can also try removing the battery and reinstalling it.

>> KEY TERMS

For explanations of key terms, see the Glossary for this text.

AC adapter
auto-switching
blue screen of death
   (BSOD)
case fan

chassis air guide (CAG)
cooler
discolored capacitor
driver store
dual rail

fanless CPU cooler
file recovery software
heat sink
lithium ion
Memory Diagnostics

passive CPU cooler
processor thermal trip
   error
sheet battery
Windows pinwheel

>> REVIEWING THE BASICS

1. What are the two major components of a processor cooler assembly?

2. How many pins does the CPU fan header on a motherboard have?

3. If the power connector from the CPU fan has only three pins, it can still connect to the 4-pin header, but what functionality is lost?

4. How do you determine the wattage capacity needed by a power supply?

5. Which one component in a high-end gaming computer is likely to draw the most power?

6. When you first turn on a computer and you don't hear a spinning drive or fan or see indicator lights, is the problem hardware or software related?

7. What is a Windows error message called that appears on a blue screen?

8. How many beeps does startup UEFI/BIOS give to indicate a successful POST?

9. Which two components in a system might give out a loud whining noise?

10. What Windows utility can you use to test RAM?

11. Which Windows tool is best to use to verify that hardware components installed in Windows are working properly?

12. What is the purpose of standoffs installed between the bottom of the case and the motherboard?

13. If a system hangs after being used for several hours and you suspect overheating, what can you do to easily monitor the CPU and system temperature?

14. What are two reasons to tie cables up and out of the way inside a computer case?

15. Why should a tower case not sit on thick carpet?

16. For most computer cases, does air flow from front to rear or rear to front?

17. Which type of CPU cooler contains heat pipes?

18. What can you do if a port on the motherboard is faulty and a device requires this type of port?

19. What can you do to stop a computer from repeatedly restarting in a continuous loop?

20. When a cell phone overheats, why is it important to find out whether the heat is coming from the bottom of the phone or from other areas of the phone?

>> THINKING CRITICALLY

1. How much power is consumed by a load drawing 5 A with 120 V across it?

2. What is a reasonable wattage capacity for a power supply to be used with a system that contains a DVD drive, three hard drives, and a high-end video card?

   a. 250 W

   b. 1000 W

   c. 700 W

   d. 150 W

3. You upgrade a faulty PCIe video card to a recently released higher-performing card. Now the user complains that Windows 8 hangs a lot and gives errors. Which is the most likely source of the problem? Which is the least likely source?

   a. Overheating

   b. Windows does not support the new card

   c. The drivers for the card need updating

   d. Memory is faulty

4. What should you immediately do if you turn on a computer and smell smoke or a burning odor?

   a. Unplug the computer.

   b. Dial 911.

   c. Find a fire extinguisher.

   d. Press a key on the keyboard to enter BIOS setup.

5. When you boot up a computer and hear a single beep, but the screen is blank, what can you assume is the source of the problem?

   a. The video card or onboard video

   b. The monitor or monitor cable

   c. Windows startup

   d. The processor

6. You suspect that a power supply is faulty, but you use a power supply tester to measure its voltage output and find it to be acceptable. Why is it still possible that the power supply may be faulty?

7. Someone asks you for help with a computer that hangs at odd times. You turn it on and work for about 15 minutes, and then the computer freezes and powers down. What do you do first?

   a. Replace the surge protector.

   b. Replace the power supply.

   c. Wait about 30 minutes for the system to cool down and try again.

   d. Install an additional fan.

>> REAL PROBLEMS, REAL SOLUTIONS

REAL PROBLEM 5-1 Replacing a Power Supply

Suppose you turn on a system and everything is dead—no lights, nothing on the monitor screen, and no spinning fan or hard drive. You verify the power to the system works, all power connections and power cords are securely connected, and all pertinent switches are turned on. You can assume the power supply has gone bad. It's time to replace it. To prepare for this situation in a real work environment, exchange power supplies with another student in your lab who is using a computer that has a power supply rated at about the same wattage as yours. Then verify that your system starts up and works.

REAL PROBLEM 5-2 Using Event Viewer to Troubleshoot a Hardware Problem

Just about anything that happens in Windows is recorded in Event Viewer (Eventvwr.msc). You can find events such as a hardware or network failure, OS error messages, or a device that has failed to start. When you first encounter a Windows, hardware, application, or security problem, get in the habit of checking Event Viewer as one of your first steps toward investigating the problem. To save time, first check the Administrative Events log because it filters out all events except Warning and Error events, which are the most useful for troubleshooting. Do the following to practice using Event Viewer:

1. For Windows 8, press **Win+X**, click **Run**, and enter **eventvwr.msc**. For Windows 7, enter **eventvwr.msc** in the Search box. Event Viewer opens. Drill down into the **Custom Views** list in the left pane and click **Administrative Events**. Scroll through the list of Error or Warning events and list any that indicate a possible hardware problem. Make note of the first event in the list.

2. Disconnect the network cable.

3. In the Event Viewer menu bar, click **Action** and **Refresh** to refresh the list of events. How many new events do you see? Click each new event to see its details below the list of events until you find the event that tells you the network cable was unplugged. Figure 5-42 shows Event Viewer for Windows 7. Describe the details of the event about the network cable.

4. Tinker around with other hardware on your computer. What actions did you take that triggered a Warning or Error event in Event Viewer?

Figure 5-42 Use Event Viewer to find logs that can help with troubleshooting hardware problems

REAL PROBLEM 5-3 Troubleshooting a Hung System

A user complains to you that her system hangs for no known reason. After asking her a few questions, you identify these symptoms:

▲ The system hangs after about 15–20 minutes of operation.

▲ When the system hangs, it doesn't matter what application is open or how many applications are open.

▲ When the system hangs, it appears as though power is turned off: There are no lights, spinning drives, or other evidence of power.

You suspect overheating might be the problem. To test your theory, you decide to do the following:

1. You want to verify that the user has not overclocked the system. How do you do that?

2. You decide to check for overheating by examining the temperature of the system immediately after the system is powered up and then again immediately after the system hangs. Describe the steps you take to do this.

3. After doing the first two steps, you decide overheating is the cause of the problem. What are four things you can do to fix the problem?

Supporting Hard Drives and Other Storage Devices

The hard drive is the most important permanent storage device in a computer, and supporting hard drives is one of the more important tasks of a computer support technician. This chapter introduces the different kinds of hard drive technologies and the ways a computer interfaces with a hard drive. You learn how to select and install the different types of hard drives and how to troubleshoot hard drive problems. You also learn about tape drives and how to select and install optical drives in desktops and laptops. The chapter also covers flash memory cards, including which type of card to buy for a particular need.

HARD DRIVE TECHNOLOGIES AND INTERFACE STANDARDS

A+
220-901
1.5, 1.7,
1.11

A hard disk drive (HDD), most often called a hard drive, comes in two sizes for personal computers: the 2.5" size is used for laptop computers and the 3.5" size is used for desktops. See Figure 6-1. In addition, a smaller 1.8" size hard drive (about the size of a credit card) is used in some low-end laptops and other equipment such as MP3 players.

3.5" magnetic hard drive

2.5" SSD drive

2.5" magnetic hard drive

Figure 6-1 A hard drive for a desktop is larger than those used in laptops

> **Notes** In technical documentation, you might see a hard drive abbreviated as HDD (hard disk drive). However, this chapter uses the term *hard drive*.

Now let's look at the technologies used inside a hard drive and then we'll turn to how the drive interfaces with the computer.

TECHNOLOGIES USED INSIDE A HARD DRIVE

A+
220-901
1.5, 1.7,
1.11

The two types of hardware technologies used inside the drive are solid-state and magnetic. In addition, some drives use a combination of both technologies. Here are important details about each:

▲ **Solid-state drive.** A solid-state drive (SSD), also called a solid-state device (SSD), is called solid-state because it has no moving parts. The drives are built using nonvolatile memory, which is similar to that used for USB flash drives. Recall that this type of memory does not lose its data even after the power is turned off.

In an SSD drive, flash memory is stored on EEPROM (Electronically Erasable Programmable Read-Only Memory) chips inside the drive housing. The chips contain grids of rows and columns with two transistors at each intersection that hold a 0 or 1 bit. One of these transistors is called a floating gate and accepts the 0 or 1 state according to a logic test called NAND (stands for "Not AND"). Therefore, the memory in an SSD is called NAND flash memory. EEPROM chips are limited as to the number of times transistors can be reprogrammed. Therefore, the life span of an SSD drive is based on the number of write operations to the drive. (The number of read operations does not affect the life span.) For example, one SSD manufacturer guarantees its SSD drives for 20 GB of write operations per day for three years. For normal use, a drive would not be used that much and would last much longer.

6

> ✏ **Notes** Many solid-state drive manufacturers reserve blocks on the drive that are used when blocks begin to prove they are no longer reliable. Also, a technique called wear leveling assures that the logical block addressing does not always address the same physical blocks in order to distribute write operations more evenly across the device.

Because flash memory is expensive, solid-state drives are much more expensive than magnetic hard drives, but they are faster, more reliable, last longer, and use less power than magnetic drives. Figure 6-2 shows two sizes of solid-state drives (2.5" and 1.8") and what the inside of an SSD hard drive looks like. The 1.8" drives are used in some laptops and other small mobile devices.

1.8" solid-state drive

Inside an SSD drive

2.5" solid-state drive

Courtesy of Toshiba America Electronic Components

Figure 6-2 Solid-state drives by Toshiba

� *Magnetic hard drive.* A magnetic hard drive has one, two, or more platters, or disks, that stack together and spin in unison inside a sealed metal housing that contains firmware to control reading and writing data to the drive and to communicate with the motherboard. The top and bottom of each disk have a read/write head that moves across the disk surface as all the disks rotate on a spindle (see Figure 6-3). All the read/write heads are controlled by an actuator, which moves the read/write heads across the disk surfaces in unison. The disk surfaces are covered with a magnetic medium that can hold data as magnetized spots. The spindle rotates at 5400, 7200, or 10,000 RPM (revolutions per minute). The faster the spindle, the better performing the drive.

Actuator

Drive spindle
Platters or disks

Read-write head

Figure 6-3 Inside a magnetic hard drive

Data is organized on a magnetic hard drive in concentric circles called tracks (see Figure 6-4). Each track is divided into segments called sectors (also called records). Older hard drives used sectors that contained 512 bytes. Most current hard drives use 4096-byte sectors.

Figure 6-4   A hard drive is divided into tracks and sectors; several sectors make one cluster

▲ *Hybrid hard drives.* A hybrid hard drive (H-HDD), sometimes called a solid-state hybrid drive (SSHD), uses both technologies. The flash component serves as a buffer to improve drive performance. Some hybrid drives perform just as well as an SSD drive. For a hybrid drive to function, the operating system must support it.

Before a magnetic drive leaves the factory, sector markings are written to it in a process called low-level formatting. (This formatting is different from the high-level formatting that Windows does after a drive is installed in a computer.) The hard drive firmware, UEFI/BIOS on the motherboard, and the OS use a simple sequential numbering system called logical block addressing (LBA) to address all the sectors on the drive. SSD drives are marked into blocks, which are communicated to the motherboard and OS, which read/write to the drive in blocks just as with magnetic drives.

The size of each block and the total number of blocks on the drive determine the drive capacity. Today's drive capacities are usually measured in GB (gigabytes) or TB (terabytes, each of which is 1024 gigabytes). Magnetic drives are generally much larger in capacity than SSD drives.

You need to be aware of one more technology supported by both SSD and magnetic hard drives called S.M.A.R.T. (Self-Monitoring Analysis and Reporting Technology), which is used to predict when a drive is likely to fail. System UEFI/BIOS uses S.M.A.R.T. to monitor drive performance, temperature, and other factors. For magnetic drives, it monitors disk spin-up time, distance between the head and the disk, and other mechanical activities of the drive. Many SSD drives report to the UEFI/BIOS the number of write operations, which is the best measurement of when the drive might fail. If S.M.A.R.T. suspects a drive failure is about to happen, it displays a warning message. S.M.A.R.T. can be enabled and disabled in UEFI/BIOS setup.

> ✎ **Notes**   Malware has been known to give false S.M.A.R.T. alerts.

Now let's look at how the drive's firmware or controller communicates with the motherboard.

SATA INTERFACE STANDARDS USED BY A HARD DRIVE

A+
220-901
1.5, 1.7,
1.11

All hard drives in today's personal computers use the SATA interface standards to connect to the motherboard. The serial ATA or SATA (pronounced "*say*-ta") standard uses a serial data path, and a SATA data cable can accommodate a single SATA drive (see Figure 6-5).

Figure 6-5 A SATA cable connects a single SATA drive to a motherboard SATA connector

> ✎ **Notes** Years ago, hard drives used the Parallel ATA (PATA) standards, also called the IDE (Integrated Drive Electronics) standards, to connect to a motherboard. PATA allowed for one or two IDE connectors on a motherboard, each using a 40-pin data cable. Two drives could connect to one cable. In addition, a few personal computer hard drives used the SCSI (pronounced "scuzzy") interface standard.

External hard drives can connect to a computer by way of external SATA (eSATA), FireWire, or USB. Be sure the port provided by the computer uses the same standard that the external drive uses, for example, SuperSpeed USB 3.0 or eSATA III. If the port is not fast enough, you can install an expansion card to provide faster ports.

A consortium of manufacturers, called the Serial ATA International Organization (SATA-IO; see *sata-io.org*) and led by Intel, developed the SATA standards, and the standards also have the oversight of the T13 Committee (*t13.org*). SATA has had three major revisions, which are summarized in Table 6-1.

> ✎ **Notes** Interface standards for drives define data speeds and transfer methods between the drive controller, the UEFI/ BIOS, the chipset on the motherboard, and the OS. The standards also define the type of cables and connectors used by the drive and the motherboard or expansion cards.

SATA Standard	Data Transfer Rate	Comments
SATA Revision 1.x* **SATA I or SATA1** **Serial ATA-150** **SATA/150** **SATA-150**	1.5 Gb/sec	**SATA, first introduced as an ATA/ATAPI-7 standard, was published as part of a revision to the older PATA standards managed by the T13 Committee (*t13.org*) that governed the PATA standards.**
SATA Revision 2.x* **SATA II or SATA2** **Serial ATA-300** **SATA/300** **SATA-300**	3 Gb/sec	**The first SATA II standards were published by the T13 Committee (*t13.org*) within ATA/ATAPI-8; later revisions of SATA II were published by SATA-IO (*sata-io.org*), which now manages SATA standards.** **The standard first came out in 2006. Most motherboards used it by 2010.**
SATA Revision 3.x* **SATA III or SATA3** **Serial ATA-600** **SATA/600** **SATA-600**	6 Gb/sec	**SATA III was first published by SATA-IO in 2009. Most new motherboards today use this standard.**

*Name assigned by the SATA-IO organization

Table 6-1   SATA standards

> ★ **A+ Exam Tip** The A+ 220-901 exam expects you to know the speeds used by SATA1, SATA2, and SATA3, also known as SATA I, SATA II, and SATA III. These speeds apply to internal (SATA) and external (eSATA) devices.

SATA interfaces are used by all types of drives, including hard drives, CD, DVD, Blu-ray, and tape drives. SATA supports hot-swapping, also called hot-plugging. With hot-swapping, you can connect and disconnect a drive while the system is running. Hard drives that can be hot-swapped cost significantly more than regular hard drives.

A SATA drive connects to one internal SATA connector on the motherboard by way of a 7-pin SATA data cable and uses a 15-pin SATA power connector (see Figure 6-6). An internal SATA data cable can be up to 1 meter in length. A motherboard might have two or more SATA connectors; use the connectors in the order recommended in the motherboard user guide. For example, for the four connectors shown in Figure 6-7, you are told to use the red ones before the black ones.

SATA power connectors

SATA data connectors

Figure 6-6   A SATA data cable and SATA power cable

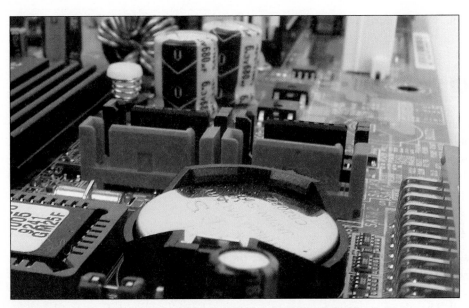

Figure 6-7   This motherboard has two black and two red SATA II ports

Figure 6-8   Two eSATA ports on a motherboard

In addition to internal SATA connectors, the motherboard or an expansion card can provide external SATA (eSATA) ports for external drives (see Figure 6-8). External SATA drives use a special external shielded SATA cable up to 2 meters long. Seven-pin eSATA ports run at the same speed as the internal ports using SATA I, II, or III standards. The eSATA port is shaped differently from an internal SATA connector so as to prevent people from using the unshielded internal SATA data cables with the eSATA port.

When purchasing a SATA hard drive, keep in mind that the SATA standards for the drive and the motherboard need to match. If either the drive or the motherboard uses a slower SATA standard than the other device, the system will run at the slower speed. Other hard drive characteristics to consider when selecting a drive are covered later in the chapter.

Hands-On | Project 6-1   Examine UEFI/BIOS Settings for a Hard Drive

A+
220-901
1.5

Following the directions given in the chapter, "All About Motherboards," view the UEFI/BIOS setup information on your computer, and write down all the UEFI/BIOS settings that apply to your hard drive. Explain each setting that you can. What is the size of the installed drive? Does your system support S.M.A.R.T.? If so, is it enabled?

Now that you know about the various hard drive technologies and interfaces, let's see how to select and install a hard drive.

HOW TO SELECT AND INSTALL HARD DRIVES

In this part of the chapter, you learn how to select a hard drive for your system. Then, you learn the details of installing a SATA drive. Next, you learn how to deal with using removable bays, the problem of installing a hard drive in a bay that is too wide for it, and special considerations to install a hard drive in a laptop. You also learn how to set up a RAID system.

SELECTING A HARD DRIVE

When selecting a hard drive, keep in mind that to get the best performance from the system, the system UEFI/BIOS and the hard drive must support the same standard. If they don't support the same standard, they revert to the slower standard that both can use, or the drive will not work at all. There's no point in buying an expensive hard drive with features that your system cannot support.

Therefore, when making purchasing decisions, you need to know what standards the motherboard or controller card providing the drive interface can use. To find out, see the documentation for the board or the card. For the motherboard, you can look at UEFI/BIOS setup screens to see which standards are mentioned. However, know that when installing a drive, you don't need to know which SATA standard a hard drive supports because the startup UEFI/BIOS uses autodetection. With autodetection, the UEFI/BIOS detects the new drive and automatically selects the correct drive capacity and configuration, including the best possible standard supported by both the hard drive and the motherboard.

> ✎ **Notes** To learn how to match up and install really old motherboards or drives, see the content "Selecting and Installing Hard Drives using Legacy Motherboards" in the online content that accompanies this text. For more information, see the Preface.

When purchasing a hard drive, consider the following factors that affect performance, use, and price:

▲ *The capacity of the drive.* Today's hard drives for desktop systems are in the range of 1 TB for SSD drives to more than 6 TB for magnetic drives. The more gigabytes or terabytes, the higher the price. Magnetic drives have larger capacity for the money than solid-state drives.

▲ *The spindle speed.* Magnetic hard drives for desktop systems run at 5400, 7200, or 10,000 RPM (revolutions per minute). The most common is 7200 RPM. The higher the RPMs, the faster the drive.

▲ *The interface standard.* Use the standards your motherboard supports. For SATA, most likely that will be SATA II or SATA III. For external drives, common standards are eSATA, FireWire 800 or 400, and SuperSpeed or Hi-Speed USB.

▲ *The cache or buffer size.* For magnetic hard drives, buffer memory improves hard drive performance and can range in size from 2 MB to 128 MB. The more the better, though the cost goes up as the size increases. A buffer helps because the hard drive reads ahead of the requested data and stores the extra data in the buffer. If the next read is already in the buffer, the controller does not need to return to the spinning platters for the data. Buffering especially improves performance when managing large files, such as when working with videos or movies.

A hard drive manufacturer might produce both magnetic drives and solid-state drives. Some hard drive manufacturers are listed in Table 6-2. Most manufacturers of memory also make solid-state drives.

Manufacturer	Website
Crucial	*www.crucial.com*
Kingston Technology	*www.kingston.com*
Samsung	*www.samsung.com*
Seagate Technology and Maxtor	*www.seagate.com* or *www.maxtor.com*
Western Digital	*www.wdc.com*

Table 6-2   Hard drive manufacturers

Now let's turn our attention to the step-by-step process of installing a SATA drive.

STEPS TO INSTALL A SATA DRIVE

A+
220-901
1.4, 1.5,
1.11

In Figure 6-9, you can see the back of a SATA hard drive. A SATA drive might have jumpers used to set features such as the ability to power up from standby mode. Most likely, if jumpers are present on a SATA drive, the factory has set them as they should be and advises you not to change them.

SATA jumper block

SATA data connector

SATA power connector

Figure 6-9   Rear of a SATA drive

★ **A+ Exam Tip**   The A+ 220-901 exam expects you to know how to configure SATA devices in a system. What you learn in this chapter about installing a SATA hard drive in a system also applies to installing a SATA optical drive or tape drive. Hard drives, optical drives, and tape drives use a SATA data connector and a power connector.

Some SATA drives have two power connectors, as does the one in Figure 6-10. Choose between the SATA power connector (which is the preferred connector) or the legacy 4-pin Molex connector, but never install two power cords to the drive at the same time because this could damage the drive.

Figure 6-10　Rear of a SATA drive with two power connectors

You can also purchase a SATA controller card that can provide internal SATA connectors and external eSATA connectors. You might want to use a controller card when (1) the motherboard drive connectors are not functioning, or (2) the motherboard does not support a fast SATA standard that your hard drives use. Figure 6-11 shows a PCIe storage controller card that offers two internal SATA III connections and two eSATA III ports.

Figure 6-11　SATA storage controller card by SYBA has two external and two internal ports and supports 6 Gbps SATA III speeds

Here is the step-by-step process of installing a SATA drive in a desktop system.

STEP 1: KNOW YOUR STARTING POINT

As with installing any other devices, before you begin installing a hard drive, make sure you know where your starting point is. Do this by answering these questions: How is your system configured? Is everything working properly? Verify which of your system's devices are working before installing a new one. Later, if a device does not work, the information will help you isolate the problem. Keeping notes is a good idea whenever you install new hardware or software or make any other changes to your computer system. Write down what you know about the system that might be important later.

> ✎ **Notes**　When installing hardware and software, don't install too many things at once. If something goes wrong, you won't know what's causing the problem. Install one device, start the system, and confirm that the new device is working before installing another.

STEP 2:READ THE DOCUMENTATION AND PREPARE YOUR WORK AREA

Before you take anything apart, carefully read all the documentation for the drive and controller card, as well as the part of your motherboard documentation that covers hard drive installation. Make sure that you can visualize all the steps in the installation. If you have any questions, keep researching until you locate the answer. You can also call technical support, or ask a knowledgeable friend for help. As you get your questions answered, you might discover that what you are installing will not work on your computer, but that is better than coping with hours of frustration and a disabled computer. You cannot always anticipate every problem, but at least you can know that you made your best effort to understand everything in advance. What you learn with thorough preparation pays off every time!

You're now ready to set out your tools, documentation, new hardware, and notebook. Remember the basic rules concerning static electricity. Be sure to protect against electrostatic discharge (ESD) by wearing an ESD strap during the installation. You need to also avoid working on carpet in the winter when there's a lot of static electricity.

Some added precautions for working with a hard drive are as follows:

- Handle the drive carefully.
- Do not touch any exposed circuitry or chips.
- Prevent other people from touching exposed microchips on the drive.
- When you first take the drive out of the static-protective package, touch the package containing the drive to a screw holding an expansion card or cover, or to a metal part of the computer case, for at least two seconds. This drains the static electricity from the package and from your body.
- If you must set down the drive outside the static-protective package, place it component-side-up on a flat surface.
- Do not place the drive on the computer case cover or on a metal table.

If you're assembling a new system, in most situations, it's best to install drives before you install the motherboard so that you will not accidentally bump sensitive motherboard components with the drives.

STEP 3: INSTALL THE DRIVE

So now you're ready to get started. Follow these steps to install the drive in the case:

1. Shut down the computer and unplug it. Then press the power button for three seconds to drain residual power. Remove the computer case cover. Check that you have an available power cord from the power supply for the drive.

> ✎ **Notes** If there are not enough power cords from a power supply, you can purchase a Y connector that can add an additional power cord.

2. Decide which bay will hold the drive. To do that, examine the locations of the drive bays and the length of the data cables and power cords. Bays designed for hard drives do not have access to the outside of the case, unlike bays for optical drives and other drives in which discs are inserted. Also, some bays are wider than others to accommodate wide drives such as a DVD drive. Will the data cable reach the drives and the motherboard connector? If not, rearrange your plan for locating the drive in a bay, or purchase a custom-length data cable. Some bays are stationary, meaning the drive is installed inside the bay because it stays in the case. Other bays are removable; you remove the bay and install the drive in the bay, and then return the bay to the case.

3. For a stationary bay, slide the drive in the bay, and using a screwdriver, secure one side of the drive with one or two short screws (see Figure 6-12). It's best to use two screws so the drive will not move in the bay, but sometimes a bay only provides a place for a single screw on each side. Some drive bays provide one or two tabs that you can pull out before you slide the drive in the bay and then push the

tabs in to secure the drive. Another option is a sliding tab (see Figure 6-13) that is used to secure the drive. Pull the tab back, slide in the drive, and push the tab forward to secure the drive.

Figure 6-12   Secure one side of the drive with one or two screws

> ⚡ **Caution**   Be sure the screws are not too long. If they are, you can screw too far into the drive housing, which will damage the drive itself.

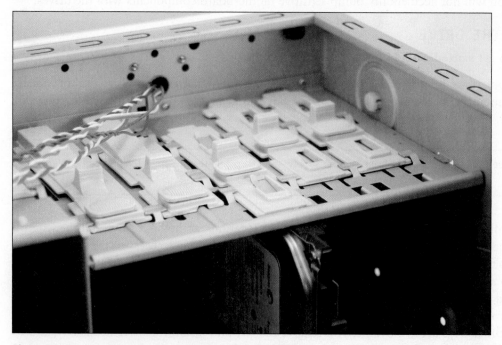

Figure 6-13   This drive bay uses tabs to secure the drive

4. When using screws to secure the drive, carefully, without disturbing the drive, turn the case over and put one or two screws on the other side of the drive (see Figure 6-14). To best secure the drive in the case, use two screws on each side of the drive.

Hard drive

Figure 6-14 Secure the other side of the drive with one or two screws

✎ Notes Do not allow torque to stress the drive. In other words, don't force a drive into a space that is too small for it. Also, placing two screws in diagonal positions across the drive can place pressure diagonally on the drive.

5. Check the motherboard documentation to find out which SATA connectors on the board to use first. For example, five SATA connectors are shown in Figure 6-15. The documentation says the two blue SATA connectors support 6.0 Gb/s and slower speeds, and the two black and one red SATA connectors support 3.0 Gb/s and slower speeds. On this board, be sure to connect your fastest hard drive to a blue connector. For some boards, the hard drive that has the bootable OS installed must be connected to the first SATA connector, which is usually labeled SATA 0. For both the drive and the motherboard, you can only plug the cable into the connector in one direction. A SATA cable might provide a clip on the connector to secure it (see Figure 6-16).

Figure 6-15 Five SATA connectors support different SATA standards

Figure 6-16   A clip on a SATA connector secures the connection

6. Connect a 15-pin SATA power connector or 4-pin Molex power connector from the power supply to the drive (see Figure 6-17).

Figure 6-17   Connect the SATA power cord to the drive

7. Check all your connections and power up the system.

8. To verify the drive was recognized correctly, enter UEFI/BIOS setup and look for the drive. Figure 6-18 shows a UEFI setup screen on one system that has four SATA connectors. A hard drive is installed on one of the faster yellow SATA connectors and a DVD drive is installed on one of the slower brown SATA connectors.

> ✎ **Notes** If the drive light on the front panel of the computer case does not work after you install a new drive, try reversing the LED wire on the front panel header on the motherboard.

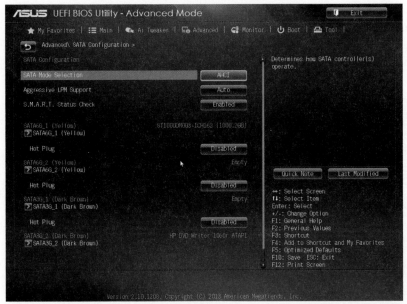

Source: American Megatrends, Inc.

Figure 6-18   UEFI setup screen showing a SATA hard drive and DVD drive installed

You are now ready to prepare the hard drive for first use. If you are installing a new hard drive in a system that is to be used for a new Windows installation, boot from the Windows setup DVD, and follow the directions on the screen to install Windows on the new drive. If you are installing a second hard drive in a system that already has Windows installed on the first hard drive, you use the Disk Management utility in Windows to prepare the drive for first use (called partitioning and formatting the drive).

INSTALLING A DRIVE IN A REMOVABLE BAY

A+
220-901
1.4, 1.5,
1.11

Now let's see how a drive installation goes when you are dealing with a removable bay. Figure 6-19 shows a computer case with a removable bay that has a fan at the front of the bay to help keep the drives cool. (The case manufacturer calls the bay a fan cage.) The bay is anchored to the case with three black locking pins. The third locking pin from the bottom of the case is disconnected in the photo.

Three locking pins used to hold the bay in the case

Figure 6-19   The removable bay has a fan in front and is anchored to the case with locking pins

Unplug the cage fan from its power source. Turn the handle on each locking pin counterclockwise to remove it. Then slide the bay to the front and out of the case. Insert the hard drive in the bay, and use two screws on each side to anchor the drive in the bay (see Figure 6-20). Slide the bay back into the case, and reinstall the locking pins. Plug in the cage fan power cord.

Figure 6-20   Install the hard drive in the bay using two screws on each side of the drive

INSTALLING A SMALL DRIVE IN A WIDE BAY

A+
220-901
1.4, 1.5,
1.11

If you are mounting a hard drive into a bay that is too large, a universal bay kit can help you securely fit the drive into the bay. These inexpensive kits should create a tailor-made fit. In Figure 6-21, you can see how the universal bay kit adapter works. The adapter spans the distance between the sides of the drive and the bay. Figure 6-22 shows a SATA SSD drive with the brackets connected. Because SSD drives are usually smaller than magnetic drives, you're likely to need a bay kit to fit these drives into most desktop computer cases.

Side brackets
connect to hard
drive

Figure 6-21   Use the universal bay kit to make the drive fit the bay

Figure 6-22 SSD drive with bay kit connected

INSTALLING A HARD DRIVE IN A LAPTOP

When purchasing and installing an internal hard drive or optical drive in a laptop, see the laptop manufacturer's documentation about specific sizes and connectors that will fit the laptop. Also be aware of voiding a warranty if you don't follow the laptop manufacturer's directions. Here is what you need to know when shopping for a laptop hard drive:

- A desktop hard drive is 3.5 inches wide and a laptop drive is 2.5 inches or 1.8 inches wide. Because the form factor of a laptop drive is more compact, it costs more than a desktop drive holding the same amount of data. Some laptop hard drives use SSD (solid-state device) technology.
- Today's laptop hard drives use a SATA interface, and older laptops used a PATA interface. Check your laptop manual to know which type of hard drive to buy, or remove the old drive and see which interface it uses. SATA data and power connectors on a laptop hard drive look the same as those in a desktop installation.

Before deciding to replace a hard drive, consider these issues:

- If the old drive has crashed, you'll need the recovery media to reinstall Windows and the drivers. Make sure you have the recovery media before you start.
- If you are upgrading from a low-capacity drive to a higher-capacity drive, you need to consider how you will transfer data from the old drive to the new one. One way to do that is to use a USB-to-SATA converter. Using this converter, both drives can be up and working on the laptop at the same time, so you can copy files.

To replace a hard drive, older laptop computers required that you disassemble the laptop. With newer laptops, you should be able to easily replace a drive. For example, for one laptop, first power down the system, remove peripherals, including the AC adapter, and remove the battery pack. Then remove a screw that holds the drive in place (see Figure 6-23).

⚡ **Caution** To protect sensitive components, never open a laptop case without first unplugging the AC adapter and removing the battery pack.

Figure 6-23   This one screw holds the hard drive in position

Open the lid of the laptop slightly so that the lid doesn't obstruct your removing the drive. Turn the laptop on its side and push the drive out of its bay (see Figure 6-24). Then remove the plastic cover from the drive. Move the cover to the new drive, and insert the new drive in the bay. Next, replace the screw and power up the system.

Figure 6-24   Push the drive out of its bay

When the system boots up, if UEFI/BIOS setup is set to autodetect hard drives, UEFI/BIOS recognizes the new drive and searches for an operating system. If the drive is new, boot from the Windows recovery DVD and install the OS.

Notes It is possible to give general directions on desktop computer repair that apply to all kinds of brands, models, and systems. Not so with laptops. Learning to repair laptops involves learning unique ways to assemble, disassemble, and repair laptop components for specific brands and models of laptops.

For some laptops, such as the one shown in Figure 6-25, you remove a cover on the bottom of the computer to expose the hard drive. Then remove one screw that anchors the drive. You can then remove the drive.

6

Figure 6-25 Remove a cover on the bottom of the laptop to exchange the hard drive, which is attached to a proprietary bracket

SETTING UP HARDWARE RAID

A+
220-901
1.5, 1.11

For most personal computers, a single hard drive works independently of any other installed drives. A technology that configures two or more hard drives to work together as an array of drives is called RAID (redundant array of inexpensive disks or redundant array of independent disks). Two reasons you might consider using RAID are:

▲ To improve fault tolerance, which is a computer's ability to respond to a fault or catastrophe, such as a hardware failure or power outage, so that data is not lost. If data is important enough to justify the cost, you can protect the data by continuously writing two copies of it, each to a different hard drive. This method is most often used on high-end, expensive file servers, but it is occasionally appropriate for a single-user workstation.
▲ To improve performance by writing data to two or more hard drives so that a single drive is not excessively used.

TYPES OF RAID

Several types of RAID exist; the four most commonly used are RAID 0, RAID 1, RAID 5, and RAID 10. Following is a brief description of each, including another method of two disks working together, called spanning. The first four methods are diagrammed in Figure 6-26:

Figure 6-26 Ways that hard drives can work together

◢ Spanning, sometimes called JBOD (just a bunch of disks), uses two hard drives to hold a single Windows volume, such as drive E:. Data is written to the first drive, and, when it is full, the data continues to be written to the second.

◢ RAID 0 also uses two or more physical disks to increase the disk space available for a single volume. RAID 0 writes to the physical disks evenly across all disks so that no one disk receives all the activity and therefore improves performance. Windows calls RAID 0 a striped volume. To understand that term, think of data striped—or written across—several hard drives. RAID 0 is preferred to spanning.

◢ RAID 1 is a type of mirroring that duplicates data on one drive to another drive and is used for fault tolerance. Each drive has its own volume, and the two volumes are called mirrors. If one drive fails, the other continues to operate and data is not lost. Windows calls RAID 1 a mirrored volume.

◢ RAID 5 stripes data across three or more drives and uses parity checking, so that if one drive fails, the other drives can re-create the data stored on the failed drive by using the parity information. Data is not duplicated, and, therefore, RAID 5 makes better use of volume capacity. RAID-5 drives increase performance and provide fault tolerance. Windows calls these drives RAID-5 volumes.

◢ RAID 10, also called RAID 1+0 and pronounced "RAID one zero" (*not* "RAID ten"), is a combination of RAID 1 and RAID 0. It takes at least four disks for RAID 10. Data is mirrored across pairs of disks, as shown at the top of Figure 6-27. In addition, the two pairs of disks are striped, as shown at the bottom of Figure 6-27. To help you better understand RAID 10, in the figure notice the data labeled as A, A, B, B across the first stripe. RAID 10 is the most expensive solution that provides the best redundancy and performance.

RAID 1: Two pairs of mirrored disks

RAID 10: Mirrored and striped

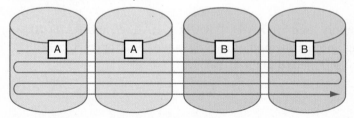

Figure 6-27   RAID 1 and RAID 10

⭐ **A+ Exam Tip** The A+ 220-901 exam expects you to be able to contrast RAID 0, RAID 1, RAID 5, and RAID 10.

All RAID configurations can be accomplished at the hardware level (called hardware RAID) or at the operating system level (called software RAID). Using Windows 7 to implement software RAID, the Disk Management utility is used to configure a group of hard drives in a RAID array. In Windows 8, you can use the Disk Management utility or the new Windows 8 Storage Spaces utility to implement software RAID. However, software RAID is considered an unstable solution and is not recommended by Microsoft. Configuring RAID at the hardware level is considered best practice because if Windows gets corrupted, the hardware might still be able to protect the data. Also, hardware RAID is generally faster than software RAID.

HOW TO IMPLEMENT HARDWARE RAID

Hardware RAID can be set up by using a RAID controller that is part of the motherboard UEFI/BIOS or by using a RAID controller storage card. Figure 6-28 shows a RAID controller card by Sabrent that provides four SATA ports.

Figure 6-28 RAID controller card provides four SATA internal connectors

★ **A+ Exam Tip** The A+ 220-901 exam expects you to be able to set up hardware RAID.

When installing a hardware RAID system, for best performance, all hard drives in an array should be identical in brand, size, speed, and other features. Also, if Windows is to be installed on a hard drive that is part of a RAID array, RAID must be implemented before Windows is installed. As with installing any hardware, first read the documentation that comes with the motherboard or RAID controller and follow those specific directions rather than the general guidelines given here. Make sure you understand which RAID configurations the board supports.

For one motherboard that has six SATA connectors that support RAID 0, 1, 5, and 10, here are the general directions to install the RAID array using three matching hard drives in a RAID-5 array:

1. Install the three SATA drives in the computer case and connect each drive to a SATA connector on the motherboard (see Figure 6-29). To help keep the drives cool, the drives are installed with an empty bay between each drive.

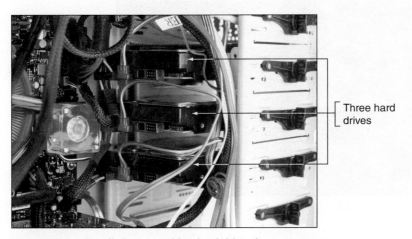

Figure 6-29 Install three matching hard drives in a system

2. Boot the system and enter UEFI/BIOS setup. On the Advanced setup screen, verify the three drives are recognized. Select the option to configure SATA and then select RAID from the menu (see Figure 6-30).

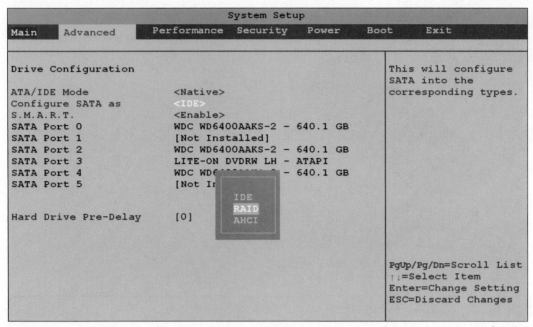

Source: Intel

Figure 6-30 Configure SATA ports on the motherboard to enable RAID

3. Reboot the system and a message is displayed on screen: "Press <Ctrl+I> to enter the RAID Configuration Utility." Press **Ctrl** and **I** to enter the utility (see Figure 6-31). Notice in the information area that the three drives are recognized and their current status is Non-RAID Disk.

Source: Intel

Figure 6-31 BIOS utility to configure a RAID array

4. Select option 1 to **Create RAID Volume**. On the next screen shown in Figure 6-32, enter a volume name (FileServer in our example).

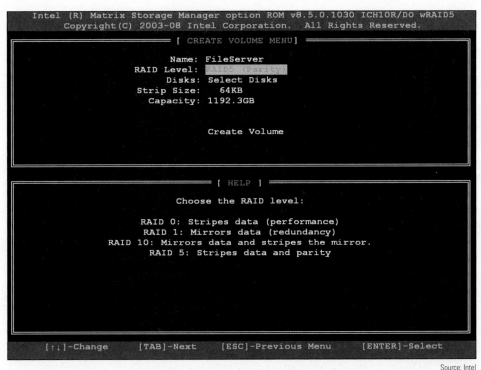

Source: Intel

Figure 6-32 Make your choices for the RAID array

5. Under RAID Level, select **RAID5 (Parity)**. Because we are using RAID 5, which requires three hard drives, the option to select the disks for the array is not available. All three disks will be used in the array.

6. Select the value for the Strip Size. (This is the amount of space devoted to one strip across the striped array. Choices are 32 KB, 64 KB, or 128 KB.)

7. Enter the size of the volume. The available size is shown in Figure 6-32 as 1192 GB, but you don't have to use all the available space. The space you don't use can later be configured as another array. (In this example, I entered 500 GB.)

8. Select **Create Volume** to complete the RAID configuration. A message appears warning you that if you proceed, all data on all three hard drives will be lost. Type **Y** to continue. The array is created and the system reboots.

You are now ready to install Windows. Windows 8/7/Vista have built-in hardware RAID drivers and, therefore, automatically "see" the RAID array as a single 500-GB hard drive. After Windows is installed on the drive, Windows will call it drive C:.

APPLYING | CONCEPTS   TROUBLESHOOT HARD DRIVE INSTALLATIONS

**A+
220-901
4.2**

Sometimes, trouble crops up during an installation. Keeping a cool head; thinking things through carefully a second, third, and fourth time; and using all available resources will most likely get you out of any mess.

Installing a hard drive is not difficult, unless you have an unusually complex situation. For example, your first hard drive installation should not involve the extra complexity of installing a RAID array. If a complicated installation is necessary and you have never installed a hard drive, ask for expert help.

(continues)

The following list describes errors that cropped up during a few hard drive installations; the list also includes the causes of the errors and what was done about them. Everyone learns something new when making mistakes, and you probably will, too. You can then add your own experiences to this list:

⏴ Shawn physically installed a SATA hard drive. He turned on the machine and accessed UEFI/BIOS setup. The hard drive was not listed as an installed device. He checked and discovered that autodetection was not enabled. He enabled it and rebooted. Setup recognized the drive.

⏴ When first turning on a previously working computer, Susan received the following error message: "Hard drive not found." She turned off the machine, checked all cables, and discovered that the data cable from the motherboard to the drive was loose. She reseated the cable and rebooted. POST found the drive.

⏴ Lucia physically installed a new hard drive, replaced the cover on the computer case, and booted the computer with a Windows setup DVD in the drive. POST beeped three times and stopped. Recall that diagnostics during POST are often communicated by beeps if the tests take place before POST has checked video and made it available to display the messages. Three beeps on some computers signal a memory error. Lucia turned off the computer and checked the memory modules on the motherboard. A module positioned at the edge of the motherboard next to the cover had been bumped as she replaced the cover. She reseated the module and booted again, this time with the cover still off. The error disappeared.

⏴ Jason physically installed a new hard drive and turned on the computer. He received the following error: "No boot device available." He forgot to insert a Windows setup DVD. He put the disc in the drive and rebooted the machine successfully.

⏴ The hard drive did not physically fit into the bay. The screw holes did not line up. Juan got a bay kit, but it just didn't seem to work. He took a break, went to lunch, and came back to make a fresh start. Juan asked others to help view the brackets, holes, and screws from a fresh perspective. It didn't take long to discover that he had overlooked the correct position for the brackets in the bay.

> **⚡ Caution**   When things are not going well, you can tense up and make mistakes more easily. Be certain to turn off the machine before doing anything inside! Not doing so can be a costly error. For example, a friend had been trying and retrying to boot for some time and got frustrated and careless. She plugged the power cord into the drive without turning the computer off. The machine began to smoke and everything went dead. The next thing she learned was how to replace a power supply!

EXTERNAL ENCLOSURES

**A+
220-901
1.5, 1.11**

Hard drives are sometimes stored in external enclosures such as the one shown in Figure 6-33. These enclosures make it easy to expand the storage capacity of a single computer or to make available hard drive storage to an entire network. For network attached storage (NAS), the enclosure connects to the network using an Ethernet port. When the storage is used by a single computer, the connection is made using a USB or eSATA port. Regardless of how the enclosure connects to a computer or network, the hard drives inside the enclosure might use a SATA connection.

Courtesy of D-Link Corporation

Figure 6-33 The NAS ShareCenter Pro 1100 by D-Link can hold four hot-swappable SATA hard drives totaling 12 TB of storage, has a dual-core processor and 512 MB of RAM, and supports RAID

Here is what you need to know about supporting these external enclosures:

▲ An enclosure might contain firmware that supports RAID. For example, a switch on the rear of one enclosure for two hard drives can be set for RAID 0, RAID 1, or stand-alone drives. Read the documentation for the enclosure to find out how to manage the RAID volumes.

▲ To replace a hard drive in an enclosure, see the documentation for the enclosure to find out how to open the enclosure and replace the drive.

▲ If a computer case is overheating, one way to solve this problem is to remove the hard drives from the case and install them in an external enclosure. However, it's better to leave the hard drive that contains the Windows installation in the case.

6

Hands-On | Project 6-2 Select a Replacement Hard Drive

A+
220-901
1.5

Suppose one of the 640-GB Western Digital hard drives installed in the RAID array and shown in Figure 6-29 has failed. Search the Internet and find a replacement drive as close to this drive as possible. Print three webpages showing the sizes, features, and prices of three possible replacements. Which drive would you recommend as the replacement drive and why?

Hands-On | Project 6-3 Prepare for Hard Drive Hardware Problems

A+
220-901
4.2

1. Boot your PC and make certain that it works properly. Turn off your computer, remove the computer case, and disconnect the data cable to your hard drive. Turn on the computer again. Write down the message that appears.

2. Turn off the computer and reconnect the data cable. Reboot and make sure the system is working again.

3. Turn off the computer and disconnect the power supply cord to the hard drive. Turn on the computer. Write down the error message that appears.

4. Turn off the computer, reconnect the power supply, and reboot the system. Verify the system is working again.

Hands-On | Project 6-4   Install a Hard Drive

A+
220-901
1.5

In a lab that has one hard drive per computer, you can practice installing a hard drive by removing a drive from one computer and installing it as a second drive in another computer. When you boot up the computer with two drives, verify that both drives are accessible in Windows 8 File Explorer or Windows 7/Vista Windows Explorer. Then remove the second hard drive, and return it to its original computer. Verify that both computers and drives are working.

Now let's move on to other types of storage devices, including tape drives, optical drives, and flash cards.

Courtesy of Quantum Corporation

Figure 6-34   The LTO-5 HH tape drive by Quantum writes to LTO Ultrium 5 and LTO Ultrium 4 tapes and reads from LTO Ultrium 5, LTO Ultrium 4, and LTO Ultrium 3 tapes. It provides AES 256-bit data encryption security, WORM functionality, and partitioning capability.

IDENTIFYING TAPE DRIVES

A+
220-901
1.5, 1.11

Tape drives (see Figure 6-34) are an inexpensive way of backing up an entire hard drive or portions of it. Because tape drives are less expensive for backups than external hard drives, CDs, DVDs, or USB flash drives, they are still used for backups even though other methods are more convenient. Tapes currently have up to 185 TB true tape capacity and come in several types and formats. Some tape drives and tape cartridges support WORM (write once and read many). WORM drives and cartridges assure that data written on the tape will not be deleted or overwritten. Most tape drives come bundled with backup software to use them.

★ **A+ Exam Tip**   The A+ 220-901 exam expects you to know how to install a tape drive and how to select the right tapes for the drive.

The biggest disadvantage of using tape drives is that data is stored on tape by sequential access; to read data from anywhere on the tape, you must start at the beginning of the tape and read until you come to the sought-after data. Sequential access makes recovering files slow and inconvenient, which is why tapes are not used for general-purpose data storage.

✎ **Notes**   Two basic ways computers access data is random access and sequential access. As an analogy, "pick a card, any card" is random access and "take the first card in the stack" is sequential access.

Tape drives accommodate one of two kinds of tapes: full-sized data cartridges are $4 \times 6 \times \frac{5}{8}$ inches, and the smaller minicartridges, like the one shown in Figure 6-35, are $3\frac{1}{4} \times 2\frac{1}{2} \times \frac{3}{5}$ inches. Minicartridges are more popular because their drives can fit into a standard 3-inch drive bay of a computer case.

Write-protect switch

Figure 6-35 Minicartridge for a tape drive has a write-protect switch

Here is a list of some of the more common types of tape cartridges:

▲ *DDS (Digital Data Storage).* DDS-1, DDS-2, DDS-3, DDS-4, and DDS-5 are popular types. DDS-5 holds up to 36 GB of native or 72 GB of compressed data. DDS-5 is also called DAT72.

▲ *LTO (Linear Tape-Open).* LTO Ultrium 2, LTO Ultrium 3, LTO Ultrium 4, and LTO Ultrium 5 are sometimes referred to as LTO cartridges. LTO Ultrium 5 holds up to 1.5 TB of native or 3.0 TB of compressed data. Figure 6-36 shows an LTO Ultrium 3 tape.

Figure 6-36 This Maxel LTO Ultrium 3 data tape cartridge can hold up to 800 GB of compressed data

▲ *DLT (Digital Linear Tape).* DLT IV or DLT-4 holds up to 40 GB of native or 80 GB of compressed data.

▲ *SDLT (Super Digital Linear Tape).* Super DLT II holds up to 300 GB of native or 600 GB of compressed data.

▲ *Travan.* Travan cartridges vary from TR-1 through TR-7. The TR-7 holds 20 GB of native and 40 GB of compressed data.

▲ *AIT (Advanced Intelligent Tape).* AIT types have been around a long time and include AIT Turbo, AIT-1 through AIT-5, and S-AIT. S-AIT holds up to 1.3 TB of compressed data.

▲ *SLR (Scalable Linear Recording).* SLR types include SLR1 through SLR140. SLR140 holds 70 GB of native or 140 GB of compressed data.

When selecting a tape drive, consider how many and what type of cartridges the drive can use and how it interfaces with the computer. The drive might be able to read from more types of cartridges than it can write to. A tape drive can be external or internal. An external tape drive costs more but can be used by more than one computer. An internal tape drive can interface with a computer using a SATA, PATA, or SCSI connection. An external tape drive can connect to a computer using a USB, FireWire, SCSI, SAS, or eSATA port.

> ✏️ **Notes** For an interesting photo gallery of tape media, see *backupworks.com*.

SUPPORTING OTHER TYPES OF STORAGE DEVICES

A+
220-901
1.5, 1.11

Before we explore the details of several other types of storage devices, including optical discs, USB flash drives, and memory cards, let's start with the file systems they might use.

FILE SYSTEMS USED BY STORAGE DEVICES

A+
220-901
1.5, 1.11

A storage device, such as a hard drive, CD, DVD, USB flash drive, or memory card, uses a file system to manage the data stored on the device. A file system is the overall structure the OS uses to name, store, and organize files on a drive. In Windows, each storage device is assigned a drive letter. In Windows 8 File Explorer or Windows 7/Vista Windows Explorer, to see what file system a device is using, right-click the device and select **Properties** from the shortcut menu. The device Properties box appears, which shows the file system and storage capacity of the device (see Figure 6-37).

Figure 6-37 This 4-GB SD card is using the FAT32 file system

Installing a new file system on a device is called *formatting* the device, and the process erases all data on the device. One way to format a device is to right-click the device and select **Format** from the shortcut menu. In the box that appears, you can select the file system to use (see Figure 6-38). The New Technology file system (NTFS) is primarily used by hard drives. The exFAT file system is used by large-capacity removable storage devices such as large-capacity USB flash drives, memory cards, and some external hard drives. In addition, the older FAT32 and FAT file systems are used by smaller-capacity devices. If you have problems with a device, make sure it's using a file system appropriate for your situation.

Figure 6-38   A storage device can be formatted using Windows Explorer

Now let's look at the types of optical drives you might be called on to support.

STANDARDS USED BY OPTICAL DRIVES AND DISCS

**A+
220-901
1.5, 1.11**

CDs, DVDs, and Blu-ray discs use similar laser technologies. Tiny lands and pits on the surface of a disc represent bits, which a laser beam can read. This is why they are called optical storage technologies. CD (compact disc) drives use the CDFS (Compact Disc File System) or the UDF (Universal Disk Format) file system, while DVD (digital versatile disc or digital video disc) drives and Blu-ray Disc (BD) drives use the newer UDF file system.

Blu-ray drives are backward compatible with DVD and CD technologies, and DVD drives are backward compatible with CD technologies. Depending on the drive features, an optical drive might be able to read and write to BDs, DVDs, and CDs. An internal optical drive can interface with the motherboard by way of a SATA connection. An external drive might use an eSATA, FireWire, or USB port. Figure 6-39 shows an internal DVD drive, and Figure 6-40 shows an external DVD drive.

Courtesy of Plextor

Figure 6-39   This internal DVD drive uses a SATA connection

Figure 6-40   The PX-610U external DVD±RW drive by Plextor uses a USB 2.0 port

Data is written to only one side of a CD, but can be written to one or both sides of a DVD or Blu-ray disc. Also, a DVD or Blu-ray disc can hold data in two layers on each side. This means these discs can hold a total of four layers on one disc (see Figure 6-41).

The breakdown of how much data can be held on CDs, DVDs, and BDs is shown in Figure 6-42. The capacities for DVDs and BDs depend on the sides and layers used to hold the data.

Figure 6-41   A DVD can hold data in double layers on both the top and bottom of the disc, yielding a maximum capacity of 17 GB

Figure 6-42   Storage capacities for CDs, DVDs, and BD discs

★ **A+ Exam Tip**   The A+ 220-901 exam expects you to know the capacities of CDs, DVDs, and Blu-ray discs. These capacities are all listed in Figure 6-42.

✎ **Notes**   The discrepancy in the computer industry between one billion bytes (1,000,000,000 bytes) and 1 GB (1,073,741,824 bytes) exists because 1 KB equals 1024 bytes. Even though documentation might say that a DVD holds 17 GB, in fact, it holds 17 billion bytes, which is only 15.90 GB.

When shopping for an optical drive, suppose you see a couple of ads like those shown in Figure 6-43. To sort out the mix of disc standards, Table 6-3 can help. The table lists the popular CD, DVD, and Blu-ray disc standards.

Source: *tigerdirect.com*

Figure 6-43   Ads for internal and external DVD burners

Disc Standard	Description
CD-ROM disc or drive	*CD-read-only memory.* A CD-ROM disc burned at the factory can hold music, software, or other data. The bottom of a CD-ROM disc is silver. A CD-ROM drive can read CDs.
CD-R disc	*CD recordable.* A CD-R disc is a write-once CD.
CD-RW disc or drive	*CD rewriteable.* A CD-RW disc can be written to many times. A CD-RW drive can write to a CD-RW or CD-R disc and also overwrite a CD-RW disc.
DVD-ROM drive	*DVD read-only memory.* A DVD-ROM drive can also read CDs or DVDs.
DVD-R disc	*DVD recordable, single layer.* A DVD-R disc can hold up to 4.7 GB of data and is a write-once disc.
DVD-R DL disc	*DVD recordable in dual layers.* Doubles storage to 8.5 GB of data on one disc surface.
DVD-RW disc or drive	*DVD rewriteable.* A DVD-RW disc is also known as an erasable, recordable drive or a write-many disc. The speeds in an ad for an optical drive indicate the maximum speed supported when burning this type of disc, for example, DVD-RW 6X.
DVD-RW DL disc or drive, aka DL DVD drive	*DVD rewriteable, dual layers.* A DVD-RW DL disc doubles storage capacity to 8.5 GB.
DVD+R disc or drive	*DVD recordable.* Similar to but faster than DVD-R. Discs hold about 4.7 GB of data.
DVD+R DL disc or drive	*DVD recordable, dual layers.* Doubles disc storage to 8.5 GB on one surface.
DVD+RW disc or drive	*DVD rewriteable.* Faster than DVD-RW.
DVD-RAM disc or drive	*DVD Random Access Memory.* Rewriteable and erasable. You can erase or rewrite certain sections of a DVD-RAM disc without disturbing other sections of the disc, and the discs can handle many times over the number of rewrites (around 100,000 rewrites), compared with about a thousand rewrites for DVD-RW and DVD+RW discs. DVD-RAM discs are popular media used in camcorders and set-top boxes.
BD-ROM drive	*BD read-only memory.* A Blu-ray BD-ROM drive can also read DVDs, and some can read CDs.
BD-R disc or drive	*BD recordable.* A BD-R drive might also write to DVDs or CDs.
BD-RE disc or drive	*BD rewriteable.* A BD-RE drive might also write to DVDs or CDs.

Table 6-3   Optical discs and drive standards

⭐ **A+ Exam Tip** The A+ 220-901 exam expects you to know about the combo optical drives and burners, including CD, CD-RW, DVD, DVD-RW, DVD DL, Blu-ray, BD-R, and BD-RE combo drives.

✎ **Notes** CDs, DVDs, and BDs are expected to hold their data for many years; however, you can prolong the life of a disc by protecting it from exposure to light.

Hands-On | Project 6-5 Learn How Optical Drives Work

A+ 220-901 1.5 Optical drives and other removable storage technologies are interesting to study. Check out the animated explanation at the website *howstuffworks.com*. Search on "How Removable Storage Works." List 10 facts you learned about optical drives.

INSTALLING AN OPTICAL DRIVE

A+ 220-901 1.5, 1.11 Internal optical drives on today's computers use a SATA interface. Figure 6-44 shows the rear of a SATA optical drive. An optical drive is usually installed in the drive bay at the top of a desktop case (see Figure 6-45). After the drive is installed in the bay, connect the data and power cables.

SATA power connector

SATA data connector

Figure 6-44   Rear of a SATA optical drive

Figure 6-45   Slide the drive into the bay flush with the front panel

★ A+ Exam Tip The A+ 220-901 exam expects you to know how to install a CD, DVD, or Blu-ray drive.

Windows 8/7/Vista supports optical drives using its own embedded drivers without add-on drivers. Therefore, when Windows first starts up after the drive is installed, it recognizes the drive and installs drivers. Use Device Manager to verify the drive installed with no errors and is ready to use.

REPLACING AN OPTICAL DRIVE ON A LAPTOP

A+
220-901
1.5, 1.11

Some of the newest laptops do not have an optical drive in order to save on the size and weight of a laptop, but instead use an external optical drive. However, several new laptops still include the optical drive, and if it goes bad on a laptop, it is likely cheaper to replace the optical drive than to replace the laptop. For some systems, you'll need to first remove the keyboard to expose an optical drive. Follow along as we remove the DVD drive from one laptop system:

1. *Very important:* Unplug the AC adapter and remove the battery pack.

2. For this laptop, to remove the keyboard, you first remove one screen on the bottom of the case and then turn the case over and pry up the keyboard. You can then move the keyboard to one side. You can leave the ribbon cable from the motherboard to the keyboard connected. When you move the keyboard out of the way, the DVD drive is exposed, as shown in Figure 6-46.

Figure 6-46   Remove the keyboard to expose the optical drive

3. Remove the screw that holds the DVD drive to the laptop (see Figure 6-47).

Figure 6-47   Remove the screw that holds the DVD drive

4. Slide the drive out of the bay (see Figure 6-48).

5. When you slide the new drive into the bay, make sure you push it far enough into the bay so that it solidly connects with the drive connector at the back of the bay. Replace the screw.

For other systems, the optical drive can be removed by first removing a cover from the bottom of the laptop. Then you remove one screw that secures the drive. Next, push the optical drive out of the case (see Figure 6-49).

Figure 6-48   Slide the drive out of the bay

Figure 6-49   Push the optical drive out the side of the case

SOLID-STATE STORAGE

Types of solid-state storage include SSD hard drives, USB flash drives, and memory cards. USB flash drives currently for sale range in size from 128 MB to 1 TB and go by many names, including a flash pen drive, jump drive, thumb drive, and key drive. Several USB flash drives are shown in Figure 6-50. Flash drives might work at USB 2.0 or USB 3.0 speed and use the FAT (for small-capacity drives) or exFAT file system (for large-capacity drives). Windows 8/7/Vista has embedded drivers to support flash drives. To use one, simply insert the device in a USB port. It then shows in Windows 8 File Explorer or Windows 7/Vista Windows Explorer as a drive with an assigned letter.

Figure 6-50   USB flash drives come in a variety of styles and sizes

To make sure that data written to a flash drive is properly saved before you remove the flash drive from the computer, double-click the **Safely Remove Hardware** icon in the notification area of the Windows taskbar (see Figure 6-51). The Safely Remove Hardware box opens, also shown in Figure 6-51. After you click the device listed, it is then safe to remove it.

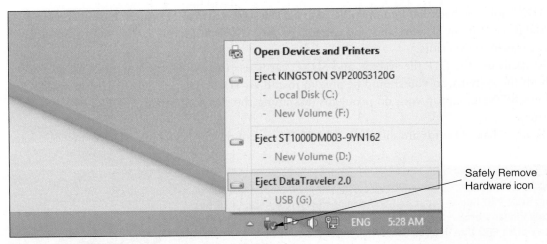

Figure 6-51 Safely Remove Hardware icon and dialog box

Memory cards might be used in digital cameras, tablets, cell phones, MP3 players, digital camcorders, and other portable devices, and most laptops have memory card slots provided by a built-in smart card reader. If there is not a memory card slot included in the device, you can add an external smart card reader that uses a USB connection. The most popular memory cards are Secure Digital (SD) cards, which follow the standards of the SD Association (*sdcard.org*), and are listed in Table 6-4. The three standards used by SD cards are 1.x (regular SD), 2.x (SD High Capacity or SDHC), and 3.x (SD eXtended Capacity or SDXC). In addition, these cards come in three physical sizes.

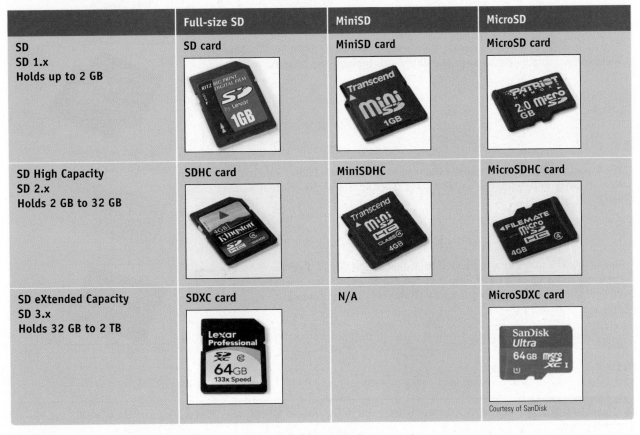

	Full-size SD	MiniSD	MicroSD
SD SD 1.x Holds up to 2 GB	SD card	MiniSD card	MicroSD card
SD High Capacity SD 2.x Holds 2 GB to 32 GB	SDHC card	MiniSDHC	MicroSDHC card
SD eXtended Capacity SD 3.x Holds 32 GB to 2 TB	SDXC card	N/A	MicroSDXC card Courtesy of SanDisk

Table 6-4 Flash memory cards that follow the SD Association standards

SDHC and SDXC slots are backward compatible with earlier standards for SD cards. However, you cannot use an SDHC card in an SD slot, and you cannot use an SDXC card in an SDHC slot or SD slot. Only use SDXC cards in SDXC slots.

SD and SDHC cards use the FAT file system, and SDXC cards use the exFAT file system. Windows 8/7/Vista support both file systems, so you should be able to install an SD, SDHC, or SDXC card in an SD slot on a Windows 8/7/Vista laptop with no problems (assuming the slot supports the SDHC or SDXC card you are using).

Memory cards other than SD cards are shown in Table 6-5. Some of the cards in Table 6-5 are now obsolete.

Flash Memory Device	Example
The Sony Memory Stick PRO Duo is about half the size of the Memory Stick PRO but is faster and has a higher storage capacity (up to 2 GB). You can use an adapter to insert the Memory Stick PRO Duo in a regular Memory Stick slot.	
Compact Flash (CF) cards come in two types, Type I (CFI) and Type II (CFII). Type II cards are slightly thicker. CFI cards will fit a Type II slot, but CFII cards will not fit a Type I slot. The CF standard allows for sizes up to 137 GB, although current sizes range up to 32 GB. UDMA CompactFlash cards are faster than other CompactFlash cards. UDMA (Ultra Direct Memory Access) transfers data from the device to memory without involving the CPU.	
MultiMediaCard (MMC) looks like an SD card, but the technology is different and they are not interchangeable. Generally, SD cards are faster than MMC cards.	
Embedded MMC (eMMC) is internal storage used instead of using an SSD drive in inexpensive mobile devices such as cell phones, tablets, and laptops.	 Courtesy of SanDisk
The Memory Stick is used in Sony cameras and camcorders. A later version, the Memory Stick PRO, improved on the slower transfer rate of the original Memory Stick.	
The xD-Picture Card has a compact design (about the size of a postage stamp), and currently holds up to 2 GB of data. You can use an adapter to insert this card into a PC Card slot on a laptop computer or a CF slot on a digital camera.	

Table 6-5   Flash memory cards

★ **A+ Exam Tip**   The A+ 220-901 exam expects you to know about SD, MicroSD, MiniSD, Compact Flash, eMMC, and xD memory cards.

Figure 6-52 shows several flash memory cards together so you can get an idea of their relative sizes. Sometimes a memory card is bundled with one or more adapters so that a smaller card will fit a larger card slot.

Figure 6-52 Flash memory cards

Hands-On | Project 6-6 Shop for Storage Media

A+
220-901
1.5

Shop online and print or save webpages showing the following devices. Two online sites you can use are Micro Center (*microcenter.com*) and TigerDirect (*tigerdirect.com*):

1. DVD+R DL discs, which are usually sold in packs. What is the storage capacity of each disc? How many discs are in the pack? What is the price per disc?

2. DVD+RW disc, which is usually sold as a single. What is the price per disc? How many more times expensive is a DVD+RW disc than a DVD+R disc?

3. The largest-capacity USB flash drive you can find. What is its capacity and price?

4. The eight types of SD memory cards in Table 6-4. What is the storage capacity and price of each card? Which type of SD card gives you the most storage per dollar?

TROUBLESHOOTING HARD DRIVES

A+
220-901
4.2

In this part of the chapter, you learn how to troubleshoot problems with hard drives. Problems caused by the hard drive during the boot can be caused by the hard drive subsystem, by the file system on the drive, or by files required by Windows when it begins to load. When trying to solve a problem with the boot, you need to decide if the problem is caused by hardware or software. All the problems discussed in this section are caused by hardware.

SLOW PERFORMANCE

A+
220-901
4.2

One of the most common complaints about a computer is that it is running slowly. When files are physically written over a magnetic hard drive in disconnected fragments on the drive, slow performance can result. (SSD drives don't suffer from slow performance when files are fragmented on the drive.) A quick fix for fragmented files is to run the defragmentation tool on the hard drive. Windows 8/7/Vista automatically defragments a magnetic hard drive once a week, but you can run the defragmentation tool independently of the scheduled maintenance. The Windows defragmentation tool rearranges fragments or parts of files in contiguous clusters so that, when the computer is searching for files, they are easier and faster to find. To run the defragmentation tool, right-click the **Start** button in Windows 8, click **Run**, and enter the **dfrgui** command. In Windows 7, click **Start** and enter the **dfrgui** command in the Search box. Select the drive to defrag (see Figure 6-53 for Windows 8). Windows will tell you if the drive is fragmented and will benefit from defragmentation. Notice in the figure that solid-state drives are not marked as fragmented, but Windows 8 can optimize these drives to release unused space to reduce the number of write operations to the drive. (Windows 7 does not optimize SSD drives.)

Figure 6-53   Windows reports the selected volume D: is not fragmented

HARD DRIVE PROBLEMS DURING THE BOOT

Hardware problems usually show up at POST, unless there is physical damage to an area of the hard drive that is not accessed during POST. Hardware problems often make the hard drive totally inaccessible. If UEFI/BIOS cannot find a hard drive at POST, it displays an error message similar to these:

```
No boot device available
Hard drive not found
OS not found
Read/write failure
Fixed disk error
Invalid boot disk
Inaccessible boot device
```

```
Drive not recognized
RAID not found
RAID stops working
Numeric error codes in the 1700s or 10400s
S.M.A.R.T. errors during the boot
```

The reasons UEFI/BIOS cannot access the drive can be caused by the drive, the data cable, the electrical system, the motherboard, or a loose connection. Here is a list of things to do and check before you open the case:

1. If UEFI/BIOS displays numeric error codes or cryptic messages during POST, check the website of the UEFI/BIOS manufacturer for explanations of these codes or messages.

2. Check UEFI/BIOS setup for errors in the hard drive configuration. If you suspect an error, set UEFI/BIOS to default settings, make sure autodetection is turned on, and reboot the system.

3. Try booting from another bootable media such as the Windows setup DVD or a USB flash drive or CD with the Linux OS and diagnostics software installed (for example, Hiren's BootCD software at *hirensbootcd.org*). If you can boot using another media, you have proven that the problem is isolated to the hard drive subsystem. You can also use the bootable media to access the hard drive, run diagnostics on the drive, and possibly recover its data.

4. For a RAID array, use the firmware utility to check the status of each disk in the array and to check for errors. Press a key at startup to access the RAID UEFI/BIOS utility. This utility lists each disk in the array and its status. You can search the website of the motherboard or RAID controller manufacturer for an interpretation of the messages on this screen and what to do about them. If one of the disks in the array has gone bad, it might take some time for the array to rebuild using data on the other disks. In this situation, the status for the array is likely to show as Caution.

   After the array has rebuilt, your data should be available. However, if one of the hard drives in the array has gone bad, you need to replace the hard drive. After you have replaced the failed drive, you must add it back to the RAID array. This process is called rebuilding a RAID volume. How to do this depends on the RAID hardware you are using. For some motherboards or RAID controller cards, you use the RAID firmware. For others, you use the RAID management software that came bundled with the motherboard or controller. You install this software in Windows and use the software to rebuild the RAID volume using the new hard drive.

If the problem is still not solved, open the case and check these things. Be sure to protect the system against ESD as you work:

1. Remove and reattach all drive cables.

2. If you're using a RAID or SATA controller card, remove and reseat it or place it in a different slot. Check the documentation for the card, looking for directions for troubleshooting.

3. Inspect the drive for damage, such as bent pins on the connection for the cable.

4. Determine if a magnetic hard drive is spinning by listening to it or lightly touching the metal drive (with the power on).

5. Check the cable for frayed edges or other damage.

6. Check the installation manual for things you might have overlooked. Look for a section about system setup, and carefully follow all directions that apply.

7. S.M.A.R.T. errors that display during the boot result from UEFI/BIOS reporting that the drive has met a threshold point of failure. Back up the data and replace the drive as soon as possible.

8. When Windows installed on a hard drive cannot launch, it might present a BSOD (blue screen of death) screen with error messages or it might hang and you see a never-ending spinning Windows pinwheel or wait icon. Windows includes several tools for checking a hard drive for errors and repairing a corrupted

Windows installation. Without getting into these details of supporting Windows, here are a few simple things you can try:

a. *Use Windows 8/7/Vista Startup Repair.* The Startup Repair utility restores many of the Windows files needed for a successful boot. Following directions given in the chapter, "Supporting the Power System and Troubleshooting Computers," boot from the Windows setup DVD. For Windows 8, on the opening screen, select your language, and click **Repair your computer**. Next choose **Troubleshoot**, then choose **Advanced options**. On Advanced options (see Figure 6-54), click **Startup Repair** and follow the on-screen instructions. In Windows 7, boot from the Windows setup DVD, click **Repair your computer**, and sign in to the Windows system installed on the hard drive. Next, on the System Recovery Options menu (see Figure 6-55), select **Startup Repair**.

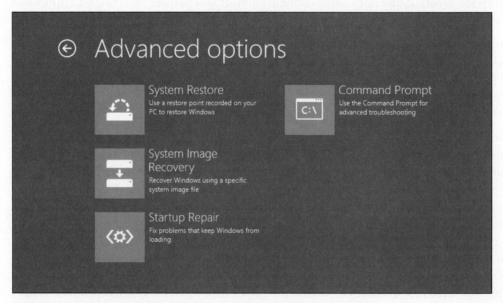

Figure 6-54   Select Startup Repair to fix problems with Windows startup

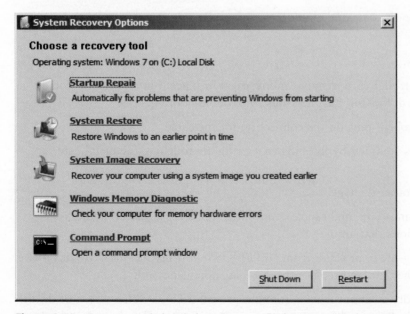

Figure 6-55   Recovery tools in Windows Recovery Environment (Windows RE) for a Windows 7 installation

b. *Use the chkdsk command.* To make sure the hard drive does not have bad sectors that can corrupt the file system, you can use the chkdsk command. To use the command in Windows 8, select Command Prompt from the Advanced options menu (refer back to Figure 6-54). In Windows 7, select Command Prompt from the System Recovery Options menu (refer back to Figure 6-55). At the command prompt that appears, use this chkdsk command to search for bad sectors on drive C: and recover data:

```
chkdsk C: /r
```

c. *Repair the BCD.* The BCD (Boot Configuration Data) is a small database that holds parameters Windows needs for a successful boot. At a command prompt, use this bootrec command to rebuild the BCD:

```
bootrec /RebuildBCD
```

d. *Repair the MBR.* When a hard drive is using the MBR method to manage partitions on the drive, the bootrec command can be used to fix problems with the MBR program that is needed to start Windows. Use this command:

```
bootrec /FixMBR
```

e. *Repair the boot sector.* The boot sector holds the MBR partition table. To repair a corrupted boot sector, use this command:

```
bootrec /FixBoot
```

9. Check the drive manufacturer's website for diagnostic software. Sometimes this software can be run from a bootable CD. Run the software to test the drive for errors.

10. If it is not convenient to create a bootable CD with hard drive diagnostic software installed, you can move the drive to a working computer and install it as a second drive in the system. Then you can use the diagnostic software installed on the primary hard drive to test the problem drive. While you have the drive installed in a working computer, be sure to find out if you can copy data from it to the good drive, so that you can recover any data not backed up. Remember that you set the drive on the open computer case (see Figure 6-56) or use a SATA-to-USB converter to connect the drive to a USB port. If you have the case open with the computer turned on, be *very careful* to not touch the drive or touch inside the case.

Figure 6-56 Temporarily connect a faulty hard drive to another system to diagnose the problem and try to recover data

11. After you have tried to recover the file system on the drive and before you decide to replace the hard drive, try these things to clean the drive and get a fresh start:

    a. *Format a hard drive volume.* If you decide the hard drive volume is corrupted and you want to start over, open a Windows command prompt and use the format command to erase everything on the volume. In this example, D: is the drive letter for the volume:

    ```
    format D:
    ```

    b. *Use diskpart to start over with a fresh file system.* If formatting the volume doesn't work, you can erase the hard drive partitions using the diskpart command. When you enter diskpart at a command prompt, the DISKPART> prompt appears. Then use these commands to wipe everything off the hard drive. In the example, you are erasing partition 1 on disk 0.

    ```
    list disk
    select disk 0
    list partition
    select partition 1
    clean
    ```

    Use the **exit** command to exit the diskpart utility. You can then reinstall Windows, which partitions the hard drive again. If Windows cannot recognize the drive, it's probably time to replace hardware in the hard drive subsystem.

12. If the drive still does not boot, exchange the three field replaceable units—the data cable, the storage card (if the drive is connected to one), and the hard drive itself—for a hard drive subsystem. Do the following, in order, and test the hard drive after each step:

    a. Reconnect or swap the drive data cable.

    b. Reseat or exchange the drive controller card, if one is present.

    c. Exchange the hard drive for a known good drive.

13. Sometimes older drives refuse to spin at POST or a failing drive can make a loud clicking noise. Drives that have trouble spinning often whine at startup for several months before they finally refuse to spin altogether. If your drive whines loudly when you first turn on the computer, never turn off the computer and replace the drive as soon as possible. One of the worst things you can do for a drive that is having difficulty starting up is to leave the computer turned off for an extended period of time. Some drives, like old cars, refuse to start if they are unused for a long time. A drive making a loud clicking noise most likely is not accessible and must be replaced.

14. A bad power supply or a bad motherboard also might cause a disk boot failure.

If the problem is solved by exchanging the hard drive, take the extra time to reinstall the old hard drive to verify that the problem was not caused by a bad connection.

>> CHAPTER SUMMARY

Hard Drive Technologies and Interface Standards

▲ A hard disk drive (HDD) comes in three sizes: 3.5" for desktop computers and 2.5" and 1.8" for laptops.

▲ A hard drive can be a magnetic drive, a solid-state drive, or a hybrid drive. A solid-state drive contains flash memory and is more expensive, faster, more reliable, and uses less power than a magnetic drive.

▲ Most hard drives, tape drives, and optical drives use the SATA interface standards. External SATA ports are called eSATA ports.

▲ Three SATA standards provide data transfer rates of 1.5 Gb/sec (using SATA I), 3.0 Gb/sec (using SATA II), and 16.0 Gb/sec (using SATA III).

▲ S.M.A.R.T. is a self-monitoring technology whereby the UEFI/BIOS monitors the health of the hard drive and warns of an impending failure.

How to Select and Install Hard Drives

▲ When selecting a hard drive, consider the storage capacity, technology (solid-state or magnetic), spindle speed, interface standard, and buffer size (for hybrid drives).

▲ SATA drives require no configuration and are installed using a power cord and a single SATA data cable.

▲ Laptop hard drives plug directly into a SATA connection on the system board.

▲ RAID technology uses an array of hard drives to provide fault tolerance and/or improvement in performance. Choices for RAID are RAID 0 (striping using two drives), RAID 1 (mirroring using two drives), RAID 5 (parity checking using three drives), and RAID 10 (striping and mirroring combined using four drives).

▲ Hardware RAID is implemented using the motherboard UEFI/BIOS or a RAID controller card. Software RAID is implemented in Windows. Best practice is to use hardware RAID rather than software RAID.

▲ Multiple hard drives can be installed in a single external enclosure to expand the storage capacity of a single computer or to make hard drive storage available on a network.

Identifying Tape Drives

▲ Tape drives are an inexpensive way to back up an entire hard drive or portions of it. Tape drives are more convenient for backups than   drives. The disadvantage of tape drives is that data can only be accessed sequentially.

Supporting Other Types of Storage Devices

▲ File systems a storage device might use in Windows include NTFS, exFAT, FAT32, and FAT.

▲ CDs, DVDs, and BDs are optical discs with data physically embedded into the surface of the disc. Laser beams are used to read data off the disc by measuring light reflection.

▲ Optical discs can be recordable (such as a CD-R disc) or rewriteable (such as a DVD-RW disc).

▲ Flash memory cards are a type of solid-state storage. Types of flash memory card standards by the SD Association include SD, MiniSD, MicroSD, SDHC, MiniSDHC, MicroSDHC, SDXC, and MicroSDXC. Other memory cards include Memory Stick PRO Duo, Memory Stick PRO, Sony Memory Stick Micro M2, CompactFlash I and II, eMMC, and xD-Picture Card.

Troubleshooting Hard Drives

▲ Defragmenting a magnetic hard drive can sometimes improve slow performance of the drive.

▲ Problems caused by the hard drive during the boot can be caused by the hard drive subsystem, by the file system on the drive, or by files required by Windows when it begins to load. After the boot, bad sectors on a drive can cause problems with corrupted files.

▲ To determine if the hard drive is the problem when booting, try to boot from another media, such as the Windows setup DVD.

▲ For problems with a RAID volume, use the RAID controller firmware (on the motherboard or on the RAID controller card) or RAID management software installed in Windows to report the status of the array and to rebuild the RAID volume.

▲ To determine if a drive has bad sectors, use the chkdsk command. You can run the command after booting to the System Recovery Options menu using the Windows setup DVD.

▲ The bootrec command can be used to rebuild the BCD, repair the MBR, or repair the boot sector of a hard drive.

▲ Use the format command to erase everything on a Windows volume.

▲ Use commands within the diskpart utility to completely erase a partition on a hard drive.

▲ Field replaceable units in the hard drive subsystem are the data cable, optional storage card, and hard drive.

>> KEY TERMS

For explanations of key terms, see the Glossary for this text.

autodetection
BCD (Boot Configuration Data)
BD-R
BD-RE
Blu-Ray Disc (BD)
bootrec
CD (compact disc)
CDFS (Compact Disc File System)
CD-ROM
CD-RW
chkdsk
CompactFlash (CF) card
data cartridge
defragmentation tool
diskpart

DVD (digital versatile disc or digital video disc)
DVD-ROM
DVD-RW
DVD-RW DL
embedded MMC (eMMC)
external enclosure
external SATA (eSATA)
fault tolerance
file system
format
formatting
hard disk drive (HDD)
hard drive
hot-swapping
hybrid hard drive (H-HDD)

low-level formatting
magnetic hard drive
minicartridge
mirrored volume
MultiMediaCard (MMC)
NAND flash memory
RAID (redundant array of inexpensive disks or redundant array of independent disks)
RAID 0
RAID 1
RAID 1+0
RAID 10
RAID 5
RAID-5 volume
read/write head

Secure Digital (SD) card
sequential access
serial ATA (SATA)
S.M.A.R.T. (Self-Monitoring Analysis and Reporting Technology)
smart card reader
solid-state device (SSD)
solid-state drive (SSD)
spanning
Startup Repair
storage card
striped volume
UDF (Universal Disk Format) file system
wear leveling
xD-Picture Card

>> REVIEWING THE BASICS

1. What three types of technologies are used inside hard drives?

2. At what three speeds in revolutions per minute might the spindle inside a hard drive rotate?

3. When the OS addresses the sectors on a hard drive as one long list of sequential sectors, what is this technology called?

4. What is the transfer speed for SATA I? SATA II? SATA III?

5. How many pins does a SATA internal data cable have? How many pins does a SATA power cable have?

6. What term describes the technology that allows you to exchange a hard drive without powering down the system?

7. Which RAID level mirrors one hard drive with a second drive so that the same data is written to both drives?

8. Which RAID level stripes data across multiple drives to improve performance and also provides fault tolerance?

9. How many hard drives are necessary to implement RAID 10?

10. When implementing RAID on a motherboard, where do you enable the feature?

11. What type of file system is used by Blu-ray discs?

12. What type of file system is used by SDXC memory cards?

13. How much data can a CD hold?

14. How much data can a double-sided, dual-layer DVD hold?

15. How much data can a double-sided, single-layer BD hold?

16. Which costs more, a CD-R or a CD-RW disc?

17. Which type of flash memory card is currently the smallest type of card?

18. What command-prompt command do you use to determine if a drive has bad sectors?

19. What command can you use to rebuild the BCD?

20. What physical sizes of hard drives are installed in laptops?

>> THINKING CRITICALLY

1. You install a SATA hard drive and then turn on the computer for the first time. You access UEFI/BIOS setup and see that the drive is not recognized. Which of the following do you do next?

   a. Turn off the computer, open the case, and verify that memory modules on the motherboard have not become loose.

   b. Turn off the computer, open the case, and verify that the data cable and power cable are connected correctly and jumpers on the drive are set correctly.

   c. Verify that UEFI/BIOS autodetection is enabled.

   d. Reboot the computer and enter UEFI/BIOS setup again to see if it now recognizes the drive.

2. You want to install an SSD drive in your desktop computer, but the drive is far too narrow to fit snugly into the bays of your computer case. Which of the following do you do?

   a. Install the SSD in a laptop computer.

   b. Buy a bay adapter that will allow you to install the narrow drive in a desktop case bay.

   c. This SSD is designed for a laptop. Flash UEFI/BIOS so that your system will support a laptop hard drive.

   d. Use a special SATA controller card that will support the narrow hard drive.

3. Mark each statement as true or false:

   a. PATA hard drives are older and slower than SATA hard drives.

   b. SATA 1 is about 10 times faster than SATA 3.

   c. RAID 0 can be implemented using only a single hard drive.

   d. RAID 5 requires five hard drives working together at the same speed and capacity.

   e. You can use an internal SATA data cable with an eSATA port.

   f. A SATA internal data cable has 7 pins.

>> REAL PROBLEMS, REAL SOLUTIONS

REAL PROBLEM 6-1 Recovering Data

Your friend has a Windows 8 desktop system that contains important data. He frantically calls you to say that when he turns on the computer, the lights on the front panel light up and he can hear the fan spin for a moment and then all goes dead. His most urgent problem is the data on his hard drive, which is not backed up. The data is located in several folders on the drive. What is the quickest and easiest way to solve the most urgent problem, recovering the data? List the major steps in that process.

REAL PROBLEM 6-2 Using Hardware RAID

You work as an IT support technician for a boss who believes you are really bright and can solve just about any problem he throws at you. Folks in the company have complained one time too many that the file server downtime is just killing them, so he asks you to solve this problem. He wants you to figure out what hardware is needed to implement hardware RAID for fault tolerance.

You check the file server's configuration and discover it has a single hard drive using a SATA connection with Windows Server 2012 installed. There are four empty bays in the computer case and four extra SATA power cords. You also discover an empty PCIe x4 slot on the motherboard. UEFI/BIOS setup does not offer the option to configure RAID, but you think the slot might accommodate a RAID controller.

Complete the investigation and do the following:

1. Decide what hardware you must purchase and print webpages showing the products and their cost.

2. What levels of RAID does the RAID controller card support? Which RAID level is best to use? Print any important information in the RAID controller documentation that supports your decisions.

3. What is the total hardware cost of implementing RAID? Estimate how much time you think it will take for you to install the devices and test the setup.

Supporting I/O Devices

After completing this chapter, you will be able to:

- Describe the general approach technicians use to install and support I/O devices

- Install and configure several I/O devices, such as barcode readers, biometric devices, digital cameras, webcams, graphic tablets, and touch screens

- Install and configure adapter cards

- Support the video subsystem, including selecting a monitor and video card and supporting dual monitors and video memory

- Troubleshoot common problems with I/O devices

This chapter is packed full of details about the many I/O (input/output) devices an IT support technician must be familiar with and must know how to install and support. Most of us learn about new technologies as we need to use a device or when a client or customer requests our help with purchasing decisions or solving a problem with a device. Good technicians soon develop the skills of searching the web for explanations, reviews, and ads about a device and can quickly turn to support websites for how to install, configure, or troubleshoot a device. This chapter can serve as your jump start toward learning about many computer parts and devices used to enhance a system. It contains enough information to get you started toward becoming an expert at computer devices.

We begin with the basic skills common to supporting any device, including how to use Device Manager and how to select the right port for a new peripheral device. Then you learn to install I/O devices and adapter cards and to support the video subsystem. Finally, you learn how to troubleshoot problems with I/O devices.

BASIC PRINCIPLES FOR SUPPORTING DEVICES

A+
220-901
1.4, 1.7

An I/O or storage device can be either internal (installed inside the computer case) or external (installed outside the case and called a peripheral device). These basic principles apply to supporting both internal and external devices:

▲ *Every device is controlled by software.* When you install a new device, such as a barcode reader or scanner, you must install both the device and the device drivers to control the device. These device drivers must be written for the OS you are using. Recall from earlier chapters that the exceptions to this principle are some simple devices, such as the keyboard, which are controlled by the system UEFI/BIOS. Also, Windows has embedded device drivers for many devices. For example, when you install a video card, Windows can use its embedded drivers to communicate with the card, but to use all the features of the card, you can install the drivers that came bundled with the card.

▲ *When it comes to installing or supporting a device, the manufacturer knows best.* In this chapter, you learn a lot of principles and procedures for installing and supporting a device, but when you're on the job installing a device or fixing a broken one, read the manufacturer's documentation and follow those guidelines first. For example, for most installations, you install the device before you install the device driver. However, for some devices, such as a digital camera and a wireless keyboard, you might need to install the device driver first. Check the device documentation to know which to do first.

▲ *Some devices need application software to use the device.* For example, after you install a scanner and its device drivers, you might also need to install Adobe Photoshop to use the scanner.

▲ *A device is no faster than the port or slot it is designed to use.* When buying a new external device, pay attention to the type of port for which it is rated. For example, an external hard drive designed to use a USB 2.0 port will work using a USB 3.0 port, but will work at the USB 2.0 speed even when it's connected to a faster USB 3.0 port. For another example, a TV tuner card in a PCI slot will not work as fast as a TV tuner card in a PCI Express slot because of the different speeds of the slots.

▲ *Use an administrator account in Windows.* When installing hardware devices under Windows, you need to be signed in to the system with a user account that has the highest level of privileges to change the system. This type of account is called an administrator account.

▲ *Problems with a device can sometimes be solved by updating the device drivers.* Device manufacturers often release updates to device drivers. Update the drivers to solve problems with the device or to add new features. You can use Device Manager in Windows to manage devices and their drivers.

▲ *Install only one device at a time.* If you have several devices to install, install one and restart the system. Make sure that device is working and all is well with the system before you move on to install another device.

Device Manager (its program file is named devmgmt.msc) is your primary Windows tool for managing hardware. It lists almost all installed hardware devices and the drivers they use. (Printers and many USB devices are not listed in Device Manager.) Using Device Manager, you can disable or enable a device, update its drivers, uninstall a device, and undo a driver update (called a driver rollback).

Before we move on to installing devices, you need to be familiar with the ports on a computer. When selecting a new device, to get the best performance, select one that uses the fastest port available on your computer.

PORTS AND WIRELESS CONNECTIONS USED BY PERIPHERAL DEVICES

A+
220-901
1.7

Many ports used by peripheral or external devices are pictured in Table 1 in the chapter, "First Look at Computer Parts and Tools." When deciding what type of port a new device should use, the speed of the port is often a tiebreaker. Table 7-1 shows the speeds of various ports, from fastest to slowest. Because wireless connections are sometimes an option, they are also included in the table for comparison. For example, you might need to decide between a USB 2.0 printer connection and a Bluetooth wireless connection. This table can help you decide if speed should be a consideration.

> **★ A+ Exam Tip** The A+ 220-901 exam expects you to be able to compare the speeds and distances among USB (1.1, 2.0, and 3.0), FireWire 400 and 800 ports, and Bluetooth, Infrared, and NFC wireless connections. The facts you need to know are found in Table 7-1.

7

Port or Wireless Type	Maximum Speed	Maximum Cable Length or Wireless Range
eSATA Version 3 (eSATA-600)	6.0 Gbps (gigabits per second)	Cable lengths up to 2 meters
SuperSpeed USB (USB 3.0)	5.0 Gbps	Cable lengths up to 3 meters
eSATA Version 2 (eSATA-300)	3.0 Gbps	Cable lengths up to 2 meters
eSATA Version 1 (eSATA-150)	1.5 Gbps or 1500 Mbps (megabits per second)	Cable lengths up to 2 meters
FireWire 800 (also called 1394b)	1.2 Gbps or 800 Mbps	Cable lengths up to 100 meters
Wi-Fi 802.11n RF (radio frequency) of 2.4 GHz or 5.0 GHz	Up to 500 Mbps	Range up to 70 meters
Hi-Speed USB (USB 2.0)	480 Mbps	Cable lengths up to 5 meters
FireWire 400 (also called 1394a)	400 Mbps	Cable lengths up to 4.5 meters
Original USB (USB 1.1)	12 Mbps or 1.5 Mbps	Cable lengths up to 3 meters
Wi-Fi 802.11g RF of 2.4 GHz	Up to 54 Mbps	Range up to 100 meters
Wi-Fi 802.11a RF of 5.0 GHz	Up to 54 Mbps	Range up to 50 meters
Wi-Fi 802.11b RF of 2.4 GHz	Up to 11 Mbps	Range up to 100 meters
Bluetooth wireless RF of 2.4 GHz	Up to 3 Mbps	Range up to 10 meters
Infrared (IR) wireless Invisible light; frequency range of 100 to 400 THz (terahertz or 1 trillion hertz), just above red light	Up to 4 Mbps for fast speed IR; up to 1.15 Mbps for medium speed IR, and up to 115 Kbps (kilobits per second) for slow speed IR	Range up to 5 meters
Near Field Communication (NFC) RF of 13.56 MHz	Up to 424 kbps	Range up to 10 centimeters

Table 7-1 Data transmission speeds for various port types and wireless connections

USB CONNECTIONS

Here is a summary of important facts you need to know about USB connections:

1. The USB Implementers Forum, Inc. (*www.usb.org*), the organization responsible for developing USB, uses the symbols shown in Figure 7-1 to indicate SuperSpeed USB (USB 3.0), Hi-Speed USB (USB 2.0), or Original USB (USB 1.1).

Source: USB Forum

Figure 7-1 SuperSpeed, Hi-Speed, and Original USB logos appear on products certified by the USB Forum

2. As many as 127 USB devices can be daisy-chained together using USB cables. In a daisy chain, one device provides a USB port for the next device.

3. USB uses serial transmissions, and USB devices are hot-swappable, meaning that you can plug or unplug one without first powering down the system.

4. A USB cable has four wires, two for power and two for communication. The two power wires (one is hot and the other is ground) allow the host controller to provide power to a device. Table 7-2 shows the different USB connectors on USB cables.

> ✏️ **Notes**   Sometimes a mouse that uses USB 2.0 gives problems when plugged into a USB 3.0 port. If a mouse refuses to work or is unstable, try moving it to a USB 2.0 port.

Cable and Connectors	Description
A-Male to B-Male cable 	The A-Male connector on the left is flat and wide and connects to an A-Male USB port on a computer or USB hub. The B-Male connector on the right is square and connects to a USB 1.x or 2.0 device such as a printer.
Mini-B to A-Male cable 	The Mini-B connector has five pins and is often used to connect small electronic devices, such as a digital camera, to a computer.
A-Male to Micro-B cable 	The Micro-B connector has five pins and has a smaller height than the Mini-B connector. It's used on digital cameras, cell phones, and other small electronic devices.
A-Male to Micro-A cable 	The Micro-A connector has five pins and is smaller than the Mini-B connector. It's used on digital cameras, cell phones, and other small electronic devices.
USB 3.0 A-Male to USB 3.0 B-Male cable 	This USB 3.0 B-Male connector is used by SuperSpeed USB 3.0 devices such as printers or scanners. Devices that have this connection can also use regular B-Male connectors, but this USB 3.0 B-Male connector will not fit the connection on a USB 1.1 or 2.0 device. USB 3.0 A-Male and B-Male connectors and ports are blue.
USB 3.0 A-Male to USB 3.0 Micro-B cable 	The USB 3.0 Micro-B connector is used by SuperSpeed USB 3.0 devices. The connectors are not compatible with regular Micro-B connectors.

Table 7-2   USB connectors

> ✎ **Notes** A USB 3.0 A-Male connector or port has additional pins compared with USB 1.1 or 2.0 ports and connectors but still is backward compatible with USB 1.1 and 2.0 devices. A USB 3.0 A-Male or B-Male connector or port is usually blue. Take a close look at the blue and black USB ports shown in Figure 4 in the chapter "First Look at Computer Parts and Tools."

FIREWIRE (IEEE 1394) CONNECTIONS

USB and FireWire competed as a solution for fast I/O connections for a few years, but USB clearly won that contest, and now FireWire is hardly used in new devices. FireWire standards are managed by the 1394 Trade Association (*www.1394ta.org*). The official name of these standards is IEEE 1394, and other names used are FireWire (first used by Apple) and i.LINK (first used by Sony). The most common name used today is FireWire. Here are the key facts you need to know about FireWire:

⊿ FireWire uses serial transmissions, and FireWire devices are hot-swappable.
⊿ FireWire 800 (1394b) allows for up to 63 FireWire devices to be daisy-chained together. FireWire 400 (1394a) allows for up to 16 daisy-chained devices.
⊿ FireWire 400 (1394a) supports two types of connectors and cables: a 4-pin connector that does not provide voltage to a device and a 6-pin connector that does. Figure 7-2 shows a cable that plugs into a 6-pin FireWire port to provide a 4-pin connector for a FireWire device.

> ✎ **Notes** IEEE 1394a ports with six pins are the most common FireWire ports on motherboards.

Figure 7-2   IEEE 1394a cable provides a smaller 4-pin and larger 6-pin connectors

⊿ FireWire 800 (1394b) uses a 9-pin rectangular connector. Figure 7-3 shows a FireWire 800 adapter card that provides three 1394 ports: two 1394b 9-pin ports and one 1394a 6-pin port. The power cable connected to the card plugs into a 4-pin Molex power cable from the power supply to provide extra power to the card. The latest 1394 standard is 1394c, which allows FireWire 800 to use a standard network port and network cable.

6-pin 1394a
port

9-pin 1394b
ports

Figure 7-3   This 1394 adapter card supports both 1394a and 1394b and uses a 32-bit PCI slot

Figure 7-4   This remote control is an Infrared device
that uses an IR transceiver connected to
a laptop by way of a USB port

INFRARED CONNECTIONS

Infrared (IR) is an outdated wireless technology
to connect personal devices that has been mostly
replaced by Bluetooth. IR requires an unobstructed
"line of sight" between the transmitter and receiver.
Today, the most common use of Infrared is by remote
controls. Figure 7-4 shows a remote control that can
be used with multimedia applications installed on a
laptop computer. The remote communicates with the
laptop by way of an IR transceiver connected to a
USB port. To use the remote, the device drivers that
came bundled with the device are installed and then
the IR transceiver is connected to the USB port.

> ✎ **Notes**   Infrared standards are defined by the Infrared
> Data Association (IrDA). Its website is *www.irda.org*.

Now that you know about the ports and wireless
connections used for external devices, let's see how
to install them.

INSTALLING I/O PERIPHERAL DEVICES

A+
220-901
1.12
Installing peripheral or external devices is easy to do and usually goes without a hitch. All devices need device drivers or UEFI/BIOS to control them and to interface with the operating system. Simple input devices, such as the mouse and keyboard, can be controlled by the UEFI/BIOS or have embedded device drivers built in to the OS. For these devices, you usually don't have to install additional device drivers.

Peripheral devices you might be called on to install include a keyboard, mouse, touch pad, barcode reader, biometric device (for example, a fingerprint reader), touch screen, motion controller, scanner, microphone, game pad, joystick, digitizer, digital camera, smart card reader, webcam, camcorder, MIDI-enabled devices, speakers, and display devices. These installations are similar, so learning to do one will help you do another. Here are the general procedures to install any peripheral device:

1. *Read the manufacturer's directions.* I know you don't want to hear that again, but when you follow these directions, the installation goes better. If you later have a problem with the installation and you ask the manufacturer for help, being able to say you followed the directions exactly as stated goes a long way toward getting more enthusiastic help and cooperation.

2. *Make sure the drivers provided with the device are written for the operating system (OS) you are using.* Know that 64-bit drivers are required for a 64-bit operating system, and 32-bit drivers are required for a 32-bit OS. You can sometimes use drivers written for older Windows versions in newer Windows versions, but for best results, use drivers written for the OS installed. You can download the drivers you need from the manufacturer's website.

3. *Make sure the motherboard port you are using is enabled.* Most likely it is enabled, but if the device is not recognized when you plug it in, go into UEFI/BIOS setup and make sure the port is enabled. In addition, UEFI/BIOS setup might offer the option to configure a USB port to use SuperSpeed (USB 3.0), Hi-Speed USB (USB 2.0), or original USB (USB 1.1). Figure 7-5 shows the BIOS setup screen for one system where you can enable or disable onboard devices. In addition, if you are having problems with a motherboard port, don't forget to update the motherboard drivers that control the port.

Figure 7-5 Use BIOS setup to enable or disable onboard ports

4. *Install drivers or plug in the device.* Some devices, such as a USB printer, require that you plug in the device before installing the drivers, and some devices require you to install the drivers before plugging in the device. For some devices, it doesn't matter which is installed first. Carefully read and follow the device documentation. For example, the documentation for one digital camera says that if you install the camera before installing the driver, the drivers will not install properly.

If you plug in the device first, Device Setup launches and steps you through the installation of drivers (see Figure 7-6). As Device Setup works, an icon appears in the taskbar. To see the Device Setup box, as shown in the figure, click the icon.

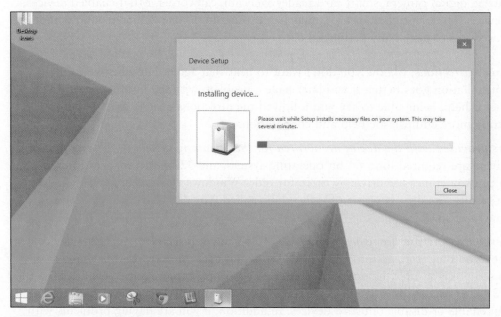

Figure 7-6 Device Setup begins installing a new device

If you need to install the drivers first, run the setup program on CD or DVD. If you downloaded drivers from the web, double-click the driver file and follow the directions on screen. It might be necessary to restart the system after the installation. After the drivers are installed, plug the device into the port. The device should immediately be recognized by Windows. If you have problems using the device, turn to Device Manager for help.

5. *Install the application software to use the device.* For example, a FireWire camcorder is likely to come bundled with video-editing software. Run the software to use the device.

Now let's look at some key features and installation concerns for several peripheral devices.

MOUSE OR KEYBOARD

Plug a mouse or keyboard into a USB port and Windows should immediately recognize it and install generic drivers. Because PS/2 ports are not hot-pluggable, you must restart Windows after plugging a mouse or keyboard into a PS/2 port. For keyboards with special features such as the one shown in Figure 7-7, you need to install the drivers that came with the keyboard before you can use these features. Also notice in Figure 7-7 a green USB to PS/2 adapter and a purple PS/2 to USB adapter, which can solve the problem when a case has PS/2 ports and doesn't have enough USB ports.

Figure 7-7 The mouse and keyboard require drivers to use the extra buttons and zoom bar

You can later use Device Manager to uninstall, disable, or enable most devices. However, USB devices are managed differently. To uninstall a USB device such as the USB keyboard shown in Figure 7-7, use the Programs and Features window. To open the window in Windows 8, press **Win+X** and click **Programs and Features**. For Windows 7, click **Start**, click **Control Panel**, and click **Programs and Features**. In the Programs and Features window (see Figure 7-8), select the device and click **Uninstall**. Follow the directions on screen to uninstall the device.

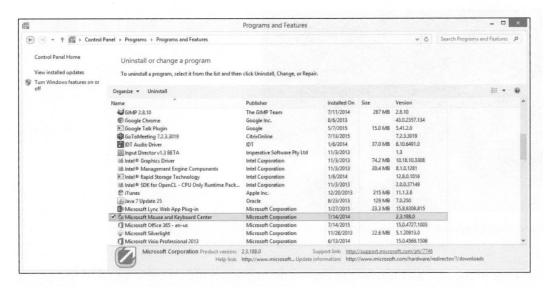

Figure 7-8 USB devices are listed as installed programs

> ✎ **Notes** The A+ 220-901 exam expects you to use Control Panel in Classic view, which presents a list of individual items. If Control Panel is in Category view, which presents items in groups, to get Classic view, click **Category** and then click **Small icons** or **Large icons**.

REPLACING THE KEYBOARD AND TOUCH PAD IN A LAPTOP

Replacing the keyboard is pretty easy to do. Before you begin any disassembly of a laptop, refer to the manufacturer documentation. Here are typical steps that are similar to many models of laptops:

1. Power down the laptop and remove the AC adapter and the battery pack.

2. Remove two or more screws on the bottom of the laptop (see Figure 7-9). (Only the manufacturer documentation can tell you which ones because there are probably several of them used to hold various components in place.)

Figure 7-9 Remove screws on the bottom of the laptop

3. Turn the laptop over and open the lid. Gently push the keyboard toward the lid while pulling it up to release it from the case (see Figure 7-10).

Figure 7-10 Pry up and lift the keyboard out of the laptop case

4. Bring the keyboard out of the case and forward to expose the keyboard ribbon cable attached underneath the board. Use a screwdriver to lift the cable connector up and out of its socket (see Figure 7-11).

Figure 7-11 Disconnect the keyboard cable from the motherboard

5. Replace the keyboard following the steps in reverse order.

Sometimes the touch pad and keyboard are one complete field replaceable unit (FRU). If the touch pad is a separate component, it might be part of the keyboard bezel, also called the palm rest. This bezel is the flat cover that surrounds the keyboard. Most likely you have to remove the keyboard before you can remove the keyboard bezel.

BARCODE READERS

A+
220-901
1.12

A barcode reader is used to scan barcodes on products at the point of sale (POS) or when taking inventory. The reader might use a wireless connection, a serial port, a USB port, or a keyboard port. If the reader uses a keyboard port, most likely it has a splitter (called a keyboard wedge) on it for the keyboard to use, and data read by the barcode reader is input into the system as though it were typed using the keyboard. Figure 7-12 shows a barcode reader by Intermec that is a laser scanner and uses Bluetooth to connect wirelessly to the computer.

Courtesy of Intermec Technologies

Figure 7-12 Handheld or hands-free barcode scanner by Intermec Technologies

BIOMETRIC DEVICES

A+
220-901
1.12

A biometric device is an input device that inputs biological data about a person, used to identify a person's fingerprint, handprint, face, voice, eye, or handwritten signature. For example, you can use a fingerprint reader to sign in to Windows or to access an iPhone using Touch ID technology. These fingerprint readers should not be considered the only authentication to control access to sensitive data: for that, use a strong password, which is a password that is not easy to guess.

Fingerprint readers can look like a mouse and use a wireless or USB connection, such as the one shown in Figure 7-13, or they can be embedded on a keyboard, flash drive, or laptop case. For mobile devices, the fingerprint reader can be activated by pressing a button or touch screen. Most fingerprint readers that are not embedded in other devices use a USB connection. As with other USB devices, read the documentation to know if you should install the drivers first or the device first.

Figure 7-13   Fingerprint readers can (a) look like a mouse, but smaller, or (b) be embedded on a keyboard

DIGITAL CAMERAS AND CAMCORDERS

A digital camera or camcorder can hold images and videos both in embedded memory that cannot be removed or exchanged and in removable flash memory cards. Both of these types of memory retain data without a battery. Here are two ways to transfer images from your camera or camcorder to a computer:

▲ *Connect the camera or camcorder to the computer using a cable.* Using embedded memory or flash memory cards, you can connect the device to your computer using a USB or FireWire port and cable. To connect the device to the computer, you might need to first install the software and then connect the device, or you might need to connect the device and then install the software. Read the camera or camcorder documentation to find out which order to use. After the device and software are installed, the software displays a menu to download images or video to your computer.

▲ *Install the memory card in the computer.* If images or video are stored on a flash memory card installed in your device, you can remove the card and then insert it in a flash memory card slot on your computer. Most laptop computers have one or more of these slots (see Figure 7-14).

Card in SD slot

PRO Duo slot

Figure 7-14   This laptop has two flash memory card slots

If your computer doesn't have this slot, or the slot is not compatible with the type of card you are using, you have two choices:

▲ Perhaps you can purchase an adapter so that your smaller memory card will fit into a larger card slot. Figure 7-15 shows examples of these adapters.

Figure 7-15   MicroSDHC card with four adapters

▲ You can install a USB smart card reader that provides a memory card slot to fit your card. Figure 7-16 shows one reader that connects to a computer using a USB port.

Figure 7-16   This Hi-Speed USB card reader/writer by Targus can read CompactFlash I and II, MicroDrive, SDHC, SD, MMC, xD, Memory Stick, PRO Duo, and Mini SD cards

When the memory card is recognized by Windows, it is assigned a drive letter and you can see it listed in Windows 8 File Explorer or Windows 7 Windows Explorer. Use Explorer to copy, move, and delete files from the card.

📝 **Notes** It's interesting to know that TWAIN (Technology Without An Interesting Name) is a standard format used by scanners and digital cameras and other devices for transferring images.

⭐ **A+ Exam Tip** The A+ 220-901 exam expects you to know how to install the software bundled with your digital camera before attaching the camera to your computer.

WEBCAMS

A webcam (web camera) is embedded in most laptops and can also be installed as a peripheral device using a USB port or some other port. For example, the webcam shown in Figure 7-17 works well for personal chat sessions and videoconferencing and has a built-in microphone. First, use the setup CD to install the software and then plug in the webcam to a USB port.

A webcam comes with a built-in microphone. You can use this microphone or use the microphone port on the computer. Most software allows you to select these input devices. For example, Figure 7-18 shows the Tools Options box for Camtasia Recorder by TechSmith (*www.techsmith.com*).

Source: Camtasia Recorder by TechSmith

© iStockphoto/Eric Ferfuson

Figure 7-17   This personal web camera clips to the top of your laptop and has a built-in microphone

Figure 7-18   The Camtasia Recorder application allows you to change the input devices used for video and sound

GRAPHICS TABLETS

Another input device is a graphics tablet, also called a digitizing tablet or digitizer, that is used to hand draw and is likely to connect by a USB port (see Figure 7-19). It comes with a stylus that works like a pencil on the tablet. The graphics tablet and stylus can be a replacement to a mouse or touch pad on a laptop, and some graphics tablets come with a mouse. Graphics tablets are popular with graphic artists and others who use desktop publishing applications.

Figure 7-19 A graphics tablet and stylus are used to digitize a hand drawing

Install the graphics tablet the same way you do other USB devices. Additional software might be bundled with the device to enhance its functions, such as inputting handwritten signatures into Microsoft Word documents.

MOTION CONTROLLERS

A+
220-901
1.12

A motion controller, sometimes called a motion sensor, provides input to the computer by sensing the motion of your fingers and hands. Figure 7-20 shows an example of a motion controller that uses a USB connection. It senses the space just above the controller where motions by your hands and fingers are used to control the computer. Motion controllers are commonly used with gaming consoles such as Xbox One or the Wii. Graphic designers or engineers who work with 3D images might also use a motion controller to manipulate designs, and motion controllers are also used in hospitals to allow surgeons access to vital data while maintaining a sterile environment. As with other USB devices, read the documentation to know if you should install the drivers first or the device first.

Site: https://www.leapmotion.com/

Figure 7-20 Leap Motion offers an affordable motion controller

MIDI DEVICES

A+
220-901
1.12

MIDI (musical instrument digital interface), pronounced "middy," is a set of standards that are used to represent music in digital form. Using the MIDI format, each individual note played by each individual instrument is digitally stored. MIDI standards are used to connect electronic music equipment, such as musical keyboards and mixers, or to connect this equipment to a computer for input, output, and editing. Most sound cards can play MIDI files, and most electronic instruments have MIDI ports.

A MIDI port is a 5-pin DIN port that looks like a PS/2 keyboard port, only larger. Figure 7-21 shows MIDI ports on electronic drums. A MIDI port is either an input port or an output port, but not both. Normally, you would connect the MIDI output port to a mixer, but you can also use it to connect to a computer.

Figure 7-21   MIDI ports on an electronic drum set

Here are ways to connect a musical instrument to a computer using the MIDI standards:

▲ **MIDI to MIDI.** A few sound cards provide MIDI ports. Use two MIDI cables to connect output jack to input jack and to connect input jack to output jack.

▲ **MIDI to USB.** If your computer does not have MIDI ports, you can use a MIDI-to-USB cable like the one shown in Figure 7-22. The two MIDI connectors on the cable are for input and output.

Figure 7-22   MIDI-to-USB cable lets you connect an electronic musical instrument to your computer

▲ **USB to USB.** Newer instruments have a USB port to interface with a computer using MIDI data transmissions.

▲ **USB to MIDI.** A USB port on an instrument can also connect to MIDI ports on a computer sound card.

⭐ **A+ Exam Tip**   The A+ 220-901 exam expects you to know how to install and configure MIDI devices.

To mix and edit music using MIDI on your computer, you'll need MIDI editing software such as JAMMER Pro by SoundTrek (*www.soundtrek.com*). Before connecting the instrument to your computer, install the software that you intend to use to manage the music. Then, connect the instrument.

TOUCH SCREENS

A+
220-901
1.12

A touch screen is an input device that uses a monitor or LCD panel as the backdrop for input options. In other words, the touch screen is a grid that senses taps, finger pinches, and slides and sends these events to the computer by way of a USB port or other type of connection. Some laptops have built-in touch screens, and you can also install a touch screen on top of a monitor screen as an add-on device. As an add-on device, the touch screen has its own AC adapter to power it. Some monitors for desktop systems have built-in touch screen capability.

For add-on desktop monitors, clamp the touch screen over the monitor. For most installations, you install the drivers before you connect the touch screen to the computer by way of a USB port. After you install the drivers and the touch screen, you must use management software that came bundled with the device to decide how much of the monitor screen is taken up by the touch screen and to calibrate the touch screen. Later, if the monitor resolution is changed, the touch screen must be recalibrated.

KVM SWITCHES

A+
220-901
1.12

A KVM (Keyboard, Video, and Mouse) switch allows you to use one keyboard, monitor, and mouse for multiple computers. A KVM switch can be useful in a server room or testing lab where you use more than one computer and want to keep desk space clear of multiple keyboards, mice, and monitors or you simply want to lower the cost of peripherals. Figure 7-23 shows a KVM switch that can connect a keyboard, monitor, mouse, microphone, and speakers to two computers. The device uses USB ports for the keyboard and mouse.

Connectors for computer 1

Connectors for computer 2

Press button to toggle between computers

Connectors for monitor, keyboard, and mouse

Figure 7-23   This KVM switch connects two computers to a keyboard, mouse, monitor, microphone, and speakers and uses USB for the keyboard and mouse

A KVM switch does not require that you install device drivers to use it. Just plug in the cables from each computer to the device. Also plug in one set of a monitor, mouse, keyboard, and possibly a microphone and speakers to the device. Switch between computers by using a hot key on the keyboard, buttons on the top of the KVM switch, or a wired remote such as the one shown in Figure 7-23.

INSTALLING AND CONFIGURING ADAPTER CARDS

In this part of the chapter, you learn to install and configure adapter cards. These cards include a video card, sound card, storage controller card, serial and parallel port card, Thunderbolt card, FireWire card, USB card, storage card, TV tuner card, and video capture card. The purpose of adding an adapter card to a system is to have available the external ports or internal connectors the card provides.

Regardless of the type of card you are installing, when preparing to install an adapter card, be sure to verify and do the following:

▲ *Verify the card fits an empty expansion slot.* Recall that there are several PCI and PCI Express standards; therefore, make sure the card will fit the slot. To help with airflow, try to leave an empty slot between cards. Especially try to leave an empty slot beside the video card, which puts off a lot of heat.

▲ *Verify the device drivers for your OS are available.* Check the card documentation and make sure you have the drivers for your OS. For example, you need to install 64-bit Windows 8 device drivers in a 64-bit installation of Windows 8. It might be possible to download drivers for your OS from the website of the card manufacturer.

▲ *Back up important data that is not already backed up.* Before you open the computer case, be sure to back up important data on the hard drive.

▲ *Know your starting point.* Know what works and doesn't work on the system. Can you connect to the network and the Internet, print, and use other installed adapter cards without errors?

Here are the general directions to install an adapter card. They apply to any type of card.

1. Read the documentation that came with the card. For most cards, you install the card first and then the drivers, but some adapter card installations might not work this way.

2. If you are installing a card to replace an onboard port, access UEFI/BIOS setup and disable the port.

3. Wear an ESD strap as you work to protect the card and the system against ESD. Shut down the system, unplug power cords and cables, and press the power button to drain the power. Remove the computer case cover.

4. Locate the slot you plan to use and remove the faceplate cover from the slot if one is installed. Sometimes a faceplate punches or snaps out, and sometimes you have to remove a faceplate screw to remove the faceplate. Remove the screw in the top of the expansion slot or raise the clip on the top of the slot. Save the screw; you'll need it later.

5. Remove the card from its antistatic bag and insert it into the expansion slot. Be careful to push the card straight down into the slot, without rocking the card from side to side. Rocking it from side to side can widen the expansion slot, making it difficult to keep a good contact. If you have a problem getting the card into the slot, resist the temptation to push the front or rear of the card into the slot first. You should feel a slight snap as the card drops into the slot.

Recall that PCIe x16 slots use a retention mechanism in the slot to help stabilize a heavy card (see Figure 7-24). For these slots, you might have to use one finger to push the stabilizer to the side as you push the card into the slot. Alternately, the card might snap into the slot and then the retention mechanism snaps into position. Figure 7-25 shows a PCIe video card installed in a PCIe x16 slot.

Figure 7-24 A white retention mechanism on a PCIe x16 slot pops into place to help stabilize a heavy video card

Regular PCI slots

Video card

PCI Express x16 slot

PCI Express x1 slots

Figure 7-25 A PCIe video card installed in a PCIe x16 slot

6. Insert the screw that anchors the card to the top of the slot (see Figure 7-26). Be sure to use this screw. If it's not present, the card can creep out of the slot over time.

Figure 7-26 Secure the card to the case with a single screw

7. Connect any power cords or data cables the card might use. For example, a video card might have a 6-pin or 8-pin PCIe power connector for a power cord from the power supply to the card (see Figure 7-27). (If the power supply does not have the right connector, you can buy an inexpensive adapter to convert a 4-pin Molex connector to a PCIe connector.) In another example, look at Figure 7-3 shown earlier in the chapter. This FireWire card requires a power connection using a 4-pin Molex power cable from the power supply.

Figure 7-27   Connect a power cord to the PCIe power connector on the card

8. Make a quick check of all connections and cables, and then replace the case cover. (If you want, you can leave the case cover off until you've tested the card, in case it doesn't work and you need to reseat it.) Plug up the external power cable and essential peripherals.

9. Start the system. When Windows starts, it should detect a new hardware device is present and attempt to automatically install the drivers. As the drivers are installed, a message might appear above the taskbar. When you click the message, the Device Setup window appears (refer back to Figure 7-6). You can cancel the wizard and manually install the drivers.

10. Insert the CD that came bundled with the card and launch the setup program on the CD. The card documentation will tell you the name of the program (examples are Setup.exe and Autorun.exe). Figure 7-28 shows the opening menu for one setup program for a video card. Click **Install Video Drivers** and follow the on screen instructions to install the drivers. If you are using downloaded driver files, double-click the file to begin the installation and follow the directions on screen.

> **Notes**   All 64-bit drivers must be certified by Microsoft to work in Windows. However, some 32-bit drivers might not be. During the driver installation, if you see a message that says 32-bit drivers have not been certified, go ahead and give permission to install the drivers if you obtained them from the manufacturer or another reliable source.

Figure 7-28 Opening menu to install video drivers

Source: EVGA

11. After the drivers are installed, you might be asked to restart the system. Then you can configure the card or use it with application software. If you have problems with the installation, turn to Device Manager and look for errors reported about the device. The card might not be properly seated in the slot.

> **Notes** Some motherboards provide extra ports that can be installed in faceplate openings off the back of the case. For example, Figure 7-29 shows a module that has a game port and two USB ports. To install the module, remove a faceplate and install the module in its place. Then connect the cables from the module to the appropriate connectors on the motherboard.

Figure 7-29 This I/O module provides two USB ports and one game port

Now let's turn our attention to a little information about three types of cards you might be called on to install. As with any adapter card you install, be sure to get familiar with the user guide before you start the installation so that you know the card's hardware and software requirements and what peripheral devices it supports.

SOUND CARDS AND ONBOARD SOUND

A+
220-901
1.4

A sound card (an expansion card with sound ports) or onboard sound (sound ports embedded on a motherboard) can play and record sound, and save it in a file. Figure 7-30 shows a sound card by Creative (*us.creative.com*). This Sound Blaster card uses a PCIe x1 slot and supports up to eight surround sound version 7.1 speakers. The color-coded speaker ports are for these speakers: front left and right, front center, rear left and right, subwoofer, and two additional rear speakers. The two S/PDIF (Sony/Philips Digital InterFace) ports are used to connect to external sound equipment such as a CD or DVD player.

Courtesy of Creative Technology Ltd.

Figure 7-30   Sound Blaster X-Fi Titanium sound card by Creative uses a PCIe x1 slot

✎ Notes If you are using a single speaker or two speakers with a single sound cable, connect the cable to the lime-green sound port on the motherboard, which is usually the middle port.

TV TUNER AND VIDEO CAPTURE CARDS

A+
220-901
1.4

A TV tuner card can turn your computer into a television. A port on the card receives input from a TV cable and lets you view television on your computer monitor. If the TV signal is analog, the TV tuner card can convert it to digital. A video capture card lets you capture this video input and save it to a file on your hard drive. Some cards are a combination TV tuner card and video capture card, making it possible for you to receive television input and save that input to your hard drive (see Figure 7-31). A high-end TV tuner/video capture card might also serve as your video card. Also, some motherboards and laptop computers have onboard TV tuners and TV captures.

Courtesy of AVerMedia Technologies, Inc. USA.

Figure 7-31 The AVerMedia AVerTV PVR 150 Plus TV tuner and video capture card uses a PCIe x1 slot and works alongside a regular video card

When installing a TV tuner or capture card, most likely you will install the drivers, install the card, and then install the application software that comes bundled with the card. You can then configure and manage the card using the applications.

Hands-On | Project 7-1 Install a Device

A+
220-901
1.4

Install a device on a computer. If you are working in a classroom environment, you can simulate an installation by moving a device from one computer to another. Devices that you might consider installing are a video card, webcam, or fingerprint reader.

REPLACING EXPANSION CARDS IN A LAPTOP

A+
220-901
1.4, 3.1

A laptop does not contain the normal PCI Express or PCI slots found in desktop systems. Newer laptops are likely to use the Mini PCI Express slots (also called Mini PCIe slots) that use the PCI Express standards applied to laptops. Mini PCI Express slots use 52 pins on the edge connector. These slots can be used by many kinds of Mini PCIe cards. These cards are often used to enhance communications options for a laptop, including Wi-Fi wireless, cellular WAN, and Bluetooth Mini PCIe cards. Figure 7-32 shows a Mini PCI Express Sierra Wireless mobile broadband Internet card. Older laptops use a Mini PCI slot (see Figure 7-33), which uses PCI standards. Mini PCI cards are about twice the size of Mini PCI Express cards. Figure 7-34 shows a Wi-Fi Mini PCI card by MikroTik.

Source: Sierra Wireless

Figure 7-32 MC8775 PCI Express Mini card by Sierra Wireless used for voice and data transmissions on cellular networks

Figure 7-33 A Mini PCI slot follows PCI standards applied to laptops

Courtesy of MikroTik

Figure 7-34 Wireless IEEE 802.11a/b/g/n Mini PCI card by MikroTik

For many laptops, you can remove a cover on the bottom of the laptop to expose expansion cards so that you can exchange them without an extensive disassemble. For example, to remove the cover on the bottom of one Lenovo laptop, first remove several screws and then lift the laptop cover up and out. Several internal components are exposed, as shown in Figure 7-35.

Figure 7-35   Removing the cover from the bottom of a laptop exposes several internal components

The half-size Mini PCIe wireless Wi-Fi card shown in Figure 7-36 has two antennas. To remove the card, first remove the one screw shown in the photo and disconnect the two black and white antenna wires. Then slide the card forward and out of the slot. You can then install a new card.

Figure 7-36   This half-size Mini PCIe wireless card is anchored in the expansion slot with one screw

Figure 7-37 shows a full-size Mini PCIe card installed in a different laptop. First disconnect the one antenna and remove the one screw at the top of the card, and then pull the card forward and out of the slot.

Wireless antenna

2. Remove screw
1. Disconnect antenna

3. Pull and lift card from slot

Figure 7-37   How to remove a Mini PCI Express card

★ **A+ Exam Tip**   The A+ 220-901 exam expects you to be able to replace a Mini PCIe card in a laptop.

After you have installed a Mini PCIe card that is a Bluetooth, cellular WAN, or other wireless adapter, try to connect the laptop to the wireless network. If you have problems making a connection, verify that Device Manager reports the device is working properly and that Event Viewer has not reported error events about the device.

SUPPORTING THE VIDEO SUBSYSTEM

| A+ |
| 220-901 |
| 1.4, 1.7, |
| 1.10, 1.11 |

The primary output device of a computer is the monitor. The two necessary components for video output are the monitor and the video card (also called the video adapter and graphics adapter) or a video port on the motherboard. In this part of the chapter, you learn about monitors, video cards, the video connectors they use, and how to support the video subsystem.

MONITOR TECHNOLOGIES AND FEATURES

| A+ |
| 220-901 |
| 1.10 |

The most popular type of monitor for laptop and desktop systems is an LCD flat-screen monitor (see Figure 7-38), but you have other choices as well. Here is a list and description of each type of monitor:

▲ *LCD monitor.* The LCD (liquid crystal display) monitor, also called a flat-panel monitor, was first used in laptops. The monitor produces an image using a liquid crystal material made of large, easily polarized molecules. Figure 7-39 shows the layers of the LCD panel that together create the image. At the center of the layers is the liquid crystal material. Next to it is the layer responsible for providing color to the image. These two layers are sandwiched between two grids of electrodes forming columns and rows. Each intersection of a row electrode and a column electrode forms one pixel on the LCD panel. Software can address each pixel to create an image.

Figure 7-38   An LCD monitor

Polarizer Glass Column electrodes
Color layer
Liquid crystal layer
(this layer blocks
or allows light to
pass for each pixel)
Row electrodes
Glass
Polarizer
Image formed
on screen

Backlighting

A pixel is formed by the
intersection of the row and
column electrodes

Figure 7-39 Layers of an LCD panel

Two common classes of LCD monitors are:

▲ Twisted Nematic (TN) LCD monitors are preferred by gamers because they have fast response times to keep fast-moving images crisp. However, TN monitors are brighter, consume more power, and have limited viewing angles.

▲ In-Plane Switching (IPS) monitors are a newer technology that offers truer color images and better viewing angles. However, IPS monitors are expensive and have slower response times.

The LCD panel does not produce any light so it needs a source of light, called backlighting. There are two common types of backlighting:

▲ Cold Cathode Fluorescent Lamp (CCFL) backlighting, also called fluorescent backlighting, is an older technology first used in laptop monitors. It uses one or two fluorescent tubes to light the panel. An inverter circuit board provides power to the fluorescent light. Two fluorescent tubes (CCFL-2) requires two inverter boards.

▲ LED (light-emitting diode) backlighting receives its DC power directly from the motherboard and doesn't use an inverter. The growing trend for most monitor manufacturers is to use LED backlighting, which provides a better range and accuracy of color and uses less power than fluorescent backlighting. LED technology also uses less mercury, and is, therefore, kinder to the environment when an LCD monitor is disposed of. When you see a monitor advertised as an LED monitor, know the monitor is an LCD monitor that uses LED backlighting.

▲ *Plasma monitor.* A plasma monitor provides high contrast with better color than LCD monitors. They work by discharging xenon and neon plasma on flat glass and don't contain mercury. Plasma monitors are expensive and heavy and are generally available only in large commercial sizes.

▲ *Projector.* A digital projector (see Figure 7-40) is used to shine a light that projects a transparent image onto a large screen and is often used in classrooms or with other large groups. Several types of technologies are used by projectors, including LCD. A projector is often installed on a computer as a dual monitor, which you learn how to do later in the chapter.

Figure 7-40   Portable XGA projector by Panasonic

◢ *OLED monitor.* An OLED (organic light-emitting diode) monitor uses a thin LED layer or film between two grids of electrodes and does not use backlighting. It does not emit as much light as an LCD monitor does, and, therefore, can produce deeper blacks, provide better contrast, work in darker rooms, and use less power than can an LCD monitor. On the other hand, LED monitors give less glare than OLED monitors. OLED screens are used by digital cameras, camcorders, mobile devices, and other small portable electronic devices. OLED monitors are just now appearing for desktop systems.

> ★ **A+ Exam Tip**   The A+ 220-901 exam expects you to know about these monitor types and technologies: LCD, LED, plasma, projector, and OLED.

A laptop display almost always uses LCD technology, although laptops that use OLED display are available. It is expected that laptops will one day use plasma display because plasma is expected to use only about 20 percent as much power as LCD and gives better quality display than LCD. Some laptop LCD panels use LED backlighting to improve display quality and conserve power.

> ★ **A+ Exam Tip**   The A+ 220-901 exam expects you to know about the components within the display of a laptop, including LCD, LED, OLED, and plasma types. You also need to know about backlighting and the function of an inverter.

For desktops, by far the most popular monitor type is LCD. Figure 7-41 shows an ad for one high-end LCD monitor. Table 7-3 explains the features mentioned in the ad.

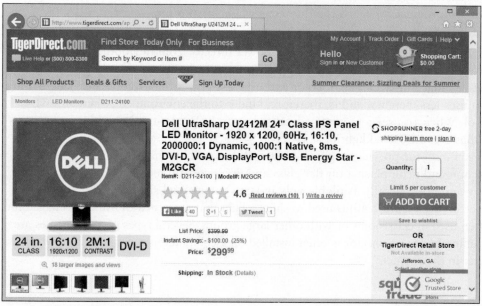

Figure 7-41   An ad for a monitor lists cryptic monitor features

⭐ **A+ Exam Tip** The A+ 220-901 exam expects you to know about these monitor features: refresh rate, resolution, native resolution, brightness in lumens, and analog and digital connectors used.

7

Monitor Characteristic	Description
Screen size	The screen size is the diagonal length of the screen surface in inches.
Aspect ratio	The aspect ratio is the proportional relationship between width and height. Common aspect ratios are 4:3, 16:9, and 16:10. Sometimes, an image must be converted from one aspect ratio to another. Three ways to convert a standard 4:3 image to a wide screen 16:9 is to add black bars to either side of the image to fill in the space; stretch the image horizontally, which creates distortion; or zoom without distorting the image until the image touches the sides, which will crop the top and bottom of the image.
Refresh rate	The refresh rate is the number of times a monitor screen is built or refreshed in one second, measured in Hz (cycles per second). The ad in Figure 7-41 shows the monitor refresh rate as 60 Hz (60 frames per second)—the higher, the better. Related to refresh rate, the response time is the time it takes to build one frame, measured in ms (milliseconds)—the lower, the better. The ad in Figure 7-41 shows a response time of 8 ms (time to build one frame).
Pixel pitch	A pixel is a spot or dot on the screen that can be addressed by software. The pixel pitch is the distance between adjacent pixels on the screen—the smaller the number, the better. An example of a pixel pitch is .283mm.
Resolution	The resolution is the number of spots or pixels on a screen that can be addressed by software. Values can range from 640 × 480 up to 4096 × 2160 for high-end monitors. Popular resolutions are 1920 × 1080 and 1366 × 768.
Native resolution	The native resolution is the number of pixels built into the LCD monitor. Using the native resolution usually gives the highest-quality image.
Contrast ratio	Contrast ratio is the contrast between true black and true white on the screen—the higher the contrast ratio, the better. 1000:1 is better than 700:1. An advertised dynamic contrast ratio is much higher than the contrast ratio, but is not a true measurement of contrast. Dynamic contrast adjusts the backlighting to give the effect of an overall brighter or darker image. For example, in Figure 7-41, the contrast ratio is 1000:1, and the dynamic ratio is 20,000,000:1. When comparing quality of monitors, pay attention to the contrast ratio, more so than the dynamic ratio.
Viewing angle	The viewing angle is the angle of view when a monitor becomes difficult to see. A viewing angle of 170 degrees is better than 140 degrees.
Backlighting or brightness	Brightness is measured in cd/m² (candela per square meter), which is the same as lumens/m² (lumens per square meter). In addition, the best LED backlighting for viewing photography is class IPS, which provides the most accurate color.
Connectors	Options for connectors are VGA, DVI-I, DVI-D, HDMI, DisplayPort, and Apple's Thunderbolt. Some monitors offer more than one connector (see Figure 7-42). These and other connectors used by video cards and monitors are discussed later in the chapter.
Other features	LCD monitors can also provide a privacy or antiglare surface, tilt screens, microphone input, speakers, USB ports, adjustable stands, and perhaps even a port for your iPod. Some monitors are also touch screens, so they can be used with a stylus or finger touch.

Table 7-3 Important features of a monitor

⚡ **Caution** If you spend many hours in front of a computer, you may strain your eyes. To protect your eyes from strain, look away from the monitor into the distance every few minutes. Use a good monitor with a high refresh rate or low response time. The lower refresh rates that cause monitor flicker can tire and damage your eyes. When you first install a monitor, set the refresh rate at the highest value the monitor can support.

Power port

Sound ports

Analog VGA connector

DVI-D connector

Figure 7-42   The rear of this LCD monitor shows digital and analog video ports to accommodate a video cable with either a 15-pin analog VGA connector or a digital DVI connector

VIDEO CARDS AND CONNECTORS

A+
220-901
1.4, 1.7,
1.10, 1.11

Video cards (see Figure 7-43) are sometimes called graphics adapters, graphics cards, or display cards. Most motherboards sold today have one or more video ports integrated into the motherboard. If you are buying a motherboard with a video port, make sure that you can disable the video port on the motherboard if it gives you trouble. You can then install a video card and use its video port rather than the port on the motherboard. Recall that a video card can use a PCI or PCI Express slot on the motherboard. The fastest slot to use is a PCIe x16 slot.

Cooling fan

Heat sink

Tab used to stabilize the card

PCI Express x16 connector

15-pin analog video port

S-Video connector

DVI-I video port

Figure 7-43   The PCX 5750 graphics card by MSI Computer Corporation uses the PCI Express x16 local bus

Recall that types of video ports include VGA, S-Video, DVI, DisplayPort, and HDMI connectors. In addition to these ports, you also need to know about a composite video, miniHDMI, Mini-DIN-6, DVI-I, DVI-D, and DVI-A ports. All these ports are described here:

▲ **VGA.** The 15-pin VGA port is the standard analog video port and transmits three signals of red, green, and blue (RGB). A VGA port is sometimes called a DB-15 port.

▲ **DVI ports.** DVI ports were designed to replace VGA, and variations of DVI can transmit analog and/ or digital data. The five DVI standards for pinouts are shown in Figure 7-44. Three DVI connectors are shown in Figure 7-45. The DVI standards specify the maximum length for DVI cables is 5 meters, although some video cards produce a strong enough signal to allow for longer DVI cables.

DVI-D (Digital Only)	DVI-I (Digital or Analog)	DVI-A (Analog Only)
DVI-D Single Link	DVI-I Single Link	DVI-A
DVI-D Dual Link	DVI-I Dual Link	

Figure 7-44   Five pinout arrangements for DVI ports and connectors

Figure 7-45   Three types of DVI connectors: (left) DVI-I, (middle) DVI-D, and (right) DVI-A

Here are the variations of DVI:

▲ **DVI-D.** The DVI-D port only transmits digital data. Using an adapter to convert a VGA cable to the port won't work. You can see a DVI-D port in Figure 7-46a.

(a)   (b)

Figure 7-46   Two types of DVI ports: (a) DVI-D, (b) DVI-I

▲ *DVI-I.* The DVI-I port (see Figure 7-46b) supports both analog and digital signals. If a computer has this type of port, you can use a digital-to-analog adapter to connect an older analog monitor to the port using a VGA cable (see Figure 7-47). If a video card has a DVI port, most likely it will be the DVI-I port (the one with the four extra holes) so that you can use an adapter to convert the port to a VGA port.

▲ *DVI-A.* The DVI-A port only transmits analog data. You don't see these very often.

Figure 7-47   Digital-to-analog video port converter using DVI-I connector with extra four pins

▲ *Composite video.* Using a composite video port, also called an RGB port, the red, green, and blue (RGB) are mixed together in the same signal. This is the method used by television and can be used by a video card that is designed to send output to a TV. Composite video uses a round RCA connector that is usually yellow and has a single pin in the center. Figure 7-48 shows a laptop that has a composite video input port so that you can use the laptop as your display for a game box. Composite video does not produce as sharp an image as VGA video or S-Video.

Figure 7-48   This laptop designed for multimedia applications has an embedded TV tuner and can also receive audio and video input from game boxes

▲ *S-Video (Super-Video) ports.* An S-Video port is a 4-pin or 7-pin round port used by some televisions and video equipment. An S-Video cable is shown in Figure 7-49. A few older video cameras use a 6-pin variation of S-Video. The connector is called a Mini-DIN -6 connector and looks like a PS/2 connector used by a keyboard or mouse. (In general, a DIN connector is always round with multiple pins in the connector.)

Figure 7-49 An S-Video cable used to connect a video card to an S-Video port on a television

▲ *Component video.* Whereas composite video has the red, green, and blue mixed in the same signal, component video has been split into different components and carried as separate signals. Figure 7-50 shows five RCA connectors on one component video and audio cable. Three lines carry video (red, blue, and green), and the red and white lines are used for audio (audio in and audio out).

Red, green, blue video connectors

Red and white audio connectors

Figure 7-50 Component video and audio cable uses five RCA connectors

▲ *DisplayPort.* DisplayPort was designed to replace DVI and can transmit digital (not analog) video and audio data. It uses data packet transmissions similar to those of Ethernet, USB, and PCI Express, and is expected to ultimately replace VGA, DVI, and HDMI on desktop and laptop computers. Besides the regular DisplayPort used on video cards and desktop computers, laptops might use the smaller Mini DisplayPort. Figure 7-51 shows a DisplayPort to Mini DisplayPort cable. Some DisplayPort controllers allow you to use a DisplayPort-to-HDMI adapter so the port can be used with an HDMI connection. Maximum length for DisplayPort cables is 15 meters.

Figure 7-51   DisplayPort to Mini DisplayPort cable

UEFI/BIOS setup can be used to manage onboard DisplayPort and HDMI ports. For example, look at Figure 7-5 shown earlier in the chapter, where you can enable or disable the audio transmissions of DisplayPort and HDMI ports and still use these ports for video.

◢ *HDMI and HDMI mini connectors.* HDMI transmits both digital video and audio (not analog), and was designed to be used by home theater equipment. The HDMI standards allow for several types of HDMI connectors. The best known, which is used on most computers and televisions, is the Type A 19-pin HDMI connector. Small mobile devices can use the smaller Type C 19-pin HDMI mini connector, also called the mini-HDMI connector. Figure 7-52 shows a cable with both connectors that is useful when connecting some devices like a smart phone to a computer. Figure 7-53 shows an HDMI to DVI-D cable. Because HDMI does not transmit analog data, the connector works only on DVI-D and DVI-I ports, not DVI-A ports. To connect HDMI to VGA, you need an HDMI to VGA adapter with signal conversion because VGA is analog and HDMI is digital. The maximum length of an HDMI cable depends on the quality of the cable; no maximum length has been specified.

Figure 7-52   HDMI to miniHDMI cable

Courtesy of Belkin Corporation

Figure 7-53   An HDMI to DVI cable can be used to connect a computer that has a DVI port to home theater equipment that uses an HDMI port

Digital Rights Management (DRM) is meant to protect digital content and prevent piracy. DRM involves both software and hardware. HDMI and DVI allow for protected content to stay encrypted until it is on the presentation device. If you end up with a blank screen when playing a movie or no sound when listening to a CD, the problem may be that DRM is blocking the signal to prevent it from being pirated. In addition to protecting content from being pirated, DRM also limits quality of content based on its authorization. For example, a high-definition movie must be limited to DVD quality on video outputs that are not approved by DRM.

⭐ **A+ Exam Tip** The A+ 220-901 exam expects you to know about these video connector types: VGA (DB-15), HDMI, Mini HDMI, DisplayPort, S-Video, Mini-DIN-6, composite (RGB), component, RCA, DVI-D, DVI-I, and DVI-A.

Hands-On | Project 7-2 Research Video Port Adapters

Research the web and find devices that can be used as solutions to these problems. Print or save the webpage showing the device and price:

1. Find an adapter that allows you to connect a Thunderbolt port on a computer to a DVI monitor using a DVI cable.

2. Find an adapter that allows you to connect a Mini DisplayPort on your laptop to a DVI-D port on your monitor. Also find a cable that will work with the adapter.

3. Find an adapter that will allow you to connect a DVI-I port on your desktop to a VGA monitor, using a VGA cable.

7

Now let's see how to configure a monitor or dual monitors connected to a Windows computer.

CHANGING MONITOR SETTINGS

A+
220-901
1.4, 1.7,
1.10, 1.11

Settings that apply to the monitor can be managed by using the monitor buttons and Windows utilities. Using the monitor buttons, you can adjust the horizontal and vertical position of the screen on the monitor surface and change the brightness and contrast settings. For laptops, the brightness and contrast settings can be changed using function keys on the laptop.

APPLYING | CONCEPTS INSTALL DUAL MONITORS

A+
220-901
1.10

To increase the size of your Windows desktop, you can install more than one monitor for a single computer. To install dual monitors, you need two video ports on your system, which can come from motherboard video ports, a video card that provides two video ports, or two video cards.
To install a second monitor in a dual-monitor setup using two video cards, follow these steps:

1. Verify the original video card works properly and decide whether it is to be the primary monitor.

2. Boot the computer and enter UEFI/BIOS setup. If UEFI/BIOS setup has the option to select the order in which video cards are initialized, verify the currently installed card is configured to initialize first. For example, for the UEFI/BIOS system in Figure 7-54, the video adapter in the PCIe slot initializes first before other video adapters. If it does not initialize first, then, when you install the second card, video might not work at all when you first boot with two cards.

(continues)

Figure 7-54   In UEFI/BIOS setup, verify the currently installed video adapter is set to initialize first

3. Install a second video card in an empty slot. A computer might have a second PCIe slot or an unused PCI slot you can use. Attach the second monitor.

4. Boot the system. Windows recognizes the new hardware and launches Device Setup. You can use the utility to install the video card drivers or cancel the utility and install them manually as you learned to do earlier in the chapter.

Here are the steps to configure dual monitors:

1. Connect two monitors to your system. Open **Control Panel** in Classic view, click **Display**, and then click **Adjust resolution**. The Screen Resolution window appears (see Figure 7-55).

Figure 7-55   Configure each monitor in a dual-monitor configuration

2. Notice the two numbered boxes that represent your two monitors. When you click one of these boxes, the drop-down menu changes to show the selected monitor, and the screen resolution and orientation (Landscape, Portrait, Landscape flipped, or Portrait flipped) follow the selected monitor. This lets you customize the settings for each monitor. If necessary, use drag-and-drop to arrange the boxes so that they represent the physical arrangement of your monitors.

Notes In Figure 7-55, if you arrange the two boxes side by side, your extended desktop will extend left or right. If you arrange the two boxes one on top of the other, your extended desktop will extend up and down.

3. Adjust the screen resolution according to your preferences. For the sharpest images, use the native resolution for each monitor. Most often, the native resolution is the highest resolution listed, but this is not always the case. To know for certain the native resolution, see the documentation that came with the monitor.

4. The Screen Resolution window (refer back to Figure 7-55) allows you to select how to handle multiple displays. You can extend your desktop onto the second monitor, duplicate displays, or disable display on either monitor. To save the settings, click **Apply**. The second monitor should initialize and show the extended or duplicated desktop.

5. Close the **Screen Resolution** window. For an extended desktop, open an application and verify you can use the second monitor by dragging the application window over to the second monitor's desktop.

After you add a second monitor to your system, you can move from one monitor to another simply by moving your mouse over the extended desktop. Switching from one monitor to the other does not require any special keystroke or menu option.

Most laptop computers are designed to be used with projectors and provide a VGA, DisplayPort, or HDMI port for this purpose. To use a projector, plug in the projector to the extra port and then turn it on. For a laptop computer, use a function key to activate the video port and toggle between extending the desktop to the projector, using only the projector, duplicating the screen on the projector, or not using the projector. When giving a presentation, most presenters prefer that they see their presentation duplicated on the LCD screen and the projector.

Notes For group presentations that require a projector, the software used for the presentations is likely to be Microsoft PowerPoint. If you configure your projector as a dual monitor, you can use PowerPoint to display a presentation to your audience on the projector at the same time you are using your LCD display to manage your PowerPoint slides. To do so, for PowerPoint, select the **SLIDE SHOW** tab. In the Set Up group, click **Set Up Slide Show**. In the Set Up Show box under Multiple monitors, check **Show Presenter View** or **Use Presenter View** and click **OK**.

VIDEO MEMORY AND WINDOWS

A+
220-901
1.4, 1.7,
1.10, 1.11

Video cards have their own processor called a graphics processing unit (GPU) or visual processing unit (VPU). These processors use graphics RAM installed on the card so that RAM on the motherboard is not tied up with video data. (If a motherboard offers a video port rather than using a video card, the GPU is part of the onboard video controller and is called integrated video. For integrated video, RAM on the motherboard is used for video data, or some video RAM is embedded on the motherboard.)

The more RAM installed on the card, the better the performance. Most video cards used and sold today use DDR2, DDR3, Graphics DDR3 (GDDR3), GDDR4, or GDDR5 memory. Graphics DDR memory is faster than regular DDR memory and does a better job of storing 3D images. Some video cards have as much as 2 GB of graphics memory.

Most Windows 7/Vista editions offer the Aero user interface (also called Aero glass), which has a 3D appearance. Windows 8 removed Aero glass, but kept a few of the same features. The hardware must qualify for Aero glass before Windows can enable it. These requirements include onboard video or a video card that supports DirectX 9 or higher, has at least 128 MB of video memory, and uses the Windows Display Driver Model (WDDM). The Windows Display Driver Model is a Windows component that manages graphics. DirectX is a Microsoft software development tool that software developers can use to write multimedia applications such as games, video-editing software, and computer-aided design software. Components of DirectX include DirectDraw, DirectMusic, DirectPlay, and Direct3D. The video firmware on the video card or motherboard chipset can interpret DirectX commands to build 3D images as presented to them by the WDDM. In addition, Windows relies on DirectX and the WDDM to produce the Aero user interface.

If an application, such as a game or desktop publishing app, that relies heavily on graphics is not performing well or giving errors, the problem might be video memory or the version of DirectX the system is using. You can use the dxdiag.exe command to display information about hardware and diagnose problems with DirectX. To use the command in Windows 8, press **Win+X** and click **Run**. Then type **dxdiag.exe** in the Run box and press **Enter**. For Windows 7, click **Start**, type **dxdiag.exe** in the Search box, and press **Enter**. Respond to a message box that appears asking if you want to check if your drivers are digitally signed. Then the opening window shown in Figure 7-56 appears. Look for the version of DirectX installed (version 11 in the figure).

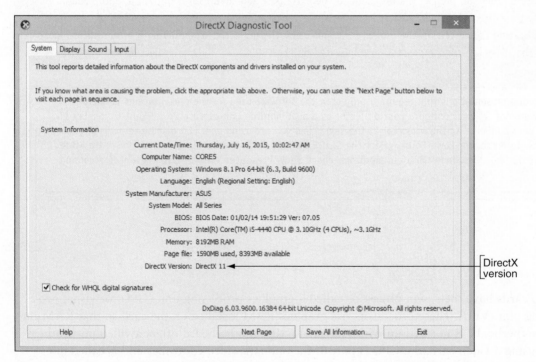

Figure 7-56   The DirectX Diagnostic tool reports information about DirectX components

To find out the latest version of DirectX published by Microsoft, go to *www.microsoft.com* and search on "DirectX End-User Runtime Web Installer." The download page similar to Figure 7-57 appears. If you want to install a new version of DirectX, click **Download** and follow the directions on screen.

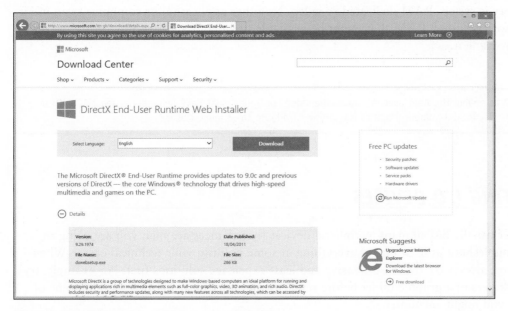

Figure 7-57   Download the latest version of DirectX

Video memory available to the graphics processor can be the graphics memory embedded on the video card or on the motherboard, system memory, or a combination of both. To see the video memory available to Windows, use Control Panel to open the **Screen Resolution** window (refer back to Figure 7-55). Click **Advanced settings.** The video properties box appears. Figure 7-58 shows two properties boxes for two systems. Figure 7-58a is for a laptop computer, and Figure 7-58b is for a desktop computer.

Figure 7-58   Memory allocated to video under Windows 8 (a) for a laptop computer, and (b) for a desktop computer

Here is an explanation of the four entries in the dialog box that concern video memory:

- ◢ Total Available Graphics Memory is total memory that may be available to the video subsystem.
- ◢ Dedicated Video Memory is found on a video card or embedded on the motherboard. The motherboard in both the laptop and desktop have 32 MB of graphics memory.
- ◢ System Video Memory is system RAM dedicated to video. No other application or component can use it.
- ◢ Shared System Memory is system RAM that might be available to video if another application or component is not already using it.

> ✎ **Notes** For Windows 7 to enable the Aero user interface, the video controller must have available at least 128 MB of video memory. In other words, Total Available Graphics Memory must add up to at least 128 MB.

TROUBLESHOOTING I/O DEVICES

| A+ 220-901 3.1, 3.2, 4.3, 4.5 | A computer usually has so many peripheral devices that chances are high you are going to have to troubleshoot at least one of everything at some point in your technical career. When this happens, always try the least invasive and least expensive solutions first. For example, try updating drivers of a graphic tablet before replacing it. So let's learn how to handle some of |

the errors or problems you might encounter.

NUMLOCK INDICATOR LIGHT

| A+ 220-901 4.3, 4.5 | If a user complains she cannot sign in to Windows even when she's certain she is entering the correct password, ask her to make sure the NumLock key is set correctly. Laptops use this key to toggle between the keys interpreted as letters and numbers. Most laptops have a NumLock indicator light near the keyboard. |

DEVICE MANAGER

| A+ 220-901 4.3, 4.5 | Device Manager is usually a good place to start troubleshooting. A Device Manager window is shown on the left side of Figure 7-59. Click a white arrow to expand the view of an item, and click a black arrow to collapse the view. Notice the yellow triangle beside the SM Bus Controller, which indicates a problem with this motherboard component. To see a device's |

properties box, right-click the device and click **Properties**.

Figure 7-59 Use Device Manager to solve problems with hardware devices

First try updating the drivers. (Click **Update Driver** on the General tab or the Driver tab.) If a driver update creates a problem, you can roll back (undo) the driver update if the previous drivers were working. (Windows does not save drivers that were not working before the driver update.) If you are still having a problem with a device, try uninstalling it and installing it again. (To uninstall the device, click **Uninstall** on the Driver tab.) Then reboot and reinstall the device, looking for problems during the installation that point to the source of the problem. Sometimes reinstalling a device is all that is needed to solve the problem.

If Windows is not able to locate new drivers for a device, locate and download the latest driver files from the manufacturer's website to your hard drive. Be sure to use 64-bit drivers for a 64-bit OS and 32-bit drivers for a 32-bit OS. If possible, use Windows 8 drivers for Windows 8, Windows 7 drivers for Windows 7, and Vista drivers for Vista. You can double-click the downloaded driver files to launch the installation.

UPDATING PORT OR SLOT DRIVERS ON A LAPTOP

If you ever have a problem with a port or slot on a laptop, first turn to Device Manager to see if errors are reported and to update the drivers for the port or slot. The laptop manufacturer has probably stored backups of the drivers on the hard drive under support tools and on the recovery media if the recovery media is available. You can also download the latest drivers from the manufacturer's website. If the problem is still not solved after updating the drivers, try using Device Manager to uninstall the port or slot drivers and then use the support tools to reinstall the drivers.

Hands-On | Project 7-3 Update Device Drivers

A+
220-901
4.5

Using your home or lab computer connected to the Internet, go to Device Manager and attempt to update the drivers on all your installed devices. Which devices did Windows find newer drivers for?

TROUBLESHOOTING MONITORS AND VIDEO

For monitor and video problems, as with other devices, try doing the easy things first. For instance, try to make simple hardware and software adjustments. Many monitor problems are caused by poor cable connections or bad contrast/brightness adjustments. Typical monitor and video problems and how to troubleshoot them are described next, and then you learn how to troubleshoot video problems on laptop computers.

> ✎ **Notes**   A user very much appreciates a support technician who takes a little extra time to clean a system being serviced. When servicing a monitor, take the time to clean the screen with a soft dry cloth or monitor wipe.

PROBLEMS WITH VIDEO CARD INSTALLATIONS

When you install a video card, here is a list of things that can go wrong and what to do about them:

◢ *When you first power up the system, you hear a whining sound.* This is caused by the card not getting enough power. Make sure a 6-pin or 8-pin power cord is connected to the card if it has this connector. The power supply might be inadequate.

◢ *When you first start up the system, you see nothing but a black screen.* Most likely this is caused by the onboard video port not being disabled in UEFI/BIOS setup. Disable the port.

◢ *When you first start up the system, you hear a series of beeps.* UEFI/BIOS cannot detect a video card. Make sure the card is securely seated. The video slot or video card might be bad.

◢ *Error messages about video appear when Windows starts.* This can be caused by a conflict in onboard video and the video card. Try disabling onboard video in Device Manager.

◢ *Games crash or lock up.* Try updating drivers for the motherboard, the video card, and the sound card. Also install the latest version of DirectX. (You learn about DirectX later in the chapter.) Then try uninstalling the game and installing it again. Then download all patches for the game.

MONITOR INDICATOR LIGHT IS NOT ON; NO IMAGE ON SCREEN

If you hear one or no beep during the boot and you see a blank screen, then UEFI/BIOS has successfully completed POST, which includes a test of the video card or onboard video. You can then assume the problem must be with the monitor or the monitor cable. Ask these questions and try these things:

1. Is the monitor power cable plugged in?

2. Is the monitor turned on? Try pushing the power button on the front of the monitor. An indicator light on the front of the monitor should turn on, indicating the monitor has power.

3. Is the monitor cable plugged into the video port at the back of the computer and the connector on the rear of the monitor?

4. Try a different monitor and a different monitor cable that you know are working.

> ✎ **Notes**   When you turn on your computer, the first thing you see on the screen is the firmware on the video card identifying itself. You can use this information to search the web, especially the manufacturer's website, for troubleshooting information about the card.

MONITOR INDICATOR LIGHT IS ON; NO IMAGE ON SCREEN

For this problem, try the following:

1. Make sure the video cable is securely connected at the computer and the monitor. Most likely the problem is a bad cable connection.

2. If the monitor displays POST but goes blank when Windows starts to load, the problem is Windows and not the monitor or video. Boot from the Windows setup DVD and perform a Startup Repair, which you learned to do in the chapter, "Supporting the Power System and Troubleshooting Computers." If this works, change the driver and resolution.

3. The monitor might have a switch on the back for choosing between 110 volts and 220 volts. Check that the switch is in the correct position.

4. The problem might be with the video card. If you have just installed the card and the motherboard has onboard video, go into BIOS setup and disable the video port on the motherboard.

5. Verify the video cable is connected to the video port on the video card and not to a disabled onboard video port.

6. Using buttons on the front of the monitor, check the contrast adjustment. If there's no change, leave it at a middle setting.

7. Check the brightness or backlight adjustment. If there's no change, leave it at a middle setting.

8. If the monitor-to-computer cable detaches from the monitor, exchange it for a cable you know is good, or check the cable for continuity. If this solves the problem, reattach the old cable to verify that the problem was not simply a bad connection.

9. Test a monitor you know is good on the computer you suspect to be bad. If you think the monitor is bad, make sure that it also fails to work on a good computer.

10. Open the computer case and reseat the video card. If possible, move the card to a different expansion slot. Clean the card's edge connectors, using a contact cleaner purchased from a computer supply store.

11. If there are socketed chips on the video card, remove the card from the expansion slot and then use a screwdriver to press down firmly on each corner of each socketed chip on the card. Chips sometimes loosen because of temperature changes; this condition is called chip creep.

12. Trade a good video card for the video card you suspect is bad. Test the video card you think is bad on a computer that works. Test a video card you know is good on the computer that you suspect is bad. Whenever possible, do both.

13. Test the RAM on the motherboard with memory diagnostic software.

14. For a motherboard that is using a PCI-Express video card, try using a PCI video card in a PCI slot or a PCIe ×1 video card in a PCIe ×1 slot. A good repair technician keeps an extra PCI video card around for this purpose.

15. Trade the motherboard for one you know is good. Sometimes, though rarely, a peripheral chip on the motherboard can cause the problem.

SCREEN GOES BLANK 30 SECONDS OR ONE MINUTE AFTER THE KEYBOARD IS LEFT UNTOUCHED

A Green motherboard (one that follows energy-saving standards) used with an Energy Saver monitor can be configured to go into standby or sleep mode after a period of inactivity. Using this feature can also help prevent burn-in. Burn-in is when a static image stays on a monitor for many hours leaving a permanent impression of that image on the monitor. An alternate method to avoid burn-in is to use a screen saver that has a moving image or a rotation of varying images. To wake up the computer, press any key on the keyboard or press the power button. Use the Power Options applet in Control Panel to configure the sleep settings on a computer.

> ✎ **Notes** Problems might occur if the motherboard power-saving features are turning off the monitor, and Windows screen saver is also turning off the monitor. If the system hangs when you try to get the monitor going again, try disabling one or the other. If this doesn't work, disable both.

POOR DISPLAY

In general, you can solve problems with poor display by using controls on the monitor and using Windows settings. Do the following:

▲ *LCD monitor controls.* Use buttons on the front of an LCD monitor to adjust color, brightness, contrast, focus, and horizontal and vertical positions.

▲ *Windows display settings.* Use Windows settings to adjust font size, screen resolution, brightness, color, and Clear Type text. Open Control Panel in Classic view and click **Display**. Use these settings to adjust the display:

    ▲ To make sure Clear Type text is selected, click **Adjust ClearType text** and turn on ClearType (see Figure 7-60). Then follow the steps in the wizard to improve the quality of text displayed on the screen.

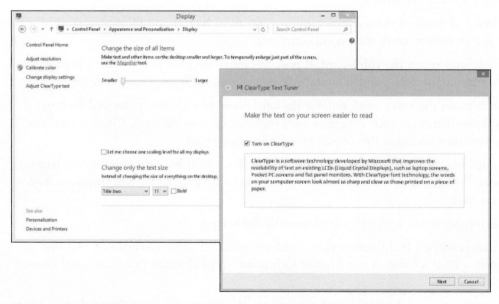

Figure 7-60 ClearType in Windows improves the display of text on the screen

    ▲ LCD monitors will not experience distorted geometry if the resolution is set to the native resolution. So if monitor shows distorted geometry where images are stretched inappropriately, adjust the resolution. Also a low resolution can cause oversized images or icons. To adjust screen resolution, click **Change display settings** in the Display window.

> ✎ **Notes** If adjusting the resolution doesn't correct oversized images or icons, try updating the video drivers.

◢ To calibrate colors, click **Calibrate color** in the Display window and follow the directions on screen. As you do so, color patterns appear (see Figure 7-61). Use these screens to adjust the gamma settings, which define the relationships among red, green, and blue as well as other settings that affect the display.

Figure 7-61 Two screens in the Windows 8 color calibration wizard

◢ *Update the video drivers.* The latest video drivers can solve various problems with the video subsystem, including poor display.

Here are a few other display problems and their solutions:

◢ *Dead pixels.* An LCD monitor might have pixels that are not working called dead pixels, which can appear as small white, black, or colored spots on your screen. A black or white pixel is likely to be a broken transistor, which cannot be fixed. Having a few dead pixels on an LCD monitor screen is considered acceptable and usually not covered under the manufacturer's warranty.

> ✎ **Notes** A pixel might not be a dead pixel (a hardware problem), but only a stuck pixel (a software problem). You might be able to use software to fix stuck pixels. For example, run the online software at *www.flexcode.org/lcd2.html* to fix stuck pixels. The software works by rapidly changing all the pixels on the screen. (Be aware the screen flashes rapidly during the fix.)

◢ *Dim image.* A laptop computer dims the LCD screen when the computer is running on battery to conserve the charge. You can brighten the screen using the Windows display settings. To do so, open **Control Panel** in Classic view, click **Display**, and then click **Adjust brightness** (see Figure 7-62). To check if settings to conserve power are affecting screen brightness, note the power plan that is selected. Click **Change plan settings** for this power plan. On the next screen, you can adjust when or if the screen will dim (see Figure 7-63). If the problem is still not resolved, it might be a hardware problem. How to troubleshoot hardware in laptops is covered later in this chapter.

7

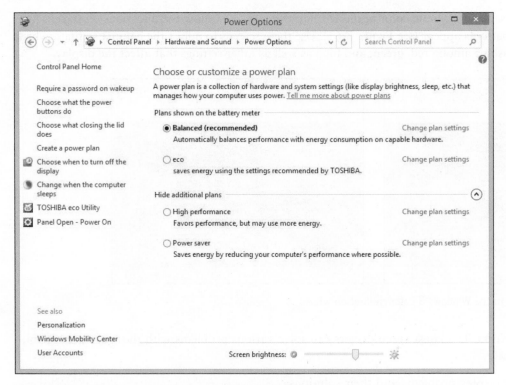

Figure 7-62   Adjust screen brightness at the bottom of this screen

Figure 7-63   Change power plan options to affect how or if the screen dims

A dim image in a desktop monitor might be caused by a faulty video card or a faulty monitor. To find out which is the problem, connect a different monitor. If the monitor is the problem, most likely the backlighting in the LCD monitor is faulty and the monitor needs replacing.

▲ *Artifacts.* Horizontally torn images on screen are called artifacts (see Figure 7-64), and happen when the video feed from the video controller gets out of sync with the refresh of the monitor screen. The problem can be caused by hardware or software. A common cause is when the GPU on the video card overheats. You can test that possibility by downloading and running freeware to monitor the temperature of the CPU and the GPU while you're playing a video game. If you notice the problem occurs when the GPU

Figure 7-64 A simulation of horizontal tears on an image called artifacts

TechPowerUp GPU-Z 0.8.4

| Graphics Card | Sensors | Validation | PowerColor Giveaway |

GPU Core Clock	600.0 MHz
GPU Memory Clock	666.7 MHz
GPU Temperature	34.0 °C
GPU Power	0.1 W
GPU Load	2 %
Memory Usage (Dedicated)	16 MB
Memory Usage (Dynamic)	52 MB

☐ Log to file   Sensor refresh rate: 1.0 sec
☑ Continue refreshing this screen while GPU-Z is in the background

Intel(R) HD Graphics 4600   Close

Source: GPU-Z by TechPowerUp

Figure 7-65 GPU-Z monitors the GPU temperature

temp is high, install extra fans around the video card to keep it cool. Two freeware programs to monitor temperatures are CPU-Z by CPUID (*www.cpuid.com/softwares/cpu-z.html*) and GPU-Z by TechPowerUp (*www.techpowerup.com/gpuz*). See Figure 7-65.

Notes In this text, we've given several options for various freeware utilities. It's a good idea to know about your options for several reasons. Each freeware utility has different options; owners of freeware might not update their utility in a timely manner, and websites might decide to include adware with their downloads.

Try updating the video drivers. However, if you see artifacts on the screen before Windows loads, then you know the problem is not caused by the drivers. The problem might be caused by the monitor. Try using a different monitor to see if the problem goes away. If so, replace the monitor.

Overclocking can cause artifacts. Other causes of artifacts are the motherboard or video card going bad, which can happen if the system has been overheating or video RAM on the card is faulty. Try replacing the video card. The power supply also might be the problem.

In general, to improve video quality, upgrade the video card and/or monitor. Poor display might be caused by inadequate video RAM. Your video card might allow you to install additional video RAM. See the card's documentation.

APPLYING | CONCEPTS CORRECT WINDOWS DISPLAY SETTINGS WHEN THE SCREEN IS UNREADABLE

A+ 220-901 4.3, 4.5

When the display settings don't work, you can easily return to standard VGA settings called VGA mode, which includes a resolution of 640 × 480 or 800 × 600 for some systems.

To use VGA mode when Windows 8 is able to boot and you can use at least one monitor, do the following:

1. Press **Win+X** and click **Run**. In the Run box, type **msconfig.exe** and press **Enter**. The System Configuration box appears. Click the **Boot** tab (see Figure 7-66).

(continues)

2. On the Boot tab, check **Base video** and click **OK**. In the box that appears, click **Restart**. The system will restart in VGA mode. You can now adjust display settings or reinstall video drivers.

3. After you fix any problems with video, open the System Configuration box and click **Normal startup** on the General tab. Then restart Windows.

Figure 7-66   Control how Windows boots

To use VGA mode in Windows 7/Vista, do the following:

1. Reboot the system and press the **F8** key after the first beep. The Advanced Boot Options menu appears.

2. Select **Safe Mode** to boot up with minimal configurations of Windows, which includes standard VGA mode. Alternately, to boot Windows normally and use VGA mode, select **Enable low-resolution video (640 × 480)**.

Change the display settings and then restart Windows.

Hands-On | Project 7-4   Adjust Windows Display Settings

A+
220-901
4.3, 4.5

To practice changing display settings, do the following:

1. Using the Windows 8 Display window, calibrate the color displayed on your monitor screen. Verify ClearType text is enabled.

2. Try different screen resolutions supported by your monitor. Then verify the monitor is set to use the highest refresh rate it supports.

3. To view your Windows desktop in VGA mode, use the instructions given earlier to boot to Windows 8 Basic video or Windows 7 Enable low-resolution video (640 x 480). Then restart Windows and return your system to normal Windows display settings.

VIDEO SYSTEM IN A LAPTOP

A+
220-901
3.1, 3.2,
4.3, 4.5

If the LCD panel shows a black screen, but the power light indicates that power is getting to the system, the video subsystem might be the source of the problem. Do the following:

1. Look for an LCD cutoff switch or button on the laptop (see Figure 7-67). The switch must be on for the LCD panel to work.

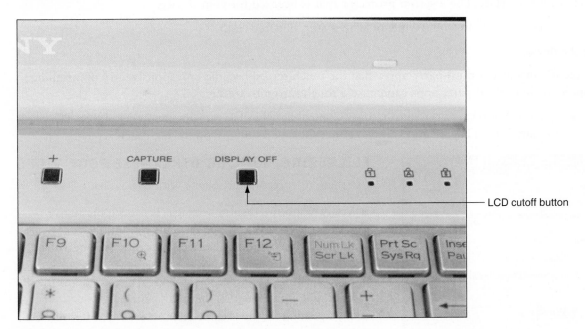

CAPTURE   DISPLAY OFF

— LCD cutoff button

Figure 7-67 LCD cutoff button on a laptop

2. If using an onboard video port, try to use the video port to connect it to an external monitor. After you connect the monitor, use a function key to toggle between the LCD panel, the external monitor, and both the panel and monitor. If the external monitor works, but the LCD panel does not work, try these things using the external monitor:

   ◢ Check Device Manager for warnings about the video controller and to update the video drivers.
   ◢ Check Event Viewer for reported problems with the video subsystem. You learned about Event Viewer in the chapter, "Supporting the Power System and Troubleshooting Computers."

3. If you still can't get the LCD panel on a laptop to work, but the external monitor does work, you have proven the problem is with the LCD panel assembly. In a laptop, a dim screen or no display can be caused by a bad inverter. If replacing the inverter does not help, the next task is to replace the LCD panel. Be aware the replacement components might cost more than the laptop is worth. Steps to replace the LCD panel in a laptop are covered later in the chapter.

CANNOT CONNECT TO EXTERNAL MONITOR

When wanting to expand desktop space or possibly troubleshoot video problems, you need to be able to use an external monitor with a laptop. If the connection to the external monitor fails, try the following solutions:

1. Make sure the monitor is getting power.

2. Use the Function keys to toggle between the laptop display and the external monitor. (Alternately, you can press Win+P to toggle between displays.)

3. Try using a different cable.

4. Try using a different connection if the laptop and monitor have another option available.

TOUCH SCREEN IS NONRESPONSIVE

Smart phones, tablets, and some laptops offer a touch screen. If the touch screen becomes unresponsive, try the following solutions:

1. Wash and thoroughly dry your hands.

2. If there is a case or screen protector, remove it. Some screen protectors are too thick and interfere with the touch screen interface. Use a screen protector that is licensed for your device.

3. Clean the screen with an electronic wipe, or with a soft, lint-free cloth.

4. Restart the device.

5. If you recently installed a third-party app when the touch screen became unresponsive, try uninstalling that app. Sometimes third-party apps can cause a touch screen to freeze.

6. Recalibrate the touch screen. For a laptop, open Control Panel in Classic view and click **Tablet PC Settings**. See Figure 7-68. (The item in Control Panel shows up only if you have a touch screen.)

Figure 7-68   Calibrate the touch screen on a laptop

FLICKERING, DIM, OR OTHERWISE POOR VIDEO

Use these tips to solve problems with bad video:

- Verify Windows display settings. Try using the native resolution for the LCD panel. This resolution will be the highest resolution available unless the wrong video drivers are installed.
- Try adjusting the brightness, which is a function of the backlight component of the LCD panel.
- Try updating the video drivers. Download the latest drivers from the laptop's manufacturer's website. Bad drivers can cause an occasional ghost cursor on screen. A ghost cursor is a trail left behind when you move the mouse.
- A flickering screen can be caused by bad video drivers, a low refresh rate, a bad inverter, or loose connections inside the laptop. To adjust the refresh rate, use Control Panel to open the Display window. In the Display window, click **Change display settings**. In the Screen Resolution window, click **Advanced settings**. On the Monitor tab, select the highest refresh rate available (see Figure 7-69).

Figure 7-69   Use the highest refresh rate the system supports

REPLACING THE LCD PANEL IN A LAPTOP

Because the LCD panel is so fragile, it is one component that is likely to be broken when a laptop is not handled properly. If the LCD display is entirely black, most likely you'll have to replace the entire LCD assembly. However, for a laptop that uses fluorescent backlighting, if the screen is dim, but you can make out that some display is present, the problem might be the inverter. The inverter board converts DC to AC used to power the backlighting of the LCD panel (see Figure 7-70). Check with the laptop manufacturer to confirm that it makes sense to first try replacing just the relatively inexpensive inverter board before you replace the more expensive entire LCD panel assembly. If the entire assembly needs replacing, the cost of the assembly might exceed the value of the laptop.

Figure 7-70 A ThinkPad inverter board

Sometimes, a laptop LCD panel, including the entire cover and hinges, is considered a single field replaceable unit, and sometimes components within the LCD assembly are considered FRUs. For example, the field replaceable units for the display panel in Figure 7-71 are the LCD front bezel, the hinges, the LCD

Figure 7-71 Components in an LCD assembly

panel, the inverter board, the LCD interface cables, the LCD USB cover, and the rear cover. Also know that an LCD assembly might include a microphone, webcam, or speakers that are embedded in the laptop lid. For other laptops, the microphone and speakers are inside the case. The speakers are considered a field replaceable unit. In addition, a Wi-Fi antenna might be in the lid of the laptop, which is why if you need a better Wi-Fi signal, you should raise the lid of the laptop. When you disassemble the lid, you must disconnect the antenna from the bottom part of the laptop.

Some high-end laptops contain a video card that has embedded video memory. This video card might also need replacing. In most cases, you would replace only the LCD panel and perhaps the inverter board.

Before you begin any disassembly of a laptop, refer to the manufacturer documentation. The following are some general directions to replace an LCD panel:

1. Remove the AC adapter and the battery pack.

2. Remove the upper keyboard bezel. (A bezel is a band that holds a device in place and the keyboard bezel is a band around the keyboard that holds it in place.) You might also need to remove the keyboard.

3. Remove the screws holding the hinge in place and remove the hinge cover. Figure 7-72 shows a laptop with a metal hinge cover, but some laptops use plastic covers that you can easily break as you remove them. Be careful with the plastic ones.

Figure 7-72   Remove the hinge cover from the laptop hinge

4. Remove the screws holding the LCD panel to the laptop.

5. You're now ready to remove the LCD panel from the laptop. Be aware there might be wires running through the hinge assembly, cables, or a pin connector. Cables might be connected to the motherboard using ZIF connectors. As you remove the LCD top cover, be careful to watch for how the panel is connected. Don't pull on wires or cables as you remove the cover, but first carefully disconnect them.

6. Next, remove screws that hold the top cover and LCD panel together. Sometimes, these screws are covered with plastic or rubber circles or pads that match the color of the case. First use a dental pick or small screwdriver to pick off these covers. You should then be able to remove the front bezel and separate the rear cover from the LCD panel. For one LCD panel, when you separate the LCD assembly from the lid cover, you can see the inverter board. Figure 7-73 shows the inverter being compared with the new one to make sure they match. The match is not identical but should work.

Figure 7-73 The inverter is exposed and is compared with the new one

7. Disconnect the old inverter and install the new one. When disconnecting the ribbon cable from the old inverter, notice you must first lift up on the lock holding the ZIF connector in place, as shown in Figure 7-74.

8. Install the new inverter. Reassemble the LCD panel assembly. Make sure the assembly is put together with a tight fit so that all screws line up well.

9. Reattach the LCD panel assembly to the laptop.

Figure 7-74 Lift up on the ZIF connector locking mechanism before removing the ribbon cable

SPEAKERS IN A LAPTOP

A+
220-901
3.1, 3.2,
4.3, 4.5

Laptops and other mobile devices have built-in speakers. If you're not getting any sound from the speakers, try the following solutions:

- Make sure the volume is turned up.
- Update the audio output drivers.
- Run the Playing Audio troubleshooting tool. Open Control Panel in Classic view and select **Troubleshooting**. In the Hardware and Sound group, select **Troubleshoot audio playback**. Follow the on-screen instructions for the Playing Audio troubleshooting wizard.

Sometimes speakers might get cracks or tears in the membrane that creates the sound, but also consider that laptop speakers are generally quieter than external speakers. When laptop speakers start sounding weak or unclear, first try updating the speaker drivers using Device Manager. You can also try plugging an external set of speakers to the audio port of the laptop. If using external speakers isn't convenient for the user, then you can replace the broken speakers.

Hands-On | Project 7-5   Research Replacing Speakers in a Laptop

Your friend Andrea has an old laptop, an HP Pavilion zd8000, and it is still serving her well. The only complaint she has is the left speaker has a static sound to it. The other speaker sounds good. She asks you to help her out. You know that, because the other speaker is still good, you need to replace the one bad speaker. Research on the Internet to find the speaker replacement part, find an online tutorial on how to replace the speaker for Andrea's laptop, then answer the following questions:

1. What is the price for the replacement speaker? Cite your source.

2. Is the cost of replacement worth more than what the laptop is worth?

3. Provide your source for the online tutorial.

4. After reviewing an online tutorial explaining the steps to replace the speaker, how long would you guess it would take you to replace the speaker, assuming everything goes as planned?

5. List the tools needed to replace the speaker.

>> CHAPTER SUMMARY

Basic Principles for Supporting Devices

◢ Adding new devices to a computer requires installing hardware and software. Even if you know how to generally install an I/O device, always follow the specific instructions of the product manufacturer.

◢ Use Device Manager under Windows to manage hardware devices and to solve problems with them.

◢ Popular I/O ports on a motherboard include eSATA (Versions 1, 2, and 3), FireWire 800 and 400, and USB (Versions 1, 2, and 3). Older ports include parallel, serial, and PS/2 ports.

◢ Wireless connections can use Wi-Fi 802.11a/b/g/n, Bluetooth, and Infrared standards.

◢ USB connectors include the A-Male, B-Male, Mini-B, Micro-B, Micro-A, USB 3.0 B-Male, and USB 3.0 Micro-B connectors.

Installing I/O Peripheral Devices

◢ When installing devices, use 32-bit drivers for a 32-bit OS and 64-bit drivers for a 64-bit OS.

◢ A touch screen is likely to use a USB port. Software is installed to calibrate the touch screen to the monitor screen and receive data input.

◢ Biometric input devices, such as a fingerprint reader, collect biological data and compare it with that recorded about the person to authenticate the person's access to a system.

◢ A KVM switch lets you use one keyboard, monitor, and mouse with multiple computers.

Installing and Configuring Adapter Cards

◢ Generally, when an adapter card is physically installed in a system and Windows starts up, it detects the card and then you install the drivers using the Windows wizard. However, always follow specific instructions from the device manufacturer when installing an adapter card because the order of installing the card and drivers might be different.

▲ A TV tuner card turns your computer or laptop into a television. A video capture card allows you to capture input from a camcorder or directly from TV. Combo cards have both abilities. A sound card allows you to input audio and use multispeaker systems.

Supporting the Video Subsystem

▲ Types of monitors include LCD monitor, plasma monitor, projector, and OLED monitor. An LCD monitor can use two types of backlighting: fluorescent and LED.

▲ Technologies and features of LCD monitors include screen size, refresh rate, pixel pitch, resolution, native resolution, contrast ratio, viewing angle, backlighting, and connectors that a monitor uses.

▲ Video ports that a video card or motherboard might provide are VGA, DVI-I, DVI-D, DVI-A, composite video, S-Video, component video, DisplayPort, HDMI, and HDMI mini ports.

▲ Use the Screen Resolution window to configure a monitor resolution and configure dual monitors.

▲ To use the Aero user interface, Windows 7/Vista requires a video card or onboard video to have at least 128 MB of video RAM, support DirectX version 9 or higher, and use the Windows Display Driver Model (WDDM).

▲ The dxdiag.exe command is used to report information about hardware, including the video card and which version of DirectX it is using.

Troubleshooting I/O Devices

▲ Use Device Manager to update drivers on I/O devices giving trouble.

▲ Video problems can be caused by the monitor, video cable, video card, onboard video, video drivers, or Windows display settings.

▲ To bypass Windows display settings, boot the system to the Advanced Boot Options menu and select Safe Mode or Enable low-resolution video (640 × 480).

▲ A few dead pixels on an LCD monitor screen are considered acceptable by the manufacturer.

▲ Artifacts on the monitor screen can be caused by hardware, software, overheating, or overclocking. Try updating video drivers and checking for high temperatures.

>> KEY TERMS

For explanations of key terms, see the Glossary for this text.

1394a	Device Manager	flat-panel monitor	LED (light-emitting diode)
1394b	Digital Rights Management (DRM)	fluorescent backlighting	Micro-A connector
A-Male connector	digitizer	ghost cursor	Micro-B connector
artifact	digitizing tablet	graphics tablet	MIDI (musical instrument digital interface)
B-Male connector	DirectX	HDMI connector	Mini-B connector
barcode reader	DisplayPort	HDMI mini connector	Mini-DIN-6 connector
biometric device	distorted geometry	hot-swappable	Mini DisplayPort
burn-in	DVI-A	Infrared (IR)	mini-HDMI connector
Cold Cathode Fluorescent Lamp (CCFL)	DVI-D	In-Plane Switching (IPS)	Mini PCI Express
composite video port	DVI-I	inverter circuit board	Mini PCIe
contrast ratio	dxdiag.exe	KVM (Keyboard, Video, and Mouse) switch	motion controller
DB-15	FireWire 400	LCD (liquid crystal display)	motion sensor
dead pixel	FireWire 800		

native resolution	plasma monitor	response time	TV tuner card
OLED (organic light-emitting diode)	projector	RGB port	Twisted Nematic (TN)
	RCA connector	sound card	USB 3.0 Micro-B connector
pixel	refresh rate	stylus	VGA mode
pixel pitch	resolution	touch screen	video capture card

>> REVIEWING THE BASICS

1. Which is faster, an eSATA-600 port or a FireWire 800 port?

2. What is the speed for Hi-Speed USB?

3. How many times faster is a Hi-Speed USB port than an Original USB port running at 12 Mbps?

4. Which is faster, USB 3.0 or eSATA 600?

5. Which is faster, Wi-Fi 802.11n or Bluetooth?

6. How many pins does a FireWire 800 port have?

7. What type of wireless transmission requires a line-of-sight clearance?

8. Will a printer rated to use USB 3.0 work when you connect the printer's USB cable into a USB 2.0 port on your computer?

9. What is the easiest way to tell if a USB port on a laptop computer is using the USB 3.0 standard?

10. For an LCD monitor, what is the best resolution to use?

11. Which gives less glare, an LED monitor or an OLED monitor?

12. Which gives a better measurement for the quality of an LCD monitor, the contrast ratio or the dynamic contrast ratio?

13. What command do you use to find out which version of DirectX your video card is using?

14. Name two types of ports a keyboard might use.

15. Which Windows utility is most likely the one to use when uninstalling an expansion card?

16. Would you expect all the devices listed in UEFI/BIOS setup to also be listed in Device Manager? Would you expect all devices listed in Device Manager to also be listed in UEFI/BIOS setup?

17. Why is it best to leave a slot empty between two expansion cards?

18. Which speaker port should you use when connecting a single speaker to a PC?

19. What type of adapter card allows you to connect your computer to cable so that you can watch TV on your computer?

20. Which is faster, SuperSpeed USB or FireWire 800?

21. Why might a musical keyboard have two MIDI ports?

22. What can you do if a port on the motherboard is faulty and a device requires this type of port?

23. What are two screen resolutions that might be used by VGA mode?

24. What is another name for a VGA port?

25. Which type of drivers must always be certified in order to be installed in Windows?

>> THINKING CRITICALLY

1. If a PS/2 keyboard does not work on your system and yet you know the keyboard is good, what is the best solution?

   a. Disable the PS/2 port in UEFI/BIOS setup and use a PS/2 splitter to install a keyboard and mouse using the PS/2 mouse port.

   b. Install a USB keyboard on a USB port.

   c. Exchange the PS/2 port on your motherboard.

   d. Replace the motherboard.

2. You plug a new scanner into a USB port on your Windows 7 system. When you first turn on the scanner, what should you expect to see?

   a. A message displays by the scanner software telling you to reboot your system.

   b. Windows Device Setup launches to install drivers.

   c. Your system automatically reboots.

   d. An error message from the USB controller appears.

3. You turn on your Windows 7 computer and see the system display POST messages. Then the screen turns blue with no text. Which of the following items could be the source of the problem?

   a. The video card

   b. The monitor

   c. Windows

   d. Microsoft Word software installed on the system

4. You have just installed a new sound card in your system, and Windows says the card installed with no errors. When you plug up the speakers and try to play a music CD, you hear no sound. What is the first thing you should do? The second thing?

   a. Check Device Manager to see if the sound card is recognized and has no errors.

   b. Reinstall Windows 7.

   c. Use Device Manager to uninstall the sound card.

   d. Identify your sound card by opening the case and looking on the card for the manufacturer and model.

   e. Check the volume controls on the speaker amplifier and in Windows.

   f. Use Device Manager to update the sound card drivers.

5. You have just installed a new DVD drive and its drivers under Windows 8. The drive will read a CD but not a DVD. You decide to reinstall the device drivers. What is the first thing you do?

   a. Open Control Panel and click Add New Hardware.

   b. Open Device Manager and choose Update Driver.

   c. Remove the data cable from the DVD drive so Windows will no longer recognize the drive and allow you to reinstall the drivers.

   d. Open Device Manager and uninstall the drive.

7

6. Match the following ports to the diagrams in Figure 7-75. Note that some ports are not used: Dual Link DVI-I, Single Link DVI-D, parallel, USB Type A, USB Type B, FireWire 400, VGA, DisplayPort, Mini Display Port, 4-pin S-Video, HDMI, PS/2, and serial.

Figure 7-75   Identify ports

>> REAL PROBLEMS, REAL SOLUTIONS

REAL PROBLEM 7-1 Helping with Upgrade Decisions

Upgrading an existing system can sometimes be a wise thing to do, but sometimes the upgrade costs more than the system is worth. Also, if existing components are old, they might not be compatible with components you want to use for the upgrade. A friend, Renata, asks your advice about several upgrades she is considering. Answer these questions:

1. Renata has a four-year-old desktop computer that has a Core2 Duo processor and 2 GB of memory. It does not have a FireWire port. She wants to use a camcorder that has a FireWire 400 interface to a PC. How would she perform the upgrade, and what is the cost? Save or print webpages to support your answers.

2. Her computer has one USB port, but she wants to use her USB printer at the same time she uses her USB scanner. How can she do this, and how much will it cost? Save or print webpages to support your answers.

3. Renata also uses her Windows 8 computer for gaming and wants to get a better gaming experience. The computer is using onboard video and has an empty PCI Express video slot. What is the fastest and best graphics card she can buy? How much does it cost? Save or print webpages to support your answer.

4. What is the total cost of all the upgrades Renata wants? Do you think it is wise for her to make these upgrades or would it be wiser to purchase a new system? How would you explain your recommendation to her?

REAL PROBLEM 7-2 Using Input Director

Input Director is software that lets you use one keyboard and mouse to control two or more computers that are networked together. You can download the free software from *www.inputdirector.com*. To use the software, you need to know the host name of each computer that will share the keyboard and mouse. To find out the host name, in Windows 8, right-click **Start** and select **System**. In Windows 7 right-click **Computer** and select **Properties**. The host name is listed as the Computer name.

Working with a partner, download and install Input Director and configure it so that you and your partner are using the same keyboard and mouse for your computers.

REAL PROBLEM 7-3 Researching a Computer Ad

Pick a current website or magazine ad for a complete, working desktop computer system, including computer, monitor, keyboard, and software, together with extra devices such as a mouse or printer. Research the details of the ad and write a two- to four-page report describing and explaining these details. This project provides a good opportunity to learn about the latest offerings on the market as well as current pricing.

REAL PROBLEM 7-4 Working with a Monitor

Do the following to practice changing monitor settings and troubleshooting monitor problems:

1. Practice changing the display settings, including the wallpaper, screen saver, and appearance. If you are not using your own computer, be sure to restore each setting after making changes.

2. Pretend you have made a mistake and selected a combination of foreground and background colors that makes reading the screen impossible. Solve the problem by booting Windows into Safe Mode. Correct the problem and then reboot.

3. Change the monitor resolution. Try several resolutions. Make a change and then make the change permanent. You can go back and adjust it later if you want.

4. Work with a partner who is using a different computer. Unplug the monitor in the computer lab or classroom, loosen or disconnect the computer monitor cable, or turn the contrast and brightness all the way down while your partner does something similar to the other computer. Trade computers and troubleshoot the problems.

5. Wear an ESD strap. Turn off the computer, press the power button, remove the case cover, and loosen the video card. Turn on the computer and write down the problem as a user would describe it. Turn off the computer, reseat the card, and verify that everything works.

6. Turn off your system. Insert into the system a defective video card provided by your instructor. Turn on the system. Describe the resulting problem in writing, as a user would.

Connecting To and Setting Up a Network

In this chapter, you learn how Windows uses TCP/IP protocols and standards to create and manage network connections, including how computers are identified and addressed on a network. You also learn to connect a computer to a network and how to set up and secure a small wired or wireless network.

This chapter prepares you to assume total responsibility for supporting both wired and wireless networks in a small-office/home-office (SOHO) environment. In the chapter, "Supporting Network Hardware," you learn more about the hardware used in networking, including network devices, connectors, cabling, networking tools, and the types of networks used for Internet connections. So let's get started by looking at how TCP/IP works in the world of Windows networking.

> ★ **A+ Exam Tip** Much of the content in this chapter applies to both the A+ 220-901 exam and the A+ 220-902 exam. This text includes icons for the A+ 220-901 (hardware) exam only. For markup of content relating to the A+ 220-902 (software) exam, see the companion volume to this text, *A+ Guide to Software, 9th ed.*

UNDERSTANDING TCP/IP AND WINDOWS NETWORKING

A+
220-901
2.3, 2.4 When two computers communicate using a local network or the Internet, communication happens at three levels (hardware, operating system, and application). The first step in communication is one computer must find the other computer. The second step is both computers must agree on the methods and rules for communication (called protocols). Then one computer takes on the role of making requests from the other computer. A computer making a request from another is called the client and the one answering the request is called the server. Most communication between computers on a network or the Internet uses this client/server model. For example, in Figure 8-1, someone uses a web browser on a client to request a webpage from a web server. To handle this request, the client computer must first find the web server, the protocols for communication are established, and then the request is made and answered. Hardware, the OS, and the applications on both computers are all involved in this process.

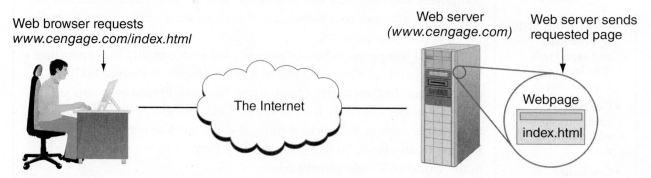

Figure 8-1 A web browser (client software) requests a webpage from a web server (server software); the web server returns the requested data to the client

Let's first look at the layers of communication that involve hardware, the OS, and applications and then see how computers are addressed and found on a network or the Internet. Then we'll see how a client/server request is made by the client and answered by the server.

LAYERS OF NETWORK COMMUNICATION

A+
220-901
2.3, 2.4 When your computer at home is connected to your Internet service provider (ISP) off somewhere in the distance, your computer and a computer on the Internet must be able to communicate. When two devices communicate, they must use the same protocols so that the communication makes sense. For almost all networks today, including the Internet, the group or suite of protocols used is called TCP/IP (Transmission Control Protocol/ Internet Protocol).

Communication between two computers happens in layers. In Figure 8-2, you can see how communication starts with an application (browser) passing a request to the OS, which passes the request to the network card and then on to the network. When the request reaches the network card on the server, the network card passes it on to the OS and then the OS passes it on to the application (the web server).

Figure 8-2 Network communication happens in layers

Listed next is a description of each level of communication:

▲ **Level 1: Hardware level.** At the root level of communication is hardware. The hardware or physical connection might be wireless or might use network cables, phone lines (for DSL or dial-up), or TV cable lines (for a cable modem). For local wired or wireless networks, a network adapter (also called a network card, a network interface card, or a NIC) inside your computer is part of this physical network. Every network adapter (including a network card, network port on a motherboard, onboard wireless, or wireless NIC) has a 48-bit (6-byte) number hard-coded on the card by its manufacturer that is unique for that device (see Figure 8-3). The number is written in hexadecimal, and is called the MAC (Media Access Control) address, hardware address, physical address, adapter address, or Ethernet address. Part of the MAC address identifies the manufacturer that is responsible for making sure that no two network adapters have the same MAC address. MAC addresses are used to locate a computer on a local area network (LAN). A local area network (LAN) is a network bound by routers or other gateway devices. A router is a device that manages traffic between two or more networks and can help find the best path for traffic to get from one network to another. A gateway is any device or computer that network traffic can use to leave one network and go to a different network.

MAC address

Figure 8-3   This Gigabit Ethernet adapter by Intel uses a PCIe x1 slot

◢ *Level 2: Operating system level.* Operating systems use IP addresses to find other computers on a network. An IP address is a 32-bit or 128-bit string that is assigned to a network connection when the connection is first made. Whereas a MAC address is only used to find a computer on a local network, an IP address can be used to find a computer anywhere on the Internet (see Figure 8-4) or on an intranet. An intranet is any private network that uses TCP/IP protocols. A large enterprise might support an intranet that is made up of several local networks. A local network can further be divided into smaller networks and each of these smaller networks is called a subnetwork or subnet. IP addresses are used to find computers on subnets, an intranet, or the Internet.

Communication
is by MAC address

Communication
is by IP address

Internet

LAN A   LAN B

Figure 8-4   Computers on the same LAN use MAC addresses to communicate, but computers on different LANs use IP addresses to communicate over the Internet

▲ *Level 3: Application level.* Most applications used on the Internet or a local network are client/server applications. Client applications, such as Internet Explorer, Google Chrome, or Outlook, communicate with server applications such as a web server or email server. Each client and server application installed on a computer listens at a predetermined address that uniquely identifies the application on the computer. This address is a number and is called a port number, port, or port address. For example, you can address a web server by entering into a browser address box an IP address followed by a colon and then 80, which is the port number for a web server application. Suppose a computer with an IP address of 136.60.30.5 is running both an email server, which listens at port 25, and a web server application listening at port 80. If a client computer sends a request to 136.60.30.5:25, the email server that is listening at that port responds. On the other hand, if a request is sent to 136.60.30.5:80, the web server listening at port 80 responds (see Figure 8-5).

Figure 8-5 Each server running on a computer is addressed by a unique port number

Figure 8-6 shows how communication moves from a browser to the OS to the hardware on one computer and on to the hardware, OS, and web server on a remote computer. As you connect a computer to a network, keep in mind that the connection must work at all three levels. And when things don't work right, it helps to understand that you must solve the problem at one or more levels. In other words, the problem might be with the physical equipment, with the OS, or with the application.

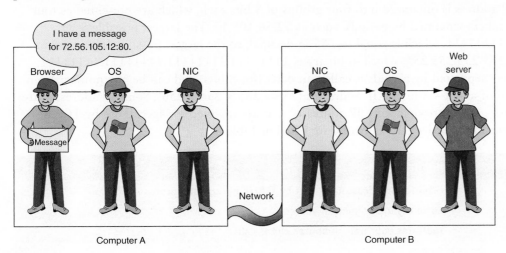

Figure 8-6 How a message gets from a browser to a web server using three levels of communication

Before a message is transmitted on a network, if it is too long, it's broken up into segments. Also, header and trailer information are added, including the IP addresses of the source computer and destination computer, the application's port number, and the protocols for communication the message uses on the network. When this information is added, the message is called a segment, datagram, packet, or frame depending on what information has been added to the header and trailer and which layer of communication added the information.

HOW IP ADDRESSES GET ASSIGNED

A+
220-901
2.3, 2.4

An IP address has 32 bits or 128 bits. When the Internet and TCP/IP were first invented, it seemed that 32 bits were more than enough to satisfy any needs we might have for IP addresses because this standard, called Internet Protocol version 4 (IPv4), created about four billion potential IP addresses. Today we need many more than four billion IP addresses over the world. Partly because of a shortage of 32-bit IP addresses, Internet Protocol version 6 (IPv6), which uses an IP address with 128 bits, was developed. Currently, the Internet uses a mix of 32-bit and 128-bit IP addresses. The Internet Assigned Numbers Authority (IANA at *iana.org*) is responsible for keeping track of assigned IP addresses and has already released all its available 32-bit IP addresses. IP addresses leased from IANA today are all 128-bit addresses.

A MAC address is embedded on a network adapter at the factory, but IP addresses are assigned manually or by software. An IP address can be a dynamic IP address (IP address is assigned by a server each time the computer or device connects to the network) or a static IP address (IP address is permanently assigned to the computer or device).

> ★ **A+ Exam Tip** The A+ 220-901 exam expects you to know what a DHCP server is and to understand how to use static and dynamic IP addressing.

For dynamic IP addresses, a DHCP (Dynamic Host Configuration Protocol) server gives an IP address to a computer when it first attempts to initiate a connection to the network and requests an IP address. A computer or other device (such as a network printer) that requests an address from a DHCP server is called a DHCP client. It is said that the client is leasing an IP address. A DHCP server that serves up IPv6 addresses is often called a DHCPv6 server. How to configure a Windows computer to use dynamic or static IP addressing is covered later in the chapter.

Next, let's see how IPv4 addresses are used, and then you'll learn about IPv6 addresses.

HOW IPv4 ADDRESSES ARE USED

A 32-bit IP address is organized into four groups of 8 bits each, which are presented as four decimal numbers separated by periods, such as 72.56.105.12. The largest possible 8-bit number is 11111111, which is equal to 255 in decimal, so the largest possible IP address in decimal is 255.255.255.255, which in binary is 11111111.11111111.11111111.11111111. Each of the four numbers separated by periods is called an octet (for 8 bits) and can be any number from 0 to 255, making a total of about 4.3 billion IP addresses ($256 \times 256 \times 256 \times 256$). Some IP addresses are reserved, so these numbers are approximations. IP addresses that are reserved for special use by TCP/IP and should not be assigned to a device on a network are listed in Table 8-1.

IP Address	How It Is Used
255.255.255.255	Used for broadcast messages by TCP/IP background processes
0.0.0.0	Currently unassigned IP address
127.0.0.1	Indicates your own computer and is called the loopback address

Table 8-1 Reserved IP addresses

The first part of an IP address identifies the network, and the last part identifies the host. When messages are routed over the Internet, the network portion of the IP address is used to locate the right local network. After the message arrives at the local network, the host portion of the IP address is used to identify the one computer on the network that is to receive the message. How does a computer or other network device know what part of an IP address identifies the network and what part identifies the host? It relies on a subnet mask for this information.

SUBNET MASKS

The subnet mask identifies which part of an IP address is the network portion and which part is the host portion. A computer or other device can use its subnet mask to know if an IP address of another computer is on its network or another network (see Figure 8-7).

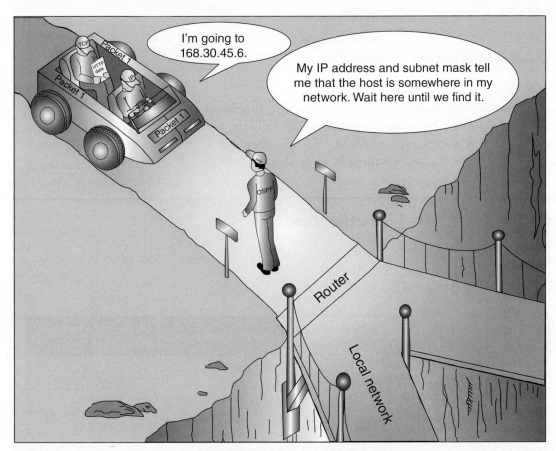

Figure 8-7 A host (router, in this case) can always determine if an IP address is on its network

A subnet mask has 32 bits and is a string of 1s followed by a string of 0s, for example, 11111111.1111 1111.11110000.00000000. The 1s in a subnet mask say, "On our network, this part of an IP address is the network part," and the group of 0s says, "On our network, this part of an IP address is the host part." On Windows screens, a subnet mask is displayed in decimal, for example the subnet mask of 11111111.11111 111.00000000.00000000 is 255.255.0.0 in decimal.

Suppose the IP address of a computer on Network A is 201.18.20.160 and the subnet mask is 11111111 .11111111.00000000.00000000. The subnet mask tells Windows that the first 16 bits or two octets of the IP address is the network ID. Therefore, when Windows is deciding how to communicate with a computer that has an IP address of 201.18.20.208, it knows the computer is on its own network, but a computer with an IP address of 201.19.23.160 is on another network.

Let's look at one more example. Suppose the IP address of a computer is 19.200.60.6 and its subnet mask is 255.255.240.0. Is a computer with the IP address 19.200.51.100 on its network? Here's the logic to find out:

Question	Answer
1. What is my IP address in binary?	19.200.60.6 in binary is: 00010011.11001000.00111100.00000110.
2. What is the other IP address in binary?	19.200.51.100 in binary is: 00010011.11001000.00110011.01100100.
3. Based on my subnet mask, how many bits in my IP address identify my network?	255.255.240.0 in binary is: 11111111.11111111.11110000.00000000. 20 bits identify the network.
4. Do the first 20 bits in my IP address match the first 20 bits in the other IP address?	Compare the 20 red bits in the two IP addresses: 00010011.11001000.00111100.00000110 00010011.11001000.00110011.01100100 Yes, they match.
5. Is the other IP address on my network?	Yes.

Sometimes an IP address and subnet mask are written using a shorthand notation like 15.50.212.59/20, where the /20 means that the first 20 bits in the IP address identify the network. This notation is sometimes called slash notation or CIDR notation (pronounced "*cider notation*"), named after the CIDR (Classless Interdomain Routing) standards that were written in 1993 about subnetting.

Hands-On | Project 8-1   Practice Using Subnet Masks

A+
220-901
2.3, 2.4

To practice your skills using subnet masks, fill in Table 8-2. First, convert decimal values to binary and then record your decisions in the last column.

Local IP Address	Subnet Mask	Other IP Address	On the Same Network? (Yes or No)
15.50.212.59 Binary: _____	255.255.240.0 Binary: _____	15.50.235.80 Binary: _____	
192.168.24.1 Binary: _____	255.255.248.0 Binary: _____	192.168.31.198 Binary: _____	
192.168.0.1 Binary: _____	255.255.255.192 Binary: _____	192.168.0.63 Binary: _____	
192.168.0.10 Binary: _____	255.255.255.128 Binary: _____	192.168.0.120 Binary: _____	

Table 8-2   Practice using subnet masks

That brings us to a fun way of explaining subnet masks. Suppose all the tall sticks shown in Figure 8-8 belong to the same large network that has been subnetted. The short stick represents the subnet mask for all subnets. How many subnets are in the network? Which sticks belong in the same subnet as Stick 5? As Stick 6?

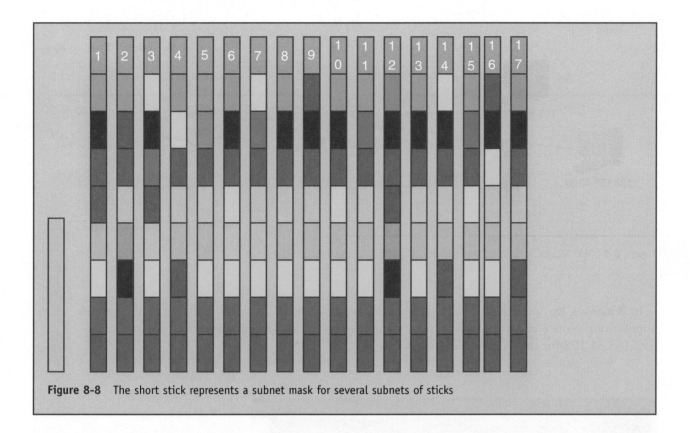

Figure 8-8 The short stick represents a subnet mask for several subnets of sticks

PUBLIC, PRIVATE, AND AUTOMATIC PRIVATE IP ADDRESSES

IP addresses available to the Internet are called public IP addresses. To conserve the number of public IP addresses, some blocks of IP addresses have been designated as private IP addresses that are not allowed on the Internet. Private IP addresses are used within a company's private network, and computers on this network can communicate with one another using these private IP addresses.

IEEE recommends that the following IP addresses be used for private networks:

- 10.0.0.0 through 10.255.255.255
- 172.16.0.0 through 172.31.255.255
- 192.168.0.0 through 192.168.255.255

If a computer first connects to the network that is using dynamic IP addressing and is unable to lease an IP address from the DHCP server, it generates its own Automatic Private IP Address (APIPA) in the address range 169.254.*x*.*y*.

> **Notes** IEEE, a nonprofit organization, is responsible for many Internet standards. Standards are proposed to the networking community in the form of an RFC (Request for Comment). RFC 1918 outlines recommendations for private IP addresses. To view an RFC, visit the website *www.rfc-editor.org*.

NAT (Network Address Translation) is a technique designed to conserve the number of public IP addresses needed by a network. A router or other gateway device stands between a private network and the Internet and substitutes the private IP addresses used by computers on the private network with its own public IP address when these computers need access to the Internet. See Figure 8-9. Besides conserving public IP addresses, another advantage of NAT is security; the gateway hides the entire private network behind this one address.

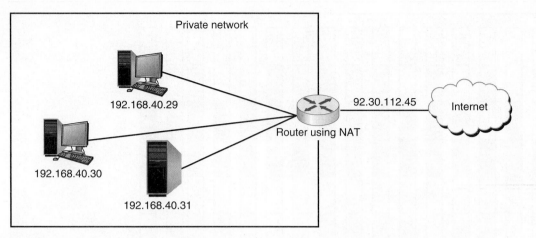

Figure 8-9   NAT allows computers with private IP addresses to access the Internet

In Windows, the ipconfig command can be used to show the IP addresses assigned to all network connections. Notice in Figure 8-10 that the computer has been assigned a private IPv4 address of 192.168.31.198 for the wireless connection.

Figure 8-10   The wireless network connection has been assigned a private IPv4 address

HOW IPv6 ADDRESSES ARE USED

Using the IPv6 standards, more has changed than just the number of bits in an IP address. To improve routing capabilities and speed of communication, IPv6 changed the way IP addresses are used to find computers on the Internet. Let's begin our discussion of IPv6 by looking at how IPv6 addresses are written and displayed:

◢ An IPv6 address has 128 bits that are written as eight blocks of hexadecimal numbers separated by colons, like this: 2001:0000:0B80:0000:0000:00D3:9C5A:00CC.

◢ Each block is 16 bits. For example, the first block in the address above is 2001 in hex, which can be written as 0010 0000 0000 0001 in binary.

◢ Leading zeros in a four-character hex block can be eliminated. For example, the IP address above can be written as 2001:0000:B80:0000:0000:D3:9C5A:CC.

⏵ If blocks contain all zeros, they can be written as double colons (::). The IP address above can be written two ways:

⏵ 2001::B80:0000:0000:D3:9C5A:CC

⏵ 2001:0000:B80::D3:9C5A:CC

To avoid confusion, only one set of double colons is used in an IP address. In this example, the preferred method is the second one: 2001:0000:B80::D3:9C5A:CC because the address is written with the fewest zeros.

The way computers communicate using IPv6 has changed the terminology used to describe TCP/IP communication. Here are a few terms used in the IPv6 standards:

⏵ A link, sometimes called the local link, or local network, is a local area network (LAN) or wide area network (WAN) bounded by routers.

⏵ A node is any device that connects to the network, such as a computer, printer, or router. An interface is a node's attachment to a link. The attachment can be a logical attachment, such as when a virtual machine connects to the network, or a physical attachment, such as when a network adapter connects to the wired network.

⏵ The last 64 bits or 4 blocks of an IP address identify the interface and are called the interface ID or interface identifier. These 64 bits uniquely identify an interface on the local network.

⏵ Neighbors are nodes on the same local network.

So far, very few networks solely use IPv6. Most networks, including the Internet, rely on IPv4 protocols. On IPv4 networks, tunnels are used to allow IPv6 messages to travel on the network. A tunnel works by encapsulating an IPv6 message inside an IPv4 message. Two common tunneling protocols are ISATAP (pronounced "eye-sa-tap" and stands for Intra-Site Automatic Tunnel Addressing Protocol) and Teredo (pronounced "ter-EE-do"), which is named after the Teredo worm that bores holes in wood. Teredo IPv6 addresses begin with 2001.

IPv6 supports these three types of IP addresses:

⏵ A unicast address is used to send messages to a single node on a network. Three types of unicast addresses are link-local addresses, unique local addresses, and global addresses.

⏵ A multicast address is used to deliver messages to all nodes in a targeted, multicast group, such as when video is streaming from a server to multiple nodes on a network.

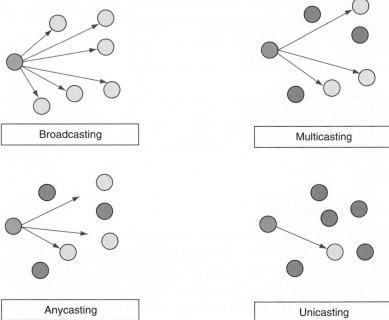

⏵ An anycast address is used by routers and can identify multiple destinations and a message is delivered only to the closest destination.

With IPv4 broadcasting, messages are sent to every node on a local network. However, IPv6 doesn't use broadcasting, which reduces network traffic. The concepts of broadcasting, multicasting, anycasting, and unicasting are illustrated in Figure 8-11.

Table 8-3 lists the currently used address prefixes for these types of IP addresses. In the future, we can expect more prefixes to be assigned as they are needed.

Figure 8-11   Concepts of broadcasting, multicasting, anycasting, and unicasting

IP Address Type	Address Prefix
Link-local address	FE80::/64 (First 64 bits are always 1111 1110 1000 0000...)
Unique local address	FC00::/7 (First 7 bits are always 1111 1100)
Global address	2000::/3 (First 3 bits are always 001)
Multicast	FF00::/8 (First 8 bits are always 1111 1111)
Unassigned address	0::0 (All zeroes)
Loopback address	0::1, also written as ::1 (127 zeroes followed by 1)

Table 8-3 Address prefixes for types of IPv6 addresses

★ **A+ Exam Tip** The A+ 220-901 exam expects you to know the prefixes listed in Table 8-3 and to know the IPv6 loopback address.

Three types of unicast addresses are link-local, unique link-local, and global addresses, which are graphically shown in Figure 8-12.

Link-Local Address

64 bits	64 bits
Prefix 1111 1110 1000 0000 0000 0000 ... 0000 FE80::/64	Interface ID

Unique Local Address

48 bits	16 bits	64 bits
Network ID	Subnet ID	Interface ID

Global Address

48 bits	16 bits	64 bits
Global Routing Prefix	Subnet ID	Interface ID

Figure 8-12 Three types of IPv6 addresses

Here is a description of the three types of unicast addresses:

◢ A link-local unicast address, also called a link-local address or local address, can be used for communicating with neighboring nodes in the same link (the local network). These local addresses are similar to IPv4 private IP addresses and most begin with FE80::/64. (This prefix notation means the address begins with FE80 followed by enough zeros to make 64 bits.) Link-local addresses are not allowed on the Internet or allowed to travel outside private networks. Look back at Figure 8-10 to see an example of a link-local address where the wireless interface has the IPv6 address of fe80::dcc8:2a19:e752:769f. The first 64 bits are fe80:: and the interface ID is dcc8:2a19:e752:769f.

◢ A unique local address is a private address that can travel across subnets within the private network. These addresses are used by network administrators when subnetting a large network.

◢ A global unicast address, also called a global address, can be routed on the Internet. These addresses are similar to IPv4 public IP addresses. The first 48 bits of the address is the Global Routing Prefix. When an ISP assigns a global address to a customer, it's these 48 bits that it assigns. An organization that leases one Global Routing Prefix from its ISP can use it to generate many IPv6 global addresses.

SUBNETS

IPv6 uses subnetting but doesn't need a subnet mask because the subnet ID that identifies a subnet is part of the IPv6 address. The subnet ID is the 16 bits following the first 48 bits of the address. When a large IPv6 network is subnetted, a DHCPv6 server assigns a node in a subnet a global address or unique local address that contains the correct subnet ID for the node's subnet.

> **Notes** An excellent resource for learning more about IPv6 and how it works is the e-book, *TCP/IP Fundamentals for Microsoft Windows*. To download the free PDF, search for it at *www.microsoft.com/download*.

8

VIEW IP ADDRESS SETTINGS

A+
220-901
2.3, 2.4

In summary, let's use the ipconfig command to take a look at the IPv4 and IPv6 addresses assigned to all network connections on a computer (see Figure 8-13).

Figure 8-13   The ipconfig command showing IPv4 and IPv6 addresses assigned to this computer

Notice in the figure the four IP addresses that have been assigned to the physical connections:

◢ Windows has assigned the wireless connection two IP addresses, one IPv4 address and one IPv6 address.

◢ The Ethernet LAN connection has also been assigned an IPv4 address and an IPv6 address.

The IPv6 addresses are followed by a % sign and a number; for example, %5 follows the first IP address. This number is called the zone ID or scope ID and is used to identify the interface in a list of interfaces for this computer.

IPv6 addressing is designed so that a computer can self-configure its own link-local IP address, which is similar to how IPv4 uses an Automatic Private IP Address (APIPA). Here's what happens when a computer using IPv6 first makes a network connection:

1. The computer creates its IPv6 address by using the FE80::/64 prefix and uses its MAC address to generate an interface ID for the last 64 bits.

2. It then performs a duplicate address detection process to make sure its IP address is unique on the network.

3. Next, it asks if a DHCPv6 server is present on the network to provide configuration information. If a server responds with DHCP information, the computer uses whatever information this might be, such as the IP addresses of DNS servers or its own IP address. Because a computer can generate its own link-local IP address, a DHCPv6 server usually serves up only global or unique local addresses.

CHARACTER-BASED NAMES IDENTIFY COMPUTERS AND NETWORKS

A+
220-901
2.3, 2.4

Remembering an IP address is not always easy, so character-based names are used to substitute for IP addresses. Here are the possibilities:

▲ A host name, also called a computer name, is the name of a computer and can be used in place of its IP address. The name can have up to 63 characters, including letters, numbers, and special characters. Examples of computer names are www, ftp, Jean's Computer, TestBox3, and PinkLaptop. You can assign a computer name while installing Windows. In addition, you can change the computer name at any time using the System window:

1. For Windows 8, press **Win+X** and click **System**. For Windows 7, open Control Panel in Classic view and click **System**. In the System window, click **Advanced system settings**.

2. In the System Properties box, on the Computer Name tab (see Figure 8-14), click **Change**. You will need to restart your computer for the change to take effect.

Figure 8-14   View and change the computer name

▲ A workgroup is a group of computers on a peer-to-peer network that are sharing resources. The workgroup name assigned to this group is only recognized within the local network.

▲ A domain name identifies a network. Examples of domain names are the names that appear before the period in *microsoft.com*, *course.com*, and *mycompany.com*. The letters after the period are called the top-level domain and tell you something about the domain. Examples are .com (commercial), .org (nonprofit), .gov (government), and .info (general use).

▲ A fully qualified domain name (FQDN) identifies a computer and the network to which it belongs. An example of an FQDN is *www.cengage.com*. The host name is *www* (a web server), *cengage* is the domain name, and *com* is the top-level domain name of the Cengage network. Another FQDN is *joesmith.mycompany.com*.

On the Internet, a fully qualified domain name must be associated with an IP address before this computer can be found. This process of associating a character-based name with an IP address is called name resolution. The DNS (Domain Name System or Domain Name Service) protocol is used by a DNS server to find an IP address for a computer when the fully qualified domain name is known. On home or small company networks, the ISP is responsible for providing access to one or more DNS servers as part of the service it provides for Internet access. Larger corporations have their own DNS servers to perform name resolution for the enterprise network. When an individual or organization, which has its own DNS servers, leases a public IP address and domain name and sets up a website, it is responsible for entering the name resolution information into its primary DNS server. This server can present the information to other DNS servers on the web and is called the authoritative name server for the website.

⭐ **A+ Exam Tip** The A+ 220-901 exam expects you to be familiar with client-side DNS.

📝 **Notes** When you enter a fully qualified domain name such as *www.cengage.com* in a browser address bar, that name is translated into an IP address followed by a port number. It's interesting to know that you can skip the translation step and enter the IP address and port number in the address box. See Figure 8-15.

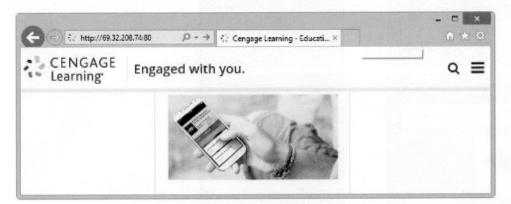

Figure 8-15 A website can be accessed by its IP address and port number: http://69.32.208.74:80

When Windows is trying to resolve a computer name to an IP address, it first looks in the DNS cache it holds in memory. If the computer name is not found in the cache, Windows then turns to a DNS server if it has the IP address of the server. When Windows queries the DNS server for a name resolution, it is called the DNS client.

TCP/IP PROTOCOL LAYERS

A+
220-901
2.3, 2.4

A protocol is an agreed-to set of rules for communication between two parties. Operating systems and client/server applications on the Internet all use protocols that are supported by TCP/IP. The left side of Figure 8-16 shows these different layers of protocols and how they relate to one another. As you read this section, this figure can serve as your road map to the different protocols.

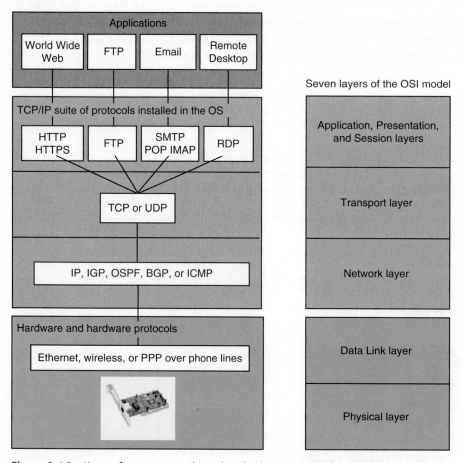

Figure 8-16   How software, protocols, and technology on a TCP/IP network relate to
each other

Notes When studying networking theory, the OSI model is used, which divides network communication into seven layers. In the OSI model, protocols used by hardware are divided into two layers (Data Link and Physical layers), and TCP/IP protocols used by the OS are divided into five layers (Network, Transport, Session, Presentation, and Application layers). These seven layers are shown on the right side of Figure 8-16.

In the following sections, the more significant applications and operating system protocols are introduced. However, you should know that the TCP/IP protocol suite includes more protocols than just those mentioned in this chapter; only some of them are shown in Figure 8-16.

TCP/IP PROTOCOLS USED BY THE OS

Looking back at Figure 8-16, you can see three layers of protocols between the applications and the hardware protocols. These three layers make up the heart of TCP/IP communication. In the figure, TCP or UDP manages communication with the applications protocols above them as well as the protocols shown underneath TCP and UDP, which control communication on the network.

TCP Guarantees Delivery

All communication on a network happens by way of messages delivered from one location on the network to another. In TCP/IP, the protocol that guarantees message delivery is TCP (Transmission Control Protocol). TCP makes a connection, sends the data, checks whether the data is received, and resends it if it is not. TCP is, therefore, called a connection-oriented protocol. TCP is used by applications such as web browsers and email. Guaranteed delivery takes longer and is used when it is important to know that the data reached its destination.

For TCP to guarantee delivery, it uses protocols at the IP layer to establish a session between client and server to verify that communication has taken place. When a TCP message reaches its destination, an acknowledgment is sent back to the source (see Figure 8-17). If the source TCP does not receive the acknowledgment, it resends the data or passes an error message back to the higher-level application protocol.

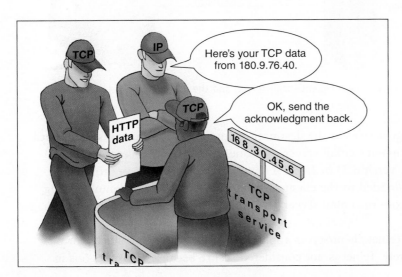

Figure 8-17 TCP guarantees delivery by requesting an acknowledgment

★ **A+ Exam Tip** The A+ 220-901 exam expects you to be able to contrast the TCP and UDP protocols.

UDP Provides Fast Transmissions

On the other hand, UDP (User Datagram Protocol) does not guarantee delivery by first connecting and checking whether data is received; thus, UDP is called a connectionless protocol or best-effort protocol. UDP is used for broadcasting, such as streaming video or sound over the web, where guaranteed delivery is not as important as fast transmission. UDP is also used to monitor network traffic.

TCP/IP PROTOCOLS USED BY APPLICATIONS

Some common applications that use the Internet are web browsers, email, chat, FTP, Telnet, Remote Desktop, and Remote Assistance. Here is a bit of information about several of the protocols used by these and other applications:

▲ *HTTP.* HTTP (Hypertext Transfer Protocol) is the protocol used for the World Wide Web and used by web browsers and web servers to communicate. You can see when a browser is using this protocol by looking for http at the beginning of a URL in the address bar of a browser, such as *http://www.microsoft.com.*

▲ *HTTPS.* HTTPS (HTTP secure) refers to the HTTP protocol working with a security protocol such as Secure Sockets Layer (SSL) or Transport Layer Security (TLS), which is better than SSL, to create a secured socket. A socket is a connection between a browser and web server. HTTPS is used by web browsers and servers to secure the socket by encrypting the data before it is sent and then decrypting it before the data is processed. To know a secured protocol is being used, look for https in the URL, as in *https://www.wellsfargo.com*.

▲ *SMTP.* SMTP (Simple Mail Transfer Protocol) is used to send an email message to its destination (see Figure 8-18). The email server that takes care of sending email messages (using the SMTP protocol) is often referred to as the SMTP server.

Figure 8-18   The SMTP protocol is used to send email to a recipient's mail server, and the POP3 or IMAP4 protocol is used by the client to receive email

▲ *POP and IMAP.* After an email message arrives at the destination email server, it remains there until the recipient requests delivery. The recipient's email server uses one of two protocols to deliver the message: POP3 (Post Office Protocol, version 3) or IMAP4 (Internet Message Access Protocol, version 4). Using POP3, email is downloaded to the client computer and, unless the default setting is changed, the email is then deleted from the email server. Using IMAP, the client application manages the email stored on the server.

▲ *Telnet.* The Telnet protocol is used by Telnet client/server applications to allow an administrator or other user to control a computer remotely. Telnet is not considered secure because transmissions in Telnet are not encrypted.

▲ *LDAP.* Lightweight Directory Access Protocol (LDAP) is used by various client applications when the application needs to query a database. For example, an email client on a corporate network might query a database that contains the email addresses for all employees or an application might query a database of printers looking for a printer on the corporate network or Internet. Data sent and received using the LDAP protocol is not encrypted; therefore, an encryption layer is sometimes added to LDAP transmissions.

▲ *SMB.* Server Message Block (SMB) is a file access protocol originally developed by IBM and used by Windows to share files and printers on a network. The current release of the SMB protocol is CIFS, also called SMB2.

▲ *AFP.* AFP (Apple Filing Protocol) is a file access protocol used by early editions of the Mac operating system by Apple and is one protocol in the suite of Apple networking protocols called AppleTalk. (TCP/IP has replaced AppleTalk for most networking protocols in the Mac OS.) Current Mac OS releases use SMB2 for file access, and support AFP for backward compatibility with earlier versions of the Mac OS.

▲ **CIFS.** CIFS (Common Internet File System), also called SMB2, is a file access protocol and the cross-platform version of SMB used between Windows, Linux, Mac OS, and other operating systems.

▲ **FTP.** FTP (File Transfer Protocol) is used to transfer files between two computers. Web browsers can use the protocol. Also, third-party FTP client software, such as CuteFTP by GlobalSCAPE (*www.cuteftp.com*) and others, offers more features for file transfer than does a browser. By default, FTP transmissions are not secure. Secure FTP (SFTP) uses SSH encryption.

▲ **SSH.** The Secure Shell (SSH) protocol encrypts transmission so they cannot be intercepted by a hacker. SSH is used in various situations for encryption, such as SFTP. SSH is commonly used in Linux to pass sign-in information to a remote computer and control that computer over a network. Because it's secure, SSH is preferred over Telnet on Linux systems.

▲ **SNMP.** Simple Network Management Protocol (SNMP) is used to monitor network traffic. It is used by the Microsoft SNMP Agent application that monitors traffic on a network and helps balance that traffic.

▲ **RDP.** Remote Desktop Protocol (RDP) is used by the Windows Remote Desktop and Remote Assistance utilities to connect to and control a remote computer.

> ★ **A+ Exam Tip** The A+ 220-901 exam expects you to know about the following application protocols: FTP, SSH, Telnet, SMTP, DNS, HTTP, POP3, IMAP, HTTPS, RDP, SMB, AFP, DHCP, LDAP, SNMP, and CIFS.

8

APPLYING | CONCEPTS   INTERNET EXPLORER AND FTP

A+
220-901
2.3, 2.4

To use FTP in Internet Explorer, enter the address of an FTP site in the address box, for example, *ftp.cengage.com*. A logon dialog box appears where you can enter a user name and password (see Figure 8-19). When you click **Log on**, you can see folders on the FTP site and the FTP protocol displays in the address bar, as in *ftp://ftp.cengage.com*. It's easier to use File Explorer or Windows Explorer to transfer files rather than Internet Explorer.

Figure 8-19   Log on to an FTP site

After you have located the FTP site, to use Explorer for file transfers, press **Alt**, which causes the menu bar to appear. In the menu bar, click **View, Open FTP site in File Explorer** (see Figure 8-20). Explorer opens, showing files and folders on the FTP site. You can copy and paste files and folders from your computer to the site.

(continues)

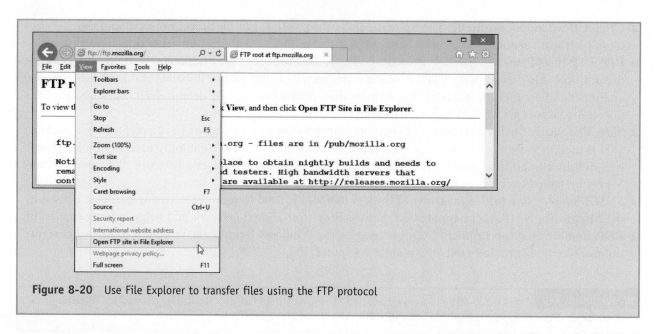

Figure 8-20   Use File Explorer to transfer files using the FTP protocol

Client/server applications use ports to address each other. Table 8-4 lists the port assignments for common applications.

> ★ **A+ Exam Tip**   The A+ 220-901 exam expects you to know the common port assignments of the FTP, SSH, Telnet, SMTP, DNS, HTTP, POP3, IMAP, HTTPS, RDP, SMB, and AFP protocols. Before sitting for this exam, be sure to memorize these ports listed in Table 8-4.

Port	Protocol and App	Description
20	FTP client	The FTP client receives data on port 20 from the FTP server.
21	FTP server	The FTP server listens on port 21 for commands from an FTP client.
22	SSH server	A server using the SSH protocol listens at port 22.
23	Telnet server	A Telnet server listens at port 23.
25	SMTP email server	An email server listens at port 25 to receive email from a client computer.
53	DNS server	A DNS server listens at port 53.
80	Web server using HTTP	A web server listens at port 80 when receiving HTTP requests.
110	POP3 email client	An email client using POP3 receives email at port 110.
143	IMAP email client	An email client using IMAP receives email at port 143.
443	Web server using HTTPS	A web server listens at port 443 when receiving HTTPS transmissions.
3389	RDP apps, including Remote Desktop and Remote Assistance	Remote Desktop and Remote Assistance listen at port 3389.
137, 138, and 139	SMB over NetBIOS	NetBIOS is a legacy suite of protocols used by Windows before TCP/IP. To support legacy NetBIOS applications on a TCP/IP network, TCP offers NetBIOS over TCP/IP. Earlier versions of SMB required NetBIOS over TCP/IP be enabled. Ports used on these networks are: ◢ SMB over UDP uses ports 137 and 138. ◢ SMB over TCP uses ports 137 and 139. Current versions of SMB don't require NetBIOS over TCP.

Table 8-4   Common TCP/IP port assignments for client/server applications (continues)

Port	Protocol and App	Description
445	SMB direct over TCP/IP	Current releases of SMB and SMB2 use port 445 for both TCP and UDP traffic.
427	SLP and AFP	Service Location Protocol (SLP) uses port 427 to find printers and file sharing devices on a network. AFP relies on SLP and port 427 to find resources on a local network.
548	AFP	AFP over TCP/IP is used for file sharing and file services.

Table 8-4 Common TCP/IP port assignments for client/server applications (continued)

Now that you have an understanding of TCP/IP and Windows networking, let's apply that knowledge to making network connections.

CONNECTING A COMPUTER TO A NETWORK

Connecting a computer to a network is quick and easy in most situations. We begin with a summary of how to connect to a wired or wireless network and then you learn to connect to a WWAN (cellular network), how to make a dial-up connection, and how to connect to a VPN.

CONNECT TO AN ETHERNET WIRED OR WIRELESS WI-FI LOCAL NETWORK

To connect a computer to a network using an Ethernet wired or Wi-Fi wireless connection, follow these steps:

1. In general, before you connect to any network, the network adapter and its drivers must be installed and Device Manager should report no errors.

2. Do one of the following to connect to the network:

   ▲ For a wired network, plug in the network cable to the Ethernet port. The port is also called an RJ-45 port (RJ stands for registered jack) and looks like a large phone jack. Indicator lights near the network port should light up to indicate connectivity and activity. For Ethernet, Windows should automatically configure the connection.

   ▲ For a wireless network, in Windows 8, you can use the charms bar or the Network icon in the taskbar on the Windows 8/7 desktop. On the desktop, click the Network icon in the taskbar and select a wireless network. Click **Connect**. If the network is secured, you must enter the security key to the wireless network to connect.

3. Open your browser and make sure you can access the web. For wireless connections, some hotspots provide a home page where you must enter a code or agree to the terms of use before you can use the network. On a private network, open File Explorer or Windows Explorer and drill down into the Network group to verify network resources are available (see Figure 8-21).

Figure 8-21   File Explorer shows resources on the network

For wireless connections, you can view the status of the connection, including the security key used to make the connection. Do the following:

1. For Windows 8/7, open **Control Panel** in Classic view and open the **Network and Sharing Center**. Alternately, you can right-click the Network icon in the desktop taskbar and click **Open Network and Sharing Center**. The Network and Sharing Center is shown in Figure 8-22. Click **Change adapter settings**. The Network Connections window appears (see Figure 8-23).

Figure 8-22   The Network and Sharing Center reports two healthy network connections

Figure 8-23   The Network Connections window can be used to repair broken connections

✎ Notes For Windows 8, a shortcut to open the Network Connections window is to press **Win+X** and click **Network Connections**.

2. In the Network Connections window, right-click the **Wi-Fi** connection and click **Status**. In the Wi-Fi Status box (see Figure 8-24), click **Wireless Properties**. On the Wireless Properties box, select the **Security** tab. To view the security key, check **Show characters**. You can also see the security and encryption types that Windows automatically sensed and applied when it made the connection.

Figure 8-24 Verify the Network security key for the wireless network is correct

If you have a problem making a network connection, you can reset the connection. Open the Network Connections window and right-click the network connection. Select **Disable** from the shortcut menu as shown in Figure 8-25. Right-click the connection again and select **Enable**. The connection is reset. Try again to browse the web or access resources on the network. If you still don't have local or Internet access, it's time to dig a little deeper into the source of the problem. More networking troubleshooting tools and solutions are covered in the chapter, "Supporting Network Hardware."

Figure 8-25   To repair a connection, disable and then enable the connection

CONNECT TO A WIRELESS WAN (CELLULAR) NETWORK

To connect a computer using mobile broadband to a wireless wide area network (WWAN), also called a cellular network, such as those provided by Verizon or AT&T, you need the hardware and software to connect and, for some networks, a SIM card. A cellular network can support both voice and data and currently uses one of two technologies: GSM (Global System for Mobile Communications) or CDMA (Code Division Multiple Access). Most carriers in the United States use CDMA, but GSM is more popular globally. Long Term Evolution (LTE) and Voice over LTE (VoLTE) provide data and voice transmissions and are expected to ultimately replace both GSM and CDMA. Many carriers use a combination of GSM and LTE or CDMA and LTE.

Those cellular devices that use GSM or LTE require a SIM (Subscriber Identification Module) card be installed in the device, which contains the information that identifies your device to the carrier (see Figure 8-26).

Back cover of the phone is removed to reveal the SIM card

Battery must be removed to install or remove the SIM card

SIM card installed in slot

Figure 8-26   A SIM card contains proof that your device can use a cellular network

Here are your options for software and hardware devices that can connect to a cellular network:

▲ **Use an embedded mobile broadband modem.** A laptop or other mobile device might have an embedded broadband modem. In this situation, you still need to subscribe to a carrier.

▲ **Tether your cell phone to your computer.** You can tether your cell phone to your computer. The cell phone connects to the cellular network and provides communication to your computer. The phone and computer can connect by way of a USB cable (see Figure 8-27), a proprietary cable provided by your cell phone manufacturer, or a Bluetooth or Wi-Fi wireless connection. Your contract with the carrier must allow tethering.

▲ **Use a USB broadband modem.** For any computer, you can use a USB broadband modem (sometimes called an air card), such as the one shown in Figure 8-28. The device requires a contract with a cellular carrier.

When you purchase any of these devices from a carrier or manufacturer, most likely detailed instructions are included for connecting to the cellular network. Follow those instructions rather than the generic ones presented here. Generally, here's how you can connect to a cellular network:

Figure 8-27 Tether your cell phone to your laptop using a USB cable

▲ **Use an embedded broadband modem.** For laptops or other mobile devices that have an embedded modem, if a SIM card is required, insert the card in the device. For some laptops, the card slot might be in the battery bay, and you must remove the battery to find the slot. Then use

LED light indicates power

LED light indicates network activity

Figure 8-28 A USB broadband modem by Sierra Wireless

a program installed on the device to connect to the cellular network. In addition, the mobile operator might provide software for you to use.

▲ *Tether your cell phone.* To tether your cell phone to your computer, your carrier is likely to provide you software to make the connection. If software is provided, install the software first and then tether your cell phone to your computer. Use the software to make the connection.

▲ *Use a USB broadband modem.* When using a USB broadband modem, if needed, insert the SIM card in the modem (see Figure 8-29). When you insert the modem into a USB port, Windows finds the device, and the software stored on the device automatically installs and runs. A window then appears provided by the software that allows you to connect to the cellular network.

Slot for SIM card

Remove the back cover to reveal the SIM card

Figure 8-29   A SIM card with subscription information on it might be required to use a cellular network

The software might prompt you to go to the website of your carrier and activate the phone number used by the modem. Figure 8-30 shows the software provided by one modem. Notice you can connect to the mobile network or the Wi-Fi network, but not both at the same time.

Source: AT&T Communications Manager

Figure 8-30   Use the management software to connect and disconnect from the Mobile (cellular) or Wi-Fi network

CREATE A DIAL-UP CONNECTION

You never know when you might be called on to support an older dial-up connection. Here are the bare-bones steps you need to set up and support this type of connection:

1. Install an internal or external dial-up modem. Make sure Device Manager recognizes the card without errors.

2. Plug the phone line into the modem port on your computer and into the wall jack.

3. Open the **Network and Sharing Center** window. In the Network and Sharing Center window (refer back to Figure 8-22), click **Set up a new connection or network**. In the dialog box that appears (see Figure 8-31), select **Connect to the Internet - Set up a broadband or dial-up connection to the Internet** and click **Next**.

Figure 8-31 Create a dial-up connection to an ISP

4. In the next box, click **Dial-up.** In the next box (see Figure 8-32), enter the phone number to your ISP, your ISP user name and password, and the name you decide to give the dial-up connection, such as the name and city of your ISP. Then click **Create.**

Figure 8-32 Enter phone number and account information to your ISP

To use the connection, click your Network icon in the taskbar. In the list of available connections, select your dial-up connection (see Figure 8-33a) and click **Connect**. The Connect dialog box appears, where you can enter your password (see Figure 8-33b). Click **Dial**. You will hear the modem dial up the ISP and make the connection.

(a)   (b)

Figure 8-33 (a) Select your dial-up connection, and (b) enter the password to your ISP

If the dial-up connection won't work, here are some things you can try:

⊿ Is the phone line working? Plug in a regular phone and check for a dial tone. Is the phone cord securely connected to the computer and the wall jack?

⊿ Does the modem work? Check Device Manager for reported errors about the modem. Does the modem work when making a call to another phone number (not your ISP)?

⊿ Check the Dial-up Connection Properties box for errors. To do so, click **Change adapter settings** in the Network and Sharing Center, and then right-click the dial-up connection and select **Properties** from the shortcut menu. Is the phone number correct? Does the number need to include a 9 to get an outside line? Has a 1 been added in front of the number by mistake? If you need to add a 9, you can put a comma in the field like this "9,4045661200", which causes a slight pause after the 9 is dialed.

⊿ Try dialing the number manually from a phone. Do you hear beeps on the other end? Try another phone number.

⊿ When you try to connect, do you hear the number being dialed? If so, the problem is most likely with the phone number, the phone line, or the user name and password.

⊿ Try removing and reinstalling the dial-up connection.

CREATE A VPN CONNECTION

A virtual private network (VPN) is often used by employees when they telecommute to connect to the corporate network by way of the Internet. A VPN protects data by encrypting it from the time it leaves the remote computer until it reaches a server on the corporate network. The encryption technique is called a tunnel or tunneling (see Figure 8-34).

Figure 8-34 With a VPN, tunneling is used to send encrypted data over wired and wireless networks and the Internet

A VPN can be managed by operating systems, routers, or third-party software such as OpenVPN (*openvpn.net*). A VPN connection is a virtual connection, which means you are really setting up the tunnel over an existing connection to the Internet. When creating a VPN connection on a personal computer, always follow directions given by the network administrator who set up the VPN. The company website might provide VPN client software to download and install on your computer.

Here are the general steps to use Windows to connect to a VPN:

1. In the Network and Sharing Center (refer back to Figure 8-22), click **Set up a new connection or network**. Then select **Connect to a workplace - Set up a dial-up or VPN connection to your workplace** (refer back to Figure 8-31) and click **Next**.

2. In the Connect to a Workplace box, click **Use my Internet connection (VPN)**. In the next box, enter the IP address or domain name of the network (see Figure 8-35). Your network administrator can provide this information. Name the VPN connection and click **Create**.

Figure 8-35   Enter logon information to the VPN network

> **◇ OS Differences**   Windows 8 requires you to enter your user name and password at the time you connect to a VPN. Windows 7 gives you the option to enter this information when you set up the VPN or as you connect to it.

    Whenever you want to use the VPN connection, click the Network icon in the taskbar. In the list of available networks, click the **VPN connection** and click **Connect**. Enter your user name and password (for Windows 8, see Figure 8-36) and click **OK**. Your user name and password are likely to be the network ID and password you use to connect to the Windows domain on the corporate network.

Figure 8-36 Enter your user name and password to connect to your VPN

After the connection is made, you can use your browser to access the corporate secured intranet websites or other resources. The resources you can access depend on the permissions assigned the user account.

Problems connecting to a VPN can be caused by the wrong authentication protocols used when passing the user name and password to the VPN. To configure these settings, in the Network and Sharing Center, click **Change adapter settings**. In the Network Connections window, right-click **VPN Connection** and click **Properties**. In the Properties box, select the **Security** tab (see Figure 8-37). Here you can select the authentication protocols given to you by the network administrator.

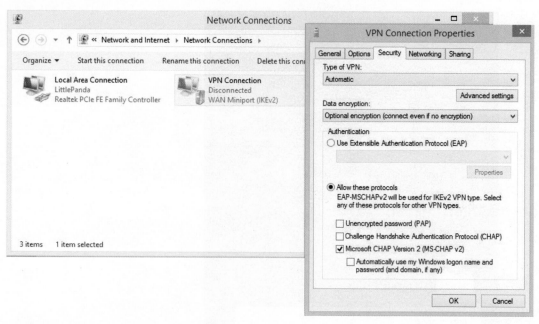

Figure 8-37   Select the VPN's authentication protocol

Now let's turn our attention to how to configure TCP/IP settings for a network connection, including dynamic, static, and alternate address configurations.

DYNAMIC AND STATIC IP CONFIGURATIONS

By default, Windows assumes dynamic IP addressing and automatically configures the network connection. However, some networks use static IP addresses.

To configure dynamic and static IP addresses, follow these steps:

1. Open the **Network Connections** window. Right-click the network connection and click **Properties**. In the Properties box, click the **Networking** tab, which is the middle box shown in Figure 8-38 for the Local Area Connection (Ethernet). Select **Internet Protocol Version 4 (TCP/IPv4)** and click **Properties**. The TCP/IPv4 Properties box appears (see the right side of Figure 8-38).

Figure 8-38   Configure TCP/IPv4 for static or dynamic addressing

2. By default, dynamic IP addressing is used, which selects *Obtain an IP address automatically* and *Obtain DNS server address automatically*. To change the settings to static IP addressing, select **Use the following IP address**. Then enter the IP address, subnet mask, and default gateway. (A default gateway is the gateway a computer uses to access another network if it does not have a better option.)

3. If you have been given the IP addresses of DNS servers, select **Use the following DNS server addresses** and enter up to two IP addresses. If you have other DNS IP addresses, click **Advanced** and enter them on the **DNS** tab of the Advanced TCP/IP Settings box.

> ✎ **Notes** Notice in Figure 8-38 that you can select Internet Protocol Version 6 (TCP/IPv6) and click Properties to change IPv6 properties, including static and dynamic address configuration.
> You can also uncheck Internet Protocol Version 6 (TCP/IPv6) to disable it. For most situations, you need to leave it enabled. A bug in Windows 7 might prevent you from joining a homegroup if IPv6 is disabled.

ALTERNATE IP ADDRESS CONFIGURATION

Suppose an employee with a laptop often travels, and her work network uses static IP addressing, and, as you know, most public networks use dynamic IP addressing. How do you configure her computer's TCP/IP settings? For travel, you would configure the computer to use dynamic IP addressing for public networks. However, when the computer attempts to connect to the corporate network, the computer won't be able to find a DHCP server to get an IP address, subnet mask, default gateway, and DNS server addresses, and it will default to an Automatic Private IP Address (APIPA) and won't have the information it needs to connect to the network or Internet. The solution is to create an alternate configuration that the computer will use if it cannot find a DHCP server.

To create an alternate configuration, on the TCP/IPv4 Properties box shown in Figure 8-38, click the **Alternate Configuration** tab. By default, the alternate configuration is Automatic private IP address. See Figure 8-39. Select **User configured**. Then enter a static IP address, subnet mask, default gateway, and DNS server addresses for the alternate configuration to be used on the company network. Click **OK** and close all boxes.

Figure 8-39 Create an alternate static IP address configuration

MANAGE NETWORK ADAPTERS

A computer makes a direct connection to a local wired network by way of a network adapter, which might be a network port embedded on the motherboard or a network interface card (NIC) designed for installation in an expansion slot on the motherboard (refer back to Figure 8-3). In addition, the adapter might also be an external device plugged into a USB port (see Figure 8-40). The wired network adapter provides a network port. A network adapter is often called a NIC, even when it's not really a card but a USB device or a network port embedded on the motherboard, which can be called an onboard NIC.

Figure 8-40 USB device provides an Ethernet port

Here are the features you need to be aware of that might be included with a network adapter:

▲ **The drivers a NIC uses.** A NIC usually comes bundled with drivers on CD and can be downloaded from the web. Windows has several embedded NIC drivers. After you install a NIC, you can install its drivers. Problems with the network adapter can sometimes be solved by using Device Manager to update the drivers or uninstall the drivers and then reinstall them.

▲ **Ethernet speeds.** For wired networks, the four speeds for Ethernet are 10 Mbps, 100 Mbps (Fast Ethernet; technical name is 100BaseT), 1 Gbps (Gigabit Ethernet or 1000BaseT), and 10 Gbps (10-gigabit Ethernet or 10GBaseT). Most network adapters sold today for local networks use Gigabit Ethernet and also support the two slower speeds. To see the speeds supported, open the Ethernet network adapter's Properties box in Device Manager. Select the Advanced tab. In the list of properties, select Speed & Duplex. You can then see available speeds in the Value dropdown list (see the right side of Figure 8-41). If the adapter connects with slower network devices on the network, the adapter works at the slower speed. Notice in the dropdown list choices for half duplex or full duplex. Full duplex sends and receives transmissions at the same time. Half duplex works in only one direction at a time. Select Auto Negotiation for Windows to use the best possible speed and duplex.

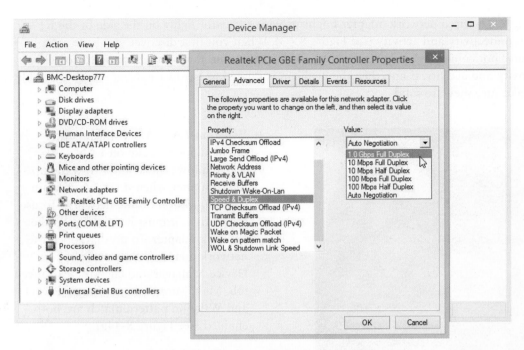

Figure 8-41 Set the speed and duplex for the network adapter

> **Notes** The speed of a network depends on the speed of each device on the network and how well a router manages that traffic. Routers, switches, and network adapters currently run at three speeds: Gigabit Ethernet (1000 Mbps or 1 Gbps), Fast Ethernet (100 Mbps), or Ethernet (10 Mbps). If you want your entire network to run at the fastest speed, make sure all your devices are rated for Gigabit Ethernet.

▲ *MAC address.* Every network adapter (wired or wireless) has a 48-bit (6-byte) identification number, called the MAC address or physical address, hard-coded on the card by its manufacturer that is unique for that adapter, and this number is used to identify the adapter on the network. An example of a MAC address is 00-0C-6E-4E-AB-A5. Most likely, the MAC address is printed on the device. You can also have Windows tell you the MAC address by entering the **ipconfig /all** command in a command prompt window (see Figure 8-42).

Figure 8-42 Use the ipconfig /all command to show the MAC address of a network adapter

▲ *Status indicator lights.* A wired network adapter might provide indicator lights on the side of the RJ-45 port that indicate connectivity and activity (see Figure 8-43). When you first discover you have a problem with a computer not connecting to a network, be sure to check the status indicator lights to verify you have connectivity and activity. If not, then the problem is related to hardware. Next, check the cable connections to make sure they are solid.

Figure 8-43 Status indicator lights for the onboard network port

▲ *Wake-on-LAN.* A network adapter might support Wake-on-LAN, which allows the adapter to wake up the computer when it receives certain communication on the network. To use the feature, it must be enabled on the network adapter. To do that, open the network adapter's Properties box in Device Manager and click the **Advanced** tab. Make sure **Wake on Magic Packet** and **Wake on pattern match** are both enabled (see Figure 8-44a).

> 🖊 **Notes** Some network adapters provide a Power Management tab in the Properties box. To use the Power Management tab to enable Wake-on-LAN, check **Allow this device to wake the computer** (see Figure 8-44b).

(a)

(b)

Figure 8-44 Enable Wake-on-LAN (a) using the Advanced tab, or (b) using the Power Management tab of the network adapter Properties box

For an onboard NIC, you must also enable Wake-on-LAN in UEFI/BIOS setup. Reboot the computer and enter UEFI/BIOS setup and look for the option on a power-management screen in UEFI/BIOS setup. Figure 8-45 shows the BIOS screen for one onboard NIC. It is not recommended that you enable Wake-on-LAN for a wireless network adapter.

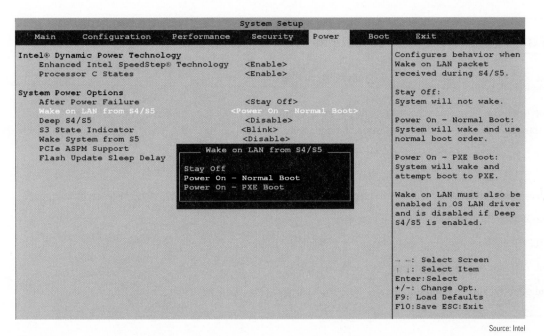

Source: Intel

Figure 8-45 Use the Power screen in the BIOS setup to enable Wake-on-LAN

Figure 8-46 Select Priority Enabled to allow the network adapter to support QoS on the network

▲ *Quality of Service (QoS).* Another feature of a network adapter is the ability to control which applications have priority on the network. The feature must be enabled and configured on the router and also enabled on the network adapters and configured in Windows for every computer on the network using the high-priority applications. To enable Quality of Service (QoS) for a NIC, open the network adapter Properties box in Device Manager. On the Advanced tab, make sure **Priority Enabled** is selected, as shown in Figure 8-46. (If the option is not listed, the adapter does not support QoS.) Later in this chapter, you learn how to configure a router to use QoS. To configure an application to use QoS, you can use Group Policy in professional and business editions of Windows. How to use Group Policy is covered in the companion volume to this text, *A+ Guide to Software.*

Hands-On | Project 8-3   Investigate TCP/IP Settings

Using a computer connected to a network, answer these questions:

1. What is the hardware device used to make this connection (network card, onboard port, wireless)? List the device's name as Windows sees it in the Device Manager window.

2. What is the MAC address of the wired or wireless network adapter? What command or window did you use to get your answer?

3. For a wireless connection, is the network secured? If so, what is the security type? What is the encryption type?

4. What is the IPv4 address of the network connection?

5. Are your TCP/IP version 4 settings using static or dynamic IP addressing?

6. What is the IPv6 address of your network connection?

7. Disable and enable your network connection. Now what is your IPv4 address?

SETTING UP A MULTIFUNCTION ROUTER FOR A SOHO NETWORK

A+
220-901
2.5, 2.6

An IT support technician is likely to be called on to set up a small office or home office (SOHO) network. As part of setting up a small network, you need to know how to configure a multipurpose router to stand between the network and the Internet. You also need to know how to set up and secure a wireless access point. Most SOHO routers are also a wireless access point.

★ A+ Exam Tip The A+ 220-901 exam expects you to be able to install, configure, and secure a SOHO wired and wireless router.

FUNCTIONS OF A SOHO ROUTER

A+
220-901
2.5, 2.6

Routers can range from small ones designed to manage a SOHO network connecting to an ISP (costing around $75 to $200) to those that manage multiple networks and extensive traffic (costing several thousand dollars). On a small office or home network, a router stands between the ISP network and the local network (see Figure 8-47), and the router is the gateway to the Internet. Note in the figure that computers can connect to the router using wired or wireless connections.

Figure 8-47   A router stands between a local network and the ISP network and manages traffic between them

A typical SOHO router is usually several devices in one:

◢ *Function 1:* As a router, it stands between two networks, the ISP network and the local network, and routes traffic between the two networks.

◢ *Function 2:* As a switch, it manages several network ports that can be connected to wired computers or to a switch that provides more ports for more computers.

◢ *Function 3:* As a DHCP server, it can provide IP addresses to networked computers.

◢ *Function 4:* As a wireless access point (WAP), it enables a wireless computer to connect to the network. This wireless connection can be secured using wireless security features.

◢ *Function 5:* As a firewall, it blocks unwanted traffic initiated from the Internet and can restrict Internet access for local computers behind the firewall. Restrictions on local computers can apply to days of the week, time of day, keywords used, or certain websites. It can limit network and Internet access to only specified computers, based on their MAC addresses. It also provides Network Address Translation (NAT) so that computers on the LAN can use private or link-local IP addresses.

◢ *Function 6:* As an FTP server, you can connect an external hard drive to the router, and the FTP firmware on the router can be used to share files with network users.

An example of a multifunction router is the Nighthawk AC1900 by NETGEAR shown in Figures 8-48 and 8-49. It has one Internet port for the broadband modem (cable modem or DSL modem) and four ports for computers on the network. The USB port can be used to plug in a USB external hard drive for use by any computer on the network. The router is also a wireless access point having multiple antennas to increase speed and range.

Source: Amazon.com

Figure 8-48   NETGEAR Nighthawk AC1900 Dual band Wi-Fi Gigabit router

Source: NETGEAR

Figure 8-49   Connections and ports on the back of the NETGEAR router

INSTALL AND CONFIGURE A ROUTER ON THE LOCAL NETWORK

A+
220-901
2.5, 2.6

When deciding where to physically place a router, consider the physical security of the router and, as a wireless access point, make sure the router is centrally located to create the best Wi-Fi hotspot for users. For physical security, don't place the router in a public location in a small business, such as the lobby. For best security, place the router behind a locked door accessible only to authorized personnel in a location with access to network cabling. The indoor range for a Wi-Fi hotspot is up to 70 meters; the range is affected by many factors, including interference from walls, furniture, electrical equipment, and other nearby hotspots. For the best Wi-Fi strength, position your router or a stand-alone wireless access point in the center of where you want your hotspot and know that a higher position (near the ceiling) works better than a lower position (on the floor).

✎ **Notes** Some wireless access points are plenum rated, meaning that, according to fire codes, they can be installed in the plenum area between floors in a building or above a suspended ceiling. For these types of installation, network technicians are careful to follow local fire codes and must take into account how the device might affect airflow in the plenum.

For routers that have external antennas, raise the antennas to vertical positions. Plug in the router and connect network cables to the local network. Connect the network cable from the ISP modem or other device to the uplink port on the router.

To configure a router for the first time or change its configuration, always follow the directions of the manufacturer rather than the general directions given here. You can use any computer on the network that uses a wired connection (it doesn't matter which one) to configure the firmware on the router. You'll need the IP address of the router and the default user name and password to the router setup. To find this information, look in the router documentation or search online for your model and brand of router.

Here are the general steps for one router, the Nighthawk AC1900 by NETGEAR, although the setup screens for your router may be different:

1. Open your browser and enter the IP address of the router in the address box. In our example, the address is 192.168.1.1. The Windows Security box appears (see Figure 8-50). For our router, the default user name and password is **admin**, although yours might be different.

Figure 8-50 Enter the user name and password to the router firmware utility

2. The main setup page of the router firmware appears in your browser window. Figure 8-51 shows the main page for a router that has already been configured. Notice the BASIC tab is selected. Most of the settings you'll need are on the ADVANCED tab. Begin by poking around to see what's available and to find the setting you need. If you make changes, be sure to save your changes. When finished, click **Logout** and close the browser window.

Source: NETGEAR

Figure 8-51 Main screen for router firmware setup

Following are some changes that you might need to make to the router's configuration. The first setting should always be done.

CHANGE THE ROUTER PASSWORD

It's extremely important to protect access to your network and prevent others from hijacking your router. If you have not already done so, change the default password to your router firmware. For our router, click the **ADVANCED** tab, click **Administration**, and click **Set Password** (see Figure 8-52). Change the password and click **Apply**. If the firmware offers the option, disable the ability to configure the router from over the wireless network. Know that this password to configure the router firmware is different from the password needed to access the router's wireless network.

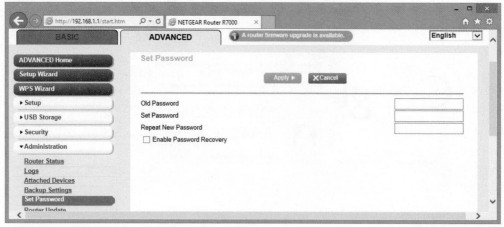

Source: NETGEAR

Figure 8-52   Change the router firmware password

> ⚡ **Caution**   Changing the router password is especially important if the router is a wireless router. Unless you have disabled or secured the wireless access point, anyone outside your building can use your wireless network. If they guess the default password to the router, they can change the password to hijack your router. Also, your wireless network can be used for criminal activity. When you first install a router, before you do anything else, change your router password and disable the wireless network until you have time to set up and test the wireless security. And, to give even more security, change the default user name to another user name if the router utility allows that option.

CONFIGURE THE DHCP SERVER

To configure the DHCP server for our sample router, click the **ADVANCED** tab and then **LAN Setup** in the Setup group (see Figure 8-53). On this page, you can enable or disable the DHCP server and set the IP address of the router and subnet mask for the network. For the DHCP server, set the starting and ending IP addresses, which determines the number of IP addresses DHCP can serve up. Be sure the router and all the IP addresses are on the same subnet, according to the subnet mask. After making changes on this page, click **Apply** to save your changes.

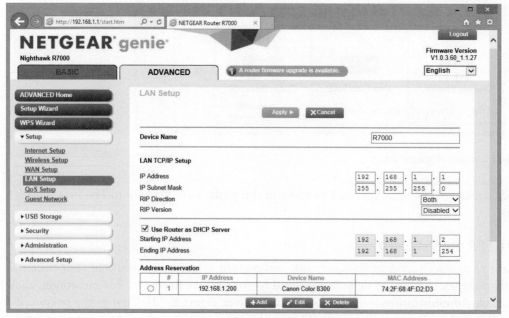

Source: NETGEAR

Figure 8-53   Configure the DHCP server in the router firmware

ASSIGN STATIC IP ADDRESSES

A computer or network printer might require a static IP address, which is called address reservation. For example, when a computer is running a web server on the local network, it needs a static IP address so that other computers on the network that need access to this intranet website can find the web server. A network printer also needs a static IP address so computers will always be able to find the printer. Do the following:

1. To identify the computer or printer, you'll need its MAC address. When the client is connected to the network, on the ADVANCED tab, click **Attached Devices** in the Administration group (see Figure 8-54). Copy the MAC address (select it and press **CTRL+C**) or write it down.

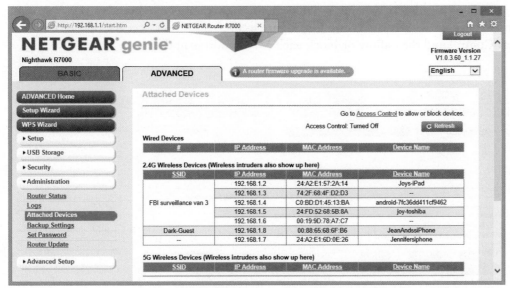

Source: NETGEAR

Figure 8-54   View the MAC addresses of devices connected to the network

2. To assign a static IP address to the client, on the LAN Setup page shown in Figure 8-53, click **Add** under **Address Reservation**. In the IP address field, enter the IP address to assign to the computer or printer. Be sure to use an IP address in the LAN's subnet, such as 192.168.1.200 in our example. Select the MAC address from the list of attached devices or copy or type the MAC address in the field. Click **Apply** to save your changes. In Figure 8-55, a Canon network printer is set to receive the IP address 192.168.1.200 each time it connects to the network.

Source: NETGEAR

Figure 8-55   Use address reservation to assign a static IP address to a computer or other device

> ✏ **Notes**   If you are running a web server on the Internet, you will need a public IP address for your router and a static private IP address for the web server. For this situation, you can lease a public IP address from your ISP at an additional cost. You will also need to enable port forwarding to the server, which is discussed later in this chapter.

MAC ADDRESS FILTERING

MAC address filtering allows you to control access to your network to only certain computers or devices. If a MAC address is not entered in a table of MAC addresses, the computer is not allowed to connect to the network. For our sample router, the MAC address table can be viewed and edited on the ADVANCED tab on the Access Control page in the Security group (see Figure 8-56). To turn on Access Control, check the box **Turn on Access Control** and then allow or block each MAC address in the table.

Source: NETGEAR

Figure 8-56   Use MAC address filtering to allow and block devices on the network

IMPROVE QoS FOR AN APPLICATION

As you use your network and notice that one application is not getting the best service, you can improve network performance for this application using the Quality of Service (QoS) feature discussed earlier in this chapter. For example, suppose you routinely use Skype to share your desktop with collaborators over the Internet. To assign a high priority to Skype for our sample router, do the following:

1. On the ADVANCED tab, select the **QoS Setup** page in the Setup group. This router configures both upstream QoS and downstream QoS. For Skype, click the **Upstream QoS** tab and then click **Setup QoS rule**.

2. Select **Skype** and click **Apply** (see Figure 8-57). If your application is not listed, scroll to the bottom of the list and click **Add Priority Rule**. On the page that appears, you can name the application and the port(s) it uses.

Source: NETGEAR

Figure 8-57 Apply a QoS rule to the selected app

8

UNIVERSAL PLUG AND PLAY

Universal Plug and Play (UPnP) helps computers on the local network automatically discover and communicate with services provided by other computers on the local network. Enable UPnP if computers on the network use applications, such as messaging, gaming, or Windows Remote Assistance, which run on other local computers and there is a problem establishing communication. Basically, a computer can use the router to advertise its service and automatically communicate with other computers on the network. UPnP is considered a security risk because shields between computers are dropped, which hackers might exploit. Therefore, use UPnP with caution.

For our sample router, UPnP is enabled on the UPnP page in the Advanced Setup group on the ADVANCED tab (see Figure 8-58). Any computers and their ports that are currently using UPnP are listed.

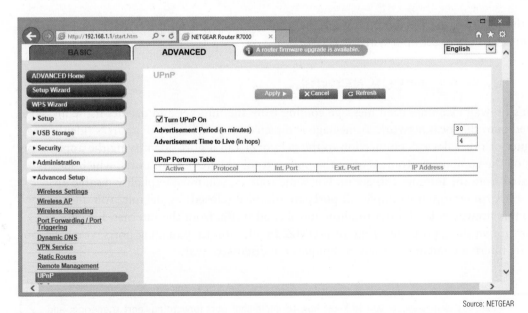

Source: NETGEAR

Figure 8-58 Turn on UPnP

UPDATE ROUTER FIRMWARE

As part of maintaining a router, know the router manufacturers often release updates to the router firmware. The router setup utility can be used to download and apply these updates. For our sample router, when you click **A router firmware update is available** on any of the setup screens (for example, see Figure 8-58), the Firmware Upgrade Assistant page appears (see Figure 8-59). Use this page to perform the upgrade.

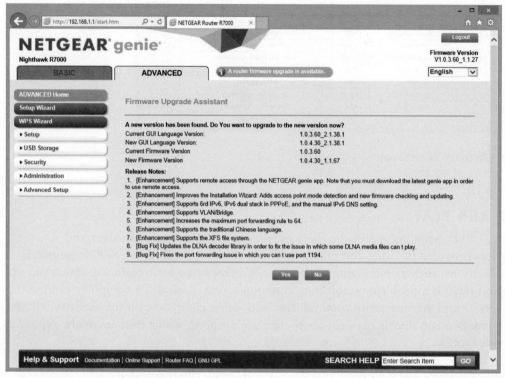

Source: NETGEAR

Figure 8-59   Update router firmware

Now let's look at the concepts and steps to allow certain activity initiated from the Internet past your firewall. Then we'll look at how to set up a wireless network.

LIMIT INTERNET TRAFFIC ON YOUR NETWORK

**A+
220-901
2.5, 2.6**

A router's firewall examines each message coming from the Internet and decides if the message is allowed onto the local network. A message is directed to a particular IP address (identifying a computer or other device's connection to the network) and a port (identifying the application running on the computer). Routers offer the option to disable (close) all ports, which means that no activity initiated from the Internet can get in. For some routers, you must explicitly disable all ports. For the NETGEAR router in our example, all ports are disabled (closed) by default. You must specify exceptions to this firewall rule in order to allow unsolicited traffic from the Internet. Exceptions are allowed using port forwarding, port triggering, or a DMZ. In addition to managing ports, you can also limit Internet traffic by filtering content. All these techniques are discussed next.

⭐ **A+ Exam Tip**   The A+ 220-901 exam expects you to know how to implement port forwarding, port triggering, and a DMZ.

PORT FORWARDING

Suppose you're hosting an Internet game or website or want to use Remote Desktop to access your home computer from the Internet. In these situations, you need to enable (open) certain ports to certain computers so that activity initiated from the Internet can get past your firewall. This technique, called port forwarding or port mapping, means that when the firewall receives a request for communication from the Internet to the specific computer and port, the request will be allowed and forwarded to that computer on the network. The computer is defined to the router by its static IP address. For example, in Figure 8-60a, port 80 is open and requests to port 80 are forwarded to the web server that is listening at that port. This one computer on the network is the only one allowed to receive requests at port 80.

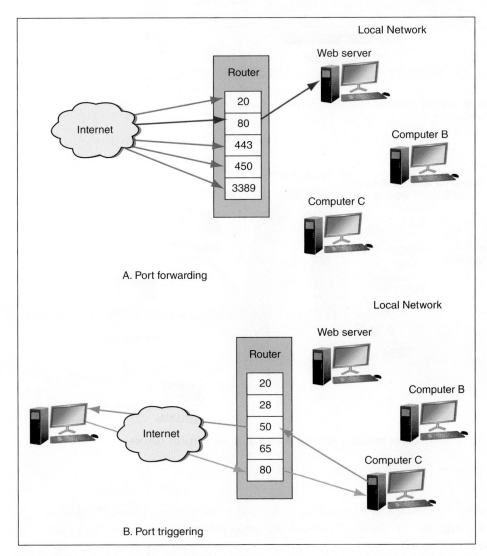

Figure 8-60   Port forwarding and port triggering

To configure port forwarding for our sample router, on the ADVANCED tab, click **Port Forwarding/ Port Triggering** in the Advanced Setup group (see Figure 8-61) and verify **Port Forwarding** is selected. Select the **Service Name** and enter the static IP address of the computer providing the service in the Server IP Address field and click **Add**. Notice in the figure that the Remote Desktop application outside the network can use port forwarding to communicate with the computer whose IP address is 192.168.1.90 using port 3389. The situation is illustrated in Figure 8-62. This computer is set to support the Remote Desktop server application.

Source: NETGEAR

Figure 8-61   Using port forwarding, activity initiated from the Internet is allowed access to a computer on the network

Figure 8-62   With port forwarding, a router allows messages past the firewall that are initiated outside the network

Also notice the IP address for the message in Figure 8-62 is directed to the router's public IP address. The router is using NAT and computers on the local network are using private IP addresses. With port forwarding, the router forwards all traffic to port 3389 to the one computer with this open port even though traffic is directed to the router's public IP address. For this reason, port forwarding is sometimes called Destination Network Address Translation (DNAT).

✎ **Notes**   By the way, if you want to use a domain name rather than an IP address to access a computer on your network from the Internet, you'll need to purchase the domain name and register it in the Internet name space to associate it with your static IP address assigned by your ISP. Several websites on the Internet let you do both; one site is by Network Solutions at *networksolutions.com*.

PORT TRIGGERING

Port triggering opens a port when a computer on the network initiates communication through another port, and is often used with Internet gaming. For example, in Figure 8-60b, Computer C sends a message to port 50 to a computer on the Internet. The router is configured to open port 80 for communication from this remote computer. Port 80 is closed until this trigger occurs. Port triggering does not require a static IP address for the computer inside the network, and any computer can initiate port triggering. The router will leave port 80 open for a time. If no more data is received from port 50, then it closes port 80.

To configure port triggering on our sample router, select **Port Triggering** on the page shown in Figure 8-61. Click **Add Service**. In the Port Triggering page that appears (see Figure 8-63), type a descriptive name for the service. For Service User, selecting **Any** allows any computer to use the service or you can enter a specific IP address of a remote computer. Select the Service Type (TCP, UDP, or both) and enter the triggering port (the outbound traffic port that will open the inbound ports). Under Inbound Connection, select the Connection Type (TCP, UDP, or both) and the range of ports that will be open for inbound traffic. This information about types of service and ports should be available from the documentation for the application you are using.

Source: NETGEAR

Figure 8-63   For port triggering, identify the service, the triggering port, and the ports to open

Here are some tips to keep in mind when using port forwarding or port triggering:

▲ You must lease a static IP address for your router from your ISP so that people on the Internet can find you. Most ISPs will provide you a static IP address for an additional monthly fee.

▲ For port forwarding to work, the computer on your network must have a static IP address so that the router knows where to send the communication.

▲ If the computer using port triggering stops sending data, the router might close the triggered port before communication is complete. Also, if two computers on the network attempt to trigger the same port, the router will not allow data to pass to either computer.

▲ Using port forwarding, your computer and network are more vulnerable because you are allowing external users directly into your private network. For better security, turn on port forwarding only when you know it's being used.

DMZ

A DMZ (demilitarized zone) in networking is a computer or network that is not protected by a firewall or has limited protection. You can drop all your shields protecting a computer by putting it in a DMZ and the firewall no longer protects it. If you are having problems getting port forwarding or port triggering to work, putting a computer in a DMZ can free it to receive any communication from the Internet. All unsolicited traffic from the Internet that the router would normally drop is forwarded to the computer designated as the DMZ server.

> ⚡ **Caution** If a DMZ computer is compromised, it can be used to attack other computers on the network. Use it only as a last resort when you cannot get port forwarding or port triggering to work. It goes without saying to not leave the DMZ enabled unless you are using it.

To set up a DMZ server for our sample router, on the ADVANCED tab, select **WAN Setup** in the Setup group (see Figure 8-64). Check **Default DMZ Server** and enter the static IP address of the computer.

Source: NETGEAR

Figure 8-64 Set up an unprotected DMZ server for the network

CONTENT FILTERING AND PARENTAL CONTROLS

Routers normally provide a way for employers or parents to limit the content that computers on the local network can access on the Internet. Filtering can apply to specific computers, users, websites, categories of websites, keywords, services, time of day, and day of week. Filters can apply to black lists (lists what cannot be accessed) or white lists (lists what can be accessed).

For our sample router, content filtering and parental controls are managed in the Security group on the ADVANCED tab. Here are the options:

◢ The Parental Controls page provides access to the Live Parental Controls application and website at *www.netgear.com/lpc* where parents can manage content allowed from the Internet and monitor websites and content accessed.

◢ The Block Sites page (see Figure 8-65) allows you to enter keywords or websites to block. Notice you can also specify a trusted IP address of a computer on the network that is allowed access to this content.

Figure 8-65 Block sites by keyword or domain names

Source: NETGEAR

▲ The Block Services page can block services on the Internet. For example, you can block Internet gaming services or email services or allow the service based on a schedule. You will need to know the ports these services use. You can also specify the IP addresses of computers to which the block applies.

▲ The Schedule page allows you to specify the schedule of time and day a blocked service can be used.

▲ The E-mail page gives you the option for the router to email to you a log of router activities.

Now let's turn our attention to configuring a wireless access point provided by a router.

SET UP A WIRELESS NETWORK

<table>
<tr><td>A+
220-901
2.5, 2.6</td><td>A wireless network is created by a wireless access point (WAP). The standards for a local wireless network are called Wi-Fi (Wireless Fidelity), and their technical name is IEEE 802.11. The IEEE 802.11 standards, collectively known as the 802.11 a/b/g/n/ac standards, have evolved over the years and are summarized in Table 8-5.</td></tr>
</table>

★ **A+ Exam Tip** The A+ 220-901 exam expects you to know about 802.11 a/b/g/n/ac standards, their speeds, distances, and frequencies.

Wi-Fi Standard	Speeds, Distances, and Frequencies
IEEE 802.11a	◢ Speeds up to 54 Mbps (megabits per second). ◢ Short range up to 50 meters with radio frequency of 5.0 GHz. ◢ 802.11a is no longer used.
IEEE 802.11b	◢ Up to 11 Mbps with a range of up to 100 meters. (Indoor ranges are less than outdoor ranges.) ◢ The radio frequency of 2.4 GHz experiences interference from cordless phones and microwaves.
IEEE 802.11g	◢ Same as 802.11b, but with a speed up to 54 Mbps.
IEEE 802.11n	◢ Up to 600 Mbps depending on the configuration. ◢ Indoor range up to 70 meters and outdoor range up to 250 meters. ◢ Can use either 5.0-GHz or 2.4-GHz radio frequency. ◢ Uses multiple input/multiple output (MIMO), which means a WAP can have up to four antennas to improve performance.
IEEE 802.11ac	◢ Standard supports up to 7 Gbps, although current actual speeds are about 1300 Mbps. ◢ Same ranges as 802.11n except performance does not weaken at long range as does 802.11n. ◢ Uses the 5.0-GHz radio frequency. ◢ Supports up to eight antennas. ◢ Supports beamforming, which detects the locations of connected devices and increases signal strength in that direction.

Table 8-5 Older and current Wi-Fi standards

Wireless computers and other devices on the wireless LAN (WLAN) must support the latest wireless standard for it to be used. If not, the connection uses the latest standard both the WAP and client support. Figure 8-66 shows a wireless adapter that has two antennas and supports the 802.11n standard. Most new adapters, wireless computers, and mobile devices support 802.11ac and are backward compatible with older standards.

Figure 8-66 Wireless network adapter with two antennas supports 802.11b/g/n Wi-Fi standards

Now let's look at the various features and settings of a wireless access point and how to configure them.

Notes When configuring your wireless access point, it's important you are connected to the router by way of a wired connection. If you change a wireless setting and you are connected wirelessly, your wireless connection will immediately be dropped and you cannot continue configuring the router until you connect again.

SECURITY KEY

The most common and effective method of securing a wireless network is to require a security key before a client can connect to the network. By default, a network that uses a security key encrypts data on the network. Use the router firmware to set the security key. For best security, enter a security key that is different from the password you use to the router utility.

Notes To make the strongest passphrase or security key, use a random group of numbers, uppercase and lowercase letters, and, if allowed, at least one symbol. Also use at least eight characters in the passphrase.

For our sample router, the security key can be set on the ADVANCED tab, Wireless Setup page in the Setup group (see Figure 8-67) and is called the Password or Network Key. Click **Apply** to save your changes.

Source: NETGEAR

Figure 8-67 Configure the router's wireless access point

SET ENCRYPTION

When you set a security key, routers by default encrypt wireless transmissions, and you can change the encryption protocols used or disable encryption. (Encrypting transmissions slows down the network; disabling encryption can improve performance and might be appropriate when you are not concerned about transmissions being hacked.) The three main protocols for encryption for 802.11 wireless networks are:

▲ **WEP.** WEP (Wired Equivalent Privacy) is no longer considered secure because the key used for encryption is static (it doesn't change).
▲ **WPA.** WPA (Wi-Fi Protected Access), also called TKIP (Temporal Key Integrity Protocol) encryption, is stronger than WEP and was designed to replace it. With WPA encryption, encryption keys are constantly changing.
▲ **WPA2.** WPA2 (Wi-Fi Protected Access 2), also called the 802.11i standard, is the latest and best wireless encryption standard. It is based on the AES (Advanced Encryption Standard), which improved on the way TKIP generated encryption keys. All wireless devices sold today support the WPA2 standard.

To configure encryption for our sample router, first, notice in Figure 8-67 that this router supports two wireless frequencies: 2.4 GHz used by 802.11 b/g/n standards and 5 GHz used by 802.11 a/n/ac. The security key applies to either band, but each band can have its own encryption type. For the best security, set both bands to **WPA-PSK [TKIP] + WPA2-PSK [AES]** encryption. This setting means a wireless connection will use WPA2 encryption unless an older device does not support it, in which case the connection reverts to WPA encryption. Click **Apply** to save your changes.

CHANGE THE DEFAULT SSID AND DISABLE SSID BROADCASTING

The Service Set Identifier (SSID) is the name of a wireless network. When you look at Figure 8-67, you can see that each frequency band has its own SSID and you can change that name. Each band is its own wireless network, which the access point (router) connects to the local wired network. When you give each band its own SSID and connect a wireless computer to your network, you can select the band by selecting the appropriate SSID. If your computer supports 802.11ac, you would want to select the SSID for the 5-GHz band in order to get the faster speeds of the 802.11ac standard. If you selected the SSID for the 2.4-GHz band, the connection would revert to the slower 802.11n standard.

> **Notes** Notice in Figure 8-67 the option to select the mode a wireless network will use, which determines the speed of the wireless network. The 802.11ac standard currently supports the speed of 1300 Mbps. If you select a slower mode for the 5-GHz band, such as 600 Mbps, in effect you are preventing the 802.11ac standard from being used on the network and connections will revert to the 802.11n standard that uses the 600-Mbps speed. For best results, use the fastest mode the band supports.

Also notice in Figure 8-67 the option to Enable SSID Broadcast. When you disable SSID broadcasting, the wireless network will appear as Unnamed or Unknown Network. When a client selects this network, you are given the opportunity to enter the SSID. If you don't enter the name correctly, you will not be able to connect. This security method is not considered strong security because software can be used to discover an SSID that is not broadcasted.

SELECT CHANNELS FOR THE WLAN

A channel is a specific radio frequency within a broader frequency. For example, two channels in the 5-GHz band are 5.180-GHz and 5.200-GHz channels. In the United States, eleven channels are available for wireless communication in the 5-GHz or 2.4-GHz bands. In North America, the 5-GHz band uses channels 36, 40, 44, and 48, and the 2.4-GHz band uses channels 1 through 14 (preferred nonoverlapping channels are 1, 6, and 11). For most networks, you can allow auto channel selection so that any channel in the frequency range (5-GHz or 2.4-GHz) will work. The device scans for the least-busy channel. However, if you are trying to solve a problem with interference from a nearby wireless network, you can set each network to a different channel and make the channels far apart to reduce interference. For example, for the 2.4-GHz band, set the network on one WAP to channel 1 and set the other WAP's network to channel 11.

RADIO POWER LEVELS

Some high-end access points allow you to adjust the radio power levels the wireless network can use. To reduce interference, limit the range of the network, or to save on electricity, reduce the power level.

WI-FI PROTECTED SETUP (WPS)

You also need to know about Wi-Fi Protected Setup (WPS), which is designed to make it easier for users to connect their computers to a wireless network when a hard-to-remember SSID and security key are used. WPS generates the SSID and security key using a random string of hard-to-guess letters and numbers. The SSID is not broadcasted, so both the SSID and security key must be entered to connect. Rather than having to enter these difficult strings, a user presses a button on a wireless computer or on the router or enters an eight-digit PIN assigned to the router (see Figure 8-68). All computers on the wireless network must support WPS for it to be used, and you must enable WPS on the router, as shown in the figure.

Source: NETGEAR

Figure 8-68 Enable WPS and decide how the router's PIN is used

WPS might be a security risk if it's not managed well. To improve WPS security, turn on auto disable so that WPS will disable after a few failed PIN entries. If routers don't have the auto disable feature, don't use WPS because an eight-digit PIN is easy to hack with repeated attempts. In addition, if the router has a WPS button to push, don't use WPS unless the router is in a secured physical location. For improved security, turn on WPS only when you are working with a user to connect to the wireless network and then turn it off.

> ★ **A+ Exam Tip** The A+ 220-901 exam expects you to know about installing and configuring a wireless network, including Wi-Fi 802.11 standards, speeds, distances, and frequencies, Wi-Fi channels (1–11), and WEP, WPA, WPA2, TKIP, and AES encryption.

Hands-On | Project 8-4   Research a Wireless LAN

A+
220-901
2.5, 2.6

Suppose you have a DSL connection to the Internet in your home and you want to connect two laptops and a desktop computer in a wireless network to the Internet. You need to purchase a multifunction wireless router like the one you learned to configure in this chapter. You also need a wireless adapter for the desktop computer. (The two laptops have built-in wireless networking.) Use the web to research the equipment needed to create the wireless LAN and answer the following:

1. Save or print two webpages showing two different multifunctional wireless routers. What are the brand, model, and price of each router?

2. Save or print two webpages showing two different wireless adapters a desktop computer can use to connect to the wireless network. Include one external device that uses a USB port and one internal device. What are the brand, model, and price of each device?

3. Which router and wireless adapter would you select for your home network? What is the total cost of both devices?

>> CHAPTER SUMMARY

Understanding TCP/IP and Windows Networking

▲ Networking communication happens at three levels: hardware, operating system, and application levels.

▲ At the hardware level, a network adapter has a MAC address that uniquely identifies it on the network.

▲ Using the TCP/IP protocols, the OS identifies a network connection by an IP address. At the application level, a port address identifies an application.

▲ IP addresses can be dynamic or static. A dynamic IP address is assigned by a DHCP server when the computer first connects to a network. A static IP address is manually assigned.

▲ An IP address using IPv4 has 32 bits, and an IP address using IPv6 has 128 bits. Some IP addresses are private IP addresses that can be used only on intranets.

▲ Using IPv4, a subnet mask determines the number of left most bits in an IP address that identify the local network. The remaining right most bits identify the host.

▲ Using IPv6, three types of IP addresses are a unicast address (used by a single node on a network), multicast address (used for one-to-many transmissions), and anycast address (used by routers).

▲ Types of unicast addresses are a global address (used on the Internet), a link-local address (used on a private network), and a unique local address (used on subnets in a large enterprise).

▲ A computer can be assigned a computer name (also called a host name), and a network can be assigned a domain name. A fully qualified domain name (FQDN) includes the computer name and the domain name. An FQDN can be used to find a computer on the Internet if this name is associated with an IP address kept by DNS servers.

▲ TCP/IP uses protocols at the application level (such as FTP, HTTP, and Telnet) and at the operating system level (such as TCP and UDP).

Connecting a Computer to a Network

▲ An IT support person needs to know how to configure TCP/IP settings and make a wired or wireless connection to an existing network.

▲ To connect to a wireless WAN or cellular network, you need a mobile broadband modem and a subscription to the cellular network. For some carriers, a SIM card is also required.

▲ A dial-up connection uses a telephone modem to make a connection to an ISP.

Setting Up a Multifunction Router for a SOHO Network

▲ A multifunction router for a small office/home office network might serve several functions, including a router, a switch, a DHCP server, a wireless access point, a firewall using NAT, and an FTP server.

▲ It's extremely important to change the password to configure your router as soon as you install it, especially if the router is also a wireless access point.

▲ To allow certain network traffic initiated on the Internet past your firewall, you can use port forwarding, port triggering, and a DMZ.

▲ To secure a wireless access point, you can require a security key, disable SSID broadcasting, and enable encryption (WPA2, WPA, or WEP). As with wired networks, you can also enable MAC address filtering.

8

>> KEY TERMS

For explanations of key terms, see the Glossary for this text.

802.11 a/b/g/n/ac
adapter address
address reservation
AES (Advanced Encryption Standard)
AFP (Apple Filing Protocol)
anycast address
AppleTalk
Automatic Private IP Address (APIPA)
beamforming
best-effort protocol
CDMA (Code Division Multiple Access)
channel
CIDR notation
CIFS (Common Internet File System)
client/server
computer name
connectionless protocol
connection-oriented protocol
default gateway
Destination Network Address Translation (DNAT)
DHCP (Dynamic Host Configuration Protocol)

DHCP client
DHCPv6 server
DMZ (demilitarized zone)
DNS (Domain Name System or Domain Name Service)
DNS client
DNS server
domain name
dynamic IP address
firewall
FTP (File Transfer Protocol)
FTP server
full duplex
fully qualified domain name (FQDN)
gateway
global address
global unicast address
GSM (Global System for Mobile Communications)
half duplex
hardware address
host name
HTTP (Hypertext Transfer Protocol)
HTTPS (HTTP secure)
IEEE 802.11ac

IEEE 802.11n
IMAP4 (Internet Message Access Protocol, version 4)
interface
interface ID
Internet Protocol version 4 (IPv4)
Internet Protocol version 6 (IPv6)
intranet
IP address
ipconfig
ISATAP
Lightweight Directory Access Protocol (LDAP)
link (local link)
link-local address
link-local unicast address
local area network (LAN)
Long Term Evolution (LTE)
loopback address
MAC (Media Access Control) address
MAC address filtering
multicast address
multiple input/multiple output (MIMO)
name resolution

NAT (Network Address Translation)
neighbors
NetBIOS
NetBIOS over TCP/IP
network adapter
network interface card (NIC)
node
octet
onboard NIC
OSI model
physical address
POP3 (Post Office Protocol, version 3)
port
port address
port forwarding
port mapping
port number
port triggering
private IP address
protocol
public IP address
Quality of Service (QoS)
Remote Desktop Protocol (RDP)
RJ-45
router

Secure FTP (SFTP)

Secure Shell (SSH)

Server Message
Block (SMB)

Service Set Identifier
(SSID)

SIM (Subscriber
Identification
Module) card

Simple Network
Management
Protocol (SNMP)

SMB2

SMTP (Simple Mail
Transfer Protocol)

socket

static IP address

subnet

subnet ID

subnet mask

switch

TCP (Transmission
Control Protocol)

TCP/IP (Transmission
Control Protocol/Internet
Protocol)

Telnet

Teredo

TKIP (Temporal Key
Integrity Protocol)

UDP (User Datagram
Protocol)

unicast address

unique local address

Universal Plug and
Play (UPnP)

virtual private
network (VPN)

Voice over LTE (VoLTE)

Wake-on-LAN

WEP (Wired Equivalent
Privacy)

Wi-Fi (Wireless Fidelity)

Wi-Fi Protected
Setup (WPS)

wireless access point (WAP)

wireless LAN (WLAN)

wireless wide area
network (WWAN)

WPA (Wi-Fi Protected
Access)

WPA2 (Wi-Fi Protected
Access 2)

>> REVIEWING THE BASICS

1. How many bits are in a MAC address?

2. How many bits are in an IPv4 address? In an IPv6 address?

3. How does a client application identify a server application on another computer on the network?

4. What are IP addresses called that begin with 10, 172.16, or 192.168?

5. Describe the difference between public and private IPv4 addresses. If a network is using private IP addresses, how can the computers on that network access the Internet?

6. Why is it unlikely that you will find the IP address 192.168.250.10 on the Internet?

7. If no DHCP server is available when a computer configured for dynamic IP addressing connects to the network, what type of IPv4 address is assigned to the computer?

8. If a computer is found to have an IP address of 169.254.1.1, what can you assume about how it received that IP address?

9. What are the last 64 bits of an IPv6 address called? How are these bits used?

10. Name two tunneling protocols that are used for IPv6 packets to travel over an IPv4 network.

11. How is an IPv6 address used that begins with 2000::? That begins with FE80::?

12. How many bits are in the Subnet ID block? What are the values of these bits for a link-local IP address?

13. Which type of IPv6 address is used to create multiple subnets within a large organization?

14. What type of server serves up IP addresses to computers on a network?

15. Which TCP/IP protocol that manages packet delivery guarantees that delivery? Which protocol does not guarantee delivery, but is faster?

16. At what port does an SMTP email server listen to receive email from a client computer?

17. Which protocol(s) does a web server use when transmissions are encrypted for security?

18. What type of server resolves fully qualified domain names to IP addresses?

19. Which email protocol allows a client application to manage email stored on an email server?

20. What technology is used to present a public IP address to computers outside the LAN to handle requests to use the Internet from computers inside the LAN?

21. Which protocol is used when an application queries a database on a corporate network such as a database of printers?

22. What type of encryption protocol does Secure FTP (SFTP) use to secure FTP transmissions?

23. What two Windows applications use the RDP protocol and port 3389?

24. Which two versions of the 802.11 technologies can use multiple antennas at both the access point and the network adapter?

25. Which wireless encryption standard is stronger, WEP or WPA?

26. When securing a Wi-Fi wireless network, which is considered better security: to filter MAC addresses, use encryption, or not broadcast the SSID?

27. Would you expect WPS to be used when a wireless network is using strong security, weak security, or no security (as in a public hotspot)?

>> THINKING CRITICALLY

1. You have just installed a network adapter and have booted up the system, installing the drivers. You open File Explorer on a remote computer and don't see the computer on which you just installed the NIC. What is the first thing you check?

   a. Has TCP/IPv6 been enabled?

   b. Is the computer using dynamic or static IP addressing?

   c. Are the lights on the adapter functioning correctly?

   d. Has the computer been assigned a computer name?

2. Your boss asks you to transmit a small file that includes sensitive personnel data to a server on the network. The server is running a Telnet server and an FTP server. Why is it not a good idea to use Telnet to reach the remote computer?

   a. Telnet transmissions are not encrypted.

   b. Telnet is not reliable and the file might arrive corrupted.

   c. FTP is faster than Telnet.

   d. FTP running on the same computer as Telnet causes Telnet to not work.

3. You have just installed a SOHO router in a customer's home and the owner has called you saying his son is complaining that Internet gaming is too slow. His son is using a wireless connection to the network. Which possibilities should you consider in order to speed up the son's gaming experience? Select all that apply.

   a. Verify the wireless connection is using the fastest wireless standard the router supports.

   b. Disable encryption on the wireless network to speed up transmissions.

   c. Suggest the son use a wired Gigabit Ethernet connection to the network.

   d. Enable QoS for the gaming applications on the router and on the son's computer.

>> REAL PROBLEMS, REAL SOLUTIONS

REAL PROBLEM 8-1 Setting Up a Small Network

The simplest possible wired network is two computers connected together using a crossover cable. In a crossover cable, the send and receive wires are crossed so that one computer can send and the other computer receive on the same wire. At first glance, a crossover cable looks just like a regular network cable (also called a patch cable) except for the labeling (see Figure 8-69). (In the chapter, "Supporting Network Hardware," you learn how to distinguish between the cables by examining their connectors.)

Figure 8-69   A patch cable and crossover cable look the same but are labeled differently

Do the following to set up and test the network:

1. Connect two computers using a crossover cable. Using the Network and Sharing Center, verify your network is up. What is the IPv4 address of Computer A? Of Computer B?

2. Join the two computers to the same homegroup. Then use File Explorer or Windows Explorer to view the files on the other computer shared with the homegroup.

3. Convert the TCP/IP configuration to static IP addressing. Assign a private IP address to each computer. Make sure the two computers are in the same subnet. What is the subnet mask? What is the IP address of Computer A? Of Computer B?

4. Verify you can still see files shared with the homegroup on each computer.

5. Assign a new IP address to each computer so they are not in the same subnet. What are the two IP addresses? Can you still see files shared with the homegroup on each computer?

6. Return the computers to the same subnet and verify each computer can find the other and its shared resources.

REAL PROBLEM 8-2 Using the Hosts File

The hosts file in the C:\Windows\System32\drivers\etc folder has no file extension and contains computer names and their associated IP addresses on the local network. An IT support technician can manually edit the hosts file when the association is needed for address resolution on the local network and a DNS server is not available on the local network.

> ✎ **Notes** For an entry in the hosts file to work, the remote computer must always use the same IP address. One way to accomplish this is to assign a static IP address to the computer. Alternately, if your DHCP server supports this feature, you can configure it to assign the same IP address to this computer each time it connects to the network.

Using your small network you set up in Real Problem 8-1, do the following to use the hosts file:

1. The ping command sends a request to a remote computer and the computer responds to verify communication. On Computer A, open a command prompt window and ping Computer B using its IP address. For example, if the IP address is 192.168.10.10, use this command: ping 192.168.10.10.

2. Try to ping Computer B, this time using its computer name. Did the ping work?

3. Use Notepad to edit the hosts file on Computer A and add the entry that associates the IP address of Computer B with its computer name.

4. Try to ping Computer B, this time using its computer name rather than IP address. Did the ping work?

8

Supporting Network Hardware

After completing this chapter, you will be able to:

- Describe network types and the Internet connections they use
- Identify, compare, and contrast hardware used to build local networks
- Set up and troubleshoot the wiring in a small network

I n the chapter, "Connecting To and Setting Up a Network," you learned how to connect a computer to a network and how to set up and secure a wired and wireless router for a small network. This chapter takes you one step further in supporting networks. You learn about the types of networks and the technologies used to build these networks. You also learn about the hardware devices, cables, and connectors used to construct a network. Finally, you learn about networking tools, how to terminate network cables, and how to troubleshoot problems with network hardware.

TYPES OF NETWORKS AND THE INTERNET CONNECTIONS THEY USE

A+
220-901
2.1, 2.2,
2.7

A computer network is created when two or more computers can communicate with each other. Networks can be categorized by several methods, including the technology used and the size of the network. When networks are categorized by size or physical area they cover, these are the categories used:

▲ *PAN.* A PAN (personal area network) consists of personal devices communicating at close range such as a cell phone and laptop computer. PANs can use wired connections (such as USB or FireWire) or wireless connections (such as Bluetooth or Infrared).

▲ *LAN.* A LAN (local area network) covers a small local area, such as a home, office, other building, or small group of buildings. LANs can use wired (most likely Ethernet) or wireless (most likely Wi-Fi, also called 802.11) technologies. A LAN is used for workstations, servers, printers, and other devices to communicate and share resources.

▲ *Wireless LAN.* A wireless LAN (WLAN) covers a limited geographical area, and is used in businesses, homes, restaurants, public parks, airports, schools, and many other places where network cabling is inconvenient to install or use.

▲ *MAN.* A MAN (metropolitan area network) covers a large campus or city. (A small MAN is sometimes called a CAN or campus area network.) Network technologies used can be wireless (most likely LTE) and/or wired (for example, Ethernet with fiber-optic cabling).

▲ *WAN.* A WAN (wide area network) covers a large geographical area and is made up of many smaller networks. The best-known WAN is the Internet. Some technologies used to connect a single computer or LAN to the Internet include DSL, cable Internet, satellite, cellular WAN, and fiber optic.

> ★ **A+ Exam Tip**   The A+ 220-901 exam expects you to know about a LAN, WAN, PAN, and MAN.

Now let's look at network technologies used for Internet connections.

NETWORK TECHNOLOGIES USED FOR INTERNET CONNECTIONS

A+
220-901
2.1, 2.2,
2.7

To connect to the Internet, a network first connects to an Internet service provider (ISP), such as Earthlink or Comcast. The most common types of connections are DSL and cable Internet (commonly called cable or cable modem). See Figure 9-1. When connecting to an ISP, know that upload speeds are generally slower than download speeds. These rates differ because users generally download more data than they upload. Therefore, an ISP devotes more of the available bandwidth to downloading and less of it to uploading.

Figure 9-1   An ISP stands between a LAN and the Internet

Networks are built using one or more technologies that provide varying degrees of bandwidth. Bandwidth (the width of the band) is the theoretical number of bits that can be transmitted over a network at one time, similar to the number of lanes on a highway. In practice, however, the networking industry refers to bandwidth as a measure of the maximum rate of data transmission in bits per second (bps), thousands of bits per second (Kbps), millions of bits per second (Mbps), or billions of bits per second (Gbps). Bandwidth is the theoretical or potential speed of a network, whereas data throughput is the average of the actual speed. In practice, network transmissions experience delays, called latency, that result in slower network performance. For example, too many splitters can cause signal strength degradation, resulting in latency. Latency is measured by the round-trip time it takes for a data packet to travel from source to destination and back to source.

Table 9-1 lists network technologies used by local networks to connect to the Internet. The table is more or less ordered from slowest to fastest maximum bandwidth within each category, although latency can affect the actual bandwidth of a particular network.

Technology (Wireless or Wired)	Maximum Speed	Common Uses
Wireless Internet connection: Cellular		
2G cellular (second-generation cellular)	Up to 50 Kbps	Uses the mobile phone service on a cellular network for voice and data (digital) transmissions. Most 2G networks use an improved version of the GSM mobile phone service, although some use CDMA, which is a competing service.
2G EDGE or 2G E cellular	Up to 384 Kbps	Improved over 2G and uses the GSM mobile phone service. (EDGE stands for Enhanced Data for GSM Evolution.)
3G cellular (third-generation cellular)	At least 200 Kbps, but can be up to 4 Mbps	Improved over 2G EDGE and allows for transmitting data and video. Uses either CDMA or GSM mobile phone services. Speeds vary widely according to the revision standards used.
4G cellular (fourth-generation cellular)	100 Mbps to 1 Gbps	Higher speeds are achieved when the client stays in a fixed position. A 4G network uses either LTE (Long Term Evolution) or WiMAX technology. LTE is more popular and faster.
Wireless Internet connection: Satellite		
Satellite	Up to 15 Mbps	Requires a dish to send and receive from a satellite, which is in a relative fixed position with the Earth.
Wired Internet connection: Telephone		
Dial-up or regular telephone (POTS, for plain old telephone service)	Up to 56 Kbps	Slow access to an ISP using a modem and dial-up connection over phone lines.
ISDN	64 Kbps or 128 Kbps	ISDN (Integrated Services Digital Network) is an outdated business-use access to an ISP over dial-up phone lines.
SDSL (Symmetric Digital Subscriber Line)	Up to 22 Mbps	Equal bandwidth in both directions. SDSL is a type of broadband technology. (Broadband refers to a networking technology that carries more than one type of signal, such as DSL and telephone or cable Internet and TV.) DSL uses regular phone lines and is an always-up or always-on connection that does not require a dial-up.
ADSL (Asymmetric DSL)	640 Kbps upstream and up to 24 Mbps downstream	Most bandwidth is from ISP to user. Slower versions of ADSL are called ADSL Lite or DSL Lite. ISP customers pay according to a bandwidth scale.
VDSL (very-high-bit-rate DSL)	Up to 70 Mbps	A type of asymmetric DSL that works only a short distance.

Table 9-1 Networking technologies (continues)

Technology (Wireless or Wired)	Maximum Speed	Common Uses
Other wired Internet connections		
Cable Internet	Up to 160 Mbps, depends on the type of cable	Connects a home or small business to an ISP, and usually comes with a cable television subscription and shares cable TV lines. Fiber-optic cable gives highest speeds.
Dedicated line using fiber optic	Up to 43 Tbps	Dedicated fiber-optic line from ISP to business or home. Speeds widely vary with price.
Wired local network: Ethernet		
Fast Ethernet (100BaseT)	100 Mbps	Used for local networks.
Gigabit Ethernet (1000BaseT)	1000 Mbps or 1 Gbps	Fastest Ethernet standard for a local network.
Wireless local network: Wi-Fi		
Wi-Fi 802.11g wireless	Up to 54 Mbps	Compatible with and has replaced 802.11b.
802.11n wireless	Up to 600 Mbps	Compatible with and has replaced 802.11g.
802.11ac wireless	1.3 Gbps	Latest Wi-Fi technology.

Table 9-1   Networking technologies (continued)

Currently, cable Internet and DSL are the two most popular ways to make an Internet connection. Let's first compare these two technologies and then we'll look at satellite, fiber-optic dedicated lines, and cellular WANs.

> ★ **A+ Exam Tip**   The A+ 220-901 exam expects you to be able to compare these network types used for Internet connections: cable, dial-up, DSL, fiber, satellite, ISDN, and cellular (mobile hotspot).

COMPARE CABLE INTERNET AND DSL

Here are the important facts about cable Internet and DSL:

- ◢ Cable Internet is a broadband technology that uses cable TV lines and is always connected (always up). With cable Internet, the TV signal to your television and the data signals to your computer or LAN share the same coaxial (coax) cable. The cable modem converts a computer's digital signals to analog when sending them and converts incoming analog data to digital.
- ◢ DSL (Digital Subscriber Line) is a group of broadband technologies that covers a wide range of speeds. DSL uses ordinary copper phone lines and a range of frequencies on the copper wire that are not used by voice, making it possible for you to use the same phone line for voice and DSL at the same time. When you make a regular phone call, you dial in as usual. However, the DSL part of the line is always connected (always up) for most DSL services.

When deciding between cable Internet and DSL, consider these points:

- ◢ Both cable Internet and DSL can sometimes be purchased on a sliding scale, depending on the bandwidth you want to buy. Subscriptions offer residential and the more-expensive business plans. Business plans are likely to have increased bandwidth and better support when problems arise.
- ◢ With cable Internet, you share the TV cable infrastructure with your neighbors, which can result in service becoming degraded if many people in your neighborhood are using cable Internet at the same time. I once used cable Internet in a neighborhood where I found I needed to avoid web surfing between 5:00 and 7:00 P.M. when folks were just coming in from work and using the Internet. With DSL, you're using a dedicated phone line, so your neighbors' surfing habits are not important.

◢ With DSL, static over phone lines in your house can be a problem. The DSL company provides filters to install at each phone jack (see Figure 9-2), but still the problem might not be fully solved. Also, your phone line must qualify for DSL; some lines are too dirty (too much static or noise) to support DSL. Figure 9-3 shows a DSL modem that can connect directly to a computer or to a router.

Figure 9-2 When DSL is used in your home, filters are needed on every phone jack except the one used by the DSL modem

Figure 9-3 This DSL modem connects to a phone jack and a computer or router to provide a broadband connection to an ISP

SATELLITE

People who live in remote areas and want high-speed Internet connections often are limited in their choices. DSL and cable options might not be available where they live, but satellite access is available from pretty much anywhere. Internet access by satellite is available even on airplanes. Passengers can connect to the Internet using a wireless hotspot and satellite dish on the plane. A satellite dish mounted on top of your house or office building communicates with a satellite used by an ISP offering the satellite service (see Figure 9-4). One disadvantage of satellite is that it requires line-of-sight connectivity without obstruction from mountains, trees, and tall buildings. Another disadvantage is that it experiences delays in transmission (called latency), especially when uploading, and is, therefore, not a good solution for an Internet connection that is to be used for videoconferencing or voice over Internet.

Figure 9-4 Communication by satellite can include television and Internet access

DEDICATED LINE USING FIBER OPTIC

Another broadband technology used for Internet access is fiber optic. The technology uses a dedicated line from your ISP to your place of business or residence. This dedicated line is called a point-to-point (PTP) connection because no other business or residence shares the line with you. Television, Internet data, and voice communication all share the broadband fiber-optic cable. Verizon calls the technology FiOS (Fiber Optic Service), and the fiber-optic cabling is used all the way from the ISP to your home. A provider might provide fiber-optic cabling up to your neighborhood and then use coaxial cable (similar to that used in cable Internet connections) for the last leg of the connection to your business or residence. Upstream and downstream speeds and prices vary.

CELLULAR WAN

A cellular network or cellular WAN consists of cells, and each cell is controlled by a base station (see Figure 9-5). The base station might include more than one transceiver and antenna on the same tower to support multiple technologies (such as LTE and GSM). Cell phones are called that because they use a cellular network.

A laptop or tablet might have an embedded cellular adapter to connect to a cellular network. If not, you can use a USB broadband modem to make the connection, which is sometimes called an air card. Recall from the chapter, "Connecting To and Setting Up a Network," that you can also tether (by cable or Bluetooth) your smart phone or other mobile device to your computer so that the computer can connect to the ISP. Some mobile devices can create a mobile hotspot that computers and other mobile devices can connect by Wi-Fi to your device and on to the Internet.

Figure 9-5   A cellular WAN is made up of many cells that provide coverage over a wide area

---

Hands-On | Project 9-1   Investigate Verizon FiOS

**A+
220-901
2.1, 2.2,
2.7**

Verizon (*verizon.com*) offers FiOS, an alternative to DSL and cable for wired broadband Internet access to a residence or small business. FiOS is a fiber-optic Internet service that uses fiber-optic cable all the way to your house or business for both your telephone service and Internet access. Search the web for answers to these questions about FiOS:

1. Give a brief description of FiOS and how it is used for Internet access.

2. What downstream and upstream speeds can FiOS support?

3. When using FiOS, does your telephone voice communication share the fiber-optic cable with Internet data?

4. What does Verizon say about FiOS cabling used for television?

5. Is FiOS available in your area?

HARDWARE USED BY LOCAL NETWORKS

A+
220-901
1.4, 1.11,
2.1, 2.2,
2.8

In this part of the chapter, you learn about the hardware devices that create and connect to networks. We discuss desktop and laptop devices, hubs, switches, bridges, and other network devices, and the cables and connectors these devices use.

DIAL-UP MODEMS

A+
220-901
1.4, 1.11,
2.1, 2.2

Of all the types of networking connections, dial-up or POTS (plain old telephone service) is the least expensive and slowest connection to the Internet. Dial-up connections are painfully slow, but you might still need them when traveling, and they're good at home when your broadband connection is down or when you just plain want to save money.

Modem cards in desktop computers provide two phone jacks, called RJ-11 jacks, so that one can be used for dial-up networking and the other jack can be used to plug in an extension telephone. Figure 9-6 shows a modem card that comes bundled with drivers on CD and a phone cord. Phone cords are a type of twisted-pair cable and use an RJ-11 connector. Twisted-pair cabling uses pairs of wires twisted together to reduce crosstalk. The RJ-11 jack has four connectors, and a phone cord can have one or two twisted pairs for a total of two or four wires in the cord. The cord carries power on the lines that can be used to power a simple telephone. Laptop computers that have embedded dial-up modem capability generally have only a single phone jack. Dial-up standards are no longer being revised, and the last dial-up modem standard is the V.92 standard.

Figure 9-6 This 56K V.92 PCI modem card comes bundled with a phone cord and setup CD

When installing a modem card, be sure to follow manufacturer directions. Most directions say to install the drivers on CD before you physically install the modem. How to configure a modem card and set up a dial-up connection are covered in the chapter, "Connecting To and Setting Up a Network."

SWITCHES AND HUBS

A+
220-901
1.4, 1.11,
2.1, 2.2,
2.8

Today's Ethernet networks use a design called a star bus topology, which means that nodes are connected to one or more centralized devices, which are connected to each other (see Figure 9-7). A centralized device can be a switch or a hub. Each device handles a network message differently.

Figure 9-7   A star bus network formed by nodes connected to multiple switches

> ✎ **Notes**   In the chapter, "Connecting To and Setting Up a Network," you learned about packets, which are messages sent over a TCP/IP network with IP address header information added. Just before a packet is put on the network, the network adapter adds additional information to the beginning and end of the packet, and this information includes the source and destination MAC addresses. The packet, with this additional information, is now called a frame.

Here are the **differen**ces between a hub and a switch:

▲ An Ethernet **hub** transmits the data frame to every device, except the device that sent the frame, as shown in Figure 9-8a. A hub is just a pass-through and distribution point for every device connected to it, without regard for what kind of data is passing through and where the data might be going. Hubs are outdated technology, having been replaced by switches. Figure 9-9 shows a hub that supports 10 Mbps and 100 Mbps Ethernet speeds.

Figure 9-8   (a) A hub is a simple pass-through device to connect nodes on a network, and (b) a switch sends a frame to the destination node based on its MAC address

Figure 9-9   A hub is a pass-through device to connect nodes on a network

◢ A switch (see Figure 9-10) is smarter and more efficient than a hub because it keeps a table of all the MAC addresses for devices connected to it. When the switch receives a frame, it searches its MAC address table for the destination MAC address of the frame and sends the frame only to the device or interface using this MAC address (see Figure 9-8b). At first, a switch does not know the MAC addresses of every device connected to it. It learns this information as it receives frames and records the source MAC addresses in its MAC address table. When it receives a frame destined to a MAC address not in its table, the switch acts like a hub and broadcasts the frame to all devices except the one that sent it.

Figure 9-7, shown earlier in the chapter, uses three switches in sequence. Physically, the network cables that run between two switches or a switch and a computer might be inside a building's walls

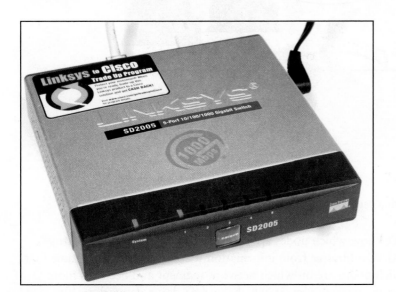

with a network jack on the wall providing an RJ-45 connector. You plug a network cable into the jack to make the connection. In practice, a small network might begin as one switch and three or four computers. As the need for more computers grows, new switches are added to provide these extra connections.

Another reason to add a switch to a network is to regenerate the network signal. An Ethernet cable should not exceed 100 meters (about 328 feet) in length. If you need to reach distances greater than that, you can add a switch in the line, which regenerates the signal.

Figure 9-10   A five-port Gigabit Ethernet switch by Linksys

WIRELESS ACCESS POINTS AND BRIDGES

A+
220-901
1.4, 1.11,
2.1, 2.2,
2.8

In the chapter, "Connecting To and Setting Up a Network," you learned that a router can also be a wireless access point. In addition, a wireless access point can be a dedicated device. The wireless access point, such as the one shown in Figure 9-11, can also be a bridge. A bridge is a device that stands between two segments of a network and manages network traffic between them. For example, one network segment might be a wireless network and the other segment might be a wired network; the wireless access point (AP) connects these two segments. Functioning as a

Figure 9-11   Xtreme N Duo Wireless Bridge/Access Point by D-Link

bridge, the AP helps to reduce the overall volume of network traffic by not allowing data frames across the bridge if it knows that the frame is addressed to a destination on its own segment. Figure 9-12 demonstrates the concept of a network bridge. (Logically, you can think of a switch as a multiport bridge.)

Figure 9-12 A bridge is an intelligent device making decisions concerning network traffic

Similar to a switch, a bridge at first doesn't know which nodes are on each network segment. It learns that information by maintaining a table of MAC addresses from information it collects from each frame that arrives at the bridge. Eventually, it learns which nodes are on which network segment and becomes more efficient at preventing frames from getting on the wrong segment, which can bog down network traffic.

> ✎ **Notes** If your wireless access point does not reach the entire area you need to cover, you can add a repeater or an extender, which amplifies and retransmits the signal to a wider coverage area. Repeaters and extenders capture the Wi-Fi signal, boost it, and retransmit it to the new area. The difference between a repeater and an extender is that a repeater rebroadcasts the signal using a new network name, whereas an extender keeps the original network name.

> ★ **A+ Exam Tip** The A+ 220-901 exam expects you to know the functions and features of a hub, switch, router, access point, bridge, and modem.

ETHERNET CABLES AND CONNECTORS

A+
220-901
2.1, 2.2,
2.8
Several variations of Ethernet cables and connectors have evolved over the years and are primarily identified by their speeds and the types of connectors used to wire these networks. Table 9-2 compares cable types and Ethernet versions.

> ★ **A+ Exam Tip** The A+ 220-901 exam expects you to know the details listed in Table 9-2.

As you can see from Table 9-2, the three main types of cabling used by Ethernet are twisted-pair, coaxial, and fiber optic. Coaxial cable is older and almost never used for current networking cable. Within each category, there are several variations discussed next.

Cable System	Speed	Cables and Connectors	Example of Connectors	Maximum Cable Length
10Base2 (ThinNet)	10 Mbps	Coaxial cable uses a BNC connector.	Courtesy of Cables4Computer.com	185 meters or 607 feet
10Base5 (ThickNet)	10 Mbps	Coaxial uses an AUI 15-pin D-shaped connector.	Courtesy of Black Box Corporation	500 meters or 1640 feet
10BaseT, 100BaseT (Fast Ethernet), 1000BaseT (Gigabit Ethernet), and 10GBaseT (10-Gigabit Ethernet)	10 Mbps, 100 Mbps, 1 Gbps, or 10 Gbps	Twisted pair (UTP or STP) uses an RJ-45 connector.	Courtesy of Tyco Electronics	100 meters or 328 feet
10BaseF, 10BaseFL, 100BaseFL, 100BaseFX, 1000BaseFX, or 1000BaseX (fiber optic)	10 Mbps, 100 Mbps, 1 Gbps, or 10 Gbps	Fiber-optic cable uses ST or SC connectors (shown to the right) or LC and MT-RJ connectors (not shown).	Courtesy of Black Box Corporation	Up to 2 kilometers (6562 feet)

Table 9-2   Variations of Ethernet and Ethernet cabling

TWISTED-PAIR CABLE

Twisted-pair cable is the most popular cabling method for local networks and uses an RJ-45 connector. The cable comes in two varieties: unshielded twisted-pair (UTP) cable and shielded twisted-pair (STP) cable. UTP cable is the least expensive and is commonly used on LANs. UTP is rated by twisted-pair category as listed in Table 9-3.

Twisted-Pair Category	Cable System	Frequency	Shielded or Unshielded	Comment
CAT-3	10BaseT	Up to 16 MHz	Unshielded	Currently used for phone lines.
CAT-5	10/100BaseT	Up to 100 MHz	Both	Has two cable pairs and seldom used today.
CAT-5e (Enhanced)	10/100BaseT, Gigabit Ethernet	Up to 100 MHz	Both	Has four twisted pairs and heavy duty sheath to help reduce crosstalk.
CAT-6	10/100BaseT, Gigabit Ethernet	Up to 250 MHz	Both	Less crosstalk because it has a plastic core that keeps the twisted pairs separated. CAT-6 and its variations are the most popular category used today.
CAT-6a	10/100BaseT, Gigabit Ethernet, 10Gig Ethernet	Up to 500 MHz	Both	Doubles the frequency of CAT-6. CAT-6a is sometimes unofficially called CAT-6e.
CAT-7	10/100BaseT, Gigabit Ethernet, 10Gig Ethernet	Up to 600 MHz	Individual pair shield and overall cable shield	Shielding almost completely eliminates crosstalk and improves noise reduction. Expected to have a longer life expectancy than previous twisted-pair categories.

Table 9-3   Twisted-pair categories

Figure 9-13 shows unshielded twisted-pair cables and the RJ-45 connector. Twisted-pair cable has four pairs of twisted wires for a total of eight wires. You learn more about how the eight wires are arranged later in the chapter.

PVC-grade
CAT-5e cable

Plenum-grade
CAT-5e cable

CAT-6 cable

Plastic core
in CAT-6 cable

RJ-45 connector

Figure 9-13 Unshielded twisted-pair cables and RJ-45 connector used for local wired networks

STP cable uses a covering or shield around each pair of wires inside the cable that protects it from electromagnetic interference caused by electrical motors, transmitters, or high-tension lines. It costs more than unshielded cable, so it's used only when the situation demands it.

> ✎ **Notes** Normally, the plastic covering of a cable is made of **PVC (polyvinyl chloride)**, which is not safe when used inside **plenums** (areas between the floors of buildings). In these situations, plenum cable covered with Teflon is used because it does not give off toxic fumes when burned. Plenum cable is two or three times more expensive than PVC cable. Figure 9-13 shows plenum cable and PVC cable, which are unshielded twisted-pair cables.

COAXIAL CABLE

Coaxial cable has a single copper wire down the middle and a braided shield around it (see Figure 9-14). The cable is stiff and difficult to manage, and is no longer used for networking. RG-6 coaxial cable is used for cable TV, having replaced the older and thinner RG-59 coaxial cable once used for cable TV. RG-6 cables use an F connector shown in Figure 9-15.

Figure 9-14 Coaxial cable and a BNC connector are used with ThinNet Ethernet

Figure 9-15 An RG-6 coaxial cable with an F connector used for connections to TV has a single copper wire

★ **A+ Exam Tip** The A+ 220-901 exam expects you to know about these cables and connectors: BNC, RJ-45, coaxial, SC, ST, LC, RJ-11, F connector, STP, UTP, CAT-3, CAT-5, CAT-5e, CAT-6, CAT-6e, plenum, PVC, RG-6, and RG-59.

FIBER OPTIC

Fiber-optic cables transmit signals as pulses of light over glass or plastic strands inside protected tubing, as illustrated in Figure 9-16. Fiber-optic cable comes in two types: single-mode (thin, difficult to connect, expensive, and best performing) and multimode (most popular). A single-mode cable uses a single path for light to travel in the cable and multimode cable uses multiple paths for light. Both single-mode and multimode fiber-optic cables can be constructed as loose-tube cables for outdoor use or tight-buffered cables for indoor or outdoor use. Loose-tube cables are filled with gel to prevent water from soaking into the cable, and tight-buffered cables are filled with synthetic or glass yarn, called strength wires, to protect the fiber-optic strands, as shown in Figure 9-16.

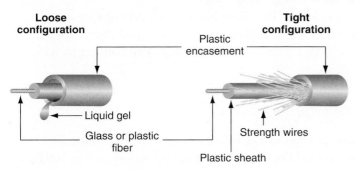

Figure 9-16 Fiber-optic cables contain a glass or plastic core for transmitting light

Fiber-optic cables can use one of four connectors, all shown in Figure 9-17. The two older types are ST (straight tip) connectors and SC (subscriber connector or standard connector) connectors. Two newer types are LC (local connector) connectors and MT-RJ (mechanical transfer registered jack) connectors. Any one of the four connectors can be used with either single-mode or multimode fiber-optic cable.

(a) ST (straight tip)

(b) SC (standard connector)

(c) LC (local connector)

(d) MT-RJ (mechanical transfer RJ)

Courtesy Fiber Communications, Inc.

Figure 9-17   Four types of fiber-optic connectors: (a) ST, (b) SC, (c) LC, and (d) MT-RJ

ETHERNET STANDARDS AND CABLES

Ethernet can run at four speeds. Each version of Ethernet can use more than one cabling method. Here is a brief description of the transmission speeds and the cabling methods they use:

▲ *10-Mbps Ethernet.* This first Ethernet specification was invented by Xerox Corporation in the 1970s, and later became known as Ethernet.

▲ *100-Mbps Ethernet or Fast Ethernet.* This improved version of Ethernet (sometimes called 100BaseT or Fast Ethernet) operates at 100 Mbps and uses STP or UTP cabling rated CAT-5 or higher. 100BaseT networks can support slower speeds of 10 Mbps so that devices that run at either 10 Mbps or 100 Mbps can coexist on the same LAN. Two variations of 100BaseT are 100BaseTX and 100BaseFX. The most popular variation is 100BaseTX. 100BaseFX uses fiber-optic cable.

▲ *1000-Mbps Ethernet or Gigabit Ethernet.* This version of Ethernet operates at 1000 Mbps and uses twisted-pair cable and fiber-optic cable. Gigabit Ethernet is becoming the most popular choice for LAN technology. Because it can use the same cabling and connectors as Fast Ethernet, a company can upgrade from Fast Ethernet to Gigabit without rewiring the network.

▲ *10-Gigabit Ethernet.* This version of Ethernet operates at 10 billion bits per second (10 Gbps) and uses fiber-optic cable. It can be used on LANs, MANs, and WANs, and is also a good choice for backbone networks. (A backbone network is a channel whereby local networks can connect to wide area networks or to each other.)

POWERLINE NETWORKING OR ETHERNET OVER POWER (EOP)

If you need network access to a remote location in a building where network cabling and Wi-Fi cannot reach, you have another option. The HomePlug standard introduced in 2001, powerline networking or Ethernet over Power (EoP), uses the power lines in a building to transmit data. Powerline networking is simple to set up, inexpensive, and can run at Gigabit speeds. Like Wi-Fi, the data is sent out on a network that you cannot necessarily contain because power lines are not confined to a single building. If a building or apartment is sharing a phase (electrical signal) with another building or apartment, the data might leak and be intercepted by a neighbor. For this reason, powerline adapters offer encryption (128-bit AES encryption) that is activated by pairing the adapters to each other. Alternately, you can install the manufacturer's utility on your computer to create a network key.

To use powerline networking, you need at least two powerline adapters (see Figure 9-18), which can be bought in pairs called a kit.

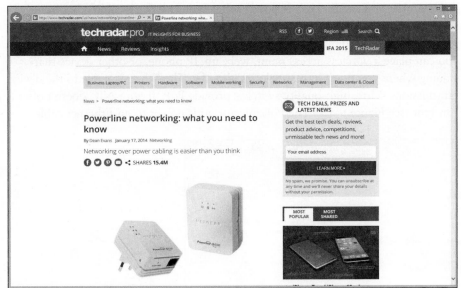

Figure 9-18   A starter kit for powerline networking includes two adapters

To install powerline networking, follow these steps:

1. Connect a powerline adapter to your router using an Ethernet cable, then plug it directly into a wall outlet.

2. In the same room, connect a second adapter to your computer using an Ethernet cable and then plug it directly into a wall outlet.

3. To pair the two devices, press and hold the security button on the first adapter for a couple seconds. When the LED lights flash, you have less than two minutes to press and hold the security button on the second adapter until the LED lights flash. The two adapters are now paired using security encryption. For additional adapters, simply repeat this step with a new adapter one at a time.

4. You can now move the second adapter to its final destination in the building knowing that you have a secured connection.

Powerline networks are not without problems. Consider the following issues powerline networking presents:

◢ Powerline adapters must be plugged directly into a wall outlet. Plugging a powerline adapter into a power strip or surge protector or sharing an outlet with an energy hog like a space heater hinders the function of the device.

◢ Powerline adapters might be large and cover both outlets on a single wall plate. A few powerline adapters offer a pass-through outlet, but most do not.

◢ Sometimes people forget to use the encryption options and end up with an unsecured network.

◢ Distance degrades quality. If you have a map of the building's circuits, try to keep the two adapters as close on the same circuit as possible. Jumping circuits decreases signal strength.

When shopping for powerline adapters, consider these things:

◢ Most powerline manufacturers belong to the Homeplug Alliance group (*www.homeplug.org*). Make sure the adapter you are considering is Homeplug certified.
◢ Make sure the adapter is rated for the latest Homeplug AV2 speed standard for Gigabit-class data transfers.
◢ If you have limited wall outlets, you might need a powerline adapter that offers a pass-through outlet.

POWER OVER ETHERNET (POE)

> **A+**
> **220-901**
> **2.8**

If you have the opposite problem of needing to get power where your network cabling has gone, you can use Power over Ethernet (PoE). Power over Ethernet (PoE) is a feature that might be available on high-end wired network adapters to allow power to be transmitted over Ethernet cable. Using this feature, you can place a wireless access point, webcam, IP phone, or other device that needs power in a position in a building where you don't have an electrical outlet. The Ethernet cable to the device provides both power and data transmissions. Most high-quality switches provide PoE. If your NIC doesn't offer PoE, you can add it using a PoE injector (see Figure 9-19). The PoE injector adds power to an Ethernet cable.

Source: https://www.google.com/webhp?hl=en#q=power+over+ethernet+injector&hl=en&tbm=shop

Figure 9-19   A PoE injector introduces power to an Ethernet cable

Some devices, such as a webcam, are designed to receive both power and data from the Ethernet cable. For other devices, you must use a splitter that splits the data and power transmissions before connecting to the device. PoE can provide up to 25.5 W from a single Ethernet port. The amount of power that reaches a device degrades with the length of the cable. Figure 9-20 shows a PoE switch and a splitter used to provide power to a non-PoE access point. When setting up a device to receive power by PoE, make sure the device sending the power, the splitter, and the device receiving the power are all compatible. Pay special attention to the voltage and wattage requirements and the type of power connector of the receiving device.

Figure 9-20   Use a PoE splitter if the receiving device is not PoE compatible

Hands-On | Project 9-2   Research a Network Upgrade

A+
220-901
1.4, 2.8

An IT support technician is often called on to research equipment to maintain or improve a computer or network and make recommendations for purchase. Suppose you are asked to upgrade a small network that consists of one switch and four computers from 100BaseT to Gigabit Ethernet. The switch connects to a router that already supports Gigabit Ethernet. Do the following to price the hardware needed for this upgrade:

1. Find three switches by different manufacturers that support Gigabit Ethernet and have at least five ports. Save or print the webpages describing each switch.

2. Compare the features and prices of the three switches. What additional information might you want to know before you make your recommendation for a small business network?

3. Find three network adapters by different manufacturers to install in the desktop computers to support Gigabit Ethernet. Save or print webpages for each NIC.

4. Compare features of the three network adapters. What additional information do you need to know before you make your recommendation?

5. Make your recommendations based on the moderate (middle-of-the-road) choices. What is the total price of the upgrade, including one switch and four network adapters?

6. What is one more question you need to have answered about other equipment before you can complete the price of the upgrade? Explain how you would find the answer to your question.

9

SETTING UP AND TROUBLESHOOTING NETWORK WIRING

A+
220-901
1.4, 2.1,
2.2, 2.9,
4.4, 4.5

To set up a small network, you'll need computers, switches, network cables, a router, and whatever device (for example, a DSL or cable modem) that provides Internet access. Some network cables might be wired inside walls of your building with wall jacks that use RJ-45 ports. These cables might converge in an electrical closet or server room. If network cables are lying on the floor, be sure to install them against the wall so they won't be a trip hazard. Take care that cables don't exceed the recommended length (100 meters for twisted pair). For best results, always use twisted-pair cables rated at CAT-5e or higher. (CAT-6 gives better performance than CAT-5e for Gigabit Ethernet, but it is a lot harder to wire and also more expensive.) To connect multiple computers, use switches rated at the same speed as your router and network adapters. For Gigabit speed on the entire network, you need to use all Gigabit switches and network adapters and a Gigabit router. However, if some devices run at slower speeds, most likely a switch or router can still support the higher speeds for other devices on the network.

If your router is also your wireless access point, take care in planning where to place it. Place the wireless access point near the center of the area where you want your wireless hotspot. The router also needs to have access to your cable modem or DSL modem. The modem needs access to the cable TV or phone jack where it receives service. Figure 9-21 shows a possible inexpensive wiring job where two switches and a router are used to wire two rooms for five workstations and a network printer. The only inside-wall wiring that is required is two back-to-back RJ-45 wall jacks on either side of the wall between the two rooms. The plan allows for all five desktop computers and a network printer to be wired with cabling neatly attached to the baseboards of the office without being a trip hazard.

Figure 9-21   Plan the physical configuration of a small network

Now let's look at the tools you need to solve problems with network cabling, the details of how a network cable is wired, and how you can create your own network cables by installing RJ-45 connectors on twisted-pair cables.

TOOLS USED BY NETWORK TECHNICIANS

A+
220-901
2.9, 4.4

Here's a list of tools a network technician might want in his or her toolbox:

▲ **Loopback plug.** A loopback plug can be used to test a network cable or port. To test a port or cable, connect one end of the cable to a network port on a computer or other device, and connect the loopback plug to the other end of the cable (see Figure 9-22). If the LED light on the loopback plug lights up, the cable and port are good. Another way to use a loopback plug is to find out which port on a switch in an electrical closet matches up with a wall jack. Plug the loopback plug into the wall jack. The connecting port on the switch in the closet lights up. When buying a loopback plug, pay attention to the Ethernet speeds it supports. Some only support 100 Mbps; others support 100 Mbps and 1000 Mbps.

Figure 9-22   A loopback plug verifies the cable and network port are good

▲ *Cable tester.* A cable tester is used to test a cable to find out if it is good or to find out what type of cable it is if the cable is not labeled. You can also use a cable tester to locate the ends of a network cable in a building. A cable tester has two components, the remote and the base (see Figure 9-23).

Figure 9-23   Use a cable tester pair to determine the type of cable and/or if the cable is good

To test a cable, connect each component to the ends of the cable and turn on the tester. Lights on the tester will show you if the cable is good and what type of cable you have. You'll need to read the user manual that comes with the cable tester to know how to interpret the lights.

You can also use the cable tester to find the two ends of a network cable installed in a building. Suppose you see several network jacks on walls in a building, but you don't know which jacks connect. Install a short cable in each of the two jacks or a jack and a port in a patch panel. Then use the cable tester base and remote to test the continuity, as shown in Figure 9-24. Whereas a loopback plug works with live cables and ports, a cable tester works on cables that are not live. You might damage a cable tester if you connect it to a live circuit, so before you start connecting the cable tester to wall jacks, be sure that you turn off all devices on the network.

Figure 9-24   Use cable testers to find the two ends of a network cable in a building

▲ *Network multimeter.* You learned about multimeters in the chapter, "First Look at Computer Parts and Tools." A network multimeter (see Figure 9-25) is a multifunctional tool that can test cables, ports, and network adapters. When you connect it to your network, it can also detect the Ethernet speed, duplex status, default router on the network, length of a cable, voltage levels of PoE, and other network statistics and details. Many network multimeters can document test results and upload results to a computer. Good network multimeters can cost several hundred dollars.

▲ *Wi-Fi analyzer.* A Wi-Fi analyzer is software that can find Wi-Fi networks, determine signal strengths, help optimize Wi-Fi signal settings, and help identify Wi-Fi security threats. For example, you can use a Wi-Fi analyzer to find out which Wi-Fi channels are being used before you pick your channels. You can turn your smart phone into a Wi-Fi analyzer by installing a free or inexpensive app through your phone's app store (see Figure 9-26).

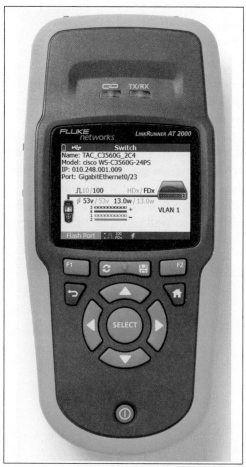

Courtesy of Fluke Corporation

Figure 9-25   The LinkRunner Pro network multimeter by Fluke Corporation works on Gigabit Ethernet networks using twisted-pair copper cabling

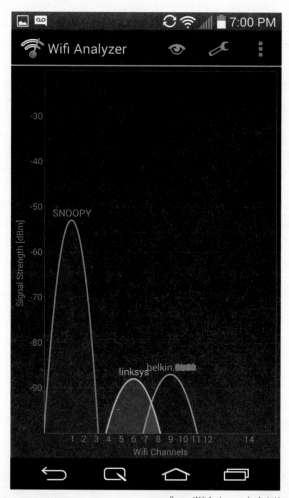

Source: Wifi Analyzer app for Android

Figure 9-26   This Wi-Fi Analyzer app detected three wireless networks

▲ *Toner probe.* A toner probe, sometimes called a tone probe, is a two-part kit that is used to find cables in the walls of a building. See Figure 9-27. The toner connects to one end of the cable and puts out a continuous or pulsating tone on the cable. While the toner is putting out the tone, you use the probe to search the walls for the tone. The probe amplifies the tone so you hear it as a continuous or pulsating beep. The beeps get louder when you are close to the cable and weaker when you move the probe away from the cable. With a little patience, you can trace the cable through the walls. Some toners can put out tones up to 10 miles on a cable and offer a variety of ways to connect to the cable, such as clips and RJ-45 and RJ-11 connectors.

Figure 9-27 A toner probe kit by Fluke Corporation

▲ *Wire stripper.* A wire stripper is used to build your own network cable or repair a cable. Use the wire stripper to cut away the plastic jacket or coating around the wires inside a twisted-pair cable so that you can install a connector on the end of the cable. How to use wire strippers is covered later in the chapter.

▲ *Crimper.* A crimper is used to attach a terminator or connector to the end of a cable. It applies force to pinch the connector to the wires in the cable to securely make a solid connection. Figure 9-28 shows a multifunctional crimper that can crimp a RJ-45 or RJ-11 connector. It also serves double-duty as a wire cutter and wire stripper.

Figure 9-28 This crimper can crimp RJ-45 and RJ-11 connectors

◢ *Punchdown tool.* A punchdown tool, also called an impact tool (see Figure 9-29), is used to punch individual wires in a network cable into their slots in a keystone RJ-45 jack that is used in an RJ-45 wall jack. Later in the chapter, you learn how to use the tool with a keystone jack.

Blade that cuts
the wire

Figure 9-29 A punchdown tool forces a wire into a slot and cuts off the wire

Another use of a punchdown tool is to terminate network cables in a patch panel. A patch panel (see Figure 9-30) provides multiple network ports for cables that converge in one location such as an electrical closet or server room. Each port is numbered on the front of the panel. On the back side, keystone jacks are color-coded for the wires to be inserted.

Courtesy of Tripp Lite

Figure 9-30 A patch panel provides Ethernet ports for cables converging in an electrical closet

When terminating a cable in a keystone jack, you first gently push each wire down into the color-coded slot of the keystone jack and then you use the punchdown tool to punch the wire down all the way into the slot. A small blade on the tip of one prong cuts off the wire at the side of the slot.

Now that you know about the tools you'll need to wire networks, let's see how the cables and connectors are wired.

HOW TWISTED-PAIR CABLES AND CONNECTORS ARE WIRED

A+
220-901
2.1, 2.2

Recall from the chapter, "Connecting To and Setting Up a Network," that two types of network cables can be used when building a network: a straight-through cable and a crossover cable. A straight-through cable (also called a patch cable) is used to connect a computer to a switch or other network device. A crossover cable is used to connect two like devices such as a hub to a hub or a computer to a computer (to make the simplest network of all).

The difference between a straight-through cable and a crossover cable is the way the transmit and receive lines are wired in the connectors at each end of the cables. A crossover cable has the transmit and receive lines reversed so that one device receives off the line to which the other device transmits. Before the introduction of Gigabit Ethernet, 10BaseT and 100BaseT required that a crossover cable be used to connect two like devices such as a switch to a switch. Today's devices that support Gigabit Ethernet use auto-uplinking, which means you can connect a switch to a switch using a straight-through cable. Crossover cables are seldom used today except to connect a computer to a computer to create this simple two-node network.

Twisted-pair copper wire cabling uses an RJ-45 connector that has eight pins, as shown in Figure 9-31. 10BaseT and 100BaseT Ethernet use only four of these pins: pins 1 and 2 for transmitting data and pins 3 and 6 for receiving data. The other pins can be used for phone lines or for power (using PoE). Gigabit Ethernet uses all eight pins to transmit and receive data and can also transmit power on these same lines.

9

Figure 9-31 Pinouts for an RJ-45 connector

Twisted-pair cabling used with RJ-45 connectors is color-coded in four pairs, as shown in Figure 9-31. Pair 1 is blue, pair 2 is orange, pair 3 is green, and pair 4 is brown. Each pair has one solid wire and one striped wire. Two standards have been established in the industry for wiring twisted-pair cabling and RJ-45 connectors: T568A and T568B standards. Both are diagrammed in Figure 9-31 and listed in Table 9-4. The T568A standard has the green pair connected to pins 1 and 2 and the orange pair connected to pins 3 and 6. The T568B standard has the orange pair using pins 1 and 2 and the green pair using pins 3 and 6, as shown in the diagram and the table. For both standards, the blue pair uses pins 4 and 5, and the brown pair uses pins 7 and 8.

Pin	100BaseT Purpose	T568A Wiring	T568B Wiring
1	Transmit+	Pair 3: White/green	Pair 2: White/orange
2	Transmit-	Pair 3: Green	Pair 2: Orange
3	Receive+	Pair 2: White/orange	Pair 3: White/green
4	(Used only on Gigabit Ethernet)	Pair 1: Blue	Pair 1: Blue
5	(Used only on Gigabit Ethernet)	Pair 1: White/blue	Pair 1: White/blue
6	Receive-	Pair 2: Orange	Pair 3: Green
7	(Used only on Gigabit Ethernet)	Pair 4: White/brown	Pair 4: White/brown
8	(Used only on Gigabit Ethernet)	Pair 4: Brown	Pair 4: Brown

Table 9-4   The T568A and T568B Ethernet standards for wiring RJ-45 connectors

It doesn't matter which standard you use so long as you're *consistent*. The important thing is that the wiring on one end of the cable match the wiring on the other end, be it T568A or T568B standards. Either way, you have a straight-through cable.

> **✎ Notes**   The T568A and T568B standards as well as other network wiring standards and recommendations are overseen by the Telecommunications Industry Association (TIA), Electronics Industries Alliance (EIA), and American National Standards Institute (ANSI).

For 10BaseT and 100BaseT networks, if you use T568A wiring on one end of the cable and T568B on the other end of the cable, you have a crossover cable (see the diagram on the left side of Figure 9-32). For Gigabit Ethernet (1000BaseT) that transmits data on all four pairs, you must not only cross the green and orange pairs but also cross the blue and brown pairs to make a crossover cable (see the diagram on the right side of Figure 9-32). Recall, however, that crossover cables are seldom used on Gigabit Ethernet. When you buy a crossover cable, most likely it is wired only for 10BaseT or 100BaseT networks. If you ever find yourself needing to make a crossover cable, be sure to cross all four pairs so the cable will work on 10BaseT, 100BaseT, and 1000BaseT networks. You can also buy an adapter to convert a straight-through cable to a crossover cable. But most likely the adapter only crosses two pairs and works only for 10BaseT or 100BaseT networks, such as the adapter shown in Figure 9-33.

Figure 9-32   Two crossed pairs in a crossover cable is compatible with 10BaseT or 100BaseT Ethernet; four crossed pairs in a crossover cable is compatible with Gigabit Ethernet

Figure 9-33 A crossover adapter converts a patch cable to a crossover cable for a 10BaseT or 100BaseT network

When you are wiring a network in a building that already has network wiring, be sure to find out if the wiring is using T568A or T568B. And then be sure you always use that standard. If you don't know which to use, use T568B because it's the most common, unless, however, you are working for the U.S. government, which requires T568A for all its networking needs.

APPLYING | CONCEPTS MAKE A STRAIGHT-THROUGH CABLE USING T568B WIRING

A+
220-901
2.1, 2.2,
2.9, 4.4

It takes a little practice to make a good network straight-through cable, but you'll get the hang of it after doing only a couple of cables. Figure 9-34 shows the materials and tools you'll need to make a network cable.

Eight-wire twisted-pair cable

Wire stripper

Crimper

RJ-45 connectors and boots

Wire cutter

Figure 9-34 Tools and materials to make a network cable

Here are the steps to make a straight-through cable using the T568B standard:

1. Use wire cutters to cut the twisted-pair cable the correct length plus a few extra inches.

2. If your RJ-45 connectors include boots, slide two boots onto the cable.

3. Use wire strippers to strip off about two inches of the plastic jacket from the end of the wire. To do that, put the wire in the stripper and rotate the stripper around the wire to score the jacket (see Figure 9-35). You can then pull off the jacket.

(continues)

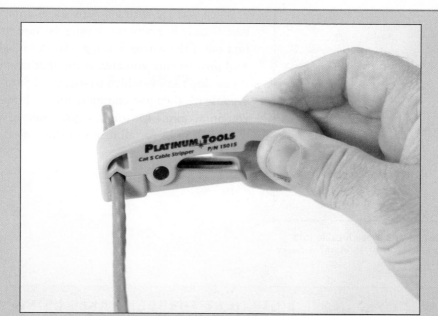

Figure 9-35   Rotate a wire stripper around the jacket to score it so you can slide it off the wire

4. Use wire cutters to start a cut into the jacket, and then use the rip cord to pull the jacket back a couple of inches (see Figure 9-36). Next, cut off the rip cord and the jacket. You take this extra precaution of removing the jacket because you might have nicked the wires with the wire strippers.

Figure 9-36   Rip back the jacket, and then cut off the extra jacket and rip cord

5. Untwist each pair of wires so you have the eight separate wires. Smooth each wire out, straightening out the kinks. Line up the wires in the T568B configuration (refer to Table 9-4).

6. Holding the tightly lined-up wires between your fingers, use wire cutters to cut the wires off evenly, leaving a little over an inch of wire. See Figure 9-37. To know how short to cut the wires, hold the RJ-45 connector up to the wires. The wires must go all the way to the front of the connector. The jacket must go far enough into the connector so that the crimp at the back of the connector will be able to solidly pinch the jacket.

Figure 9-37 Evenly cut off wires measured to fit in the RJ-45 connector with the jacket protruding into the connector

7. Be sure you have pin 1 of the connector lined up with the orange and white wire. Then insert the eight wires in the RJ-45 connector. Guide the wires into the connector, making sure they reach all the way to the front. (It helps to push up a bit as you push the wires into the connector.) You can jam the jacket firmly into the connector. Look through the clear plastic connector to make sure the wires are lined up correctly and they all reach the front and that the jacket goes past the crimp.

8. Insert the connector into the crimper tool. Use one hand to push the connector firmly into the crimper as you use the other hand to crimp the connector. See Figure 9-38. Use plenty of force to crimp. The eight blades at the front of the connector must pierce through to each copper wire to complete each of the eight connections, and the crimp at the back of the connector must solidly crimp the cable jacket to secure the cable to the connector (see Figure 9-39). Remove the connector from the crimper and make sure you can't pull the connector off the wire.

Figure 9-38 Use the crimper to crimp the connector to the cable

(continues)

The cable is crimped here

Blades pierce each wire

Figure 9-39 The crimper crimps the cable and cable jacket, and eight blades pierce the jacket of each individual copper wire

9. Slide the boot into place over the connector. Now you're ready to terminate the other end of the cable. Configure it to also use the T568B wiring arrangement. Figure 9-40 shows the straight-through cable with only one boot in place.

Figure 9-40 Finished patch cable with one boot in place

10. Use a cable tester to make sure the cable is good.

Notes You'll find several YouTube videos on network wiring. An excellent one of making a straight-through cable by CableSupply.com is posted at *www.youtube.com/watch?v=h7TjqnRl3QQ.*

Notes Networking standards that apply to wiring a keystone RJ-45 jack and a straight-through panel say that, to avoid crosstalk, the cable jacket should be removed to expose no more than three inches of twisted-pair wires, and that exposed twisted-pair wires should be untwisted no more than a half inch.

APPLYING | CONCEPTS   WIRE A KEYSTONE JACK

A+
220-901
2.1, 2.2,
2.9, 4.4

A keystone RJ-45 jack is used in a network wall jack. Here are the instructions to wire one:

1. Using a wire stripper and wire cutter, strip and trim back the jacket from the twisted-pair wire, leaving about two inches of wire exposed. Untwist the wires only so far as necessary so each wire can be inserted in the color-coded slot in the jack. The twists are needed to prevent crosstalk, and the untwisted wire should be no longer than a half inch. Figure 9-41 shows the wires in position for T568B wiring. Notice how the cable jacket goes into the keystone jack.

Figure 9-41   Eight wires are in position in a keystone jack for T568B wiring

2. Using the punchdown tool, make sure the blade side of the tool is on the outside of the jack. (The punchdown tool has Cut embedded on the blade side of the tool.) Push down with force to punch each wire into its slot and cut off the wire on the outside edge of the slot. It might take a couple of punches to do the job. See the left side of Figure 9-42. Place the jack cover over the jack, as shown in the right side of Figure 9-42.

3. The jack can now be inserted into the back side of a wall faceplate (see Figure 9-43). Make sure the wires in the jack are at the top of the jack. If you look closely at the faceplate, you can see the arrow pointing up. It's important the wires in the jack be at the top so that over the years dust doesn't settle on these wires. Use screws to secure the faceplate to the wall receptacle. Be sure to use a cable tester to check the network cable from its jack to the other end to make sure the wiring is good. When wiring a building, testing the cable and its two connections is called certifying the cable.

(continues)

Figure 9-42   Use a punchdown tool to punch the wires into the keystone jack, and then place the cover in position

Figure 9-43   Insert the jack in the faceplate, making sure the wire connectors are at the top of the jack

> ✎ **Notes** To see a video by CableSupply.com of using a punchdown tool to make an RJ-45 keystone jack, see *www.youtube.com/watch?v=sHy8mtW9eak*.

Some guidelines to follow when troubleshooting a network problem related to hardware are outlined in Figure 9-44 and listed here:

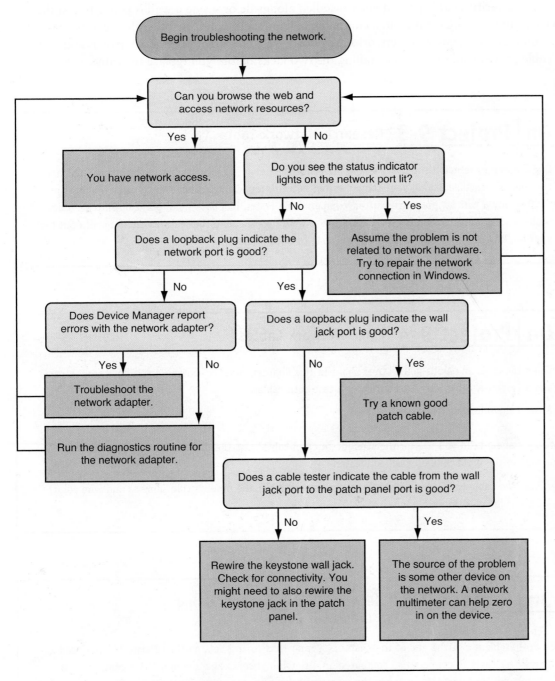

Figure 9-44 Flowchart to troubleshoot networking problems related to hardware

1. First check the status indicator lights on the network ports for connectivity and activity.
2. Use a loopback plug to verify each port. The loopback plug can work on ports provided by a computer, wall jack, patch panel, switch, router, or other device that is turned on. If you find a bad port, try a different port on a switch, router, or patch panel. You might need to replace the device.

3. For short straight-through cables connecting a computer to a wall jack or other nearby device, exchanging the straight-through cable for a known good one is easier and quicker than using a cable tester to test the cable.

4. Use a cable tester to verify a cable permanently installed alongside or inside a wall is good. To test the cable, you have to first disconnect it from a computer, patch panel, switch, or other device at both ends of the cable. Common problems with networks are poorly wired termination in patch panels and wall jacks. If the cable proves bad, first try reinstalling the two jacks before you replace the cable.

Hands-On | Project 9-3   Research Network Tools

A+
220-901
2.9, 4.4

Use the web to research the features and prices for the network tools you learned about in this chapter that you can include among your computer and network repair tools. Suppose you have a budget of $200 to buy a wire stripper, wire cutter, crimper, cable tester, loopback plug, punchdown tool, toner probe, and/or network multimeter. Save or print webpages showing the features and price of each tool you select for your toolkit. Which, if any tools, did you decide to not purchase? Why?

Hands-On | Project 9-4   Make Network Cables

A+
220-901
2.1, 2.2,
2.9, 4.4

Using the tools and skills you learned about in this chapter, practice making a straight-through cable and a crossover cable. Use a cable tester to test both cables.

Answer the following questions:

1. Which wiring standard did you use for the straight-through cable? List the pinouts (pin number and wire color) for each of the eight pins on each connector.

2. Will your crossover cable work on a Gigabit Ethernet network? List the pinouts (pin number and wire color) for each of the eight pins on each connector.

Hands-On | Project 9-5   Network Two Computers Using a Crossover Cable

A+
220-901
2.1, 2.2

In Real Problem 1 at the end of the chapter, "Connecting To and Setting Up a Network," you used a crossover cable to connect two computers in a simple network. Again connect two computers in a simple network, but this time use the crossover cable you just made. What are the Ethernet speeds that each computer supports? Which speed is the network using? Verify the network connectivity by copying a file from one computer to the other.

To wrap up the chapter, we turn our attention to software tools you can use for troubleshooting network problems and the strategies for solving these problems.

TCP/IP UTILITIES USED FOR TROUBLESHOOTING

Windows includes several TCP/IP utilities you can use to troubleshoot networking problems. In this part of the chapter, you learn to use ping, ipconfig, ifconfig, nslookup, tracert, the net commands, nbtstat, netstat, and netcom. Most of these program files are found in the \Windows\ System32 folder.

> ★ **A+ Exam Tip** The A+ 220-901 exam expects you to know about these TCP/IP utilities: ping, ipconfig, ifconfig, tracert, netstat, nbtstat, net, netdom, and nslookup. You need to know when and how to use each utility and how to interpret results.

> ✎ **Notes** Only the more commonly used parameters or switches for each command are discussed. For several of these commands, you can use the /? or /help parameter to get more help with the command. And for even more information about each command, search the *technet.microsoft.com* site.

Now let's see how to use each utility.

PING [-A] [-T] [*TARGETNAME*]

The ping (Packet InterNet Groper) command tests connectivity by sending an echo request to a remote computer. If the remote computer is online, detects the signal, and is configured to respond to a ping, it responds. (Responding to a ping is the default Windows setting.) Use ping to test for connectivity or to verify name resolution is working. A few examples of ping are shown in Table 9-5. Two examples are shown in Figure 9-45.

Ping Command	Description
ping 69.32.142.109	To test for connectivity using an IP address. If the remote computer responds, the round-trip times are displayed.
ping -a 69.32.142.109	The –a parameter tests for name resolution. Use it to display the host name and verify DNS is working.
ping -t 69.32.142.109	The –t parameter causes pinging to continue until interrupted. To display statistics, press Ctrl+Break. To stop pinging, press Ctrl+C.
ping 127.0.0.1	A loopback address test. The IP address 127.0.0.1 always refers to the local computer. If the local computer does not respond, you can assume there is a problem with the TCP/IP configuration.
ping www.cengage.com	Use a host name to find out the IP address of a remote computer. If the computer does not respond, assume there is a problem with DNS. On the other hand, some computers are not configured to respond to pings.

Table 9-5   Examples of the ping command

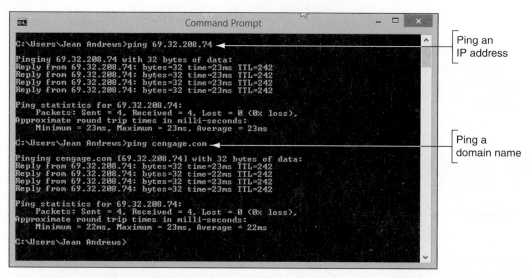

Figure 9-45 Use ping to test for connectivity and name resolution

IPCONFIG [/ALL] [/RELEASE] [/RENEW] [/DISPLAYDNS] [/FLUSHDNS]

The ipconfig (IP configuration) command can display TCP/IP configuration information and refresh the TCP/IP assignments to a connection, including its IP address. Some examples of the command are listed in Table 9-6.

Ipconfig Command	Description
ipconfig /all	Displays TCP/IP information.
ipconfig /release	Releases the IP address when dynamic IP addressing is being used.
ipconfig /release6	Releases an IPv6 address.
ipconfig /renew	Leases a new IP address from a DHCP server. Make sure you release the IP address before you renew it.
ipconfig /renew6	Leases a new IPv6 address from a DHCP IPv6 server. Make sure you release the IPv6 address before you renew it.
ipconfig /displaydns	Displays information about name resolutions that Windows currently holds in the DNS resolver cache.
ipconfig /flushdns	Flushes the name resolver cache, which might solve a problem when the browser cannot find a host on the Internet.

Table 9-6 Examples of the ipconfig command

IFCONFIG [-A] [INTERFACE] [UP] [DOWN]

The ifconfig (interface configuration) command is similar to ipconfig, and is used on UNIX, Linux, and Mac OS X operating systems. Some examples of the command are listed in Table 9-7.

Notes Commands entered in Linux, UNIX, and OS X are case sensitive: Upper- and lowercase matter.

Ifconfig Command	Description
`ifconfig`	Displays details of active interfaces and their assigned IP addresses. If a computer has only a single NIC, its interface name is most likely eth0.
`ifconfig -a`	Displays a list of active and inactive network interfaces.
`ifconfig <interface name>`	Displays details of a specific network interface. For example: `ifconfig eth0`
`ifconfig <interface name> up`	Enables a network interface. For example: `ifconfig eth0 up`
`ifconfig <interface name> down`	Disables a network interface. Disabling and enabling the network interface can sometimes solve a problem with network connectivity in Linux, UNIX, or OS X.

Table 9-7 Examples of the ifconfig command

Notes You cannot use the ifconfig command to disable or enable the network interface without root access to the OS.

9

NSLOOKUP [COMPUTERNAME]

The nslookup (namespace lookup) command lets you read information from the Internet namespace by requesting information about domain name resolutions from the DNS server's zone data. Zone data is information about domain names and their corresponding IP addresses kept by a DNS server. For example, to find out what your DNS server knows about the domain name *www.microsoft.com*, use this command:

`nslookup www.microsoft.com`

Figure 9-46 shows the results. Notice in the figure that the DNS server reports one IPv4 address and two IPv6 addresses assigned to *www.microsoft.com*. It also reports that this information is nonauthoritative, meaning that it is not the authoritative, or final, name server for the *www.microsoft.com* computer name.

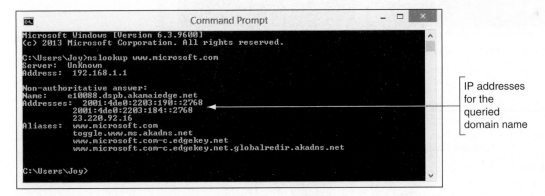

Figure 9-46 The nslookup command reports information about the Internet namespace

A reverse lookup is when you use the nslookup command to find the host name when you know a computer's IP address, such as:

`nslookup 192.168.1.102`

To find out the default DNS server for a network, enter the nslookup command with no parameters.

TRACERT [TARGETNAME]

The tracert (trace route) command can be useful when you're trying to resolve a problem reaching a destination host such as an FTP site or website. The command sends a series of requests to the destination computer and displays each hop to the destination. (A hop happens when a packet moves from one router to another.) For example, to trace the route to the *www.cengage.com* site, enter this command in a command prompt window:

```
tracert www.cengage.com
```

The results of this command are shown in Figure 9-47. A packet is assigned a Time to Live (TTL), which is the number of hop counts it can make before a router drops the packet and sends an ICMP message back to the host that sent the packet (see Figure 9-48). Internet Control Message Protocol (ICMP) messages are used by routers and hosts to communicate error messages and updates, and some routers don't send this information. The tracert command creates its report from these messages. If a router doesn't respond, the *Request timed out* message appears.

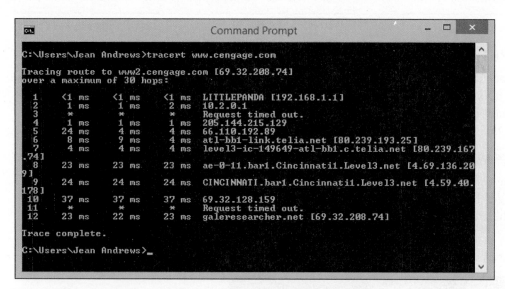

Figure 9-47   The tracert command traces a path to a destination computer

Figure 9-48   A router eliminates a packet that has exceeded its TTL

THE NET COMMANDS

The net command is several commands in one, and most of the net commands require an elevated command prompt window. In this section, you learn about the net use, net user, and net localgroup commands. The net use command connects or disconnects a computer from a shared resource or can display information about connections. For example, the following command makes a new connection to a remote computer and to a shared folder on that computer:

```
net use \\bluelight\Medical
```

> **Notes** Other important net commands are net accounts, net config, net print, net share, and net view. You might want to do a Google search on these commands to find out how they work.

Use the following command to pass a user name and password to the \\bluelight remote computer and then map a network drive to the \Medical folder on that computer:

```
net use \\bluelight\Medical /user:"Jean Andrews" mypassword
```

```
net use z: \\bluelight\Medical
```

The double quotation marks are needed in the first command above because the user name has a space in it.
A persistent network connection is one that happens at each logon. To make the two commands persistent, add the /persistent parameter like this:

```
net use \\bluelight\Medical /user:"Jean Andrews" mypassword /persistent:yes
```

```
net use z: \\bluelight\Medical /persistent:yes
```

The net user command manages user accounts. For example, the built-in administrator account is disabled by default. To activate the account, use this net user command:

```
net user administrator /active:yes
```

The net localgroup command adds, displays, or modifies local user groups. To display available local groups, use the following command:

```
net localgroup
```

To change a standard user account, Tom Jones, to an administrator account, use the following command:

```
net localgroup administrators "Tom Jones" /add
```

To change an administrator account, Tom Jones, to a standard account, use the following command:

```
net localgroup administrators "Tom Jones" /delete
```

NBTSTAT [-N] [-R] [-RR]

The nbtstat (NetBIOS over TCP/IP statistics) command is used to display statistics about the NetBT (NetBIOS over TCP/IP) protocol. NetBIOS is an older network protocol suite used before TCP/IP. Occasionally, you find a legacy application still in use that relies on NetBIOS and NetBIOS computer names. The NetBT protocol was developed to allow NetBIOS to work over a TCP/IP network.

Whereas TCP/IP uses a Hosts file on the local computer and a DNS server to resolve computer names, NetBIOS uses an Lmhosts file on the local computer and a WINS (Windows Internet Name Service) server to resolve NetBIOS computer names. Table 9-8 lists some nbtstat commands that you might use when a legacy application cannot access resources on the network.

Command	Description
nbtstat -n	Displays the NetBIOS name table on the local computer
nbtstat -r	Purges and rebuilds the NetBIOS name cache on the local computer using entries in the Lmhosts file
nbtstat -RR	Releases and renews the NetBIOS names kept by the WINS server

Table 9-8 Nbtstat commands

NETSTAT [-a] [-b] [-o]

The netstat (network statistics) command gives statistics about TCP/IP and network activity and includes several parameters. Table 9-9 lists a few netstat commands.

Command	Description
netstat	Lists statistics about the network connection, including the IP addresses of active connections.
netstat >>netlog.txt	Directs output to a text file.
netstat -b	Lists programs that are using the connection (see Figure 9-49) and is useful for finding malware that might be using the network. The -b switch requires an elevated command prompt.
netstat -b -o	Includes the process ID of each program listed. When you know the process ID, you can use the taskkill command to kill the process.
netstat -a	Lists statistics about all active connections and the ports the computer is listening on.

Table 9-9 Netstat commands

Figure 9-49 Netstat -b lists programs that are using a network connection

Notes Many commands other than netstat can use the >> parameter to redirect output to a text file. For example, try the ping or tracert command with this parameter.

NETDOM [ADD] [MOVE] [RESETPWD] [VERIFY]

The netdom (network domain) command allows administrators to manage Active Directory domains and trust relationships for Windows Server from the command prompt on the server or remotely from a Windows 8/7 workstation. The netdom command must be run using an elevated command prompt. Table 9-10 lists a few netdom commands.

Command	Description
netdom add	Adds a workstation to the domain
netdom move	Moves a workstation to a new domain
netdom resetpwd	Resets the password of the computer account for a domain controller
netdom verify	Verifies the connection is secure between a workstation and a domain controller

Table 9-10 Netdom commands

> ★ **A+ Exam Tip** Normally, the A+ exams don't require you to know about commands that are used only in Windows Server. This one netdom command is an exception and the A+ 220-901 exam expects you to be familiar with the command.

STRATEGIES FOR TROUBLESHOOTING NETWORK CONNECTIONS

A+
220-901
1.4, 4.4,
4.5

With tools in hand, you're now ready to tackle network troubleshooting, including problem solving when there is no connectivity and limited or intermittent connectivity. Here is how to find out the extent of the problem:

1. To check for local connectivity, use File Explorer in Windows 8 or Windows Explorer in Windows 7 to try to access shared folders on the network. No connectivity might be caused by the network cable or its connection, a wireless switch not turned on, a bad network adapter, or TCP/IP settings in Windows.

2. Determine whether other computers on the network are having trouble with their connections. If the entire network is down, the problem is not isolated to the computer you are working on.

3. If you can access some, but not all, shared resources on the network, this limited connectivity problem might be caused by cables or a switch on the network or a problem at the computer sharing the resources you're trying to reach.

4. To test for Internet access, use a browser to surf the web. Problems with no Internet access can be caused by cables, a SOHO router, a broadband modem, or problems at the ISP.

5. To find out if a computer with limited or no connectivity was able to initially connect to a DHCP server on the network, check for an Automatic Private IP Address (APIPA). Recall from the chapter, "Connecting To and Setting Up a Network," that a computer assigns itself an APIPA if it is unable to find a DHCP server at the time it first connects to the network. Use the ipconfig command to find out the IP address (see Figure 9-50). In the results, an APIPA presents itself as the Autoconfiguration IPv4 Address, and the address begins with 169.254.

9

Indicates
an APIPA IP
address is
assigned

Figure 9-50   The network connection was not able to lease an IP address

Now let's see how to handle problems with no or intermittent connectivity and then we'll look at problems with Internet access.

PROBLEMS WITH NO CONNECTIVITY OR INTERMITTENT CONNECTIVITY

When a computer has no network connectivity or intermittent connectivity, begin by checking hardware and then move on to checking Windows network settings.

Follow these steps to solve problems with hardware:

1. Check the status indicator lights on the NIC or the motherboard Ethernet port. A steady light indicates connectivity and a blinking light indicates activity (see Figure 9-51). Check the indicator lights on the router or switch at the other end. Try a different port on the device. If the router or switch is in a server closet and the ports are not well labeled, you can use a loopback plug to find out which port the computer is using. If you don't see either light, this problem must be resolved before you consider OS or application problems.

Figure 9-51   Status indicator lights verify connectivity for a network port

2. Check the network cable connection at both ends. Is the cable connected to a port on the motherboard that is disabled? It might need to be connected to the network port provided by a network card. A cable tester can verify the cable is good or if it is the correct cable (patch cable or crossover cable). Try a different network cable.

3. For wireless networking, make sure the wireless switch on a laptop is turned on. If you have no connectivity, limited connectivity, or intermittent connectivity, move the laptop to a new position in the hotspot. Use a wireless locator to find the best position. Rebooting a laptop might solve the problem of not receiving a signal. Problems with a low RF signal can sometimes be solved by moving the laptop or connecting to a different wireless access point with a stronger RF signal.

4. After you've checked cable connections and the wireless switch and the problem still persists, turn to Windows to repair the network connection. Use one of these methods:

   ◢ In an elevated command prompt window, use these two commands: **ipconfig /release** followed by **ipconfig /renew**.

   ◢ In the Network and Sharing Center, click **Troubleshoot problems** to access a Windows network connectivity diagnostic tool (see Figure 9-52).

   ◢ If that doesn't work, return to the Network and Sharing Center, click **Change adapter settings**, right-click the connection, and click **Disable**. Then right-click the connection again and click **Enable**.

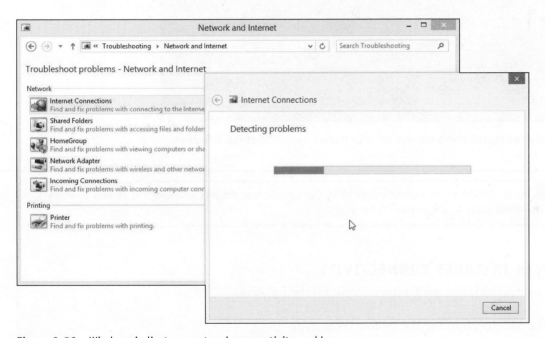

Figure 9-52 Windows indicates a network connectivity problem

If the problem is still not resolved, you need to dig deeper. Perhaps the problem is with the network adapter drivers. To solve problems with device drivers, which might also be related to a problem with the NIC, follow these steps:

1. Make sure the network adapter and its drivers are installed by checking for the adapter in Device Manager. Device Manager should report the device is working with no problems.

2. If errors are reported, try updating the device drivers. (Use another computer to download new drivers to a USB flash drive and then move the flash drive to this computer.) If the drivers still install with errors, look on the manufacturer's website or installation CD that came bundled with the adapter for diagnostic software that might help diagnose the problem.

3. If Device Manager still reports errors, try running anti-malware software and updating Windows. Then try replacing your network adapter. If that does not work, the problem might be a corrupted Windows installation.

Intermittent connectivity on a wired network might happen when a network device such as a VoIP phone is sensitive to electrical interference. You can solve this problem by attaching a ferrite clamp (see Figure 9-53) on the network cable near the port. This clamp helps to eliminate electromagnetic interference (EMI). Some cables come with preinstalled clamps, and you can also buy ferrite clamps to attach to other cables.

Clamp not yet installed

Clamp installed

Figure 9-53   Install a ferrite clamp on a network cable to protect against electrical interference

⭐ **A+ Exam Tip**   The A+ 220-901 exam expects you to be able to troubleshoot network problems that present themselves as no connectivity or limited, local, or intermittent connectivity.

PROBLEMS WITH INTERNET CONNECTIVITY

If you have local connectivity, but not Internet access, do the following:

1. Try recycling the connection to the ISP. Follow these steps:

- ◢ Unplug from the power source the cable modem, DSL modem, or other device that you use to connect to your ISP. Unplug the router. Wait about five minutes for the connection to break at the ISP.
- ◢ Plug in the cable modem, DSL modem, or other ISP device. Wait until the lights settle. Then plug in your router.
- ◢ On any computer on your network, use the Network and Sharing Center to repair the network connection. Open your browser and try to browse some websites.

2. For a cable modem, check to make sure your television works. The service might be down. For a DSL connection, check to make sure your phone gives a dial tone. The phone lines might be down.

3. To eliminate the router as the source of the problem, connect one computer directly to the broadband modem. If you can access the Internet, you have proven the problem is with the router or cables going to it. Connect the router back into the network and check all the router settings. The problem might be with DHCP, the firewall settings, or port forwarding. Try updating the firmware on the router. If you are convinced all settings on the router are correct, but the connection to your ISP works without the router and does not work with the router, it's time to replace the router.

4. To eliminate DNS as the problem, follow these steps:

   ◢ Try substituting a domain name for the IP address in a ping command:

   `ping www.cengage.com`

   If this ping works, then you can conclude that DNS works. If an IP address works, but the domain name does not work, the problem lies with DNS.

   ◢ Try pinging your DNS server. To find out the IP address of your DNS server, use the nslookup command with no parameters or open the firmware utility of your router and look on a status screen.

5. If you're having a problem accessing a particular computer on the Internet, try using the tracert command, for example:

   `tracert www.cengage.com`

   The results show computers along the route that might be giving delays.

6. If one computer on the network cannot access the Internet but other computers can, make sure MAC address filtering on the router is disabled or this computer is allowed access.

7. Perhaps the problem is with your router firewall or Windows Firewall. How to verify router firewall settings is covered in the chapter, "Connecting To and Setting Up a Network."

8. If you still cannot access the Internet, contact your ISP.

If some computers on the network have both local and Internet connectivity, but one computer does not, move on to checking problems on that computer, which can include TCP/IP settings and problems with applications.

USE TCP/IP UTILITIES TO SOLVE CONNECTIVITY PROBLEMS

No connectivity or no Internet access can be caused by Windows TCP/IP configuration and connectivity. Follow these steps to verify that the local computer is communicating over the network:

1. Using the Network and Sharing Center or the ipconfig command, try to release the current IP address and lease a new address. This process solves the problem of an IP conflict with other computers on the network or your computer's failure to connect to the network.

2. To find out if you have local connectivity, try to ping another computer on the network. To find out if you have Internet connectivity and DNS is working, try to ping a computer on the Internet using its host address. Try **ping www.cengage.com**. If this last command does not work, try the tracert command to find out if the problem is outside or inside your local network. Try **tracert www.cengage.com**.

3. In a command prompt window, enter **ipconfig /all**. Verify the IP address, subnet mask, and default gateway. For dynamic IP addressing, if the computer cannot reach the DHCP server, it assigns itself an APIPA, which is listed as an Autoconfiguration IPv4 Address that begins with 169.254 (refer back to Figure 9-50). In this case, suspect that the computer is not able to reach the network or the DHCP server is down.

4. Next, try the loopback address test. Enter the command **ping 127.0.0.1** (with no period after the final 1). Your computer should respond. If you get an error, assume the problem is TCP/IP settings on your computer. Compare the configuration with that of a working computer on the same network.

5. If you're having a problem with slow transfer speeds, suspect a process is hogging network resources. Use the **netstat –b** command to find out if the program you want to use to access the network is actually running.

6. Firewall settings might be wrong. Are port forwarding settings on the router and in Windows Firewall set correctly?

7. Two computers on the network might have the same computer name. This command reports the error:

```
net view \\computername
```

8. If the net view command using a computer name does not work, try the command using the remote computer's IP address, as in:

```
net view 192.168.1.102
```

If this command works, the problem is likely with name resolution. Make sure the computer name you are using is correct.

9. If you're having problems getting a network drive map to work, try making the connection with the net use command like this:

```
net use z: \\computername\folder
```

To disconnect a mapped network drive, use this command:

```
net use z: /delete
```

Now we move on to problems with wireless connectivity.

NO WIRELESS CONNECTIVITY

In a laptop, an internal wireless adapter uses an internal antenna, and the laptop might have a switch to turn on the internal wireless adapter or might use a key combination for that purpose. Look for the switch near the keyboard or on the side of the laptop (see Figure 9-54). Make sure the switch is set to the on position when you want to use wireless. The internal antenna might be embedded in the lid of the laptop. Raising the lid to a vertical position can sometimes improve the signal and solve a problem with intermittent connectivity.

Figure 9-54   This switch controls an internal wireless adapter

Following is a list of more things you can try. After each step, see if you can connect to the wireless network; if not, continue on to the next step.

1. Make sure you are within range of the wireless access point.

2. Click your wireless icon in the system tray. Turn the wireless connection off, wait a few seconds, then turn it back on.

3. Using the Network and Sharing Center, disable and then enable the wireless network adapter.

4. Reboot the computer.

5. Update the device drivers for the wireless card.

6. Replace the wireless card (see Figure 9-55). For instructions on how to replace the Mini PCIe wireless card, refer to the chapter, "Supporting I/O Devices."

Figure 9-55 This half-size Mini PCIe wireless card is anchored in the expansion slot with one screw

WI-FI NETWORK NOT FOUND

A wireless access point broadcasts an SSID. Your computer typically will easily find the SSID of a Wi-Fi network and connect after entering the security key, if one is needed. If your computer does not detect an SSID that you know should be available, it might be because the SSID is hidden. If you know the SSID name and the security key, you can still connect to the network by following these steps:

1. Open the Network and Sharing Center.

2. Click **Set up a new connection or network**.

3. Select **Manually connect to a wireless network** (see Figure 9-56), and click **Next**.

Figure 9-56 Set up a manual connection to a hidden SSID

4. Enter the network name, choose the security type, and enter the security key. Click **Next**.

5. Your wireless network is set up and you should be connected. Click **Close**.

NO BLUETOOTH CONNECTIVITY

If your laptop supports Bluetooth, read the documentation for configuring the Bluetooth connection that came with the laptop because Bluetooth setups differ from one laptop to another. Following the directions for your laptop, turn on Bluetooth. After Bluetooth is turned on, set your Bluetooth device near the laptop and it should pair up with it. Pairing up is the term used when the two devices begin to communicate and a passcode is requested to complete the connection.

If you are having problems getting the Bluetooth connection to work, try the following:

◢ Make sure Bluetooth is turned on (for some laptops, Bluetooth and Wi-Fi wireless are controlled by a function key or a wireless switch).

◢ Verify that Windows sees Bluetooth enabled. You might do this by using an applet in Control Panel, by using a program on the Windows 8 Start screen or Windows 7 Start menu, or by using the Bluetooth icon in the notification area of the desktop taskbar.

> ✎ **Notes** Be aware that a laptop might show the Bluetooth icon in the taskbar even when the laptop does not support Bluetooth.

◢ Be sure you have downloaded and installed all Windows updates.

◢ Look in Device Manager to make sure the Bluetooth component is recognized with no errors. For some laptops, even though the component is an internal device, it is seen in Device Manager as a USB device.

◢ Make sure the other device has Bluetooth turned on. For example, when trying to communicate with a smart phone, you must use the menu on the phone to activate Bluetooth connections. Windows should see the Bluetooth device when you click the Bluetooth icon in the taskbar and then click **Add a Bluetooth Device,** as shown in Figure 9-57a. You can also manage Bluetooth devices from the *PC and devices* page in Windows 8, as shown in Figure 9-57b.

Figure 9-57   (a) Bluetooth icon on the taskbar used to control Bluetooth devices and settings, and (b) the PC and devices page shows a Bluetooth device ready to pair

◢ Try uninstalling and reinstalling the Bluetooth drivers that come bundled with your laptop.

◢ Try uninstalling and reinstalling the drivers for your Bluetooth device. For example, if you are trying to connect to a printer using a Bluetooth wireless connection, try first turning on Bluetooth and then uninstalling and reinstalling the printer. During the printer installation, select the Bluetooth connection for the printer port, which might be called Bluetooth COM or something similar.

For more ideas for solving a Bluetooth problem, try the website of the laptop manufacturer or the website of the device you are trying to connect to your laptop using Bluetooth.

GPS NOT FUNCTIONING

A Global Positioning System (GPS) allows your laptop to be used as a navigation device with mapping software. The advantages to using your laptop as a GPS device instead of a compact GPS device, like Garmin or TomTom, is a larger screen, more detailed routing, and better routing analysis. A GPS receiver connects to your laptop using a USB port. If your GPS is not working, try the following:

◢ Sometimes the GPS receiver does not work well when plugged directly in to the USB port on a laptop. Instead, try using a short USB extension cable that is usually included with the GPS receiver. This gives the GPS receiver some distance from your laptop so there is less interference caused by the laptop.

◢ Because a GPS uses satellites, a clear view of the sky is necessary for the GPS receiver to lock signal with the satellite. Make sure you are positioned so that the receiver is able to "see" a clear sky. Buildings, mountains, and trees can all be blocks.

Hands-On | Project 9-6 Use a Port Scanner

A+
220-901
4.4, 4.5

Port scanning software can be used to find out how vulnerable a computer is with open ports. This project requires the use of two computers on the same network to practice using port scanning software. Do the following:

1. On Computer 1, download and install Advanced Port Scanner by Famatech at **http://www.advanced-port-scanner.com**. (Be careful to not accept other software offered while downloading.)

2. On Computer 2, set the network location to **Public network**. (For Windows 8, open the **Settings** charms, click the **Network** icon, click **View Connection Settings**, click **Connections**, select the network connection, and turn off **Find devices and content**. For Windows 7, open the **Network and Sharing Center** and click the network location to change it.)

3. On Computer 1, start Advanced Port Scanner and make sure that the range of IP addresses includes the IP address of Computer 2. Change the default port list to 0 through 6000. Then click **Scan**.

4. Browse the list and find Computer 2. List the number and purpose of all open ports found on Computer 2.

5. On Computer 2, set the network location to Private for Windows 8 and Home for Windows 7. Open the **System** window, click **Remote settings**, and allow Remote Assistance connections to this computer. Close all windows.

6. On Computer 1, rescan and list the number and purpose of each port now open on Computer 2. Figure 9-58 shows the results for one computer, but yours might be different.

(continues)

9

Figure 9-58 Advanced Port Scanner shows open ports on networked computers

>> *CHAPTER SUMMARY*

Types of Networks and the Internet Connections They Use

◢ Networks are categorized by size as a PAN, LAN, Wireless LAN, MAN, or WAN.

◢ Performance of a network technology is measured in bandwidth and latency.

◢ The two most popular ways to connect to the Internet are cable Internet and DSL. Other methods used include satellite, dedicated fiber optic, dial-up, and cellular wireless technologies (2G, 3G, 4G, and/or LTE).

Hardware Used by Local Networks

◢ Networking hardware used on local networks can include dial-up modems, hubs, switches, routers, wireless access points, bridges, cables, and connectors.

◢ The most popular Ethernet cable is twisted pair using an RJ-45 connector. Phone lines use an RJ-11 connector.

◢ Switches and older hubs are used as a centralized connection for devices on a wired network. A bridge stands between two network segments and controls traffic between them.

◢ Most wired local networks use twisted-pair cabling that can be unshielded twisted-pair (UTP) cable or shielded twisted-pair (STP) cable. UTP is rated by category: CAT-3, CAT-5, CAT-5e, CAT-6, CAT-6a, and CAT-7. CAT-6e is an unofficial name for CAT-6a.

⊿ Fiber-optic cables can use one of four connectors: ST, SC, LC, or MT-RJ. Any one of the four connectors can be used with single-mode or multimode fiber-optic cable.

⊿ Powerline networking, also called Ethernet over Power (EoP), sends Ethernet transmissions over the power lines of a building or house. Power over Ethernet (PoE) sends power over Ethernet cables.

Setting Up and Troubleshooting Network Wiring

⊿ Tools used to manage and troubleshoot network wiring and connectors are a loopback plug, cable tester, multimeter, toner probe, wire stripper, crimper, and punchdown tool.

⊿ The RJ-45 connector has eight pins. Four pins (pins 1, 2, 3, and 6) are used to transmit and send data using the 10BaseT and 100BaseT speeds. Using 1000BaseT speed, all eight pins are used for transmissions.

⊿ Two standards used to wire network cables are T568A and T568B. The difference between the T568A and T568B standards is the orange twisted-pair wires are reversed in the RJ-45 connector from the green twisted-pair wires.

⊿ A straight-through cable uses the T568A or T568B standard on both connectors. A crossover cable for 10BaseT or 100BaseT uses T568A for one connector and T568B for the other connector. Crossover cables are generally not used on Gigabit Ethernet networks.

⊿ Either T568A or T568B can be used to wire a network. To avoid confusion, don't mix the two standards in a building.

⊿ Use wire strippers, wire cutters, and a crimper to make network cables. A punchdown tool is used to terminate cables in a patch panel or keystone RJ-45 jack. Be sure to use a cable tester to test or certify a cable you have just made.

⊿ When troubleshooting network wiring, tools that can help are status indicator lights, loopback plugs, cable testers, Wi-Fi analyzers, toner probes, and network multimeters.

⊿ Useful Windows TCP/IP utilities for network troubleshooting are ping, ipconfig, nslookup, tracert, net use, net user, net localgroup, nbtstat, netstat, and netdom. The Linux ifconfig command is similar to the Windows ipconfig command.

⊿ When troubleshooting network problems, check hardware, device drivers, Windows, and the client or server application, in that order.

>> KEY TERMS

For explanations of key terms, see the Glossary for this text.

100BaseT	CAT-7	ferrite clamp	latency
bandwidth	cellular network	fiber optic	LC (local connector) connector
base station	cellular WAN	fiber-optic cable	line-of-sight connectivity
BNC connector	coaxial cable	Gigabit Ethernet	loopback plug
bridge	crimper	hub	MAN (metropolitan area network)
broadband	crossover cable	ifconfig (interface configuration)	mobile hotspot
cable Internet	data throughput	Internet service provider (ISP)	MT-RJ (mechanical transfer registered jack) connector
cable tester	DSL (Digital Subscriber Line)	ipconfig (IP configuration)	nbtstat (NetBIOS over TCP/IP statistics)
CAT-3	Ethernet over Power (EoP)	ISDN (Integrated Services Digital Network)	net localgroup
CAT-5	extender	keystone RJ-45 jack	net use
CAT-5e	F connector	LAN (local area network)	
CAT-6	Fast Ethernet		
CAT-6a			
CAT-6e			

net user
netdom (network domain)
netstat (network statistics)
network multimeter
nslookup (namespace lookup)
PAN (personal area network)
patch cable
patch panel
ping (Packet InterNet Groper)

plenum
PoE injector
Power over Ethernet (PoE)
powerline networking
punchdown tool
PVC (polyvinyl chloride)
repeater
reverse lookup
RG-59 coaxial cable
RG-6 coaxial cable

RJ-11 jack
SC (subscriber connector or standard connector) connector
shielded twisted-pair (STP) cable
ST (straight tip) connector
straight-through cable
switch
T568A
T568B
tether

tone probe
toner probe
tracert (trace route)
twisted-pair cabling
unshielded twisted-pair (UTP) cable
WAN (wide area network)
Wi-Fi analyzer
wire stripper
wireless LAN (WLAN)

>> REVIEWING THE BASICS

1. Place the following networking technologies in the order of their highest speed, from slowest to fastest: dial-up networking, cable Internet, Fast Ethernet, and 3G.

2. What is the difference between ADSL and SDSL?

3. Among satellite, cable Internet, and DSL, which technology experiences more latency?

4. When using DSL to connect to the Internet, the data transmission shares the cabling with what other technology?

5. When using cable Internet, the data transmission shares the cabling with what other technology?

6. What is the name of the port used by an Ethernet cable? What is the name of the port used by a dial-up modem?

7. If you want to upgrade your 100BaseT Ethernet network so that it will run about 10 times the current speed, what technology would you use?

8. What is the maximum length of a cable on a 100BaseT network?

9. What does the 100 in the name 100BaseT indicate?

10. Which type of networking cable is more reliable, STP or UTP? Which is normally used on LANs?

11. Which is more expensive, UTP CAT-6 cabling or STP CAT-6 cabling?

12. When looking at a network cable that is not labeled, describe how you can tell if the cable is a straight-through cable or a crossover cable.

13. What technology is used when power is transmitted on a network cable?

14. Describe the difference between a hub and a switch.

15. How is a wireless access point that is also a bridge more efficient in handling network traffic than a wireless access point that is not a bridge?

16. What type of cable uses an F connector?

17. Why does a CAT-6 cable have a plastic core? Which types of cabling are recommended for Gigabit Ethernet?

18. How many wires does a CAT-6 cable have? A CAT-6e cable? A coaxial cable?

19. Which tool can you use to verify that a network port on a computer is good?

20. After making a straight-through cable, which tool can you use to certify the cable?

21. Which tool can help you find a network cable in the walls of a building?

22. Which tool is used to firmly attach an RJ-45 connector to a network cable?

23. Which tool can help you find out which wall jack connects to which port on a switch in an electrical closet?

24. Name two types of devices or equipment where you might find a keystone RJ-45 jack.

25. List the number assigned to each pair and the color of each pair used in twisted-pair networking cables.

26. What two standards are used to wire networking cables?

27. Of the two standards in the previous question, which standard is the most common? Which is required for all U.S. government installations?

28. Using either of the two wiring standards, what are the colors of the two pairs used to send and/or receive data on a 100BaseT network?

29. How many pairs of wires are crossed in a crossover cable that will work on a 100BaseT network? On a 1000BaseT network?

30. To prevent crosstalk in a keystone RJ-45 jack, what is the maximum length of wire that should be untwisted?

9

>> THINKING CRITICALLY

1. Linda has been assigned the job of connecting five computers to a network. The room holding the five computers has three network jacks that connect to a switch in an electrical closet down the hallway. Linda decides to install a second switch in the room. The new switch has four network ports. She uses one port to connect the switch to a wall jack. Now she has five ports available (two wall jacks and three switch ports). While installing and configuring the NICs in the five computers, she discovers that the PCs connected to the two wall jacks work fine, but the three connected to the switch refuse to communicate with the network. What could be wrong and what should she try next?

2. If a Gigabit Ethernet NIC is having a problem communicating with a 100BaseT switch that only supports half duplex, what steps can you take to manually set the NIC to the speed and duplex used by the switch? Which speed and duplex should you choose?

3. You connect a computer to an RJ-45 wall jack using a straight-through cable. When you first open the browser on the computer, you discover it does not have Internet access. Put the following steps in the correct order to troubleshoot the problem:

   a. Use a loopback plug to verify the network port on the computer.

   b. Rewire the keystone RJ-45 wall jack.

   c. Use a loopback plug to verify the network port in the wall jack.

   d. Exchange the straight-through cable for a known good one.

   e. Verify the status indicator lights on the NIC.

   f. Use a cable tester to test the network cable and termination from the switch in the electrical closet to the wall jack.

>> REAL PROBLEMS, REAL SOLUTIONS

REAL PROBLEM 9-1 Setting Up a Wireless Access Point

As a computer and networking consultant to small businesses, you are frequently asked to find solutions to increasing demands for network and Internet access at a business. One business rents offices in a historical building that has strict rules for wiring. They have come to you asking for a solution for providing Wi-Fi access to their guests in the lobby of the building. Research options for a solution and answer the following questions:

1. Print or save webpages showing two options for a Wi-Fi wireless access point that can mount on the wall or ceiling. For one option, select a device that can receive its power by PoE from the network cable run to the device. For the other option, select a device that requires an electrical cable to the device as well as a network cable.

2. Print or save two webpages for a splitter that can be mounted near the second wireless access point that splits the power from data on the network cable. Make sure the power connectors for the splitter and the access point can work together.

3. To provide PoE from the electrical closet on the network cable to the wireless access point, print or save the webpage for an injector that injects power into a network cable. Make sure the voltage and wattage output for the injector are compatible with the needs of both wireless access points.

4. You estimate the distance for network cabling from the switch to the wireless access point is about 200 feet (61 meters). What is the cost of 200 feet of PVC CAT-6a cabling? For 200 feet of plenum CAT-6a cabling? For 200 feet of plenum CAT-7 cabling?

5. Of the options you researched, which option do you recommend? Using this option, what is the total cost of the Wi-Fi hotspot?

Supporting Printers
and Customizing a System

After completing
this chapter, you
will be able to:

- Discuss printer types and features

- Install and share printers and manage printer features, add-on devices, and the printer queue

- Perform routine maintenance tasks necessary to support printers

- Troubleshoot printer problems

- Customize a computer system to meet customer needs

This chapter discusses the most popular types of printers and how to support them. As you work through the chapter, you learn about printer types and features, how to install a local or network printer, and how to share a printer with others on a network. You learn how to manage printer features, add-on devices, shared printers, and print jobs. Then, you learn about maintaining and troubleshooting printers. Finally, we wrap up the chapter with a discussion of how to select appropriate parts for a customized computer system to satisfy the specifications given by your customer.

PRINTER TYPES AND FEATURES

> **A+**
> **220-901**
> **1.14,**
> **1.15**

The major categories of printer types include laser, inkjet (ink dispersion), impact, and thermal printers. In the following sections, we look at the different types of printers for desktop computing.

> ✎ **Notes** For heavy business use, sometimes it's best to purchase one machine for one purpose, instead of bundling many functions into a single machine. For example, if you need a scanner and a printer, purchase a good printer and a good scanner rather than a combo machine. Routine maintenance and troubleshooting are easier and less expensive on single-purpose machines, although the initial cost is higher. On the other hand, for home or small office use, a combo device can save money and counter space.

LASER PRINTERS

> **A+**
> **220-901**
> **1.14,**
> **1.15**

A laser printer is a type of electro-photographic printer that can range from a small, personal desktop model to a large, network printer capable of handling and printing large volumes continuously. Figure 10-1 shows an example of a typical laser printer for a small office.

Figure 10-1   Oki Data C3200n color laser printer

> ★ **A+ Exam Tip**   The A+ 220-901 exam expects you to be familiar with these types of printers: laser, inkjet, thermal, and impact. You also need to know about virtual printers.

Laser printers require the interaction of mechanical, electrical, and optical technologies. Laser printers work by placing toner on an electrically charged rotating drum (sometimes called the imaging drum) and then depositing the toner on paper as the paper moves through the system at the same speed the drum is turning. Figure 10-2 shows the seven steps of laser printing.

Figure 10-2   The seven progressive steps of laser printing

Note that Figure 10-2 shows only a cross-section of the drum, mechanisms, and paper. Remember that the drum is as wide as a sheet of paper. The mirror, blades, and rollers in the drawing are also as wide as paper. Also know that toner responds to a charge and moves from one surface to another if the second surface has a more positive charge than the first.

> ★ **A+ Exam Tip** The A+ 220-901 exam expects you to know the seven steps of laser printing.

The seven steps of laser printing are listed next:

1. *Processing the image.* A laser printer processes and prints an entire page at one time. The page comes to the printer encoded in a language the printer understands and the firmware inside the printer processes the incoming data to produce a bitmap (a bunch of bits in rows and columns) of the final page, which is stored in the printer's memory. One bitmap image is produced for monochrome images. For color images, one bitmap is produced for each of four colors. (The colors are blue, red, yellow, and black, better known as cyan, magenta, yellow, and black, and sometimes written as CMYK.)

2. *Charging or conditioning.* During charging, the drum is conditioned by a roller that places a high uniform electrical charge of -600 V on the surface of the drum. The roller is called the primary charging roller or primary corona, which is charged by a high-voltage power supply assembly. For some printers, a corona wire is used instead of the charging roller to charge the drum.

3. *Exposing or writing.* A laser beam controlled by motors and a mirror scans across the drum until it completes the correct number of passes. The laser beam is turned on and off continually as it makes a single pass down the length of the drum, once for each raster line, so that dots are exposed only where toner should go to print the image. For example, for a 1200 dots per inch (dpi) printer, the beam makes 1200 passes for every one inch of the drum circumference. For a 1200-dpi printer, 1200 dots are exposed or not exposed along the drum for every inch of linear pass. The 1200 dots per inch down this single pass, combined with 1200 passes per inch of drum circumference, accomplish the resolution of 1200 × 1200 dots per square inch of many laser printers. The laser beam writes an image to the drum surface as a -100 V charge. The -100 V charge on this image area will be used in the developing stage to transmit toner to the drum surface.

> 📝 **Notes** A laser printer can produce better quality printouts than a dot matrix printer, even when printing at the same dpi, because it can vary the size of the dots it prints, creating a sharp, clear image. Hewlett-Packard (HP) calls this technology of varying the size of dots REt (Resolution Enhancement technology).

4. *Developing.* The developing cylinder applies toner to the surface of the drum. The toner is charged and sticks to the developing cylinder because of a magnet inside the cylinder. A control blade prevents too much toner from sticking to the cylinder surface. As the cylinder rotates very close to the drum, the toner is attracted to the part of the surface of the drum that has a -100 V charge and repelled from the -600 V part of the drum surface. The result is that toner sticks to the drum where the laser beam has hit and is repelled from the area where the laser beam has not hit.

5. *Transferring.* In the transferring step (shown in Figure 10-2), a strong electrical charge draws the toner off the drum onto the paper. This is the first step that takes place outside the cartridge and the first step that involves the paper. The soft, black transfer roller puts a positive charge on the paper to pull the toner from the drum onto the paper. Then the static charge eliminator (refer again to Figure 10-2) weakens the charges on both the paper and the drum so that the paper does not stick to the drum. The stiffness of the paper and the small radius of the drum also help the paper move away from the drum and toward the fusing assembly. Very thin paper can wrap around the drum, which is why printer manuals usually instruct you to use only paper designated for laser printers.

10

6. *Fusing.* The fuser assembly uses heat and pressure to fuse the toner to the paper. Up to this point, the toner is merely sitting on the paper. The fusing rollers apply heat to the paper, which causes the toner to melt, and the rollers apply pressure to bond the melted toner into the paper. The temperature of the rollers is monitored by the printer. If the temperature exceeds an allowed maximum value (410 degrees F for some printers), the printer shuts down.

7. *Cleaning.* A sweeper strip cleans the drum of any residual toner, which is swept away by a sweeping blade. The charge left on the drum is then neutralized. Some printers use erase lamps in the top cover of the printer for this purpose. The lamps use red light so as not to damage the photosensitive drum.

For color laser printers, the writing process repeats four times, one for each toner color of cyan, magenta, yellow, and black. Each color requires a separate image drum. Then, the paper passes to the fusing stage, when the fuser bonds all toner to the paper and aids in blending the four tones to form specific colors.

> ★ **A+ Exam Tip**   The A+ 220-901 exam expects you to be familiar with these laser printer terms: imaging drum, fuser assembly, transfer belt, transfer roller, pickup roller, separate pads, and duplexing assembly.

CARTRIDGES AND OTHER REPLACEABLE PARTS

The charging, exposing, developing, and cleaning steps use the printer components that undergo the most wear. To make the printer last longer, these steps are done inside a removable cartridge that can be replaced. For older printers, all four steps were done inside one cartridge. For newer printers, the cleaning, charging, and exposing steps are done inside the image drum cartridge. The developing cylinder is located inside the toner cartridge. The transferring is done using a transfer belt that can be replaced, and the fusing is done inside a fuser cartridge.

By using these multiple cartridges inside laser printers, the cost of maintaining a printer is reduced. You can replace one cartridge without having to replace them all. The toner cartridge needs replacing the most often, followed by the image drum, the fuser cartridge, and the transfer assembly, in that order.

Other printer parts that might need replacing include the pickup roller that pushes forward a sheet of paper from the paper tray and the separation pad (also called separate pad) that keeps more than one sheet of paper from moving forward. If the pickup roller is worn, paper misfeeds into the printer. If the separation pad is worn, multiple sheets of paper will be drawn into the printer. Sometimes you can clean a pickup roller or separation pad to prolong its life before it needs replacing.

> ✎ **Notes**   Before replacing expensive parts in a printer, consider whether a new printer might be more cost effective than repairing the old one.

DUPLEXING ASSEMBLY

A printer that is able to print on both sides of the paper is called a duplex printer or a double-sided printer. Many laser printers and a few inkjet printers offer this feature. After the front of the paper is printed, a duplexing assembly, which contains several rollers, turns the paper around and draws it back through the print process to print on the back of the paper. Alternately, some high-end printers have two print engines so that both sides of the paper are printed at the same time.

INKJET PRINTERS

A+ 220-901 1.14, 1.15

An inkjet printer (see Figure 10-3) uses a type of ink-dispersion printing and doesn't normally provide the high-quality resolution of laser printers. Inkjet printers are popular because they are small and can print color inexpensively. Most inkjet printers today can print high-quality photos, especially when used with photo-quality paper.

Figure 10-3   An example of an inkjet printer

Figure 10-4   The ink cartridges of an inkjet printer

An inkjet printer uses a print head that moves across the paper, creating one line of the image with each pass. The printer puts ink on the paper using a matrix of small dots. Different types of inkjet printers form their droplets of ink in different ways. Printer manufacturers use several technologies, but the most popular is the bubble-jet. Bubble-jet printers use tubes of ink that have tiny resistors near the end of each tube. These resistors heat up and cause the ink to boil. Then, a tiny air bubble of ionized ink (ink with an electrical charge) is ejected onto the paper. A typical bubble-jet print head has 64 or 128 tiny nozzles, all of which can fire a droplet simultaneously. (High-end printers can have as many as 3,000 nozzles.) Plates carrying a magnetic charge direct the path of ink onto the paper to form shapes.

Inkjet printers include one or more ink cartridges to hold the different colors of ink for the printer. Figure 10-4 shows two ink cartridges. A black cartridge is on the left and a three-color cartridge is on the right. For this printer, a print head is built into each ink cartridge.

A stepper motor moves the print head and ink cartridges across the paper using a carriage and belt to move the assembly and a stabilizing bar to control the movement (see Figure 10-5). A paper tray can hold a stack of paper, or a paper feeder on the back of the printer can hold a few sheets of paper. The sheets stand up in the feeder and are dispensed one at a time. Rollers pull a single sheet into the printer from the paper tray or paper feeder. A motor powers these rollers and times the sheet going through the printer in the increments needed to print the image. When the printer is not in use, the assemblage sits in the far-right position shown in Figure 10-4, which is called the home position or parked position. This position helps protect the ink in the cartridges from drying out.

Some inkjet printers offer duplex printing. These printers are larger than normal inkjet printers because of the added space required for the duplexing assembly. For duplex printing, be sure to use heavy paper (rated at 24-pound paper or higher) so the ink doesn't bleed through.

10

Extra, unused cartridge stored here

Belt

Print head and ink cartridge assembly in parked position

Stabilizing bar

Figure 10-5   The belt and stabilizing bar used to move the print head across the page

> ✎ **Notes**   Weight and brightness are the two primary ways of measuring paper quality. The rated weight of paper (for example, 20 pounds to 32 pounds) determines the thickness of the paper. Brightness is measured on a scale of 92 to 100.

When purchasing an inkjet printer, look for the kind that uses two or four separate cartridges. One cartridge is used for black ink. Three cartridges, one for each color, give better quality color than one cartridge that holds all three colors. Some low-end inkjet printers use a single three-color cartridge and don't have a black ink cartridge. These printers must combine all colors of ink to produce a dull black. Having a separate cartridge for black ink means that it prints true black and, more important, does not use the more expensive colored ink. To save money, you should be able to replace an empty cartridge without having to replace all cartridges.

> ✎ **Notes**   To save money, you can refill an ink cartridge, and many companies will sell you the tools and ink you need as well as show you how to do it. You can also purchase refilled cartridges at reduced prices. When you purchase ink cartridges, make sure you know if they are new or refilled. Also, for best results, don't refill a cartridge more than three times.

Inkjet printers tend to smudge on inexpensive paper, and they are slower than laser printers. If a printed page later gets damp, the ink can run and get quite messy. The quality of the paper used with inkjet printers significantly affects the quality of printed output. You should use only paper that is designed for an inkjet printer, and you should use a high-grade paper to get the best results.

> ✎ **Notes**   Photos printed on an inkjet printer tend to fade over time, more so than photos produced professionally. To make your photos last longer, use high-quality paper (rated at high gloss or studio gloss) and use fade-resistant ink (such as Vivera ink by HP). Then protect these photos from exposure to light, heat, humidity, and polluted air. To best protect photos made by an inkjet printer, keep them in a photo album rather than displayed and exposed to light.

IMPACT PRINTERS

A+ 220-901 1.14, 1.15

An impact printer creates a printed page by using some mechanism that touches or hits the paper. The best-known impact printer is a dot matrix printer, which prints only text that it receives as raw data. It has a print head that moves across the width of the paper, using pins to print a matrix of dots on the page. The pins shoot against a cloth ribbon, which hits the paper, depositing the ink. The ribbon provides both the ink for printing and the lubrication for the pinheads. The quality of the print is poor compared with other printer types. However, three reasons you see impact printers still in use are: (1) They use continuous tractor feeds and fanfold paper (also called computer paper) rather than individual sheets of paper, making them useful for logging ongoing events or data, (2) they can use carbon paper to print multiple copies at the same time, and (3) they are extremely durable, give little trouble, and seem to last forever.

★ **A+ Exam Tip** The A+ 220-901 exam expects you to know about the print head, ribbon, and tractor feed in an impact printer and about impact paper used in the printer.

Maintaining a dot matrix impact printer is easy to do. The impact paper used by impact printers comes as a box of fanfold paper or in rolls (used with receipt printers). When the paper is nearing the end of the stack or roll, a color on the edge alerts you to replace the paper. Occasionally, you should replace the ribbon of a dot matrix printer. If the print head fails, check on the cost of replacing the head versus the cost of buying a new printer. Sometimes, the cost of the head is so high it's best to just buy a new printer. Overheating can damage a print head (see Figure 10-6), so keep it as cool as possible to make it last longer. Keep the printer in a cool, well-ventilated area, and don't use it to print more than 50 to 75 pages without allowing the head to cool down.

Print head

Figure 10-6 Keep the print head of a dot matrix printer as cool as possible so that it will last longer

THERMAL PRINTERS

A+ 220-901 1.14, 1.15

Thermal printers use heat to create an image. Two types of thermal printers are a direct thermal printer and a thermal transfer printer. The older direct thermal printer burns dots onto special coated paper, called thermal paper, as was done by older fax machines. The process requires no ink and does not use a ribbon. Direct thermal printers are often used as receipt printers that use rolls of thermal paper (see Figure 10-7). The printed image can fade over time.

A thermal transfer printer uses a ribbon that contains wax-based ink. The heating element melts the ribbon (also called

Courtesy of EPSON America, Inc.

Figure 10-7 The TM-T88V direct thermal printer by EPSON

10

foil) onto special thermal paper so that it stays glued to the paper as the feed assembly moves the paper through the printer. Thermal transfer printers are used to print receipts, barcode labels, clothing labels, or container labels. Figure 10-8 shows a thermal transfer printer used to make barcodes and other labels.

Thermal printers are reliable and easy to maintain. When you are responsible for a thermal printer, you know it's time to replace the paper roll when the roll shows the color down one edge. It's important to regularly clean the print head because build up can harden over time and permanently damage the head. Follow the printer manufacturer's directions to clean the print head. Some thermal printer ribbons have a print head cleaning stripe at the end of the ribbon, and it's a good idea to clean the head each time you replace the ribbon. Additionally, some manufacturers suggest cleaning the head with isopropyl alcohol wipes.

When cleaning, remove any dust and debris that gets down in the print head assembly. As you work, ground yourself to protect the sensitive heating element against static electricity. Don't touch the heating element with your fingers. Also, to prolong the life of the print head, use the lowest heat setting for the heating element that still gives good printing results.

Table 10-1 lists some printer manufacturers.

Courtesy of Zebra Technologies

Figure 10-8   The GC420 printer by Zebra is both a thermal transfer printer and a direct thermal printer

Printer Manufacturer	Website
Brother	brother-usa.com
Canon	usa.canon.com
Hewlett-Packard	hp.com
Konica Minolta	kmbs.konicaminolta.us
Lexmark	lexmark.com
Oki Data	okidata.com
Samsung	samsung.com
Seiko Epson	epson.com
Xerox	xerox.com
Zebra Technologies	zebra.com

Table 10-1   Printer manufacturers

> ★ **A+ Exam Tip**   The A+ 220-901 exam expects you to know about the feed assembly and heating element used in thermal printers and about the need for special thermal paper used in the older direct thermal printers.

Hands-On | Project 10-1 Research Printer Websites

A+ 220-901 1.14   Your company plans to purchase a new printer, and you want to evaluate the printer manufacturers' websites to determine which site offers the best support. Research three websites listed in Table 10-1 and answer these questions, supporting your answers with pages that you have saved or printed from the website:

1. Which website made it easiest for you to select a new printer, based on your criteria for its use?

2. Which website made it easiest for you to find help for troubleshooting printer problems?

3. Which website gave you the best information about routine maintenance for its printers?

4. Which website gave you the best information about how to clean its printers?

Now let's turn our attention to using Windows to install, share, and manage printers.

USING WINDOWS TO INSTALL, SHARE, AND MANAGE PRINTERS

 In this part of the chapter, you learn to install local and network printers, share an installed printer, and remotely use a shared printer. You also learn about virtual printing and how to configure printer add-ons and features. We begin with learning about a local printer and network printer.

LOCAL OR NETWORK PRINTER

 A printer connects to a single computer or to the network. A local printer connects directly to a computer by way of a USB port, serial port, or wireless connection (Bluetooth or Wi-Fi). Some printers support more than one method. A network printer has an Ethernet port to connect directly to the network or uses Wi-Fi to connect to a wireless access point. Some printers have both an Ethernet port and a USB port (see Figure 10-9). These printers can be installed as either a network printer (connecting directly to the network) or a local printer (connecting directly to a computer).

Status indicator lights for the Ethernet port

Ethernet port

USB port

Figure 10-9   This printer has an Ethernet and USB port

The two ways to install a printer and make it available on a network are:

▲ *Local printer.* A local printer can be attached to a computer using a port (for example, USB, serial, or wireless) on the computer (see Computer A in Figure 10-10). For some network printers, it is possible to set up a local printer by using an Ethernet cable connected to the Ethernet port on the network printer and the Ethernet port on the computer. The printer can be dedicated to only this one computer, or you can share the printer for network users. For a shared local printer to be available to other computers on the network, the host computer must be turned on and not in sleep or standby mode. For another computer on the network to use the shared printer, the printer drivers must be installed on the remote computer.

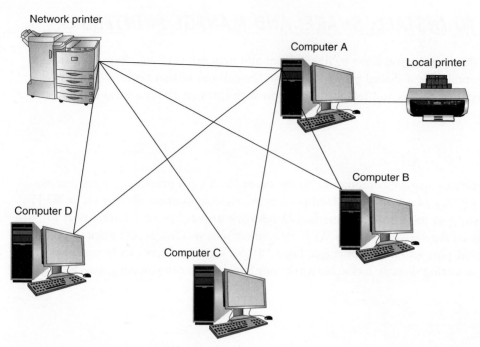

Figure 10-10 A shared local printer and a network printer

▲ *Network printer.* A network printer can connect directly to a network with its own NIC (see the network printer in Figure 10-10). A network printer is identified on the network by its IP address. To use the printer, any computer on the network can install this printer and print to it, which is called remote printing.

> ✎ **Notes** A computer can have several printers installed. Of these, Windows designates one printer to be the default printer, which is the one Windows prints to unless another is selected.

WIRED OR WIRELESS PRINTER CONNECTIONS

A+
220-901
1.12,
1.13

Connecting a wired printer (USB or Ethernet) is easy:

  ▲ *USB.* Plug the USB cable into the printer and computer and Windows installs the printer automatically.

  ▲ *Serial.* For a printer with a serial port, plug the serial cable into the printer and computer and install the printer as a local printer.

▲ *Ethernet.* Plug the Ethernet cable into the printer and network wall jack, switch, or router and install the printer as a network printer on any computer on the network.

Connecting a wireless printer is a little more complex:

▲ *Bluetooth.* For a Bluetooth printer, which is installed as a local printer, turn on Bluetooth in Windows, move the printer within range of the computer, and watch as the two Bluetooth devices pair up.

▲ *Wi-Fi ad hoc network.* For a Wi-Fi printer, you can connect the printer and computer directly to each other in a Wi-Fi ad hoc mode network. Put the printer within 30 feet of the computer. Then, in Windows 7, open the **Network and Sharing Center**, click **Set up a new connection or network**, click **Set up a wireless ad hoc (computer-to-computer) network**, and follow directions on screen. Windows 8 does not support ad hoc Wi-Fi; however, you can use third-party software to do the job. When using an ad hoc network, next, install the printer as a local printer. Some printers can handle up to four computers connected in an ad hoc Wi-Fi network.

▲ *Wi-Fi infrastructure network.* In infrastructure mode, Wi-Fi devices connect to a Wi-Fi access point, such as a SOHO router. Put the Wi-Fi printer within range of the access point and use controls on the printer to select the Wi-Fi network and enter the security key to the network if one is required. All Wi-Fi printers support infrastructure connections and some Wi-Fi printers can handle ad hoc connections.

Notes Apple computers and mobile devices can print to AirPrint printers without having to first install the printer. For a Mac or iOS device to use an AirPrint printer, simply open the Print menu in any app. If an AirPrint printer is on the network, it will appear in the list of printers. An AirPrint printer is always capable of Wi-Fi connections to a wireless network and some have a USB or Ethernet port for wired connections. AirPrint printers are also capable of cloud printing, discussed later in this chapter.

INSTALL A LOCAL OR NETWORK PRINTER

A+
220-901
1.12,
1.13

When you install a printer, printer drivers are required that are compatible with the installed operating system. Be sure to use 32-bit drivers for a 32-bit OS and 64-bit drivers for a 64-bit OS. Windows has many printer drivers built in. The drivers also come on a CD bundled with the printer or you can download them from the printer manufacturer's website.

Also, for some types of printers, you can launch the installation program that came bundled on CD with the printer or downloaded from the printer manufacturer's website. On the other hand, you can use the Windows 8/7 Devices and Printers window to install a printer. These windows are also used to manage and uninstall printers.

APPLYING | CONCEPTS   INSTALL A PRINTER

A+
220-901
1.12,
1.13

Installing a network printer is sometimes called mapping a printer. Follow these steps to install a wired or Wi-Fi network printer, serial-port printer, or Bluetooth printer in Windows:

1. Make sure the printer is connected to the network or the computer. In Control Panel in Classic view, click **Devices and Printers**. In the Devices and Printers window, click **Add a printer**. Windows searches for available printers and lists them (see Figure 10-11).

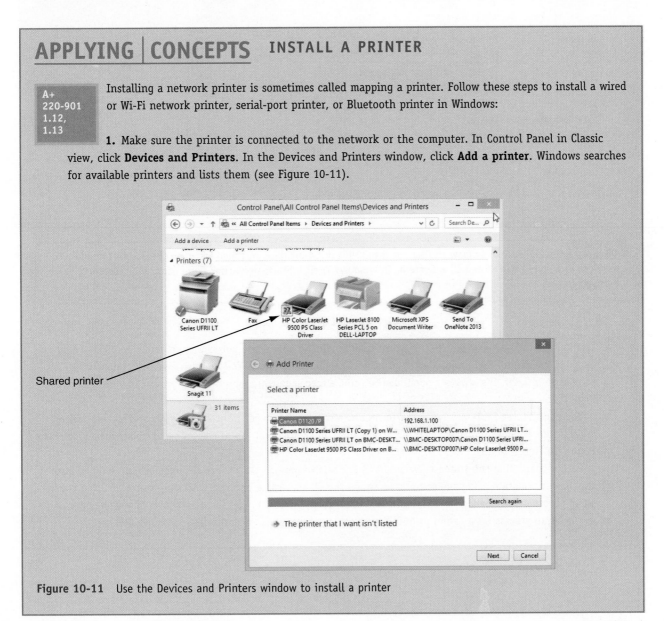

Figure 10-11 Use the Devices and Printers window to install a printer

(continues)

2. Select the printer and click **Next**. If your printer isn't listed, click **The printer that I want isn't listed** and select the printer from a list of printers for which Windows has drivers.

3. In the next box (see the left side of Figure 10-12), select the brand and model printer to use the drivers kept by Windows. To use drivers stored on CD or previously downloaded from the web, click **Have Disk**. The Install From Disk box appears (see the right side of Figure 10-12). Click **Browse** to locate the drivers; Windows is looking for an .inf file. Be sure to select 32-bit or 64-bit drivers, depending on which type of OS you are using.

Figure 10-12   Locate printer drivers on CD or downloaded from the web

> ✎ **Notes** Use the System window to find out if a 32-bit or 64-bit OS is installed. To open the System window in Windows 8, press **Win+X** and click **System**. In Windows 7, click **Start**, right-click **Computer**, and select **Properties**.

4. Continue to follow the wizard to install the printer. Dialog boxes give you the opportunity to change the name of the printer and designate the printer as the default printer. You are also given the opportunity to test the printer. It's always a good idea to print a test page when you install a printer to verify the installation works.

   You can also send a test page to the printer at any time. To do so, right-click the printer in the Devices and Printers window and select **Printer properties**. On the General tab of the Properties box, click **Print Test Page** (see Figure 10-13).

   Rather than using the Windows Devices and Printers window to start a printer installation, you can also start the installation using the setup program on the CD that came bundled with the printer or using the setup program downloaded from the printer manufacturer's website. Figure 10-14 shows one such window in the setup process for a Canon printer. This method might work when the first method fails.

Figure 10-13 Send a test page to the printer to test connectivity to the printer, the printer, and the printer installation

Source: Canon

Figure 10-14 Menu provided by a setup program that came bundled with a printer

★ **A+ Exam Tip** The A+ 220-901 exam expects you to know how to install a local and network printer in Windows.

10

SHARE A PRINTER ON A NETWORK

Each computer on a network can connect directly to a network printer. On the other hand, one computer or device can share the printer with other computers. Three general ways to share a printer on a network are to use a:

▲ *Computer as a print server.* When your computer hosting a printer shares the printer with other computers on the network, the computer is called a print server. One reason to require that all computers connect to a shared network printer rather than mapping directly to the network printer is so that you can manage all print jobs from one centralized location. In this situation, you can use Print Management in the Administrative Tools group of Control Panel to monitor the printer and solve printer problems from a centralized location.

▲ *Hardware print server.* To connect a USB, Bluetooth, or serial-port printer to the network, you can use a hardware print server, such as the one shown in Figure 10-15. This device has a USB port for a USB printer and can connect to a Wi-Fi or Ethernet network. Plug the USB cable from the printer into the USB port of the hardware print server and connect the device to the network, using either a wired or wireless connection. The printer appears as a network printer on the network, and any computer on the network can connect to it.

Source: newegg.com

Figure 10-15   This hardware print server lets you connect a USB printer to the network without first installing the printer on a local computer

▲ *Printer firmware print server.* Some advanced printers have print server programs included in the printer firmware that allow you to manage print protocols, start or stop jobs in the print queue, reorder jobs in the queue, cancel specific jobs coming from a particular computer on the network, and set up your email address so the printer alerts you by email when it has a problem.

When using a computer as the print server, before you share an installed printer, verify these Windows settings for shared resources:

▲ *Security settings.* To share resources on a network, make sure the Windows 8 network security is set to Private or the Windows 7 network security is set to Work or Home. In addition, in the Network and Sharing Center, you can click **Change advanced sharing settings** and verify **Turn on file and printer sharing** is selected, which is the default setting for a Windows 8 Private or Windows 7 Home or Work network.

▲ *Wake-on-LAN.* Remote users will not be able to use a shared printer if the computer sharing the printer is asleep. You can configure Wake-on-LAN to cause network activity to wake up a sleeping computer. How to do that is covered in the chapter, "Connecting To and Setting Up a Network."

APPLYING | CONCEPTS   CONFIGURE AND USE A SHARED PRINTER

To share an installed local or network printer with others on the network, follow these steps:

1. In the printer Properties box, click the **Sharing** tab. Check **Share this printer** (see the left side of Figure 10-16).

Figure 10-16 Share the printer and make decisions as to how printer sharing is handled

2. You can then change the share name of the printer. Notice in Figure 10-16 the option to control where print jobs are rendered. A print job can be prepared (rendered) on the remote computer (client computer) or this computer (print server). Your choice depends on which computer you think should carry this burden. You can test several print jobs on remote computers with rendering done at either location and see which method best uses computing resources on the network.

> **Notes** Group Policy under Windows 7/Vista can be used to limit and control all kinds of printer-related tasks, including the number of printers that can be installed, how print jobs are sent to print servers (rendered or not rendered), which print servers the computer can use, and which printers on a network the computer can use.

3. If you want to make drivers for the printer available to remote users who are using an operating system other than the OS on this computer, click **Additional Drivers**.

4. The Additional Drivers box opens (see the right side of Figure 10-16). For 32-bit operating systems, select **x86**. For 64-bit operating systems, select **x64**. Click **OK** to close the box. You might be asked for the Windows setup DVD or other access to the installation files.

5. Click **OK** to close the Properties box. A shared printer shows a two-friends icon under it or in the status bar in the Devices and Printers window, and the printer is listed in the Network group in File Explorer or Windows Explorer of other computers on the network.

SECURE A SHARED PRINTER

Consider the security of your shared printer and the security of documents printed:

◢ *Secure the printer.* On the printer's Properties box (refer back to Figure 10-16), click the **Security** tab to manage who has access to the printer and permissions allowed. Notice in Figure 10-17 that the Everyone group can print but is not allowed to manage the printer or documents sent to it. Just as with shared files and folders, you can share the printer with specific users and/or set up a customized user group that is allowed to use a printer.

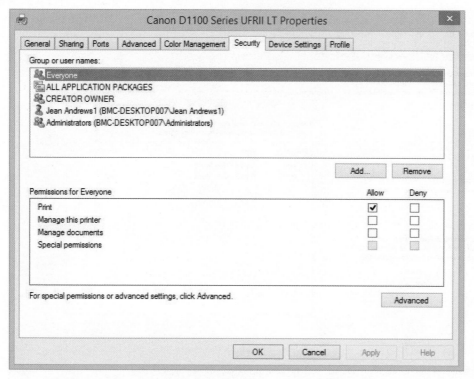

Figure 10-17   Security settings for a printer

▲ *Secure the data.* By default, documents sent to the printer are cached (spooled) to the hard drive of the print server and also cached on a hard drive that might be installed in a high-end printer. To prevent these print jobs from being hacked, don't allow caching to either hard drive. In Windows, to change the default setting for spooling, click the **Advanced** tab of the printer's Properties box (see Figure 10-18). Select **Print directly to the printer.** Not spooling to the hard drive slows down the printing process.

Figure 10-18   For best security, bypass caching print jobs to the hard drive

Notes When print jobs are spooled and the printer is not working or is turned off, the documents can back up in the printer queue. To manage the printer queue, double-click the printer in the Devices and Printers window. Click the queue link and use the menu bar in the queue window to manage the printer's queue.

USE A SHARED PRINTER

To install a shared printer on a remote computer, you can (1) Use the Devices and Printers window or (2) use File Explorer or Windows Explorer. Here are the general steps for both methods:

◢ *Devices and Printers window.* On a remote computer, in the Devices and Printers window, click **Add a printer** and follow the directions on screen to add a network printer. Select the shared printer, which has a host name in the printer address column (refer back to Figure 10-11). Windows attempts to use printer drivers found on the host computer. If it doesn't find the drivers, you will be given the opportunity to provide them on CD or another media.

If you don't see a shared printer in the list of printers to add, the user account might not be authorized to access resources on the remote computer. In this situation, use the File Explorer or Windows Explorer method discussed next, which allows the user to authenticate to the remote computer.

Notes If you don't see a shared printer in the list of printers, consider if the printer is shared by a Mac computer on the network and Bonjour is not running on your Windows computer. Bonjour is an Apple program that is used to interface between computers and devices and share content and services between them, and is used by Windows to discover a printer shared by a Mac computer. If you suspect a Mac is sharing a printer, open the Services tab of Task Manager in Windows and verify Bonjour is running. You can download the Bonjour Print Services for Windows from the Apple website at *https://support.apple.com/downloads/bonjour%20for%20windows*.

◢ *File Explorer or Windows Explorer.* In the Explorer window, drill down into the computer that is sharing the printer. If the Windows Security box appears, you need to authenticate to the remote computer with a valid user account and password on the remote computer, as shown in Figure 10-19a. (For the user name to work, the printer must be shared with this specific user or user group and the password much match the password of this user on the remote computer.) After authentication, you can see the shared printer. Right-click the printer and select **Connect**. A warning box appears (see Figure 10-19b). Click **Install driver** and follow directions on screen.

(a) (b)

Figure 10-19 (a) Authenticate to the remote computer sharing the printer; (b) allow Windows to install drivers stored on the remote computer

After the printer is installed, be sure to send a test page to the printer to verify the installation is successful.

VIRTUAL PRINTING

Printing to a file instead of producing a hard copy at a printer is called virtual printing. The types of files you can virtually print depends on the software installed on your system. To see your options for virtual printing, open the Print menu or dialog box for an application. For example, Figure 10-20 shows the results for one system.

Figure 10-20   The file types available for virtual printing depend on software installed in the system

The items of interest listed in the figure are these types of files:

▲ **PDF file.** Because Adobe Acrobat is installed on this system, it is possible to virtually print to a PDF file.

▲ **Image file, also called a bitmap file.** Snagit is imaging software normally used to take screen shots. When you print to Snagit, you create an image that appears in the Snagit window. Then, you can use Snagit to save the image as a PNG, GIF, JPG, BMP, TIF, or another image file format.

▲ **XPS file.** Windows includes the Microsoft XPS Document Writer, which creates an XPS file. The file is similar to a PDF and can be viewed, edited, printed, faxed, emailed, or posted on websites. In Windows, the file is viewed in a browser window.

▲ **Print to file.** When you check **Print to file** on a Print menu, the print job is created for the currently selected printer and saved to a PRN file. The file contains the information a printer needs to print the document. Saving a print job to a PRN file and later printing it worked with older printers, but doesn't work with modern printers. Today, it's better to create a PDF or XPS document.

> ★ **A+ Exam Tip**   The A+ 220-901 exam expects you to know about virtual printing to PDF, XPS, and image files, and about the option, Print to file.

CLOUD PRINTING

With cloud printing, you can print to a printer anywhere on the Internet from a personal computer or mobile device connected to the Internet. Cloud printing is a type of client/server application. Client software on a computer or mobile device sends a document (which might be encrypted) or a print job to server software on the local network that funnels the print jobs to a printer on its network. The computer or mobile device with the client software installed can be anywhere on the Internet. Examples of cloud printing software, also called web-based printing software or web-to-print software, are Web to Print by B2Cprint (*b2cprint.com*) and Print Manager Plus by Print Manager (*printmanager.com*). For best security, make sure your software can encrypt a document or print job sent over the Internet.

Hands-On | Project 10-2 Print in the Cloud

A+
220-901
1.12,
1.13

To practice cloud printing using Google Cloud Print, you'll need a computer with an installed printer and another computer somewhere on the Internet. For the easiest solution to using Google Cloud Print, both computers need Google Chrome installed. You'll also need a Google account.

On the computer with an installed printer, do the following:

1. If you don't already have Google Chrome, go to **google.com/chrome/browser/desktop**, download, and install it.

2. Open Google Chrome and enter **chrome://devices** in the address box. Click **Add printers**. Sign in to Google with your Google account. If you don't already have an account, you can click **Create account** to create one.

3. The list of installed printers appears. Uncheck all printers except the one you want to use for cloud printing. Click **Add Printer(s)**.

On a computer anywhere on the Internet, do the following:

4. If necessary, install Google Chrome.

5. Open Google Chrome and sign in with your Google account. Navigate to a webpage you want to print. Click the menu icon in the upper-right corner of the Chrome window and click **Print**.

6. On the Print page, click **Change** and select the printer, which is listed in the Google Cloud Print group. Click **Print**. The page prints over the web to your printer.

> ✎ **Notes** You can share your cloud printer with others who have a Google account. To do so, sign in to your Google account and go to **google.com/cloudprint**. There you'll see a list of print jobs sent to your printer. Click **Printers**. Select the printer you want to share and click **Share**. Enter the email address of your friend and click **Share**. Click **Close**. When your friend is signed in to Google, he can print to your printer from anywhere on the web.

10

CONFIGURE PRINTER FEATURES AND ADD-ON DEVICES

A+
220-901
1.12,
1.13

After the printer is installed, use the printer Properties box to manage printer features and hardware devices installed on the printer. To open the box, right-click the printer and choose **Printer properties**. On the Properties box, click the **Device Settings** tab. The options on this tab depend on the installed printer. Figure 10-21 shows the box for an HP printer. As you can see in the figure, duplex printing (2-sided printing) is available. You can also control the size of the paper installed in each input tray bin and various add-on devices for this printer, such as a printer hard drive, stapler, or stacker unit.

Figure 10-21   The Device Settings for an HP printer

After you have installed new printer add-on equipment or a feature, the equipment or feature is listed as an option in the printer Properties box for the application used for printing a document. Options can include page orientation (landscape or portrait), collated or uncollated, 1-sided or 2-sided, and quality of printing (for example, general, graphics, or photo quality). For example, Figure 10-22 shows the printer Properties box for a laser printer when printing from Microsoft Word.

Figure 10-22   Choose options in a printer Properties dialog box

Hands-On | Project 10-3 Share a Local Printer

A+
220-901
1.12,
1.13

Practice printer-sharing skills using Windows and a printer:

1. Install and share a local printer with others on the network.

2. Install a shared printer on a remote computer. Verify you can print to the printer from the remote computer.

3. Turn off the shared printer. Print again from the remote computer. On which computer is the print job queued? Cancel this print job.

Now let's turn our attention to tasks you might be called on to do when maintaining and upgrading a printer.

PRINTER MAINTENANCE AND UPGRADES

A+
220-901
1.15, 4.6

Printers generally last for years if they are properly used and maintained. To get the most out of a printer, it's important to follow the manufacturer's directions when using the device and to perform the necessary routine maintenance. For example, the life of a printer can be shortened if you allow the printer to overheat, don't use approved paper, or don't install consumable maintenance kits when they are required.

ONLINE SUPPORT FOR PRINTERS

A+
220-901
1.15, 4.6

The printer manufacturer's website is an important resource when supporting printers. Here are some things to look for:

▲ *Online documentation.* Expect the printer manufacturer's website to include documentation on installing, configuring, troubleshooting, using, upgrading, and maintaining the printer. Also look for information on printer parts and warranty, compatibility information, specifications and features of your printer, and how to recycle or dispose of a printer.

▲ *A knowledge base of common problems and what to do about them.* Some websites offer a forum where you can communicate with others responsible for supporting a particular printer. Also look for an online chat link or email address for technical support.

▲ *Updated device drivers.* Sometimes you can solve printer problems by downloading and installing the latest drivers. Also, a manufacturer makes new features and options available through these drivers. Be sure you download files for the correct printer and OS.

▲ *Replacement parts.* When a printer part breaks, buy only parts made by or approved by the printer manufacturer. Manufacturers also sell consumable supplies such as toner and ink cartridges.

▲ *Printer maintenance kits.* The best practice is to buy everything you need for routine maintenance either from the printer manufacturer or an approved vendor. If you buy from a nonapproved vendor, you risk damaging the printer, voiding its warranty, or shortening its life span.

▲ *Firmware updates.* Some high-end printers have firmware that can be flashed to solve problems and add features. Be careful to download the correct update for your printer.

Here are a few safety tips when working with printers:

▲ *Hot to touch.* Some laser printer parts can get hot enough to burn you while in operation. Before you work inside a laser printer, turn it off, unplug it, and wait about 30 minutes for it to cool down.

10

▲ *Dangerous electricity.* A printer might still keep power even when the printer on/off switch is turned off. To ensure that the printer has no power, unplug it. Even when a laser printer is unplugged, internal components might still hold a dangerous electrical charge for some time.

▲ *Laser beam.* For your protection, laser printers use a laser beam that is always enclosed inside a protective case inside the printer. Therefore, when servicing a laser printer, you should never have to look at the laser beam, which can damage your eyes.

▲ *Static electricity.* To protect memory modules and hard drives inside printers, be sure to use an ESD strap to protect these sensitive components when installing them. You don't need to wear an ESD strap when exchanging consumables such as toner cartridges, fuser assembles, or image drums.

▲ *When no one is around.* Here's one more tip to stay safe, but I don't want it to frighten you: When you work inside high-voltage equipment such as a laser printer, don't do it when no one else is around. If you have an emergency, someone needs to be close by to help you.

> **✎ Notes** When working with laser printer toner cartridges, if you get toner dust on your clothes or hands while exchanging the cartridge, don't use hot water to clean it up. Remember that heat sets the toner. Go outdoors and use a can of compressed air to blow off the toner. Then use cold water to clean your hands and clothes. It's a good idea to wear a smock or apron when working on printers.

Figure 10-23 shows an ink cartridge being installed in an inkjet printer. To replace a cartridge, turn on the printer and open the front cover. The printer releases the cartridges. You can then open the latch on top of the cartridge and remove it. Install the new cartridge as shown in the figure.

Figure 10-23   Installing an ink cartridge in an inkjet printer

CLEAN A PRINTER

A+
220-901
1.15, 4.6

A printer gets dirty inside and outside as stray toner, ink, dust, and bits of paper accumulate. As part of routine printer maintenance, you need to regularly clean the printer. How often depends on how much the printer is used and the work environment. Some manufacturers suggest a heavily used printer be cleaned weekly, and others suggest you clean it whenever you exchange the toner, ink cartridges, or ribbon.

Clean the outside of the printer with a damp cloth. Don't use ammonia-based cleaners. Clean the inside of the printer with a dry cloth and remove dust, bits of paper, and stray toner. Picking up stray toner can be a problem. Don't try to blow it out with compressed air because you don't want the toner in the air. Also, don't use an antistatic vacuum cleaner. You can, however, use a vacuum cleaner designed to pick up toner, called a toner vacuum. This type of vacuum does not allow the toner that it picks up to touch any conductive surface.

Some printer manufacturers also suggest you use an extension magnet brush. The long-handled brush is made of nylon fibers that are charged with static electricity and easily attract the toner like a magnet. For a laser printer, wipe the rollers from side to side with a dry cloth to remove loose dirt and toner. Don't touch the soft black roller (the transfer roller), or you might affect the print quality. You can find specific instructions for cleaning a printer on the printer manufacturer's website.

CALIBRATE A PRINTER

A+
220-901
1.15, 4.6

An inkjet printer might require calibration to align and/or clean the inkjet nozzles, which can solve a problem when colors appear streaked or out of alignment. To calibrate the printer, you might use the menu on the control panel of the printer or use software that came bundled with the printer. How to access these tools differs from one printer to another. See the printer manual to learn how to perform the calibration. For some printers, a Services tab is added to the printer Properties window. Other printer installations might put utility programs in the Start menu. The first time you turn on a printer after installing ink cartridges, it's a good idea to calibrate the printer.

If an inkjet printer still does not print after calibrating it, you can try to manually clean the cartridge nozzles. Check the printer manufacturer's website for directions. For most inkjet printers, you are directed to use clean, distilled water and cotton swabs to clean the face of the ink cartridge, being careful not to touch the nozzle plate. To prevent the inkjet nozzles from drying out, don't leave the ink cartridges out of their cradle for longer than 30 minutes. Here are some general directions:

1. Following the manufacturer's directions, remove the inkjet cartridges from the printer and lay them on their sides on a paper towel.

2. Dip a cotton swab in distilled water (not tap water) and squeeze out any excess water.

3. Hold an ink cartridge so that the nozzle plate faces up and use the swab to wipe clean the area around the nozzle plate, as shown in Figure 10-24. Do not clean the plate itself.

10

Nozzle head should not be cleaned

Figure 10-24   Clean the area around the nozzle plate with a damp cotton swab

4. Hold the cartridge up to the light and make sure that no dust, dirt, ink, or cotton fibers are left around the face of the nozzle plate. Make sure the area is clean.

5. Clean all the ink cartridges the same way and replace the cartridges in the printer.

6. Print a test page. If print quality is still poor, try calibrating the printer again.

7. If you still have problems, you need to replace the ink cartridges.

Laser printers automatically calibrate themselves periodically. You can instruct a laser printer to calibrate at any time by using the controls on the front of the printer or the browser-based utility program that is included in the firmware of a network printer. To access the utility, enter the IP address of the printer in the browser address box.

PRINTER MAINTENANCE KITS

A+
220-901
1.15, 4.6
Manufacturers of high-end printers provide printer maintenance kits, which include specific printer components, step-by-step instructions for performing maintenance, how often maintenance should be done, and any special tools or equipment you need to do maintenance. For example, the maintenance plan for the HP Color LaserJet 4600 printer says to replace the transfer roller assembly after printing 120,000 pages and replace the fusing assembly after 150,000 pages. The plan also says the black ink cartridge should last for about 9,000 pages and the color ink cartridge for about 8,000 pages. HP sells the image transfer kit, the image fuser kit, and the ink cartridges designed for this printer.

Figure 10-25   Use buttons on the front of the printer to display information, including the page count

To find out how many pages a printer has printed so that you know if you need to do the maintenance, you need to have the printer give you the page count since the last maintenance. You can tell the printer to display the information or print a status report by using buttons on the front of the printer (see Figure 10-25) or you can use utility software from a computer connected to the printer. See the printer documentation to know how to get this report. For network printers that offer a browser-based utility, enter the IP address of the printer in your browser and use the utility to find the counters (Figure 10-26 shows such a utility for a Canon network printer).

Source: Canon

Figure 10-26   Use the web-based printer utility to read the printer counters

After you have performed the maintenance, be sure to reset the page count so it will be accurate to tell you when you need to do the next routine maintenance. Keep a written record of the maintenance and other service done.

The A+ 220-901 exam expects you to know about the importance of resetting the page count after installing a printer maintenance kit.

As examples of replacing printer consumables, let's look at how to replace a toner cartridge, image drum, and fuser for the Oki Data color laser printer shown earlier in Figure 10-1.

The A+ 220-901 exam expects you to know how to replace a toner cartridge and apply a maintenance kit that can include an image drum or a fuser assembly.

A toner cartridge for this printer generally lasts for about 1,500 pages. Here are the steps to replace a color toner cartridge:

1. Turn off and unplug the printer. Press the cover release button on the upper-left corner of the printer and open the printer cover (see Figure 10-27).

2. Figure 10-28 shows the cover up. Notice the four erase lamps on the inside of the cover. Look inside the printer for the four toner cartridges and the fuser assembly labeled in Figure 10-29. Pull the blue toner cartridge release button forward to release the cartridge from the image drum below it and to which it is connected (see Figure 10-30).

Figure 10-27 Open the printer cover

Four erase lamps

Figure 10-28 Cover lifted

Four toner cartridges

Fuser assembly

Figure 10-29   Inside the Oki Data printer

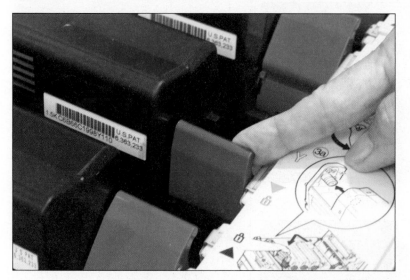

Figure 10-30   Push the blue lever forward to release the toner cartridge

Figure 10-31   Remove the toner cartridge

3. Lift the cartridge out of the printer, lifting up on the right side first and then removing the left side (see Figure 10-31). Be careful not to spill loose toner.

4. Unpack the new cartridge. Gently shake it from side to side to loosen the toner. Remove the tape from underneath the cartridge, and place the cartridge in the printer by inserting the left side first and then the right side. Push the cartridge lever back into position to lock the cartridge in place. Close the printer cover.

The printer has four image drums, one for each color. The drums are expected to last for about 15,000 pages. When you purchase a new drum, the kit comes with a new color toner cartridge. Follow these steps to replace the cartridge and image drum. In these steps, we are using the yellow drum and cartridge:

1. Turn off and unplug the printer. Wait about 30 minutes after you have turned off the printer for it to cool down. Then open the printer cover. The toner car-

tridge is inserted into the image drum. Lift the drum together with the toner cartridge out of the printer (see Figure 10-32). Be sure to dispose of the drum and cartridge according to local regulations.

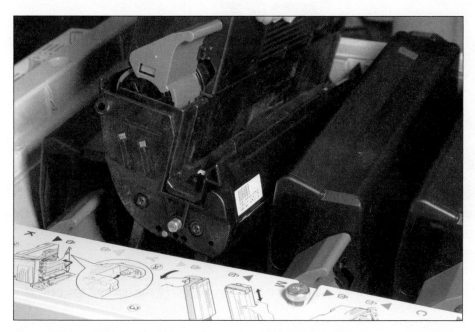

Figure 10-32 Remove the image drum and toner cartridge as one unit

2. Unpack the new image drum. Peel the tape off the drum and remove the plastic film around it. As you work, be careful to keep the drum upright so as not to spill the toner. Because the drum is sensitive to light, don't allow the drum to be exposed to bright light or direct sunlight. Don't expose it to normal room lighting for longer than five minutes.

3. Place the drum in the printer. Install the new toner cartridge in the printer. Close the printer cover.

The fuser should last for about 45,000 pages. To replace the fuser, follow these steps:

1. Turn off and unplug the printer. Allow the printer to cool and open the cover.

2. Pull the two blue fuser levers forward to unlock the fuser (see Figure 10-33).

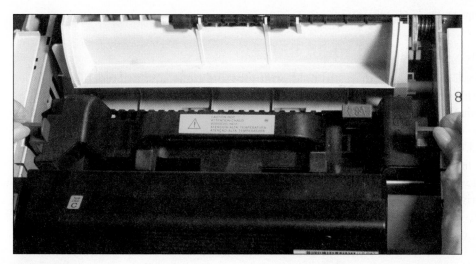

Figure 10-33 Pull the two fuser levers forward to release the fuser

3. Lift the fuser out of the printer using the handle on the fuser, as shown in Figure 10-34.

Figure 10-34   Remove the fuser

4. Unpack the new fuser and place it in the printer. Push the two blue levers toward the back of the printer to lock the fuser in place.

Whenever you service the inside of this printer, as a last step always carefully clean the LED erase lamps on the inside of the top cover (see Figure 10-35). The printer maintenance kits you've just learned to use all include a wipe to clean these strips.

Figure 10-35   Clean the LED strips on the inside top cover

UPGRADE THE PRINTER MEMORY OR HARD DRIVE

A+
220-901
1.15, 4.6

Some printers have internal hard drives to hold print jobs and fonts, and printers might also give you the option to install additional memory in the printer. Extra memory can speed up performance, reduce print errors, and prevent Out of Memory or Low Memory errors. Check the user guide to determine how much memory the printer can support and what kind of memory to buy or what kind of internal hard drive the printer might support.

As you work with printer hardware, be sure you turn off the printer and disconnect it from the power source. Also, use an antistatic ground bracelet to protect memory modules from static electricity. Most likely, you will use a screwdriver to remove a cover plate on the printer to expose a cavity where memory or a drive can be installed. To access memory on one printer, you remove thumbscrews on the back of the printer and then pull out the formatter board shown in Figure 10-36. Memory modules are installed on this board (see Figure 10-37). You can also install a hard drive in one of the two empty bays on the board. The hard drive comes embedded on a proprietary board that fits in the bay. After this equipment is installed, you must enable and configure it using the printer Properties window.

Figure 10-36 Remove the formatter board from the printer

PRINTER FIRMWARE

A+
220-901
1.15, 4.6

Most high-quality printers offer a utility embedded in the firmware that you can use to manage print jobs, view the status of the printer, see a job history, and check counters, such as the number of pages printed. These utilities are accessed through a browser. For one Canon printer, when you enter the IP address of the printer in a browser window and log on to the firmware utility, the window in Figure 10-38 appears.

10

Two empty
DIMM slots

Two installed
DIMMs

Bays for hard
drives or other
components

Figure 10-37 Memory is installed on the formatter board

Source: Canon

Figure 10-38 Use the printer's web-based utility to view the printer status and manage print jobs

TROUBLESHOOTING PRINTERS

A+ 220-901 1.15, 4.6

In this part of the chapter, you learn some general and specific printer troubleshooting tips. If you need more help with a printer problem, turn to the manufacturer's website for additional information and support.

APPLYING | CONCEPTS

A+ 220-901 1.15, 4.6

Jill is the computer support technician responsible for supporting 10 users, their peer-to-peer network, printers, and computers. Everything was working fine when Jill left work one evening, but the next morning three users meet her at the door, complaining that they cannot print to the network printer and that important work must be printed by noon. What do you think are the first three things Jill should check?

As with all computer problems, begin troubleshooting by interviewing the user, finding out what works and doesn't work, and making an initial determination of the problem. When you think the problem is solved, ask the user to check things out to make sure he is satisfied with your work. And, after the problem is solved, be sure to document the symptoms of the problem and what you did to solve it.

PRINTER DOES NOT PRINT

A+ 220-901 1.15, 4.6

When a printer does not print, the problem can be caused by the printer, the computer hardware or Windows, the application using the printer, the printer cable, or the network. Follow the steps in Figure 10-39 to isolate the problem.

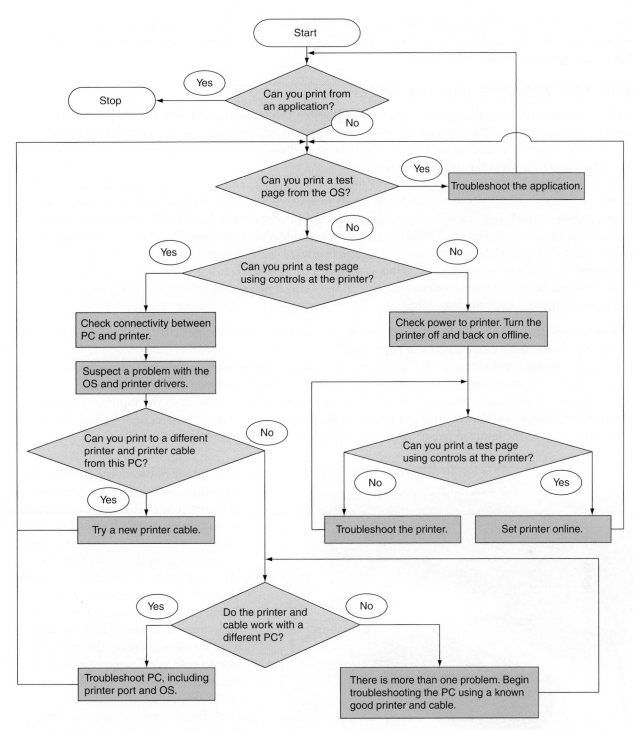

Figure 10-39   How to isolate a printer problem

As you can see in the figure, the problem can be isolated to one of the following areas:

▲ The printer itself
▲ Connectivity between the computer and its local printer
▲ Connectivity between the computer and a network printer
▲ The OS and printer drivers
▲ The application attempting to use the printer

10

In addition, if this is the first time you have tried to print after installing the printer, the printer drivers or the printer installation might be the problem. The following sections address printer problems caused by all of these categories, starting with hardware.

PROBLEMS WITH THE PRINTER ITSELF

To eliminate the printer as the problem, first check that the printer is on, and then print a printer self-test page by using controls at the printer. For directions to print a self-test page, see the printer's user guide. For example, you might need to hold down a button or buttons on the printer's front panel. If this test page prints correctly, then the printer is working.

A printer self-test page generally prints some text, some graphics, and some information about the printer, such as the printer resolution and how much memory is installed. Verify that the information on the test page is correct. For example, if you know that the printer should have 2 MB of onboard printer memory, but the test only reports 1 MB, then there is a problem with memory. If the information reported is not correct and the printer allows you to upgrade firmware on the printer, try doing that next.

If the self-test page does not print or prints incorrectly (for example, it has missing dots or smudged streaks through the page), then troubleshoot the printer until it prints correctly. When the printer self-test page does not print, check the following:

◢ Does the printer have paper? Is the paper installed correctly? Are the printer cover and rear access doors properly closed and locked? Is there a paper jam?

◢ If paper is jammed inside the printer, follow the directions in the printer documentation to remove the paper. Don't jerk the paper from the printer mechanism, but pull evenly on the paper, with care. You don't want to leave pieces of paper behind. Check for jammed paper from both the input tray and the output bin. Check both sides. An inkjet printer is likely to have a door in the back that you can open to gently remove the jammed paper, as shown in Figure 10-40.

Figure 10-40   Open the door on the back of an inkjet printer to remove jammed paper

◢ Is the paper not feeding? Remove the paper tray and check the metal plate at the bottom of the tray. Can it move up and down freely? If not, replace the tray. When you insert the tray in the printer, does the printer lift the plate as the tray is inserted? If not, the lift mechanism might need repair.

◢ Damp paper can cause paper jams or the printer to refuse to feed the paper or to wrinkle or crease the paper. Be sure to only use dry paper in a printer. Paper that is too thin can also crease or wrinkle in the printer.

◢ Look for an error message or error code in the control panel on the front of the printer. You might need to search the printer documentation or website to find out the meaning of a code. For example, error codes in the 79.xx range for HP printers can indicate a variety of problems from a print job with characters it does not understand to a failed memory module in the printer.

◢ For some error codes, the problem might be with a print job the printer cannot process. Cancel all print jobs and disconnect the printer from the network. If the control panel reports "Ready" or "Online," then you can assume the problem is with the network, computers, or print jobs, and not with the printer.

If the error code is still displayed, the problem is with the printer. Follow the directions on the printer manufacturer's website to address the error code.

◢ Try resetting the printer (for some printers, press the Reset button on the printer). Try powering down or unplugging the printer and starting it again. Check that power is getting to the printer. Try another power source.

◢ For an inkjet printer, check if nozzles are clogged. Sometimes, leaving the printer on for a while will heat up the ink nozzles and unclog them.

◢ For an impact printer, if the print head moves back and forth but nothing prints, check the ribbon. Is it installed correctly between the plate and print head? Is it jammed? If the ribbon is dried out, it needs to be replaced.

◢ Check the service documentation and printer page count to find out if routine maintenance is due or if the printer has a history of similar problems. Check the user guide for the printer and the printer manufacturer's website for other troubleshooting suggestions.

If you still cannot get a printer to work, you might need to take the printer to a certified repair shop. Before you do, though, try contacting the manufacturer. You might also be able to open a chat session on the printer manufacturer's website.

APPLYING | CONCEPTS

A+
220-901
1.15, 4.6

Now back to Jill and her company's network printer problem. Generally, Jill should focus on finding out what works and what doesn't work, always remembering to check the simple things first. Jill should first go to the printer and check that the printer is online and has no error messages, such as a Paper Out message. Then, Jill should ask, "Can anyone print to this printer?" To find out, she should go to the closest computer and try to print a Windows test page. If the test page prints, she should next go to one of the three computers that do not print and begin troubleshooting that computer's connection to the network. If the test page did not print at the closest computer, the problem is still not necessarily the printer. To eliminate the printer as the problem, the next step is to print a self-test page at the printer. If that self-test page prints, then Jill should check other computers on the network. Is the entire network down? Can one computer see another computer on the network? Perhaps part of the network is down (maybe because of a switch serving one part of the network).

PROBLEMS WITH CONNECTIVITY FOR A NETWORK PRINTER OR SHARED PRINTER

If the self-test page prints but the Windows test page does not print and the printer is a network printer or shared printer, the problem might be with connectivity between the computer and the network printer or with the host computer that is sharing the printer.

★ **A+ Exam Tip** The A+ 220-901 exam expects you to know how to determine if connectivity between the printer and the computer is the problem when troubleshooting printer issues.

Follow these steps to solve problems with network printers:

◢ Is the printer online?

◢ Turn the printer off and back on. Try rebooting the computer.

◢ Verify that the correct default printer is selected.

◢ Consider the IP address of the printer might have changed, which can happen if the printer is receiving a dynamic IP address. Using Windows, delete the printer, and then install the printer again. If this solves the problem, assign a static IP address to the printer to keep the problem from reoccurring.

◢ Can you print to another network printer? If so, there might be a problem with the printer. Look at the printer's configuration.

◢ Try pinging the printer. To do that, open a command prompt window and enter **ping 192.168.1.100** (substitute the IP address of your printer). If the printer replies (see Figure 10-41), the problem is not network connectivity.

```
Command Prompt                                    -  □  ×

Microsoft Windows [Version 6.3.9600]
(c) 2013 Microsoft Corporation. All rights reserved.

C:\Users\Jean Andrews>ping 192.168.1.100

Pinging 192.168.1.100 with 32 bytes of data:
Reply from 192.168.1.100: bytes=32 time<1ms TTL=255
Reply from 192.168.1.100: bytes=32 time<1ms TTL=255
Reply from 192.168.1.100: bytes=32 time<1ms TTL=255
Reply from 192.168.1.100: bytes=32 time<1ms TTL=255

Ping statistics for 192.168.1.100:
    Packets: Sent = 4, Received = 4, Lost = 0 (0% loss),
Approximate round trip times in milli-seconds:
    Minimum = 0ms, Maximum = 0ms, Average = 0ms

C:\Users\Jean Andrews>
```

Figure 10-41 Use the ping command to determine if you have network connectivity with the printer

◢ If pinging doesn't work, try using another network cable for the printer. Check status indicator lights on the printer network port and on the switch or router to which the printer connects.

◢ Use the printer's browser-based utility and check for status reports and error messages. Run diagnostic software that might be available on the utility menu.

◢ Try flashing the network printer's firmware.

Even though you are using a network printer, the printer might have been installed as a printer that has been shared on the network. Let's look at an example of this situation. Figure 10-42 shows a Devices and Printers window with several installed printers. Notice the two installations of the Canon D1100 Series UFRII LT printer. The first installation was done installing the Canon D1100 as a network printer addressed by its IP address. The second installation was done by using a shared printer that was shared by another computer on the network named WHITELAPTOP. When you print using the first installation of the Canon D1100, you print directly over the network to the printer. But when you print to the second installation of the Canon D1100, you print by way of the WHITELAPTOP computer. If this computer is offline, the print jobs back up in the print queue until the computer is available.

Figure 10-42 A network printer installed using two methods

When a computer has shared a local or network printer with others on the network, follow these steps to solve problems with these shared printers:

◢ Check that you can print a test page from the computer that has the printer attached to it locally or is sharing a network printer. If you cannot print from the host computer, solve the problem there before attempting to print from other computers on the network.

◢ Is enough hard drive space available on the client or host computer?

◢ Did you get an "Access denied" message when you tried to print from the remote computer? If so, you might not have access to the host computer. On the remote computer, go to File Explorer or Windows Explorer and attempt to drill down into resources on the printer's computer. Perhaps you have not entered a correct user account and password to access this computer; if so, you will be unable to use the computer's resources. Make sure you have a matching Windows user account and password on each computer.

◢ On the host computer, open the printer's Properties box and click the **Security** tab. Select **Everyone** and make sure Permissions for Everyone includes permission to print (refer back to Figure 10-17).

◢ Using Windows on the remote computer, delete the printer, and then install the printer again. Watch for and address any error messages that might appear.

PROBLEMS PRINTING FROM WINDOWS

If a self-test page works and you have already stepped through checking the printer connectivity, but you still cannot print a test page from Windows, try the following:

◢ The print spool might be stalled. Try deleting all print jobs in the printer's queue. In the Devices and Printers window, double-click the printer and click **document(s) in queue**. To cancel one document, right-click it and click **Cancel** in the shortcut menu (see Figure 10-43). To cancel all documents, click **Printer** and click **Cancel All Documents**. If the printer is still hung, try using buttons on the front of the printer to cancel print jobs. You can also power cycle the printer (turn it off and back on). Some printers have a Reset button for this purpose.

Source: Canon

Figure 10-43   Cancel the first print job in the printer queue

⭐ **A+ Exam Tip**   The A+ 220-901 exam expects you to know how to solve problems with the print spool.

▲ Verify that the correct printer is used.

▲ Verify that the printer is online. See the printer documentation for information on how to determine the status from the control panel of the printer. For many printers, "Ready" appears in this control panel.

▲ Verify that the printer cable or cable connections are solid.

▲ Stop and restart the Windows Print Spooler service. Windows uses the Services console to stop, start, and manage background services used by Windows and applications. Do the following:

1. To stop the service, enter **services.msc** in the Windows 8 Run box or the Windows 7 Search box. In the Services console, select **Print Spooler** (see Figure 10-44). Click **Stop** to stop the service.

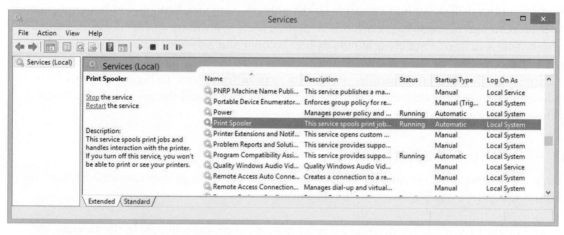

Figure 10-44   Use the Services console to stop and start the print spooler

2. To delete any print jobs left in the queue, open File Explorer or Windows Explorer and delete all files in the C:\Windows\System32\spool\PRINTERS folder.

3. Start the print spooler back up. To start up the print spooler, return to the Services console. With Print Spooler selected, click **Start**. Close the Services console window.

▲ If you still cannot print, reboot the computer. Try deleting the printer and then reinstalling it.

▲ Check the printer manufacturer's website for an updated printer driver. Download and install the correct driver.

▲ Try disabling printer spooling, which you learned to do earlier in the chapter, so that print jobs are not cached, but are sent directly to the printer.

▲ If you have trouble printing from an application, try to print to a file. For example, you can print to an XPS document by selecting Microsoft XPS Document Writer in the list of installed printers. Then you can double-click the .xps file, which opens in the XPS Viewer window, and you can print from this window.

▲ Verify that enough hard drive space is available for the OS to create temporary print files.

▲ Boot Windows into Safe Mode and attempt to print. If this step works, there might be a conflict between the printer driver and another driver or application.

APPLYING | CONCEPTS   SOLVE PROBLEMS WITH PRINTER INSTALLATIONS

**A+
220-901
1.15, 4.6**

Here are some steps you can take if the printer installation fails or installs with errors:

1. If you still have problems, consider that Windows might be using the wrong or corrupted printer drivers. Try removing the printer and then installing it again. To remove a printer, right-click the printer in the Devices and Printers window and click **Remove device**. Try to install the printer again.

2. If the problem is still not solved, completely remove the printer drivers by using the printui command. The Printer User Interface command, printui, is used by administrators to manage printers and printer drivers on remote computers. You can also use it to delete drivers on the local computer. Follow these steps:

a. If the printer is listed in the Devices and Printers window, remove it. (Sometimes Windows automatically puts a printer there when it finds printer drivers are installed.)

b. Before you can delete printer drivers, you must stop the print spooler service. Open the Services console and use it to stop the Print Spooler (refer to Figure 10-44). To delete any print jobs left in the queue, open Explorer and delete all files in the C:\Windows\System32\spool\PRINTERS folder.

c. You can now start the print spooler back up. Because the printer is no longer listed in the Devices and Printers window, starting the spooler will not tie up these drivers.

d. Open an elevated command prompt window, which is a window used to enter commands that have administrator privileges. To open the window, in Windows 8, press **Win+X** and click **Command Prompt (Admin)**. In Windows 7, click **Start**, **All Programs**, **Accessories**. Right-click **Command Prompt** and click **Run as administrator**. Respond to the UAC box.

e. At the command prompt (see the left side of Figure 10-45), enter the command: `printui /s /t2` (In the command line, the /s causes the Print Server Properties box to open and the /t2 causes the Drivers tab to be the selected tab.)

Figure 10-45 Use the printui command to delete printer drivers and possibly delete the driver package (driver store)

f. The Print Server Properties box opens, as shown in the middle of Figure 10-45. Select the printer and click **Remove**. In the Remove Driver And Package box (see the right side of Figure 10-45), select **Remove driver only** and click **OK**. It is not necessary to remove the driver package. (This driver package, also called the driver store, can be installed on this computer or a remote computer and holds a backup of the printer drivers.)

g. When a warning box appears, click **Yes**. Close all windows.

3. Try to install the printer again. Start the installation from the CD that came bundled with the printer or by using the printer setup program downloaded from the printer manufacturer's website.

POOR PRINT QUALITY

Poor print quality can be caused by the printer drivers, the application, Windows, or the printer. Let's start by looking at what can cause poor print quality with laser printers and then move on to other problems that affect printouts.

> ⭐ **A+ Exam Tip** The A+ 220-901 exam expects you to know how to resolve problems with streaks, faded prints, ghost images, garbled characters on a page, vertical lines, low memory errors, and wrong print colors. All these problems are covered in this part of the chapter.

POOR PRINT QUALITY FOR LASER PRINTERS

For laser printers, poor print quality, including faded, smeared, wavy, speckled, or streaked printouts, often indicates that the toner is low. All major mechanical printer components that normally create problems are conveniently contained within the replaceable toner cartridge. In most cases, the solution to poor-quality printing is to replace this cartridge.

Follow these general guidelines to fix poor print quality with laser printers:

- If you suspect the printer is overheated, unplug it and allow it to cool for 30 minutes.
- The toner cartridge might be low on toner or might not be installed correctly. Remove the toner cartridge and gently rock it from side to side to redistribute the toner. Replace the cartridge. To avoid flying toner, don't shake the cartridge too hard.
- If this doesn't solve the problem, try replacing the toner cartridge immediately.
- Econo Mode (a mode that uses less toner) might be on; turn it off.
- The paper quality might not be high enough. Try a different brand of paper. Only use paper recommended for use with a laser printer. Also, some types of paper can receive print only on one side.
- The printer might need cleaning. Clean the inside of the printer with a dry, lint-free cloth. Don't touch the transfer roller, which is the soft, spongy black roller.
- If the transfer roller is dirty, the problem will probably correct itself after several sheets print. If not, take the printer to an authorized service center.
- Does the printer require routine maintenance? Check the website of the printer's manufacturer for how often to perform the maintenance and to purchase the required printer maintenance kit.

> 🖉 **Notes** Extreme humidity can cause the toner to clump in the cartridge and give a Toner Low message. If this is a consistent problem in your location, you might want to invest in a dehumidifier for the room where your printer is located.

- Streaking is usually caused by a dirty developer unit or corona wire. The developer unit is contained in the toner cartridge. Replace the cartridge or check the printer documentation for directions on how to remove and clean the developer unit. Allow the corona wire to cool and clean it with a lint-free swab.
- Speckled printouts can be caused by the laser drum. If cleaning the printer and replacing the toner cartridge don't solve the problem, replace the laser drum.

> 🖉 **Notes** If loose toner comes out with your printout, the fuser is not reaching the proper temperature and toner is not being fused to the paper. Professional service is required.

- Distorted images can be caused by foreign material inside the printer that might be interfering with the mechanical components. Check for debris that might be interfering with the printer operation.
- If the page has a gray background or gray print, the image drum is worn out and needs to be replaced.

◢ A ghosted image appears a few inches below the actual darker image on the page. Ghosted images are usually caused by a problem with the image drum or toner cartridge. The drum is not fully cleaned in the cleaning stage, and toner left on it causes the ghost image. If the printer utility installed with the printer offers the option to clean the drum, try that first. The next solution is to replace the less expensive toner cartridge. If the problem is still not solved, replace the image drum.

POOR PRINT QUALITY FOR INKJET PRINTERS

To troubleshoot poor print quality for an inkjet printer, check the following:

1. Is the correct paper for inkjet printers being used? The quality of paper determines the final print quality, especially with inkjet printers. In general, the better the quality of the paper used with an inkjet printer, the better the print quality. Don't use less than 20-pound paper in any type of printer, unless the printer documentation specifically says that a lower weight is satisfactory.

2. Is the ink supply low, or is there a partially clogged nozzle?

3. Remove and reinstall the cartridge(s).

4. Follow the printer's documentation to clean each nozzle. Is the print head too close to or too far from the paper?

5. There is a little sponge in some printers near the carriage rest that can become clogged with ink. It should be removed and cleaned.

6. If you are printing transparencies, try changing the fill pattern in your application.

7. Missing lines or dots on the printed page can be caused by the ink nozzles drying out, especially when the printer sits unused for a long time. Follow the directions given earlier in the chapter for cleaning inkjet nozzles.

8. Streaks or lines down the page can be caused by dust or dirt in the print head assemblage. Follow the manufacturer's directions to clean the inkjet nozzles.

GARBLED CHARACTERS ON PAPER

If scrambled or garbled characters print on all or part of a page, the problem can be caused by the document being printed, the application, connectivity between the computer and the printer, or the printer. Follow these steps to zero in on the problem:

1. First, cancel all print jobs in the print queue. Then try printing a different document from the same application. If the second document prints correctly, the problem is with the original document.

2. Try printing using a different application. If the problem is resolved, try repairing or reinstalling the application.

3. For a USB printer, the problem might be with a USB hub, port, or cable. Is the USB cable securely connected at both ends? If you are using a USB hub, remove the hub, connecting the printer directly to the computer. Try a different USB cable or USB port.

4. Recycle the printer by powering it down and back up or pressing a Reset button.

5. Update the printer drivers. To do that, go to the website of the printer manufacturer to find the latest drivers and follow their directions to install the drivers.

6. If the problem is still not solved, the printer might need servicing. Does the printer need maintenance? Search the website of the printer manufacturer for other solutions.

LOW MEMORY ERRORS

For some printers, an error occurs if the printer does not have enough memory to hold the entire page. For other printers, only a part of the page prints. Some might signal this problem by flashing a light or displaying

10

an error message on their display panels, such as "20 Mem Overflow," "Out of memory," or "Low Memory." The solution is to install more memory or to print only simple pages with few graphics. Print a self-test page to verify how much memory is installed. Some printers give you the option to install a hard drive in the printer to give additional printer storage space.

WRONG PRINT COLORS

For a printer that is printing the wrong colors, do the following:

1. Some paper is designed to print on only one side. You might need to flip the paper in the printer.

2. Try adjusting the quality of print. How to do so varies by printer. For one color laser printer, open the **Printing Preferences** box and click the **Quality** tab (see the left side of Figure 10-46). You can try different selections on this box. To manually adjust the color, check **Manual Color Settings** and then click **Color Settings**. The box on the right side of Figure 10-46 appears.

Source: Canon

Figure 10-46   Adjust printing quality and color

3. For an inkjet printer, try cleaning the ink cartridges and calibrating the printer. One step in doing that prints a self-test page. If the self-test page shows missing or wrong colors, the problem is with the ink cartridges. Try cleaning the ink nozzles. If that doesn't work, replace the ink cartridges.

4. For a laser printer, try calibrating the printer.

Now we wrap up the chapter with a discussion of customizing computer systems.

CUSTOMIZING COMPUTER SYSTEMS

A+ 220-901 1.9, 1.12 Many computer vendors and manufacturers offer to build customized systems to meet specific needs of their customers. As a technical retail associate, you need to know how to recommend to a customer which computer components are needed for his or her specific needs. You also might be called on to select and purchase components for a customized system and perhaps even build this system from parts. In this part of the chapter, we focus on several types of customized systems you might be expected to know how to configure and what parts to consider when configuring these systems.

Here are important principles to keep in mind when customizing a system to meet customer needs:

- *Meet applications requirements.* Consider the applications the customer will use and make sure the hardware meets or exceeds the recommended requirements for these applications. Consider any special hardware the applications might require such as a joystick for gaming or a digital tablet for graphics applications.
- *Balance functionality and budget.* When working with a customer's budget, put the most money on the hardware components that are most needed for the primary intended purposes of the system. For example, if you are building a customized gaming PC, a RAID hard drive configuration is not nearly as important as the quality of the video subsystem.
- *Consider hardware compatibility.* When selecting hardware, start with the motherboard and processor. Then select other components that are compatible with this motherboard.

Now let's look at the components you need to consider when building these eight types of customized systems: graphics or CAD/CAM design workstation, audio and video editing workstation, virtualization workstation, gaming PC, home theater PC, home server PC, thick client, and thin client.

> ★ **A+ Exam Tip** The A+ 220-901 exam expects you to know how to customize each of the eight types of computers covered in this part of the chapter.

GRAPHICS OR CAD/CAM DESIGN WORKSTATION

**A+
220-901
1.9**

You might be called on to configure a graphics or CAD/CAM (computer-aided design/computer-aided manufacturing) workstation. People who use these systems might be an engineer working with CAD software to design bridges, an architect who designs skyscrapers, a graphics designer who creates artistic pages for children's books, or a landscape designer who creates lawn and garden plans. Examples of the applications these people might use include AutoCAD Design Suite by Autodesk (*usa.autodesk.com*) or Adobe Illustrator by Adobe Systems (*www.adobe.com*).

These graphics-intensive, advanced applications perform complex calculations, use large and complex files, and can benefit from the most powerful of workstations. Because rendering 3D graphics is a requirement, a high-end or ultra-high-end video card is needed. Figure 10-47 shows one ultra-high-end customized CAD workstation by CAD Computers (*www.cadcomputers.com*).

Source: cadcomputers.com

Figure 10-47 A high-end CAD workstation customized for maximum performance

Here is a breakdown of the requirements for these high-end workstations:

▲ *Use a motherboard that provides quad channels for memory and plenty of memory slots and install a generous amount of RAM.* In the ad shown in Figure 10-47, the system has 64 GB of installed RAM. For best performance, you can install the maximum amount of RAM the board supports.

▲ *Use a powerful multicore processor with a large CPU cache.* In the ad shown in Figure 10-47, the Intel Fourth Generation i7 processor, which is rated for high-end workstations and servers, has six cores and a 15-MB cache. This processor can handle the high demands of complex calculations performed by advanced software.

▲ *Use fast hard drives with plenty of capacity.* Notice the system in Figure 10-47 has two hard drives. The solid-state drive holds the Windows installation. The moderately fast second hard drive has a capacity of 2 TB to accommodate large amounts of data. For best hard drive performance in any system, be sure the motherboard and hard drives are all using SATA III.

▲ *Use a high-end video card.* To provide the best 3D graphics experience, use a high-end video card. Probably the best chipset manufacturer for high-end video cards is NVIDIA (*www.nvidia.com*). The ad in Figure 10-47 mentions the Quadro 6000. The Quadro family of graphics processors has the best-performing GPUs on the market, and the Quadro 6000 is the best Quadro currently sold (see Figure 10-48). It uses a PCIe ×16 slot and has 12 GB of GDDR5 video memory using a 384-bit video bus. The card has four HDMI ports and one DVI port. The card alone costs almost $4,000 and accounts for a major portion of the total system cost, which is almost $10,000.

Source: www.nvidia.com

Figure 10-48   This ultra-high-end video card by NVIDIA costs almost $4,000

Wouldn't it be fun to build this system? However, not all graphics workstations need to be this powerful or this expensive. You can still get adequate performance in a system for less than half the cost if you drop the RAM down to 16 GB and use an NVIDIA Quadro 2000 GPU on the video card, along with a motherboard that supports dual-channel memory.

AUDIO AND VIDEO EDITING WORKSTATION

A+
220-901
1.9

Examples of professional applications software used to edit music, audio, video, and movies include Camtasia by TechSmith (*techsmith.com*), Adobe Production Premium by Adobe Systems (*adobe.com*), Media Composer by Avid (*avid.com*), and Final Cut Pro by Apple Computers (*apple.com*). (Final Cut Pro is used only on Macs, which are popular computers in the video-editing industry.) Audio- and video-editing applications are not usually as power-hungry as CAD/CAM and graphics applications. The major difference in requirements is that most audio and video editing does not require rendering 3D graphics; therefore, you can get by with a not-so-expensive graphics card and processor. Customers might require a Blu-ray drive and dual monitors. Recall that the best LCD monitors that provide the most accurate color are LED monitors with a class IPS rating. Figure 10-49 shows the specs for one customized video-editing workstation by ADK Media Group (*adkvideoediting.com*).

Source: www.adkvideoediting.com

Figure 10-49   This mid range video-editing workstation uses a Core i7 processor and GeForce graphics processor

Here is what you need for a mid range to high-end audio/video-editing workstation:

- Use a motherboard that supports dual, triple, or quad channel memory running at least at 1600-MHz RAM speed.
- Use a Core i7 or higher processor.
- Install at least 16 GB of RAM; more is better.
- Select a good video card that has a GeForce GTX graphics processor or better. GeForce is a family of graphics processors designed by NVIDIA that is not as high end as the Quadro graphics processors but still gives good video performance. Most users will require dual or triple monitors. You might need to consider dual video cards for optimum video performance or for more than two video ports.
- Use a good sound card, such as the Creative Sound Blaster Zx sound card. This sound card uses a PCIe slot. Before you purchase, research reviews online for a good sound card.
- Use a double-sided, dual-layer DVD burner and possibly a Blu-ray burner.
- Install one or more fast and large hard drives, running at least 7200 RPM.

VIRTUALIZATION WORKSTATION

A+
220-901
1.9

Virtualization is when one physical machine hosts multiple activities that are normally done on multiple machines. One way to implement virtualization is to use virtual machine management software, called a hypervisor, which creates and manages multiple virtual machines (VMs).

Examples of hypervisors used on a desktop computer include VMware Workstation or Player, Windows Virtual PC by Microsoft, and Oracle VirtualBox. Each VM managed by a hypervisor has its own virtual hardware (virtual motherboard, processor, RAM, hard drive, and so forth) and can act like a physical computer. You can install an OS in each VM and then install applications in the VM. Figure 10-50 shows a Windows 8.1 Professional desktop with two virtual machines running that were created by Oracle VirtualBox. One VM is running Windows 8.1 Pro, and the other VM is running Windows 7 Home Premium.

Source: Oracle VirtualBox

Figure 10-50   Two virtual machines running, each with its own virtual hardware and OS (Windows 8 and Windows 7) installed

Here are the requirements for a desktop computer that will be used to run multiple virtual machines:

◢ Each VM has its own virtual processor, so it's important the processor is a multicore processor. All dual-core or higher processors and all motherboards sold today support hardware-assisted virtualization (HAV). This technology enhances the processor support for virtual machines and is enabled in UEFI/BIOS setup.

◢ Some virtual machine management programs are designed so that each VM that is running ties up all the RAM assigned to it. Therefore, you need extra amounts of RAM when a computer is running several VMs.

◢ Each VM must have an operating system installed, and it takes about 20 GB for a Windows 8/7/Vista installation. In addition, you need hard drive space for each application installed in each VM. Make sure you have adequate hard drive space for each VM.

When deciding how to use the overall budget for a virtualization workstation, maximize the number of CPU cores and the amount of installed RAM.

GAMING PC

A+
220-901
1.9

Gaming computers benefit from a powerful multicore processor and a high-end video card and sound card. Gamers who are also computer hobbyists might want to overclock their CPUs or use dual video cards for extra video performance. Take extra care to make sure the cooling methods are adequate. Because of the heat generated by multiple video cards and overclocking, liquid cooling is sometimes preferred. Also recall that when using the LGA2011 socket, liquid cooling is a

Microsoft recommendation. Most gaming computers use onboard surround sound, or you can use a sound card to improve sound. A lighted case with a clear plastic side makes for a great look.

Figure 10-51 shows a group of gaming PCs built by iBUYPOWER (*ibuypower.com*). A couple of the PCs use liquid cooling, and all use a powerful processor with at least 8 GB of RAM. The video card uses a GeForce GTX or GT graphics processor or an AMD Radeon HD graphics processor. The Radeon line of graphics processors by AMD are comparable to the NVIDIA GeForce graphics processors.

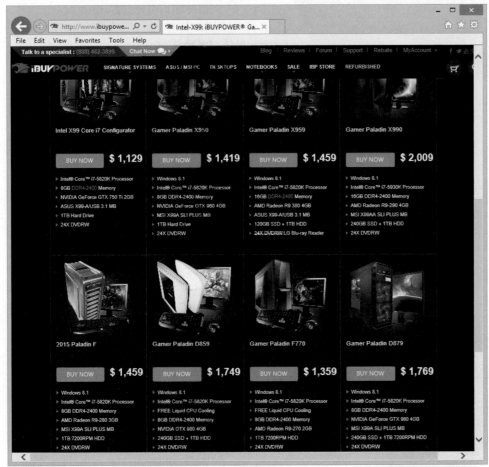

Source: www.ibuypower.com

Figure 10-51   A group of Intel Core i5 or Core i7 gaming PCs

HOME THEATER PC

**A+
220-901
1.9, 1.12**

A Home Theater PC (HTPC) is designed to play and possibly record music, photos, movies, and video on a television or extra-large monitor screen. Because these large screens are usually viewed from across the room, application software is used to control output display menus and other clickable items in fonts large enough to read at a distance of 10 feet. This interface is called a 10-foot user interface. An HTPC is also known as a media center appliance.

A custom-built HTPC needs to include these features:

▲ *Application software.* The application controls the user interface and plays and records music and video. Examples of HTPC software include Windows Media Center, which is a free upgrade for Windows 8 Pro and integrated into Windows 7/Vista, Kodi (*kodi.tv*), and Plex (*plex.tv*).

▲ **HDMI** *port to connect video output to television.* And be sure to use a high-quality HDMI cable.

▲ *Cable TV input.* The best solution is to use a TV tuner card to connect the TV coax cable directly to the computer. Most TV tuner cards include a remote (see Figure 10-52). Some TV tuner cards are also

Figure 10-52   Dual TV tuner card with IR remote lets you watch and record two TV programs at the same time

Figure 10-53   The AVerMedia AVerTV HD DVR (C027) video capture card has two HDMI input ports and uses a PCIe × 1 expansion slot

video capture cards that offer the ability to record video and audio input. If the customer plans to use a TV cable box between the TV coax cable and the HTPC, you need to provide a way to make the connection. Most TV cable boxes have an HDMI output port. Realize this won't work with the HDMI port on a motherboard because these ports are output ports and you need an input port. To input to the computer using an HDMI port, you can use a video capture card that has an HDMI input port (see Figure 10-53).

▲ *Satellite TV input.* This setup requires a satellite set-top box supplied by the company providing the satellite TV service. The best solution is to use a TV tuner card to receive input from the satellite set-top box. Make sure the types of ports on the computer and the box match up.

▲ *Internet access.* A way to receive streaming video from the Internet. To connect to the Internet, use a Gigabit Ethernet port or Wi-Fi connection.

▲ *Remote control.* A way to remotely control the HTPC because most likely the user will be sitting across the room from the computer. You can use a wireless keyboard and mouse, although the range for these devices might be too short. Some TV tuner cards include a remote. Also consider an app you can download to a smart phone to make it work as the remote.

▲ *Low background noise.* Because these computers don't perform complex calculations, you don't need as much processor or RAM power as in other systems. For example, you can use the small Intel Atom processor with 4 GB of RAM. Therefore, you won't need an extensive cooling system. You do, however, want a system that runs quietly. You can reduce noise by using SSD hard drives and low-speed fans or no fans at all.

Figure 10-54   Speaker locations for surround sound

Courtesy of Silverstone Technology Co. Ltd.

Figure 10-55   The HTPC case by Silverstone is less than six inches high and has three silent fans

▲ *Surround sound.* The system should support surround sound using at least six speakers located around the room. In Figure 10-54, you can see the preferred location for six speakers. Three popular variations of surround sound are 5.1 (uses up to six channels and speakers), 7.1 (uses up to eight channels and speakers), and 9.1 (uses up to 10 channels and speakers). Most sound cards and motherboards support six channels or ports for sound.

▲ *Case form factor.* An HTPC should be small enough to fit on a shelf in an entertainment center, and several companies make HTPC cases specifically for this purpose. The HTPC case shown in Figure 10-55 accommodates a MicroATX, mini-ITX, or mini-DTX motherboard and power supply. (A mini-DTX motherboard is slightly wider than the mini-ITX board.) The case has drive bays for 3.5-inch and 2.5-inch drives.

Alternatives to the HTPC are to use a smart TV or a set-top box. A smart TV is a television that has the ability to run apps, store data, and connect to the Internet. A set-top box offers a regular television the ability to be "smart." Manufacturers such as Roku (*roku.com*), Amazon Fire TV (*amazon.com/fire-tv-stick*), and Google Chromecast (*google.com/chromecast*) sell set-top boxes complete with a remote control.

HOME SERVER PC

A+
220-901
1.9

A home server PC is useful when you have several computers on a small home network and want to share files among them. You can use the computer to serve up these files and to stream video files and movies to client computers. One popular type of home server PC is Slingbox by Sling Media (*slingbox.com*). The device can serve up streaming media that you have stored on it not only to other computers in your home but also to a client computer anywhere on the Internet.

Here are the features and hardware you need to consider when customizing a home server computer:

▲ *Use a processor with moderate power.* The Intel Core i5 or Core i3 works well. A moderate amount of RAM is sufficient, for example, 6 to 8 GB.

▲ *Storage speed and capacity need to be maximized.* Use hardware RAID implemented on the motherboard to provide fault tolerance and high performance. Make sure the motherboard supports hardware RAID. Use fast hard drives (at least 7200 RPM) with plenty of storage capacity. Make sure the case has plenty of room for all the hard drives a customer might require.

▲ *Network transfers need to be fast, especially for streaming videos and movies.* Make sure the network port is rated for Gigabit Ethernet (1000 Mbps). All other devices and computers on the LAN should also use Gigabit Ethernet.

▲ *Printer sharing needs to be an available resource.* A USB printer can be connected directly to the computer and then you can use Windows to share the printer with others on the network. Alternately, some routers and switches provide a USB port that can be used to connect a USB printer to other computers on the network.

▲ *Onboard video works well.* Recall that onboard video is a video port embedded on the motherboard and does not perform as well as a good video card. Because the computer is not likely to be used as a workstation, you don't need powerful video.

▲ *Windows 7 can be used as the OS, but Windows 8 provides additional features.* Windows 8 offers Storage Spaces, which can hold large multimedia files on multiple hard drives. In addition, if the customer plans to use the computer to back up files on client computers, know that Windows 8 File History is easier to implement and use than the Windows 7 Backup and Restore utility.

THICK CLIENT AND THIN CLIENT

A+
220-901
1.9 A desktop computer can use virtual machine management software (called a hypervisor) to provide one or more VMs, and in this situation the computer is called a virtualization workstation. In a corporate environment, the VM can also be provided by a virtualization server, which serves up a virtual machine to a client computer. The virtualization server provides a virtual desktop for users on multiple client machines. Most, if not all, processing is done on the server, which provides to the client the Virtual Desktop Infrastructure (VDI). See Figure 10-56.

Tablet or smartphone   Laptop   Desktop   Wyse Zero Client
© Sergiy Zavgorodny/Shutterstock.com

Figure 10-56 A virtualization server provides a desktop to each client computer or appliance

These VM clients that receive the virtual desktop from the server can be a thick client, thin client, or zero client. You might be called on to customize a thick client or thin client computer for a customer. (A zero client, also called a dumb terminal, is built by the manufacturer. It does not have an OS and is little more than an interface to the network with a keyboard, monitor, and mouse.) Here are the details for a thick client and thin client computer:

◢ A thick client, also called a fat client, is a regular desktop computer or laptop that is sometimes used as a client by a virtualization server. It can be a low-end or high-end desktop or laptop. It should meet the recommended requirements to run Windows 8/7 and any applications the user might require when it is being used as a stand-alone computer rather than a VM client.

◢ A thin client is a computer that has an operating system but has little computer power and might only need to support a browser used to communicate with the server. The server does most of the processing for the thin client. To reduce the cost of the computer, configure it to meet only the minimum requirements for Windows.

Hands-On | Project 10-4 Research a Customized System

**A+
220-901
1.9**

Working with a partner, design a gaming computer or a Home Theater PC by doing the following:

1. Search the web for a prebuilt system that you like. Print or save the webpage showing the detailed specifications for the system and its price. Which parts in the system do you plan to use for your system? Which parts would you not use or upgrade for your own system?

2. Search the web for the individual parts for your system. Save or print webpages showing all the parts you need to build this computer. Don't forget the case, power supply, motherboard, processor, RAM, hard drive, and other specialized components.

3. Make a list of each part with links to the webpage that shows the part for sale. What is the total cost of all parts?

4. Exchange your list and webpages with a partner and have your partner check your work to make sure each part is compatible with the entire system and nothing is missing. Do the same for your partner's list of parts.

5. After you are both convinced your list of parts is compatible and nothing is missing, submit your work to your instructor.

10

>> CHAPTER SUMMARY

Printer Types and Features

◢ The two most popular types of printers are laser and inkjet. Other types of printers are thermal printers and impact printers (dot matrix). Laser printers produce the highest quality, followed by inkjet printers. Dot matrix printers have the advantage of being able to print multicopy documents.

◢ The seven steps that a laser printer performs to print are processing, charging, exposing, developing, transferring, fusing, and cleaning. The charging, exposing, developing, and cleaning steps take place inside removable cartridges, which makes the printer easier to maintain.

◢ Inkjet printers print by shooting ionized ink at a sheet of paper. The quality of the printout largely depends on the quality of paper used with the printer.

◢ Dot matrix printers are a type of impact printer. They print by projecting pins from the print head against an inked ribbon that deposits ink on the paper.

◢ Direct thermal printers use heat to burn dots into special paper, and thermal transfer printers melt the ribbon or foil during printing.

Using Windows to Install, Share, and Manage Printers

◢ A printer is installed as a local printer connected directly to a computer or a network printer that works as a device on the network. Local printers can connect to a computer via a USB, serial, Bluetooth, or Wi-Fi connection. Network printers can connect to the network via an Ethernet or Wi-Fi connection. USB printers are installed automatically in Windows.

◢ Windows installs, manages, and removes a printer using the Devices and Printers windows. You can also install a printer using a setup program provided by the printer manufacturer. Always print a test page after installing a printer.

◢ A print server can be a computer on the network, a hardware device, or firmware embedded in a network printer.

◢ A printer can be shared in Windows so that others on the network can use it. To use a shared printer, the printer drivers must be installed on the remote computer.

◢ Network printers are identified on the network by their IP address.

◢ The Windows print queue is managed from the Devices and Printers window.

◢ Virtual printing prints to a file, and cloud printing prints to a printer via the Internet.

◢ Printer features, such as duplexing, collating, or page orientation, are managed in a printer properties box.

Printer Maintenance and Upgrades

◢ An inkjet or laser printer can be calibrated to align the color on the page. The nozzles of an inkjet printer tend to clog or dry out, especially when the printer remains unused. The nozzles can be cleaned automatically by means of printer software or buttons on the front panel of the printer.

◢ Check the page count of the printer to know when service is due and you need to order a printer maintenance kit. The page count can be reported on the printer panel or through a web-based utility in the printer firmware.

◢ Memory and a hard drive can be added to a printer to improve performance and prevent errors.

Troubleshooting Printers

◢ When troubleshooting printers, first isolate the problem. Narrow the source to the printer, connectivity between the computer and its local printer, the network, Windows, printer drivers, the application using the printer, or the printer installation. Test pages printed directly at the printer or within Windows can help narrow down the source of the problem.

◢ Poor print quality can be caused by the printer drivers, the application, Windows, or the printer. For a laser printer, consider that low toner can be the problem. For an inkjet printer, consider that the ink cartridges need cleaning or replacing. The quality of paper can also be a problem.

◢ A printer needs memory to render a print job. Low memory can cause part of the page not to print or a printer error.

Customizing Computer Systems

◢ As a technician, you might be called on to customize a system for a customer, including a graphics or CAD/CAM workstation, audio- and video-editing workstation, virtualization workstation, gaming PC, Home Theater PC (HTPC), home server PC, thick client, or thin client.

◢ A high-end video card is a requirement in a graphics, CAD/CAM, video-editing workstation, or a gaming PC. These systems also need powerful processors and ample RAM.

▲ A TV tuner card is needed in a Home Theater PC.

▲ A thick client needs to meet recommended requirements for Windows and applications, and a thin client is a low-end computer that only needs to meet the minimum requirements for Windows.

>> KEY TERMS

For explanations of key terms, see the Glossary for this text.

10-foot user interface	extension magnet	laser printer	set-top box
ad hoc mode	brush	local printer	smart TV
AirPrint	fuser assembly	network printer	thermal paper
bitmap	hardware-assisted	pickup roller	thermal printer
Bonjour	virtualization (HAV)	print head	thermal transfer
calibration	hardware print server	print server	printer
charging	Home Theater PC	printer maintenance kit	thick client
cloud printing	(HTPC)	printer self-test page	thin client
default printer	HTPC case	printui	toner vacuum
Devices and Printers	hypervisor	remote printing	tractor feed
window	imaging drum	REt (Resolution	transfer belt
direct thermal printer	impact paper	Enhancement	transfer roller
duplex printer	impact printer	technology)	virtual printing
duplexing assembly	infrastructure mode	separate pad	virtualization server
elevated command prompt	ink cartridge	separation pad	XPS Document
window	inkjet printer	Services console	Writer

>> REVIEWING THE BASICS

1. List the seven steps used by a laser printer to print a page.

2. During the laser printing process, what determines when the toner sticks to the drum and when it does not stick to the drum?

3. What type of printer is most dependent on the quality of paper it uses to get the best printing results?

4. What should you do if an inkjet printer prints with missing dots or lines on the page?

5. What can you do to help a dot matrix printer last longer?

6. What feature on a printer must be enabled so that a printer can automatically print on both sides of the paper?

7. What is likely to be the problem when a laser printer consistently produces pages with gray print?

8. What kind of printer is assigned an IP address?

9. What two tools can you use to remove loose toner from inside a printer?

10. How can you prove a printer problem is not with the printer itself, but lies with the network, computer, OS, or application?

11. When you get a toner-low message, what can you do to extend the life of the toner cartridge before you replace the cartridge?

12. What causes a ghosted image on a printout?

13. What is likely the problem when a portion of a complicated page does not print?

14. What can you do to verify a printing problem is with an application or a document and not with Windows?

15. In a Home Theater PC, what is the purpose of an HDMI output port?

16. In a Home Theater PC, why might you need an HDMI input port? Which type of adapter card might provide this port?

17. Which system requires the best graphics card, a CAD workstation or a virtualization workstation?

18. Which is generally a better GPU, one in the NVIDIA Quadro family or one in the NVIDIA GeForce family?

19. Which socket mentioned in the chapter does Intel recommend you use with liquid cooling?

20. How many speakers or sound channels does surround sound version 5.1 use?

>> THINKING CRITICALLY

1. You are not able to print a Word document on a Windows 8 computer to a network printer. The network printer is connected directly to the network, but when you look at the Devices and Printers window, you see the name of the printer as \\SMITH\HP LaserJet 8100. In the following list, select the possible sources of the problem.

   a. The SMITH computer is not turned on.

   b. The HP LaserJet 8100 printer is not online.

   c. The SMITH printer is not online.

   d. The Windows 8 computer has a stalled print spool.

   e. The HP LaserJet 8100 computer is not logged on to the workgroup.

2. You are not able to print a test page from your Windows 8 computer to your USB local HP DeskJet printer. Which of the following are possible causes of the problem?

   a. The network is down.

   b. The printer cable is not connected properly.

   c. The Windows print spool is stalled.

   d. You have the wrong printer drivers installed.

   e. File and Printer Sharing is not enabled.

>> REAL PROBLEMS, REAL SOLUTIONS

REAL PROBLEM 10-1 Selecting a Color Printer for a Small Business

Jack owns a small real estate firm and has come to you asking for help with his printing needs. Currently, he has a color inkjet printer that he is using to print flyers, business cards, brochures, and other marketing materials. However, he is not satisfied with the print quality and wants to invest in a printer that produces more professional looking hard copy. He expects to print no more than 8,000 sheets per month and needs the ability to print envelopes, letter-size and legal-size pages, and business cards. He wants to be able to automatically print on both sides of a legal-size page to produce a three-column brochure. Research printer solutions and do the following:

1. Save or print webpages showing three printers to present to Jack that satisfy his needs. Include at least one laser printer and at least one printer technology other than laser in your selections.

2. Save or print webpages showing the routine maintenance requirements of these printers.

3. Save or print webpages showing all the consumable products (other than paper) that Jack should expect to have to purchase in the first year of use.

4. Calculate the initial cost of the equipment and the total cost of consumables for one year (other than paper) for each printer solution.

5. Prepare a list of advantages and disadvantages for each solution.

6. Based on your research, which of the three solutions do you recommend? Why?

10

APPENDIX A

Safety Procedures and Environmental Concerns

This appendix covers how to stay safe and protect the equipment and the environment as you perform the duties of an IT support technician. We begin by understanding the properties and dangers of electricity.

MEASURES AND PROPERTIES OF ELECTRICITY

**A+
220-902
5.1, 5.2**

In our modern world, we take electricity for granted, and we miss it terribly when it's cut off. Nearly everyone depends on it, but few really understand it. A successful hardware technician is not one who tends to encounter failed processors, fried motherboards, smoking monitors, or frizzed hair. To avoid these excitements, you need to understand how to measure electricity and how to protect computer equipment from its damaging power.

Let's start with the basics. To most people, volts, ohms, joules, watts, and amps are vague terms that simply mean electricity. All these terms can be used to measure some characteristic of electricity, as listed in Table A-1.

Unit	Definition	Computer Example
Volt (for example, 115 V)	A measure of electrical force measured in volts. The symbol for volts is V.	A power supply steps down the voltage from the 115 V house current to 3.3, 5, and 12 V that computer components can use.
Amp or ampere (for example, 1.5 A)	An amp is a measure of electrical current. The symbol for amps is A.	An LCD monitor requires about 5 A to operate. A small laser printer uses about 2 A. An optical drive uses about 1 A.
Ohm (for example, 20 Ω)	An ohm is a measure of resistance to electricity. The symbol for ohm is Ω.	Current can flow in typical computer cables and wires with a resistance of near zero Ω (ohm).
Joule (for example, 500 J)	A measure of work or energy. One joule (pronounced "jewel") is the work required to push an electrical current of 1 A through a resistance of 1 Ω. The symbol for joule is J.	A surge suppressor (see Figure A-1) is rated in joules—the higher the better. The rating determines how much work it can expend before it can no longer protect the circuit from a power surge.
Watt (for example, 20 W)	A measure of electrical power. One watt is one joule per second and measures the total electrical power needed to operate a device. Watts can be calculated by multiplying volts by amps. The symbol for watts is W.	The power consumption of an LCD computer monitor is rated at about 14 W. A DVD burner uses about 25 W when burning a DVD.

Table A-1 Measures of electricity

Rating is 720 joules

Figure A-1 A surge suppressor protects electrical equipment from power surges and is rated in joules

Notes To learn more about how volts, amps, ohms, joules, and watts measure the properties of electricity, see the content "Electricity and Multimeters" in the online content that accompanies this text at *cengagebrain.com*. To find out how to access this content, see the Preface to this text.

Now let's look at how electricity gets from one place to another and how it is used in house circuits and computers.

AC AND DC

A+
220-902
5.1, 5.2

Electricity can be either AC, alternating current, or DC, direct current. Alternating current (AC) goes back and forth, or oscillates, rather than traveling in only one direction. House current in the United States is AC and oscillates 60 times in one second (60 hertz). Voltage in the system is constantly alternating from positive to negative, which causes the electricity to flow first in one direction and then in the other. Voltage alternates from +115 V to 115 V. AC is the most economical way to transmit electricity to our homes and workplaces. By decreasing current and increasing voltage, we can force alternating current to travel great distances. When alternating current reaches its destination, it is made more suitable for driving our electrical devices by decreasing voltage and increasing current.

Direct current (DC) travels in only one direction and is the type of current that most electronic devices require, including computers. A rectifier is a device that converts AC to DC, and an inverter is a device that converts DC to AC. A transformer is a device that changes the ratio of voltage to current. The power supply used in computers is both a rectifier and a transformer.

Large transformers reduce the high voltage on power lines coming to your neighborhood to a lower voltage before the current enters your home. The transformer does not change the amount of power in this closed system; if it decreases voltage, it increases current. The overall power stays constant, but the ratio of voltage to current changes, as illustrated in Figure A-2.

Figure A-2 A transformer keeps power constant but changes the ratio of current to voltage

Direct current flows in only one direction. Think of electrical current like a current of water that flows from a state of high pressure to a state of low pressure or rest. Electrical current flows from a high-pressure state (called hot) to a state of rest (called ground or neutral). For a power supply, a power line may be either +5 or -5 volts in one circuit, or +12 or -12 volts in another circuit. The positive or negative value is determined by how the circuit is oriented, either on one side of the power output or the other. Several circuits coming from the power supply accommodate different devices with different power requirements.

HOT, NEUTRAL, AND GROUND

A+
220-902
5.1, 5.2

AC travels on a hot line from the power station to a building and returns to the power station on a neutral line. When the two lines reach the building and enter an electrical device, such as a lamp, the device controls the flow of electricity between the hot and neutral lines. If an easier path (one with less resistance) is available, the electricity follows that path. This can cause a short, a sudden increase in flow that can also create a sudden increase in temperature—enough to start a fire and injure both people and equipment. Never put yourself in a position where you are the path of least resistance between the hot line and ground!

> ⚡ **Caution** It's very important that PC components be properly grounded. Never connect a PC to an outlet or use an extension cord that doesn't have the third ground plug. The third line can prevent a short from causing extreme damage. In addition, the bond between the neutral and ground helps eliminate electrical noise (stray electrical signals) within the PC that is sometimes caused by other electrical equipment sitting very close to the computer.

To prevent uncontrolled electricity in a short, the neutral line is grounded. Grounding a line means that the line is connected directly to the earth, so that, in the event of a short, the electricity flows into the earth and not back to the power station. Grounding serves as an escape route for out-of-control electricity because the earth is always capable of accepting a flow of current. With computers, a surge suppressor can be used to protect a computer and its components against power surges.

> ⚡ **Caution** Beware of the different uses of black wire. In desktop computers and in DC circuits, black is used for ground, but in home wiring and in AC circuits, black is used for hot!

The neutral line to your house is grounded many times along its way (in fact, at each electrical pole) and is also grounded at the breaker box where the electricity enters your house. You can look at a three-prong plug and see the three lines: hot, neutral, and ground (see Figure A-3).

Figure A-3 A polarized plug showing hot and neutral, and a three-prong plug showing hot, neutral, and ground

> **Notes** House AC voltage in the United States is about 110–120 V, but know that in other countries, this is not always the case. In many other countries, the standard is 220 V. Outlet styles also vary from one country to the next.

Now that you know about electricity, let's turn our attention to protecting yourself against the dangers of electricity and other factors that might harm you as you work around computers.

PROTECTING YOURSELF

A+
220-902
5.1, 5.2

To protect yourself against electrical shock, when working with any electrical device, including computers, printers, scanners, and network devices, disconnect the power if you notice a dangerous situation that might lead to electrical shock or fire. When you disconnect the power, do so by pulling on the plug at the AC outlet. To protect the power cord, don't pull on the cord itself. Also, don't just turn off the on/off switch on the device; you need to actually disconnect the power. Note that any of the following can indicate a potential danger:

- The power cord is frayed or otherwise damaged in any way.
- Water or other liquid is on the floor around the device or spilled on it.
- The device has been exposed to excess moisture.
- The device has been dropped or you notice physical damage.
- You smell a strong electronics odor.
- The power supply or fans are making a whining noise.
- You notice smoke coming from the computer case or the case feels unusually warm.

SAFELY WORK INSIDE COMPUTERS, PRINTERS, AND OTHER ELECTRICAL DEVICES

A+
220-902
5.1, 5.2

To personally stay safe, always do the following, before working inside computers, printers, and other electrical devices:

- *Remove jewelry.* Remove your jewelry that might come in contact with components. Jewelry is made of metal and might conduct electricity if it touches a component. It can also get caught in cables and cords inside computer cases.
- *Power down the system and unplug it.* For a computer, unplug the power, monitor, mouse, and keyboard cables, and any other peripherals or cables attached and move them out of your way.
- *For a computer, press and hold down the power button for a moment.* After you unplug the computer, press the power button for about three seconds to completely drain the power supply. Sometimes when you do so, you'll hear the fans quickly start and go off as residual power is drained. Only then is it safe to work inside the case.

ELECTRICAL FIRE SAFETY

A+
220-902
5.1

Never use water to put out a fire fueled by electricity because water is a conductor and you might get a severe electrical shock. A computer lab needs a fire extinguisher that is rated to put out electrical fires. Fire extinguishers are rated by the type of fires they put out:

- Class A extinguishers can use water to put out fires caused by wood, paper, and other combustibles.
- Class B extinguishers can put out fires caused by liquids such as gasoline, kerosene, and oil.
- Class C fire extinguishers use nonconductive chemicals to put out a fire caused by electricity. See Figure A-4.

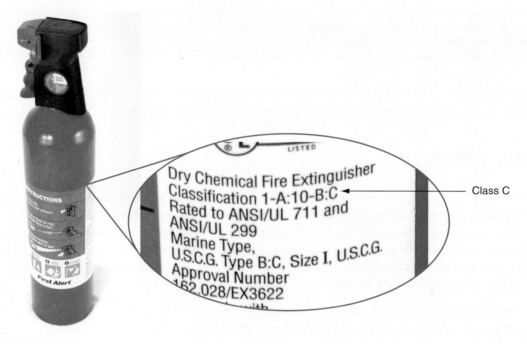

Class C

Figure A-4   A Class C fire extinguisher is rated to put out electrical fires

PROPER USE OF CLEANING PADS AND SOLUTIONS

**A+
220-902
5.1, 5.2**

As a support technician, you'll find yourself collecting different cleaning solutions and cleaning pads to clean a variety of devices, including the mouse and keyboard, CDs, DVDs, Blu-ray discs and their drives, tapes and tape drives, and monitors. Figure A-5 shows a few of these products. For example, the contact cleaner in the figure is used to clean the contacts on the edge connectors of expansion cards; the cleaning can solve a problem with a faulty connection.

Figure A-5   Cleaning solutions and pads

Most of these cleaning solutions contain flammable and poisonous materials. Take care when using them so that they don't get on your skin or in your eyes. To find out what to do if you are accidentally exposed to a dangerous solution, look on the instructions printed on the can or check out the material safety data sheet (see Figure A-6). A material safety data sheet (MSDS) explains how to properly handle substances such as chemical solvents and how to dispose of them.

An MSDS includes information such as physical data, toxicity, health effects, first aid, storage, shipping, disposal, and spill procedures. It comes packaged with the chemical; you can order one from the manufacturer, or you can find one on the Internet (see *www.ilpi.com/msds*).

> ⭐ **A+ Exam Tip** The A+ 220-901 exam expects you to know how to use MSDS documentation to find out how to dispose of chemicals so as to help protect the environment. You also need to know that you must follow all local government regulations when disposing of chemicals and other materials dangerous to the environment.

Figure A-6 Each chemical you use should have a material safety data sheet available

If you have an accident with these or other dangerous products, your company or organization might require you to report the accident to your company and/or fill out an incident report. Check with your organization to find out how to handle reporting these types of incidents.

MANAGING CABLES

A+
220-902
5.1

People can trip over cables or cords left on the floor, so be careful that cables are in a safe place. If you must run a cable across a path or where someone sits, use a cable or cord cover that can be nailed or screwed to the floor. Don't leave loose cables or cords in a traffic area where people can trip over them (called a trip hazard).

LIFTING HEAVY OBJECTS

A+
220-902
5.1

Back injury, caused by lifting heavy objects, is one of the most common injuries that happen at work. Whenever possible, put heavy objects, such as a large laser printer, on a cart to move them. If you do need to lift a heavy object, follow these guidelines to keep from injuring your back:

1. Looking at the object, decide which side of the object to face so that the load is the most balanced.

2. Stand close to the object with your feet apart.

3. Keeping your back straight, bend your knees and grip the load.

4. Lift with your legs, arms, and shoulders, and not with your back or stomach.

5. Keep the load close to your body and avoid twisting your body while you're holding it.

6. To put the object down, keep your back as straight as you can and lower the object by bending your knees.

Don't try to lift an object that is too heavy for you. Because there are no exact guidelines for when heavy is too heavy, use your best judgment as to when to ask for help.

SAFETY GOGGLES AND AIR FILTER MASK

If you are required to work in an environment such as a factory where flying fragments, chips, or other particles are about, your employer might require you wear safety goggles to protect your eyes. In addition, if the air is filled with dust or other contaminants, your employer might require you to wear an air-purifying respirator, commonly called an air filter mask, which filters the dust and other contaminants from the air you breathe. If safety goggles or a mask is required, your employer is responsible for providing you one that is appropriate for the environment in which you are working.

PROTECTING THE EQUIPMENT

As you learn to troubleshoot and solve computer problems, you gradually begin to realize that many problems you face could have been avoided by good computer maintenance that includes protecting the computer against environmental factors such as humidity, dust, and out-of-control electricity.

PROTECT THE EQUIPMENT AGAINST STATIC ELECTRICITY OR ESD

Suppose you come indoors on a cold day, pick up a comb, and touch your hair. Sparks fly! What happened? Static electricity caused the sparks. Electrostatic discharge (ESD), commonly known as static electricity, is an electrical charge at rest. When you came indoors, this charge built up on your hair and had no place to go. An ungrounded conductor (such as wire that is not touching another wire) or a nonconductive surface (such as your hair) holds a charge until the charge is released. When two objects with dissimilar electrical charges touch, electricity passes between them until the dissimilar charges become equal.

To see static charges equalizing, turn off the lights in a room, scuff your feet on the carpet, and touch another person. Occasionally, you can see and feel the charge in your fingers. If you can feel the charge, you discharged at least 1500 volts of static electricity. If you hear the discharge, you released at least 6000 volts. If you see the discharge, you released at least 8000 volts of ESD. A charge of only 10 volts can damage electronic components! *You can touch a chip on an expansion card or motherboard, damage the chip with ESD, and never feel, hear, or see the electrical discharge.*

ESD can cause two types of damage in an electronic component: catastrophic failure and upset failure. A catastrophic failure destroys the component beyond use. An upset failure damages the component so that it does not perform well, even though it may still function to some degree. Upset failures are more difficult to detect because they are not consistent and not easily observed. Both types of failures permanently affect the device. Components are easily damaged by ESD, but because the damage might not show up for weeks or months, a technician is likely to get careless and not realize the damage he or she is doing.

> ⚡ **Caution**   Unless you are measuring power levels with a multimeter or power supply tester, never, ever touch a component or cable inside a computer case while the power is on. The electrical voltage is not enough to seriously hurt you but more than enough to permanently damage the component.

Before touching or handling a component (for example, a hard drive, motherboard, expansion card, processor, or memory modules), to protect it against ESD, always ground yourself first. You can ground yourself and the computer parts by using one or more of the following static control devices or methods:

▲ *ESD strap.* An ESD strap, also called a ground bracelet, antistatic wrist strap, or ESD bracelet, is a strap you wear around your wrist. The strap has a cord attached with an alligator clip on the end. Attach the clip to the computer case you're working on, as shown in Figure A-7. Any static electricity between you and the case is now discharged. Therefore, as you work inside the case, you will not damage the components with static electricity. The bracelet also contains a resistor that prevents electricity from harming you.

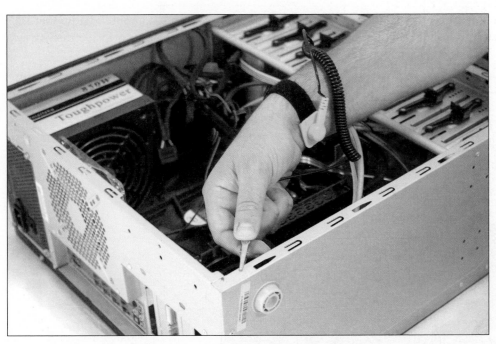

Figure A-7   A ground bracelet, which protects computer components from ESD, can clip to the side of the computer case and eliminate ESD between you and the case

A

> ⚡ **Caution**   When working on a laser printer, *don't* wear the ESD strap because you don't want to be the ground for these high-voltage devices.

◢ *Ground mats.* A ground mat, also called an ESD mat, dissipates ESD and is commonly used by bench technicians (also called depot technicians) who repair and assemble computers at their workbenches or in an assembly line. Ground mats have a connector in one corner that you can use to connect the mat to the ground (see Figure A-8). If you lift a component off the mat, it is no longer grounded and is susceptible to ESD, so it's important to use an ESD strap with a ground mat.

Figure A-8   An ESD mat dissipates ESD and should be connected to the ground

◢ *Static shielding bags.* New components come shipped in static shielding bags, also called antistatic bags. These bags are a type of Faraday cage, named after Michael Faraday, who built the first cage in 1836. A Faraday cage is any device that protects against an electromagnetic field. Save the bags to store other devices that are not currently installed in a computer. As you work on a computer, know that a device is not protected from ESD if you place it on top of the bag; the protection is inside the bag (see Figure A-9).

Figure A-9   An antistatic bag help protect components from ESD

> ⚡ **Caution**   A CRT monitor can also damage components with ESD. Don't place or store expansion cards on top of or next to a CRT monitor, which can discharge as much as 29,000 volts onto the screen.

The best way to guard against ESD is to use an ESD strap together with a ground mat. Consider an ESD strap essential equipment when working on a computer. However, if you are in a situation in which you must work without one, touch the computer case or the power supply before you touch a component in the case, which is called self-grounding. Self-grounding dissipates any charge between you and whatever you touch. Here are some rules that can help protect computer parts against ESD:

- ◢ *Rule 1:* When passing a circuit board, memory module, or other sensitive component to another person, ground yourself and then touch the other person before you pass the component.
- ◢ *Rule 2:* Leave components inside their protective bags until you are ready to use them.
- ◢ *Rule 3:* Work on hard floors, not carpet, or use antistatic spray on the carpets.
- ◢ *Rule 4:* Don't work on a computer if you or the computer have just come in from the cold because there is more danger of ESD when the atmosphere is cold and dry.
- ◢ *Rule 5:* When unpacking hardware or software, remove the packing tape and cellophane from the work area as soon as possible because these materials attract ESD.
- ◢ *Rule 6:* Keep components away from your hair and clothing.

> ★ **A+ Exam Tip**   The A+ 220-901 exam emphasizes that you should know how to protect computer equipment as you work on it, including how to protect components against damage from ESD.

Hands-On | Project A-1 Practice Handling Computer Components

Working with a partner, you'll need some computer parts and the antistatic tools you learned about in this part of the chapter. Practice touching, picking up, and passing the parts between you. As you do so, follow the rules to protect the parts against ESD. Have a third person watch as you work and point out any ways you might have exposed a part to ESD. As you work, be careful to not touch components on circuit boards or the gold fingers on the edge connector of an expansion card. When you are finished, store the parts in antistatic bags.

PHYSICALLY PROTECT YOUR EQUIPMENT FROM THE ENVIRONMENT

**A+
220-902
5.2**

When you protect equipment from ongoing problems with the environment, you are likely to have fewer problems later, and the less troubleshooting and repair you will have to do. Here is how you can physically protect a computer:

◢ *Protect a computer against dust and other airborne particles.* When a computer must sit in a dusty environment, around those who smoke, or where pets might leave hair, you can:

◢ Use a plastic keyboard cover to protect the keyboard. When the computer is turned off, cover the entire system with a protective cover or enclosure.

◢ Install air filters over the front or side vents of the case where air flows into the case. Put your hand over the case of a running computer to feel where the air flows in. For most systems, air flows in from the front vents or vents on the side of the case that is near the processor cooler. The air filter shown in Figure A-10 has magnets that hold the filter to the case when screw holes are not available.

Figure A-10   This air filter is designed to fit over a case fan, power supply fan, or panel vent on the case

◢ Whenever you have the case cover open, be sure to use compressed air or an antistatic vacuum (see Figure A-11) to remove dust from inside the case. Figure A-12 shows a case fan that jammed because of dust and caused a system to overheat. And while you're cleaning up dust, don't forget to blow or vacuum out the keyboard.

A

✎ **Notes** When working at a customer site, be sure to clean up any mess you created by blowing dust out of a computer case or keyboard.

Figure A-11 An antistatic vacuum designed to work inside sensitive electronic equipment such as computers and printers

Figure A-12 This dust-jammed case fan caused a system to overheat

▲ *Allow for good ventilation inside and outside the system.* Proper air circulation is essential to keeping a system cool. Don't block air vents on the front and rear of the computer case or on the monitor. Inside the case, make sure cables are tied up and out of the way so as to allow for airflow and not obstruct fans from turning. Put covers on expansion slot openings on the rear of the case and put face-plates over empty bays on the front of the case. Don't set a tower case directly on thick carpet because the air vent on the bottom front of the case can be blocked. If you are concerned about overheating, monitor temperatures inside and outside the case.

⭐ **A+ Exam Tip** The A+ 220-901 exam expects you to know how to keep computers and monitors well ventilated and to use protective enclosures and air filters to protect the equipment from airborne particles.

▲ *High temperatures and humidity can be dangerous for hard drives.* I once worked in a basement with PCs, and hard drives failed much too often. After we installed dehumidifiers, the hard drives became more reliable. If you suspect a problem with humidity, you can use a hygrometer to monitor the humidity in a room. High temperatures can also damage computer equipment, and you should take precautions to not allow a computer to overheat.

📝 **Notes** A server room where computers stay and people generally don't stay for long hours is set to balance what is good for the equipment and to conserve energy. Low temperature and moderate humidity are best for the equipment, although no set standards exist for either. Temperatures might be set from 65 to 70 degrees F, and humidity between 30 percent and 50 percent, although some companies keep their server rooms at 80 degrees F to conserve energy. A data center where both computers and people stay is usually kept at a comfortable temperature and humidity for humans.

▲ *Protect electrical equipment from power surges.* Lightning and other electrical power surges can destroy computers and other electrical equipment. If the house or office building does not have surge protection equipment installed at the breaker box, be sure to install a protective device at each computer. The least expensive device is a power strip that is also a surge suppressor, although you might want to use a UPS for added protection.

Lightning can also get to your equipment across network cabling coming in through an Internet connection. To protect against lightning, use a surge suppressor such as the one shown in Figure A-13 in line between the ISP device (for example, a DSL modem or cable modem) and the computer or home router to protect it from spikes across the network cables. Notice the cord on the surge suppressor, which connects it to ground.

Figure A-13 Surge protector by APC for Ethernet lines

An uninterruptible power supply (UPS) is a device that raises the voltage when it drops during brownouts or sags (temporary voltage reductions). A UPS also does double-duty as a surge suppressor to protect the system against power surges or spikes. In addition, a UPS can serve as a battery backup to provide power for a brief time during a total blackout long enough for you to save your work and shut down the system.

A UPS is not as essential for a laptop computer as it is for a desktop because a laptop has a battery that can sustain it during a blackout.

A common UPS device is a rather heavy box that plugs into an AC outlet and provides one or more outlets for the computer and the monitor (see Figure A-14). It has an on/off switch, requires no maintenance, and is very simple to install. Use it to provide uninterruptible power to your desktop computer and monitor. It's best not to connect it to nonessential devices such as a laser printer or scanner.

Figure A-14 Uninterruptible power supply (UPS)

> ✎ **Notes** Whenever a power outage occurs, unless you have a reliable power conditioner installed at the breaker box in your house or building, unplug all power cords to the computers, printers, monitors, and the like. Sometimes when the power returns, sudden spikes are accompanied by another brief outage. You don't want to subject your equipment to these surges. When buying a surge suppressor, look for those that guarantee against damage from lightning and that reimburse for equipment destroyed while the surge suppressor is in use.

Hands-On | Project A-2 Safely Clean Computer Equipment

Practice some preventive maintenance tasks by following these steps to clean a computer:

1. Shut down the computer and unplug it. Press the power button to drain power.

2. Clean the keyboard, monitor, and mouse. For a wheel mouse, remove the ball and clean the wheels. Clean the outside of the computer case. Don't forget to clean the mouse pad.

3. Open the case and using a ground bracelet, clean the dust from the case. Make sure all fans move freely.

4. Verify the cables are out of the way of airflow. Use cable ties as necessary.

5. Check that each expansion card and memory module is securely seated in its slot.

6. Power up the system and make sure all is working.

7. Clean up around your work area. If you left dust on the floor as you blew it out of the computer case, be sure to clean it up.

PROTECTING THE ENVIRONMENT

**A+
220-902
5.1, 5.2**
IT support technicians need to be aware that we can do damage to the environment if we carelessly dispose of used computer equipment improperly. As a support technician, one day you're sure to face an assortment of useless equipment and consumables (see Figure A-15).

Before you decide to trash it all, take a moment and ask yourself if some of the equipment can be donated or at least recycled. Think about fixing up an old computer and donating it to a needy middle school student. If you don't have the time for that, consider donating to the local computer repair class. The class can fix the computers up as a class project and donate them to young students.

Figure A-15 Keep, trash, recycle, or donate?

When disposing of any type of equipment or consumables, make sure to comply with local government environmental regulations. Table A-2 lists some items and how to dispose of them.

Part	How to Dispose
Alkaline batteries, including AAA, AA, A, C, D, and 9-volt	Dispose of these batteries in the regular trash. First check to see if there are recycling facilities in your area.
Button batteries used in digital cameras and other small equipment; battery packs used in notebooks	These batteries can contain silver oxide, mercury, lithium, or cadmium and are considered toxic waste that require special toxic waste handling. Dispose of them by returning them to the original dealer or by taking them to a recycling center. To recycle, pack them separately from other items. If you don't have a recycling center nearby, contact your county for local regulations for disposal.
Laser printer toner cartridges	Return these to the manufacturer or dealer to be recycled.
Ink-jet printer cartridges, computer cases, power supplies, and other computer parts, monitors, chemical solvents, and their containers	Check with local county or environmental officials for laws and regulations in your area for proper disposal of these items. The county might have a recycling center that will receive them. Discharge a CRT monitor before disposing of it. See the MSDS documents for chemicals to know how to dispose of them.
Storage media such as hard drives, CDs, DVDs, and BDs	Do physical damage to the device so it is not possible for sensitive data to be stolen. Then the device can be recycled or put in the trash. Your organization might be required to meet legal requirements to destroy data. If so, make sure you understand these requirements and how to comply with them.

Table A-2 Computer parts and how to dispose of them

> **★ A+ Exam Tip**   The A+ 220–901 exam expects you to know to follow environmental guidelines to dispose of batteries, laser printer toner, and CRT monitors, chemical solvents, and containers. If you're not certain how to dispose of a product, see its MSDS document.

Be sure a CRT monitor is discharged before you dispose of it. Most CRT monitors are designed to discharge after sitting unplugged for 60 minutes. It can be manually discharged by using a high-voltage probe with the monitor case opened. Ask a technician trained to service monitors to do this for you.

> **✎ Notes**   Go to *www.youtube.com* and search on "discharge a CRT monitor" to see some interesting videos that demonstrate the charge inside a monitor long after the monitor is turned off and unplugged. As for proper procedures, I'm not endorsing all these videos; just watch for fun.

Hands-On | Project A-3   Research Disposal Rules

Research the laws and regulations in your community concerning the disposal of batteries and old computer parts. Answer these questions regarding your community:

1. How do you properly dispose of a monitor?

2. How do you properly dispose of a battery pack used by a notebook computer?

3. How do you properly dispose of a large box of assorted computer parts, including hard drives, optical drives, computer cases, and circuit boards?

>> KEY TERMS

For explanations of key terms, see the Glossary for this text.

air filter mask	direct current (DC)	joule	static electricity
alternating current (AC)	electrostatic	material safety data	surge suppressor
amp	discharge (ESD)	sheet (MSDS)	transformer
antistatic bag	ESD mat	ohm	trip hazard
antistatic wrist strap	ESD strap	rectifier	uninterruptible power
brownout	ground bracelet	safety goggles	supply (UPS)
Class C fire	ground mat	sag	volt
extinguisher	inverter	self-grounding	watt

APPENDIX
B

Entry Points for Startup Processes

This appendix contains a summary of the entry points that can affect
Windows 8/7/Vista startup. The entry points include startup folders,
Group Policy folders, the Scheduled Tasks folder, and registry keys.

Programs and shortcuts to programs are stored in these startup folders:

◢ C:\Users*username*\AppData\Roaming\Microsoft\Windows\Start\Menu\Programs\Startup
◢ C:\ProgramData\Microsoft\Windows\Start Menu\Programs\Startup

Startup and shutdown scripts used by Group Policy are stored in these folders:

◢ C:\Windows\System32\GroupPolicy\Machine\Scripts\Startup
◢ C:\Windows\System32\GroupPolicy\Machine\Scripts\Shutdown
◢ C:\Windows\System32\GroupPolicy\User\Scripts\Logon
◢ C:\Windows\System32\GroupPolicy\User\Scripts\Logoff

Scheduled tasks are stored in this folder:

◢ C:\Windows\System32\Tasks

To see a list of scheduled tasks, enter the **schtasks** command in a command prompt window. These keys cause an entry to run once and only once at startup:

◢ HKLM\Software\Microsoft\Windows\CurrentVersion\RunOnce
◢ HKLM\Software\Microsoft\Windows\CurrentVersion\RunServiceOnce
◢ HKLM\Software\Microsoft\Windows\CurrentVersion\RunServicesOnce
◢ HKCU\Software\Microsoft\Windows\CurrentVersion\RunOnce

Group Policy places entries in the following keys to affect startup:

◢ HKCU\Software\Microsoft\Windows\CurrentVersion\Policies\Explorer\Run
◢ HKLM\Software\Microsoft\Windows\CurrentVersion\Policies\Explorer\Run

Windows loads many DLL programs from the following key, which is sometimes used by malicious software. Don't delete one unless you know it's causing a problem:

◢ HKLM\Software\Microsoft\Windows\CurrentVersion\ShellServiceObjectDelayLoad

Entries in the keys listed next apply to all users and hold legitimate startup entries. Don't delete an entry unless you suspect it to be bad:

◢ HKLM\Software\Microsoft\Windows\CurrentVersion\Run
◢ HKCU\Software\Microsoft\Windows NT\CurrentVersion\Windows
◢ HKCU\Software\Microsoft\Windows NT\CurrentVersion\Windows\Run
◢ HKCU\Software\Microsoft\Windows\CurrentVersion\Run

These keys and their subkeys contain entries that pertain to background services that are sometimes launched at startup:

◢ HKLM\Software\Microsoft\Windows\CurrentVersion\RunService
◢ HKLM\Software\Microsoft\Windows\CurrentVersion\RunServices

The following key contains a value named BootExecute, which is normally set to autochk. It causes the system to run a type of Chkdsk program to check for hard drive integrity when it was previously shut down improperly. Sometimes another program adds itself to this value, causing a problem. For more information about this situation, see the Microsoft Knowledge Base article 151376, "How to Disable Autochk If It Stops Responding During Reboot," at *support.microsoft.com*.

◢ HKLM\System\CurrentControlSet\Control\Session Manager

Here is an assorted list of registry keys that have all been known to cause various problems at startup. Remember, before you delete a program entry from one of these keys, research the program file name so that you won't accidentally delete something you want to keep:

- HKCU\Software\Microsoft\Command
- HKCU\Software\Microsoft\Command Processor\AutoRun
- HKCU\Software\Microsoft\Windows\CurrentVersion\RunOnce\Setup
- HKCU\Software\Microsoft\Windows NT\CurrentVersion\Windows\load
- HKLM\Software\Microsoft\Windows NT\CurrentVersion\Windows\AppInit_DLLs
- HKLM\Software\Microsoft\Windows NT\CurrentVersion\Winlogon\System
- HKLM\Software\Microsoft\Windows NT\CurrentVersion\Winlogon\Us
- HKCR\batfile\shell\open\command
- HKCR\comfile\shell\open\command
- HKCR\exefile\shell\open\command
- HKCR\htafile\shell\open\command
- HKCR\piffile\shell\open\command
- HKCR\scrfile\shell\open\command

Finally, check out the subkeys in the following key, which apply to 32-bit programs installed in a 64-bit version of Windows:

- HKLM\Software\Wow6432Node

Other ways in which processes can be launched at startup:

- Services can be set to launch at startup. To manage services, use the Services Console (services.msc).
- Device drivers are launched at startup. For a listing of installed devices, use Device Manager (devmgmt.msc) or the System Information Utility (msinfo32.exe).

CompTIA A+ Acronyms

CompTIA provides a list of acronyms that you need to know before you sit for the A+ exams. You can download the list from the CompTIA website at *www.comptia.org*. The list is included here for your convenience. However, CompTIA occasionally updates the list, so be sure to check the CompTIA website for the latest version.

Acronym	Spelled Out
AC	alternating current
ACL	access control list
ACPI	advanced configuration power interface
ACT	activity
ADSL	asymmetrical digital subscriber line
AGP	accelerated graphics port
AHCI	Advanced host controller interface
AP	Access point
APIPA	automatic private internet protocol addressing
APM	advanced power management
ARP	address resolution protocol
ASR	automated system recovery
ATA	advanced technology attachment
ATAPI	advanced technology attachment packet interface
ATM	asynchronous transfer mode
ATX	advanced technology extended
AUP	Acceptable Use Policy
A/V	Audio Video
BIOS	basic input/output system
BNC	Bayonet-Neill-Concelman or British Naval Connector
BTX	balanced technology extended
CAPTCHA	Completely Automated Public Turing Test To Tell Computers and Humans Apart
CCFL	Cold Cathode Fluorescent Lamp
CD	compact disc
CD-ROM	compact disc-read-only memory
CD-RW	compact disc-rewritable
CDFS	compact disc file system
CFS	Central File System, Common File System, Command File System
CIFS	Common Internet File System
CMOS	complementary metal-oxide semiconductor
CNR	Communications and Networking Riser
COMx	communication port (x=port number)
CPU	central processing unit
CRT	cathode-ray tube
DAC	discretionary access control
DB-25	serial communications D-shell connector, 25 pins
DB-9	9 pin D shell connector
DC	direct current
DDOS	distributed denial of service
DDR	double data-rate
DDR RAM	double data-rate random access memory
DDR SDRAM	double data-rate synchronous dynamic random access memory

Acronym	Spelled Out
DFS	distributed file system
DHCP	dynamic host configuration protocol
DIMM	dual inline memory module
DIN	Deutsche Industrie Norm
DLT	digital linear tape
DLP	digital light processing
DMA	direct memory access
DMZ	demilitarized zone
DNS	domain name service or domain name server
DOS	denial of service
DRAM	dynamic random access memory
DRM	Digital Rights Management
DSL	digital subscriber line
DVD	digital video disc or digital versatile disc
DVD-RAM	digital video disc-random access memory
DVD-ROM	digital video disc-read only memory
DVD-R	digital video disc-recordable
DVD-RW	digital video disc-rewritable
DVI	digital visual interface
ECC	error correcting code/error checking and correction
ECP	extended capabilities port
EEPROM	electrically erasable programmable read-only memory
EFS	encrypting file system
EIDE	enhanced integrated drive electronics
EMI	electromagnetic interference
EMP	electromagnetic pulse
EPROM	erasable programmable read-only memory
EPP	enhanced parallel port
ERD	emergency repair disk
ESD	electrostatic discharge
EULA	End User License Agreement
EVGA	extended video graphics adapter/array
EVDO	evolution data optimized or evolution data only
FAT	file allocation table
FAT12	12-bit file allocation table
FAT16	16-bit file allocation table
FAT32	32-bit file allocation table
FDD	floppy disk drive
Fn	Function (referring to the function key on a laptop)
FPM	fast page-mode
FRU	field replaceable unit
FSB	Front Side Bus

C

Acronym	Spelled Out
FTP	file transfer protocol
FQDN	fully qualified domain name
Gb	gigabit
GB	gigabyte
GDI	graphics device interface
GHz	gigahertz
GUI	graphical user interface
GPS	global positioning system
GSM	global system for mobile communications
HAL	hardware abstraction layer
HAV	Hardware Assisted Virtualization
HCL	hardware compatibility list
HDD	hard disk drive
HDMI	high definition media interface
HPFS	high performance file system
HTML	hypertext markup language
HTPC	home theater PC
HTTP	hypertext transfer protocol
HTTPS	hypertext transfer protocol over secure sockets layer
I/O	input/output
ICMP	internet control message protocol
ICR	intelligent character recognition
IDE	integrated drive electronics
IDS	Intrusion Detection System
IEEE	Institute of Electrical and Electronics Engineers
IIS	Internet Information Services
IMAP	internet mail access protocol
IMEI	International Mobile Equipment Identity
IMSI	International Mobile Subscriber Identity
IP	internet protocol
IPCONFIG	internet protocol configuration
IPP	internet printing protocol
IPS	In-plane Switching
IPSEC	Internet Protocol Security
IR	Infrared
IrDA	Infrared Data Association
IRP	Incident Response Plan
IRQ	Interrupt Request
ISDN	Integrated Services Digital Network
ISO	International Organization for Standardization/Industry Standards Organization
ISP	Internet Service Provider
JBOD	Just a Bunch of Disks

Acronym	Spelled Out
Kb	Kilobit
KB	Kilobyte or Knowledge Base
LAN	Local Area Network
LBA	Logical Block Addressing
LC	Lucent Connector
LCD	liquid Crystal Display
LDAP	lightweight directory access protocol
LED	light emitting diode
Li-on	lithium-ion
LPD/LPR	line printer daemon / line printer remote
LPT	line printer terminal
LVD	low voltage differential
MAC	media access control / mandatory access control
MAPI	messaging application programming interface
MAU	media access unit, media attachment unit
Mb	megabit
MB	megabyte
MBR	master boot record
MBSA	Microsoft Baseline Security Analyzer
MFD	multi-function device
MFP	multi-function product
MHz	megahertz
MicroDIMM	micro dual inline memory module
MIDI	musical instrument digital interface
MIME	multipurpose internet mail extension
MIMO	Multiple Input Multiple Output
MMC	Microsoft management console
MP3	Moving Picture Experts Group Layer 3 Audio
MP4	Moving Picture Experts Group Layer 4
MPEG	Moving Picture Experts Group
MSCONFIG	Microsoft configuration
MSDS	material safety data sheet
MUI	multilingual user interface
NAC	network access control
NAS	network-attached storage
NAT	network address translation
NetBIOS	networked basic input/output system
NetBEUI	networked basic input/output system extended user interface
NFS	network file system
NIC	network interface card
NiCd	nickel cadmium
NiMH	nickel metal hydride

C

Acronym	Spelled Out
NLX	new low-profile extended
NNTP	network news transfer protocol
NTFS	new technology file system
NTLDR	new technology loader
NTP	Network Time Protocol
OCR	optical character recognition
OEM	original equipment manufacturer
OLED	Organic Light Emitting Diode
OS	operating system
PAN	personal area network
PATA	parallel advanced technology attachment
PC	personal computer
PCI	peripheral component interconnect
PCIe	peripheral component interconnect express
PCIX	peripheral component interconnect extended
PCL	printer control language
PCMCIA	Personal Computer Memory Card International Association
PE	Preinstallation Environment
PGA	pin grid array
PGA2	pin grid array 2
PII	Personally Identifiable Information
PIN	personal identification number
PKI	public key infrastructure
PnP	plug and play
POP3	post office protocol 3
PoS	Point of Sale
POST	power-on self test
POTS	plain old telephone service
PPP	point-to-point protocol
PPTP	point-to-point tunneling protocol
PRI	primary rate interface
PROM	programmable read-only memory
PS/2	personal system/2 connector
PSTN	public switched telephone network
PSU	power supply unit
PVC	permanent virtual circuit
PXE	preboot execution environment
QoS	quality of service
RAID	redundant array of independent (or inexpensive) discs
RAM	random access memory
RAS	remote access service
RDP	Remote Desktop Protocol

Acronym	Spelled Out
RF	radio frequency
RFI	radio frequency interference
RGB	red green blue
RIP	routing information protocol
RIS	remote installation service
RISC	reduced instruction set computer
RJ-11	registered jack function 11
RJ-45	registered jack function 45
RMA	returned materials authorization
ROM	read only memory
RTC	real-time clock
SAN	storage area network
SAS	Serial Attached SCSI
SATA	serial advanced technology attachment
SC	subscription channel
SCP	secure copy protection
SCSI	small computer system interface
SCSI ID	small computer system interface identifier
SD card	secure digital card
SDRAM	synchronous dynamic random access memory
SEC	single edge connector
SFC	system file checker
SFF	Small Form Factor
SLI	scalable link interface or system level integration or scanline interleave mode
S.M.A.R.T.	self-monitoring, analysis, and reporting technology
SMB	server message block or small to midsize business
SMTP	simple mail transfer protocol
SNMP	simple network management protocol
SoDIMM	small outline dual inline memory module
SOHO	small office/home office
SP	service pack
SPDIF	Sony-Philips digital interface format
SPGA	staggered pin grid array
SRAM	static random access memory
SSH	secure shell
SSID	service set identifier
SSL	secure sockets layer
ST	straight tip
STP	shielded twisted pair
SXGA	super extended graphics array
TB	terabyte
TCP	transmission control protocol

C

Acronym	Spelled Out
TCP/IP	transmission control protocol/internet protocol
TDR	time domain reflectometer
TFTP	trivial file transfer protocol
TKIP	Temporal Key Integrity Protocol
TPM	trusted platform module
UAC	user account control
UDF	user defined functions or universal disk format or universal data format
UDP	user datagram protocol
UEFI	Unified Extensible Firmware Interface
UNC	universal naming convention
UPS	uninterruptible power supply
URL	uniform resource locator
USB	universal serial bus
USMT	user state migration tool
UTP	unshielded twisted pair
UXGA	ultra extended graphics array
VESA	Video Electronics Standards Association
VFAT	virtual file allocation table
VGA	video graphics array
VM	Virtual Machine
VoIP	voice over internet protocol
VPN	virtual private network
VRAM	video random access memory
WAN	wide area network
WAP	wireless access protocol/wireless access point
WEP	wired equivalent privacy
WIFI	wireless fidelity
WINS	windows internet name service
WLAN	wireless local area network
WPA	wireless protected access
WPS	WiFi Protected Setup
WUXGA	wide ultra extended graphics array
XGA	extended graphics array
ZIF	zero-insertion-force
ZIP	zigzag inline package

GLOSSARY

Hardware Key Terms

100BaseT An Ethernet standard that operates at 100 Mbps and uses twisted-pair cabling up to 100 meters (328 feet). *Also called* Fast Ethernet. Variations of 100BaseT are 100BaseTX and 100BaseFX.

4-pin 12-V connector An auxiliary motherboard connector used for extra 12-V power to the processor.

8-pin 12-V connector An auxiliary motherboard connector used for extra 12-V power to the processor, providing more power than the older 4-pin auxiliary connector.

10-foot user interface Application software used on large screens to control output display menus and other clickable items in fonts large enough to read at a distance of 10 feet.

20-pin P1 connector Used by an older ATX power supply and motherboard and provided +3.3 volts, +5 volts, +12 volts, –12 volts, and an optional and rarely used –5 volts.

24-pin P1 connector Used by ATX Version 2.2 power supply and motherboard and provides additional power for PCI Express slots.

1394a *See* FireWire 400.

1394b *See* FireWire 800.

802.11 a/b/g/n/ac The collective name for the IEEE 802.11 standards for local wireless networking, which is the technical name for Wi-Fi.

A+ Certification A certification awarded by CompTIA (The Computer Technology Industry Association) that measures an IT technician's knowledge and skills.

AC adapter A device that converts AC to DC and can use regular house current to power a laptop computer.

Accelerated Processing Unit (APU) An AMD technology that is a combination of a CPU and a graphics processor unit (GPU) in the same processor housing.

accelerometer A type of gyroscope used in mobile devices to sense the physical position of the device.

adapter address *See* MAC (Media Access Control) address.

address reservation When a DHCP server assigns a static IP address to a DHCP client. For example, a network printer might require a static IP address so that computers on the network can find the printer.

ad hoc mode A peer-to-peer wireless network between computers where each wireless computer serves as its own wireless access point and is responsible for securing each connection.

Advanced Boot Options menu A Windows 7/ Vista menu that appears when you press F8 when Windows starts. The menu can be used to troubleshoot problems when loading Windows.

AES (Advanced Encryption Standard) An encryption standard used by WPA2 and is currently the strongest encryption standard used by Wi-Fi.

AFP (Apple Filing Protocol) An outdated file access protocol used by early editions of the Mac operating system by Apple and is one protocol in the suite of AppleTalk networking protocols.

air filter mask A mask that filters the dust and other contaminants from the air for breathing safety. *Also called* air-purifying respirator.

airplane mode A setting within a mobile device that disables the cellular, Wi-Fi, and Bluetooth antennas so the device cannot transmit signals.

AirPrint A technology by Apple that allows Apple computers and mobile devices to print to an AirPrint-capable printer without first installing the printer.

all-in-one computer A computer that has the monitor and computer case built together and uses components that are common to both a laptop and a desktop computer.

alternate IP address When configuring TCP/IP in Windows, the static IP address that Windows uses if it cannot lease an IP address from a DHCP server.

alternating current (AC) Current that cycles back and forth rather than traveling in only one direction. In the United States, the AC voltage from a standard wall outlet is normally between 110 and 115 V. In Europe, the standard AC voltage from a wall outlet is 220 V.

A-Male connector A common type of USB connector that is flat and wide and connects an A Male USB port on a computer or USB hub.

amp (A) A measure of electrical current.

analog A continuous signal with infinite variations. *Compare with* digital, which is a series of binary values—1s and 0s.

ANSI (American National Standards Institute) A nonprofit organization dedicated to creating trade and communications standards.

antistatic bag Static shielding bags that new computer components are shipped in.

antistatic wrist strap *See* ESD strap.

anycast address Using TCP/IP version 6, a type of IP address used by routers and identifies multiple destinations. Packets are delivered to the closest destination.

AppleTalk An outdated suite of networking protocols used by early editions of the Apple Mac OS, and has been replaced by the TCP/IP suite of protocols.

artifact Horizontally torn images on a computer screen.

ATAPI (Advanced Technology Attachment Packet Interface) An interface standard, part of the IDE/ATA standards, that allows tape drives, optical drives, and other drives to be treated like an IDE hard drive by the system.

ATX (Advanced Technology Extended) The most common form factor for computer systems presently in use, originally introduced by Intel in 1995. ATX motherboards and cases make better use of space and resources than did the earlier AT form factor.

ATX12V power supply An ATX Version 2.1 power supply that provides an extra 12 V power cord with a 4-pin connector to be used by the auxiliary 4-pin power connector on motherboards used to provide extra power for processors.

audio port A port that can be used by a microphone, audio in, audio out, and stereo audio out. *Also called* a sound port.

autodetection A feature of UEFI/BIOS that detects a new drive and automatically selects the correct drive capacity and configuration, including the best possible standard supported by both the hard drive and the motherboard.

Automatic Private IP Address (APIPA) In TCP/IP Version 4, IP address in the address range 169.254.x.y, used by a computer when it cannot successfully lease an IP address from a DHCP server.

auto-switching A function of a laptop computer AC adapter that is able to automatically switch between 110 V and 220 V AC power.

B-Male connector A USB connector that connects a USB 1.x or 2.0 device such as a printer.

ball grid array (BGA) A connection via a processor that is soldered to the motherboard, and the two are always purchased as a unit.

bandwidth In relation to analog communication, the range of frequencies that a communications channel or cable can carry. In general use, the term refers to the volume of data that can be transmitted on a bus or over a cable stated in bits per second (bps), kilobits per second (Kbps), megabits per second (Mbps), or gigabits per second (Gbps). *Also called* data throughput or line speed.

barcode reader Used to scan barcodes on products at the points of sale or when taking inventory.

base station A fixed transceiver and antenna used to create one cell within a cellular network.

BD-R Stands for BD (Blu-ray Disc) recordable.

BD-RE Stands for BD (Blu-ray Disc) rewriteable.

beamforming A technique supported by IEEE 802.11ac Wi-Fi standard that can detect the location of connected devices and increase signal strength in that direction.

Berg power connector A type of power connector used by a power cord to provide power to a floppy disk drive.

best-effort protocol *See* connectionless protocol.

biometric device An input device that inputs biological data about a person; the data can identify a person's fingerprints, handprints, face, voice, eyes, and handwriting.

BIOS (basic input/output system) Firmware that can control much of a computer's input/output functions, such as communication with the keyboard and the monitor. *Compare with* UEFI.

BIOS setup The program in system BIOS that can change the values in CMOS RAM. *Also called* CMOS setup.

BitLocker Drive Encryption A utility in Windows 8/7/Vista that is used to lock down a hard drive by encrypting the entire Windows volume and any other volume on the drive.

bitmap Rows and columns of bits that collective represent an image.

blue screen error *See* blue screen of death (BSOD).

blue screen of death (BSOD) A Windows error that occurs in kernel mode, is displayed against a blue screen, and causes the system to halt. The error might be caused by problems with devices, device drivers, or a corrupted Windows installation. *Also called* a stop error.

Bluetooth A short-range wireless technology used to connect two devices in a small personal network.

Blu-ray Disc (BD) An optical disc technology that uses the UDF version 2.5 file system and a blue laser beam, which is shorter than any red beam used by DVD or CD discs. The shorter blue laser beam allows Blu-ray discs to store more data than a DVD.

BNC connector A connector used with thin coaxial cable. Some BNC connectors are T-shaped and called T-connectors. One end of the T connects to the NIC, and the two other ends can connect to cables or end a bus formation with a terminator.

Bonjour An Apple program that is used to interface between computers and devices and share content and services between them. When iTunes is installed on a Windows computer, the installation includes Bonjour.

Boot Configuration Data (BCD) store A small Windows database structured the same as a registry file and contains configuration information about how Windows is started. The BCD file replaces the Boot.ini file used in Windows 2000/XP.

bootrec A Windows command used to repair the BCD (Boot Configuration Data) and boot sectors.

bridge A device that stands between two segments of a network and manages network traffic between them.

broadband A transmission technique that carries more than one type of transmission on the same medium, such as voice and DSL on a regular telephone line.

brownout Temporary reductions in voltage, which can sometimes cause data loss. *Also called* sags.

buffer overflow attack Malicious software that attempts to run its code from an area of memory assigned to another program.

burn-in When a static image stays on a monitor for many hours, leaving a permanent impression of that image on the monitor.

bus The paths, or lines, on the motherboard on which data, instructions, and electrical power move from component to component.

cable Internet A broadband technology that uses cable TV lines and is always connected (always up).

cable tester A tool used to test a cable to find out if it is good or to find out what type of cable it is if the cable is not labeled.

calibration The process of checking and correcting the graduations of an instrument or device such as an inkjet printer.

CAS Latency A method of measuring access timing to memory, which is the number of clock cycles required to write or read a column of data off a memory module. CAS stands for Column Access Strobe. *Compare with* RAS Latency.

case fan A fan inside a computer case used to draw air out of or into the case.

CAT-3 (Category 3) A rating formally used for unshielded twisted-pair (UTP) cables on a network, and is currently used for phone lines.

CAT-5 (Category 5) A rating used for unshielded twisted-pair (UTP) cables and is rated for Fast Ethernet, but is seldom used today.

CAT-5e (Category 5e) A rating used for unshielded twisted-pair (UTP) cables, rated for Fast Ethernet and Gigabit Ethernet, and is popular today.

CAT-6 (Category 6) A rating used for twisted-pair cables that has less crosstalk than CAT-5e cables. CAT-6 cables might contain a plastic cord down the center of the cable that helps to prevent crosstalk, but is less flexible and more difficult to install than CAT-5e.

CAT-6a (Category 6a) A rating used for twisted-pair cables that is thicker and faster than CAT-6 and rated for 10GBase-T (10-Gigabit Ethernet).

G

CAT-6e (Category 6e) An unofficial name for CAT-6a.

CAT-7 (Category 7) A rating used for twisted-pair cables that have shielding to almost completely eliminate crosstalk and improve noise reduction.

CD (compact disc) An optical disc technology that uses a red laser beam and can hold up to 700 MB of data.

CDFS (Compact Disc File System) The 32-bit file system for CD discs and some CD-R and CD-RW discs. *Also see* Universal Disk Format (UDF).

CDMA (Code Division Multiple Access) A protocol standard used by cellular WANs and cell phones for transmitting digital data over cellular networks.

CD-ROM Stands for CD-read-only memory.

CD-RW Stands for CD rewriteable.

cellular network A network that can be used when a wireless network must cover a wide area. The network is made up of cells, each controlled by a base station. *Also called* a cellular WAN.

cellular WAN *See* cellular network.

CPU *See* central processing unit (CPU).

central processing unit (CPU) *Also called* a microprocessor or processor. The component where almost all processing of data and instructions takes place. The CPU receives data input, processes information, and executes instructions.

Centrino A technology used by Intel whereby the processor, chipset, and wireless network adapter are all interconnected as a unit, which improves laptop performance.

channel A specific radio frequency within a broader frequency.

charging In laser printing, the imaging drum is conditioned to contain a high electrical charge.

chassis A computer case for any type of computer.

chassis air guide (CAG) A round air duct that helps to pull and direct fresh air from outside a computer case to the cooler and processor.

chipset A group of chips on the motherboard that controls the timing and flow of data and instructions to and from the CPU.

chkdsk (check disk) A Windows command to verify the hard drive does not have bad sectors that can corrupt the file system.

CIDR notation A shorthand notation (pronounced "*cider notation*") for expressing an IPv4 address and subnet mask with the IP address followed by a / slash and the number of bits in the IP address that identifies the network. For example, 15.50.35.10/20.

CIFS (Common Internet File System) A file access protocol and the cross-platform version of SMB used between Windows, Linux, Mac OS, and other operating systems. *Also called* SMB2.

Class C fire extinguisher A fire extinguisher rated to put out electrical fires.

client/server Two computers communicating using a local network or the Internet. One computer (the client) makes requests to the other computer (the server), which answers the request.

cloud printing Printing to a printer anywhere on the Internet from a personal computer or mobile device connected to the Internet.

CMOS (complementary metal-oxide semiconductor) The technology used to manufacture microchips. CMOS chips require less electricity, hold data longer after the electricity is turned off, and produce less heat than earlier technologies. The configuration or setup chip is a CMOS chip.

CMOS battery The lithium coin-cell battery on the motherboard used to power the CMOS chip that holds BIOS setup data so that the data is retained when the computer is unplugged.

CMOS RAM Memory contained on the CMOS configuration chip.

coaxial cable A cable that has a single copper wire down the middle and a braided shield around it.

Cold Cathode Fluorescent Lamp (CCFL) An older backlighting technology that uses one or two fluorescent tubes to light a monitor panel.

CompactFlash (CF) card A flash memory device that allows for sizes up to 137 GB, although current sizes range up to 32 GB.

Compatibility Support Module (CSM) A feature of UEFI that allows UEFI to be backwards compatible with legacy BIOS devices and drivers.

composite video port A port used by television or by a video card that is designed to send output to a TV. A composite port is round and has only a single pin in the center of the port. *Also called* RGB port.

computer name *See* host name.

connectionless protocol A TCP/IP protocol such as UDP that works at the OSI Transport layer and does not guarantee delivery by first connecting and checking where data is received. It might be used for broadcasting, such as streaming video or sound over the web, where guaranteed delivery is not as important as fast transmission. *Also called* a best-effort protocol. *Also see* UDP (User Datagram Protocol).

connection-oriented protocol In networking, a TCP/IP protocol that confirms a good connection has been made before transmitting data to the other end, verifies data was received, and resends it if it is not. An example of a connection-oriented protocol is TCP.

contrast ratio The contrast between true black and true white on a screen.

cooler A cooling system that sits on top of a processor and consists of a fan and a heat sink.

crimper A tool used to attach a terminator or connector to the end of a cable.

crossover cable A cable used to connect two like devices such as a hub to a hub or a computer to a computer (to make the simplest network of all). A crossover cable is not rated for Gigabit Ethernet.

data bus Lines of the bus, a system of pathway used for communication on the motherboard, used for data.

data cartridge A full-sized cartridge that holds data and is used in a tape drive.

data path size The number of lines on a bus that can hold data, for example, 8, 16, 32, and 64 lines, which can accommodate 8, 16, 32, and 64 bits at a time.

Data Sources A tool in the Administrative Tools group of Control Panel that is used to allow data files to be connected to applications they normally would not use.

data throughput *See* bandwidth.

DB15 port *See* VGA (Video Graphics Array) port.

DB9 port *See* serial port.

DDR *See* Double Data Rate SDRAM.

DDR2 Memory that is faster and uses less power than DDR.

DDR3 Memory that is faster and uses less power than DDR2.

DDR3L Memory that is faster and uses less power than regular DDR3.

DDR4 Memory that is faster and uses less power than DDR3.

DE15 port *See* VGA (Video Graphics Array) port.

dead pixel A pixel on an LCD monitor that is not working and can appear as a small white, black, or colored spot on the computer screen.

default gateway The gateway a computer on a network uses to access another network unless it knows to specifically use another gateway for quicker access to that network.

default printer The designated printer to which Windows prints unless another printer is selected.

defragmentation tool A utility or command to rewrite a file to a disk in one contiguous chain of clusters, thus speeding up data retrieval.

desktop case A computer case that lies flat and sometimes serves double-duty as a monitor stand.

Destination Network Address Translation (DNAT) When a firewall using network address translation (NAT) allows uninitated communication to a computer behind the firewall through a port that is normally closed. *Also see* port forwarding.

device driver Small program stored on the hard drive and installed in Windows that tell Windows how to communicate with a specific hardware device such as a printer, network, port on the motherboard, or scanner.

Device Manager Primary Windows tool (devmgmt. msc) for managing hardware.

Devices and Printers window A window used in Windows 8/7 to manage and uninstall printers and other devices.

DHCP (Dynamic Host Configuration Protocol) A protocol used by a server to assign a dynamic IP address to a computer when it first attempts to initiate a connection to the network and requests an IP address.

DHCP client A computer or other device (such as a network printer) that requests an IP address from a DHCP server.

DHCPv6 server A DHCP server that serves up IPv6 addresses.

digital A signal consisting of a series of binary values—1s and 0s. *Compare with* analog.

G

digital rights management (DRM)   Software and hardware security limitations meant to protect digital content and prevent piracy.

digitizer   *See* graphics tablet.

digitizing tablet   *See* graphics tablet.

DIMM (dual inline memory module)   A miniature circuit board installed on a motherboard to hold memory.

direct current (DC)   Current that travels in only one direction (the type of electricity provided by batteries). Computer power supplies transform AC to low DC.

direct thermal printer   A type of thermal printer that burns dots onto special coated paper as was done by older fax machines.

DirectX   A Microsoft software development tool that software developers can use to write multimedia applications such as games, video-editing software, and computer-aided design software.

discolored capacitor   Bulging head or crusty corrosion at the base of a capacitor that might indicate a failing motherboard.

disk cloning   *See* drive imaging.

disk imaging   *See* drive imaging.

diskpart   A Windows command to manage hard drives, partitions, and volumes.

DisplayPort   A port that transmits digital video and audio (not analog transmissions) and is slowly replacing VGA and DVI ports on personal computers. *Also see* Thunderbolt port.

distorted geometry   Images are stretched inappropriately on a monitor.

DMZ (demilitarized zone)   Refers to removing firewall protection from a computer or network within an organization of protected computers and networks.

DNS (Domain Name System or Domain Name Service)   A distributed pool of information (called the name space) that keeps track of assigned host names and domain names and their corresponding IP addresses. DNS also refers to the system that allows a host to locate information in the pool and the protocol the system uses.

DNS client   When Windows queries the DNS server for a name resolution, which means to find an IP address for a computer when the fully qualified domain name is known.

DNS server   A Doman Name Service server that uses a DNS protocol to find an IP address for a computer when the fully qualified domain name is known. An Internet Service Provider is responsible for providing access to one or more DNS servers as part of the service it provides for Internet access.

docking port   A connector on a laptop to connect to a port replicator or docking station.

docking station   A device that receives a laptop computer and provides additional secondary storage and easy connection to peripheral devices.

domain name   A name that identifies a network and appears before the period in a website address such as *microsoft.com*. A fully qualified domain name is sometimes loosely called a domain name. *Also see* fully qualified domain name.

Double Data Rate SDRAM (DDR SDRAM)   A type of memory technology used on DIMMs that runs at twice the speed of the system clock, has one notch and uses 184 pins. *Also called* DDR SDRAM, SDRAM II, and DDR.

double-sided   A DIMM feature whereby memory chips are installed on both sides of a DIMM.

driver store   The location where Windows stores a copy of the driver software when first installing a device.

DSL (Digital Subscriber Line)   A telephone line that carries digital data from end to end, and is used as a type of broadband Internet access.

dual channels   A motherboard feature that improves memory performance by providing two 64-bit channels between memory and the chipset. DDR, DDR2, DDR3, and DDR4 DIMMs can use dual channels.

dual processors   Two processor sockets on a server motherboard.

dual rail   A power supply with a second +12 V circuit or rail used to ensure the first circuit is not overloaded.

dual ranked   Double-sided DIMMs that provide two 64-bit banks. The memory controller accesses first one bank and then the other. Dual-ranked DIMMs do not perform as well as single-ranked DIMMs.

dual voltage selector switch A switch on the back of the computer case where you can switch the input voltage to the power supply to 115 V used in the United States or 220 V used in other countries.

duplex printer A printer that is able to print on both sides of the paper.

duplexing assembly Used in a duplex printer, a duplexing assembly contains several rollers, turns the paper around, and draws it back through the print process to print on the back of the paper.

DVD (digital versatile disc or digital video disc) A technology used by optical discs that uses a red laser beam and can hold up to 17 GB of data.

DVD-ROM Stands for DVD read-only memory.

DVD-RW Stands for DVD rewriteable memory.

DVD-RW DL Stands for DVD rewriteable memory, dual layers. Doubles storage capacity.

DVI-A A DVI (Digital Visual Interface) video port that only transmits analog data.

DVI-D A DVI (Digital Visual Interface) video port that works only with digital monitors.

DVI-I A DVI (Digital Visual Interface) video port that supports both analog and digital monitors.

DVI (Digital Video Interface) port A port that transmits digital or analog video.

dxdiag.exe A Windows command used to display information about hardware and diagnose problems with DirectX.

dynamic IP address An IP address assigned by a DHCP server for the current session only, and is leased when the computer first connects to a network. When the session is terminated, the IP address is returned to the list of available addresses. *Compare with* static IP address.

dynamic RAM (DRAM) The most common type of system memory, it requires refreshing every few milliseconds.

ECC (error-correcting code) A chipset feature on a motherboard that checks the integrity of data stored on DIMMs or RIMMs and can correct single-bit errors in a byte. More advanced ECC schemas can detect, but not correct, double-bit errors in a byte.

EFI (Extensible Firmware Interface) The original version of UEFI that was first developed by Intel.

electrostatic discharge (ESD) Another name for static electricity, which can damage chips and

destroy motherboards, even though it might not be felt or seen with the naked eye.

elevated command prompt window A Windows command prompt window that allows commands that require administrator privileges.

embedded MMC (eMMC) Internal storage used instead of using a solid-state drive (SSD) in inexpensive mobile devices such as cell phones, tablets, and laptops.

e-reader A mobile device that holds digital versions of books, newspapers, magazines, and other printed documents, which are usually downloaded to the device from the web.

ESD mat A mat that dissipates electrostatic discharge (ESD) and is commonly used by technicians who repair and assemble computers at their workbenches or in an assembly line. *Also called* ground mat.

ESD strap A strap you wear around your wrist that is attached to the computer case, ground mat, or another ground so that electrostatic discharge (ESD) is discharged from your body before you touch sensitive components inside a computer. *Also called* antistatic wrist strap *or* ground bracelet.

Ethernet over Power (EoP) *See* powerline networking.

Ethernet port *See* network port.

Execute Disable Bit (EDB) A processor security feature that can work with the operating system to designate an area of memory for holding data or instructions.

expansion card A circuit board inserted into a slot on the motherboard to enhance the capability of the computer.

ExpressCard A PCMCIA standard for laptop I/O cards that uses the PCI Express and USB 2.0 data transfer standards. Two types of ExpressCards are ExpressCard/34 (34mm wide) and ExpressCard/54 (54mm wide). ExpressCards have been replaced by USB ports on today's laptops.

ExpressCard/34 A type of ExpressCard that is 34 mm wide. An ExpressCard/34 can fit into an ExpressCard/54 slot.

ExpressCard/54 A type of ExpressCard that is 54 mm wide.

extender A device that amplifies and retransmits a wireless signal to a wider coverage area and retains the original network name.

G

extension magnet brush   A long-handled brush made of nylon fibers that are charged with static electricity to pick up stray toner inside a laser printer.

external enclosure   A housing designed to store hard drives external from the computer.

external SATA (eSATA)   A standard for external drives based on SATA that uses a special external shielded SATA cable up to 2 meters long.

F connector   A connector used with an RG-6 coaxial cable and is used for connections to a TV and has a single copper wire.

fanless CPU cooler   A processor cooler that instead of using fans, uses heat pipes that contain a small amount of liquid that becomes vapor when heated, and the vapor draws the heat away from the processor toward the fins on the cooler. There the heat can be blown away by case fans.

Fast Ethernet   *See* 100BaseT.

fault tolerance   The degree to which a system can tolerate failures. Adding redundant components, such as disk mirroring or disk duplexing, is a way to build in fault tolerance.

ferrite clamp   A clamp installed on a network cable to protect against electrical interference.

fiber optic   As applied to Internet access technologies, a dedicated, leased line that uses fiber-optic cable from the Internet Service Provider (ISP) to a residence or place of business.

fiber-optic cable   Cable that transmits signals as pulses of light over glass or plastic strands inside protected tubing.

field replaceable unit (FRU)   A component in a computer or device that can be replaced with a new component without sending the computer or device back to the manufacturer. Examples: power supply, DIMM, motherboard, hard disk drive.

file attributes   The properties assigned to a file. Examples of file attributes are read-only and hidden status.

file recovery software   Third-party software that can help recover deleted and corrupted files.

file system   The overall structure that an OS uses to name, store, and organize files on a disk. Examples of file systems are NTFS and FAT32. Windows is always installed on a volume that uses the NTFS file system.

firewall   Hardware and/or software that blocks unwanted traffic initiated from the Internet into a private network and can restrict Internet access for local computers behind the firewall.

FireWire 400   A data transmission standard used by computers and peripherals (for example, a video camera) that transmits at 400 Mbps. *Also called* 1394a.

FireWire 800   A data transmission standard used by computers and peripherals (for example, a video camera) that transmits at 800 Mbps. *Also called* 1394b.

FireWire port   A port used for high-speed multimedia devices such as camcorders. *Also called* an IEEE 1394 port.

firmware   Software that is permanently stored in a chip. The BIOS on a motherboard is an example of firmware.

fitness monitor   A wearable computer device that can measure heart rate, count pool laps or miles jogged or biked, and a host of other activities.

fixboot   A Windows 7/Vista command that repairs the boot sector of the system partition.

fixmbr   A Windows 7/Vista command to repair the MBR (Master Boot Record).

flashing BIOS   The process of upgrading or refreshing the programming stored on a firmware chip.

flat-panel monitor   *See* LCD (liquid crystal display) monitor.

flip-chip land grid array (FCLGA)   A type of socket used by processors that has blunt protruding pins on the socket that connect with lands or pads on the bottom of the processor. The chips in the processor package are flipped over so that the top of the chip makes contact with the socket.

flip-chip pin grid array (FCPGA)   A type of socket used by processors that has holes aligned in rows to receive pins on the bottom of the processor. The chips in the processor are flipped over so that the top of the chip makes contact with the socket.

floppy disk drive (FDD)   A drive that can hold either a 5½ inch or 3¼ inch floppy disk. *Also called* floppy drive.

fluorescent backlighting   *See* Cold Cathode Fluorescent Lamp (CCFL).

format   The Windows command to prepare a hard drive volume, logical drive, or USB flash drive for use by placing tracks and sectors on its surface to store information (for example, format d:). This process erases all data on the device.

formatting *See* format.

form factor A set of specifications on the size, shape, and configuration of a computer hardware component such as a case, power supply, or motherboard.

front panel connector A group of wires running from the front or top of the computer case to the motherboard.

front panel header A group of pins on a motherboard that connect to wires that are connected to the front panel of the computer case.

Front Side Bus (FSB) *See* system bus.

FTP (File Transfer Protocol) A TCP/IP protocol and application that uses the Internet to transfer files between two computers.

FTP server A server using the FTP or Secure FTP protocol that downloads or uploads files to remote computers.

full duplex Communication that happens in two directions at the same time.

fully qualified domain name (FQDN) Identifies a computer and the network to which it belongs and includes the computer name and domain name. For example, *jsmith.amazon.com*. Sometimes loosely referred to as a domain name.

fuser assembly A component in laser printing that uses heat and pressure to fuse the toner to paper.

gateway Any device or computer that network traffic can use to leave one network and go to a different network.

geotracking A mobile device routinely reports its position to Apple, Google, or Microsoft at least twice a day, which makes it possible for these companies to track your device's whereabouts.

ghost cursor A trail on the screen left behind when you move the mouse.

Gigabit Ethernet A version of Ethernet that supports rates of data transfer up to 1 gigabit per second.

gigahertz (GHz) One thousand MHz, or one billion cycles per second. *Also see* hertz *and* megahertz.

global address *See* global unicast address.

global unicast address In TCP/IP Version 6, an IP address that can be routed on the Internet. *Also called* global address.

Globally Unique Identifier Partition Table (GUID or GPT) A partitioning system installed on a hard drive that can support 128 partitions and is recommended for drives larger than 2 TB.

GPS (Global Positioning System) A receiver that uses the system of 24 or more satellites orbiting the earth. The receiver locates four or more of these satellites, and from these four locations, calculates its own position in a process called triangulation.

graphic processing unit (GPU) A processor that manipulates graphic data to form the images on a monitor screen. A GPU can be embedded on a video card, on the motherboard, or integrated within the processor.

graphics tablet An input device that can use a stylus to hand draw. It works like a pencil on the tablet and uses a USB port.

ground bracelet *See* ESD strap.

ground mat *See* ESD mat.

GSM (Global System for Mobile Communications) An open standard for cellular networks and cell phones that uses digital communication of data and is accepted and used worldwide.

gyroscope A device that contains a disc that is free to move and can respond to gravity as the device is moved.

half duplex Communication between two devices whereby transmission takes place in only one direction at a time.

hard disk drive (HDD) *See* hard drive.

hard drive The main secondary storage device of a computer. Two technologies are currently used by hard drives: magnetic and solid state. *Also called* hard disk drive (HDD).

hardware address *See* MAC (Media Access Control) address.

hardware print server A device that can connect to a USB, Bluetooth, or serial-port printer to connect the printer to the network as a network printer.

hardware-assisted virtualization (HAV) A feature of a processor whereby it can provide enhanced support for hypervisor software to run virtual machines on a system. The feature must be enabled in UEFI/BIOS setup.

HD15 port *See* VGA (Video Graphics Array) port.

HDMI (High Definition Multimedia Interface) port A digital audio and video port currently used on televisions and other home theater equipment and is often used to connect a computer to home theater equipment.

G

HDMI connector A connector that transmits both digital video and audio and is used on most computers and televisions.

HDMI mini connector A smaller type of HDMI connector used for connecting some devices such as a smart phone to a computer. *Also called* mini-HDMI connector.

heat sink A piece of metal, with cooling fins, that can be attached to or mounted on an integrated chip package (such as the CPU) to dissipate heat.

hertz (Hz) Unit of measurement for frequency, calculated in terms of vibrations, or cycles per second. For example, for 16-bit stereo sound, a frequency of 44,000 Hz is used. *Also see* megahertz *and* gigahertz.

Home Theater PC (HTPC) A PC that is designed to play and possibly record music, photos, movies, and video on a television or extra-large monitor screen.

host name A name that identifies a computer, printer, or other device on a network, which can be used instead of the computer's IP address to address the computer on the network. The host name together with the domain name is called the fully qualified domain name. *Also called* computer name.

Hosts file A file in the C:\Windows\System32\ drivers\etc folder that contains computer names and their associated IP addresses on the local network. The file has no file extension.

hot-plugging Plugging in a device while the computer is turned on. The computer will sense the device and configure it without rebooting. In addition, the device can be unplugged without an OS error. *Also called* hot-swapping.

hotspot A small area that offers connectivity to a wireless network, such as a Wi-Fi network.

hot-swappable The ability to plug or unplug devices without first powering down the system. USB devices are hot-swappable.

hot-swapping Allows you to connect and disconnect a device while the system is running.

HTPC case A case used to accommodate a home theater PC and must be small enough to fit on a shelf in an entertainment center.

HTTP (Hypertext Transfer Protocol) The TCP/IP protocol used for the World Wide Web and used by web browsers and web servers to communicate.

HTTPS (HTTP secure) The HTTP protocol working with a security protocol such as Secure Sockets Layer (SSL) or Transport Layer Security (TLS), which is better than SSL, to create a secured socket that includes data encryption.

hub A network device or box that provides a central location to connect cables and distributes incoming data packets to all other devices connected to it. *Compare with* switch.

hybrid hard drive (H-HDD) A hard drive that uses both magnetic and solid-state drive (SSD) technologies. The bulk of storage uses the magnetic component, and a storage buffer on the drive is made of an SSD component. Windows ReadyDrive supports hybrid hard drives.

Hyper-Threading The Intel technology that allows each logical processor within the processor package to handle an individual thread in parallel with other threads being handled by other processors within the package.

Hyper Transport The AMD technology that allows each logical processor within the processor package to handle an individual thread in parallel with other threads being handled by other processors within the package.

hypervisor Software that creates and manages virtual machines on a server or on a local computer. *Also called* virtual machine manager (VMM).

I/O shield A plate installed on the rear of a computer case that provides holes for I/O ports coming off the motherboard.

iCloud A website by Apple (*www.icloud.com*) used to sync content on Apple devices in order to provide a backup of the content.

IDE (Intergrated Drive Electronics or Integrated Device Electronics) A hard drive whose disk controller is integrated into the drive, eliminating the need for a controller cable and thus increasing speed, as well as reducing price.

IEEE 1394 port *See* FireWire port.

IEEE 802.11ac The latest Wi-Fi standard that supports up to 7 Gbps (actual speeds are currently about 1300 Mbps) and uses 5.0 GHz radio frequency and beamforming.

IEEE 802.11n A Wi-Fi standard that supports up to 600 Mbps and uses 5.0 GHz or 2.4 GHz radio frequency and supports MIMO.

ifconfig (interface configuration)   A Linux and OS X command similar to the Windows ipconfig command that displays details about network interfaces and can enable and disable an interface. When affecting the interface, the command requires root privileges.

imaging drum   An electrically charged rotating drum found in laser printers.

IMAP4 (Internet Message Access Protocol, version 4)   A protocol used by an email server and client that allows the client to manage email stored on the server without downloading the email. *Compare with POP3.*

impact paper   Paper used by impact printers and comes as a box of fanfold paper or in rolls (used with receipt printers).

impact printer   A type of printer that creates a printed page by using a mechanism that touches or hits the paper.

Infrared (IR)   An outdated wireless technology that has been mostly replaced by Bluetooth to connect personal computing devices.

In-Plane Switching (IPS)   A class of LCD monitor that offers truer color images and better viewing angles, but is expensive and has slower response times.

infrastructure mode   Wi-Fi devices connect to a Wi-Fi access point, such as a SOHO router, which is responsible for securing and managing the wireless network.

ink cartridge   Cartridge in inkjet printers that holds the different colors of ink for the printer.

inkjet printer   A type of ink dispersion printer that uses cartridges of ink. The ink is heated to a boiling point and then ejected onto the paper through tiny nozzles.

interface   In TCP/IP Version 6, a node's attachment to a link. The attachment can be a physical attachment (for example, when using a network adapter) or a logical attachment (for example, when using a tunneling protocol). Each interface is assigned an IP address.

interface ID   In TCP/IP Version 6, the last 64 bits or 4 blocks of an IP address that identify the interface.

internal components   The main components installed in a computer case.

Internet Protocol version 4 (IPv4)   A group of TCP/IP standards that uses IP addresses that have 32 bits.

Internet Protocol version 6 (IPv6)   A group of TCP/IP standards that uses IP addresses that have 128 bits.

Internet Service Provider (ISP)   A commercial group that provides Internet access for a monthly fee; Charter, Earthlink, and Windstream are large ISPs.

intranet   Any private network that uses TCP/IP protocols. A large enterprise might support an intranet that is made up of several local networks.

inverter   An electrical device that converts DC to AC.

IP address   A 32-bit or 128-bit address used to uniquely identify a device or interface on a network that uses TCP/IP protocols. Generally, the first numbers identify the network; the last numbers identify a host. An example of a 32-bit IP address is 206.96.103.114. An example of a 128-bit IP address is 2001:0000:B80::D3:9C5A:CC.

ipconfig (IP configuration)   A Windows command that displays TCP/IP configuration information and can refresh TCP/IP assignments to a connection including its IP address.

ISATAP   In TCP/IP Version 6, a tunneling protocol that has been developed for IPv6 packets to travel over an IPv4 network and stands for Intra-Site Automatic Tunnel Addressing Protocol.

ISDN (Integrated Services Digital Network)   A broadband telephone line that can carry data at about five times the speed of regular telephone lines. Two channels (telephone numbers) share a single pair of wires. ISDN has been replaced by DSL.

ISO image   A file format that has an .iso file extension and holds an image of all the data, including the file system that is stored on an optical disc. ISO stands for International Organization for Standardization. *Also called* disc image.

ITX   *See* Mini-ITX.

joule   A measure of work or energy. One joule of energy produces one watt of power for one second.

jumper   Two small posts or metal pins that stick up side by side on the motherboard or other device and are used to hold configuration information. The jumper is considered closed if a cover is over the wires and open if the cover is missing.

keyboard backlight   A feature on some keyboards where the keys light up on the keyboard.

G

Key-enrollment Key (KEK)   *See* Key-exchange Key (KEK).

Key-exchange Key (KEK)   A Secure Boot database that holds digital signatures provided by OS manufacturers.

keystone RJ-45 jack   A jack that is used in an RJ-45 wall jack.

KVM (Keyboard, Video, and Mouse) switch   A switch that allows you to use one keyboard, mouse, and monitor for multiple computers. Some KVM switches also include sound ports so that speakers and a microphone can be shared among multiple computers.

LAN (local area network)   A network bound by routers that usually covers only a small area, such as one building.

land grid array (LGA)   A socket that has blunt protruding pins in uniform rows on the socket that connect with lands or pads on the bottom of the processor. *Compare with* pin grid array (PGA).

laptop   A portable computer that is designed for travel and mobility. Laptops use the same technology as desktop computers, with modifications for conserving voltage, taking up less space, and operating while on the move. *Also called* a notebook.

laser printer   A type of printer that uses a laser beam to control how toner is placed on the page and then uses heat to fuse the toner to the page.

latency   Delays in network transmissions resulting in slower network performance. Latency is measured by the round-trip time it takes for a data packet to travel from source to destination and back to source.

LC (local connector) connector   A fiber-optic cable connector that can be used with either single-mode or multimode fiber-optic cables and is easily terminated and smaller than an SC connector.

LCD (liquid crystal display) monitor   A monitor that uses LCD technology. LCD produces an image using a liquid crystal material made of large, easily polarized molecules. *Also called* flat-panel monitor.

LED (Light-Emitting Diode)   A technology used in an LCD monitor that uses less mercury than earlier technologies.

Level 1 cache (L1 cache)   Memory on the processor die used as a cache to improve processor performance.

Level 2 cache (L2 cache)   Memory in the processor package but not on the processor die. The memory is used as a cache or buffer to improve processor performance. *Also see* Level 1 cache (L1 cache).

Level 3 cache (L3 cache)   Cache memory further from the processor core than Level 2 cache but still in the processor package.

Lightning port   The connector used on newer Apple iPhones, iPods, and iPads for power and communication.

Lightweight Directory Access Protocol (LDAP)   A protocol used by various client applications when the application needs to query a database.

line-of-sight connectivity   A type of connection used by satellites that requires no obstruction from mountains, trees, and tall buildings from the satellite dish to the satellite.

link (local link)   In TCP/IP version 6, a local area network or wide area network bounded by routers. *Also called* local link.

link-local address   *See* link-local unicast address.

link-local unicast address   In TCP/IP Version 6, an IP address used for communicating among nodes in the same link and is not allowed on the Internet. *Also called* local address *and* link-local address.

lithium ion   Currently the most popular battery type for laptop computers that is more efficient than earlier types. Sometimes abbreviated as "Li-Ion" battery.

local area network (LAN)   A network bound by routers or other gateway devices.

local link   *See* link.

local printer   A printer connected to a computer by way of a port on the computer. *Compare with* network printer.

LoJack   A technology by Absolute Software used to track the whereabouts of a laptop computer and, if the computer is stolen, lock down access to the computer or erase data on it. The technology is embedded in the UEFI/BIOS of many laptops.

Long Term Evolution (LTE)   The latest standard used to transmit both voice and digital data over cellular networks and is expected to eventually replace CDMA and GSM.

loopback address   An IP address that indicates your own computer and is used to test TCP/IP configuration on the computer.

loopback plug   A device used to test a port in a computer or other device to make sure the port is working and might also test the throughput or speed of the port.

low-level formatting   A process (usually performed at the factory) that electronically creates the hard drive tracks and sectors, and tests for bad spots on the disk surface. *Compare with* high-level formatting.

LPT (Line Printer Terminal)   Assignments of system resources that are made to a parallel port and that are used to manage a print job. Two possible LPT configurations are referred to as LPT1: and LPT2:.

LPT port   *See* parallel port.

MAC (Media Access Control) address   A 48-bit (6-byte) hardware address unique to each network interface card (NIC) or onboard network controller that is assigned by the manufacturer at the factory and embedded on the device. The address is often printed on the adapter as hexadecimal numbers. An example is 00 00 0C 08 2F 35. *Also called* a physical address, an adapter address, or a hardware address.

MAC address filtering   A technique used by a router or wireless access point to allow access to a private network to only certain computers or devices identified by their MAC addresses.

magnetic hard drive   One of two technologies used by hard drives where data is stored as magnetic spots on disks that rotate at a high speed. *Compare with* solid state drive (SSD).

main board   *See* motherboard.

MAN (metropolitan area network)   A type of network that covers a large city or campus.

Master Boot Record (MBR)   On an MBR hard drive, the first sector on the drive, which contains the partition table and a program BIOS uses to boot an OS from the drive.

Material Safety Data Sheet (MSDS)   A document that explains how to properly handle substances such as chemical solvents; it includes information such as physical data, toxicity, health effects, first aid, storage, disposal, and spill procedures.

megahertz (MHz)   One million Hz, or one million cycles per second. *Also see* hertz *and* gigahertz.

memory bank   The memory a processor addresses at one time. Today's desktop and laptop processors use a memory bank that is 64 bits wide.

Memory Diagnostics   A Windows 8/7/Vista utility (mdsched.exe) used to test memory.

microATX (MATX)   A smaller version of the ATX form factor. MicroATX addresses some new technologies that were developed after the original introduction of ATX.

Micro-A connector   A USB connector that has five pins and is smaller than the Mini-B connector. It is used on digital cameras, cell phones, and other small electronic devices.

Micro-B connector   A USB connector that has five pins and has a smaller height than the Mini-B connector. It is used on digital cameras, cell phones, and other small electronic devices.

microprocessor   *See* central processing unit (CPU).

microUSB   A smaller version of the regular USB connector.

MIDI (musical instrument digital interface)   A set of standards that are used to represent music in digital form. A MIDI port is a 5-pin DIN port that looks like a keyboard port, only larger.

MIMO   *See* multiple input/multiple output (MIMO).

Mini-B connector   A USB connector that has five pins and is often used to connect small electronic devices, such as a digital camera, to a computer.

Mini-DIN-6 connector   A 6-pin variation of the S-Video port and looks like a PS/2 connector used by a keyboard or mouse.

Mini DisplayPort   A smaller version of DisplayPort that is used on laptops or other mobile devices.

mini-HDMI connector   *See* HDMI mini connector.

Mini-ITX   A smaller version of the microATX form factor. *Also called* ITX.

Mini PCI   The PCI industry standard for desktop computer expansion cards, applied to a much smaller form factor for laptop expansion cards.

Mini PCI Express (Mini PCIe)   A standard used for laptop internal expansion slots that follows the PCI Express standards applied to laptops.

minicartridge   A tape drive cartridge that is only $3\frac{1}{4} \times 2\frac{1}{2} \times 3/5$ inches. It is small enough to allow two drives to fit into a standard 5 inch drive bay of a PC case.

miniUSB   A smaller version of the regular USB connector and is smaller than microUSB.

mirrored volume   The term used by Windows for the RAID 1 level that duplicates data on one drive to another drive and is used for fault tolerance. *Also see* RAID 1.

G

mobile hotspot　Created by a mobile device so that other devices or computers can connect by Wi-Fi to the device and on to the Internet.

modem port　A port used to connect dial-up phone lines to computers.

Molex connector　A 4-pin power connector used to provide power to a PATA hard drive or optical drive.

motherboard　The main board in the computer, *also called* the system board. The CPU, ROM chips, DIMMs, RIMMs, and interface cards are plugged into the motherboard.

motion controller　An input device that senses the motion of your fingers and hands.

motion sensor　*See* motion controller.

MT-RJ (mechanical transfer registered jack) connector　A type of connector used by fiber-optic cables and can be used with either single-mode or multimode fiber-optic cables and is more difficult to connect than the smaller LC connector.

multicast address　In TCP/IP version 6, an IP address used when packets are delivered to a group of nodes on a network.

multicasting　In TCP/IP version 6, one host sends messages to multiple hosts, such as when the host transmits a video conference over the Internet.

multicore processing　A processor technology whereby the processor housing contains two or more processor cores that operate at the same frequency but independently of each other.

MultiMediaCard (MMC)　A compact storage card that looks like an SD card, but the technology is different and they are not interchangeable. Generally, SD cards are faster than MMC cards.

multimeter　A device used to measure the various attributes of an electrical circuit. The most common measurements are voltage, current, and resistance.

multiple input/multiple output (MIMO)　A feature of the IEEE 802.11n/ac standards for wireless networking whereby two or more antennas are used at both ends of transmissions to improve performance.

multiplier　The factor by which the bus speed or frequency is multiplied to get the CPU clock speed.

multiprocessing　Two processing units installed within a single processor and first used by the Pentium processor.

multiprocessor platform　A system that contains more than one processor. The motherboard has more than one processor socket and the processors must be rated to work in this multiprocessor environment.

multitouch　A touch screen on a computer or mobile device that can handle a two-finger pinch.

name resolution　The process of associating a character-based name with an IP address.

NAND flash memory　The type of memory used in solid-state drives (SSD). NAND stands for "Not AND" and refers to the logic used when storing a one or zero in the grid of rows and columns on the memory chip.

NAT (Network Address Translation)　A technique that substitutes the public IP address of the router for the private IP address of computer on a private network when these computers need to communicate on the Internet. *See also* Destination Network Address Translation (DNAT).

native resolution　The actual (and fixed) number of pixels built into an LCD monitor. For the clearest display, always set the resolution to the native resolution.

nbtstat (NetBIOS over TCP/IP Statistics)　A Windows TCP/IP command that is used to display statistics about the NetBT protocol.

Near Field Communication (NFC)　A wireless technology that establishes a communication link between two NFC devices (for example, two smart phones or a smart phone and an NFC tag) that are within 4 inches of each other.

neighbors　In TCP/IP version 6, two or more nodes on the same link.

net localgroup　A Windows TCP/IP command that adds, displays, or modifies local user groups.

net use　A Windows TCP/IP command that connects or disconnects a computer from a shared resource or can display information about connections.

net user　A Windows TCP/IP command used to manage user accounts.

NetBIOS　A legacy suite of protocols used by Windows before TCP/IP.

NetBIOS over TCP/IP　A feature of Server Message Block (SMB) protocols that allows legacy NetBIOS applications to communicate on a TCP/IP network.

netbook   A low-end, inexpensive laptop with a small 9 or 10 inch screen and no optical drive that is generally used for web browsing, email, and word processing by users on the go.

netdom (network domain)   A Windows TCP/IP command that allows administrators to manage Active Directory domains and trust relationships for Windows Server from the command prompt on the server or remotely from a Windows 8/7 workstation.

netstat (network statistics)   A Windows TCP/IP command that gives statistics about TCP/IP and network activity and includes several parameters.

network adapter   *See* network interface card (NIC).

Network Attached Storage (NAS)   A device that provides multiple bays for hard drives and an Ethernet port to connect to the network. The device is likely to support RAID.

network drive map   Mounting a drive to a computer, such as drive E:, that is actually hard drive space on another host computer on the network.

network interface card (NIC)   An expansion card that plugs into a computer's motherboard and provides a port on the back of the card to connect a computer to a network. *Also called* a network adapter.

network multimeter   A multifunctional tool that can test network connections, cables, ports, and network adapters.

network port   A port used by a network cable to connect to the wired network. *Also called* an Ethernet port.

network printer   A printer that any user on the network can access, through its own network card and connection to the network, through a connection to a stand-alone print server, or through a connection to a computer as a local printer, which is shared on the network.

node   Any device that connects to the network, such as a computer, printer, or router.

North Bridge   That portion of the chipset hub that connects faster I/O buses (for example, the video bus) to the system bus. *Compare with* South Bridge.

notebook   *See* laptop.

nslookup (name space lookup)   A TCP/IP command that lets you read information from the Internet name space by requesting information about domain name resolutions from the DNS server's zone data.

octet   In TCP/IP version 4, each of the four numbers that are separated by periods and make up a 32-bit IP address. One octet is 8 bits.

ohm (Ω)   The standard unit of measurement for electrical resistance. Resistors are rated in ohms.

OLED (Organic Light-emitting Diode) monitor   A type of monitor that uses a thin LED layer or film between two grids of electrodes and does not use backlighting.

onboard NIC   A network port embedded on the motherboard.

onboard port   Ports that are directly on the motherboard, such as a built-in keyboard port or on-board network port.

optical connector   A connector used with a fiber-optic cable.

option ROM   A Secure Boot driver required as the computer first boots, that are digitally signed and identified in the signature database.

OSI Model   A model for understanding and developing computer-to-computer communication, it divides networking functions among seven layers: Physical, Data Link, Network, Transport, Session, Presentation, and Application.

overclocking   Running a processor at a higher frequency than is recommended by the manufacturer, which can result in an unstable system, but is a popular thing to do when a computer is used for gaming.

packet   A message sent over a network as a unit that contains the data and information at the beginning that identifies the type of data, where it came from, and where it's going. *Also called* data packet or datagram.

PAN (personal area network)   A small network consisting of personal devices at close range; the devices can include smart phones, PDAs, and laptop computers.

parallel ATA (PATA)   An older IDE cabling method that uses a 40-pin flat or round data cable or an 80-conductor cable and a 40-pin IDE connector. *Also see* serial ATA.

parallel port   An outdated female 25-pin port on a computer that transmitted data in parallel, 8 bits at a time, and was usually used with a printer. Parallel ports have been replaced by USB ports. *Also called* an LPT1 port, LPT2 port and LPT port.

parity An older error-checking scheme used with SIMMs in which a ninth, or "parity," bit is added. The value of the parity bit is set to either 0 or 1 to provide an even number of ones for even parity and an odd number of ones for odd parity.

parity error An error that occurs in parity error-checking when the number of 1s in the byte is not in agreement with the expected number.

partition A division of a hard drive that can hold a volume. MBR drives can support up to four partitions on one hard drive. In Windows, GPT drives can have up to 128 partitions.

passive CPU cooler *See* fanless CPU cooler.

patch cable *See* straight-through cable.

patch panel A device that provides multiple network ports for cables that converge in one location such as an electrical closet or server room.

PC Card A card that uses a PC Card slot on a laptop, and provides a port for peripheral devices or adds memory to the laptop. A PC Card is about the size of a credit card, but thicker.

PCI (Peripheral Component Interconnect) A bus common to personal computers that uses a 32-bit wide or a 64-bit data path. Several variations of PCI exist. On desktop systems, one or more notches on a PCI slot keep the wrong PCI cards from being inserted in the PCI slot.

PCI Express (PCIe) The latest evolution of PCI, which is not backward-compatible with earlier PCI slots and cards. PCIe slots come in several sizes, including PCIe x1, PCIe x4, PCIe x8, and PCIe x16.

PCIe 6/8-pin connector A power cord connector used by high-end video cards using PCIe x16 slots to provide extra voltage to the card and can accommodate a 6-hole or 8-hole port.

PCI-X The second evolution of PCI, which is backward-compatible with conventional PCI slots and cards, except 5-V PCI cards. PCI-X is focused on the server market.

PCL (Printer Control Language) A printer language developed by Hewlett-Packard that communicates to a printer how to print a page.

PCMCIA card An card used with older laptops that was one or more variations of a PC Card to add memory to a laptop or provide ports for peripheral devices. For example, modem cards, network cards for wired or wireless network, sound cards, SCSI host adapters, FireWire

controllers, USB controllers, flash memory adapter, TV tuner, and hard disks.

phablet A mobile device that has the same capabilities of a smart phone or tablet and is smaller than a tablet and larger than a smart phone.

physical address *See* MAC (Media Access Control) address.

pickup roller A part in a printer that pushes forward a sheet of paper from the paper tray.

ping A TCP/IP command used to troubleshoot network connections. It verifies that the host can communicate with another host on the network. Stands for Packet InterNet Groper.

pin grid array (PGA) A socket that has holes aligned in uniform rows around the socket to receive the pins on the bottom of the processor. *Compare with* land grid array (LGA).

pixel A small spot on a fine horizontal scan line. Pixels are illuminated to create an image on the monitor.

pixel pitch The distance between adjacent pixels on the screen.

plasma monitor A type of monitor that provides high contrast with better color than LCD monitors. They work by discharging xenon and neon plasma on flat glass and don't contain mercury.

Platform Key (PK) A digital signature belonging to the motherboard or computer manufacturer. The PK authorizes turning on or off Secure boot and updating the KEK database.

plenum The area between floors of a building.

PoE injector A device that adds power to an Ethernet cable so the cable can provide power to a device.

POP or POP3 (Post Office Protocol, version 3) The protocol that an email server and client use when the client requests the downloading of email messages. The most recent version is POP version 3. *Compare with* IMAP4.

port (1) As applied to services running on a computer, a number assigned to a process on a computer so that the process can be found by TCP/IP. *Also called* a port address *or* port number. (2) A physical connector, usually at the back of a computer, that allows a cable from a peripheral device, such as a printer, mouse, or modem, to be attached.

port address *See* port.

port filtering   To open or close certain ports so they can or cannot be used. A firewall uses port filtering to protect a network from unwanted communication.

port forwarding   A technique that allows a computer on the Internet to reach a computer on a private network using a certain port when the private network is protected by NAT and a firewall that controls the use of ports. *Also called* port mapping.

port mapping   *See* port forwarding.

port number   *See* port.

port triggering   When a firewall opens a port because a computer behind the firewall initiates communication on another port.

POST (power-on self test)   A self-diagnostic program used to perform a simple test of the CPU, RAM, and various I/O devices. The POST is performed by startup UEFI/BIOS when the computer is first turned on.

POST card   A test card installed in a slot on the motherboard or plugged in to a USB port that is used to help discover and report computer errors and conflicts that occur when a computer is first turned on and before the operating system is launched. *Also called* POST diagnostic card.

POST diagnostic card   *See* POST card.

PostScript   A printer language developed by Adobe Systems that tells a printer how to print a page.

Power over Ethernet (PoE)   A feature that might be available on high-end wired network adapters that allows power to be transmitted over Ethernet cable to remote devices.

power supply   A box inside the computer case that receives power and converts it to provide power to the motherboard and other installed devices. Power supplies provide 3.3, 5, and 12 volts DC. *Also called* a power supply unit (PSU).

power supply tester   A device that can test the output of each power cord coming from a power supply.

power supply unit (PSU)   *See* power supply.

powerline networking   A technique to allow Ethernet transmissions over power lines. A powerline adapter is plugged into the electrical circuit(s) at both ends and the adapters connect to the Ethernet network. Because the transmissions are not contained, encryption is required for security. *Also called* Ethernet over Power (EoP).

print head   The part in an inkjet or impact printer that moves across the paper, creating one line of the image with each pass.

print server   Hardware or software that manages the print jobs sent to one or more printers on a network.

print spooler   A queue for print jobs.

printer maintenance kit   A kit purchased from a printer manufacturer that contains the parts, tools, and instructions needed to perform routine printer maintenance.

printer self-test page   A test page that prints by using controls at the printer. The page allows you to eliminate a printer as a problem and usually prints test, graphics, and information about the printer such as the printer resolution and how much memory is installed.

printui   The Windows Printer User Interface command used by administrators to manage printers on the local and remote computers.

private IP address   In TCP/IP version 4, an IP address that is used on a private network that is isolated from the Internet.

processor   *See* central processing unit (CPU).

processor frequency   The speed at which the processor operates internally. Usually expressed in GHz.

processor thermal trip error   A problem when the processor overheats and the system restarts.

projector   Used to shine a light that projects a transparent image onto a large screen and is often used in classrooms or with other large groups.

protocol   A set of rules and standards that two entities use for communication. For example, TCP/IP is a suite or group of protocols that define many types of communication on a TCP/IP network.

PS/2 port   A round 6-pin port used by a keyboard or mouse.

public IP address   In TCP/IP version 4, an IP address available to the Internet.

punchdown tool   A tool used to punch individual wires from a network cable into their slots to terminate the cable.

PVC (polyvinyl chloride)   The product used to cover Ethernet cables that is not safe to be used in a plenum because it gives off toxic fumes when burned.

G

quad channels Technology used by a motherboard and DIMMs that allows the memory controller to access four DIMMS at the same time. DDR3 and DDR4 DIMMs can use quad channels.

Quality of Service (QoS) A feature used by Windows and network hardware devices to improve network performance for an application that is not getting the best network performance. VoIP (Voice over IP) requires a high QoS.

QuickPath Interconnect (QPI) The technology used first by the Intel X58 chipset for communication between the chipset and the processor using 16 serial lanes similar to that used by PCI Express. Replaced the 64-bit wide Front Side Bus used by previous chipsets.

radio frequency (RF) The frequency of waves generated by a radio signal, which are electromagnetic frequencies above audio and below light. For example, Wi-Fi 802.11n transmits using a radio frequency of 5 GHz and 2.4 GHz.

RAID (redundant array of inexpensive disks or redundant array of independent disks) Several methods of configuring multiple hard drives to store data to increase logical volume size and improve performance, or to ensure that if one hard drive fails, the data is still available from another hard drive.

RAID 0 Using space from two or more physical disks to increase the disk space available for a single volume. Performance improves because data is written evenly across all disks. Windows calls RAID 0 a striped volume. *Also called* striping *or* striped volume.

RAID 1 A type of drive imaging that duplicates data on one drive to another drive and is used for fault tolerance. Windows calls RAID 1 a mirrored volume. *Also called* mirrored volume.

RAID 1+0 *See* RAID 10.

RAID 10 A combination of RAID 1 and RAID 0 that requires at least four disks to work as an array of drives and provides the best redundancy and performance.

RAID 5 A technique that stripes data across three or more drives and uses parity checking, so that if one drive fails, the other drives can re-create the data stored on the failed drive. RAID 5 drives increase performance and provide fault tolerance. Windows calls these drives RAID-5 volumes.

RAID-5 volume The term used by Windows for RAID 5. *See* RAID 5.

RAM (random access memory) Memory modules on the motherboard containing microchips used to temporarily hold data and programs while the CPU processes both. Information in RAM is lost when the computer is turned off.

RAS Latency A method of measuring access timing to memory, which is the number of clock cycles required to write or read a row of data off a memory module. RAS stands for Row Access Strobe. *Compare with* CAS Latency.

raw data Data sent to a printer without any formatting or processing.

RCA connector A connector used with composite and component cables that is round and has a single pin in the center.

read/write head A sealed, magnetic coil device that moves across the surface of a disk in a hard disk drive (HDD) either reading data from or writing data to the disk.

ReadyDrive The Windows 7/Vista technology that supports a hybrid hard drive.

recovery image A backup of the Windows volume.

rectifier An electrical device that converts AC to DC. A computer power supply contains a rectifier.

refresh rate As applied to monitors, the number of times in one second the monitor can fill the screen with lines from top to bottom. *Also called* vertical scan rate.

remote application An application that is installed and executed on a server and is presented to a user working at a client computer.

Remote Desktop Protocol (RDP) The Windows protocol used by Remote Desktop and Remote Assistance utilities to connect to and control a remote computer.

remote printing Printing from a computer or mobile device to a printer that is not connected directly to the computer or device.

repeater A device that amplifies and retransmits a wireless signal to a wider coverage area and uses a new network name for the rebroadcast.

resolution The number of pixels on a monitor screen that are addressable by software (example: 1024 × 768 pixels).

Resource Monitor A Windows tool that monitors the performance of the processor, memory, hard drive, and network.

response time The time it takes to build one frame.

REt (Resolution Enhancement technology) The term used by Hewlett-Packard to describe the way a laser printer varies the size of the dots used to create an image. This technology partly accounts for the sharp, clear image created by a laser printer.

retinal scanning As part of the authentication process, some systems use biometric data by scanning the blood vessels on the back of the eye and is considered the most reliable of all biometric data scanning.

reverse lookup To find the host name when you know a computer's IP address. The nslookup command can perform a reverse lookup.

revoked signature database (dbx) A Secure Boot database that is a blacklist of signatures for software that has been revoked and no longer trusted.

RG-59 coaxial cable An older and thinner coaxial cable once used for cable TV.

RG-6 coaxial cable A coaxial cable used for cable TV and replaced the older and thinner RG-59 coaxial cable.

RGB port *See* composite video port.

RIMM An older type of memory module developed by Rambus, Inc.

riser card A card that plugs into a motherboard and allows for expansion cards to be mounted parallel to the motherboard. Expansion cards are plugged into slots on the riser card.

RJ-11 *See* RJ-11 jack.

RJ-11 jack A phone line connection or port found on modems, telephones, and house phone outlets.

RJ-45 A port that looks like a large phone jack and is used by twisted-pair cable to connect to a wired network adapter or other hardware device. RJ stands for registered jack. *Also called* Ethernet port.

router A device that manages traffic between two or more networks and can help find the best path for traffic to get from one network to another.

RSA tokens A type of smart card that contains authentication information.

S1 state On the UEFI/BIOS power screen, one of the five S states used by ACPI power-saving mode to indicate different levels of power-savings functions. In the S1 state, the hard drive and monitor are turned off and everything else runs normally.

S2 state On the UEFI/BIOS power screen, one of the five S states used by ACPI power-saving mode to indicate different levels of power-savings functions. In S2 state, the hard drive and monitor are turned off and everything else runs normally. In addition, the processor is also turned off.

S3 state On the UEFI/BIOS power screen, one of the five S states used by ACPI power-saving mode to indicate different levels of power-savings functions. In S3 state, everything is shut down except RAM and enough of the system to respond to a wake-up. S3 is sleep mode.

S4 state On the UEFI/BIOS power screen, one of the five S states used by ACPI power-saving mode to indicate different levels of power-savings functions. In S4 state, everything in RAM is copied to a file on the hard drive and the system is shut down. When the system is turned on, the file is used to restore the system to its state before shut down. S4 is hibernation.

S5 state On the UEFI/BIOS power screen, one of the five S states used by ACPI power-saving mode to indicate different levels of power-savings functions. S5 state is the power off state after a normal shutdown.

safety googles Eye googles worn while working in an unsafe environment such as a factory where fragments, chips, or other particles might injure eyes.

sag *See* brownout.

SATA power connector A 15-pin flat power connector that provides power to SATA drives.

SC (subscriber connector or standard connector) connector A type of snap-in connector used by fiber-optic cables and can be used with either single-mode or multimode fiber-optic cables. It is not used with the fastest fiber-optic networking.

SCSI (Small Computer System Interface) An interface between a host adapter and the CPU that can daisy chain as many as 7 or 15 devices on a single bus.

screen orientation The layout or orientation of the screen that is either portrait or landscape.

screen resolution The number of dots or pixels on the monitor screen expressed as two numbers such as 1680×1050.

SDRAM II *See* Double Data Rate SDRAM.

Secure Boot A UEFI feature that prevents a system from booting up with drivers or an OS that are not digitally signed and trusted by the motherboard or computer manufacturer.

Secure Digital (SD) card A type of memory card used in digital cameras, tablets, cell phones, MP3 players, digital camcorders, and other portable devices. The three standards used by SD cards are 1.x (regular SD), 2.x (SD High Capacity or SDHC), and 3.x (SD eXtended Capacity or SDXC).

Secure FTP (SFTP) A TCP/IP protocol used to transfer files from an FTP server to an FTP client using encryption.

Secure Shell (SSH) A protocol that is used to pass login information to a remote computer and control that computer over a network using encryption.

self-grounding A method to safeguard against ESD that involves touching the computer case or power supply before touching a component in the computer case.

separate pad *See* separation pad.

separation pad A printer part that keeps more than one sheet of paper from moving forward.

sequential access A method of data access used by tape drives, whereby data is written or read sequentially from the beginning to the end of the tape or until the desired data is found.

serial ATA (SATA) An ATAPI interface standard for hard drives, optical drives, and other drives that uses a narrower and more reliable cable than the 80-conductor cable and is easier to configure than PATA systems. *Also see* parallel ATA.

serial port A male 9-pin or 25-pin port on a computer system used by slower I/O devices such as a mouse or modem. Data travels serially, one bit at a time, through the port. Serial ports are sometimes configured as COM1, COM2, COM3, or COM4. *Also called* DB9 port.

Server Message Block (SMB) A protocol used by Windows to share files and printers on a network.

Service Set Identifier (SSID) The name of a wireless access point and wireless network.

Services console A console used by Windows to stop, start, and manage background services used by Windows and applications.

set-top box A device that makes a regular TV function as a smart TV.

sheet battery A secondary battery that fits on the bottom of a laptop to provide additional battery charge.

shielded twisted pair (STP) cable A cable that is made of one or more twisted pairs of wires and is surrounded by a metal shield.

Short Message Service (SMS) A technology that allows users to send a test message using a cell phone.

signature database (db) A Secure Boot database that holds a list of digital signatures of approved operating systems, applications and drivers that can be loaded by UEFI.

SIM (Subscriber Identity Module) card A small flash memory card that contains all the information a device needs to connect to a GSM or LTE cellular network, including a password and other authentication information needed to access the network, encryption standards used, and the services that a subscription includes.

SIMM (single inline memory module) An outdated miniature circuit board used to hold RAM. SIMMs held 8, 16, 32, or 64 MB on a single module. SIMMs have been replaced by DIMMs.

Simple Network Management Protocol (SNMP) A TCP/IP protocol used to monitor network traffic.

single channel The memory controller on a motherboard that can access only one DIMM at a time. *Compare with* dual channel and triple channel.

single-sided A DIMM that has memory chips installed on one side of the module.

small form factor (SFF) A motherboard used in low-end computers and home theater systems. Often used with an Intel Atom processor and sometimes purchased as a motherboard-processor combo unit.

S.M.A.R.T. (Self-Monitoring Analysis and Reporting Technology) A system BIOS and hard drive feature that monitors hard drive performance, disk spin up time, temperature, distance between the head and the disk, and other mechanical activities of the drive in order to predict when the drive is likely to fail.

smart camera A digital camera that has embedded computing power to make decisions about the content of the photos or videos it records, including transmitting alerts over a wired or wireless network when it records certain content. *Also called* a vision sensor.

smart card reader A device that can read a smart card used to authenticate a person onto a network.

smart phone A cell phone that includes abilities to send text messages, text messages with photos, videos, or other multimedia content, surf the web, manage email, play games, take photos and videos, and download and use apps.

smart TV   A television that has the ability to run apps, store data, and connect to the Internet.

SMB2   *See* CIFS (Common Internet File System).

SMTP (Simple Mail Transfer Protocol)   A TCP/IP protocol used by email clients to send email messages to an email server and on to the recipient's email server. *Also see* POP and IMAP.

SMTP AUTH (SMTP Authentication)   An improved version of SMTP and used to authenticate a user to an email server when the email client first tries to connect to the email server to send email. The protocol is based on the Simple Authentication and Security Layer (SASL) protocol.

socket   An established connection between a client and a server, such as the connection between a browser and web server.

SO-DIMM (small outline DIMM)   A type of memory module used in laptop computers that uses DIMM technology. A DDR3 SO-DIMM has 204 pins. A DDR2 or DDR SO-DIMM has 200 pins. Older, outdated SO-DIMMs can have 72 pins or 144 pins.

Software Explorer   A Vista tool used to control startup programs.

solid-state device (SSD)   An electronic device with no moving parts. A storage device that uses memory chips to store data instead of spinning disks (such as those used by magnetic hard drives and CD drives). Examples of solid state devices are jump drives (also called key drives or thumb drives), flash memory cards, and solid state disks used as hard drives in notebook computers designed for the most rugged uses. *Also called* solid state disk (SSD) or solid state drive (SSD). *Compare with* magnetic hard drive.

solid-state drive (SSD)   A hard drive that has no moving parts. *Also see* solid state device (SSD).

sound card   An expansion card with sound ports.

South Bridge   That portion of the chipset hub that connects slower I/O buses (for example, a PCI bus) to the system bus. *Compare with* North Bridge.

spacer   *See* standoff.

spanning   A configuration of two hard drives which hold a single Windows volume to increase the size of a volume. Sometimes called JBOD (just a bunch of disks).

S/PDIF (Sony-Phillips Digital InterFace) sound port   A port that connects to an external home theater audio system, providing digital audio output and the best signal quality.

spooling   Placing print jobs in a print queue so that an application can be released from the printing process before printing is completed. Spooling is an acronym for simultaneous peripheral operations online.

staggered pin grid array (SPGA)   A type of socket used by processors that has pins staggered over the socket in order to squeeze more pins into a small space.

standoff   Round plastic or metal pegs that separate the motherboard from the case, so that components on the back of the motherboard do not touch the case. *Also called* spacer.

startup UEFI/BIOS   Part of UEFI or BIOS firmware on the motherboard that is responsible for controlling the computer when it is first turned on. Startup UEFI/BIOS gives control over to the OS once the OS is loaded.

startup repair   A Windows 8/7/Vista utility that restores many of the Windows files needed for a successful boot.

static electricity   *See* electrostatic discharge (ESD).

static IP address   A permanent IP address that is manually assigned to a computer.

static RAM (SRAM)   RAM chips that retain information without the need for refreshing, as long as the computer's power is on. They are more expensive than traditional DRAM.

ST (straight tip) connector   A type of connector used by fiber-optic cables and can be used with either single-mode or multimode fiber-optic cables. The connector does not support full-dupex transmissions and is not used on the fastest fiber-optic systems.

storage card   An adapter card used to manage hardware RAID rather than using the firmware on the motherboard.

straight-through cable   An Ethernet cable used to connect a computer to a switch or other network device. *Also called* a patch cable.

striped volume   The term used by Windows for RAID 0. A type of dynamic volume used for two or more hard drives that writes to the disks evenly rather than filling up allotted space on one and then moving on to the next. *Compare with* spanned volume. *Also see* RAID 0.

stylus   A device that is included with a graphics tablet that works like a pencil on the tablet.

subnet   A group of local networks when several networks are tied together in a subsystem of the larger intranet. In TCP/IP Version 6, one or more links that have the same 16 bits in the subnet ID of the IP address. *See* subnet ID.

subnet ID   In TCP/IP Version 6, the last block (16 bits) in the 64-bit prefix of an IP address. The subnet is identified using some or all of these 16 bits.

subnet mask   In TCP/IP Version 4, 32 bits that include a series of ones followed by zeroes. For example, 11111111.11111111.11110000.00000000, which can be written as 255.255.240.0. The 1s identify the network portion of an IP address, and the 0s identify the host portion of an IP address. The subnet mask tells Windows if a remote computer is on the same or different network.

surge supressor   A device designed to protect against voltage spikes by blocking or grounding excessive voltage.

S-Video port   A 4-pin or 7-pin round video port that sends two signals over the cable, one for color and the other for brightness, and is used by some high-end TVs and video equipment.

switch   A device used to connect nodes on a network in a star network topology. When it receives a packet, it uses its table of MAC addresses to decide where to send the packet.

synchronus DRAM (SDRAM)   The first DIMM to run synchronized with the system clock which has two notches, and uses 168 pins.

system UEFI/BIOS   UEFI (Unified Extensible Firmware Interface) or BIOS (basic input/output system) firmware on the motherboard that is used to control essential devices before the OS is loaded.

system board   *See* motherboard.

system bus   The bus between the CPU and memory on the motherboard. The bus frequency in documentation is called the system speed, such as 400 MHz. *Also called* the memory bus, Front Side Bus, local bus, or host bus.

system clock   A line on a bus that is dedicated to timing the activities of components connected to it. The system clock provides a continuous pulse that other devices use to time themselves.

system state data   In Windows, files that are necessary for a successful load of the operating system.

T568A   Standards for wiring twisted-pair network cabling and RJ-45 connectors and have the green pair connected to pins 1 and 2 and the orange pair connected to pins 3 and 6.

T568B   Standards for wiring twisted-pair network cabling and RJ-45 connectors and have the orange pair using pins 1 and 2 and the green pair connected to pins 3 and 6.

tablet   A computing device with a touch screen that is larger than a smart phone and has functions similar to a smart phone.

TCP (Transmission Control Protocol)   The protocol in the TCP/IP suite of protocols that works at the OSI Transport layer and establishes a session or connection between parties and guarantees packet delivery.

TCP/IP (Transmission Control Protocol/Internet Protocol)   The group or suite of protocols used for almost all networks, including the Internet. Fundamentally, TCP is responsible for error checking transmissions, and IP is responsible for routing.

Telnet   A TCP/IP protocol used by the Telnet client/server applications to allow an administrator or other user to control a computer remotely.

Teredo   In TCP/IP Version 6, a tunneling protocol to transmit TCP/IPv6 packets over a TCP/IPv4 network, named after the Teredo worm that bores holes in wood. Teredo IP addresses begin with 2001, and the prefix is written as 2001::/32.

tether   To connect a mobile device with a cellular connection to the Internet to a computer so that the computer can access the Internet by way of the mobile device.

thermal compound   A creamlike substance that is placed between the bottom of the cooler heat sink and the top of the processor to eliminate air pockets and to help to draw heat off the processor.

thermal paper   Special coated paper used by thermal printers.

thermal printer   A type of line printer that uses wax-based ink, which is heated by heat pins that melt the ink onto paper.

thermal transfer printer   A type of thermal printer that uses a ribbon that contains wax-based ink. The heating element melts the ribbon onto special thermal paper so that it stays glued to the paper as the feeder assembly moves the paper through the printer.

thick client   A regular desktop computer or laptop that is sometimes used as a client by a virtualization server. *Also called* fat client.

thin client   A computer that has an operating system, but has little computing power and might only need to support a browser used to communicate with a virtualization server.

thread   Each process that the processor is aware of; a single task that is part of a longer task or request from a program.

Thunderbolt port   A port that transmits both video and data on the same port and cable. The port is shaped the same as the DisplayPort and is compatible with DisplayPort devices.

TKIP (Temporal Key Integrity Protocol)   A type of encryption protocol used by WPA to secure a wireless Wi-Fi network. *Also see* WPA (WiFi Protected Access).

tone probe   A two-part kit that is used to find cables in the walls of a building. *Also called* a toner probe.

toner probe   *See* tone probe.

toner vacuum   A vacuum cleaner designed to pick up toner used in laser printers and does not allow it to touch any conductive surface.

touch pad   A common pointing device on a laptop computer.

touch screen   An input device that uses a monitor or LCD panel as a backdrop for user options. Touch screens can be embedded in a monitor or LCD panel or installed as an add-on device over the monitor screen.

tower case   The largest type of personal computer case. Tower cases stand vertically and can be as high as two feet tall. They have more drive bays and are a good choice for computer users who anticipate making significant upgrades.

TPM (Trusted Platform Module)   A chip on a motherboard that holds an encryption key required at startup to access encrypted data on the hard drive. Windows 8/7/Vista BitLocker Encryption can use the TPM chip.

tracert (trace route)   A TCP/IP command that enables you to resolve a connectivity problem when attempting to reach a destination host such as a website.

trace   A wire on a circuit board that connects two components or devices.

tractor feed   A continuous feed within an impact printer that feeds fanfold paper through the printer rather than individual sheets, making them useful for logging ongoing events or data.

transfer belt   A laser printer component that completes the transferring step in the printer.

transfer roller   A soft, black roller in a laser printer that puts a positive charge on the paper. The charge pulls the toner from the drum onto the paper.

transformer   An electrical device that changes the ratio of current to voltage. A computer power supply is basically a transformer and a rectifier.

trip hazard   Loose cables or cords in a traffic area where people can trip over them.

triple channels   When the memory controller accesses three DIMMs at the same time. DDR3 DIMMs support triple channeling.

TV tuner card   An adapter card that receives a TV signal and displays TV on the computer screen.

Twisted Nematic (TN)   A class of LCD monitor that has fast response times to keep fast moving images crisper, but monitors are brighter, consume more power, and have limited viewing angles.

twisted-pair cabling   Cabling, such as a network cable, that uses pairs of wires twisted together to reduce crosstalk.

UDF (Universal Disk Format)   A file system for optical media used by all DVD discs and some CD-R and CD-RW discs. *Also see* CDFS (Compact Disc File System).

UDP (User Datagram Protocol)   A connectionless TCP/IP protocol that works at the OSI Transport layer and does not require a connection to send a packet or guarantee that the packet arrives at its destination. The protocol is commonly used for broadcasting to multiple nodes on a network or the Internet. *Compare with* TCP (Transmission Control Protocol).

unicast address   Using TCP/IP version 6, an IP address assigned to a single node on a network.

Unified Extensible Firmware Interface (UEFI)   An interface between firmware on the motherboard and the operating system that improves on legacy BIOS processes for booting, handing over the boot to the OS, and loading device drivers and applications before the OS loads. UEFI also manages motherboard settings and secures the boot to ensure that no rogue operating system hijacks the system.

uninterruptible power supply (UPS)   A device that raises the voltage when it drops during brownouts.

unique local address (ULA)   In TCP/IP Version 6, an address used to identify a specific site within a large organization. It can work on multiple links within the same organization. The address is a hybrid between a global unicast address that works on the Internet and a link-local unicast address that works on only one link.

Universal Plug and Play (UPnP)   An unsecure method a router can use to allow unfiltered communication between nodes on a private network. Hackers sometimes are able to exploit UPnP, so use with caution.

unshielded twisted pair (UTP) cable   The most popular cabling method for local networks and is the least expensive and is commonly used on LANs. The cable is made of twisted pairs of wires and is not surrounded by shielding.

USB 3.0 B-Male connector   A USB connector used by SuperSpeed USB 3.0 devices such as printers or scanners.

USB 3.0 Micro-B connector   A small USB connector used by SuperSpeed USB 3.0 devices. The connectors are not compatible with regular Micro-B connectors.

USB (Universal Serial Bus) port   A type of port designed to make installation and configuration of I/O devices easy, providing room for as many as 127 devices daisy-chained together.

USB optical drive   An external optical drive that connects to a computer via a USB port.

USB to Bluetooth adapter   A device that plugs into a USB port on a computer to connect to Bluetooth devices.

USB to RJ-45 dongle   An adapter that plugs into a USB port and provides an RJ-45 port for a network cable to connect to a wired network.

USB to Wi-Fi dongle   An adapter that plugs into a USB port and provides wireless connectivity to a Wi-Fi network.

VGA (Video Graphics Adapter) port   A 15-pin analog video port popular for many years. *Also called* DB15 port, DE15 port, or HD15 port.

VGA mode   Standard VGA settings, which include a resolution of 640 x 480.

video capture card   An adapter card that captures video input and saves it to a file on the hard drive.

video memory   Memory used by the video controller. The memory might be contained on a video card or be part of system memory. When part of system memory, the memory is dedicated by Windows to video.

virtual machine (VM)   Software that simulates the hardware of a physical computer, creating one or more logical machines within one physical machine.

virtual printing   Printing to a file rather than directly to a printer.

virtual private network (VPN)   A security technique that uses encrypted data packets between a private network and a computer somewhere on the Internet.

virtualization   When one physical machine hosts multiple activities that are normally done on multiple machines.

virtualization server   A computer that serves up virtual machines to multiple client computers and provides a virtual desktop for users on these client machines.

vision sensor   *See* smart camera.

Voice over LTE (VoLTE)   A technology used on cellular networks for LTE to support voice communication.

VoIP (Voice over Internet Protocol)   A TCP/IP protocol and an application that provides voice communication over a TCP/IP network. *Also called* Internet telephone.

volt (V)   A measure of potential difference or electrical force in an electrical circuit. A computer ATX power supply usually provides five separate voltages: 112 V, 212 V, 15 V, 25 V, and 13.3 V.

wait state   A clock tick in which nothing happens, used to ensure that the microprocessor isn't getting ahead of slower components. A 0-wait state is preferable to a 1-wait state. Too many wait states can slow down a system.

Wake-on-LAN   Configuring a computer so that it will respond to network activity when the computer is in a sleep state.

WAN (wide area network)   A network or group of networks that span a large geographical area.

watt (W)   The unit of electricity used to measure power. A typical computer may use a power supply that provides 500W.

wearable technology device A device, such as a smart watch, wristband, arm band, eyeglasses, headset, or clothing, that can perform computing tasks, including making phone calls, sending text messages, recording and transmitting data, and checking email.

wear leveling A technique used on a solid-state drive (SSD) that assures the logical block addressing does not always address the same physical blocks in order to distribute write operations more evenly across the device.

WEP (Wired Equivalent Privacy) An encryption protocol used to secure transmissions on a Wi-Fi wireless network; however, it is no longer considered secure because the key used for encryption is static (it doesn't change).

Wi-Fi (Wireless Fidelity) The common name for standards for a local wireless network as defined by IEEE 802.11. *Also see* 802.11 a/b/g/n/ac.

Wi-Fi analyzer Hardware and/or software that monitors a Wi-Fi network to detect devices not authorized to use the network, identify attempts to hack transmissions, or detect performance and security vulnerabilities.

Wi-Fi Protected Setup (WPS) A method to make it easier for users to connect their computers to a secured wireless network when a hard-to-remember SSID and security key are used, and is considered a security risk that should be used with caution.

Windows Boot Manager (BootMgr) The Windows 8/7/Vista program that manages the initial startup of Windows. For a BIOS system, the program is bootmgr; for a UEFI system, the program is bootmgfw.efi. The program file is stored in the root of the system partition.

Windows Experience Index A Windows 7/Vista feature that gives a summary index designed to measure the overall performance of a system on a scale from 1.0 to 7.9.

Windows pinwheel A Windows graphic that indicates the system is waiting for a response from a program or device.

wireless access point (WAP) A wireless device that is used to create and manage a wireless network.

wireless LAN (WLAN) A type of LAN that does not use wires or cables to create connections, but instead transmits data over radio or infrared waves.

wireless locator A tool that can locate a Wi-Fi hotspot and tell you the strength of the RF signal.

wireless wide area network (WWAN) A wireless broadband network for computers and mobile devices that uses cellular towers for communication. *Also called* a cellular network.

wire stripper A tool used when terminating a cable. The tool cuts away the plastic jacket or coating around the wires in a cable so that a connector can be installed on the end of the cable.

WPA (WiFi Protected Access) A data encryption method for wireless networks that use the TKIP (Temporal Key Integrity Protocol) encryption method and the encryption keys are changed at set intervals while the wireless LAN is in use. WPA is stronger than WEP.

WPA2 (WiFi Protected Access 2) A data encryption standard compliant with the IEEE802.11i standard that uses the AES (Advanced Encryption Standard) protocol. WPA2 is currently the strongest wireless encryption standard.

x86 processor An older processor that first used the number 86 in the model number and processes 32 bits at a time.

x86-64 bit processor Hybrid processors that can process 32 bits or 64 bits.

xD-Picture Card A type of flash memory device that has a compact design and currently holds up to 8 GB of data.

XPS Document Writer A Windows 8/7/Vista feature that creates a file with an .xps file extension. The file is similar to a .pdf file and can be viewed, edited, printed, faxed, emailed, or posted on websites.

zero insertion force (ZIF) socket A socket that uses a small lever to apply even force when you install the processor into the socket.

zero-fill utility A hard drive utility that fills every sector on the drive with zeroes.

ZIF connector A ZIF (zero insertion force) connector uses a lever or latch to prevent force from being used on a sensitive connection.

G

INDEX

I

I

I